SAP PRESS e-books

Print or e-book, Kindle or iPad, workplace or airplane: Choose where and how to read your SAP PRESS books! You can now get all our titles as e-books, too:

- By download and online access
- For all popular devices
- And, of course, DRM-free

Convinced? Then go to www.sap-press.com and get your e-book today.

Materials Management with SAP S/4HANA®

SAP PRESS is a joint initiative of SAP and Rheinwerk Publishing. The know-how offered by SAP specialists combined with the expertise of Rheinwerk Publishing offers the reader expert books in the field. SAP PRESS features first-hand information and expert advice, and provides useful skills for professional decision-making.

SAP PRESS offers a variety of books on technical and business-related topics for the SAP user. For further information, please visit our website: *www.sap-press.com*.

Justin Ashlock
Sourcing and Procurement with SAP S/4HANA
2020, approx. 750 pp., hardcover and e-book
www.sap-press.com/5003

Bernd Roedel, Johannes Esser
Inventory Management with SAP S/4HANA
2019, 494 pages, hardcover and e-book
www.sap-press.com/4892

Jawad Akhtar
Quality Management with SAP S/4HANA
2019, 950 pages, hardcover and e-book
www.sap-press.com/4924

Jawad Akhtar
Production Planning with SAP S/4HANA
2019, 1010 pages, hardcover and e-book
www.sap-press.com/4821

Jawad Akhtar, Martin Murray

Materials Management with SAP S/4HANA®

Business Processes and Configuration

Rheinwerk
Publishing

Editor Meagan White
Acquisitions Editor Emily Nicholls
Copyeditor Yvette Chin
Cover Design Graham Geary
Photo Credit Shutterstock.com/104077769/© cowardlion
Layout Design Vera Brauner
Production Hannah Lane
Typesetting III-satz, Husby (Germany)
Printed and bound in the United States of America, on paper from sustainable sources

ISBN 978-1-4932-1741-0

© 2020 by Rheinwerk Publishing, Inc., Boston (MA)
1st edition 2019, 1st reprint 2020

Library of Congress Cataloging-in-Publication Data
Names: Akhtar, Jawad, author. | Murray, Martin, author.
Title: Materials management with SAP S/4HANA : business processes and
    configuration / Jawad Akhtar, Martin Murray.
Description: First edition. | Bonn : Rheinwerk Publishing, 2018. | Includes
    index.
Identifiers: LCCN 2018035401 (print) | LCCN 2018037015 (ebook) | ISBN
    9781493217427 (ebook) | ISBN 9781493217410 (alk. paper)
Subjects: LCSH: Materials management--Data processing. | SAP HANA (Electronic
    resource)
Classification: LCC TS161 (ebook) | LCC TS161 .A344 2018 (print) | DDC
    658.7--dc23
LC record available at https://lccn.loc.gov/2018035401

Contents at a Glance

Dear Reader,

Sometimes when I'm driving over the Zakim Bridge in Boston, I marvel at the materials required to construct it.

As bridges go, it doesn't seem like a particularly intricate one—and yet my mind boggles to imagine the number of parts, from small screws to steel beams, that hold the bridge together. To plan, procure, and stock the right kind and quantity of cable and concrete for this skyline icon must have been an extraordinary undertaking.

The Zakim was completed in 2003—long before the arrival of SAP S/4HANA—but its builders placed incalculable trust in their data and processes. Today's SAP customers have similarly rigorous demands, and seek to implement SAP S/4HANA systems that capture modern materials management requirements for MRP, procurement, and inventory. That's where this book comes in: to help customers and consultants set up and run SAP S/4HANA for their products or projects, however iconic.

If you have feedback about *Materials Management with SAP S/4HANA: Business Processes and Configuration* (or thoughts about bridges), reach out! Your comments and suggestions are the most useful tools to help us make our books the best they can be. Please feel free to contact me and share any praise or criticism you may have.

Thank you for purchasing a book from SAP PRESS!

Meagan White
Editor, SAP PRESS

meaganw@rheinwerk-publishing.com
www.sap-press.com
Rheinwerk Publishing · Boston, MA

Contents

1   Materials Management Overview

2   Organizational Structure

3 Configuring the Material Master

4   Material Master Data: Part 1

6   Business Partners

8   Batch Management Data

10 Purchase Requisitions

11 Requests for Quotation 401

12 Purchase Orders

13   External Services Management

14   Special Procurement Types

15   Material Requirements Planning   539

17   Inventory Management Overview — 617

20   Physical Inventory   699

22   Inventory Valuation and Account Assignment   751

25 Document Management System 849

26 Early Warning System 873

27   Reporting and Analytics

Appendices

Acknowledgments

Like my previous three books, this book is dedicated to the loving memory of my parents, who have left for their eternal abodes. If you are blessed with one or both living parents, please take great care of them and spend as much time with them as possible, for they are the true paths to all professional and personal successes in life.

Writing this book as a lead author was indeed a tall order knowing very well that the SAP world in general and the SAP materials management (MM) community in particular have very high expectations from the late Martin Murray's works and the enormous legacy he has left behind.

I wish to express my enormous admiration for my acquisitions editor at SAP PRESS, Emily Nicholls. Emily has once again trusted me to bring out and present the very best in the MM component of SAP S/4HANA.

At SAP PRESS, I have always been greatly impressed by its managing director, Florian Zimniak, who treats his authors as the greatest assets, ensuring that we authors keep coming back for many more projects. Finally, to my editor, Meagan White: It's a sheer pleasure to collaborate with her on every book or E-Bite project! Under Meagan's able editorship, I have enormous confidence that my words are in great hands—hands that know how to present information in a structured and logical way that makes perfect sense and is easy to read, hands that also know when to cut text that doesn't fit! My appreciation also goes out to the unsung and unseen publishing team, such as the copyeditor, the production team, the design team, and so on, who work tirelessly behind the scenes to bring out the very best in each book.

Last but not least: To my readers—I am truly humbled and honored for all the appreciation I've received from all of you over the years. I hope that, like my previous three books, this book also meets your expectations and becomes a useful stepping stone in your SAP career.

Preface

Welcome to the first edition of *Materials Management with SAP S/4HANA: Business Processes and Configuration*.

This book is a comprehensive review of the materials management (MM) functionality in the latest version of SAP S/4HANA, which at the time of this writing is SAP S/4HANA 1709 (on-premise).

Who Is This Book For?

The subject of this book is not just of interest to those who work directly with MM but is also relevant for those who work in related SAP areas, such as production planning (PP), quality management (QM), or plant maintenance (PM). The topics we'll cover in this book should also be of interest to those in logistics and supply chain management and to purchasing managers who want to understand more of the functionality they've implemented (or may be considering implementing), such as the material ledger and service purchasing, and want in-depth expertise in configuring the MM functionality in SAP S/4HANA.

If you are working with sales and distribution (SD), you'll benefit from a greater understanding of the material movements related to sales orders and of how material is issued for customer sales orders.

PP staff will benefit from additional familiarity with how materials are received from production and the purchasing of material for production orders.

Other staff working with SAP S/4HANA functionalities such as QM and PM will benefit from a greater understanding of the general topics within MM.

As you can see, this book on MM has wide applicability across the SAP landscape. Before going deeper into the book, let's look at how the book is organized so you can go directly to the chapter with the information you seek, or you can proceed in a more linear fashion.

How This Book Is Organized

The organization of this book is designed to best serve various individuals who work in the MM environment, whether they are SAP configuration experts or users tasked with using MM as part of their everyday work experience and want to gain more understanding of the functionality.

Each chapter focuses on a specific MM function, exploring the different facets of the function and providing related examples. The book starts by examining the MM functionality from the very basic key elements through standard MM functions such as purchasing and inventory movements to more complex functions such as material ledger and classification. Let's get an idea of what's included in each chapter:

- **Chapter 1**
  This chapter is an MM overview and discusses the role of the MM functionality within the logistics function and the supply chain management.

- **Chapter 2**
  This chapter describes the organizational structure of the MM functionality. This structure forms the basis of the building blocks in SAP S/4HANA such as procurement and inventory management (IM) and is a key to understanding the makeup of MM.

- **Chapter 3**
  In this chapter, you'll explore various organizational structures including the client, company, plant, and storage location. This chapter takes you through these key configuration elements and describes step-by-step how to set these elements up in a logical sequential order. The objects configured in this chapter will be used throughout the book.

- **Chapter 4**
  The material master is used throughout the system, and this chapter partially describes the elements that go into each material master record. In this chapter, you'll examine the master data found in the MM functionality. The material master (and its various views) and serial records are described in detail. The chapter explains how this data is created and used by showing configuration steps and examples. We'll also show you how to create a new material type, assign it a number range, and we'll discuss how this new material type is then used in creating a new material master record. We'll also carefully examine the structure and makeup of the material master file.

- **Chapter 5**
  This chapter picks up where Chapter 4 left off, covering the remaining details of the material master, including advanced planning, production resources/tools (PRTs), QM, forecasting, material planning information, and accounting and costing details.

- **Chapter 6**

  This chapter is similar in structure to Chapter 4 and Chapter 5, except that we'll examine business partner master data. Since the business partner object has a completely new look and new features in SAP S/4HANA, we'll cover all associated configuration steps as well as business processes.

- **Chapter 7**

  This chapter describes the elements and functionality of the purchasing information record and how it contains data specifically for a particular material and vendor.

- **Chapter 8**

  This chapter examines data related to batch management, including batch records for materials. We'll also show you how to select a batch using the batch determination functionality.

- **Chapter 9**

  This chapter is an overview of the purchasing functionality within MM. We'll include an overview of the purchase requisition, request for quotation (RFQ), purchase order (PO), source list, and vendor evaluation. These topics are then examined in more detail in later chapters.

- **Chapter 10**

  This chapter focuses on the purchase requisition. We'll examine how to create a purchase requisition, either entered directly or created indirectly, and how a requisition is processed. A new purchase requisition document type is created to provide an in-depth coverage to configuration and associated business processes.

- **Chapter 11**

  This chapter examines the RFQ function. While not all companies use RFQs, this chapter examines how they are created, released, and sent to selected vendors. We'll also examine the other side of the RFQ, that is, the quotation received from the vendor and how to enter quotations, compare competing quotations, and reject losing bids.

- **Chapter 12**

  With this chapter, we move into the area of the PO, including the various functions associated with the PO, such as account assignment, message output, and order type. The chapter also investigates the variations, such as outline purchase agreements, scheduling agreements, and contracts. We'll also cover the functionality of purchase release strategies.

- **Chapter 13**

  This chapter discusses external services management (ESM). The procurement of services is as important to companies as the procurement of materials, and this chapter reviews the ESM functionality. The service master record, standard service catalog (SSC), and service entry are all examined in this chapter.

- **Chapter 14**

  This chapter covers special procurement types, which enable a company to manage business processes that differ from standard and routine processes in procurement or IM.

- **Chapter 15**

  In this chapter, we'll explore the functionality of consumption-based planning by reviewing the master data required and the planning process involved. The planning evaluation, using the material requirements planning (MRP) list, is also discussed. We'll also cover how to set up an MRP area and how to use it in the planning process via MRP Live.

- **Chapter 16**

  In this chapter, we'll examine the forecasting functionality in MM. We'll provide an overview of the forecast models, parameters, and options that can be used in forecasting within SAP S/4HANA.

- **Chapter 17**

  This chapter offers you an overview of the IM functionality briefly examining goods issues, goods receipts, returns, physical inventory, reservations, and stock transfers. These items are then examined in greater detail in the following chapters.

- **Chapter 18**

  This chapter identifies the various goods issues that can be carried out within IM. We'll describe the issues most often seen in a plant, such as issue to production and issue to scrap.

- **Chapter 19**

  This chapter reviews the function of the goods receipt. The most common goods receipts, which are goods receipts from production orders and goods receipt for a PO, are examined in detail.

- **Chapter 20**

  This chapter examines the function of the physical inventory. This process is still a staple in most companies, and this chapter reviews how the physical inventory process can be completed.

- **Chapter 21**

  This chapter describes the business process of invoice verification. The chapter describes a standard three-way match as well as other invoice options, such as evaluated receipt settlement or two-way matches. The chapter also reviews the function of blocking and releasing invoices.

- **Chapter 22**

  In this chapter, we'll review the functionality of valuation and account assignment. This chapter examines the last in first out (LIFO) and first in first out (FIFO) functionalities as well as examine the lowest value determination functionality. We'll also cover the configuration steps for, as well as the business processes associated with, setting up automatic account determination.

- **Chapter 23**

  This chapter focuses on the material ledger, which may not be something that an MM consultant has used. However, as the material ledger is now a mandatory requirement in SAP S/4HANA, we'll provide a good understanding of material ledger functionality in this chapter.

- **Chapter 24**

  This chapter examines the classification system. Although not part of the MM functionality, understanding how classification works is important because this powerful tool is used, not only in the material master, but also in the PO release strategy and a number of other areas. This chapter describes the elements of classification, such as a class and characteristics and how these elements are used to classify materials and other objects.

- **Chapter 25**

  In this chapter, we'll review a subject not necessarily considered core to MM: the Document Management System (DMS). Documents are often linked to the material master record, and understanding how these documents are linked via the DMS can be useful. This chapter shows you how to create a document record and link a document record to an object.

- **Chapter 26**

  This chapter covers a latent but powerful SAP alert tool, the Early Warning System (EWS). The EWS consists of user-defined alerts that can help business users monitor and get alerts on critical business situations threatening to disrupt logistics and supply chain operations. The EWS works throughout SAP S/4HANA; thus, the concepts covered in this chapter can easily be used in other SAP functional areas such as PP, QM, SD, PM, or PS.

- **Chapter 27**

  This final chapter dives deep into covering some of the SAP-delivered standard reports, information systems, and standard analyses available in logistics in general and MM in particular. Next-generation SAP Fiori-based reporting and transactional apps in SAP S/4HANA are also covered in this chapter.

Tip

The menu paths in this book each begin with **SAP Menu • Tools • Customizing • IMG • SPRO** followed by clicking on **Display Reference IMG** or pressing F5 . For the sake of brevity, each menu path will not include that repetitive section of the path.

Conclusion

Reading this book will provide you with a comprehensive review of MM in SAP S/4HANA. The topics we'll discuss will reinforce your current knowledge and help you develop skills in areas that may be unfamiliar. This book should be a key reference for your current and future MM experience.

Let's now proceed to Chapter 1, where we'll provide a general introduction to SAP, with a focus on MM in particular, so that you can see how MM can integrate into the logistics and supply chain functions of your company.

Chapter 1
Materials Management Overview

Materials management (MM) is a core functionality of SAP S/4HANA. The functionality within MM is the engine that drives logistics and supply chain management. In this chapter, we'll describe the elements that make MM such an important part of SAP and the logistics function.

In this chapter, we'll describe the importance of the materials management (MM) functionality in SAP S/4HANA in the context of the overall functionality of SAP software and as a part of the supply chain.

MM contains many aspects of SAP functionality, including purchasing, goods receiving, material storage, consumption-based planning, and inventory. MM is highly integrated with other functionalities such as financials (FI), controlling (CO), production planning (PP), sales and distribution (SD), quality management (QM), plant maintenance (PM), and warehouse management (WM).

This chapter examines why MM is a core functionality in any SAP S/4HANA implementation. You'll learn why MM can be described as the engine that drives the supply chain within the SAP system and learn how MM is integrated with other SAP components or functionalities.

1.1 What Is Materials Management?

In this section, we'll provide a brief overview of the core SAP S/4HANA functionality and describe where MM fits into the structure. We'll also cover business suite functionality, which includes important business functionalities for supply chain management. Next, we'll dive more deeply into using MM as part of logistics and your supply chain.

1.1.1   Materials Management in SAP S/4HANA

SAP was originally developed as an enterprise software package attractive to large manufacturing companies. As the number of companies adopting SAP began to grow, a number of smaller companies in many different industries came to believe that SAP could also provide them a competitive advantage.

Many of these smaller companies required just the core SAP functionality, which usually consists of MM, FI, SD, and PP. Often, companies start their implementations with this core functionality, and then on the second and third phases of their implementations, they could introduce other functionalities such as CO, WM, human resources (HR), QM, and so on.

SAP not only continues to innovate and bring new offerings often, its vision is to make SAP software simple to run and use. SAP S/4HANA is the latest offering that not only simplifies logistics operations by combining several interconnected logistics and supply chain functionalities, but also makes the entire experience of working with SAP software user friendly.

The latest annual release of core SAP S/4HANA on-premise was in September 2017 (SAP S/4HANA on-premise 1709). Therefore, the examples and screenshots in this edition of the book are all from the SAP S/4HANA 1709 (on-premise), unless otherwise stated.

SAP has also extensively worked on the user experience side of the software, and SAP Fiori is SAP's next-generation user interface. The images and screenshots in this book are a mix of web-based SAP Fiori interfaces and SAP GUI (graphical user interface). As SAP develops more extensive solutions and tools for its customers, MM continues to be an important foundation on which subsequent functionality can be built.

Now that we've reviewed the history of MM as part of SAP S/4HANA, in the next section, we'll examine how MM works as part of the logistics function.

1.1.2   Materials Management in Logistics

Logistics in SAP incorporates a number of distinct areas that together follow the movement of materials from manufacturer to consumer. Logistics, in essence, is the management of business operations, including the acquisition, storage, transportation, and delivery of goods along the supply chain. A supply chain is a network of retailers, distributors, transporters, storage facilities, and suppliers that participate in the sale, delivery, and production of a particular product.

In this section, we'll review the MM functionality as part of logistics.

Management of the Supply Chain

Given the nature of logistics and the supply chain, MM is an integral part of the logistics function within SAP. When we look at MM in the supply chain, we should keep in mind three important flows (discussed in greater detail in Section 1.2):

- **Material flow**
  The material flow describes the movement of materials from the supplier to the company and then on to the customer (and, potentially, returns from the customer). Today, companies integrate with suppliers and customers, not just interact with them. Therefore, any improvements you can provide to the visibility of material flows will allow your company to be flexible and responsive to your customers. Customers want to do business with companies that are responsive. These companies gain a competitive advantage and increase market share by being more flexible, quicker, and more dependable.

- **Information flow**
  The information flow includes transmitting orders (i.e., electronic data interchange [EDI], etc.) and updating the status of all deliveries. Companies that can show customers and vendors viability by using real-time information have a distinct competitive advantage over others.

- **Financial flow**
  The financial flow includes the financial documents created at each material movement. If a material is valuated, then a movement—credit or debit—is made between accounts to reflect the material's value moving from, for example, inventory accounts and accounts payable (AP) clearing accounts.

SAP and Logistics

At this point, we've defined the logistics function and the flows within the supply chain. So how can SAP help you manage this supply chain to gain a competitive advantage?

SAP software ensures that the correct materials are at the correct location at the correct time in the correct quantity and at the most competitive cost. Competitive advantage is achieved when the company can manage this process, which involves managing the company's relationships with its suppliers and customers. Controlling inventory, forecasting customer demand, and receiving timely information concerning all aspects of supply chain transactions will also be involved.

When you break this structure down and look at the functionalities and components involved in the management of the supply chain, you'll see that, although MM is an integral part of logistics, it's only one part of the bigger picture. Although the old SAP ERP functionalities are still available in SAP S/4HANA, the components or modules of SAP ERP have been replaced with business processes. Some important logistics and supply chain business processes in which MM plays a central role are:

- **Procure-to-pay processes**

  In this business process, a request to procure a material is either created manually by a business user or is automatically generated through a materials planning program, such as material requirements planning (MRP). In an SAP system, this material request is created as a purchase requisition, which is converted into a request for quotations (RFQ) and sent to relevant suppliers. Upon receipt, quotes from suppliers are also maintained in the RFQs. A price comparison of all the quotations received will be performed, and one supplier will be chosen to supply the required material. The remaining quotations are marked as rejected to prevent users from mistakenly processing these quotations further. Rejected suppliers are also sent rejection letters. The successful quotation is converted into a procurement element, such as a quantity or a value contract, a scheduling agreement, or a purchase order. If this procurement element must go through an approval process, then the release strategy (approval process) triggers. Once released, the goods are received in the warehouse. The supplier's invoice is recorded and verified via a three-way matching (purchase order–goods received–invoice received), and finally, the supplier is paid.

- **Plan-to-product processes**

  In this business process, products are produced in-house and planned involves both production planning and also planning for raw materials and packing materials, which are often procured. This planning takes place using a materials planning program such as material requirements planning (MRP). The procure-to-pay business process triggers raw and packing materials procurement. Once these materials are received in the company's warehouse, the production process can begin because the raw and packing materials required to produce a product are now available in the warehouse. A goods issuance for the raw and packing materials required to produce a product involves the inventory management (IM) area of materials management. When the product is produced, it is delivered to the warehouse, which again is a part of the MM functionality.

- **Order-to-cash processes**

  The order-to-cash business process begins when a company receives an inquiry from a customer for a product that the company provides. This inquiry is maintained in sales and distribution (SD), and the sales representative issues a quotation to the customer with reference to the same inquiry. If the customer accepts the quotation, then the quotation is converted into a sales order. When ready to deliver the product to the customer, the company issues the product from its warehouse with reference to the sales order. Issuing products from the warehouse in an inventory management process is in the domain of MM. Billing to the customer takes place, and on receiving customer payment, the payment is recorded in the accounts receivables (AR) of the SAP system.

- **Maintenance management**
  In this business process, the spare parts and consumables required to maintain a plant's machinery or assets are either procured using the procure-to-pay business cycle or issued from a warehouse if in stock. This spare parts or consumables issuance from the warehouse is also an inventory management process of MM and includes reference to a maintenance order in plant maintenance (PM).

- **Project management**
  In this business process, the materials required for a project, such as for constructing a new plant or warehouse, are either procured using the procure-to-pay business cycle or issued from a warehouse if stock is available. This project's stock issuance from the warehouse, which again is part of the inventory management process in MM, includes a reference to a work breakdown structure (WBS) element of the project system (PS).

Next, let's review how MM functionality is integrated with other SAP software.

1.2   Materials Management Integration

When you look at your supply chain, you'll see where MM integrates with the other tools and functionalities within SAP S/4HANA to create an efficient landscape for managing supply chains. In the following sections, we'll further examine the supply chain flows and the ways in which MM is integrated with these flows.

1.2.1   The Material Flow of the Supply Chain

The material flow is the movement of a material from the supplier to the customer. To instigate a flow, a material requirement must be created either by the PP functionality via an MRP system or by a sales order created in SD. The need is created, and a purchase requisition is sent to the supplier, relating instructions on the delivery date, quantity, and price. The vendor sends the material, which, once received, may be subject to a quality inspection in QM. Once approved, the material may be stored in a warehouse using WM. The material could be required in a production order in PP or be part of a larger project defined in PS. After a final material is available for the customer, the material can be picked from the warehouse and shipped to the customer using the SD functionality.

Through the description of this simple flow, you can easily see that MM is highly integrated with the other SAP software.

1.2.2   The Information Flow of the Supply Chain

To more clearly understand financial flows, let's work through an example that starts with an order from a customer. This order could be transmitted via EDI to the SAP system. Information in your SAP system communicates whether the item is in stock, and, if not, the information is sent to the MRP tool. Information is sent back to the customer including a delivery date. The MRP tool takes all of the information regarding production schedules, the capacity of the production facility, and the available materials required in production and creates production orders and material requests in the procurement system.

The information in the procurement system creates orders with the required delivery dates that are transmitted to vendors. The return information from the vendor confirms the date of delivery of the material. The vendor can send EDI transmissions informing the company about the status of the delivery.

Upon receipt of the material, information is passed from the receiving documents to the warehousing system (WM) to store the material correctly. The information is passed to the production systems (PP) to calculate if the production order is ready to commence. When the material is ready to ship, SAP produces information for shipping (SD) and can send that information to the customer.

At all of these touchpoints (integration), information has been recorded and is available for review and analysis. The more information is shared across the total supply chain, the more benefits can be achieved with improvements based on the analytical data.

The logistics information system (LIS) and other standard reports in SAP can give the supply chain management team invaluable insights into how their logistics function operates.

1.2.3   The Financial Flow of the Supply Chain

The typical flow of financial information in a supply chain includes the invoices received by the company from vendors, the payments to the vendors, the billing of customers for materials, and the incoming payments. The vendor supplies materials to the company and sends an invoice to be paid.

Within SAP, you have two options for paying vendors:

- Payment on receipt of the materials (two-way match)
- Payment on receipt of the vendor invoice (three-way match)

The AP department carries out this function. The invoice verification process within the SAP system is an excellent example of the integration between MM and FI. The financial flow of the supply chain hasn't changed in magnitude, even though the information and material flows may have. However, the current SAP system allows you to analyze the financial key performance indicators (KPIs) that are part of the overall supply chain. These KPIs can include inventory turnover, days of working capital, days of inventory, days sales outstanding, and days payables outstanding. The integration of MM and the other key functionalities within the logistics function combine to provide this important information in an accurate and timely fashion.

1.3   Summary

In this chapter, we've discussed how the MM functionality in SAP is the foundation or backbone of any SAP implementation. MM can be described as the engine that drives a supply chain within SAP. MM also integrates with most other SAP offerings in some way. Our aim of the following chapters is to focus on the functionality and configuration of MM and its complex integration with other SAP tools.

Let's move on to Chapter 2 to examine the organizational structure of MM, which includes sections on client structures, company codes, plants, storage locations, and purchasing organizations.

Chapter 2
Organizational Structure

Organizational structure is the key for a successful SAP implementation. To achieve the flawless execution of business processes, an extremely important step is to accurately map your company's organizational structure into the SAP system.

In a new SAP implementation, a number of decisions must be made to ensure a successful project. Decisions such as the client structure, company codes, plants, storage locations, and purchasing organizations in SAP are all important to the project and require knowledge about the objects to include after creating among stakeholders and with the project's implementation team.

Configuring an accurate organizational structure is key to a successful SAP implementation. From a materials management (MM) perspective, purchasing organizations, plants, storage locations, and purchasing groups are important elements of an organizational structure. Separate organizational structure elements exist for financial accounting (FI), such as company codes. For sales and distribution (SD), the organizational structures are sales organizations, divisions, and distribution channels, among others. All SAP S/4HANA organizational structures are agreed upon between the customer and the project's implementation team at the beginning of the SAP project to lay the right foundations so the SAP system can meet the reporting and transactional requirements of the customer.

In this chapter, we'll review the MM organizational structure and how it's used in SAP systems. We'll also describe the configuration steps for various organizational structures possible in the SAP system. You'll learn about many different elements of the organizational structures available in various industries and how to map these elements into the organizational structure in SAP.

2.1 Mapping Business Functions of a Company in the SAP System

As shown in Figure 2.1, the different functional departments of an organization are mapped into an SAP system using organizational units. *Organizational units* are responsible for a set of business functions. An enterprise or corporate group is mapped into the SAP system as a *client*, and different companies or subsidiaries of an enterprise are referred to as the *company codes*. Clients and company codes are two types of organizational units often found at the highest level in the SAP organizational structure. When discussing the levels of an organizational structure in SAP, the client is the highest element, but many other levels may exist. A client may have one or more company codes assigned to it; each company code may have one or more plants assigned to it; and each plant may have one or more storage locations assigned to it. Furthermore, each company may have a set of purchasing groups. A *purchasing group* is a buyer or a group of buyers defined independently of the organizational structure. Therefore, a purchasing group isn't necessarily assigned to a purchasing organization or company code.

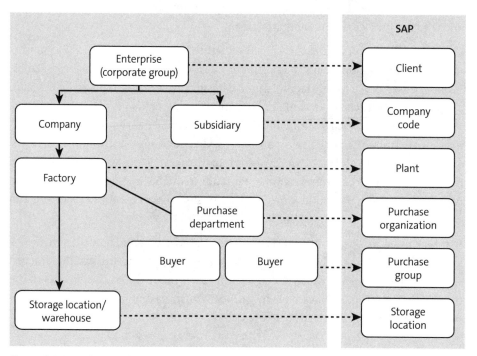

Figure 2.1 Mapping Business Functions with Organizational Units in SAP

While each section in this chapter will cover organizational units in SAP in detail, let's start with a basic and high-level understanding of these units and how the different departments and business functions of a company fit into an SAP system. For any successful implementation project, you must understand your customer's organizational structure and map this organizational structure in a way that meets all of the business process requirements. For this task, you must also understand the essential terminology used in an industry and in the SAP organizational structure, as shown in Figure 2.1 and Figure 2.2, as follows:

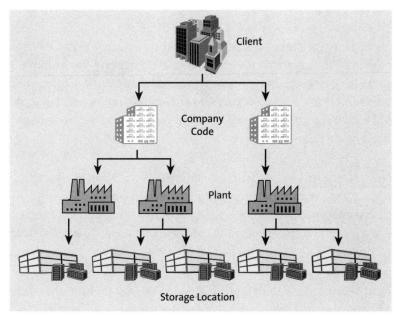

Figure 2.2 The MM Organizational Structure in an SAP System

- **Client/company**
  As the highest organizational unit in an SAP system, the *client* can be a corporate group and can represent a company or a conglomerate of companies. For example, consider a fictional corporate group called the XYZ Corporation, which has companies such as XYZ Steel, XYZ FMCG, XYZ Textile, and XYZ Pharmaceuticals. If the XYZ Corporation wants to implement an SAP system for all of its companies in a single instance, then the whole conglomerate should be represented as a single client. On the other hand, if the various companies each install SAP systems individually (i.e., each company will have one SAP instance), then the individual companies will be represented as clients.

> **Note**
>
> In an SAP system, the word *client* has a specific meaning, and a clear understanding of what this word means in this context is important. In general speech, a "client" is a customer to whom you are providing services. In an SAP system, however, a "client" refers to a corporate group, which is the highest organizational element.
>
> Clients in an SAP system are also used to differentiate among real-time data, test data, and development data, which we'll discuss in detail in Section 2.2.

- **Company code**

  A *company code* is the smallest organizational unit for which you can have an independent accounting department within external accounting. For example, a corporate group (a client) may have one or more independent companies, all of which have their own SAP General Ledger (G/L) account, balance sheet, and profit and loss (P&L) account. Each of these independent business entities must be created in the SAP system as separate company codes.

- **Plant**

  In industry terminology, a manufacturing facility is called a *plant*. In an SAP system, however, a plant can be a manufacturing facility, a sales office, a corporate head office, a maintenance plant, or a central delivery warehouse. In general, a plant can be any location within a company code that is involved in some activity for the company code.

- **Storage location**

  A *storage location* is a place within a plant where materials are kept. Inventory management on a quantity basis is carried out at the storage location level in the plant, as is physical inventory. *Physical inventory* is the process of verifying physical stock with the system stock. If any differences exist in stock quantity, system stocks are updated with actual physical stock quantity. Physical inventory is carried out at each storage location level.

- **Purchasing organization**

  In industry terminology, the purchasing department deals with vendors and is responsible for all procurement activities. The purchasing department is mapped as a *purchasing organization* in the SAP system. Purchasing organizations negotiate the conditions of purchase with vendors for one or more plants and are legally responsible for honoring purchasing contracts.

- **Purchasing group**
  A *purchasing group* is a term for a buyer or a group of buyers responsible for certain purchasing activities. Because a purchase order is a legal document, the purchasing group is represented on a purchase order or contract. The purchasing group can also play an important role in reporting various purchasing transactions. In an SAP system, a purchasing group isn't assigned to purchasing organizations or any other organizational units. Purchasing groups are defined at the client level and can create purchasing documents for any purchasing organization.

2.2   Client Structure in the SAP System

In this section, we'll examine the client, the client landscape, and some general technical consideration surrounding SAP clients.

2.2.1   What Is a Client?

A company that purchases an SAP system will install the system on its servers and then configure the SAP system to the company's specific needs. This system is called an *instance*. Companies can have more than one SAP instance, but all the instances exist on different SAP systems. A number of clients can be created within one SAP instance. A client is an organizational and legal entity in the SAP system. The master data is protected within the client because the data can't be accessed from outside the system. Master data is the data that remains in the system for a much longer period of time (than, for example, a transaction), and business users repeatedly access master data to perform business functions.

The master data in a client is only visible within that client and can't be displayed or changed from another client. Multiple clients may exist in an SAP system. Each of these clients can have a different objective, and each client represents a unique environment. A client has its own set of tables and user data. Objects can be either client dependent or client independent. SAP objects that are used by only one client are client dependent. Objects that are used by all of the clients in an SAP system, such as ABAP programs, are client independent. Figure 2.3 shows **Client 100**, which is an SAP instance, as a demo client. The same SAP system also has another client (**Client 200**), which contains SAP Best Practices (bottom-right for all available SAP clients/instances).

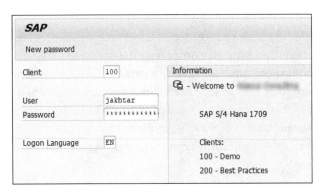

Figure 2.3 Client in an SAP System

Figure 2.4 shows the login screen if you are using the SAP Fiori launchpad to log into the same SAP system as with the SAP GUI (graphical user interface) shown in Figure 2.3.

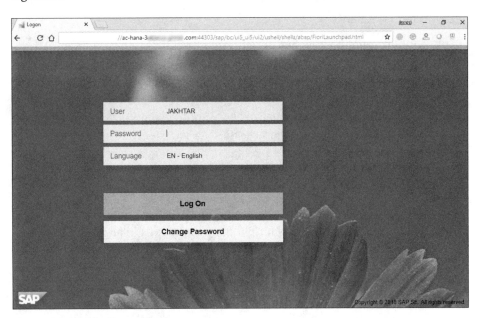

Figure 2.4 SAP Fiori Launchpad

SAP delivers two clients—client 000 and client 001—among others:

- **Client 000**
  The SAP reference client contains tables with default settings but no master data.

Client 000 can be copied, using the client copy function, to create the clients to be used in the implementation. For important configuration work, you'll need to log on to client 000. Client 000 also plays an important role in upgrade processes. Each time an SAP customer upgrades its system, client-dependent changes are automatically made in client 001, the production preparation client, and these changes then can be copied to other clients. Neither client 000 nor client 001 should be removed from the system.

- **Client 001**
  This client is initially identical to client 000 and is delivered as the preparation production client. After upgrades, client 001 won't be identical to client 000. Customizing can be performed in this client, but it can't be used as the production client. You can choose whether or not to use this client.

2.2.2   Clients in the SAP Landscape

After the SAP system has been installed with the delivered clients, the technical team or, more specifically, the system administration team (SAP NetWeaver) will need to create the number of clients that reflect the customer's needs. The general client structure for an SAP implementation includes a development client, a training client, a quality client, a preproduction client, and a production client.

The development client is where all development work should take place. You may create more than one development client. For example, you might have be a *sandbox client* for general users and SAP consultants to practice and test configurations. In addition, you may have a *clean* or *golden* development client where a specific configuration is made and from which this configuration is then transported to the quality client for review and testing before moving on to the production client.

A training client usually reflects the current production system and is used primarily for training project staff and end users. When configuration is transported to the production client, this configuration is transported to the training client at the same time. The training client is useful for training but isn't required for implementation. If no training client is available or created, then you can use the quality client for testing or training. A preproduction client is often created in SAP to test and check configurations, master data uploads, cutover balances uploads, business processes, customized objects, and reporting before these settings are finally transported to the production client.

To successfully manage this client environment, you'll need strict procedures and security measures to ensure that the integrity of clients is maintained.

2.2.3   Change and Transport System

Changes created in the development client must be moved, or transported, to the quality client for testing and then to the production client. The Change and Transport System (CTS) can be used to move objects such as programs, screens, configurations, or security settings from one client to another. CTS creates consistency between clients by maintaining log entries. CTS provides a standardized procedure for managing and recording changes made to a client.

When you're configuring functionality in a development client that has been designated as the client to migrate from, you'll find that saving the configuration will require extra steps.

On saving, the **Enter Change Request** dialog screen will require you to either add this configuration step to an existing Customizing request or to create a new request. If you opt to create a new request, another popup screen will appear that requires a short description of the change you're making and that may default the other information, such as your user ID, source client, category, and target client. If the target client is blank, make sure that you enter the correct target client for your change request, as shown in Figure 2.5.

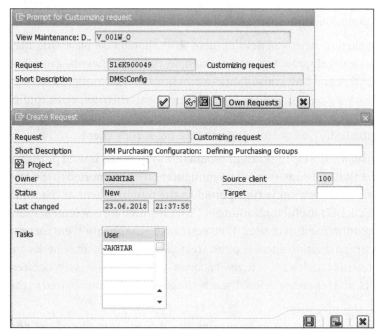

Figure 2.5 Creating and Saving a Customizing Request

On saving this change request, the system will display the change request number. The system will have saved the configuration change you've made and logged that change in the change request.

The change request can be viewed by using Transaction SE01. On the initial screen, enter the change request number or press F4 to find your request. Click on the display button to display the request. By expanding the view, you can see the changes that have been made to the tables in the current client and that will be migrated to the target client. If authorized, you may also release the change request so that these changes can be migrated. If you don't have authorization, the change request will need to be released by a designated SAP NetWeaver (SAP Basis) resource. By using Transaction SE10, you can see all requests and repairs owned by a specific user ID.

Now that you have a basic understanding of the various organizational units, let's move on to discuss how to create an organizational structure by looking at some common business scenarios.

2.3 Company Code

The company code is a familiar term in SAP, but understanding the difference between a physical company and a company as defined in the SAP system is important.

> **Example**
>
> In the following section, we'll create a new company code 1000 by copying from the SAP-delivered reference company code 0001. We'll create a new plant 6000, five new storage locations for the plant 6000, a new purchasing organization 6000, and some new purchasing groups. We'll also cover how to assign newly created organizational units with each other (for example, assigning the purchasing organization 6000 to the company code 1000).

2.3.1 What Is a Company?

The US Census Bureau (2002) defines a "company" as follows:

A company comprises all the establishments that operate under the ownership or control of a single organization. A company may be a business, service, or membership organization; it may consist of one or several establishments and operate at one or several locations. It includes all subsidiary organizations, all establishments that are majority-owned by the company or any subsidiary, and all the establishments that can be directed or managed by the company or any subsidiary.

SAP defines a "company" and a "company code" separately. SAP defines a "company" as the smallest organizational unit for which the organization must prepare legal financial statements. A company can contain one or more company codes, but these company codes must use the same chart of accounts and the same fiscal year breakdown.

SAP defines a company code as the smallest organizational unit for which a complete, self-contained set of accounts can be drawn up. You'll be able provide data for generating balance sheets and profit and loss (P&L) statements. A company code represents legally independent companies. Using more than one company code allows a customer to manage financial data for different independent companies at the same time. For example, a company that is in two different businesses (i.e., producing industrial chemicals and textile products) requires separate legal financial statements and thus will require two different company codes in the SAP system.

When deciding on an organizational structure, you can use one or many company codes. Thus, for example, if a US company has components of its organization in Canada and in Mexico, that company may decide to use two company codes. Company code currencies can be different for each component, but they must use the same chart of accounts.

2.3.2 Creating a Company Code

The creation of a company and company codes is usually part of configuring financials (FI), but you'll need to have some basic understanding of FI so as to integrate company code with MM organizational structure.

> **Tips & Tricks**
>
> In general, we *always* recommend that, when creating a company code, you copy a company code from an existing company code. In a standard system, company code 0001 is provided by SAP for this purpose. When you copy company codes, the system also copies parameters specific to company codes. If necessary, you can then change the specific data in the relevant application, which is less time consuming than creating a new company code and which also reduces the chance of error when maintaining the settings for a new company code.

The same tip of copying one SAP object to another should generally be followed for most configuration objects.

To copy a company code from an existing company code, follow the menu path **Enterprise Structure • Definition • Financial Accounting • Edit, Copy, Delete, Check Company Code**. Click on the company code **Copy** option and then click on the **Copy Organization Objects** button. As shown in Figure 2.6, enter "0001" in the **From Company Code** field (company code 0001 is SAP AG) and enter the code you want to create into the **To Company Code** field, which in our example is "1000." A company code can be alphanumeric and may have up to four characters. Click on the **OK** button, and a popup window will ask whether you want to copy the G/L account company code data. Click **Yes**. When a message appears concerning local currency, select the appropriate currency. You'll now see a message that outlines the completed activities.

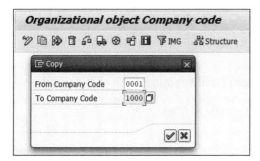

Figure 2.6 Copying a Company Code

At this point, you can edit the data in your newly created company code by following the navigation path **Enterprise Structure • Definition • Financial Accounting • Edit, Copy, Delete, Check Company Code • Select Edit Company Code Data**. By selecting your company code and clicking on the **Details** button, you can change the company name, city, country, currency, and language.

2.4   Plants

You may not think of yourself as working in a plant, but SAP uses the term "plant" to describe many different types of environments and business functions regardless of whether the plant is a physical location (such as a manufacturing unit, a head office, a warehouse) or a virtual location (such as a seaport).

2.4.1   What Is a Plant?

The definition of a plant depends on its use. From an MM view, a plant can be defined as a location that holds valuated stock. A production planning (PP) view defines a plant as an organizational unit that is central to planning production. A plant also can be defined as a location that contains service or maintenance facilities. The definition of a plant will vary depending on the needs of the customer.

The key characteristics of a plant are:

- A plant is assigned to a single company code. A company code can have several plants.
- Several storage locations in which material stocks are managed can belong to a single plant.
- A single business area is assigned to a plant and to a division.
- A plant can be assigned to several combinations of sales organization and distribution channels, which are the organizational structures in SD.
- A plant can have several shipping points. A shipping point can be assigned to several plants.
- A plant can be defined as a maintenance planning plant.

The plant plays an important role in the following areas:

- **Material valuation**
  If the valuation level is the plant, the material stocks are valuated at the plant level, and you can define the material prices for each plant. Each plant can have its own account determination.

- **Inventory management**
  The material stocks are managed within a plant.

- **Material requirements planning**
  Material requirements are planned for each plant. Each plant has its own materials requirements planning (MRP) data. Analyses for MRP can be made across plants.

- **Costing**
  In costing, valuation prices are defined only within a plant.

- **Plant maintenance**
  If a plant performs plant maintenance (PM) planning tasks, this plant defined as a maintenance planning plant. A maintenance planning plant can also carry out planning tasks for other plants (including other maintenance plants).

2.4.2 Prerequisites for a Plant

Before setting up a plant, certain other settings must be defined:

- **Factory calendar**
  We'll cover the factory calendar in Section 2.8.

- **Country key**
  A country key is required to define a plant. The system is delivered with country keys, and new country codes must be configured if they don't exist in the system. For example, the United States is represented by US, Switzerland represented by CH, Germany with DE, India with IN, and Pakistan with PK, and so on.

- **Region keys**
  A region code is required along with the country code. A region is defined as a state or province associated with a country. For example, if the country code is defined as US for the United States, the two-character region keys will represent the individual states and US protectorates such as Guam and Puerto Rico.

Let's now delve into the steps involved in defining and assigning a plant in the SAP system.

2.4.3 Defining a Plant

A four-character string defines the **Plant** field, which can be configured using Transaction OX10 or via the navigation path **Enterprise Structure • Definition • Logistics • General • Define, Copy, Delete, Check Plant**.

Tips & Tricks

We recommend creating a new plant by copying an existing one and then making the required changes (just as we discussed earlier with company codes). This method copies all of the dependent table entries into Customizing; otherwise, you'll need to maintain these manually.

To create a plant via the copy function, follow these steps:

1. Select **Copy, Delete, Check Plant**.

2. On the next screen, click on the **Copy Org Object** button and enter the **From Plant** and **To Plant** codes, as shown in Figure 2.7. For this example, create a new plant 6000 by copying the plant 1000.

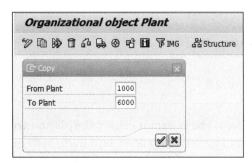

Figure 2.7 Creating Plant via Copy Function

3. Click on **OK**. Several prompts will appear to confirm the transfer of number ranges and other details from the reference plant to the new plant. Click **OK** or **Confirm** on all prompts.

4. To see the completed activities, enter the existing plant (from which data will be copied to the new plant) in the **From Plant** field and enter the new plant code in the **To Plant** field.

5. Select **Define Plant**, select the plant 6000, and either click on the details to define, as shown in Figure 2.8 and Figure 2.9, like the plant's address, the factory calendar, telephone numbers, and so on. The language can be set by clicking on the **Address** icon.

6. You can maintain a plant's material master data at the plant level for the following views on a material master record in particular: **MRP, Purchasing, Storage, Work Scheduling, Production Resources/Tools, Forecasting, Quality Management, Sales**, and **Costing**.

Note

If you are working for a US-based customer, you might have to select the tax jurisdiction code, which is used for determining tax rates in the United States. This code actually defines to which tax authority you must pay taxes. These jurisdiction codes are defined by SAP Finance consultants.

As mentioned earlier in Section 2.4.1, defining a plant as a valuation area is recommended over a company code.

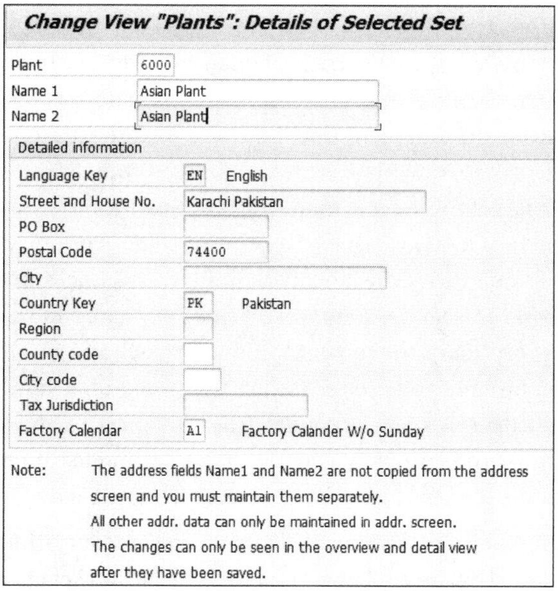

Figure 2.8 Defining a Plant

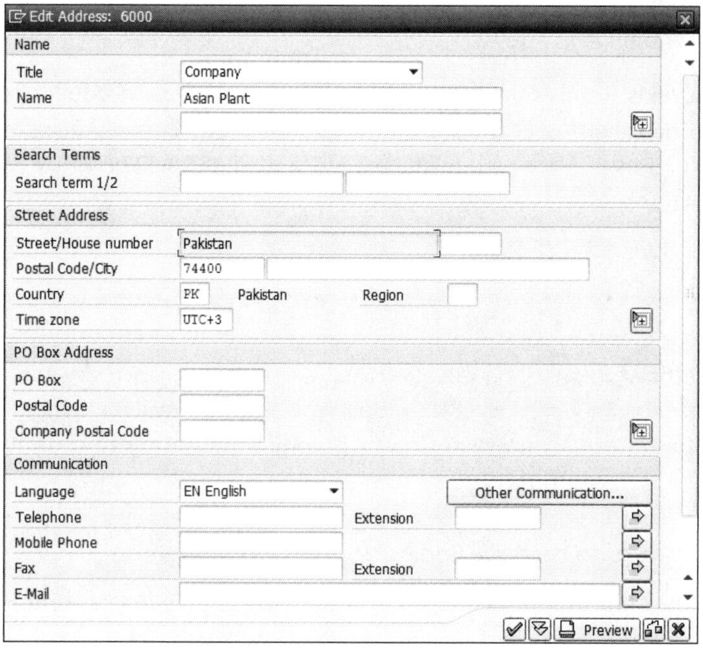

Figure 2.9 Maintaining Plant Address

2.4.4   Valuation Level

Stock materials can be managed in inventory on the basis of quantity, value, or both, depending on the material type of the material master record. For each material type, you can configure whether inventory management operates on a quantity basis, a value basis, or both. In a standard system, raw material (material type code ROH) is managed on a quantity and value basis. If the stock is managed on a quantity basis, as a result, every stock movement such as a goods issue or a goods receipt is noted in inventory management, and stock quantities are updated. Similarly, if stocks are managed on a value basis, the stock value that is a material value is updated in the financial book of accounts during every goods movement transaction such as a goods issue or a goods receipt. When you procure valuated materials (managed on a value basis), the stock value is updated into stock G/L accounts. The valuation of stock materials can be done at the plant or the company code level. Based on customer requirements, you may need to define the value area for the valuated materials.

The valuation level can be defined using Transaction OX14 or using the navigation path **Enterprise Structure • Definition • Logistics – General • Define Valuation Level**.

Two options are available:

- **Valuation Area is a Plant**
- **Valuation Level is a Company Code**

The valuation area/level is simply the level at which a company wants to valuate its inventory. If you define valuation at the plant level (recommended), you'll need to define a separate valuation area for each plant, and stock materials will be valuated separately for each plant.

Select the required option and click **Save**.

Note

SAP recommends setting the plant as a valuation area, which is necessary if you are using production planning (PP), product cost controlling (CO-PC), or SAP Retail. Once set, you cannot switch the valuation level from plant to company code, or vice versa.

2.4.5   Assigning a Plant to a Company Code

On agreeing and establishing the valuation level, you can assign a plant to an existing company code. This assignment is performed so that all plant transactions can be attributed to a single legal entity, that is, a company code. This assignment can be achieved in Transaction OX18 or by using the navigation path **Enterprise Structure • Assignment • Logistics – General • Assign Plant to Company Code**.

Figure 2.10 shows the assignment of plants to company codes. One company code can have multiple plants, so you can assign multiple plants to a company code on this screen. You can also enter multiple company codes and their respective plants and save these settings.

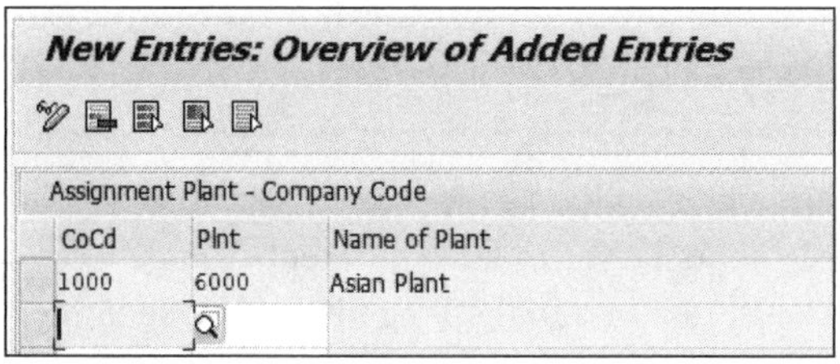

Figure 2.10 Assignment of Plants to Company Codes

In this section, we described the importance of the plant within an organizational structure. In the next section, we'll turn to storage location functionality.

2.5 Storage Locations

After the plant level, the next level in a physical structure defined in MM is the storage location. A storage location is a physical or virtual location to store a material. Each storage location is assigned to a plant. You can assign multiple storage locations to a plant, but you cannot assign a storage location to multiple plants. Let's now first define a storage location and then assign it to a plant.

2.5.1 What Is a Storage Location?

In its systems, SAP traditionally defines a storage location as a place where stock is physically kept within a plant. At least one storage location will always be defined for a plant. A storage location is the lowest level of location definition within the MM functionality. Regarding a physical storage location, no set rules limit what it should look like. Some SAP customers may have a highly developed inventory-monitoring system that uniquely defines a physical location, storage bin, an open yard, a tank, tray, drawer, cabinet, and so on, as a location that contains inventory separate from other inventory. Depending on the physical size of the materials involved, a storage location may be as small as a 5 cm^3 bin or as large as an entire building.

Some customers may not have sophisticated inventory systems, and you may be working with a location that has no obvious storage definitions. Assessing the current state of your storage and evaluating proposals for reengineering your storage facilities are appropriate tasks before trying to define storage locations. For example, when lead time is involved among various production operations or steps, storage locations are created on the shop floor (production floor) to store semifinished or semiproduced materials.

Example

In real-world business scenarios, most clients prefer to have different storage locations for different types of materials (e.g., raw material storage locations, semifinished storage locations, finished goods storage locations, and scrap material storage locations). Let's consider a real-world example involving a leading pharmaceutical manufacturing company. The company has created an expired goods storage location apart from the storage locations for raw material, semifinished materials, finished materials, and spare parts. As soon as a material's shelf-life expiration date (SLED) has been reached, the material is moved automatically, through a batch job, from the finished goods storage location to the expiry goods storage location. Stock in an expiry goods storage location is not considered for planning purposes, in other words, not included in stock and demand planning.

A storage location has the following attributes:

- One or more storage locations may exist within a plant. For example, a plant in Florida may have multiple and separate storage locations, such as for raw materials, semifinished products, and scrap materials.
- A storage location has a description and at least one address.
- Storing material data specific to a storage location is possible.
- Stocks are managed only on a quantity basis and not on a value basis at the storage location level. (Valuation is either at the plant level or at the company code level.)
- Physical inventories are carried out at the storage location level.
- A storage location can be assigned to a warehouse number in warehouse management (WM). You can assign more than one storage location to the same warehouse number within a plant.

- Storage locations are always created for a plant and cannot be created independently of a plant.

2.5.2   Defining a Storage Location

A four-character string defines a storage location, which can be configured using Transaction OX09 or via the navigation path **Enterprise Structure • Definition • Materials Management • Maintain Storage Location**.

Enter the plant number in the **Plant** field in initial screen of Transaction OX09, as shown in Figure 2.11. On the screen that opens, click the **New Entries** icon, and then you'll add the storage location number and a description. You can then highlight your new storage location and click on the addresses of storage locations in the dialog structure. Click on the **New Entries** icon to enter a number for the storage location address, which can be up to three characters. Once entered, you'll be directed to another screen to enter secondary information such as a physical address and telephone number.

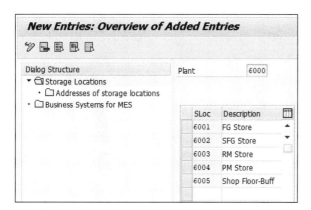

Figure 2.11 Creating Storage Locations

2.5.3   Automatic Creation of Storage Locations

You can create storage locations automatically when an inward goods movement for a material is performed. The configuration needs the plant and/or the type of movement to be defined to allow the automatic creation of storage locations. This configuration can reduce the data maintenance effort for storage locations. The automatic storage location will only be activated if the movement is for normal stock, not special stock.

This configuration can be performed using Transaction OMB3 or via the navigation path **Materials Management • Inventory Management and Physical Inventory • Goods Receipt • Create Storage Location Automatically**.

Automatic creation of storage locations can be set for each plant as needed, as shown in Figure 2.12, or for a particular goods movement, as shown in Figure 2.13.

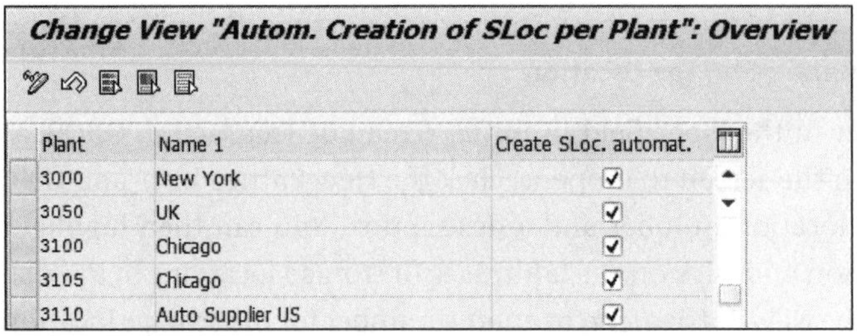

Change View "Autom. Creation of SLoc per Plant": Overview

Plant	Name 1	Create SLoc. automat.
3000	New York	✓
3050	UK	✓
3100	Chicago	✓
3105	Chicago	✓
3110	Auto Supplier US	✓

Figure 2.12 Automatic Storage Location Creation by Plant

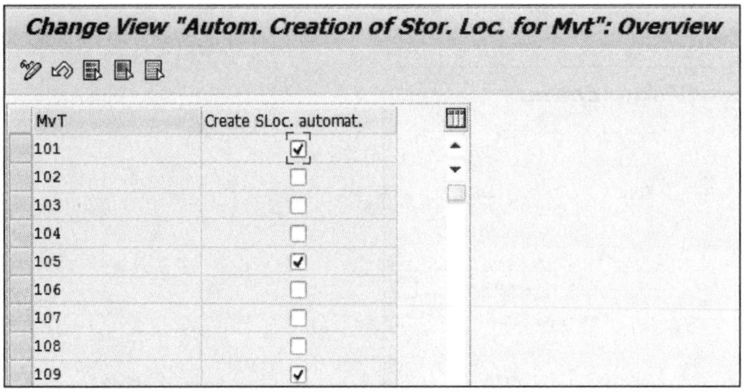

Change View "Autom. Creation of Stor. Loc. for Mvt": Overview

MvT	Create SLoc. automat.
101	✓
102	☐
103	☐
104	☐
105	✓
106	☐
107	☐
108	☐
109	✓

Figure 2.13 Automatic Storage Location Creation by Movement Type

In the next section, we'll cover setting up an organizational structure in MM that pertains to the procurement and purchasing processes of a company.

2.6   Purchasing Organization

The purchasing department of a company may be a single person calling vendors manually or may consist of hundreds of purchasing agents spread across the world using Internet-based purchasing. Thus, the purchasing organization is an important element in the procurement of materials.

In the following sections, we'll cover what a purchasing organization is and describe different types of purchasing organizations. We'll also cover how to assign a purchasing organization to our previously configured company code 1000 and plant 6000.

2.6.1   What Is a Purchasing Organization?

The purchasing function for SAP customers can range from quite simple to very complex. The largest SAP customers may spend hundreds of millions of dollars in purchasing each year and have a sophisticated purchasing department that works at many different levels, from strategic global procurement to low-level vendor relationships. SAP can be defined to allow all purchasing departments to be accurately reflected.

A *purchasing organization* is simply defined as a group of purchasing activities associated with all or a specific part of the enterprise.

2.6.2   Types of Purchasing Organizations

Several types of purchasing organizations are used, including on the enterprise, company, and plant levels. A reference purchasing organization can also be defined. Let's briefly each of these types.

Plant-Specific Purchasing Organization

Let's say you have separate purchasing departments for each plant, and each purchasing department is responsible for negotiating with vendors, creating contracts, and issuing purchase orders. This scenario is called a *plant-specific purchasing organization*. In this scenario, you'll need to define a purchasing organization for each plant in the SAP system and then assign these purchasing organizations to their respective plants. For example, let's say your customer has two different company codes, and each company code has plants assigned to it. Company code 1 has two plants, and company code 2 has one plant. Additionally, each plant has a separate purchasing organization. Purchasing organization 1, purchasing organization 2, and purchasing organization 3 are assigned to plant 1, plant 2, and plant 3, respectively.

Cross-Plant Purchasing Organization

In this scenario, a single purchasing department is responsible for procurement activities for more than one plant. In this case, you'll need to create a purchasing organization that's responsible for more than one plant in the same company code.

For example, your customer may have two different company codes, and each company code has plants assigned to it. Company code 1 has two plants, and Company code 2 has one plant. Purchasing organization 1 is assigned to plant 1 and plant 2 because this purchasing organization responsible for both of the plants in company code 1.

Cross-Company Code/Corporate Group-Wide Purchasing Organization

Some customers have just one purchasing organization for the procurement activities of multiple plants in different company codes. For example, let's say your customer has two different company codes, and each has one or more plants assigned to it. Company code 1 has two plants, and company code 2 has one plant. Purchasing organization 1 is assigned to plant 1, plant 2, and plant 3 of company code 1 and company code 2.

A world leader in printing papers, headquartered in France, has more than 15 company codes and 50 plants—and all of the plants are assigned to a single purchasing organization. In this way, this one purchasing organization controls all vendor negotiations and is thus responsible for high-volume orders, which increases their negotiation power. Using a single purchasing organization also makes it easier to maintain and track long-term contracts with vendors.

> **Note**
>
> In Customizing, you can assign a purchasing organization to a company code and plant. In cross-company code purchasing organizations, you'll need to assign purchasing organizations to plants only. Don't assign purchasing organizations to company codes.

Reference Purchasing Organization

Some customers may have a scenario where one centralized purchasing department at the corporate group level is responsible for the negotiation and creation of global agreements. These agreements are used by local purchasing organizations to create purchase orders. This business scenario helps companies negotiate better prices due to high-volume purchases. In an SAP system, such a purchasing organization is referred to as a *reference purchasing organization*.

For example, let's say a client has two different company codes, and each company code has plants assigned to it. Company code 1 has two plants, and company code 2 has one plant. Each plant has a separate purchasing organization: Purchasing organization 1, purchasing organization 2, and purchasing organization 3 are assigned to plant 1, plant 2, and plant 3, respectively.

Purchasing organization 4 is assigned to purchasing organization 1, purchasing organization 2, and purchasing organization 3. Purchasing organization 4 is the reference purchasing organization. The reference purchasing organization can negotiate with vendors and create global outline agreements (contracts and scheduling agreements). Plant-specific purchasing organizations (i.e., purchasing organization 1, purchasing organization 2, and purchasing organization 3) can issue purchase orders to vendors with reference to these global agreements.

Standard Purchasing Organization

SAP also provides a *standard purchasing organization*, which can be used to create automatic purchase orders. In the automatic purchase order creation process, the system needs to find the purchasing organization. The system gets the plant code from the purchase requisition and, from the plant code system, determines the standard purchasing organization (because the standard purchasing organization is assigned to the plant). Finally, a purchase order is created.

Now that you have a thorough understanding of the different types of purchasing organizations and their business functions, let's move forward to learning how to create them in an SAP system.

2.6.3   Creating a Purchasing Organization

To create a purchasing organization, follow the menu path **Enterprise Structure • Definition • Materials Management • Maintain Purchasing Organization**.

As shown in Figure 2.14, create a new purchasing organization (6000), give it a short description, and save your entry.

Figure 2.14 Creating a Purchasing Organization

2.6.4   Assigning a Purchasing Organization to a Company Code

In a scenario where a purchasing organization is responsible for the plants of one company code only, follow the menu path **Enterprise Structure • Assignment • Materials Management**, as shown in Figure 2.15.

Based on your business scenario, various options are available for assigning purchasing organizations. In this screen, you'll see all of the purchasing organizations you've created in previous steps and can assign the company code to the purchasing organization, as shown in Figure 2.15.

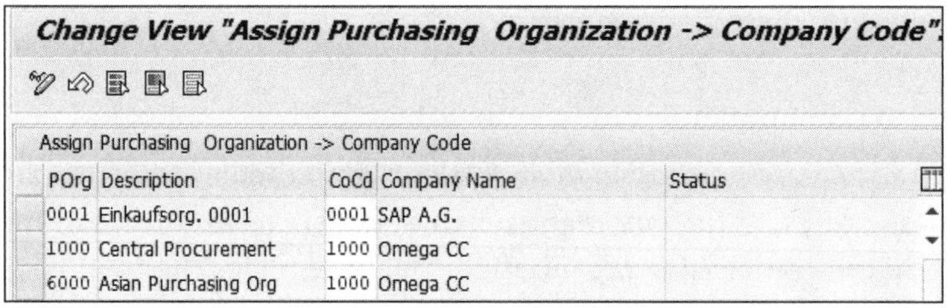

Change View "Assign Purchasing Organization -> Company Code"

Assign Purchasing Organization -> Company Code

POrg	Description	CoCd	Company Name	Status	
0001	Einkaufsorg. 0001	0001	SAP A.G.		
1000	Central Procurement	1000	Omega CC		
6000	Asian Purchasing Org	1000	Omega CC		

Figure 2.15 Assigning a Purchasing Organization to a Company Code

> **Note**
>
> Assigning a purchasing organization to a company code is required only when you want to create a purchasing organization specific to a certain company code. After you assign a purchasing organization to a company code, you can't assign this purchasing organization to any other company codes or plants.
>
> Remember that, for a cross-company code purchasing organization, you won't assign the purchasing organization to a company code. A cross-company code purchasing organization may be responsible for procurement activities for several plants, and those activities belong to different company codes.

2.6.5   Assigning a Purchasing Organization to a Plant

Assigning a purchasing organization to a plant is mandatory and will enable the creation of procurement elements, such as purchase orders, for that plant. To assign a purchasing organization to one or more plants, follow the menu path **Enterprise Structure • Assignment • Materials Management • Assign Purchasing Organization to Plant**. As shown in Figure 2.16, for our example, let's assign the purchasing organization 6000 to the plant 6000. Save your entry.

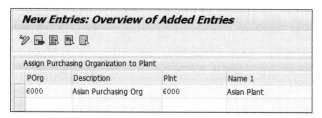

Figure 2.16 Assigning a Purchasing Organization to a Plant

In a cross-plant purchasing organization scenario, you'll assign a purchasing organization to multiple plants with the following options:

- One purchasing organization procures for one plant (plant-specific purchasing).
- One purchasing organization procures for several plants (cross-plant purchasing).
- Several purchasing organizations procure for one plant (a combination of plant-specific purchasing organization, cross-plant purchasing organization, and cross-company code purchasing organization).

If several purchasing organizations procure for a certain plant, you can define one of them as the standard purchasing organization for pipeline procurement, consignment, and stock transfer scenarios. This standard purchasing organization will be used by the system when performing source determination for stock transfers and consignment.

For goods issues of pipeline materials, the purchasing information records of the standard purchasing organization are read. To assign the standard purchasing organization to a plant, follow the path **Enterprise Structure • Assignment • Materials Management • Assign Standard Purchasing Organization to Plant**.

You can define one standard purchasing organization for each plant, and this purchasing organization is automatically proposed and selected by the system while creating automatic purchase orders.

2.6.6 Assigning a Purchasing Organization to a Reference Purchasing Organization

In your enterprise, you may have a scenario where one purchasing department wants to refer to the purchasing terms and conditions of another purchasing department. In SAP system, the referred purchasing department becomes the **Reference Purchasing Organization**. Thus, when a purchasing organization is assigned to a reference purchasing organization, the former can use the already negotiated terms of purchases, such as rate per unit, discount based on volume, payment terms, and so on.

To set this reference up, follow the path **Enterprise Structure • Assignment • Materials Management • Assign Purchasing Organization to Ref Purchasing Organization**. The screen shown in Figure 2.17 will appear.

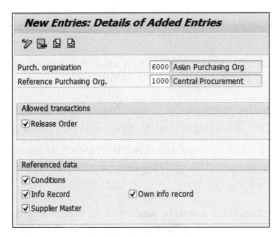

Figure 2.17 Assigning a Reference Purchasing Organization to a Purchasing Organization

In addition to the assignment, the following settings need to be configured:

- **Allowed transactions—Release Order**
  Select this checkbox when a purchasing organization is allowed to create contract release orders (purchase orders) from the contracts of the referenced purchasing organization.

- **Referenced data—Conditions**
  Select this checkbox when a purchasing organization wants to refer only to conditions from the contracts of the reference purchasing organization. (When a purchasing organization wants to refer conditions and create contract release orders from contracts of a referenced purchasing organization, select both checkboxes.)

- **Referenced data—Info Record**
  Select this checkbox to allow access to the info record of the reference purchasing organization.

- **Referenced data—Own info record**
  Selecting this checkbox will mean that the info record of the reference purchasing organization is only read if no info record has been maintained for the operative

purchasing organization. In the case of info updates from purchasing documents, the info record found is updated. A new info record for the operative purchasing organization is only created if no info record exists for the reference purchasing organization.

- **Referenced data—Supplier Master**
  Selecting this checkbox will enable access to the supplier master (vendor) of the reference purchasing organization.

2.7 Purchasing Groups

A purchasing group can be defined as a person (or a group of people) dealing with a certain material (or a group of materials) purchased by the purchasing organization. The purchasing group is defined in configuration via navigation path **Materials Management • Purchasing • Create Purchasing Groups**.

Enter a three-character alphanumeric code into **Purchasing Group** field along with a description (**Desc. Pur. Grp**), telephone number (**Tel.No. Pur.Grp**), and **Fax number**. Figure 2.18 shows details about purchasing group that have already been created.

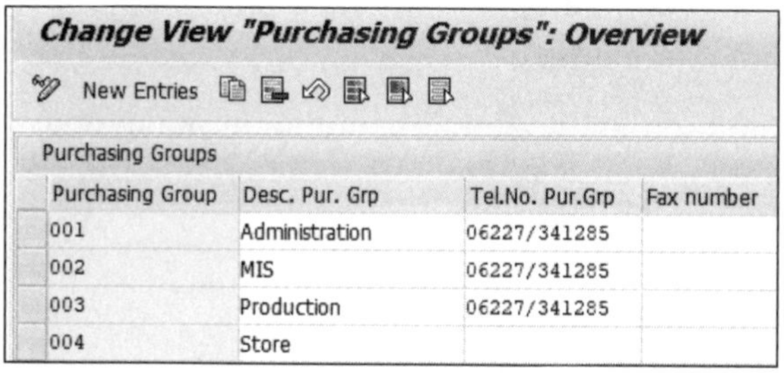

Purchasing Group	Desc. Pur. Grp	Tel.No. Pur.Grp	Fax number
001	Administration	06227/341285	
002	MIS	06227/341285	
003	Production	06227/341285	
004	Store		

Change View "Purchasing Groups": Overview

New Entries

Purchasing Groups

Figure 2.18 Creating Purchasing Groups

2.8 SAP Calendar

For all business functions of the company, such as procurement, production, materials planning and scheduling, to effectively take place, a calendar must exist in the SAP system. This calendar is then assigned to the plant. You'll have to first define each national holiday and then combine all of the individual holidays into a holiday calendar. This holiday calendar is then assigned to the factory calendar.

The SAP calendar creation function includes three individual steps:

- Defining holidays
- Creating a holiday calendar
- Defining a factory calendar and assigning a holiday calendar to it

To create a new calendar, use Transaction SCAL or follow the configuration menu path **SAP NetWeaver • General Settings • Maintain Calendar**. On the screen shown in Figure 2.19, maintain the requisite details, such as public holidays, holiday calendar, and factory calendar, in the same sequence.

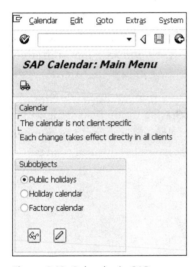

Figure 2.19 Calendar in SAP

In the following sections, we'll go into more detail about the different calendar options.

2.8.1   Public Holidays

Select the **Public holidays** radio button shown earlier in Figure 2.19 and then click the **Change** icon. Select the **New Holiday** icon, which will then allow you to indicate whether a holiday is a fixed date or a floating date. A floating public holiday depends on factors such as moon phases to determine the actual date of the holiday. As shown in Figure 2.20, selecting **Floating Public Holiday** ❶ leads to the **Floating Public Holidays** dialog box ❷, where you'll set the holiday to any specific date or day, or even set the holiday to sync with religious denominations, such as Buddhist, Christian, Islamic, or Jewish calendars.

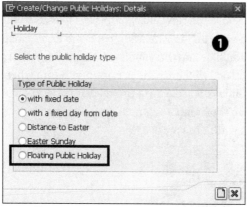

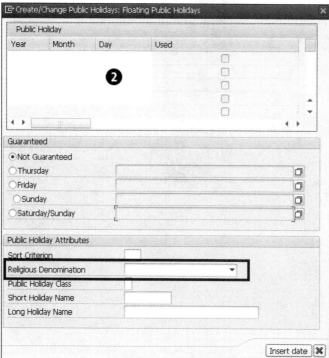

Figure 2.20 Public Holidays

2.8.2   Holiday Calendar

After defining and saving a public holiday, you'll return to the screen shown earlier in Figure 2.19, where you can select the **Holiday Calendar** radio button, which will show a list of all the holidays defined so far. Choose the **New Entry** icon, which leads to the screen shown in Figure 2.21. After you provide an identification code and a short text for the holiday calendar in this screen, you'll define the validity of the holiday calendar. Next, select the **Assign Holiday** button, which opens a popup window where you'll select all of the relevant public holidays by selecting the relevant checkboxes. Press ⌈Enter⌉ to confirm and, finally, save the holiday calendar. You'll be returned to the original **SAP Calendar** screen, shown earlier in Figure 2.19.

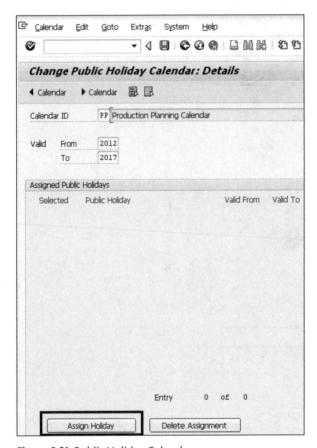

Figure 2.21 Public Holiday Calendar

2.8.3   Factory Calendar

Finally, on the screen shown earlier in Figure 2.19, select the **Factory calendar** radio button, which opens the screen shown in Figure 2.22, where you'll enter the validity date for the factory calendar, assign a **Holiday Calendar ID**, and define workdays. You can also define **Special Rules** to denote any holiday (off day) as a workday.

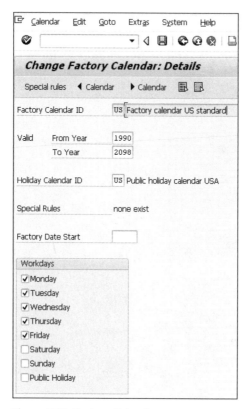

Figure 2.22 Factory Calendar

2.9   Summary

In this chapter, you've seen that knowledge of organizational structures in SAP is important to anyone working on an SAP implementation project. Each company will create its own version of the SAP landscape, including Change and Transport System (CTS) and other technical elements. Understanding these elements and how your company adopts them as well as the principles of the MM structure are important to anyone working with SAP systems, whether as an MM consultant or while advising on the organizational structure.

In the next chapter, we'll cover a wide range of master data in MM, from the material master and vendor master, to batch management data and serial number data.

Chapter 3
Configuring the Material Master

Materials management (MM) includes a number of important master data including the material master, which is at the core of the business processes for procurement, inventory management, production, quality assurance, accounting, and invoice verification.

Master data in materials management (MM) requires a significant amount of understanding, not only on the part of the SAP consultant but also on the part of the SAP customer. When implementing SAP, customers are usually transitioning from one or more legacy systems. A key aspect of any implementation is the conversion of existing data to the master data in SAP.

A fundamental indicator of a successful implementation is the level to which the data has been correctly converted into SAP master data. In this chapter, we'll examine one of the most important kinds of master data, the material master and its associated configuration, which is integral to MM.

3.1 Material Master

The material master is the repository of the data used for a material. The material master serves as a single source of information for each material; it's where all information about a material is entered and accessed from. The material master is used throughout the SAP system and by different business users.

When implementing SAP, the information contained in the material master can be overwhelming. When examining an existing system, such as a BPCS, JD Edwards, Oracle, or Lawson system, you may find that product or material files contain only a fraction of the material master data required for an SAP system to function. In the following sections, we'll discuss the factors you should consider when defining and configuring the material master. Next, we'll cover material number ranges and then delve into defining material types to meet specific business needs.

While Chapter 4 and Chapter 5 cover the material master in great detail, understanding the main attributes of material master data—the material number, industry sector, and material type, as shown in Figure 3.1—is important. The *material number* is a unique 18- to 40-character field that can be entered manually or can be created automatically by the system, based on the type of number assignment. For an external number assignment, you can enter the material number manually; for an internal number assignment, the system creates the material number automatically when you save the material master record. The *industry sector* controls the screen setup and screen sequence. The SAP system includes predefined industry sectors, but if any specific requirement doesn't match these predefined sectors, you can create your own.

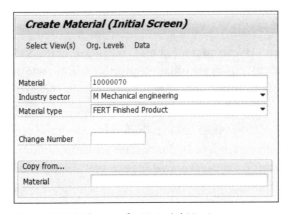

Figure 3.1 Attributes of a Material Master

Material types have many controlling functions, including the following:

- Number assignment
- Number range
- Procurement type
- Screen setup (i.e., allowed views, field selection, and screen sequence)
- Price control
- Account determination
- Quantity and value updating in plants

SAP provides preconfigured material types, but you can also create your own by copying the standard material types and making the required changes. Some of the SAP-provided material types are:

- ROH: Raw material
- HALB: Semifinished material
- FERT: Finished material
- HAWA: Trading material

3.2   Configuring a New Material Type

A material type is a definition of a group of materials with similar attributes, such as raw material, semifinished material, finished material, or consumable material. A material type must be assigned to each material record entered into the material master.

To configure a new material type, use Transaction OMS2 or follow the menu path **Logistics – General • Material Master • Basic Settings • Material Types • Define Attributes of Material Types**.

On the screen that appears, you can either make changes to an SAP-provided material type (such as ROH, HAWA, DIEN, HALB, or FERT), or you can create a new material. For the latter, click on the **New Entries** button or copy an existing material type and make the required changes. For our example, copy the existing material type ROH (raw material) to create the new material type ZCON. For example, for a confectionary, all new raw materials used in producing candy will be categorized in this new material type ZCON.

Tips & Tricks

While creating a new material type, we recommend copying an SAP-provided material type and then making changes, instead of starting from scratch. Otherwise, you'll need to maintain multiple settings and screens, which can be time consuming and has a high chance of errors or missing settings.

For additional settings, select the material type from the **MTyp** column and click on the **Details** button. The details of the selected material type ZCON are shown in Figure 3.2. Depending on your business needs, make the following key settings in material types, as shown in Figure 3.2:

- **Field reference (field reference key)**
  This setting determines the field status such as required, hidden, display, and optional. As shown in Figure 3.2, you can enter "ROH" in the **Field reference** field.

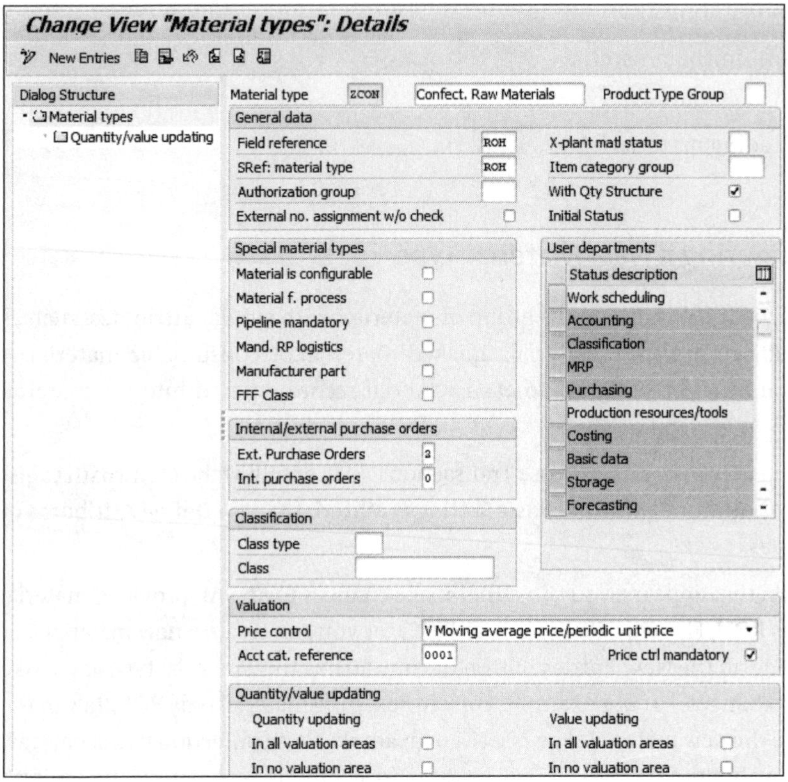

Figure 3.2 Creating a New Material Type

- **User departments (views in the material master)**

  User departments such as purchasing, sales, and production are referred to as views in the material master. This setting determines which views can be selected for the material type. For example, a sales view is essential for finished goods because the sales department needs to maintain data specific to selling materials. Similarly, a purchasing view is necessary for raw materials and packing materials to enable their purchase.

- **Pipeline mandatory**

  This setting determines whether pipeline handling is possible or mandatory. This setting also determines whether external and/or internal purchase orders or quantity and value updates are possible. Pipeline materials are used in continuous process chemical industries, such as oil refineries. Crude petroleum is issued to production for refining via a pipeline. Water or gas supplied to a fertilizer industry by the utilities companies are other examples of pipeline materials. (We'll discuss price control in more detail in Chapter 5.)

- **Ext. Purchase Orders/Int. purchase orders (type of procurement)**
  This setting determines whether internal procurement, external procurement, or both are allowed.

- **Price control**
  You can select **Standard Price** or **Moving average price/periodic unit price** for a material type, as shown in Figure 3.2. The selected price control is copied (default) when you create a material master record, but you can change the price control from a standard price to moving average price, and vice versa. If the **Price ctrl mandatory** checkbox is selected, the price control method selected in the material type can't be changed while creating a material master record.

After you've selected the material type, click on the **Quantity/value updating** folder (on the left side of the screen).

As shown in Figure 3.3, you'll need to select **Qty updating** and **Value Update** in each valuation area. The significance of these fields is as follows:

- **Qty updating**
  Specifies that the material is managed on a quantity basis in the material master record for the relevant valuation area.

- **Value Update**
  Specifies that the material is managed on a value basis in the material master record for the valuation area concerned. The values are updated in the respective general ledger (G/L) accounts at the same time.

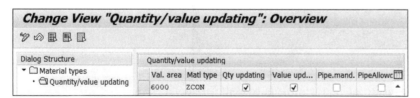

Figure 3.3 Quantity and Value Updating in a Material Type

An issue that SAP customers often face when converting their item files over to the material master is whether to keep their legacy numbering scheme, that is, whether to continue entering their own material numbers. SAP can also automatically assign incremental material numbers.

Often, legacy systems have a meaningful material numbering scheme. This numbering may have been in place for some time, and staff members will probably be most comfortable with this numbering scheme. To simplify maintenance, the automatic assignment of material numbers is the best choice. When working with relevant stakeholders, be aware that that you'll need to discuss whether to use a meaningful numbering scheme in SAP, and these discussions can lead to informed business decisions on material numbering in general.

The material number field is defined in configuration using Transaction OMSL or following the navigation path **Logistics – General • Material Master • Basic Settings • Define Output Format for Material Numbers**. Figure 3.4 shows the configuration screen for defining the output format for material numbers.

This configuration screen doesn't have many input fields but is extremely important when initially defining the material master. After deciding on material master numbering scheme, you'll first enter the length of the material number in the **Material No. Length** field.

Then, you may decide that automatically assigned material numbers must be in a certain format. In this case, you'll define the template and the special characters required. Figure 3.4 shows a template defined for internally assigned material numbers.

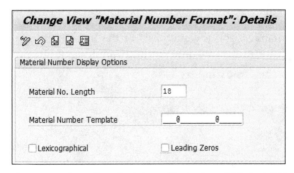

Figure 3.4 Template for Internally Assigned Material Numbers

In this case, let's say you require that material numbers follow this format: 123@45678901@23456. The only character that can't be used in a template is an underscore because that symbol is used to signify a nontemplate field.

The two other fields in Transaction OMSL deal with how a material number is stored and how SAP determines numbers.

The **Lexicographical** indicator is only relevant for numeric material numbers, either internally or externally defined. As shown in Figure 3.4, the **Lexicographical** indicator isn't set, which means that numbers are stored with leading zeros that are right justified. For example, if a user enters the number "12345678," the number will be stored as 000000000012345678, with 10 leading zeros.

If the **Lexicographical** indicator is set, then the numeric number isn't right justified and isn't padded with zeros. Instead, the field acts more like a character string, where the leading zero becomes a valid character.

In the following example, the **Lexicographical** indicator has been set. A user entering material "12345678" finds that the material number is stored as 12345678 with no padding. If the user then entered "0012345678," this value is stored as entered as a completely different material number in SAP. However, an internally assigned material number is padded with leading zeros, for example, 000000000012345678. Therefore, now three separate material numbers exist in the system.

Remember that the **Lexicographical** indicator can't be changed after numeric material numbers exist in the system, so this option must be decided before any tests are run in the system.

The other field in Transaction OMSL is the **Leading Zeros** indicator. If this indicator is set, then the material number is shown with leading zeros. However, if the **Lexicographical** indicator is set, then the **Leading Zeros** indicator is ignored by the system.

> **Note**
>
> SAP S/4HANA allows a material master number to be extended from the standard 18 characters up to 40 characters. To activate this functionality, follow the configuration path **Cross-Application Components • General Application Functions • Field Length Extension • Activate Extended Fields**. As shown in Figure 3.5, be sure to read and follow SAP Note 2232396 before activating this functionality.

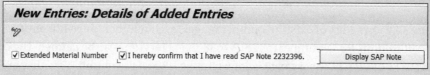

Figure 3.5 Material Master Up to 40 Characters Long in SAP S/4HANA

3.3 Defining a Number Range for a Material Type

In this step, you'll define the type of number assignments and the number of range intervals for material master records. When creating a material master record, each material must have a unique number. Two ways of defining a number range exist:

- **Internal number assignment**
  A number within the defined number range is assigned by the SAP system.

- **External number assignment**
  You'll assign a number within the defined number range interval. You can define the intervals for external number assignments numerically as well as alphanumerically.

You can also define both an internal and an external number range interval for the material type. In real-world scenarios, most companies use internal number assignment when they want numerical number ranges for materials, so that the system automatically assigns the unique material number serially and incrementally. In cases where alphanumerical number ranges are desired, use external number assignment.

To configure a number range for material types, use Transaction MMNR or follow the menu path **Logistics – General** • **Material Master** • **Basic Settings** • **Material Types** • **Define Number Range for each Material Type**. As shown in Figure 3.6, click on the change **Intervals** button (pencil), which brings up the screen shown in Figure 3.7.

Figure 3.6 Material Master Number Range Maintenance

Figure 3.7 shows a list of existing number ranges; each number range is identified in the first column, **No**. A number range up to 18 characters long can be defined. The current status of each number range is shown in the **NR Status** column. Note that number ranges cannot overlap with each other.

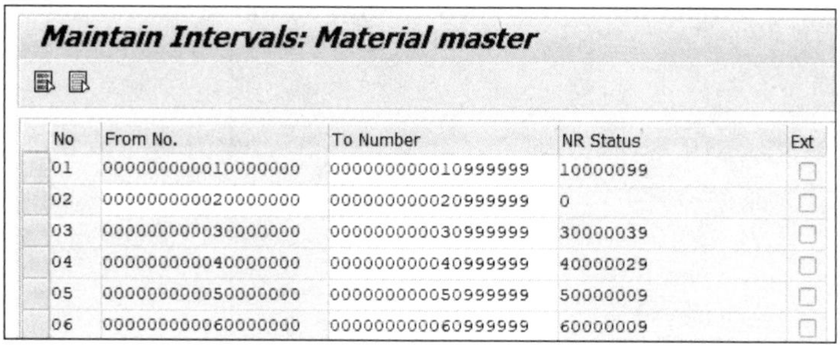

Maintain Intervals: Material master

No	From No.	To Number	NR Status	Ext
01	00000000010000000	000000000010999999	10000099	☐
02	000000000020000000	000000000020999999	0	☐
03	000000000030000000	000000000030999999	30000039	☐
04	000000000040000000	000000000040999999	40000029	☐
05	00000000050000000	000000000050999999	50000009	☐
06	00000000060000000	000000000060999999	60000009	☐

Figure 3.7 Available Number Ranges

As a first step in creating a new number range, click on the define groups icon, as shown in Figure 3.6, which brings up the screen shown in Figure 3.8. Click on the new icon ☐ to create a new number range group. Creating a number range group and then assigning individual material types to this group will enable to system to assign the defined number range each time a new material of the assigned material types is created in the SAP system.

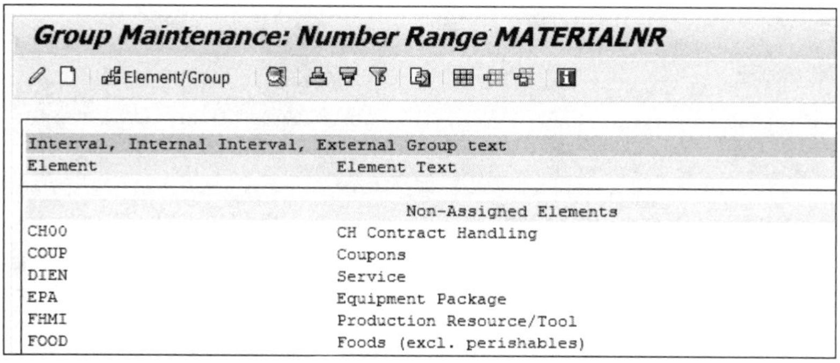

Group Maintenance: Number Range MATERIALNR

✎ ☐ ⊞ Element/Group   🔲 🖨 ▽ ▼ 🗇 ⊞ ⊞ ⊞ 🔢

Interval, Internal Interval, External Group text Element	Element Text
	Non-Assigned Elements
CH00	CH Contract Handling
COUP	Coupons
DIEN	Service
EPA	Equipment Package
FHMI	Production Resource/Tool
FOOD	Foods (excl. perishables)

Figure 3.8 Group Maintenance Numbering of the Material Master

As you'll soon see, you can have a one-to-many assignment of a number range group to a material type; that is, one number range group can have multiple material types assigned to it. However, you cannot assign one material type to multiple material number groups.

As shown in Figure 3.9, click on the **Insert Interval**, maintain the text of group name in the **Group** field, and define a new number range in the **From number** and **To number** fields by entering "10000000000" and "19999999999," respectively. Save your entry, and the system will bring up the screen shown in Figure 3.10.

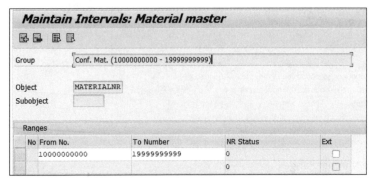

Figure 3.9 Inserting a New Number Range

In our example, the newly defined number range has the identifier **23** in the **No** column, as shown in Figure 3.10.

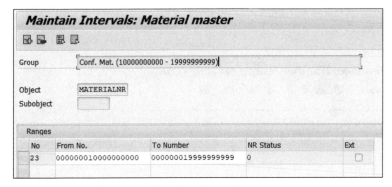

Figure 3.10 Number Range Identification Assigned

Now, to assign the newly created number range group 23 to the newly created material type ZCON, place the cursor in the material type **ZCON** and click on the **Element/ Group** button, as shown in Figure 3.11. The popup shown in Figure 3.12 will appear.

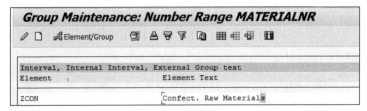

Figure 3.11 Material Type with Unassigned Number Range

As shown in Figure 3.12, select the newly created number range **23** and click **OK**.

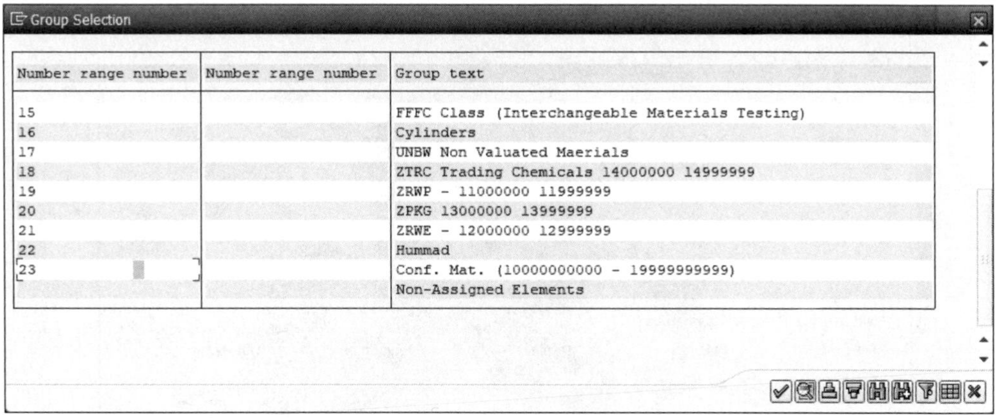

Number range number	Number range number	Group text
15		FFFC Class (Interchangeable Materials Testing)
16		Cylinders
17		UNBW Non Valuated Maerials
18		ZTRC Trading Chemicals 14000000 14999999
19		ZRWP – 11000000 11999999
20		ZPKG 13000000 13999999
21		ZRWE – 12000000 12999999
22		Hummad
23		Conf. Mat. (10000000000 – 19999999999)
		Non-Assigned Elements

(Group Selection)

Figure 3.12 Number Range Group Selection for Material Type Assignment

Figure 3.13 shows the assignment of the material type **ZCON** to the number range **23**.

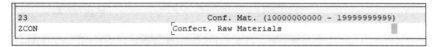

23	Conf. Mat. (10000000000 – 19999999999)
ZCON	Confect. Raw Materials

Figure 3.13 New Number Range Assigned to Material Type ZCON

3.4   Defining Field Selections

The field status of a field in material master data is controlled by the following:

- Material type
- Transaction code
- Industry sector
- Plant
- Procurement type (internal/external)

Similar fields are organized under different groups called *field selection groups*. For example, **Field selection group 1** contains two fields, **Base Unit of Measure** and **Unit of Measurement Text**, as shown in Figure 3.14.

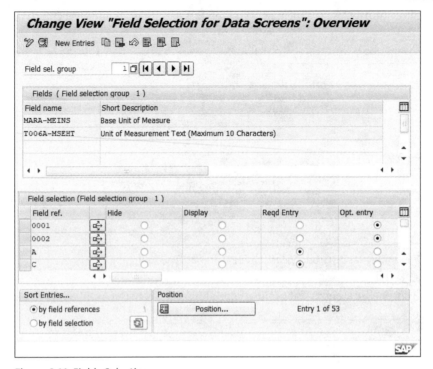

Figure 3.14 Fields Selection

A field reference key is assigned to each of the different controlling units, such as material types, transaction codes, industry sectors, plants, and procurement types. For example, field reference keys DIEN and MM03 are assigned to the service material type transaction and the display material transaction, respectively.

Maintain the field status for the combination of field selection group and field reference key, as shown in Figure 3.14. Some considerations to keep in mind:

- The field status of a field selection group for a field reference key prefixed with "SAP" must not be changed.

- The field reference key for transaction codes and certain procurement types (E: internal procurement, and F: external procurement) are already configured and can't be changed.

- New field reference keys must begin with Y or Z.

- New field selection groups, if required, can be taken from those that aren't preconfigured. For example, field selection groups 206 through 240 are available.

- The system determines how the field status should be set, as follows: The field status **Hide** has the highest priority, followed by **Display**, **Required (Mandatory)**, and **Optional**, in that order.

3.5 Configuring an Industry Sector

As mentioned earlier in Section 3.1, while SAP does provide a few standard industry sectors, you can create a new or make changes to an existing industry sector. Use Transaction OMS3 or follow the menu path **Logistics – General • Material Master • Field Selection • Define Industry Sectors**. Figure 3.15 shows that a new industry sector **F** has been created for **FMCG: Confectionary**.

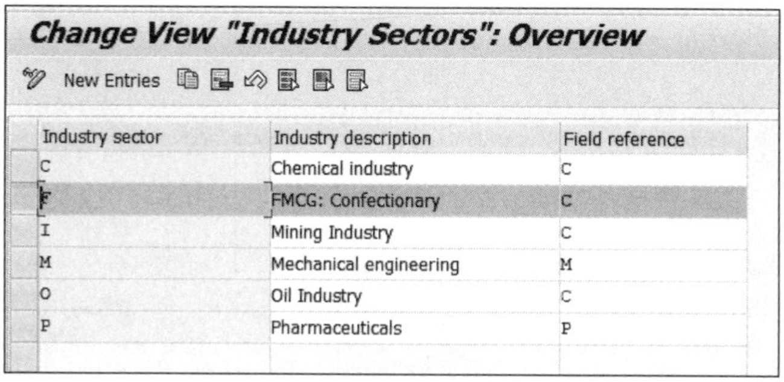

Change View "Industry Sectors": Overview		
Industry sector	Industry description	Field reference
C	Chemical industry	C
F	FMCG: Confectionary	C
I	Mining Industry	C
M	Mechanical engineering	M
O	Oil Industry	C
P	Pharmaceuticals	P

Figure 3.15 Defining an Industry Sector

3.6 Defining Material Groups

The benefits of using material groups are in reporting, such as spend analysis, distribution of roles and responsibilities in purchasing and inventory departments, and so on. For example, some companies have buyers based on the material group. One buyer may be responsible for procuring only materials under material groups for "Stationery" and "Repairs." Another buyer may be responsible for procuring materials under the material group "Steel" and so on.

Organizations, such as the United Nations Standard Products and Services Code (UNSPSC), offer precodification of materials and services. UNSPSC provides an open, global, multisector standard for efficient, accurate classification of products and services. You can configure material groups in line with UNSPSC codes (from its provided list). Many companies use UNSPSC for classifying their products and services.

You can define different material groups to distinguish among various materials. For example, an enterprise that manufactures computers can classify computers as desktops, laptops, and servers; each of these items would be its own group. To define material groups, follow the menu path **Logistics – General • Material Master • Settings for Key Fields • Define Material Groups**. As shown in Figure 3.16, you can define a material group by copying the existing material group or by clicking on the **New Entries** button. After clicking on the **New Entries** button, enter the material group code and a description for the material in the relevant fields.

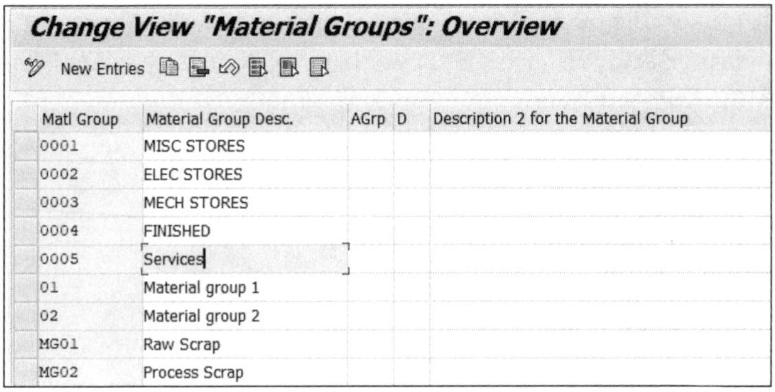

Change View "Material Groups": Overview

New Entries

Matl Group	Material Group Desc.	AGrp	D	Description 2 for the Material Group
0001	MISC STORES			
0002	ELEC STORES			
0003	MECH STORES			
0004	FINISHED			
0005	Services			
01	Material group 1			
02	Material group 2			
MG01	Raw Scrap			
MG02	Process Scrap			

Figure 3.16 Creating New Material Groups

3.7 Configuring a New Unit of Measure

SAP provides a large number of standard units of measure (UoMs) to meet almost all business needs. Using change management to convince your client to use as many standard UoMs as possible, instead of creating new ones, is imperative. However, if needed for the business or for reporting, new UoMs can be created. For example, customized UoMs can be "Enzyme," "Box," etc., which are unique or specific to a company only.

To create a new UoM, use Transaction CUNI or follow the menu path **SAP IMG • SAP NetWeaver • General Settings • Check Units of Measurement**.

Figure 3.17 shows the initial screen. The **Dimensions** button provides access to seven base dimensions, to which all other dimensions can be traced. These dimensions are length, weight, time, electrical current, temperature, molecular mass, and brightness.

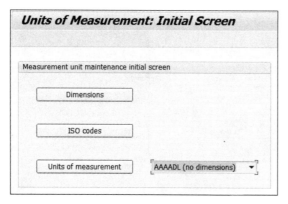

Figure 3.17 Unit of Measure: Initial Screen

Whenever a unit of measure (UoM) needs to be created, you'll first need to decide to which base dimension it belongs; otherwise, the new UoM is created under no base dimension. Dimensions help group UoMs. The system will allow you to create business-specific dimensions, but we always advise creating new UoMs under one of the seven base dimensions.

By clicking the **ISO codes** button, an ISO code can be assigned to several internal measurement units. An ISO code is important for electronic data interchange (EDI) and is used for converting SAP-internal UOMs into standard UOMs. Therefore, we always suggest assigning an ISO code to a UoM.

By clicking the **Units of Measurement** button, you can choose the particular dimension under which the new unit of measure will be created. For example, select **TIME** and then click on **Units of measurement**. All units created under the dimension **TIME** are defined with respect to S (seconds). S is the SI unit in this dimension. For our example, create a new UoM called ZBX (Box) having no dimensions (**AAAADL**).

As shown in Figure 3.18, click on the **Create** button: The screen shown in Figure 3.19 will appear where you can maintain the details for the unit of measure ZBX being created.

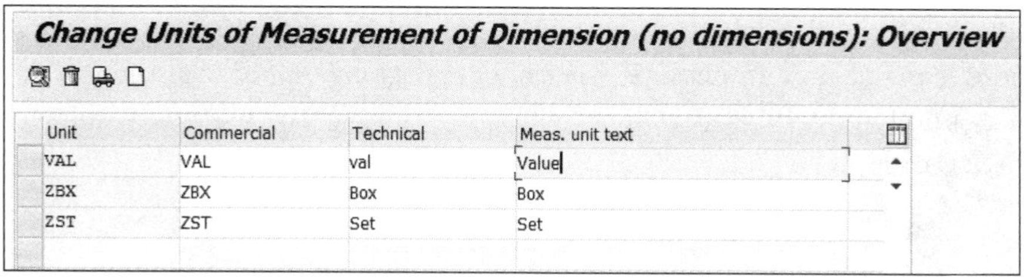

Change Units of Measurement of Dimension (no dimensions): Overview

Unit	Commercial	Technical	Meas. unit text
VAL	VAL	val	Value
ZBX	ZBX	Box	Box
ZST	ZST	Set	Set

Figure 3.18 A New Unit of Measure

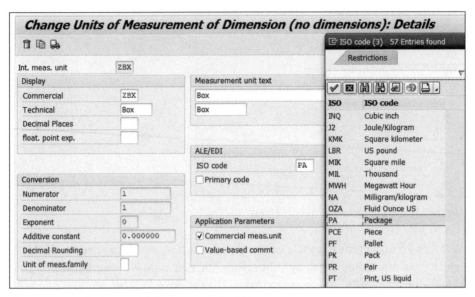

Figure 3.19 Assigning an ISO Code to a Unit of Measure

While maintaining the details shown in Figure 3.19, note the following important points:

- Maintain details like measurement text, commercial name, and technical name.

- Maintain the **Conversion factor** with respect to the SI unit, if any.

- Maintain the **Decimal Places** field (up to which decimal value should display) and **Decimal rounding** field (up to which the value should be rounded off).

- Select the **Commercial unit** checkbox if that unit will be used commercially. This unit will be displayed in the F4 help for units of measure.

- Select the **Value** checkbox if that unit will be derived from a value. If the unit is based on a quantity, then you don't need to select this checkbox.

- Select the **ISO code** for the unit and select the **Primary code** checkbox if the unit will serve as the primary unit for the ISO code. If the same **ISO code** is used for more than one unit of measure, you can only flag one unit of measure as a primary unit for one ISO code. Other units of measure will be secondary units for this ISO code.

3.8   Validating the Correctness of Configurable Objects

Together with the configuration steps described in Chapter 2 and in this chapter, let's quickly check and validate whether all the objects have been correctly and completely *configured*. Then, we can *assign* these configured objects into master data and use the master data to *perform* business transactions, such as creating purchase orders or performing goods receipts.

> **Tips & Tricks**
>
> As is always standard in testing, checking, and validating the configuration, the agreed-upon objects are first configured during SAP implementation projects. These configured objects are then assigned to the master data. The master is then used to perform business transactions. Finally, the configured objects are often used as selection criteria in various SAP standard reports. In other words, the relationship between these elements follows Configuration → Master Data → Transactions → Reports.

To recap, in Chapter 2, we configured a new plant 6000, several new storage locations (including a storage location for raw material 6003), and a new purchasing organization 6000, along with the associated configurations.

In this chapter, we created a new material type ZCON. We also created a new number range and assigned the number range to the material type ZCON. A new industry sector (F FMCG: Confectionary) was created. Finally, a new unit of measure (ZBX) was also configured, which we'll soon assign to a material master.

We'll begin the process of creating a new material master and checking to see whether all the configured objects are correctly assigned to it. When the system creates a material master number, we'll then test out the purchasing cycle by using the same material we created in the first step to create a purchase order that'll have the newly created purchasing organization 6000. A goods receipt for the created purchase order will further validate whether the objects have been correctly configured.

> **Note**
>
> Don't worry if you aren't able to perform the steps covered below in the SAP system at this time. Later chapters will cover all these steps in details. The purpose here is to show the logical connections among Configuration → Master Data → Transactions → Reports.

Access the screen shown in Figure 3.20 via Transaction MM01 and select **F FMCG: Confectionary** from the **Industry Sector** dropdown menu and then choose **ZCON** from the **Material type** dropdown menu. Next, select the **Org. Levels** button, which brings up the screen shown in Figure 3.21.

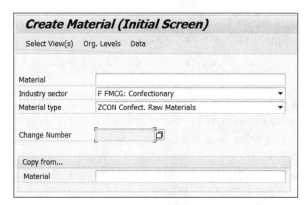

Figure 3.20 Initial Screen of the Material Master

As shown in Figure 3.21, enter the plant "6000" and the storage location "6003." Click **Continue**.

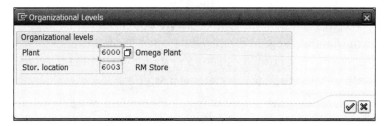

Figure 3.21 Organizational Structure of a Material

Go back to the screen shown in Figure 3.20, but this time, click **Select view(s)**. In the popup that appears, only views previously configured on the screen shown earlier in Figure 3.2 will be available for selection. Select a few views, such as **Basic data 1**, **Basic data 2**, **Purchasing**, **Plant data/Stor. 1**, and **Accounting 1**. Press ⌨Enter, and the screen shown in Figure 3.22 will appear.

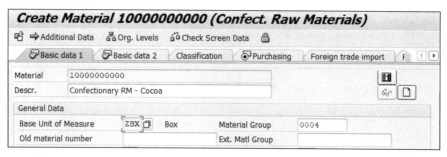

Figure 3.22 Basic Data 1 Tab of the Material Master

Notice the internal number assignment for **Material** is **100000000000**, and the **Base Unit of Measure** available and assigned is ZBX. Click on the **Purchasing** tab and maintain the available or configured purchasing group, which in this example is "0004." Next, click on the **Plant data/Stor. 1** tab, and the screen shown in Figure 3.23 will appear.

As shown in Figure 3.23, the newly created material of material type ZCON is being created for plant 6000 and storage location 6003. Click on the **Accounting 1** tab and maintain the **Valuation class**, which in this example is "3001." Save your entry, and you should see a message confirming the creation of new material 100000000000, which follows the number range we assigned to the material type ZCON.

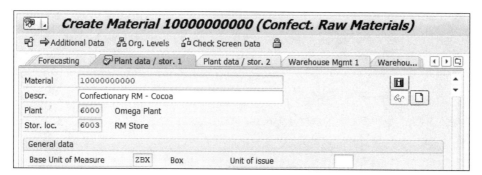

Figure 3.23 Organizational Level of the Newly Configured Material Type

Let's now also quickly test the purchasing part of configuration that we performed in Chapter 2 as well as test our newly created material 100000000000.

Figure 3.24 shows purchase order 4500000228 has been created for **Purch. Org.** 6000, belonging to the **Company Code** 1000, and for **Material** 100000000000. The fact that we are able to successfully create a purchase order for the new purchasing organization confirms the purchasing objects have been configured completely and correctly.

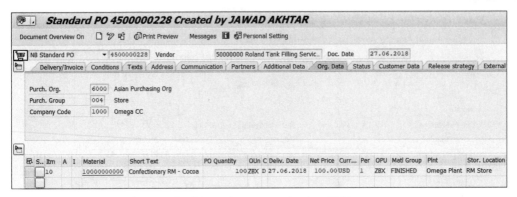

Figure 3.24 Purchase Order for Purchase Organization 6000

Figure 3.25 shows the goods receipt screen for the same purchase order 4500000228, which can be accessed via Transaction MIGO. Goods against this PO will be received in plant 6000 and storage location 6003 and can be confirmed from the message **Document is O.K.**, which appears at the bottom of the screen.

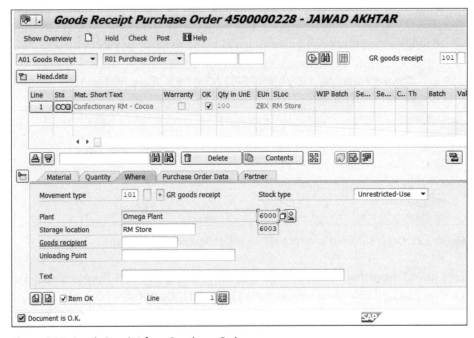

Figure 3.25 Goods Receipt for a Purchase Order

While not an exhaustive list, you should follow the configuration objects checklist below during a SAP implementation project. We recommend preparing a Microsoft Excel Control Sheet for MM so that all the information on configurable objects is available at one place. Almost all configuration topics are covered in this book at least once so you can build on the concepts and replicate these objects to your business processes in the SAP system:

1. Plants
2. Storage locations for each plant
3. Material types
4. Material groups
5. Material requirements planning (MRP) controllers
6. Base unit of measure
7. Business partners roles
8. Business partners categories
9. Suppliers account groups
10. Services groups
11. Services categories
12. Document types for purchase requisitions, PO, RFQ, scheduling agreement, outline agreements (quantity and value contracts)
13. Overdelivery and underdelivery tolerances
14. Condition schemas
15. Account determination
16. Accruals
17. Letter of credit (imports) fields
18. Purchase requisitions document types
19. Purchase orders document types
20. Purchasing organizations
21. Purchasing groups for each purchasing organization
22. Release strategies for purchase requisition, PO, RFQ, scheduling agreement, outline agreements (quantity and value contracts)
23. Customized movement types
24. Batch determination procedures

3.9   Summary

In this chapter, we described the major configurable objects to set up the material master in the SAP system, including material type, material number range, number range assignment, industry type, and a new unit of measure.

Let's move on to Chapter 4, which is the first part of our material master data coverage, encompassing material type, basic data, classification data, purchasing data, forecasting data, work scheduling data, sales organizational data, and sales general data.

Chapter 4
Material Master Data: Part 1

Data entered into the material master is extremely important to an SAP implementation. Incorrect, incomplete, or missing data can bring operations to a screeching halt. Understanding how to enter correct data into the material master is vital for all SAP components.

In this chapter, the first of two chapters focused on the material master, we'll show you the basic structure of the material master and review the data entry screens for in the basic data, classification, purchasing, sales org, and material requirements planning views. Understanding what a field in the material master is and how it relates to data in a legacy system is important.

Data conversions are often not treated with the importance that they deserve. The earlier in the implementation the team works on understanding the data in the SAP master files, the more time will be available for correctly converting legacy data and creating data that doesn't reside in the legacy files.

Prior to starting any implementation, we recommend starting parallel projects for cleansing legacy data and eradicating duplicate and redundant records. Often companies have many duplicate records for one vendor or for materials that are obsolete, which should be identified and corrected before any data is loaded into SAP. Maintaining correct, complete, and comprehensive master data is one of the keys to a successful SAP implementation project, and this data should be constantly cleansed, refined, and improved over time.

Your company may have more than one legacy system and may be combining and loading master data from several systems into one SAP system. The more complicated the data rationalization task, the earlier you'll need to start ensuring the successful loading of data into SAP before the implementation goes live. As we've mentioned before, you'll need complete, correct, and comprehensive master data to ensure that business processes run smoothly in the SAP system.

Note

During an SAP implementation project, the configuration objects are first decided and agreed upon with relevant stakeholders. These objects are configured in the SAP system by consultants. These configured objects are then assigned to the master data. Transactions or business processes then use the master data. Finally, reporting functions, whether for standard SAP reports or custom ones, will use configured objects, master data, and transactions.

For example, the logical sequence of how these four elements work is as follows:

1. As described in Chapter 2, we *configured* a new purchasing organization 6000 and a new plant 6000.

2. These two objects are then assigned to the material master, which is master data, as you'll see throughout this chapter. Supplier or vendor master data (now called business partner master data) is MM master data which can be assigned to purchasing organization 6000. We'll cover this process in Chapter 6.

3. Business processes or transactional data, such as a purchase order of a material-vendor combination, will use the master data we created in the previous step. We'll cover this process in Chapter 12.

4. Finally, a few standard purchasing or inventory reports can be created to use plant, purchasing organization, material master, or vendor master data as selection criteria. We'll cover these reporting and evaluation topics in Chapter 27.

To summarize, configuration is a backend SAP system activity and must occur only once during an SAP implementation project. Master data is a frontend input activity that also often happens only once or only occasionally. Master data remains largely unchanged for a much longer period of time and is used in routine business transactions. Transactions or business processes, such as creating a purchase requisition, a purchase order, or goods issuance or goods receipt are again input activities and take place as frequently as needed. Finally, the reporting and analysis, for example, to determine the number of open purchase orders or vendors who delivered goods but haven't been paid, are *outputs* of all these previous input activities.

As an SAP consultant, you must always stay focused on the *output* (reporting) during the SAP implementation project. Doing so means you'll need to ensure the necessary data *inputs* are in place in the system to be able to produce the necessary outputs. (Remember, when data is incorrect or missing, data outputs will be incorrect or incomplete!)

Before covering the first master data in MM, the material master, let's quickly recap the configuration information we covered in detail in Chapter 2 and Chapter 3.

4.1   Industry Sector

A *configured* industry sector must be *assigned* for each material master record added. In general, most SAP customers use just one industry sector for all their material master records, but this limit isn't mandatory.

An SAP system has four predefined industry sectors:

- P: For the pharmaceutical sector.
- C: For the chemical industry sector.
- M: For the mechanical engineering sector.
- A: For plant engineering and construction.

Defining a new industry sector requires choosing a single character to identify the industry sector and providing a description. The new industry sector must be linked to a field reference, which we discussed in Chapter 3. A *field reference* consists of a list of material master fields and an indicator determining whether an individual field is hidden or displayed, optional or required. Exercise careful consideration when configuring new field references.

4.2   Material Type

A *material type* is a group of materials with similar attributes. Material types allow you to manage different materials in a uniform manner. For example, a material type can group together materials that are purchased or produced internally or that have no value. SAP delivers a set of standard, predefined material types, but you may need to create your own material types, as we covered in Chapter 3.

4.2.1   Standard Material Types

A number of SAP-delivered material types can be used without having to configure any new material types. In this section, we'll discuss standard material types, but you may decide to configure your own, which comes with the added complication of additional configuration steps and testing.

The standard material types include:

- **CONT: Kanban container**

  This material type is delivered by SAP for creating kanban containers. A kanban container is used in a kanban container-based system, sometimes implemented at a specific manufacturing plant for just-in-time (JIT) replenishment of parts on the production line. A kanban container is used to transport the material from the supply area to the manufacturing location. Materials used as kanban containers only have the basic data view.

- **DIEN: Services**

  Services are either internally or externally supplied by a vendor. Services can involve activities such as consulting, garbage collection, or legal services. Service material master records don't have storage information.

- **ERSA: Spare parts**

  Spare parts are materials used for equipment maintenance in the plant. The material is purchased and stored like any other purchased item, but a spare part isn't sold and therefore doesn't contain sales information. If a maintenance item is sold, then the material should use a different material type, such as material type HAWA, for trading goods.

- **FERT: Finished goods**

  A finished good is a material that has been manufactured by some form of production from items, such as raw materials. A finished good isn't purchased and thus doesn't contain any purchasing information. However, a finished good is sold and thus does contain sales information.

- **FHMI: Production resources/tools (PRTs)**

  Production resources/tools (PRTs) are purchased and used by the plant maintenance department. This material type is assigned to items used in the maintenance of plant equipment, such as test machines, drill bits, or calibrating tools. The material type for PRTs doesn't contain sales information because the PRTs aren't purchased to sell. In addition, PRTs are only managed on a quantity basis.

- **HALB: Semifinished goods**

  Semifinished products are often purchased or produced and then completed and sold as finished goods. Semifinished products could come from another part of your company or from a vendor. The semifinished material type allows for purchasing and work scheduling but not sales. If a company also sells its semifinished products, then sales views can be activated.

- **HAWA: Trading goods**
  Trading goods are generally materials that are purchased from vendors and sold. This kind of material type only allows purchasing and sales information because no internal operations are carried out on these materials. An example of a trading good can be found at many computer manufacturers, who sell their own manufactured goods (computers) but also may also sell printers and routers. These trading goods aren't manufactured by the company but bought from other manufacturers and sold alongside their own manufactured computers.

- **HERS: Manufacturer parts**
  Manufacturer parts are materials that can be supplied by different vendors who may use different part numbers to identify the material. This type of material can be found in many retail stores. For example, a DIY retail store may sell a three-step ladder for $20, but the ladder can be made by three different manufacturers, each of which have a different part number. The store will then have three part numbers for the ladder, but the consumer won't be aware of this fact.

- **HIBE: Operating supplies**
  These materials are vendor-purchased operating supplies used in the production process. This type of product includes lubricants, compressed air, or solder. The HIBE material type can contain purchasing data but not sales information.

- **IBAU: Maintenance assembly**
  A maintenance assembly isn't an individual object but a set of logical elements to separate technical objects into clearly defined units for plant maintenance For example, a car can be a technical object, and the engine, transmission, axles, and so on are the maintenance assemblies. An IBAU material type contains basic data and classification data.

- **KMAT: Configurable material**
  Configurable materials form the basis for variant configuration, and the KMAT material type is used for all materials that are variant configuration materials. A material of this type can have variables that are determined by the user during the sales process. For example, automotive equipment produced by a manufacturer may have variable attributes that each car manufacturer needs to be different for each car, such as length of a chain or the height of a belt.

- **LEER: Empties**
  Empties are materials consisting of returnable transport packaging and can be subject to a nominal deposit. Examples of empties include crates, drums, bottles, or pallets. Empties can be made from several materials grouped together in a bill of material (BOM) that is assigned to a finished material.

Empties Management

The empties management functionality is available in MM. This functionality allows the use of sales BOMs in purchasing and sales, and empties can be added to full product items in purchase orders (POs). You can also process these empties during invoice verification.

This functionality allows separate valuations for full products versus related empties and is compatible with other solutions that use BOMs (e.g., a free goods discount).

- **LEIH: Returnable packaging**
  Reusable packaging material is used to pack finished goods to send to the customer. When the finished good is unpacked, the customer is obliged to return the returnable packaging material to the vendor.

- **NLAG: Nonstock material**
  The nonstock material type is used for materials that aren't held in stock and aren't inventoried. These materials can be called "consumables" and include items such as maintenance gloves, safety glasses, or grease. Items in this material type are usually purchased only when needed.

- **PIPE: Pipeline material**
  The pipeline material type is assigned to materials that are brought into the production facility via pipelines. These materials aren't usually planned because they are always on hand. This type of material type is used, for example, for oil, water, electricity, or natural gas.

- **ROH: Raw materials**
  Raw material is purchased material that is fed into the production process and may result in a finished good. No sales data exists for a raw material because this material type is not sold. To reclassify a raw material for sales, then the material type would be changed to HAWA, for trading goods.

- **UNBW: Nonvaluated material**
  This nonvaluated material type is similar to the NLAG (nonstock material) except that nonvaluated material is held by quantity and not by value. Examples of this material type are often seen in plant maintenance, where materials are extremely important to the plant's equipment but of little or no other value. Therefore, the plant maintenance department will monitor inventory to allow for planned purchases.

- **VERP: Packaging material**
  Unlike material type LEER (empties), the packaging material type is for materials that are packaged but are free of charge to the customer in the delivery process. Although free to the customer, the packaging material may still have value, and a physical inventory is recorded.

- **WETT: Competitive products**
  The sales department uses material type WETT to monitor competitors' goods. This material type is used to identify competing products. Only basic data is held for these materials.

Note

In addition to these material types, a number of additional material types are available for SAP Retail customers. These types include FRIP (perishables); NOF1 (nonfood items); FOOD (food except perishables); FGTR (beverages); MODE (apparel); VKHM (additional items, such as clothes labels); and WERB (advertising material).

4.2.2   Configuring Material Types

As we covered in Chapter 3, the best method for creating a new material type is to select an existing material type and copy it to a new one. Copying from an existing material type reduces the amount of configuration required. For user-defined material types, the four-character **Material Type** field should always start with "Z."

After a new material type is configured, the valuation areas defined for that material type can also be configured. A *valuation area* is the level at which material is valuated. The valuation area can be defined at the plant level or the company code level. A number of valuation areas can be defined for a material type.

The four fields that can be configured for each valuation area (**Val. area**)/material type (**Matl type**) combination are the following:

- **Qty updating**
  This field specifies whether a material assigned this material type can be managed on a quantity basis for this valuation area.

- **Value Update**
  This field specifies whether a material assigned this material type can be managed on a value basis for this valuation area.

- **Pipe.mand**
  This field specifies whether a material assigned this material type is subject to mandatory pipeline handling for this valuation area.

- **PipeAllowd**
  This field specifies whether a material assigned this material type can be subject to pipeline handling for this valuation area.

4.2.3   Changing a Material Type

Sometimes, the material type of a material may need to be changed. For example, if a raw material used for in-house production now needs to be sold, the material type may need to be changed from ROH (raw material) to HAWA (trading goods).

A number of caveats exist regarding unrestricted material type changes, as shown in Table 4.1. In addition, if the material has any stock, reservations, or purchasing documents against it, changing the material type may require some extra steps.

Material with Old Material Type	Material with New Material Type
No price control specification	Can only allow standard price
PRTs view maintained	PRTs view must be maintained
Not a configurable material	Must not be a configurable material
Allows inspection plans	Must allow inspection plans
Material for process indicator	Must be the same setting
Manufacturer part indicator	Must be the same setting
Stock value updated in general ledger (G/L) account	Must be the same G/L account
Quantity and value updating	Must be the same as previously
Warehouse management (WM) transfer request open	WM view must be maintained
Batch managed	Must be batch managed

Table 4.1 Changing a Material Type

Let's now cover the steps for creating a new material master in the SAP system.

4.3   Basic Data

The basic data screen is the initial screen that is displayed when a material master record is created. The basic data screen contains data that is common across the client, such as material description and basic unit of measure (UoM).

In the following sections, we'll create a new material master, discuss the importance of organizational structures in MM, and cover in detail the individual material master screens, known as *views*, in the SAP system.

4.3.1   Creating a Material Master Record: Immediately

The material master record can be created in a number of different ways. The most common way to create a material master record is to use Transaction MM01 or follow the navigation path **Logistics • Materials Management • Material Master • Material • Create (General) • Immediately**.

Figure 4.1 shows the fields you'll need to maintain to initially create a material master record.

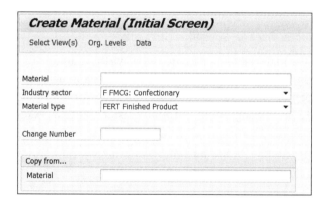

Figure 4.1 Initial Fields Required for Creating a Material Master Record

The necessary fields are described here:

- **Material**
  Leave this field blank for internal numbering or enter a material number if the number range is configured for external numbers.
- **Industry sector**
  Enter the selected industry sector.

- **Material Type**

  Enter a predefined material type or a user-defined material type.

- **Change Number (optional)**

  Enter a change number if the customer is using engineering change management (ECM).

- **Copy from Material (optional)**

  Enter a material number for the material that provides the information required for the new material.

4.3.2   Creating a Material Master Record: Schedule

If you decide to schedule the creation of the material master, you can use Transaction MM11 or follow the navigation path **Logistics • Materials Management • Material Master • Material • Create (General) • Schedule**.

This screen has the same entry fields as Transaction MM01, shown earlier in Figure 4.1, but an additional field requires you enter a date on which the material is scheduled to be created.

4.3.3   Creating a Material Master Record: Special

This particular way of creating the material master record is to have the material type already defined. For example, if you want to create a material master record using the ROH material type (raw material), then you can use Transaction MMR1 or follow the navigation path **Logistics • Materials Management • Material Master • Material • Create (Special) • Raw Material**.

Table 4.2 shows the transactions you'll use to create material masters for the various material types.

Material Type	Transaction
Raw materials (ROH)	MMR1
Semifinished materials (HALB)	MMB1
Finished products (FERT)	MMF1
Operating supplies (HIBE)	MMI1
Trading goods (HAWA)	MMH1

Table 4.2 Transactions for Creating Materials by Material Type

Material Type	Transaction
Nonvaluated material (UNBW)	MMU1
Nonstock material (NLAG)	MMN1
Packaging (VERP)	MMV1
Empties (LEER)	MML1
Services (DIEN)	MMS1
Configurable material (KMAT)	MMK1
Maintenance assembly (IBAU)	MMP1
Competitor product (WETT)	MMW1
Returnable packaging (LEIH)	MMG1

Table 4.2 Transactions for Creating Materials by Material Type (Cont.)

4.3.4 Selecting Views

After the material type, industry sector, and external material number (if applicable) are entered, a dialog box will show the **Views** available to the particular material type. Users can choose into which views they want to enter information, as shown in Figure 4.2.

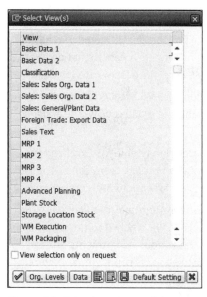

Figure 4.2 Selecting Views of the Material Master

Note

This chapter and Chapter 5 are totally focused on covering the details and options available in each of the different views of a material master. Both chapters also cover all possible views a material master can have so that users maintaining and using data in different views of material master know all the options and choices available to them.

During an SAP implementation project, a single material master file in the MS Excel format is shared with business users to fill in the relevant data belonging to their business functions. Maintaining this material master file is the collective, combined, and shared responsibility of relevant stakeholders and business users. For example, only the sales department of a company knows complete details of the sales processes, discounts, rebates, etc., and therefore, they'll need to maintain the data required in the sales views of the material master. Similarly, the production personnel knows production complexities and scenarios best and therefore are best suited to fill in the work scheduling (production) view of the material master in the MS Excel template.

While each SAP component will have its own set of master data, we recommend identifying and assigning responsibilities to the persons who will fill in the relevant views/data in the various fields of the material master data file in MS Excel format. This consolidated data will then be uploaded into the SAP system during the SAP implementation project.

The best way to fill in the data is to consider each and every field in the MS Excel file as the same field available in the SAP system. For example, evaluate each raw material in the MS Excel file that needs to be *assigned* a previously configured purchasing group code. Better yet, you can set up a validation rule for each field so that only configured objects are available for selection in the MS Excel file of the material master.

When the purchasing data of a material master from the MS Excel is uploaded in the **Purchasing** tab in the SAP system, the relevant purchasing group code will be assigned to it.

While this example covers how to manage the material master in MS Excel and then into the SAP system, you and your SAP implementation project team can adopt the same approach for all master data files using MS Excel for various SAP components.

Due to the completely integrated nature of an SAP system and the way data and information flow from one SAP component to another, we highly recommend maintaining close and complete coordination among the various departments and business functions of the company so that the most relevant, complete, and correct information is entered into the master data templates.

4.3.5   Organizational Levels

After the views have been selected on the screen shown earlier in Figure 4.2, click **Org. Levels** button on the same screen. A dialog box, shown in Figure 4.3, will appear with the organizational levels required for this material master record.

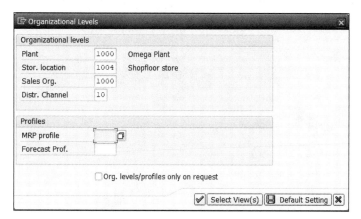

Figure 4.3 Organizational Levels for Creating a Material Master Record

During data entry, a user can enter the **Plant, Stor. Location**, **Sales Org.**, **Distr. Channel, Warehouse No.**, and **Storage Type**. The organizational levels relate to the level at which material master information is held. **Distr. Channel** is required for sales and distribution (SD) screens; **Warehouse No.** for warehouse management (WM) screens and other items.

In the **Profiles** section, the other two fields are **MRP profile** for material requirements planning (MRP) and **Forecast prof.** for forecasting, both of which we'll discuss in this section.

Materials Requirements Planning Profile

An MRP profile is a key that provides a set of field values for MRP screens to save users from having to make data entry decisions.

An MRP profile isn't part of configuration and can be defined by authorized end users by using Transaction MMD1 or following the navigation path **SAP Menu • Logistics • Materials Management • Material Master • Profile • MRP Profile • Create**.

Figure 4.4 shows some of the fields that can be defaulted for the MRP profile. The MRP profile allows you to highlight a field from the list of fields on the MRP screens. You can choose one of two options. The data from the field is entered into the material master either as a fixed value that can't be overwritten or as a default value that can be changed. After you determine which fields will be part of the MRP key, the values must be entered. The MRP profile can be changed or deleted using Transaction MMD2.

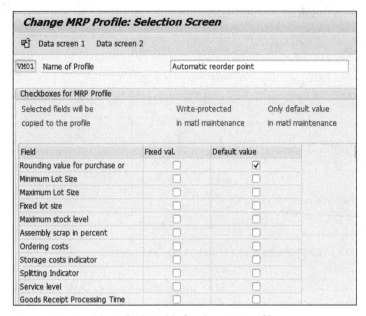

Figure 4.4 Possible Default Fields for the MRP Profile

> **Note**
>
> Chapter 15 covers MRP in greater detail.

Forecast Profile

A forecast profile is similar to the MRP profile because it's a key that provides a set of field values for the **Forecasting** screen.

The forecast profile can be defined by authorized end users by using Transaction MP80 or following the navigation path **Logistics • Materials Management • Material Master • Profile • Forecast Profile • Create**.

> **Note**
>
> Chapter 16 covers forecasting in greater detail.

4.3.6   Basic Data Tabs

After the views have been selected and the organizational levels entered, the first tab that appears is the **Basic data 1** tab, as shown in Figure 4.5.

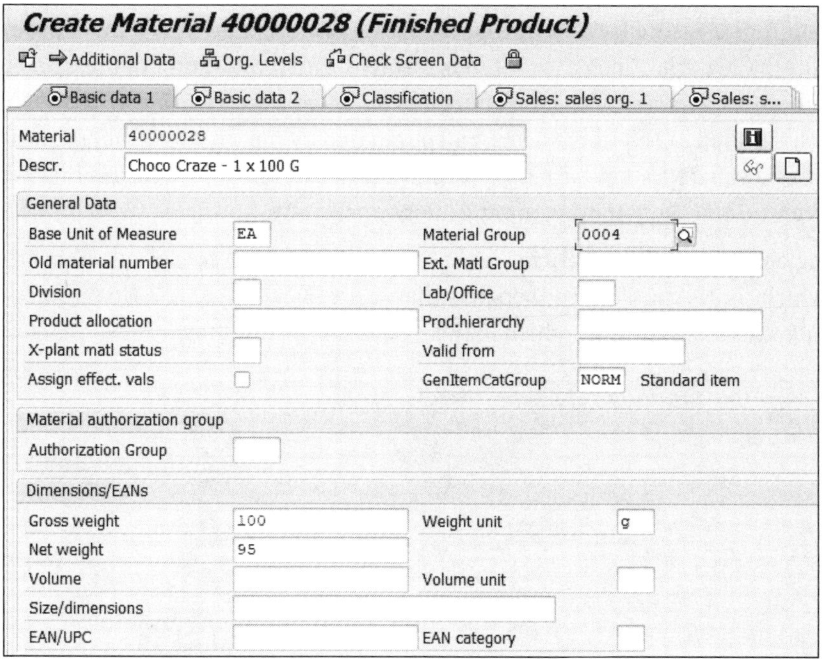

Figure 4.5 Material Master: Basic Data 1 Tab

The **Basic data 1** tab allows data entry for nonorganizational level fields. This screen doesn't require a plant or sales organization to be defined but allows the user to enter basic information about the material. The mandatory fields on this screen, as defined by configuration, are the minimum information required for creating a material master. If the complete material master is created by a number of different departments, each entering its own information, then this basic data can be used to enter materials at the client level. In the following sections, we'll describe many of the fields in the **Basic data 1** tab.

Material Description

The first field to be entered is the material description (**Descr.** field). You can add different descriptions of the material based on the language, with EN as English, DA as Danish, or NL as Dutch, for example. Since a material description can only be up to 40 characters long, a good practice would be defining a material description policy. Abbreviations and standard wording should be used where possible.

Base Unit of Measure

The **Base Unit of Measure** field is the unit of measure (UoM) that represents the lowest level for the material. The base unit of measure is the smallest unit of measure in which the company maintains its inventory. For example, sheet metal may be sold in single sheets, stored in pallets of sheets, and purchased by the truckload, but the base UoM may be a square foot. A base unit can have alternate units of measure that are multiples of the base UoM (i.e., grams and kilograms).

By clicking on the **Additional Data** in Figure 4.5, you'll access the screen shown in Figure 4.6, which shows the UoM conversions that relate back to the base UoM (that is, are multiples of the base UoM), which in this case is **EA** (each).

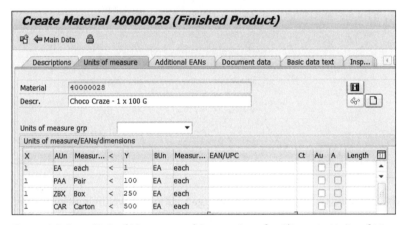

Figure 4.6 Base Unit of Measure and Conversions for Alternate Units of Measure

Material Group

The **Material Group** field reflects a method of grouping similar materials. A material group can be defined either by classification or by configuration. The material group is important not only for searching for materials but also in other areas, for example, purchasing when defining release strategies (approvals). For example, a purchasing information record can be created without a material number but must have a material group and a vendor. This material group/vendor purchasing information record is used in production orders where in-process material is sent to vendors for outside processing.

A material group can be configured using Transaction WG21 or by following the navigation path **Logistics – General • Material Group • Create Material Group**.

You can also create a material group hierarchy, which can be difficult and time-consuming. Thus, a best practice is to use an existing hierarchical material structure already defined in the implementing organization.

> **Warning**
>
> Changes to the material group hierarchy after the project has been implemented can be quite complicated and have far-reaching implications. Therefore, defining material groups and hierarchies early in the project is important.

Old Material Number

The **Old Material Number** field is useful for entering the number for the material that exists in legacy systems or in systems that are still interfacing (but not integrated) with SAP. This field is up to 18 characters in length. For example, if your company is using a legacy warehouse system for shipping materials, the material number used on that system could be entered into the **Old Material Number** field in SAP.

Division

Each material can only be assigned to one division, primarily at an SD organizational level, which is entered in the **Division** field. This value can be used to distinguish different areas of a distribution channel. A division allows a company to organize its sales structure to work with groups of similar materials. Divisions can be configured by using Transaction VOR2 or following the navigation path **Sale and Distribution • Master Data • Define Common Divisions**.

Laboratory/Design Office

The **Lab/Office** field defines the laboratory or design office responsible for the material. This field is used more frequently in PP to identify the persons responsible for a BOM. You can configure this field by following the navigation path **Logistics – General • Material Master • Settings for Key Fields • Define Laboratories/Offices**.

Cross-Plant Material Status

The material status can be entered in a number of areas. The cross-plant material status (**X-plant matl status**) field on the **Basic Data 1** tab allows a user to enter a status that will be valid across the client. Material statuses are defined using Transaction OMS4 or by following the navigation path **Logistics – General • Material Master • Settings for Key Fields • Define Material Statuses**.

A two-character field identifies the material status. The user can configure new material statuses as well. The material status shown in Figure 4.7 is user-defined and shows the process areas where either a warning message (**A**) or an error message (**B**) is given.

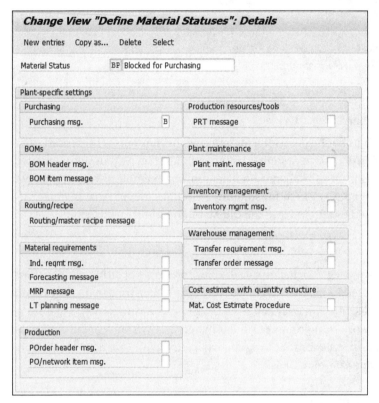

Figure 4.7 Process Area Attributes for a User-Defined Material Status

Product Hierarchy

A product hierarchy is used in the SD area for analysis and price determination. The **Prod.hierarchy** field is an alphanumeric character string that groups together materials by combining different characteristics. In a standard SAP system, the product hierarchy can have up to three levels. Levels 1 and 2 have five characters each, and level 3 has eight. The product hierarchy is defined using Transaction V/76.

General Item Category Group

The **GenItemCatGroup** field allows the system to automatically generate an item type in the sales document being created. This item type depends on the type of sales document and the general item category group. The item category group can be configured by following the navigation path **Sales and Distribution • Sales • Sales Documents • Sales Document Items • Define Item Category Groups**.

Dimensions/EANs

This section of the **Basic data 1** tab enables you to enter information in the **Gross Weight**, **Net Weight**, and **Volume** fields. The **Size/dimensions** text field allows a text description that may be required on a document. The dimensions of a material may be relevant to shipping companies when they are deciding how to pack and ship material. The dimensions may determine how the material is to be shipped.

Also included in this section of the screen are settings related to the International Article Number (EAN), which is assigned by the manufacturer of the particular material. The EAN identifies the manufacturer uniquely. In the United States, the equivalent to the EAN is the Universal Product Code (UPC). An SAP customer can configure EANs to be used internally.

Some configuration items can be found for EAN/UPC items by following the navigation path **Logistics – General • Material Master • Settings for Key Fields • International Article Numbers (EANs)**. Configuration items include the following:

- Internal and external number ranges for EAN (Transaction W4EN)
- Number ranges for perishables for EAN (four-digit and five-digit ranges)
- Prefixes for EAN/UPCs
- Attributes for EAN/UPCs

> **Note**
>
> The fields discussed in the following sections aren't displayed on the screen shown in Figure 4.5 but can be displayed depending on how the screen layout is configured. Each client's material master screens may appear slightly differently.

Click on the **Basic Data 2** tab, as shown in Figure 4.5, and the screen shown in Figure 4.8 will appear.

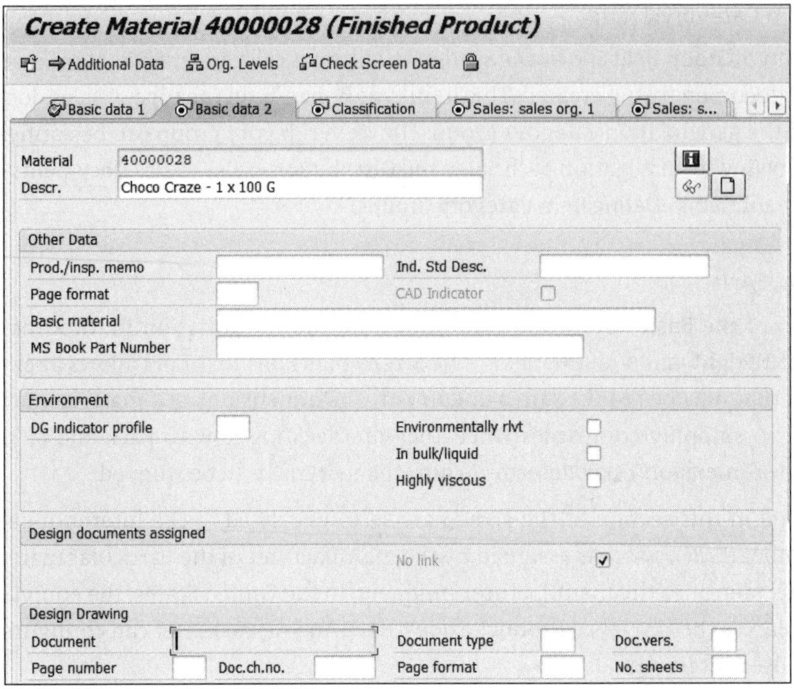

Figure 4.8 Material Master: Basic Data 2 Tab

Product/Inspection Memo and Industry Standard Description

These fields are for information only. The **Product/Inspection** field allows you to enter a product or inspection memo for the material. The **Industry Standard** field allows the entry of the industry standard description of the material. If an International Organization for Standardization (ISO) or American National Standards Institute (ANSI) standard name exists for the material, then this value can be added.

Basic Material

Under the **Basic Data 2** tab, the **Basic material** field allows you to group the material being entered under another material. The **Basic material** field has no specific control function but is often used in custom reports so end users can see the activity of a material at a basic material level.

A basic material can be configured by following the navigation path **Logistics – General • Material Master • Settings for Key Fields • Define Basic Materials**.

Dangerous Goods Indicator Profile

This field is defined in SAP Environment, Health, and Safety Management (SAP EHS Management). A **DG** indicator profile can be selected if the material being added is relevant for dangerous goods and for any documentation that accompanies that type of material.

The **DG** indicator profile can be configured in SAP EHS Management by following the navigation path **Environmental Health and Safety • Dangerous Goods Management • Dangerous Goods Checks • Common Settings • Specify Indicator Profiles for Material Master**.

Environmentally Relevant

This field is relevant for safety data shipping. If this field is checked, then during the delivery creation process, an output type of SDS (safety data sheet) is selected via the SD condition table. The output for this delivery will include a material safety data sheet (MSDS) and other documentation that may be defined in SAP EHS Management for product safety.

Highly Viscous and In Bulk/Liquid

These two indicators don't have any control features in a standard SAP system. These indicators can be used to influence the text or documentation of transportation documents if custom reports are developed.

Design Drawing Fields

The **Document Type, Document Version, Page Number, Document Chapter Page Format**, and **Number of Sheets** fields are all used for design documents that aren't controlled by the Document Management System (DMS). If users need to add a design document to the material master, then these fields will need to be maintained. These fields serve as integration points between MM and the DMS.

> **Note**
>
> In Chapter 25, we'll cover the DMS in greater detail.

Cross-Plant Configurable Material

This field is used in variant configuration to identify a configurable material that is relevant for the client, not just relevant to one plant.

Material Group: Packaging Materials

A packaging material group can be entered for a material that groups similar packaging materials. Packaging material groups can be found in table TVEGR. These fields can be configured by following the navigation path **Logistics – General • Handling Unit Management • Basics • Technical Basics • Define Material Groups for Packaging Materials**.

4.4   Classification Data

Classification data is used primarily when searching for materials. The characteristic values entered into the classes for each material can be used to search for a material with that set of characteristics. This functionality is quite powerful if you've allocated significant effort into identifying and creating characteristics and classes, as well as entering the characteristic values for materials and other objects, such as vendors or batches. Classification also finds extensive usage in the batch management functionality that we'll cover in Chapter 8.

In the following sections, we'll cover how to assign a previously created class to a material master that then brings up the characteristics associated with the class. We'll also show you how to maintain characteristic values of the class that is assigned to the material master.

4.4.1   Class Type

The **Classification** tab allows information to be entered into user-defined characteristics and classes that can be assigned to a material.

Figure 4.9 shows that, for this material, a user can choose a class that has been assigned to one of four class types. A *class type* is a predefined grouping in SAP. When a class is created, a class type is assigned depending on its function. Figure 4.9 shows class type **023**, which is for batch records, while class type **001** is for the material master. A class contains the characteristics for which values are entered. Users can view the classes of a particular class type by choosing that class type, as shown in Figure 4.9. We'll cover the classification system in more detail in Chapter 24.

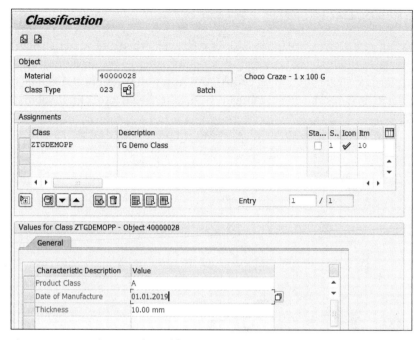

Figure 4.9 Two Classes Selected for a Material, with One Class Showing Its Characteristics

4.4.2   Classes

After a class type has been chosen for the material, in our example, class type 001, individual classes can be selected. These classes have been set up to group together characteristics that describe a material further than the usual fields in the material master.

4.4.3   Characteristics

Characteristics make up the lowest level of a classification structure. Information or a value is entered at the characteristic level. As shown in Figure 4.9, the class **ZTGDE-MOPP** is of **023** (batch) and has been selected for this material. The characteristics for the first class, **Product Class**, are shown and are available for entering values. The other two characteristics of this class are **Date of Manufacture** and **Thickness**.

Characteristics can be configured to accept certain values or a range of values, and entry can be mandatory or optional. We'll cover classification in more detail in Chapter 24.

4.5 Purchasing Data

The **Purchasing** tab, shown in Figure 4.10, is displayed when the material being entered is assigned to a material type that allows purchasing. For example, normally, a **Purchasing** tab is available for trading goods (HAWA), raw materials (ROH), and PRTs (FHMI). Some of the fields shown have already been described in other material master screens.

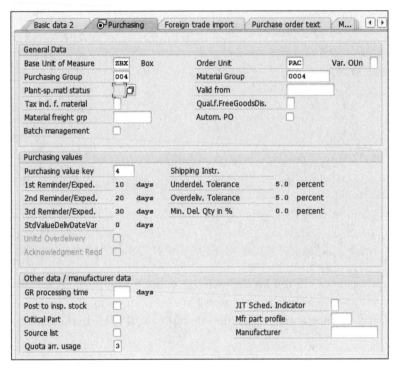

Figure 4.10 Material Master: Purchasing Tab

In the following sections, we'll cover the various areas that make up the purchasing data view of the material master. Starting with the general data and the options available, we'll cover the purchasing value key, which acts as a control function for purchasing business functions. We'll also cover foreign trade data (imports) as well as trade or legal requirements in some countries. Finally, we'll discuss the legal control options available while performing purchasing business processes.

4.5.1 General Data

The **General Data** area contains the various units of measure and other basic data that can be entered on the **Purchasing** tab of the material master. In the following sections, we'll discuss the most important fields and indicators in this area.

Base Unit of Measure

The **Base Unit of Measure** field defaults from the **Basic data 1** tab and also populates other data screens. After a **Base Unit of Measure** is entered, this data will appear as the UoM for all instances. For example, if a material has a base UoM of kilograms (kg), then this UoM will be the default for purchasing, warehousing, production, and so on. This default will be used unless another UoM is entered in those screens, for example, entering pounds ("lb") into the **Purchasing Unit of Measure** field.

Order Unit

The purchasing **Order Unit** field is the UoM in which the material can be purchased. Therefore, a material that has a **Base Unit of Measure** of **Each (EA)** may be purchased from a vendor in the **Order Unit** of **Carton (CAR)**. If the conversion between the base UoM and the order unit isn't already defined (refer to Figure 4.5 again to maintain alternate UoMs), the system will open a popup where you can maintain the conversion. If the **Order Unit** field is blank, then the **Base Unit of Measure** is used as the purchasing **Order Unit** of measure.

Variable Order Unit

Selecting the **Var. OUn** checkbox allows the purchasing UoM to be a variable. The purchasing UoM can be changed during PO creation.

Plant-Specific Material Status

The plant-specific material status (**Plant-sp.matl status**) field on the **Purchasing** tab uses the same status fields found in the **X-plant matl. status** field in the **Basic data 1** tab shown earlier in Figure 4.5. The field on this screen defines the material status at the plant level.

Tax Indicator for Material

The **Tax ind. f. material** field is used for the automatic determination of the tax code in purchasing. The tax code can be determined automatically by price determination using purchasing conditions.

Qualify for Free Goods Discount

This indicator (**Qual.f.FreeGoodsDis.**) specifies whether a material qualifies for a discount in kind. A value should appear if the material does qualify for a discount in kind from vendors.

Material Freight Group

The **Material freight grp** field is used to classify materials to provide transportation information to forwarding agents and rail transportation companies.

The configuration for freight groups and codes is completed in the transportation area of SD. To configure freight groups, follow the navigation path **Logistics Execution • Transportation • Basic Transportation Functions • Maintain Freight Code Sets and Freight Codes**.

Automatic Purchase Order

The **Autom. PO** indicator allows POs to be generated automatically when purchase requisitions are converted into POs. To make the generation automatic, a further indicator must be set in the vendor master record of the vendor associated with the PO. Chapter 12 covers this functionality.

Batch Management Requirement Indicator

The **Batch management** indicator configures the material to allow batches to be created for the material. This indicator is found on screens where the batch information is required, such as the **MRP** tabs.

4.5.2   Purchasing Value Key

The **Purchasing Value Key** field is configured to allow the entry for purchasing-related values like tolerance limits; reminder days, which are the days elapsed before a vendor is contacted regarding outstanding POs; or similar information by using one entry. Figure 4.11 shows a purchasing value key (**Pur.Val.Key**) whose attributes can be configured.

You can configure a purchase value key by following the navigation path **Materials Management • Purchasing • Material Master • Define Purchasing Value Keys**. In the following sections, we'll discuss the most important fields in this area.

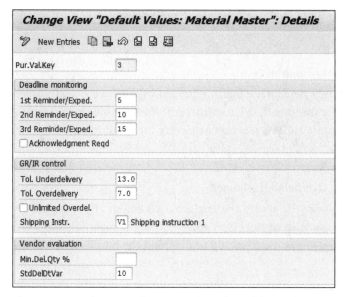

Figure 4.11 Purchasing Value Key and Configurable Attributes

Deadline Monitoring: Reminders

In the reminder fields, you'll enter the number of days after which a reminder or other message is generated and sent to the vendor. If the value entered is a positive number, then reminders are sent that number of days after the due date given by the purchasing document. If the value entered is a negative number, the reminder is sent that number of days before the due date.

The number of days in the **1st Reminder/Exped.**, **2nd Reminder/Exped.**, and **3rd Reminder/Exped.** fields are used from the purchasing information record. If no record exists, then information from the material master record is used.

Deadline Monitoring: Acknowledgement Required

If the **Acknowledgment Reqd** checkbox is selected, then the vendor is expected to supply an acknowledgement that it has received the purchasing document. Deadline monitoring is covered in Chapter 12.

GR/IR Control: Underdelivery Tolerance

In this field, you can enter a percentage figure representing the underdelivery tolerance (**Tol. Underdelivery**) for this material. For instance, if the tolerance is 13%, then on a PO to a vendor for 20 units, the customer will accept a delivery for 18 units (10%) but not 17 units (15%).

GR/IR Control: Overdelivery Tolerance

In this field, you can enter a percentage figure representing the overdelivery tolerance (**Tol. Overdelivery**) for this material. For example, if the tolerance is 7%, then on a PO to a vendor for 340 units, the you'll accept a delivery for 363 units (6.8%) but not 364 units (7.1%).

GR/IR Control: Unlimited Overdelivery Allowed

The **Unlimited Overdel.** indicator allows the customer to accept any overdelivery from the vendor. This allowance may not be acceptable for some materials and some vendors, so the purchasing department should understand the ramifications of unlimited overdelivery.

GR/IR Control: Shipping Instructions

The **Shipping Instr.** field allows a shipping instruction indicator to be chosen. The instructions describing shipping and packaging requirements are sent to the vendor if configured. The **Shipping Instr.** indicator is found in table T027A and configured by following the navigation path **Materials Management • Purchasing • Material Master • Define Shipping Instructions**.

Vendor Evaluation: Minimum Delivery Quantity Percentage

In this field (**Min.Del.Qty %**), you can enter the minimum percentage of the PO quantity that must be delivered for the goods receipt to be included in the vendor evaluation. This field prevents a vendor from receiving a good score for an on-time delivery when the delivery quantity was insufficient.

Vendor Evaluation: Standardizing Value for Delivery Time Variance

The value is entered to determine how many days from the planned delivery date will constitute 100% variance for vendor evaluation. If the entry in this field (**StdDelDt-Var**) is 10, then the vendor evaluation system calculates that the vendor will receive a 100% variance if the PO is delivered 10 or more days after the expected delivery date. Vendor evaluation is covered in Chapter 12.

4.5.3   Other Data/Manufacturer Data

The **Other data/manufacturer data** section on the **Purchasing** screen, shown earlier in Figure 4.10, contains other data required for the purchasing view of the material master. These data types will be discussed in the following sections.

Goods Receipt Processing Time in Days

The **GR Processing Time** refers to the number of working days required after receiving the material for quality inspection and movement into storage.

Post to Inspection Stock

The **Post to insp. stk** indicator allows you to indicate whether the material is subject to inspection and whether the material needs to be posted to inspection stock.

Critical Part

The **Critical Part** indicator is only used in inventory sampling and is for information purposes only. Discuss with the relevant stakeholders whether they need to use this indicator and how.

Quota Arrangement Usage

The **Quota arr. usage** field is a key that defines how quota arrangements are used in purchasing. The information for the quota arrangement usage key is configured by following the navigation path **Materials Management • Purchasing • Quota Arrangement • Define Quota Arrangement Usage**. Figure 4.12 shows purchasing functions that can be assigned to a quota arrangement usage key.

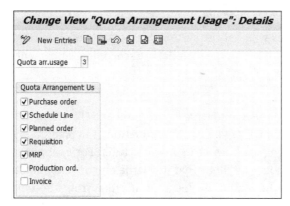

Figure 4.12 Purchasing Functions Assignable to a Quota Arrangement Usage Key

The quota arrangement usage key controls how the total order quantity is calculated in the quota arrangement and which source of supply is determined for the material. The key can be configured for the following purchasing functions:

- **Purchase order**
  The quantity of the material ordered is included in the quota arrangement.

- **Schedule Line**
  The quantity scheduled in delivery schedules for this material is included.

- **Planned order**
  The quantity planned in planned orders for this material is included.

- **requisition**
  The total quantity requested in purchase requisitions for this material is included.

- **MRP**
  Planned orders and purchase requisitions created by MRP are included.

- **Production ord.**
  The quantity of all production orders for this material is included.

- **Invoice**
  The value of all invoices is included.

Source List

The **Source list** indicator is important to the purchasing department. If this indicator is set, a source list must be maintained for procurement for the plant. This source list must be created before a PO can be entered. Maintaining source lists is described more fully in Chapter 9.

Item Relevant to Just-in-Time Delivery Schedules

The **JIT Sched. Indicator** determines whether the system can generate a JIT delivery schedule, as well as the forecast schedules, for the material in a scheduling agreement.

Manufacturer Part Number

This **Mfr Part Number** field is part of the manufacturer part number (MPN) functionality. A vendor who supplies a material that you use in production or in plant maintenance may be the supplier of the part but not its manufacturer. For example, a number of manufacturers may produce oil filters that fit a lathe on your shop floor, so your company may require that the vendor sell you a specific filter from a specific manufacturer. Let's say that the manufacturer make better filters at its plant in Latvia than at its plants in Latin America. Therefore, you, as a customer, can specify you prefer Latvian oil filters by using a specific MPN with your vendor. The way to store that information is in the **MPN** field of the material master.

Manufacturer

The **Manufact.** field is the manufacturer corresponding to the MPN number that has been entered into that field.

4.5.4   Foreign Trade Data

In this section, we'll examine the fields found under the **Foreign trade import** tab, as shown in Figure 4.13.

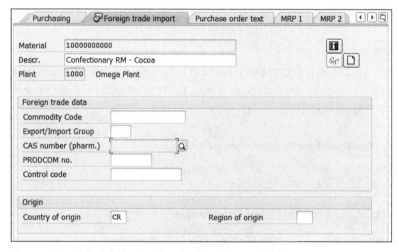

Figure 4.13 Material Master: Foreign Trade Import Tab

Commodity Code/Import Code Number for Foreign Trade

The **Commodity Code** field relates to the harmonized system for the description and coding of merchandise. If selected, the commodity code is used for statistical purposes and must be declared to the regulatory authorities for foreign trade transactions. Examples of this are Intrastat and Extrastat in the European Union and the Automated Export System (AES) in the United States.

Commodity codes are defined in table T604 and can be configured by following the navigation path **Sales and Distribution • Foreign Trade/Customs • Basic Data for Foreign Trade • Define Commodity Codes/Import Code Numbers by Country.**

Export/Import Group

This four-character code is a grouping for similar materials based on import and export attributes. Export/import group information can be found in table TVFM and can be configured by following the navigation path **Sales and Distribution • Foreign Trade/Customs • Basic Data for Foreign Trade • Define Material Groups for Import/ Export**.

CAS Number for Pharmaceutical Products

This field is only required if the material has a CAS number that is a key to the descriptions given by the World Health Organization (WHO) for customs-free materials.

A CAS number can be defined by using Transaction VI36 or by following the navigation path **Sales and Distribution • Foreign Trade/Customs • Specific Data for Customs Processing • Define CAS Numbers**.

PRODCOM Number for Foreign Trade

This field is used to enter a PRODCOM number in EU countries and allows for harmonized production statistics in the European Union. PRODCOM numbers can be configured by using Transaction VE47.

Control Code for Consumption Taxes in Foreign Trade

This field is used for consumption taxes in foreign trade.

4.5.5   Origin/EU Market Organization/Preferences

In this section, we'll cover the **Country of origin** and **Region of origin** fields, which are particularly relevant when using a Certificate of Origin document.

Country of Origin

A country of origin must be specified for export documentation. The material will often require a Certificate of Origin to be printed and included in the shipping documents. The **Country of origin** field uses country abbreviations.

Region of Origin

The region of origin—a state in the United States, a county in the United Kingdom, a province in Australia, and so on—can provide more information about where the material originated for documentation.

CAP Product List Number

The **CAP product list no.** field is the number of the material as defined in the EU market products group list. Product list numbers can be configured using Transaction VI67.

CAP Product Group

Similar materials can be grouped under a CAP product group, which is used in the European Union only. CAP product groups can be configured using Transaction VI69.

Preference Status

This field specifies whether a preference status is allowed at the plant level. A preference status identifies whether a material is eligible to receive any special or preferential treatment under the terms of a trade agreement between countries.

Vendor Declaration Status

This field specifies whether the vendor declaration status is allowed at the plant level. A vendor declaration states where the material was manufactured. The origin of the material is determined with this declaration.

4.5.6   Legal Control

The **Legal control** section relates to the details required for the exemption certificate, which we'll discuss next.

Exemption Certificate/Certificate Number/Issue Date

The **ExemptionCertificate** field is defined as an indicator for export certification information. The values for export certification include the following:

- **A – Applied for**
  The material doesn't require a license for import or export.

- **B – Accepted**
  The material doesn't require a license for import or export because a certificate has been obtained.

- **C – Rejected**
  The application for an exemption certificate has been rejected.

- **Blank – Not relevant**
  The material has no exemption and requires an import or export license.

If the field has been set to **B**, then the certificate number and the issue date must be entered using the two fields, **Exemption cert. no.** and **Iss. date of ex.cert.**

Military Goods

This field is for use only in Germany, due to weapons regulations. Outside of Germany, you can use this field for information purposes.

In the next section, we'll examine the material master fields used for forecasting purposes.

4.6   Sales Organizational Data

The tabs shown in Figure 4.14 and Figure 4.15 allow a user entering sales information to enter data relevant to a particular sales organization. A material may be sold by various sales organizations, and the data for each may differ. Many fields in these screens will default from other entry screens, such as **Base Unit of Measure**. Some fields shown in Figure 4.14 and Figure 4.15 have already been described in other material master screens. In the following sections, we'll detail the components of the major sections within these screens.

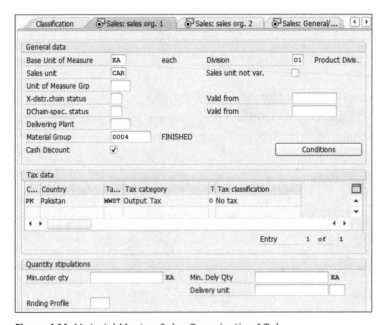

Figure 4.14 Material Master: Sales Organization 1 Tab

4.6.1   General Data

The **General data** section in the first sales organization tab in the material master includes some basic data used in sales processing for materials, such as the **Sales unit**; the **Sales unit not var.** indicator (i.e., variable sales unit not allowed); **X-distr.chain status** (cross-distribution chain material status); and **Delivering Plant**.

Sales Unit

The UoM in which the material is sold is known as the sales UoM. For each sales organization, a material can be specified in a sales UoM that is used for sales orders. This UoM can be the same as the base UoM or a multiple of the base UoM. An example is a material that has bottle as its base UoM but can be sold in the sales organization for the United States as cartons and sold through the sales organization for France as pallets.

Variable Sales Unit Not Allowed Indicator

If the **Sales unit not var.** indicator is set, then the sales UoM in the material master can't be changed in the sales order. If the indicator isn't selected, then the sales representative can change the sales UoM in the order from carton to pallet. With the indicator set, the sales representative can't change the sales unit, and the sales unit will remain as cartons.

Cross-Distribution Chain Material Status

The **X-distr.chain** status field, along with the distribution chain-specific material status field (**DChain-spec. status**), is used in SAP Retail and checks whether a material can be used in different distribution channels.

Delivering Plant

This field designates the default plant where this material is delivered. This field is automatically copied into the sales order as the delivery plant.

4.6.2   Tax Data

In the **Tax data** section of the screen, tax data can be entered for a number of countries in which a material is sold. The country is entered, along with the tax category and the relevant tax classification. A number of tax categories may exist per country.

The **Tax category** for materials is specific to the sales organization/division/plant level that defines the country-specific taxes during pricing. The configuration of the access sequences in the tax-condition tables for sales tax and use tax is made in the **Financial Accounting Global Settings** section of the IMG. That part of the IMG is cross-client and requires careful consideration before any access sequences are added. Consult with an FI specialist when considering any changes to the tax-calculation procedures.

The tax category/classification is defined in the IMG using Transaction OVK4 or by following the navigation path **Sales and Distribution • Basic Functions • Taxes • Define Tax Relevancy of Master Records**.

4.6.3   Quantity Stipulations

The fields in the **Quantity stipulations** section describe the minimum and maximum values of the material used for a particular sales organization.

Minimum Order Quantity

The **Min.order qty** value is the minimum quantity that a customer can order for this material/sales organization combination.

Minimum Delivery Quantity

The **Min. dely qty** value is the minimum quantity that a customer can have delivered for an order for this material/sales organization combination.

Delivery Unit

The **Delivery unit** is the minimum unit of quantity for a delivery. The second field is for the UoM. For example, if the delivery unit is 50 cartons, then the delivery quantity to the customer can only be 50, 100, 150, and so on. The delivery quantity can't be 125 cartons, which is not a multiple of 50.

Rounding Profile

The **Rnding Profile** field defines how a quantity is rounded up to a given value, depending on whether a static or dynamic profile is defined. The configuration for a rounding profile allows you to define the rounding quantities for different thresholds. Table 4.3 shows an example of a static rounding profile.

Threshold Value	Rounding Value
1.000	70.000
211.000	300.000
301.000	450.000
451.000	1000.000

Table 4.3 Configuration for a Rounding Profile in Transaction OWD1

Table 4.4 shows the actual rounding of quantities 1 to 1,000 based on the rounding values listed in Table 4.3. The configuration for rounding profiles can be found by using Transaction OWD1 or by following navigation path **Production • Material Requirements Planning • Planning • Lot-Size Calculation • Maintain Rounding Profile**.

Value From	Value To	Rounded Value
1.000	70.000	70.000
71.000	140.000	140.000
141.000	210.000	210.000
211.000	300.000	300.000
301.000	450.000	450.000
451.000	1000.000	1000.000

Table 4.4 Actual Rounding of Quantities

4.6.4   Grouping Items

A material can be assigned to any number of material groups, which the sales department can use in the information systems, as shown in Figure 4.15.

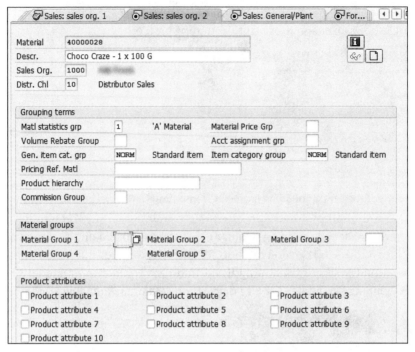

Figure 4.15 Material Master: Sales: Sales Org. 2 Tab

Material Statistics Group

The material statistics group is a grouping used in the logistics information system (LIS). This field is found in table TVSM. The values can be configured using Transaction OVRF or by following the navigation path **Logistics Information System (LIS) • Logistics Data Warehouse • Updating • Updating Control • Settings: Sales and Distribution • Statistics Groups • Maintain Statistics Groups for Material**.

Volume Rebate Group

The **Volume rebate group** field is just a way to group similar materials for rebate agreement processing. The field can be configured by following the navigation path **Logistics General • Sales and Distribution • Billing • Rebate Processing • Define Material Rebate Group**.

Commission Group

The **Commission group** field can group together materials that offer similar commissions. The commission group can be used in pricing procedures. This field can be configured by following the navigation path **Logistics – General • Material Master • Settings for Key Fields • Data Relevant to Sales and Distribution • Define Commission Groups**.

Material Pricing Group

The **Material pricing grp** is another available field that groups materials for pricing conditions. This field is found in table T178.

Account Assignment Group

The **Acct assignment grp** field can be selected to group together materials that have similar accounting requirements. For example, you can select a group for service revenues or a group for trading goods revenues. This field is used in sales billing documents and can be found in table TVKM. Account assignment groups can be defined in configuration steps by following the navigation path **Sales and Distribution • Basic Functions • Account Assignment/Costing • Revenue Account Determination • Check Master Data Relevant for Account Assignment • Materials: Account Assignment Groups**.

4.6.5   Material Groups

The material groups that can be entered on this sales organization tab aren't used in standard SAP S/4HANA processing. The sales department can use the five **Material group** fields to further define a material based on the sales organization. These fields will be available for sales department analysis.

The definition of these five material groups can be configured by following the navigation path **Logistics – General • Material Master • Settings for Key Fields • Data Relevant to Sales and Distribution • Define Material Groups**.

4.6.6   Product Attributes

The **Product attribute** indicators are available to the sales department for analysis. The ten **Product attribute** fields are found in table MVKE, which can be viewed using Transaction SE11.

In this section, we discussed the data used to define the **Sales: sales org.** data tab on the material master record. The next section goes into the material master screen for the sales general data in detail.

4.7   Sales General Data

The **General data** section for the **Sales: General/Plant** tab is specific to a material and a particular plant, as shown in Figure 4.16. In the following sections, we'll lead you through the main subsections of this area.

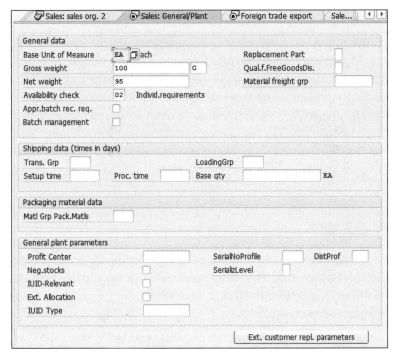

Figure 4.16 Material Master: Sales: General/Plant Tab

4.7.1   General Data

The **General data** section for the material, as it refers to sales functionality, includes the fields for **Replacement part** and **Availability check** and the approved batch record required (**Appr.batch rec. req.**) indicator.

Replacement Part

This indicator allows the sales department to specify whether a material is a replacement part. You have the options of indicating that this material isn't a replacement part, that this material must be a replacement part, or that the material is an optional replacement part.

Availability Check

The **Availability check** field is important to the sales department because it defines how an availability check is defined. The configuration can be found using Transaction OVZ2 or by following the navigation path **Sales and Distribution • Basic Functions • Availability Check and Transfer of Requirements • Availability Check • Availability Check with ATP Logic or Against Planning • Define Checking Groups**.

New availability checks can be defined based on the sales department's requirements.

Approved Batch Record Required Indicator

The **Appr.batch rec. req.** indicator is only valid when the batches are from a process order. This indicator specifies that certain activities can only be performed after a batch record has been entered.

4.7.2   Shipping Data

The many fields used in the shipping processes are described next.

Transportation Group

The **Trans. group** field is used to group together those materials that have similar transportation requirements, such as trucks, tankers, trains, and so on. This field can be used in the automatic route scheduling function in sales order and delivery. The transportation group can be configured by following the navigation path **Logistics Execution • Shipping • Basic Shipping Functions • Routes • Route Determination • Define Transportation Groups**.

Loading Group

The **LoadingGrp** field allows sales departments to group together materials that have similar loading requirements, such as cranes, forklifts, trolleys, and so on. This field is required if shipping point determination will be used. The field contents can be configured by following the navigation path **Logistics Execution • Shipping • Basic Shipping Functions • Shipping Point and Goods Receiving Point Determination • Define Loading Groups**.

Setup Time

The **Setup time** for shipping is similar to the setup times in other material master tabs such as the **Work Scheduling** tab. This setup time is strictly the setup time for getting the equipment, such as a forklift or a trolley cart, ready to move the material.

Processing Time/Base Quantity

The processing time field (**Proc. time**) for shipping is the actual time it takes to load the material from its location onto the transportation vehicle. This processing time is valid for the amount of material that is entered into the base quantity (**Base qty**) field.

Packaging Material Data

Before the **General plant parameters** area, you can find the **Packing Material Data** area. In this section, the **Ref. Mat. for Pckg** field references the packaging material of another material to be used for this material.

4.7.3   General Plant Parameters

A number of plant parameters used in sales processing are described next.

Negative Stock in Plant

The **Neg.stocks** indicator can be set if stocks of this material must allow a negative stock situation. Negative stock occurs when actual physical stock exists, but that stock has not been received into inventory. If a goods issue is made from inventory, then the stock will be negative until the missing goods receipt is made. This scenario allows stock to be shipped without waiting for paperwork to be completed. However, this situation is depends on company policy.

Profit Center

A profit center is a function of the controlling area of SAP. A profit center is a way of internally managing the company, which may have to manage and analyze financials for profit center accounting. The **Profit Center** field in this screen can be used if profit centers will be used.

Serial Number Profile

The serial number profile field (**SerialNoProfile**) is used for materials that must be serialized. For example, a fuel indicator that is sold for use on an airplane may require a unique serial number. The serial number profile determines the conditions and business transactions for issuing serial numbers. Serial numbers are covered in Chapter 12.

Distribution Profile

Companies using SAP Retail can use the distribution profile field (**DistProf**) for materials in a plant as a control profile for merchandise distribution.

Level of Explicitness for Serial Number

This field (**SerializLevel**) describes the level on which serial numbers are unique. A number of different levels can be assigned. Serial numbers can be made unique across the SAP client by entering "1" for every material. This value will also create an equipment number with the same number as the serial number. If the field is left blank, then the serial number will be unique to the material only.

In this section, we discussed the **Sales: General/Plant** tab on the material master. We'll discuss the remaining material master screens in the next chapter.

> **Note**
>
> The details of **Foreign trade exports** tab are the same as the fields we covered in **Foreign trade imports** tab in Section 4.5.4.

4.8   Material Requirements Planning Data

Planners need material planning tools to accurately plan materials for timely availability across the entire logistics and supply chain. A planner's primary concern is to ensure that enough stock is always available for sales to customers without escalating inventory carrying costs or facing a shortage of raw or packing materials needed for production processes. Material requirements planning (MRP) is a planning tool to help production and procurement planners create feasible and realistic plans so they can quickly initiate procurement or production processes.

Note

Refer to Chapter 15 on MRP, where we cover this topic in detail.

A *planned order* is a proposal that a planner can convert to a purchase requisition for external procurement or in-house production. MRP creates planned orders based on a material's net requirement quantity and its needed availability. The net requirement calculation takes into account existing warehouse stock, the quality of stock, existing or open purchase orders, and production orders to calculate the material's shortage quantity. If the system finds that a material shortage, a planned order will be created for the shortage quantity. MRP is not restricted to quantity planning; it also takes timelines into account, such as the time it takes to procure a material (known as the *replenishment lead time*, or RLT), the time required to process goods receipt in the warehouse, or the time required for quality inspection.

MRP data is divided into a number of tabs in the material master. Figure 4.17 shows the first tab, which allows data to be entered for a material/plant combination. The number of screens may depend on the version of SAP you're working on.

The information on the four MRP tabs is important in how material is made, planned, procured, and produced within the plant. Some fields from these tabs have been discussed in previous sections.

In the following sections, we'll start by covering the general MRP data to develop a basic comprehension of MRP. Then, we'll move on to discuss the MRP elements you'll need to consider and understand to make sense of the MRP results that we'll cover in Chapter 10. We'll cover procurement, production, scheduling, and material availability fields as well as fields that control repetitive manufacturing (REM).

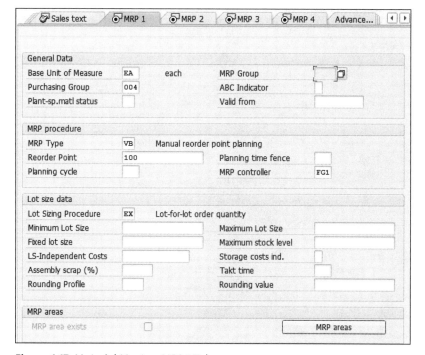

Figure 4.17 Material Master: MRP 1 Tab

4.8.1   General Data

The **General Data** section contains some fields already entered, such as **Base Unit of Measure**, but also includes the **MRP Group** and the **ABC Indicator** fields.

MRP Group

The **MRP Group** field is a combination of special control parameters specific to the total planning run. An MRP group is created at the plant level and assigned to materials with similar needs for these parameters.

The MRP group is created using Transaction OPPR or by following the navigation path **Production • Material Requirements Planning • MRP Groups • Carry Out Overall Maintenance of Material Groups**.

Figure 4.18 shows the fields available for modifying an MRP group.

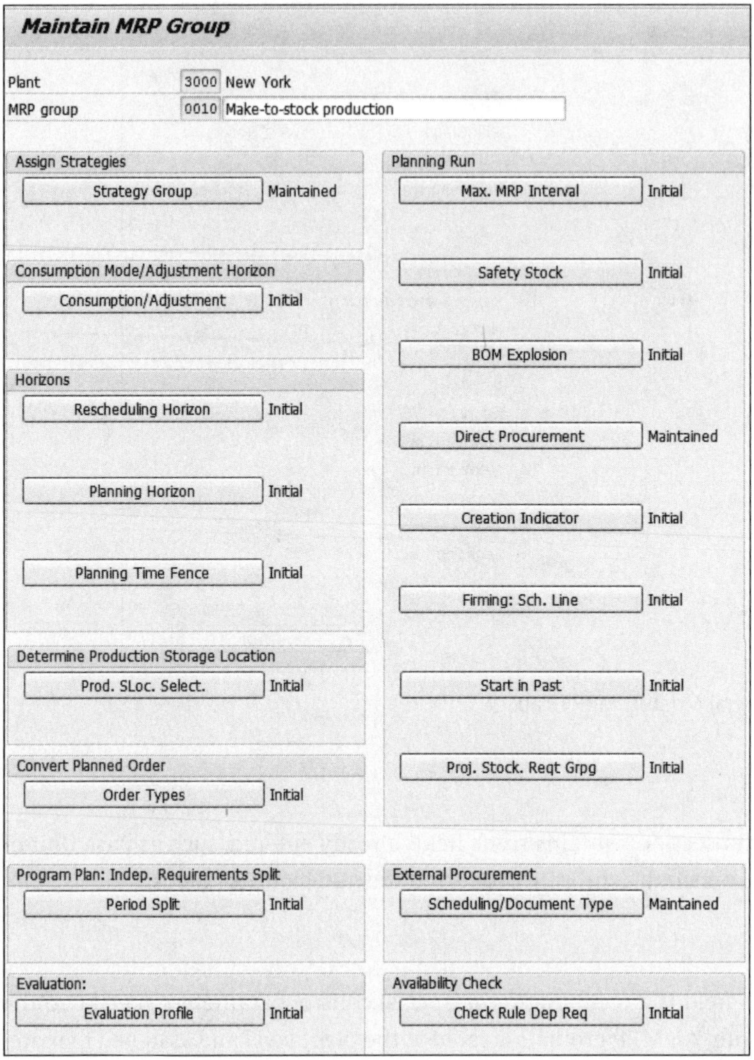

Figure 4.18 MRP Group Parameters

ABC Indicator

The **ABC Indicator** field allows a determination to be made based on consumption criteria. The higher the consumption, the more important the material is, and A represents the highest importance. The SAP system predefines the indicators **A**, **B**, and **C**, but you can also define other indicators.

The **ABC Indicator** field can be configured by following the navigation path **Logistics – General • Material Master • Settings for Key Fields • Define ABC Indicator**.

> **Note**
> Chapter 20 covers how ABC works in physical inventory.

4.8.2   Material Requirements Planning Procedure

The **MRP procedure** fields allow the entry of the **MRP Type, MRP Controller**, and other fields necessary for the MRP function.

Material Requirements Planning Type

The **MRP Type** field is a key to a procedure used to plan a material and to control which MRP parameters can be maintained for the material.

SAP predefines a number of MRP types, but you can create new MRP types in configuration. Table 4.5 shows these standard MRP types and their descriptions.

MRP Type	Description
PD	Standard MRP
VB	Manual reorder point planning
VM	Automatic reorder point planning
V1	Automatic reorder point planning (including external requirements)
V2	Automatic reorder point planning (without external requirements)
VV	Forecast-based planning
ND	No planning

Table 4.5 SAP Standard MRP Types

The planning department can create new MRP types using configuration by following the navigation path **Production • Material Requirements Planning • Master Data • Check MRP Types**.

Reorder Point

This field is used only for reorder point planning. Reorder point planning uses a reorder point to indicate to MRP that a material needs to be included in the next planning run when a requirement will be produced. The production staff determines the reorder level and enters this value into the material master. The reorder level can be calculated in a number of ways. For example, a reorder point can be calculated as the safety stock level plus the forecasted demand for the material during its replenishment lead time.

Planning Time Fence

To create a period of time when no automatic changes are made to the master plan, the planning department enters a value for the **Planning time fence**.

Planning Cycle

The **Planning cycle** field reflects a planning calendar that determines when material is ordered and planned. For this data to be relevant, the material must be assigned an MRP type that allows time-phased planning. The planning cycle can be configured for the specific planning department. To configure the planning calendar, follow the navigation path **Production • Material Requirements Planning • Master Data • Maintain Planning Calendar**. The planning calendar was covered in Chapter 2.

Material Requirements Planning Controller

The **MRP Controller** field reflects a person or persons who are responsible for the planning of the material. Since the MRP controllers of MM and PP use the same SAP table, we recommend coordinating with the PP team to ensure no overlap among MRP controller codes configured in the SAP system.

The MRP controller can be configured by following the navigation path **Production • Material Requirements Planning • Master Data • Define MRP Controllers**.

4.8.3   Lot Size Data

A number of lot size fields can be maintained under this tab, such as minimum and maximum lot sizes, if this information is relevant for the material.

Lot Size

The **Lot size** field defines the lot-sizing procedure. The procedure calculates the reorder quantity in the planning run. Lot sizes can be defined for short-term and long-term periods. The production department will determine what lot-size calculation is required for the material. The lot-size calculation can be configured by using Transaction OMI4 or following the navigation path **Production • Material Requirements Planning • Planning • Lot-Size Calculation • Check Lot-Sizing Procedure**.

Minimum Lot Size

The planning department can enter this field to determine this material's minimum lot size for procurement.

Maximum Lot Size

This field is the material's maximum lot size for procurement. This value is used in the lot-size calculation for production orders.

Fixed Lot Size

The **Fixed lot size** field is the amount of the material ordered when there is a shortage of the material. If the fixed lot size is less than the shortage, then multiples of the fixed lot size will be ordered to cover the shortage.

Maximum Stock Level

This field is only used if the **Lot size** field value "HB" (replenish to maximum) has been entered for this material. This field determines the maximum level of stock for this material at the plant.

Ordering Costs

These costs are only used with the optimum lot-sizing procedure and represent the cost of producing or purchasing the material above the normal purchasing costs. The system assumes the currency is the same as the currency used for the plant.

Storage Costs Indicator

This field is used only with the optimum lot-sizing procedure and is defined as the cost of storing material based on the quantity and the unit price.

Assembly Scrap

The **Assembly scrap (%)** field represents the amount of scrap that normally occurs during the assembly of a material. The percentage scrap will allow the lot-size calculation to increase to allow for scrap. A value should only be entered if this material is an assembly.

Takt Time

"Takt" is the German word for the baton used by an orchestra conductor to regulate the speed at which musicians play. Production uses takt time as the rate at which a material is completed. If the **Takt time** field is defined as four hours, a complete material is produced every four hours.

> **Note**
>
> Chapter 15 covers how to set up and use MRP areas in the SAP system.

The second MRP tab, as shown in Figure 4.19, allows the entry of material data for **Procurement**, such as **Procurement type** and the **Backflush** indicator; **Scheduling**, such as **In-house production** and **Planning calendar**; and **Net requirements calculations**, such as **Safety stock** of the material.

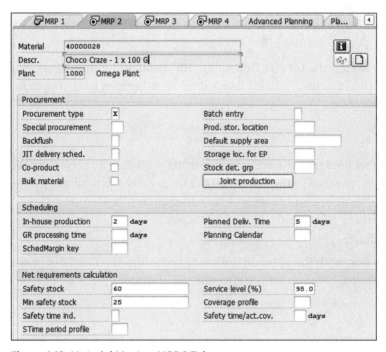

Figure 4.19 Material Master: MRP 2 Tab

4.8.4   Procurement

The first section of data fields on the second MRP tab in the material master refer to how a material can be procured for production.

Procurement Type

The **Procurement type** field describes how a material is procured. For example, a material can be purchased externally from a vendor, be produced in-house via a production or a process order, or be both produced and purchased.

Batch Entry

The **Batch entry** key is used to identify where the batches must be entered in the production process. Three options are available for the **Batch entry** field:

- Manual batch determination at release of order
- Batch not required in order; confirmation required
- Automatic batch determination upon release of order

Special Procurement

The **Special procurement** field is configured to describe a procurement scenario. This key can determine the procurement type, procurement from another plant, and bill of materials (BOM) characteristics. The configuration of the **Special procurement** field can be found by following the navigation path **Production • Material Requirements Planning • Master Data • Define Special Procurement Type**. Chapter 14 covers special procurement types.

Production Storage Location

If the material is produced in-house, the storage location entered in the **Prod. stor. location** field is used in the planned or production order, as well as for backflushing purposes.

Default Supply Area

The **Default supply area** field is used for Kanban operations. The default supply area is a defined interim storage area that supplies material to the production operation. Supply areas aren't part of configuration and can be defined using Transaction PK05 or by following the navigation path **Logistics • Production • Kanban • Supply Area • Maintain**.

Storage Location for External Procurement

The storage location for external procurement field (**Storage loc. for EP**) is used as the storage location defaulted into the planned order for material procured externally.

Just-in-Time Delivery Schedule

This indicator can be set to allow a JIT delivery schedule to be generated as well as the forecast schedules for this material.

Co-Product Indicator

A *co-product* is a material generated by the production process that has the composition or characteristics of a manufactured product or a semifinished product. Selecting the **Co-product** checkbox indicates the material is a co-product. If a by-product is produced during the production process, then you don't need to select the **Co-product** indicator. A co-product is of equal value or a high value product (while a by-product is a low-value product) and can either be sold off or used in another production process. Inventory management is possible for both co-products and by-products. This topic is covered in more detail in Chapter 19.

Bulk Material Indicator

This indicator, if selected, defines the material as a bulk material for BOM purposes.

4.8.5   Scheduling

In this section, we'll cover the scheduling aspects of materials planning.

In-House Production

The system uses this field to calculate the time (in days) required to produce a material in-house.

GR Processing Time

The system uses this field to calculate the time (in days) required to make a product available. For example, if two days are required for inspecting a procured material, this time is added to the scheduling during an MRP run.

Scheduling Margin Key

The system uses this field to create a buffer in scheduling to account for any unforeseen delays during production or procurement. This time can also provide the planner with additional time for securing approvals to procure or produce a material.

Planned Delivery Time

The system uses this field to calculate the time (in days) required to procure a material.

> **Tips & Tricks**
>
> Report WPDTC compares planned delivery times maintained in the material master, supplier master (business partner), and purchasing information record with the actual time it took for the supplier to deliver a material. This comparison between planned and actual delivery time can then be used to update the MM master data such as material master, supplier master, or purchasing information record.

Planning Calendar

While the system uses the factory calendar for most of its planning, the planning calendar provides planners with an alternate option for planning materials to meet specific business needs. We covered the planning calendar in Chapter 2.

4.8.6   Net Requirements Calculations

The net requirements calculations are for the safety stock amounts active for a material at a specific plant. For example, depending on the specific production facilities at each plant and the location of key vendors, the values for safety stock, minimum safety stock, and service level may be different for each plant in the company.

Safety Stock

The purpose of **Safety Stock** is to ensure that no material shortage occurs for production. The safety stock level is designed to offset any unexpected increase in demand.

Figure 4.20 shows how the safety stock relates to reorder point planning in the consumption-based planning method. Refer to Figure 4.17 again to maintain the reorder point in the material master.

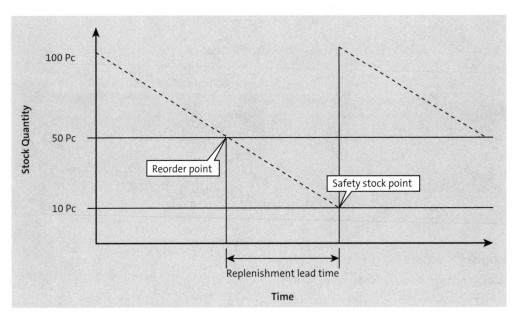

Figure 4.20 Safety Stock and Reorder Point

Service Level

This percentage field is used in the calculation of safety stock. A low **Service level** percentage will be reflected in a low safety stock level. A 95% service level will mean that a material's stock must be available 95% of the time it's required. Falling below this threshold will mean increasing the safety stock to meet the desired and expected service level.

Minimum Safety Stock

The minimum safety stock level (**Min. safety stock**) is the lower limit of the safety stock range. This field should only be used by the planning department in forecasting and calculating safety stock.

Coverage Profile

The **Coverage profile** field defines parameters used for calculating safety stock dynamically. The dynamic safety stock is calculated using daily average requirements and the range of coverage. The coverage profile can be configured by following the navigation path **Materials Management • Consumption-Based Planning • Planning • MRP Calculation • Define Range of Coverage Profile**.

Safety Time Indicator

The safety time indicator (**Safety time ind.**) allows the user to define the mechanism for safety time. Two indicators can be used. The first allows the safety time to be active for all requirements; the second is just for independent requirements. The safety time is when the MRP requirements can be brought forward. This time buffer allows more time for the delivery of materials, among other things.

Safety Time/Actual Coverage

The **Safety time/act.cov.** field contains a value representing the actual time that the MRP requirements are brought forward. This value is the number of actual coverage in workdays.

Period Profile for Safety Time

To define safety time, employing a period profile maybe more useful, given that requirements fluctuate at different times of the year. In configuration, you can create a safety time based on the dates entered for each period. You can also create a number of safety time period profiles.

The configuration can be completed using Transaction OMOD or by following the navigation path **Materials Management • Consumption-Based Planning • Planning • MRP Calculation • Define Period Profile for Safety Time**.

The third **MRP** tab on the material master, shown in Figure 4.21, allows the entry of forecast, planning, and availability check information.

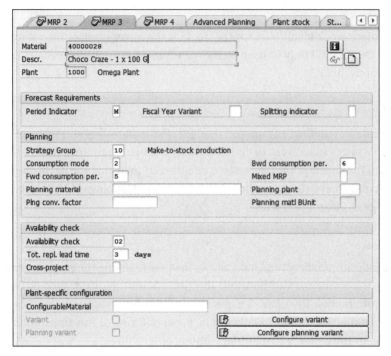

Figure 4.21 Material Master: MRP 3 Tab

4.8.7   Forecast Requirements

The **Forecast Requirements** section contains three fields: **Period Indicator**, **Fiscal Year Variant**, and **Splitting indicator**.

Period Indicator

The **Period Indicator** field specifies the time period for which consumption values are held for forecasting. The normal time period is 1 month, which is the SAP default if this field is left blank. This field is also displayed on the **Forecasting Data** tab.

Fiscal Year Variant

The **Fiscal Year Variant** is an accounting-defined field that describes the variant for the fiscal year, that is, the number of posting periods. The fiscal year variant can be configured using Transaction OB37 or by following the navigation path **Financial Accounting • Financial Accounting Global Settings • Fiscal Year • Maintain Fiscal Year Variant**. This field is also displayed on the **Forecasting Data** tab.

Splitting Indicator

The **Splitting indicator** plays an important function within forecast-based planning. The forecast for a material may determine that production needs to manufacture 1,000 units per month for the next 6 months. However, the planning function needs to split production into smaller time intervals. In this example, a planning run may be required to determine the number of units required to be produced each day for the first month, then weekly for the second month, and then monthly after that. Thus, a splitting indicator can be defined in the configuration to determine the number of days, the number of weeks, and the number of forecast periods required.

This configuration can be found by following the navigation path **Production • Basic Data • Material Requirements Planning • Forecast • Define Splitting of Forecast Requirements for MRP**.

4.8.8   Planning

This part of the screen allows the maintenance of a number of fields regarding the planning of the material at the specific plant.

Strategy Group

The **Strategy group** field groups planning strategies. The strategies used in planning are usually predefined in SAP. Some examples of strategies include **10: Make to Stock Production, 20: Make to Order Production, 30: Production by Lot Size**, and **70: Planning at Assembly Level**.

A strategy group is defined with a main strategy and can have up to seven other strategies as part of that group. For instance, strategy group 33 may have its main planning strategy defined as **30: Production by Lot Size** and then have **40: Planning with Final Assembly** defined as part of the group. The configuration for the strategy group can be found by following the navigation path **Production • Basic Data • Material Requirements Planning • Master Data • Independent Requirements Parameters • Planning Strategy • Define Strategy Group**.

Consumption Mode

The **Consumption mode** is simply the direction in which the system consumes requirements. In backward consumption, the consumption of the planned requirements occurs before the requirement date. In a forward consumption system, consumption occurs after the requirement date.

Backward Consumption Period

The **Bwd consumption per.** field relates to the consumption mode. If the consumption mode is defined as backward consumption, then this field defines the number of workdays that consumption should be carried out. A backward consumption period can last up to 999 workdays from the current date.

Forward Consumption Period

The **Fwd consumption per.** field also relates to the consumption mode. If the consumption mode is defined as forward consumption, then this field defines the number of workdays that consumption should be carried out. The forward consumption period can last up to 999 workdays from the current date.

Mixed Material Requirements Planning

The **Mixed MRP** field identifies the material as being available to one of three options: subassembly planning with final assembly, gross requirements planning, or subassembly planning without final assembly.

Planning Material

The **Planning material** field can be used when a material has a BOM that contains variant and nonvariant parts. Using another material (the planning material), the planning department can plan the nonvariant parts. When planning runs, the planning material isn't produced but is only used to plan the nonvariant parts. This planning strategy is called *planning with a planning material*.

Planning Plant

The **Planning plant** field reflects the plant associated with the planning of the material. The material is planned to be goods received into this plant.

Conversion Factor for Planning Material

If the regular material and the planning material don't have the same UoM, conversion will be needed. The **Plng conv. factor** field holds a 10-character string and can be defined as appropriate. If the field is blank, the system assumes that the conversation factor is a factor of 1.

4.8.9 Availability Check

This section allows you to review the availability check that has been identified on other entry screens and the addition of total replenishment lead time and cross-project materials.

Total Replenishment Lead Time

The **Tot. repl. lead time** field reflects the time, in workdays, that is required before a material is available to be used or sold. This field isn't a system calculation but should be the sum of the total in-house production times and the planned delivery times.

This field should be maintained if the planning department wants total replenishment lead time to be included in the availability check.

Cross-Project Material Indicator

This indicator allows the user to take into account all project stock or just stock from one project segment.

The fourth **MRP** tab, shown in Figure 4.22, shows the BOM explosion data, such as **Component Scrap (%)**; information for discontinued parts, such as **Follow-up matl**; and repetitive manufacturing, assemblies, and deployment strategy, such as **REM profile**.

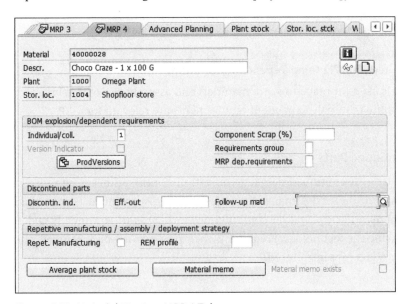

Figure 4.22 Material Master: MRP 4 Tab

4.8.10   Bill of Materials Explosion/Dependent Requirements

The information in the **BOM explosion/dependent requirements** section includes the selection method, component scrap, and requirements group.

Component Scrap

The **Component scrap (%)** value is needed to calculate the correct figure for component stock in MRP. This field is needed if a material is a component in a BOM. If a BOM for a finished material needs 400 units of material X, and material X has a component scrap figure of 10%, then the actual figure needed is 110%, that is, 440 units of material X. This figure isn't used if it's defined in the BOM.

Individual or Collective Requirements

The **Individual/coll.** indicator allows the planning department to determine whether a material is relevant for individual or collective requirements, or for both. Individual requirements are quantities of the material shown separately. Collective requirements are quantities of the material grouped together.

Requirements Group

The **Requirements group** field can be set to allow the system to group together the material requirements for a material on a daily basis.

Material Requirements Planning Dependent Requirements

This indicator is used for make-to-stock materials and assemblies. Set this indicator to indicate that the materials-dependent requirements are relevant for MRP.

4.8.11   Discontinued Parts

If a material is to be discontinued, data regarding its discontinuation can be added in this section. In some industries, many materials could be discontinued. For example, companies that manufacture and sell computer network cards are continually updating and improving the technology. Frequently, their products are discontinued, and replacement products are introduced.

Discontinuation Indicator

The **Disontin. ind.** indicator is used when a material is being discontinued. For MRP purposes, the system needs to know whether this material has dependent requirements. This indicator can be set to "1" for a single-level material and to "3" for dependent requirements.

Effective-Out Date

The **Eff.-out** field reflects the date by which the inventory of the discontinued material will be at zero. After this time, the follow-up material will be used in its place.

Follow-Up Material

This field is the material number of the material that will replace the discontinued material on the effective-out date.

4.8.12   Repetitive Manufacturing/Assembly/Deployment Strategy

Information in this section relates to repetitive manufacturing, assemblies, and deployment strategies.

Repetitive Manufacturing Indicator

This indicator allows a material to be considered in repetitive manufacturing. If this indicator is selected, a repetitive manufacturing profile must also be entered for the material.

Repetitive Manufacturing Profile

The repetitive manufacturing profile (**REM profile**) can be configured but allows the production user to determine some issues, such as the following:

- Error correction for use during backflushing
- Goods issue backflushing at goods receipt
- Planned order reduction
- Which movement types are used

A repetitive manufacturing profile can be configured by following the navigation path **Production • Repetitive Manufacturing • Control Data • Define Repetitive Manufacturing Profiles**.

4.9   Summary

This chapter on the material master discussed the elements that make up the material master for a number of screens, including the **Basic Data, Classification, Purchasing, Sales: Sales Org., Sales General/Plant,** and **Material Requirements Planning** (MRP).

Chapter 5, our second chapter on the material master, will describe the advanced planning, forecasting, work scheduling, production planning and detailed scheduling (PP-DS), production resources/tools (PRTs) data, plant data/storage location data, warehouse management (WM) data, quality management (QM) data, accounting, and costing.

Chapter 5
Material Master Data: Part 2

Complete, correct, and comprehensive master data forms the backbone of a successful SAP implementation project. Master data maintenance is also critical to efficiently and effectively run business processes in the SAP system.

In this second chapter on the material master, we'll show you the data entry screens (or views) for advanced planning, forecasting, work scheduling, production resources/tools (PRTs) data, plant data/storage location data, warehouse management (WM) data, quality management (QM) data, accounting, and costing. Understanding the fields in the material master and how they relate to the data in a customer's legacy system is important.

5.1   Advanced Planning Data

Production planning and detailed scheduling (PP-DS) with SAP S/4HANA became available with SAP S/4HANA 1610. This functionality introduces the advanced capacity planning and heuristics for materials planning that were previously only available in SAP Advanced Planning and Optimization (SAP APO).

PP-DS transactions are executed directly in SAP S/4HANA, thereby eliminating the need for a separate installation to run PP-DS transactions. The material master and the work center creation are also synchronous, which means that a material or a work center that has just been created can be immediately available for planning in PP-DS. Some PP-DS functionalities are also integrated with SAP S/4HANA. For example, MRP Live (refer to Chapter 15 on this topic) now can also plan PP-DS materials, and a single report is available to convert planned orders.

Let's now cover some of the important fields of PP-DS. Figure 5.1 shows the **Advanced Planning** tab of the material master.

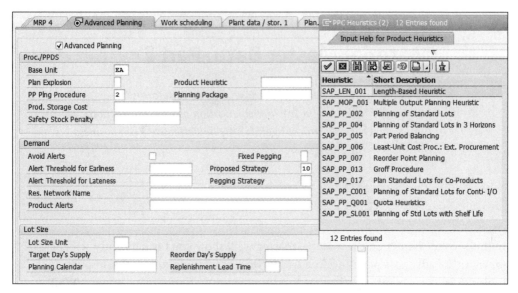

Figure 5.1 PP-DS Advanced Planning Tab

Note

To use PP-DS in SAP S/4HANA, select the **Indicator for Advanced Planning** checkbox, which supports advanced liveCache-based planning and scheduling.

5.1.1   Procurement/PP-DS

In the following sections, we'll describe some of the important fields in the **Proc./PPDS** area.

PP Planning Procedure

The **PP Plng Procedure** field defines that, for each planning-relevant material, that is, for an event occurring for a location product (which is a material), an action is triggered by PP-DS. The PP planning procedure also determines, according to customer requirements, whether the desired quantity or the confirmed quantity of a schedule line is relevant for pegging. For example, let's say a planning-relevant event such as a goods movement for a product or a change in the product master takes place. Possible actions by the PP-DS can be immediately calling up a product heuristic for the product or creating a planning file entry. A *heuristic* is a planning function in PP-DS that executes planning for selected objects such as products, resources, operations, or line networks.

Plan Explosion

This field specifies the task list type, such as a bill of materials (BOM) and routing, that the system will use to create receipts in PP-DS.

Product Heuristic

Just as MRP types in SAP S/4HANA control the type of planning a material can have, a product heuristic is the planning method for PP-DS. Notice some of the available product heuristics shown in the dropdown menu on the far right-hand side of Figure 5.1.

5.1.2 Demand

In the following sections, we'll describe some of the important fields in **Demand** area.

Avoid Alerts in Pegging

If you select this indicator, the system will attempt to create the pegging relationships between requirements and receipts, if possible, without the quantity or date alerts. First, the system links receipts and requirements that are compatible on a time and quantity basis, then the remaining receipts and requirements in a second step.

> **Warning**
> This method can reduce system performance.

Alert Threshold for Early Receipts

The system creates a date/time alert for a fixed or a dynamic pegging relationship if the earliness exceeds the alert threshold, that is, if the availability date/time is earlier than the specified timeframe before the requirements date. To specify the timeframe, use the format HHHHHH:MM (hours:minutes). For example, "1000:10" means 1,000 hours and 10 minutes, while "20:20" means 20 hours and 20 minutes. If you don't specify a value, the system uses the value "100000:00." Therefore, the system only creates an alert if an availability date/time is more than 100,000 hours before the requirements date.

Alert Threshold for Delayed Receipts

Similar to the alert threshold for early receipts, the system creates a date/time alert for a fixed or a dynamic pegging relationship if the delay exceeds the alert threshold, that is, if the availability date/time is later than the specified timeframe after the requirements date.

Pegging Strategy for Dynamic Pegging

Using the pegging strategy, you can determine in which time sequence the system should cover requirements for the product with dynamic pegging and in which time sequence the system should use the product receipts in the pegging interval to cover a requirement. Thus, the pegging strategy controls the following:

- Which requirement the system should cover first
- Which receipts the system should use first

Generally, for dynamic pegging, the system begins by covering the earliest requirement, then processes the next requirement, and so on. Since several receipts may exist for the availability dates/times within the pegging interval, you must specify which receipt the system should use first. The following options exist:

- **Use current receipts**
  With this option, the system uses the current receipt where possible to cover a requirement. Starting from the requirement date, the system first searches to the beginning of the pegging interval. If no receipts exist in this direction, the system will search to the end of the pegging interval.
- **Use the earliest receipt (first in first out)**
  With this option, the system uses the earliest receipts in the pegging interval to cover a requirement, that is, the first receipt in the pegging interval, then the second, and so on. With this strategy, excess receipts only become available later.

Resource Network

This field indicates the name of the resource network. A *resource network* describes the physical links between resources in a plant, such as processing units, reactors, vessels, and so on. A resource network explains the flow of materials through a plant.

Product Alerts

In this field, you'll specify whether:

- The system determines direct alerts for a requirement or a receipt of a product.
- The product is relevant to network alerts.

If a product is relevant to network alerts, the system evaluates the direct alerts for this product for receipts or requirements at the higher levels of the pegging structure as well.

You can hide alerts for less critical components and thus:

- Increase the clarity and transparency of network alerts
- Improve performance

If you choose the **Do Not Determine Any Alerts** option, the system will not determine any direct alerts for the product. The product is thus also not relevant with regard to the network.

> **Note**
>
> You'll need to specify whether and which alerts are actually displayed by the system in the planning interface or in the **Alert Monitor** in the PP-DS alert profile that you use for planning.

5.1.3 Lot Size

In the following sections, we'll describe some of the important fields in **Lot Size** area.

Lot Size Unit

This field indicates the valid unit of measure (UoM). The following options exist:

- No lot size units maintained: The base unit of measure maintained for the product applies.
- A unit of measure (alternate or base unit of measure) can be maintained, which can be converted to the base UoM. If you enter an alternate unit of measure, the conversion to the base UoM must be maintained on the tab **Units of Measure** (refer to Chapter 4 again). The alternate units of measure must be able to be converted to the base UoM for the product, as otherwise the unit will not be accepted.

For example, the alternate unit of measure is kilogram (kg). The base unit of measure is piece (pc). 5kg correspond to 3 pieces.

Target Days' Supply in Workdays

The PP-DS standard heuristic SAP_PP_002 (planning of standard lots) and the SNP (supply network planning) heuristic takes into account the target days' supply if you have selected one of the following target stock level methods:

- **No entry**
  Target days' supply from product master.

- **4**

  Target stock level equals maximum stock level + safety stock.

- **5**

  Maximum from maximum stock level/target days' supply (product master).

- **6**

  Total from maximum stock level/target days' supply (product master).

- **7**

  No target stock level.

To plan location products using target stock level methods, use the standard heuristic SAP_PP_002 (planning of standard lot sizes). Refer again to the far right side of Figure 5.1.

The heuristic-based planning uses the SNP heuristic. The SNP heuristic plans demand over the entire supply chain network (cross-location planning) and creates a medium-term production and distribution plan. This heuristic does not take into account any constraints or costs, which means that the plan created may not necessarily be feasible. In a second step after the heuristic run, the planner can then adjust the plan using capacity leveling in interactive SNP planning to create a plan that is feasible.

Reorder Days' Supply (in Workdays)

Specify the reorder days' supply if you have defined **Reorder Point Method 2** for the location product.

5.1.4   Goods Receipt/Goods Issue

In the following sections, we'll describe some important fields in **GR/GI** (goods receipt/goods issue) area, as shown in Figure 5.2.

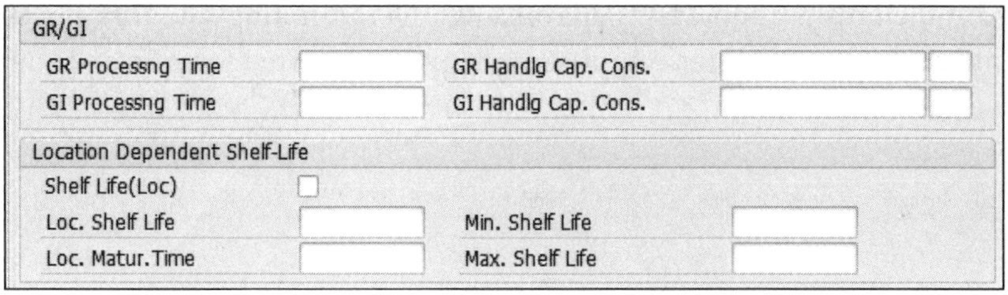

Figure 5.2 More PP-DS Master Data Maintenance Options in the Advanced Planning Tab

Goods Receipt Processing Time

This field represents the time between the delivery or the production of a product and its availability as stock. This time is used, for example, as handling time or time for quality checks and is added to the transportation duration or the production time of a product.

Handling Capacity Consumption in Unit of Measure (Goods Receipt)

Used to calculate how much handling resource capacity is consumed by the product for a particular plan. For example, if the handling resource can handle 1,000 liters per day, and you define the handling capacity consumption as 10 liters per piece, the maximum rate is 100 pieces per day.

5.1.5   Location-Dependent Shelf Life

In this area, you can control whether the system should consider the resource location-dependent shelf life of a product and, if so, the standard, minimum, and maximum shelf lives a product must have. A location in PP-DS can be a plant, a distribution center, a storage location MRP area, a customer, a transportation lane, or a business partner (vendor).

The **Advanced Planning** tab examined in this section contains specific information that is important when a material is subject to detailed planning using the newly introduced PP-DS functionality. The next section examines the information entered into the **Forecasting** tab of the material master.

5.2   Forecasting Data

The **Forecasting** tab, shown in Figure 5.3, is displayed when the material being entered is assigned to a material type applicable to forecasting. A forecast profile can be entered at the organizational level, if available. The forecasting data that can be entered into the material master comprises the initial calculated forecast and consumption values.

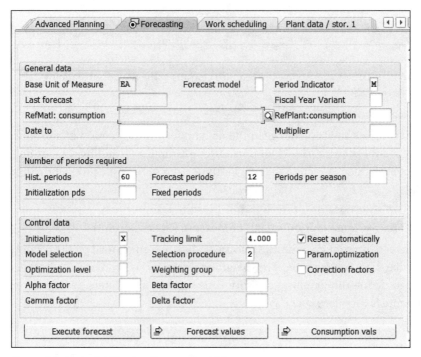

Figure 5.3 Material Master: Forecasting Tab

5.2.1   General Data

The **General data** section on the **Forecasting** tab includes a number of fields, discussed in detail in the following sections, such as the **Forecast model** to be used for the material, the **Period Indicator** used for forecasting the material, and the **Fiscal Year Variant**.

Forecast Model

The forecast model calculates the requirements forecast for the material. The forecast models and analysis of forecasting in general are discussed in Chapter 16.

Period Indicator

The **Period Indicator** field specifies the time period for which the consumption values are held for forecasting. The normal time period is 1 month, which is the SAP default if this field is left blank.

Fiscal Year Variant

The **Fiscal Year Variant** is an accounting defined field that describes the variant for the fiscal year, that is, the number of posting periods. The fiscal year variant can be configured using Transaction OB37 or by following the navigation path **Financial Accounting • Financial Accounting Global Settings • Fiscal Year • Maintain Fiscal Year Variant**.

Reference Material for Consumption

If the material you're entering has no historical data from which to create a forecast, you can define a material that may similar for use as a reference material in the **RefMatl:consumption** field. The system then uses the consumption figures for the reference material to create a forecast for the new material.

Reference Plant

The reference plant field (**RefPlant:consumption**) represents the plant from which to drive consumption figures. This field is used for new materials and used in combination with the **RefMatl:consumption** field. This field points to the plant from which you require the material to copy the consumption figures.

Date To

This field is the furthest date to which the figures for the reference material should be taken. This field is used with the **RefMatl:consumption** and the **RefPlant:consumption** fields.

Multiplier

The **Multiplier** field is a number between 0 and 1 where the value relates to the percentage of the consumption of the reference material that should be used for the new material. For example, 1 means 100% of the reference material consumption is used, whereas 0.6 indicates that 60% of the reference material consumption is used.

5.2.2   Number of Periods Required

The fields in this section include the historical periods, forecast periods, and the number of periods per seasonal cycle.

Historical Periods

The number of historical periods entered into the **Hist. periods** field is used to calculate the forecast. If left blank, no periods are used.

Forecast Periods

The number entered in the **Forecast periods** field is the number of periods over which the forecast is calculated.

Number of Periods for Initialization

This number is for the historical values that you want to be used for the forecast initialization. If the **Initialization pds** field is blank, no historical values are used to initialize the forecast.

Fixed Periods

The **Fixed periods** field is used to avoid fluctuations in the forecast calculation or because production can no longer react to changed planning figures. The forecast will be fixed for the number of periods entered.

Number of Periods per Seasonal Cycle

If you use a seasonal forecast model, then the **Periods per season** field can be used to define the number of periods that make up a season for this material.

5.2.3   Control Data

The **Control data** section of the **Forecasting** tab includes the **Initialization** indicator and the **Tracking limit**, **Model selection**, and **Weighting group** fields, among others.

Initialization Indicator

If a forecast needs to be initialized, then set this indicator to allow the system to initialize the forecast or allow forecasts to be manually initialized.

Tracking Limit

The **Tracking limit** field holds a value that specifies the amount by which the forecast value may deviate from the actual value. This figure can be entered to three decimal places.

Reset Forecast Model Automatically

If the **Reset automatically** indicator is selected, the forecast is reset if the tracking limit is exceeded.

Model Selection

This field is only active if the user did not enter a value in the **Forecast model** field, which means that the system will select a model automatically. To assist the system in choosing a forecast model, the **Model selection** field can be set to one of the following three indicators:

- **T**: Examine for a trend.
- **S**: Examine for seasonal fluctuations.
- **A**: Examine for a trend and seasonal fluctuations.

Selection Procedure

The **Selection procedure** field is used when the system is selecting a forecasting model. Two selection procedures are available:

- **1**: This procedure performs a significance test to find the best seasonal or trend pattern.
- **2**: This procedure carries out the forecast for all models and then selects the model with the smallest mean absolute deviation (MAD).

Indicator for Parameter Optimization

If the **Param.optimization** indicator is set, then the system will use the smoothing factors for the given forecast model.

Optimization Level

This indicator can be set to **Fine**, **Middle**, or **Rough**. The finer the optimization level, the more accurate the forecast becomes but at the expense of processing time and system resource consumption.

Weighting Group

This key is used with the weighted moving average forecast model. The weighting group can be configured by following the navigation path **Materials Management •** **Consumption-Based Planning • Forecast • Weighting Groups for Weighting Moving** **Average**.

Correction Factor Indicator

The **Correction factors** indicator allows you to decide whether the forecast should include the following corrector factors:

- **Alpha factor**
  This correction is the smoothing factor for the basic value. If left blank, the default for the **Alpha factor** is 0.2.

- **Beta factor**
  This correction is the smoothing factor for the trend value. If left blank, the default for the **Beta factor** is 0.1.

- **Gamma factor**
  This correction is the smoothing factor for the seasonal index. If left blank, the default for the **Gamma factor** is 0.3.

- **Delta factor**
  This correction is the smoothing factor for the mean absolute deviation. If left blank, the default for the **Delta factor** is 0.3.

In this section, we've discussed, in sufficient detail, the forecast data required for the material master record. In the next section, we'll go on to examine the data required for the **Work Scheduling** tab.

5.3   Work Scheduling Data

The **Work scheduling** tab, shown in Figure 5.4, allows you to enter information relevant to a particular plant. The material may be used in many plants. Some of the fields in this screen will be defaulted from other entry screens, such as **Base Unit of** **Measure**. In the following sections, we'll discuss the major areas of this screen. If your company produces a product, be sure to activate and maintain the work scheduling view.

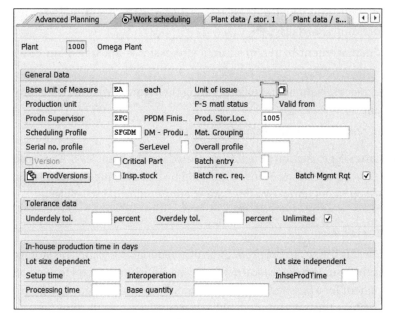

Figure 5.4 Material Master: Work Scheduling Tab

5.3.1   General Data

The **General Data** section refers to the production unit, production storage location, and the production scheduling profile.

Production Unit

The **Production unit** field reflects the UoM that is used for the material in the production process. If no production unit is entered, then the base UoM is assumed for the production UoM.

Production Supervisor

The production supervisor has an important position in production and plays many roles, including the following:

- Generating a collaborative production schedule
- Maximizing plant efficiency through the effective use of equipment and personnel
- Determining short-term labor requirements necessary to support the plan
- Creating a production plan that meets stated goals for on-time delivery

175

- Monitoring schedule adherence and schedule attainment to identify corrective actions for addressing shortfalls
- Working with management to report current order status and maintain order accuracy
- Coordinating project schedules and incorporating them into the commercial production schedule
- Identifying and resolving potential capacity constraints

In the material master, a production schedule is entered at each plant level. The **Prodn Supervisor** can be configured using Transaction OPJ9 or by following the navigation path **Production • Shop Floor Control • Master Data • Define Production Scheduler**.

Production Storage Location

The **Prod.stor.loc** field is the key to the production of a material in a plant. This storage location is used as the issuing storage location for the backflushing process for a material that is a component for a finished good. If the material is a finished good, then this storage location is where the finished goods will be received after production.

Production Scheduling Profile

The production scheduling profile can be configured using Transaction OPKP or by following the navigation path **Production • Shop Floor Control • Master Data • Define Production Scheduling Profile**.

The **Prod.Sched.Profile** field can be configured to perform automatic actions on either the release or the creation of a production or process order. The profile also provides configuration for capacity planning, availability check goods receipt, batch management, and transport and order type.

5.3.2   Tolerance Data

The **Tolerance data** section includes the fields that describe the underdelivery and overdelivery tolerances.

Underdelivery Tolerance

The **Underdely tol.** field allows you to define an underdelivery tolerance percentage for the material. Thus, if a goods receipt for a production order differs from the expected amount by more than the underdelivery tolerance, then the goods receipt won't be allowed.

Overdelivery Tolerance

The **Overdely tol.** field allows you to define an overdelivery tolerance percentage for the material. Thus, if a goods receipt for a production order differs from the expected amount by more than the overdelivery tolerance, then the goods receipt won't be allowed.

Unlimited Overdelivery

If the **Unlimited** indicator is set, then the goods receipt from a production order for this material will accept any amount over the expected goods receipt total.

5.3.3   In-House Production Time in Days

The fields in the **In-house production time in days** section include **Setup time, Processing time, Interoperation**, and **Base quantity**.

Setup Time

The **Setup time** field is used to determine the dates for planned orders. The setup time is the number of days required to configure the work centers used in the production of the material. For example, if production for material ABC in a machine shop has finished, the equipment must have the parts used for material ABC removed. After the machines have been torn down, and the setup for the next production has been run, material XYZ will start. After the run for XYZ has finished, the machines will be torn down before the next production run. The setup time for material XYZ is the setup time plus the teardown time.

This setup time doesn't take into account the quantity of the material being produced. The setup time may be a standard figure that has been calculated or negotiated. The field can be defined up to two decimal places for partial days.

Interoperation Time

The **Interoperation** field reflects the time that a material is in the state between operations in the production order. Many situations can make up the total interoperation time:

- **Move time**
  Time accumulated as the material is moved from one work center to the next.
- **Wait time**
  Time the material has to be left alone after an operation but before the move can take place on the material, for example, curing and temperature reduction.

- **Queue time**
  Time that materials are queued for work centers that are bottlenecked or because of production delays in operations. This queue time can be calculated by production staff.

- **Float before production**
  The number of days between the start date or the production order and the scheduled start date (entered by the production scheduler).

- **Float after production**
  The number of days from the end of the production order to the scheduled end date (entered by the production scheduler).

In-House Production Time

This field (**InhseProdTime**) is the number of days related to all of the individual elements of in-house production, including floats and interoperation. This value is used in material planning and is lot size independent.

Processing Time

The **Processing time** field reflects the amount of time the material consumes at the work centers used in the production order. The processing time will take into account the **Base quantity** that is entered.

Base Quantity

This processing time is entered for the base quantity and can be defined up to three decimal places.

In this section, we discussed the data used to define the **Work scheduling** tab. In the next section, we'll go into detail about maintaining production resources/tools (PRT) data in the material master.

5.4   Production Resources/Tools Data

The **Prod.resources/tools** tab, shown in Figure 5.5, allows the plant maintenance department to enter the data for a PRT material. Some of the fields shown have already been described in other material master screens. In the following sections, we'll discuss the most important elements of this tab.

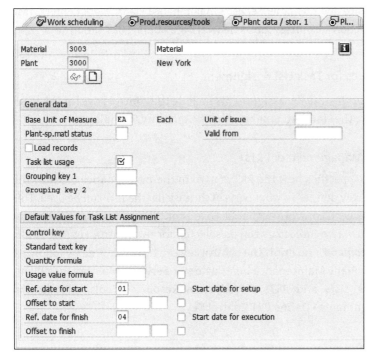

Figure 5.5 Material Master: Prod.Resources/Tools Tab

5.4.1   General Data

The **General data** section on the **Prod.resources/tools** tab allows you to enter basic plant-specific data such as **Task list usage** and **Grouping key**.

Task List Usage

This field determines on what task lists the PRT is valid for the particular plant. This field can be found in table TC23. The configuration for the **Task list usage** field is found in Transaction OP47 or via the navigation path **Plant Maintenance and Customer Service • Maintenance Plans, Work Centers, Task Lists and PRTs • Production Resources/ Tools • General Data • Define Task List Usage Keys.**

Grouping Keys 1 and 2

These fields allow the plant maintenance department to define groupings for their PRTs. The configuration for the grouping keys is found by following the navigation path **Plant Maintenance and Customer Service • Maintenance Plans, Work Centers, Task Lists and PRTs • Production Resources/Tools • General Data • Define PRT Group Keys**.

5.4.2   Default Values for Task List Assignment

The default values for the task list assignments include the control keys for the management of the PRTs, the standard text key, and the quantity formula.

Control Key for the Management of PRTs

The **Control key** field specifies how the PRT is used in the maintenance order or the task list. The control key defines in what parts of the task list the PRT can be used. This field allows you to select a control key that has been configured. During the configuration of a control key, five indicators can be selected for the control key: **Schedule, Calculate, Confirm, Expand**, and **Print**. The control key can be configured by following the navigation path **Plant Maintenance and Customer Service • Maintenance Plans, Work Centers, Task Lists and PRTs • Production Resources/Tools • Production Resource/Tool Assignments • Define PRT Control Keys**.

Standard Text Key

The **Standard text key** allows the plant maintenance department to enter a key on the material master that defines a standard text for the PRT, which is then used as a default in the task list or maintenance order. The standard texts are maintained using Transaction CA10 or by following the navigation path **Quality Management • Quality Planning • Inspection Planning • Operation • Work Center • Maintain Standard Text Keys**.

The standard text has to be maintained in the correct language. For example, the standard text key PO00010 for PRTs can be defined in a number of different languages.

Quantity Formula

This field is the formula for calculating the total of the PRTs required. This field is copied into the maintenance order or task list. The formula can be defined in configuration using Transaction OIZM or by following the navigation path **Plant Maintenance and Customer Service • Maintenance Plans, Work Centers, Task Lists and PRTs • Production Resources/Tools • Production Resource/Tool Assignments • Formulas • Configure Formula Definition**.

All formulas are defined in Transaction OIZM. For a formula to be selected in the **Quantity formula** field in the **Prod.resources/tools** tab, the formula must have the **PRT Allowed for Requirement** indicator, found on the configuration screen of Transaction OIZM, selected.

Usage Value Formula

This field calculates the total usage value of the PRT. This field is selected from the same formulas as the **Quantity formula** field.

Reference Date to Start of Production Resource/Tool Usage

The **Ref. date for start** field is used in calculating the start date/time for the PRT usage. This value is used with the **Offset to start** field, which is the next field in the material master and used in the task list or maintenance order.

Offset to Start

This field is used in conjunction with the **Ref. date for start** field for PRT scheduling. This numeric value can be positive or negative. A negative value indicates a start time before the reference date. A positive value indicates a time after the reference date. The numeric value can have a unit of measure (UoM) that indicates hours, minutes, days, and so on.

Reference Date for Finish/Offset to Finish

These fields are similar to the **Offset to start** field, except they determine the finish date rather than the start date.

In this section, we've discussed the data used to define the **PRT** tab. In the next section, we'll go into detail about maintaining plant and storage location data in the material master screen.

5.5   Plant Data/Storage Location

The **Plant data/stor.** tabs, shown in Figure 5.6 and later in Figure 5.7, allow the inventory staff to enter information relevant to storage locations and to shelf-life characteristics, including storage bins, container requirements, maximum storage periods, and total shelf life of a material, as we'll explain in the following sections.

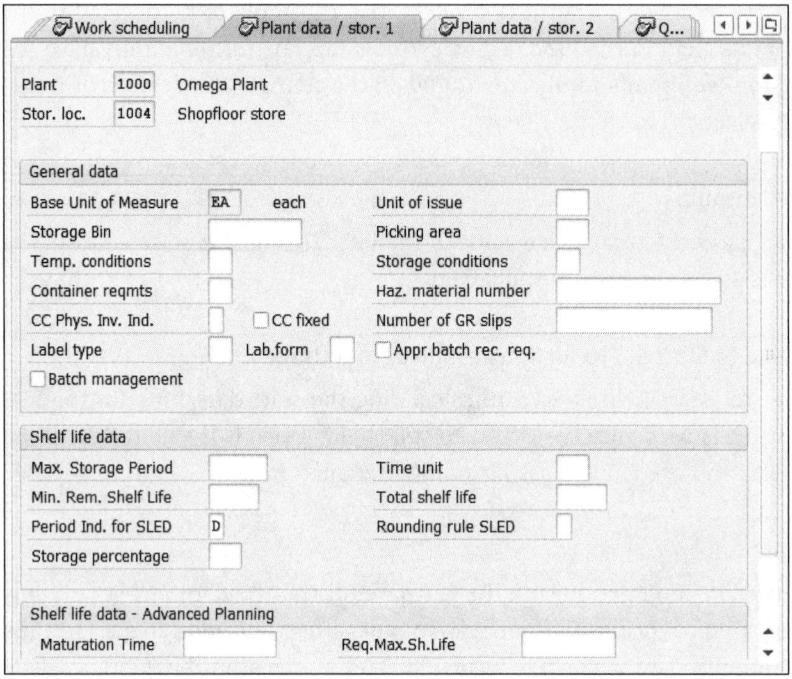

Figure 5.6 Material Master: Plant Data/Stor. 1 Tab

5.5.1   General Data

The fields in this section of the **Plant data/stor. 1** tab allow the entry of material data specifically for the storage location, such as **Storage Bin** and cycle counting indicator (**CC phys. inv. ind**). These values are referred to as general data items.

Storage Bin

The **Storage Bin** field can be entered by the warehouse staff to identify a location within the storage location where the material is always stored. This value is used when WM isn't implemented. The **Storage Bin** is a 10-character field that isn't configurable because it serves no functional purpose and is only used as a reference field. The **Storage Bin** field doesn't have any functionality within inventory management (IM).

> **Note**
>
> Only one storage bin can be defined for each material per storage location.

Picking Area

The **Picking area** field represents a group of WM storage bins that are used for picking in lean WM. The **Picking area** field is similar to the definition of storage section on the **Warehouse Management** tab. The picking area can be configured by following the navigation path **Logistics Execution • Shipping • Picking • Lean WM • Define Picking Areas**.

Temperature Conditions

The **Temp. conditions** field is simply the temperature at which the material should be stored. Certain chemicals and metals need to be stored at low temperatures to avoid chemical reactions. The **Temp. conditions** field is stored at the client level, so this value valid for all plants. The **Temp. conditions** field can be configured by following the navigation path **Logistics – General • Material Master • Settings for Key Fields • Define Temperature Conditions**.

Storage Conditions

The **Storage conditions** field is similar to the **Temp. conditions** field in that this value a client-wide field valid for all plants. The storage conditions can be defined to be relevant for specific requirements. Examples of a storage condition may be refrigeration, outside only, or in a hotbox. The **Storage conditions** field can be configured using the navigation path **Logistics – General • Material Master • Settings for Key Fields • Define Storage Conditions**.

Container Requirements

Container reqmts is another field that works at the client level and is the same for all plants. This field defines what container a material should be stored and shipped in. The **Container reqmts** field can be configured by following the navigation path **Logistics – General • Material Master • Settings for Key Fields • Define Container Requirements**.

Hazardous Material Number

A hazardous material number can be assigned to the material at the client level. This number links the material with the hazardous material information defined for that hazardous material number, such as water pollutant, hazardous storage class, or warnings. Hazardous material isn't defined in configuration but in logistics. A hazardous material can be created using Transaction VM01 or by following the navigation path **Logistics • Logistics Execution • Master Data • Material • Hazardous Material • Create**.

Cycle Counting Physical Inventory Indicator

Select the cycle counting indicator (**CC phys. inv. ind.**) if the material must be cycle counted. The indicator can also determine how the count is taken and how often. The cycle count indicator usually is an A, B, C, or D to coincide with the ABC indicators. The cycle counting indicator is defined by four characteristics:

- Number of physical inventories per fiscal year to be performed
- Maximum interval of days between counts
- Float time allowed for the planned count date after the required date
- Percentage of consumption allocated to each of the indicators (A, B, C, etc.)

The cycle counting indicator can be configured using Transaction OMCO or by following the navigation path **Materials Management • Inventory Management and Physical Inventory • Physical Inventory • Cycle Counting**.

Cycle Counting Indicator Is Fixed

If the **CC fixed** indicator is set, then **CC phys. inv. ind.**, defined previously, can't be changed by the ABC functionality that can be run periodically. If the indicator isn't set, **CC phys. inv. ind.** will be changed if the ABC functionality determines that the material has changed status. If the indicator is set, and no changes can be made via the ABC functionality, then **CC phys. inv. ind.** can still be selected by changing it in the material master.

Number of Goods Receipt Slips

The **Number of GR slips** field allows the receiving department to enter a figure to determine the number of goods receipt documents that will be printed. If the field is left blank, the system assumes that one material document will be printed.

Label Type

Some materials require labels to be printed and affixed to the product or packaging. The **Label type** field defines which labels are printed for which goods movement, how many labels are printed, and which printer they are printed on. The label type can be configured using Transaction OMCF or by following the navigation path **Materials Management • Inventory Management and Physical Inventory • Print Control • Set Label Printout • Label Type**.

Label Form

The **Lab.form** field can be used when a **Label type** has been entered for a material. The **Lab.form** field defines the dimensions and characteristics of the label. The label form can be defined using Transaction OMCF, as with the label type, or by following the navigation path **Materials Management • Inventory Management and Physical Inventory • Print Control • Set Label Printout • Label Form**.

5.5.2   Shelf Life Data

The **Shelf life data** section allows the entry of data used in shelf-life date functionality. For example, some companies use, store, and sell material that can only be used before its shelf life expires, such as food items, chemicals, and pharmaceuticals. Materials with shelf life dates need to be batch managed.

Maximum Storage Period

This field is for information and reporting only and doesn't have any functionality. Users can define the maximum storage period for a material before it expires.

Time Unit

This field is the UoM of the maximum storage period, that is, days, months, and years. For example, many foodstuffs will have a shelf life of days, whereas pharmaceuticals may have a shelf life of a year or more.

Minimum Remaining Shelf Life

The **Min. Rem. Shelf Life** field determines whether a material can be received via goods receipt based on the remaining shelf life of the material to be received. If this field has the value 100 days, and the material to be received has only 80 days of shelf life left, then the goods receipt won't be accepted. The **Min. Rem. Shelf Life** field works at the client level and is the same for the material across all plants.

Total Shelf Life

The **Total shelf life** field is at the client level, and the value doesn't vary by plant. The total shelf life is the time for which the materials will be kept, from the production date to the shelf-life expiration date (SLED). The shelf life is only checked if the expiration date check has been activated. The activation is configured at the plant level or movement type level using Transaction OMJ5 or by following the navigation path

Logistics – General • Batch Management • Shelf Life Expiration Date (SLED) • Set Expiration Date Check.

Period Indicator for Shelf-Life Expiry Date

The **Period Ind. for SLED** field is defined for the SLED fields used in this material master tab. The period can be defined as months, days, and so on. The period indicator can be configured using Transaction OO2K or by following the navigation path **Logistics – General • Batch Management • Shelf Life Expiration Date (SLED) • Maintain Period Indicator**.

Rounding Rule for Shelf-Life Expiration Date

The **Rounding rule SLED** allows SLED dates to be rounded up to the nearest unit of the time defined in the period indicator. For example, if the period indicator is months, then the rounding rule either is the first day of the month, the last day of the month, or no change if no rounding rule exists. The rounding rule is for calculated dates rather than dates entered into the record.

Figure 5.7 shows the second **Plant data/stor.** tab. The fields displayed in the **Weight/volume** section, such as the **Gross Weight** and **Net Weight** fields, and in the **General Plant Parameters** section, such as **Serial no. Profile** and **Profit Center**, can found on other material master screens.

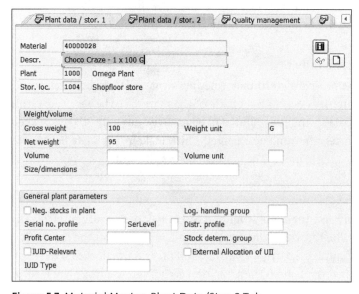

Figure 5.7 Material Master: Plant Data/Stor. 2 Tab

In the next section, we'll examine the material master screens for WM and the data that can be entered if a company uses WM.

5.6   Warehouse Management Data

The **Warehouse Mgmt** tabs of the material master allow you to enter information at the warehouse/storage type level, as shown in Figure 5.8 and in Figure 5.9. In the following sections, we'll discuss the main sections of the **Warehouse Mgmt** tabs.

5.6.1   General Data

The **General data** section, shown in Figure 5.8, allows the entry of specific WM data, including **Base Unit of Measure** and **Picking storage type**.

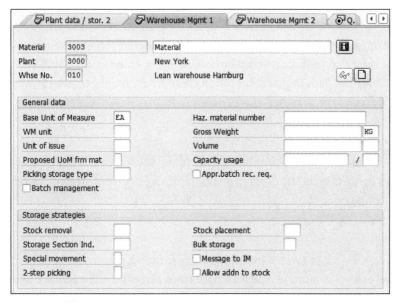

Figure 5.8 Material Master: Warehouse Mgmt 1 Tab

Warehouse Management Unit of Measure

Like other units of measure, this **WM unit** field is the UoM defined for the material as related to its movements through the warehouse.

Unit of Issue

This **Unit of issue** field allows the warehouse department to define a different UoM for items issued from the warehouse, as an alternative to the base UoM.

Picking Storage Type

This **Picking storage type** field is used by planning as the storage type that will contain material that can be used in rough-cut planning.

5.6.2   Storage Strategies

The data in this section relates to the stock placement and stock removal strategies in WM that can be attributed to the material during the material master creation.

Stock Removal

This field allows warehouse staff to enter the storage type indicator that defines the sequence in which storage types are searched for the material to be picked in the warehouse. The storage type indicator can be defined using Transaction OMLY or by following the navigation path **Logistics Execution • Warehouse Management • Strategies • Activate Storage Type Search**.

Stock Placement

The **Stock placement** field acts in a similar manner to the **Stock removal** field, except that the strategy defined in the storage type search is for a placement strategy rather than a removal strategy.

Storage Section

The storage section search is a more specific strategy for stock placement because it defines one level below the storage type search for stock placement. The **Storage Section Ind.** must be defined for each warehouse and storage type. The strategy allows up to ten storage sections to be defined in sequence for the placement strategy. The configuration can be found using Transaction OMLZ or by following the navigation path, **Logistics Execution • Warehouse Management • Strategies • Activate Storage Section Search**.

Bulk Storage

Within the placement strategies, you can define how bulk materials should be placed in stock. The **Bulk storage** indicator can be used if the bulk storage placement strategy has been activated in WM. The **Bulk storage** indicator can indicate height or width of a particular storage type. The configuration can be found using Transaction OMM4 or by following the navigation path **Logistics Execution • Warehouse Management • Strategies • Putaway Strategies • Define Strategy for Bulk Storage**.

Special Movement

The **Special movement** indicator allows a material to be identified as requiring a special goods movement. The **Special movement** indicator is configured in WM to allow special processing for a group of materials. The configuration is found by following the navigation path **Logistics Execution • Warehouse Management • Master Data • Material • Define Special Movement Indicators**.

If the **Special movement** indicator has been defined, it can be used when WM processes intersect with IM processes, where the configuration determines the WM movement type. The **Special movement** indicator can allow certain materials assigned with the indicator to behave differently during goods movements. The configuration for the warehouse goods movements can be found by following the navigation path **Logistics Execution • Warehouse Management • Interfaces • Inventory Management • Define Movement Types**.

Message to Inventory Management

This field is used if the WM system is decentralized. If this indicator is set, WM information for this material will be sent to IM immediately.

Two-Step Picking

In WM, you can choose between one-step and two-step picking for materials. If the material is large and bulky, then a one-step picking is optimal. However, if the materials to be picked are small and numerous, then one-step picking may not be an efficient use of warehouse resources. Therefore, two-step picking is used to minimize the workload. The two-step process defines an interim storage type, which is normally 200, where items are picked and transferred to; from there, the final pick takes place. The configuration for two-step picking is found by following the navigation path **Logistics Execution • Warehouse Management • Interfaces • Shipping • Define 2-Step Picking**.

Allow Addition to Stock Indicator

Setting this indicator allows material to be added to the existing stock of the same material in the same storage bin, only if the characteristics of the two quantities of material are the same. If the storage-type table doesn't allow additions to existing stock for this storage type, the indicator is redundant.

Figure 5.9 shows the data relating to palletization and storage bin stock, which we'll describe in further detail next.

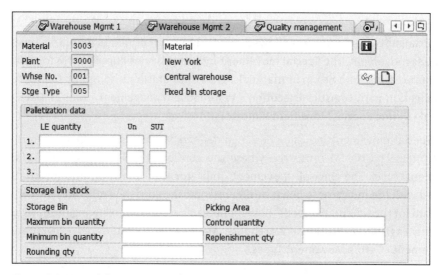

Figure 5.9 Material Master: Warehouse Mgmt 2 Tab

5.6.3   Palletization Data

Palletization is used in storage unit handling within WM. The process uses pallets to store and move material in the warehouse. The **Palletization data** section determines how the material should be entered into stock. The material can be placed into storage in different ways depending on the storage unit type being used.

Loading Equipment Quantity/Unit of Measure

The **LE quantity** represents the amount of material to be placed on the storage unit type. The storage unit type (**SUT**) described in this section is the entity used to store some material in the warehouse. This field determines the quantity of material that can be stored in the storage unit.

Storage Unit Type

The storage unit type (**SUT**) is a description of how the material is stored in the storage bin. For example, some bins may not allow a full pallet due to height restrictions, but a half-pallet may fit. Therefore, the warehouse can define a storage unit type that defines a half-pallet and the quantity of the material that can fit on that half-pallet.

> **Example**
>
> Suppose that, for material XYZ, 30 boxes are equivalent to one half-pallet. The storage unit type is configured in the IMG and must be activated in each warehouse before it can be used. A definition of the storage unit type exists for each plant. The configuration can be made by following the navigation path **Logistics Execution • Warehouse Management • Master Data • Material • Define Storage Unit Types**.

5.6.4   Storage Bin Stock

The **Storage bin stock** information entered in the **Warehouse Mgmt 2** tab is used for calculation in WM bin replenishment.

Storage Bin

The storage bin is the lowest level of storage defined in the warehouse. The **Storage Bin** field allows a warehouse user to enter a storage bin that this material will be added to for the plant/storage type combination. Pressing the F4 key shows the options for the empty storage bins.

Maximum Bin Quantity

This value can be entered to define the maximum quantity of a material that can be entered into any storage bin defined in the storage type. The quantity is defined in the base UoM, not the WM UoM.

Control Quantity

The **Control quantity** can be entered to define for this storage type the amount of material that reaches the level where stock removal can take place. Similar to the **Maximum bin quantity**, this **Control quantity** uses the material's base UoM.

Minimum Bin Quantity

This field allows warehouse users to define a minimum quantity that can be stored in the bin locations for this storage type. This requirement makes efficient use of storage bins. For example, if a material is small, the maximum bin quantity is high, and no minimum quantity is set, then you might have many bins each containing small amounts of stock. Entering a minimum bin quantity allows a bin to be used efficiently and minimizes picking. Like the other quantities, the **Minimum bin quantity** is recorded in the base quantity unit.

Replenishment Quantity

The **Replenishment qty** field is defined to suggest the quantity that should be placed in the storage bin. Like the other quantities, the **Replenishment qty** is recorded in the base quantity unit.

Rounding Quantity

This quantity is used if a material is subject to the quantity-dependent picking strategy. The **Rounding qty** field represents the figure that picking quantities are rounded down to for this material/storage type combination. This quantity is also defined in the base UoM.

In the next section, we'll examine the material master screens that contain the QM fields. Data on these screens should only be maintained if your client is using the QM functionality.

5.7   Quality Management Data

The **Quality management** tab allows the quality department to define the basic quality requirements for the material at each plant level. The following sections cover the most important fields and sections of this tab.

5.7.1   General Data

The **General data** section of the **Quality management** tab, shown in Figure 5.10, allows the entry of specific QM data, including UoM, inspection interval, and documentation.

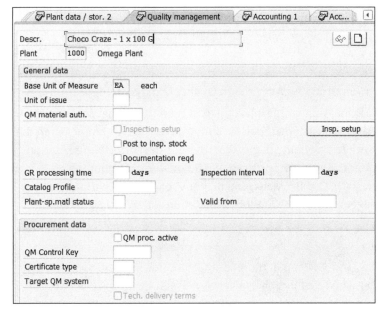

Figure 5.10 Material Master: Quality Management Tab

Inspection Setup

Inspection setup information is already determined if a QM inspection setup already exists for this material/plant combination. If a quality inspection user wants to enter the inspection setup information for this material at this plant, the **Insp. Setup** button to the right will bring up the inspection entry screen. This screen allows a number of inspection types to be entered, such as **Goods Receipt Inspection** for purchase orders or production orders, recurring (repeat) inspection, and **Stock Transfer Inspection**.

Post to Inspection Stock Indicator

This indicator can be set to force material to be posted to inspection stock. This indicator is copied into the purchase order (PO). However, this indicator is ignored if an inspection type that is stock-relevant—in other words, an inspection due to stock movement—has been entered in the inspection setup.

Tips & Tricks

If the company hasn't implemented or isn't using QM, you can still select this checkbox available in various views of material master so that the incoming stock is posted

---

to quality inspection instead of unrestricted-use stock. In other words, using this checkbox offers limited quality management functionality even when not using QM.

Material Authorization Group for Activities in Quality Management

The **QM material auth.** field allows the quality department to add a layer of security to the quality information of each material. An authorization group can be entered in the field to check whether a quality inspection user has the correct authorization to view the information. The authorization group is defined in configuration by following the navigation path **Quality Management • Environment • Central Functions • Authorization Management • Define Authorization Group and Digital Signature**.

> **Note**
>
> This field not only control who is authorized to perform quality functions but also controls the digital signature functionality in QM. A digital signature is an electronic signature and is cross-component functionality in SAP that allows the acceptance and approval of various SAP objects by requiring the business users to enter their SAP passwords to reflect their acceptance or approvals of SAP objects. These SAP objects can be, for example, results recordings and usage decisions (the decision to use a material or not) of an inspection lot.

Document Required Indicator

After the **Documentation Reqd** indicator is set, the system will record any changes to inspection lots or usage decisions. These status changes are recorded in change documents that can be viewed in the status history for the material.

Inspection Interval

This field allows the quality department to enter the number of days required between inspections of the material at this plant. This value is copied to the batch master record when a batch is created. Refer to Chapter 8 to see how this functionality works.

Catalog Profile

This field reflects a value that is relevant in quality notifications. The catalog profile is defined in configuration by following the navigation path **Quality Management • Quality Notifications • Notification Creation • Notification Content • Define Catalog Profile**.

5.7.2   Procurement Data

The procurement data on the **Quality management** tab of the material master allows the material to be flagged for quality checks in procurement.

Quality Management in Procurement Indicator

The **QM proc. active** indicator switches on the QM aspect of procurement and can be activated at a plant level or a client level. If activated at the client level, then the **QM Control Key** field should also be defined. Selecting the **QM proc. active** checkbox also means that the system must have a QM info record already created before a procurement process, such as a purchase order, can be created. Just like the purchasing information record, a QM info record has a one-to-one relationship between a vendor and a material on the quality aspects of the procurement.

Quality Management Control Key

The **QM Control Key** can be defined during configuration and determines how a material is affected by quality during the procurement cycle. The control key can determine the following:

- If technical delivery terms must exist as a document
- If a quality assurance document must exist between the company and the vendor
- If a valid purchasing information record must exist
- If a quality certificate is required from the vendor on each shipment
- If a block can be put in place against the invoice

Certificate Type

The incoming quality certificate can be required by the quality department for each goods receipt item or PO item concerning certain materials from the vendor. Many different certificate types can be defined in configuration by following the navigation path **Quality Management • QM in Logistics • QM in Procurement • Define Keys for Certificate Processing • Define Certificate Types**.

Target Quality Management System

The **Target QM system** field allows the quality department to define the type of QM system it requires from vendors. For example, the quality department may require that the vendors for the material have an ISO 9001 certification for their sites. The configuration in QM can define the requirements and, in addition, can determine what rating vendors can achieve through the quality department's evaluation.

The configuration for the target QM system can be found using Transaction OQB7 or by following the navigation path **Quality Management • QM in Logistics • QM in Procurement • Define QM Systems**.

The **Quality management** tab we've examined in this section contains specific information important when the material undergoes quality checks. Coordinate with the quality control and quality assurance staff to ensure that the correct information is entered.

In the next section, we'll examine the information entered into the accounting screens of the material master.

5.8   Accounting Data

The first **Accounting** tab in the material master, shown in Figure 5.11, allows the accounting department to enter the valuation and price data needed for inventory transactions.

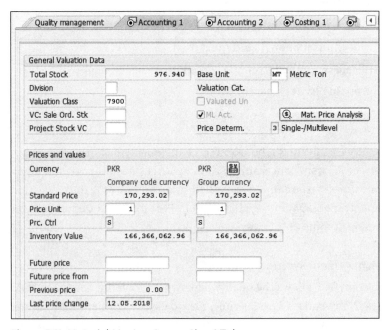

Figure 5.11 Material Master: Accounting 1 Tab

In the following sections, we'll discuss the screens and fields necessary for maintaining the accounting data of a material.

5.8.1   General Data

The **General Data** section on the first accounting tab displays some information that has been entered on other material master tabs, such as **Base Unit of Measure**.

Valuation Category

This field determines whether the material is subject to split valuation. *Split valuation* means that a material can be valuated in different ways. An example of split valuation is the valuation of separate batches, such as in the chemical industry where batches of the same material may have a different number of days left before batches expire. A batch with only 10 days before expiration may be valuated differently from a batch that has 100 days left before expiration because the batch with only 10 days left of shelf life could only be sold at a discounted price. Refer to Chapter 22 where we'll cover this topic in detail.

Material Ledger Active

The **ML act.** indicator shows whether the Material Ledger has been activated for this material. The Material Ledger is the basis of actual costing and enables material inventories to be valuated in multiple currencies and also using different valuation approaches. By default, the Material Ledger is now active in SAP S/4HANA. Chapter 23 covers the Material Ledger.

5.8.2   General Valuation Data

The **General valuation Data** section is where the valuation class is determined for the material at the specific plant and the price of the material, either standard or moving average.

Valuation Class

The **Valuation Class** field is a mechanism to assign a material to the general ledger (G/L) accounts. These G/L accounts are updated when material movements relevant to accounting occur. The valuation class is assigned to a material type via configuration.

The valuation class can be configured using Transaction OMSK or by following the navigation path **Materials Management • Valuation and Account Assignment •**

Account Determination • Account Determination without Wizard • Define Valuation Class.

Valuation Class for Sales Order Stocks

The accounting department has the option of entering a different valuation class for sales order stock in the **VC: Sales order stk** field.

Valuation Class for Project Stock

As with the valuation class for sales order stock, the accounting department can enter a different valuation class for project stock in the **Proj. stk val. class** field.

Price Control

The **Price control** field is used in the valuation of the stock. The two options are average moving price (**V**) and standard price (**S**).

Price Unit

The number entered in the **Price Unit** field is the number of units that the moving price or standard price relates to. Therefore, if the standard price for material XYZ is 3.24 USD, and the price unit is 1000, then the actual cost per unit is 0.00324 USD. The price unit is important when entering materials with small prices because it can prevent rounding errors if the number of decimal places in a report isn't sufficient.

Moving Price

The moving price, more often called the *moving average price*, is calculated by dividing the material value by the total stock. This price changes with each goods movement relevant for valuation. The accounting department can make an initial price entry if the **Price control** field is set to **V** for moving price. This field is also referred to as the *periodic unit price* (PUP) if the Material Ledger is active.

Standard Price

The **Standard price** field is a constant; once entered, this price doesn't fluctuate and doesn't take into account invoice prices or any other price-altering movements. The standard price can be entered when the **Price control** field is set to **S** for standard price.

Future Price

The **Standard price** can be changed through an entry in the **Future price** field. A future price entered in the field will become valid starting on the date entered in the **Valid from** field.

The second accounting tab, as shown in Figure 5.12, includes the **Determination of lowest value** and **LIFO data** sections. For detailed coverage on this topic, refer to Chapter 22.

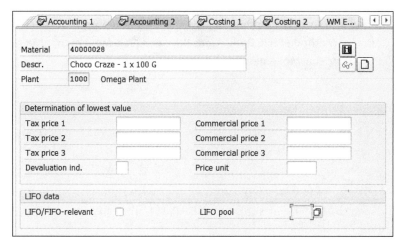

Figure 5.12 Material Master: Accounting 2 Tab

5.8.3   Determination of Lowest Value

This section contains the fields for three **Tax price** and three **Commercial price** fields, as well as the **Devaluation ind.** and **Price unit** fields.

Tax Price

This field is available for entering the price of the material for tax purposes. This field isn't used in the United States but is used in some countries. Check with the accounting department if this field is used in your particular country.

Commercial Price

This field is available for entering the price of the material for commercial valuation purposes. This field is also not used in the United States but is used in some countries. Check with the accounting department if this field is used in your particular country.

Devaluation Indicator

A value can be entered into the **Devaluation ind.** field in the material master if the company feels that the material is a slow or nonmoving item. The accounting department can configure a number of indicators for each material type per company code that has a devaluation percentage attached.

The indicator can be changed to increase or decrease the devaluation percentage depending on the movement of the material stock. The indicators can be configured using Transaction OMW6 or by following the navigation path **Materials Management • Valuation and Account Assignment • Balance Sheet Valuation Procedures • Configure Lowest-Value Method • Price Deductions Based on Non-Movement • Maintain Devaluation by Slow/Non-Movement by Company Code**.

5.8.4   Last In First Out Data

The two fields in this section are the **LIFO/FIFO-relevant** indicator and the **LIFO pool** field. For detailed coverage on this topic, refer to Chapter 22.

Last In First Out/First In Last Out Relevant

If this indicator is set, the material is subject to LIFO (last in first out) valuation and FIFO (first in first out) valuation.

LIFO valuation for stock implies that, as new stock comes in and then moves out first, the old stock doesn't change in value, and no overvaluation of the older stock occurs.

FIFO valuation calculates the valuation of the stock based on the price of the last receipt. Although this method is the most realistic valuation, older stock can be overvaluated.

Last In First Out Pool

The **LIFO pool** field is ignored if a material isn't LIFO relevant. The **LIFO pool** field can be configured to define a group of materials that can be valued together. LIFO pools can be configured using Transaction OMW2 or by following the navigation path **Materials Management • Valuation and Account Assignment • Balance Sheet Valuation Procedures • Configure LIFO/FIFO Methods • LIFO • Configure LIFO Pools**.

The accounting tabs we've examined in this section contain specific information important when the material is valuated. Check with the accounting staff to ensure that the correct information is entered.

In the next section, we'll examine the information entered into the costing tabs of the material master.

5.9   Costing Data

The costing tabs of the material master, shown in Figure 5.13 and Figure 5.14, allow the costing department to enter costing information for a material. Some of the fields on these screens have been discussed in previous sections.

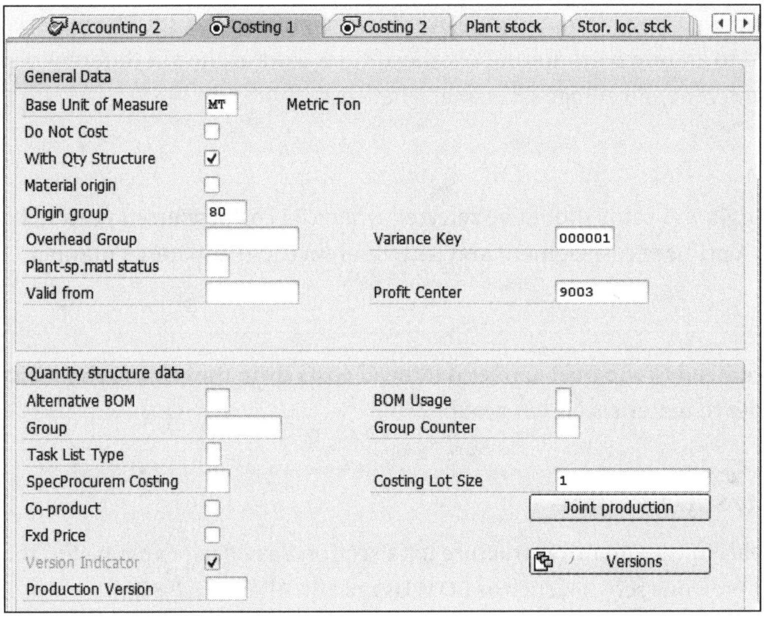

Figure 5.13 Material Master: Costing 1 Tab

5.9.1   General Data

The **General Data** section contains a number of fields, which we'll discuss in the following sections.

Do Not Cost

This checkbox should be selected if the material won't have a material cost estimate, a sales order cost estimate, or a procurement alternative. The material also won't be part of a BOM explosion.

With Quantity Structure

The costing of materials can be performed with or without a quantity structure. If you cost materials with a quantity structure, select on the **With Qty Structure** indicator. If you cost materials without a quantity structure, don't select this indicator. If this indicator isn't selected, the planned costs for the material are calculated using the cost estimate without a quantity structure. Check with staff working on the costing of materials to ensure this checkbox is set correctly.

Origin Group

The **Origin group** field is used to subdivide overhead and material costs. The material can be assigned to an origin group, and overhead costs are assigned to different origin groups at different percentage rates or at a flat cost.

Material Origin

The **Material origin** indicator should be selected when the costs incurred need to be updated under a primary cost element and with reference to the material number.

Overhead Group

The costing **Overhead Group** field applies overhead costs from the costing sheet of a production order to materials in that group.

5.9.2   Quantity Structure Data

Some of the fields in the **Quantity structure data** section have been explained in the descriptions of previous screens, such as **BOM Usage** and **Alternative BOM**.

Group

A **Group,** sometimes called a *task list group*, can combine production processes that are similar and that are for similar materials. Groups can be used to group task lists for varying lot sizes.

Group Counter

Combined with the group, the **Group Counter** identifies a unique task list for a material. A task list describes the steps needed to produce a material or perform an activity without reference to an order. The task list is comprised of a header, operations, material component allocations, PRTs, and inspection characteristics.

Task List Type

This field identifies the task list type, that is, whether the task list is for routings, rate routings, standard networks, and so on. The task list type can be maintained using Transaction OP8B or by following the navigation path **Production • Basic Data • Routing • Control Data • Maintain Task List Types**.

Costing Lot Size

This field allows the product costing department to enter a lot size for the material, which will be used in the product cost estimate.

The first section of the **Costing 2** tab, as shown in Figure 5.14, is the **Standard Cost Estimate**, which shows **Future**, **Current**, and **Previous** prices.

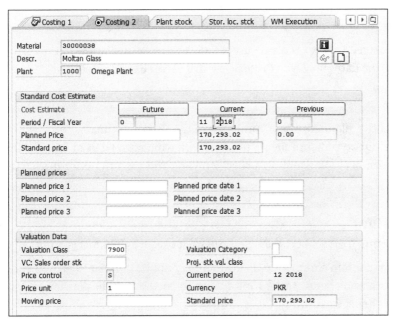

Figure 5.14 Material Master: Costing 2 Tab

5.9.3   Standard Cost Estimate

A standard cost estimate is the most important type of cost estimate in material costing. This type of cost estimate forms the basis for profit planning or product costing. The standard cost estimate is created for each material at the beginning of the company's fiscal year.

Planned Price

The **Planned price** field allows the entry of a marked standard cost estimate for a future price for the material. When a standard cost estimate for a material is marked, the cost calculated in the standard cost estimate is written to the material master record as the future planned price. A standard cost estimate must be marked before it can be released to the material. This field isn't the same as the three **Planned price** fields in the **Planned prices** section.

Standard Price

The value in the **Standard price** field means that all goods movements are valuated at that price.

5.9.4   Planned Prices

This part of the screen allows a costing user to add three planned prices to the material master and the dates on which those prices will become valid.

Planned Price 1

Subsequent to the planned price from the standard cost estimate, three other planned prices can be added to the material master, which can be used for product costing. The price becomes valid on a specified date, and then the price is used in product costing.

Planned Price Date 1

On this date, planned price 1 becomes valid and will be used by product costing.

The costing tabs contain a number of fields that may not be familiar to an MM consultant, so you should contact the costing analyst to ensure that the data entered in the material master is correct.

The section on **Valuation Data** holds information on how the system valuates a material. For example, the **Valuation Class** field controls whether a material produced in-house should be valuated differently than the material procured from external sources. Similarly, the **Price Control** field controls whether a material should be valuated at standard price or moving average. If selecting the standard price option (**S**), the system will keep the material's price the same or standard, and any deviation in valuation is recorded as a gain or a loss. With the moving average price option, the system updates the material valuation each time its value changes.

5.10   Summary

In this chapter and Chapter 4, we discussed the elements that make up the material master. At first, the SAP material master might seem daunting. Other inventory or integrated systems have item master data and files that are a fraction of the size of the material master, which is important when bringing on legacy systems. When converting legacy master files into the SAP material master, commonly the legacy master files will only hold a small number of the fields necessary for the material master.

Most companies spend a great deal of time constructing data for the material master. Therefore, you should learn about the material master structure and the implications of entering or not entering information into material master fields.

Another master file is examined in Chapter 6: the business partner master file. A business partner, as it is now known in SAP S/4HANA, was previously (and may still be) referred to as a vendor master or supplier master who supplies materials and services to a company. The information contained in the business partner master file allows the purchasing department to purchase from and pay business partners.

Chapter 6

Business Partners

The business partner function in SAP brings together the different and diverse business processes a company manages—all via a single transaction and with a consolidated view of a partner's data. A business partner can have the role of a supplier (or vendor), a customer, a person, or an employee. A business partner can be created as an organization, a person, or a group.

6

In SAP S/4HANA, the business partner has become the leading object and the single point of entry to maintain supplier (formerly known as vendor) and customer master data. This approach makes master data maintenance easier and achieves harmonization among the various business functions of a company. Compared to SAP ERP transactions, maintaining supplier and customer master data through the business partner offers the following advantages:

- A legal entity is represented with one business partner.

- A business partner allows the maintenance of multiple addresses for various uses.

- In SAP ERP, one supplier or customer could only be associated to one vendor account group. With business partners, multiple roles can be associated to the same business partner.

- Maximal data sharing and reuse of data leads to an easier and simplified data consolidation.

- The general data of a business partner is available for different business partner roles, while specific data is stored for each role.

- Multiple relationships to the same business partner can be maintained.

- Time dependency at different subentities (i.e., roles, address, relationship, bank data) can be maintained.

A business partner can be a person or a group of persons or an organization having some interest in the company's business. You can create a business partner in

207

different business partner roles. During the course of a business relationship with your company, a business partner can assume other business partner roles. You do not need to create the general data, which is the same for all business partner functions. As a result, you can use the same business partner for different applications. For example, you can interact with business partner number 10000 as a customer in a customer role *and* as a vendor in a vendor role. In this way, a business partner can play multiple roles.

In an SAP system, master data synchronization synchronizes master data objects that are similar from a business, but not from a technical, point of view. In this way, you can integrate different SAP applications seamlessly in your business processes. For example, you can use master data synchronization to set up the integration of the business partner with the vendor master. As a result, you'll be able to integrate SAP applications that make technical use of the business partner in their user interfaces and use the vendor master as a technical basis in subsequent business processes. Customer/vendor integration (CVI) for business partners is a mandatory prerequisite in SAP S/4HANA.

As in previous chapters, we'll first cover the configuration steps for a business partner and then describe how to create business partner master data in which the configured objects will be assigned. Further, we'll use the configurations covered in previous chapters, such as our example purchasing organization 6000, plant 6000, and material 10000000, among others, to create a logical links among all the configurations we've undertaken so far.

In the following sections, we'll present an example in which vendors providing high-value materials to our company are configured as a business partner in a step-by-step approach. Topics ranging from configuring a vendor account group to creating and assigning a number range to this new vendor account group are covered. We'll also configure a new business partner purchasing role for vendors supplying high-value materials to our company.

Finally, we'll also cover the configuration steps for using financials (FI) in SAP S/4HANA, which also requires configuring and setting up business partners in the SAP system. During an SAP implementation project, and due to the integrated nature of the business partner in materials management (MM) with FI, we highly recommend coordinating with the FI team to ensure that the configuration and business processes between FI and MM are completely aligned.

6.1   Configuring Vendor Account Groups (Financial Accounting)

In an SAP implementation, commonly, separate vendor account groups are created for foreign/import vendors, local vendors, and service vendors. Any logical grouping of vendor account groups should be created to meet the reporting needs of your company. This bifurcation of vendor account groups not only helps with better and more focused reporting on different vendor groups but also enables the assignment of specific pricing schemas for each vendor group.

For example, in foreign procurement, different types of charges (known as *conditions* in SAP) will have to be paid, more types than in local procurement. These different charges on imports range from a letter of credit (LC) opening fee with an opening bank, demurrage, wharf-rage, customs clearance, LC clearance charges, and shipment charges to customs agent charges. To attend to all kinds of charges in imports procurement, you'll configure a pricing scheme that is then assigned to foreign vendors (business partners). Another pricing schema with fewer conditions would be configured for local vendors and assigned to the local vendor group.

> **Note**
>
> We always recommend using the standard configuration objects predelivered by SAP instead of creating new ones. However, as is often the case with most SAP implementation projects, specific business needs, authorizations, or reporting needs will require configuring new objects.
>
> Wherever possible and available, configure new objects using the standard objects already available to save time and effort.
>
> Despite the introduction of the terms like "business partner" or "supplier" in SAP S/4HANA, be aware that you'll still frequently come across the SAP ERP term "vendor" in configuration, master data, business processes, and reporting.

In the following sections, we'll briefly cover the minimum FI configuration required for business partners in MM to effectively work. We'll show you how to create a FI vendor account group and then how to create a number range, which is then assigned to the FI vendor account group. We always recommend complete coordination with an FI consultant so that the MM-FI integration is error-free.

6.1.1 Vendor Account Groups (Financial Accounting)

A vendor account group is a way of grouping vendors with the same number range and the same attributes entered. The account group is defined to allow certain fields to be seen and maintained on the vendor master.

The vendor master record is especially relevant to a purchasing organization. When creating a vendor, a purchasing user determines what data associated with that vendor is relevant only to a single purchasing organization.

However, a vendor often deals with several purchasing departments in a single company, and the negotiations between the vendor and the company might be limited to a specific geographical area, which may relate to a single purchasing organization. For example, if a global fast-moving consumer goods (FMCG) company negotiates rates and discounts with a company, the terms may be different for the company's Canadian locations than for locations in Mexico or China. Therefore, when entering the vendor master record for this FMCG company, the differences between purchasing organizations may be significant.

To create a new vendor account group, follow the menu path **Financial Accounting (New) • Accounts Receivable and Accounts Payable • Vendor Accounts • Master Data • Preparations for Creating Vendor Master Data • Define Account Groups with Screen Layout (Vendors)**.

As shown in Figure 6.1, create a new vendor account group, **Group** HVPV, and then double-click on the **Details** icon.

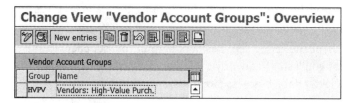

Figure 6.1 Vendor Account Group

A one-time vendor record, shown in Figure 6.2, can be used for a vendor that is only used once or very rarely. For example, you may need a material in an emergency, and perhaps your normal vendor for that material can't supply the item in the requested time. In this instance, a local vendor or an unapproved vendor may be used for this one-off purchase. Such a record can be used for a number of vendors, which reduces the amount of data entry and data maintenance required. Companies can also use one-time vendor records for travel, expense reimbursement, and vendors that can't accept the company's purchase orders (POs).

A one-time vendor record can be created in the same way as any normal vendor by using Transaction BP. The difference is that a one-time vendor uses a special account group. One-time vendor records don't usually contain any significant data or any bank and financial information. Many companies have policies in place to ensure that vendor master records aren't created for one-time or limited-use vendors. Some of these policies may include establishing a limit on the number of transactions per year and restricting the yearly spend on these vendors. For example, if a vendor has more than four transactions a year, or if the total annual spending with a vendor is more than $4,000, then company policy could require that a vendor master record be maintained for that vendor instead of that vendor being treated as a one-time vendor only.

To maintain the **Field status** of any field, as shown in Figure 6.3, click on any of the three options shown in Figure 6.2:

- **General Data**
- **Company Code Data**
- **Purchasing Data**

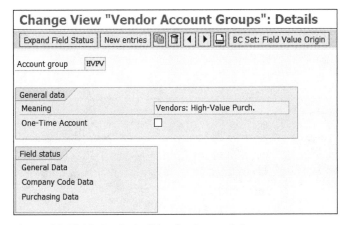

Figure 6.2 Fields Control of Vendor Account Group

The configuration screen shown in Figure 6.3 allows you to make certain fields required (**Req. Entry**), optional (**Opt. entry**), display only (**Display**), or suppressed (**Suppress**). This configuration is specific to the account group that is entered when a vendor master record is created.

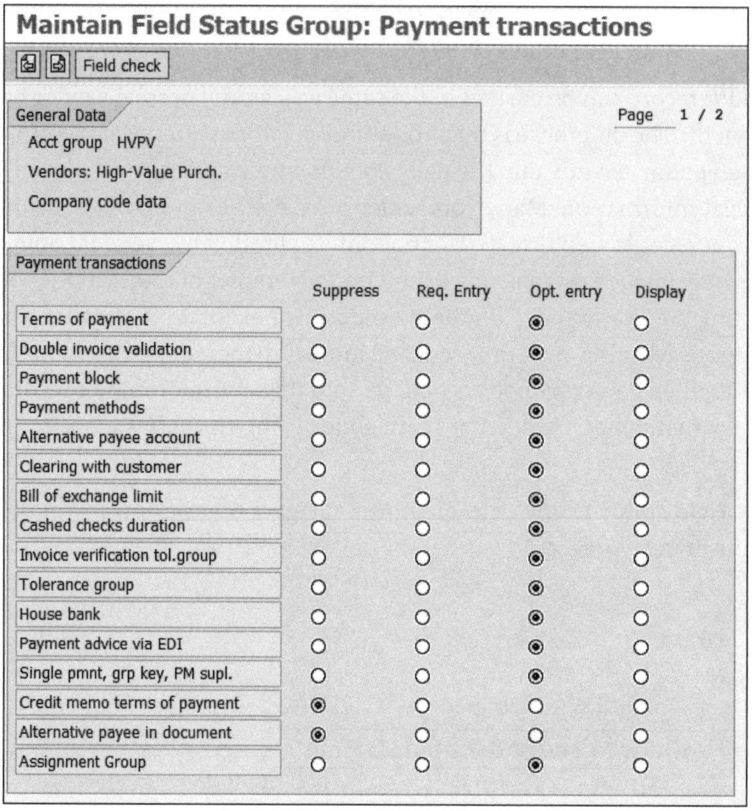

Maintain Field Status Group: Payment transactions

⌑ ⌑ | Field check

General Data				Page 1 / 2
Acct group HVPV				
Vendors: High-Value Purch.				
Company code data				

Payment transactions

	Suppress	Req. Entry	Opt. entry	Display
Terms of payment	O	O	◉	O
Double invoice validation	O	O	◉	O
Payment block	O	O	◉	O
Payment methods	O	O	◉	O
Alternative payee account	O	O	◉	O
Clearing with customer	O	O	◉	O
Bill of exchange limit	O	O	◉	O
Cashed checks duration	O	O	◉	O
Invoice verification tol.group	O	O	◉	O
Tolerance group	O	O	◉	O
House bank	O	O	◉	O
Payment advice via EDI	O	O	◉	O
Single pmnt, grp key, PM supl.	O	O	◉	O
Credit memo terms of payment	◉	O	O	O
Alternative payee in document	◉	O	O	O
Assignment Group	O	O	◉	O

Figure 6.3 Field Status Group

Note

These screen layouts can also be modified by company code by following the navigation path **Financial Accounting (New) • Vendor Accounts • Master Data • Preparations for Creating Vendor Master Data • Define Screen Layout per Company Code**.

6.1.2   Number Ranges for Vendor Account Group

When defining vendor number ranges, remember that vendor numbers, like material numbers, can be externally or internally assigned. Many SAP customers create different number ranges for each account group. Careful consideration is required when defining number ranges to prevent number ranges from overlapping.

Use Transaction XKN1 to create vendor number ranges or follow the navigation path **Financial Accounting (New) • Vendor Accounts • Master Data • Preparations for Creating Vendor Master Data • Create Number Ranges for Vendor Accounts**. Figure 6.4 shows the configuration for vendor number ranges.

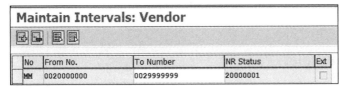

Figure 6.4 Defining Number Ranges of a Vendor Account Group

For this transaction, you should enter a unique identifier for the range, defined by a two-character field, and then enter the range of numbers to define the number range. The **NR Status** field in edit mode allows you to define the current number. The **Ext** field allows you to define whether the number range is externally defined or user defined. For our example, let's create a new number range by entering "MM" in the **NO** column, clicking the insert interval icon (**+**), and maintaining the number range by entering "20000000" in the **From No.** field and "29999999" in the **To Number** field.

After defining a number range, the next step is to assign the number range to the vendor account group, which we'll cover in the next section.

6.1.3   Assigning Number Ranges to Vendor Account Groups

After a number range is defined, you can assign it to a vendor account group by following the navigation path **Financial Accounting (New) • Vendor Accounts • Master Data • Preparations for Creating Vendor Master Data • Assign Number Ranges to Vendor Account Groups**.

A number range can be assigned to many vendor account groups, as shown in Figure 6.5. Therefore, if your company decides to use just one number range for all its vendors, the configuration will show only one number range assigned to all account groups.

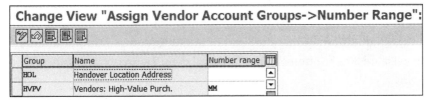

Figure 6.5 Assigning Number Ranges of a Vendor Account Group

For our example, assign the **Number range** MM to the vendor account group HVPV (**Group**).

In this section, we covered the minimum FI-related configuration required for business partner configuration to begin. In the next section, we'll cover the steps for configuring business partners.

6.2   Configuring a Business Partner

In this section, we'll cover the steps involved in setting up business partners in the SAP system.

6.2.1   Defining and Assigning Number Ranges

Just as the process of defining and assigning number ranges for vendor account groups is important, we'll need to do the same for business partner number ranges. The process of defining and assigning business partner number ranges follows the same steps we covered for vendor account groups in the previous section.

To define a business partner number range, follow the menu path **Cross-Application Components • SAP Business Partner • Business Partner • Basic Settings • Define Number Ranges**. Figure 6.6 shows the definition of business partner number range interval **MM**.

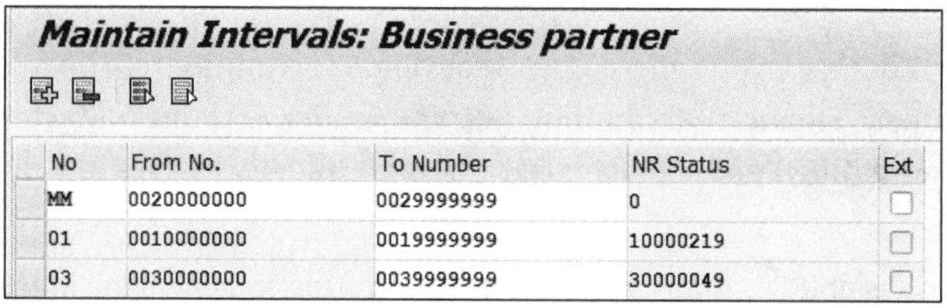

Maintain Intervals: Business partner

No	From No.	To Number	NR Status	Ext
MM	0020000000	0029999999	0	☐
01	0010000000	0019999999	10000219	☐
03	0030000000	0039999999	30000049	☐

Figure 6.6 Defining Business Partner Number Ranges

To assign a business partner number range, follow the menu path **Cross-Application Components • SAP Business Partner • Business Partner • Basic Settings • Define Groupings and Assign Number Ranges**.

As shown in Figure 6.7, the number range MM has been assigned to the business partner grouping HVPV.

Figure 6.7 Assigning Business Partner Number Ranges to a Business Partner Grouping

Tips & Tricks

We recommend creating a business partner grouping for each vendor account group. To simplify configuration and business processes, an even better method is to use the same identifiers between the FI vendor account groups and business partners.

6.2.2   Defining Business Partner Role Categories

In this step, we'll configure a new business partner role category for vendors of high-value purchases by copying from the standard available business partner category FLVN01. A business partner role category is the highest level of business partner in which various business partner roles are created for an organization, a group, or a person.

To define business partner role categories, follow the menu path **Cross-Application Components • SAP Business Partner • Business Partner • Basic Settings • Define BP Roles**.

Figure 6.8 shows the list of available business partner role categories, including the standard business partner role category FLVN01, which is used in the purchasing process. Select **FLVN01** in the **Role Cat.** column, click on **Copy As.**, and create the new **BP Role Cat.** as **ZHVPRC**, as shown in Figure 6.9.

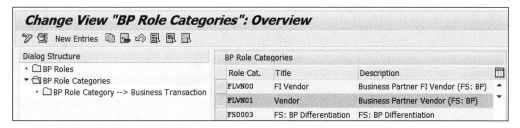

Figure 6.8 Available Business Partner Role Categories

As shown in Figure 6.9, maintain the **Title** and **Description** fields of the new business partner role category ZHVPRC. The **Diff. Type** field (differentiation type) is the controlling field, that is, the field that controls the types of data or the screens available while creating a new business partner of this specific business partner role category. Type 0 will enable maintenance of general data of a business partner. Type 2 will bring up purchasing-related fields, tabs, and screen of a business partner for data maintenance, while type 3 will enable maintenance of sales area data, wherein a business partner is a customer. You can also control which or all of the three business partner categories, that is, organization, person or a group is allowed for a particular business partner role category by selecting the relevant checkboxes.

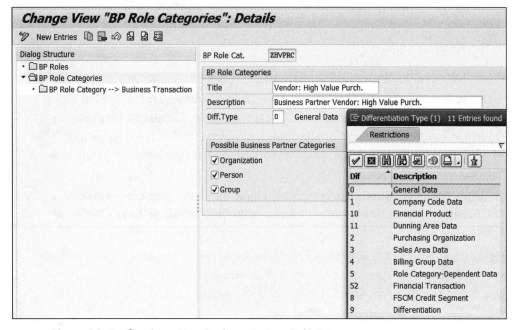

Figure 6.9 Configuring a New Business Partner Role Category

For this example, choose **Differentiation Type** 2 as we want to create a new business partner role category for the purchasing function, and the screen shown in Figure 6.10 will appear.

Figure 6.10 shows the newly configured business partner role category ZHVPRC. Select it, and click on the **BP Roles** located on the left hand side of the screen.

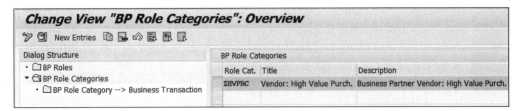

Figure 6.10 Business Partner Role Category ZHVPRC

As shown in Figure 6.11, create a new **BP Role** ZHVPO1 by clicking **New Entries** and assigning the **BP Role Category** ZHVPRC just created in the previous step. Be sure the **Std Assignment BP Role -> BP Role Cat.** checkbox has been selected so that the system assigns this specific business partner role ZHVPO1 to the business partner role category ZHVPRC.

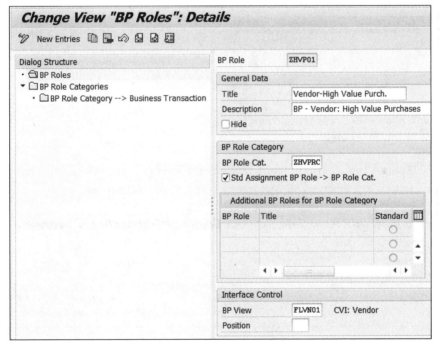

Figure 6.11 Business Partner Role and Assignment of a Business Partner Role Category

It's important to note that several business partner roles can be assigned to a business partner role category (in other words, a business partner role category can have several business partner roles assigned to it), therefore, selecting this checkbox will ensure one standard business partner role is read while creating a business partner master data. Assign the *standard* **BP view** FLVN01 in the lower half of the screen to ensure standard screens and layouts are available while creating a new business partner of the newly configured business partner role category. (Recall that we created this business partner category role by copying the standard business partner role category FLVN01.)

In the **Interface Control** section, you'll need to choose one of the predefined customer/vendor integration (**CVI**) views. If no view is assigned, the settings for the business partner view 000000 (General BP) will be used in the dialog box, and you won't be able to access the customer-/vendor-specific fields from transaction business partner.

Finally, select the **BP Role Category -- > Business Transaction** on the left hand side of the screen, and the popup shown in Figure 6.12 will appear.

As shown in Figure 6.12, enter the **BP Role Category** "ZHVPRC" and click **Continue**.

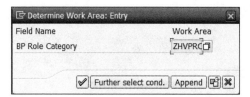

Figure 6.12 Allowed Business Transactions for Business Partner Role Category

Figure 6.13 shows the control function that either allows or disallows business partner transactions to a business partner role category. Save your entries.

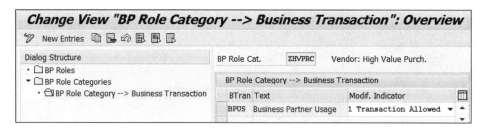

Figure 6.13 Business Transactions Control for a Business Partner Role Category

6.2.3   Field Attributes for Business Partner Role Category

You can control fields and their behaviors by choosing which fields are mandatory or optional, display only, or hidden. To control the field attributes of the business partner role category we configured in the previous step, follow the menu path **Cross-Application Components • SAP Business Partner • Field Groupings • Configure Field Attributes per BP Role • Configure Field Attributes for Each Role Category**.

As shown in Figure 6.14, choose the **BP Role** ZHVP01 and then click **Field Grouping**.

Figure 6.14 Field Group of Business Partner Role

Figure 6.15 shows a large number of **Data Sets** on the left hand side. Clicking on the relevant set will bring up the field group (**Field Grp**) where you can control the fields' attributes. This configuration screen allows you to make certain fields required (**Req. Entry**), optional (**Opt. entry**), display only (**Display**), or suppressed (**Hide**). This configuration is specific to the business partner role that is entered when a vendor master record is created.

Change View "Field Grou BP Role": Overview

BP - Vendor: High Value Purchases
Vendor-High Value Purch.

Data Set Description	Fld Groups Description	Field grp	Hide	Req.entry	Opt. entry	Display	Not spec.
Company Code	3325		○	○	○	○	●
Customer: Additional Data, PRA	Group for Calculation Schema (Supplie...	3497	○	○	○	○	●
General Data	Incoterms - Location 1	3527	○	○	○	○	●
Obsolete: General Customer Da	Incoterms - Location 2	3528	○	○	○	○	●
Obsolete: General Vendor Data	Incoterms Version	3526	○	○	○	○	●
RFM: Supplier - Basic Data	Pricing Date Control	3499	○	○	○	○	●
RFM: Supplier - Purchase Data	Suppl.: Auto Generation of Purchase O...	3498	○	○	○	○	●
Stakeholder Relationship Mana	Suppl.: Restriction Prof. for PO-Based ...	3493	○	○	○	○	●
Status	Supplier: Checkbox f. Service-Based In...	3482	○	○	○	○	●
Supplier: Purchasing Data	Supplier: Checkbox: GR-Based Invoice ...	3474	○	○	○	○	●
Vendor: Additional Data, PRA G	Supplier: Confirmation Control Key	3501	○	○	○	○	●
Vendor: CIN Details	Supplier: Customs Office: Foreign Tra...	3477	○	○	○	○	●
Vendor: General Data	Supplier: Dispatcher/Controller	3486	○	○	○	○	●
Vendor: Great Britain CIS Verif	Supplier: ERS for Return Item	3479	○	○	○	○	●

Field check

Figure 6.15 Available Controls of Business Partner Role Category

In this section, we covered business partner configuration. In the next section, we'll cover customer/vendor integration—a mandatory prerequisite to using business partners.

6.3   Customer/Vendor Integration

Setting up customer/vendor integration (CVI) is a mandatory prerequisite for using business partners in SAP S/4HANA. The vendor (now, business partner) master and customer master will be used. The business partner is the single point of entry to create, edit, and display master data for business partners, customers, and suppliers.

> **Note**
>
> The following sections cover the integration between the FI configurations of the vendor account group with the MM configuration of the business partner we covered in previous sections of this chapter.

In the following sections, we'll cover the steps involved in setting up CVI with a focus on business partner integration with our previously created vendor account group.

6.3.1   Setting the Business Partner Role Category for Business Partner to Vendor

In this step, you'll define business partner role categories, which enable vendor integration in the direction from the business partner to the vendor. You can determine how the system creates the corresponding vendor in FI when you process a business partner.

The business partner role categories entered are vendor-based, which means that the system considers vendor integration when it processes business partners with a corresponding business partner role. In this configuration activity, you'll define whether the business partner role assigned to the business partner role category is mandatory or optional for the vendor business partner role.

With mandatory vendor business partner roles, the system automatically creates corresponding vendors. With optional vendor business partner roles, you can determine whether you want to create a corresponding vendor during business partner processing.

Note

A prerequisite for this configuration step is that both business partner roles and business partner role categories must already be created.

The terms "vendor" or "FI vendor" and "customer" or "FI customer" are used interchangeably in the documentation for master data synchronization and are synonyms.

To set up the business partner role category for the direction business partner to vendor, follow the menu path **Master Data Synchronization • Customer/Vendor Integration • Business Partner Settings • Settings for Vendor Integration • Set BP Role Category for Direction BP to Vendor**.

Figure 6.16 shows the **BP role category** ZHVPRC. The **Vendor-Based** radio button will make creating a vendor mandatory when creating a business partner with the business partner role category ZHVPRC.

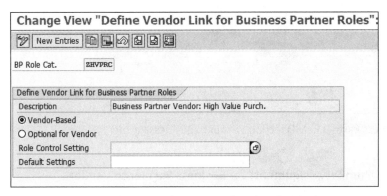

Figure 6.16 Business Partner Role Category for Direction Business Partner to Vendor

6.3.2 Defining the Business Partner Role for Vendor to Business Partner

In this configuration step, you'll assign business partner roles to the account group for the vendor master record in which the business partner is to be created when processing the vendor.

When you process a vendor as part of business partner-vendor integration, the system will create a business partner with the relevant account group in the business partner roles that are assigned to this account group.

> **Note**
>
> Before undertaking this configuration activity, ensure the following prerequisites have been met:
>
> - The vendor account groups in FI have been created.
> - The business partner roles have been defined with relevant settings already made.

To group together different business partner roles into a business partner group, follow the menu path **Master Data Synchronization** • **Customer/Vendor Integration** • **Business Partner Settings** • **Settings for Vendor Integration** • **Define BP Role for Direction Vendor to BP**.

Figure 6.17 shows the single business partner group (**Group**) HVPV has been assigned to multiple business partner roles, such as FLVN00, FLVN01, and ZHVP01.

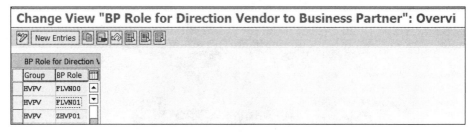

Figure 6.17 Business Partner Role Direction Vendor to Business Partner

6.3.3   Defining Number Assignments for Business Partner to Vendor

In this step, you'll assign vendor account groups for the vendor master records to the business partner grouping to ensure that the system updates the vendor at the same time during business partner processing. When you make this assignment, you'll choose whether the vendor master record should be created with both internal or external account numbers or created with identical numbers.

> **Note**
>
> Before undertaking this configuration activity, ensure the following prerequisites have been met:
>
> - You've defined and assigned number ranges and groupings for the business partners.

- You've determined the account groups and the number ranges assigned to the account groups for creating vendor accounts in customization in the FI component.

To assign business partner grouping to vendor account group, follow the menu path **Master Data Synchronization • Customer/Vendor Integration • Business Partner Settings • Settings for Vendor Integration • Field Assignment for Vendor Integration • Assign Keys • Define Number Assignment for Direction BP to Vendor**.

Figure 6.18 shows the business partner **Grouping** HVPV has been assigned the vendor account group (**Account group**) HVPV. To use the same number as the business partner number currently being processed when you create the vendor master record, set the **Same Numbers** indicator.

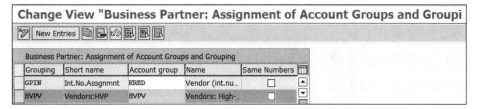

Figure 6.18 Number Assignment of Account Groups and Grouping

6.3.4   Defining Number Assignments for Vendor to Business Partner

In this configuration step, you'll assign business partner groupings to account groups for the vendor master records to ensure that, when you process vendors as part of vendor integration, the system also updates the business partners at the same time. With this assignment, you can choose whether the vendor master record should be created with an account group with internal or external number assignment or with identical numbers.

Note

Before undertaking this configuration activity, ensure the following prerequisites have been met:

- Number ranges and groupings for business partners are in place.
- Number ranges and groupings for vendor account groups are in place.

To assign the vendor account grouping from the FI component with the business partner account group, follow the menu path **Master Data Synchronization • Customer/Vendor Integration • Business Partner Settings • Settings for Vendor Integration • Field Assignment for Vendor Integration • Assign Keys • Define Number Assignment for Direction Vendor to BP**.

As shown in Figure 6.19, choose the account group for the vendor master data from **FI** and assign the required grouping for the business partner to it.

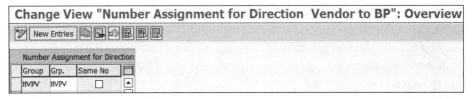

Figure 6.19 Number Assignment for Direction Vendor to Business Partner

6.4   Additional Business Partner Configurations

In the following sections, we'll cover additional business partner configuration required to ensure master data creation and business processes run smoothly.

6.4.1   Business Partner Types

You can configure a business partner type to group business partners according to your own defined criteria. You can also control fields for data entry, depending on the requirements of the relevant business partner type.

To configure a business partner type, follow the menu path **Cross-Application Components • SAP Business Partner • Business Partner • Basic Settings • Define Business Partner Types**.

Figure 6.20 shows a newly configured **Partner Type** ZHVP, which we'll assign in the **Control** tab while creating a business partner.

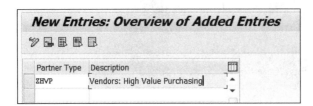

Figure 6.20 Business Partner Types

6.4.2 Partner Functions

The screen shown in Figure 6.21 allows a purchasing user to define the relationships between vendors of particular account group and partner functions. A vendor can vary in size from a sole proprietor to a large multinational company. To best describe a vendor's various operations, partner functionality can be described. Partner functions can be used for both customers and vendors.

Change View "Permissible Partner Roles per Account Group": Overview

New Entries

Funct	Name	Group	Name	
VN	Supplier	HVPV	Vendors: High-Value Purch.	▲

Figure 6.21 Permissible Partner Roles for Account Groups

Table 6.1 provides a selection of available vendor partner codes.

Partner Code	Description
AZ	Alternative payment recipient
CA	Contract address
CP	Contact person
ER	Employee responsible
GS	Goods supplier
OA	Ordering address
PI	Invoice presented by
VN	Vendor

Table 6.1 List of Partner Functions

Basically, a partner function allows the purchasing department to determine what functions a vendor performs within a larger vendor organization. For example, a multinational auto parts manufacturer may supply material to your company, so you've created a vendor number (**VN**) for them. However, the address to which you send the POs may be a separate address in a separate division of the manufacturer's business. Therefore, you'll create a vendor number for the ordering address (OA), and that record will be entered into the **Partner function** screen for the **VN Vendor**. Further, you may need to manage a separate contact address (CA) for a vendor that supplies the invoices (PI) and an alternative payee (AZ). All of these can be created and entered into the **Partner functions** screen of the VN partner.

To define permissible partner roles for an account group, follow the menu path **Materials Management • Purchasing • Partner Determination • Partner Roles • Define Permissible Partner Roles per Account Group**.

Figure 6.21 shows the partner function **VN** has been assigned to the vendor account group **HVPV**.

6.4.3   Vendor Subrange Functionality

The vendor subrange (VSR) functionality can be used to subdivide a vendor's products into different ranges. For example, a vendor could be an office supply company, and subranges could be divided into computer media, paper products, and ink products.

The VSR functionality can be entered into the purchasing information record of a particular vendor/material combination. The allocation of a material to a certain VSR allows the vendor to see items sorted on its PO in subrange order.

Configuration is required to enable VSRs. Transaction OMSG allows you to edit vendor account groups. The indicator can be set to enable VSRs for that vendor account group.

To setup vendor subrange, use Transaction OMSG or follow the navigation path **Logistics – General • Business Partner • Vendor • Control • Define Account Groups and Field Selection**.

With the necessary configuration for business partners in place, let's now assign these configured objects in the business partner master data and also explore the features and functionalities of the business partner in detail.

6.5   Maintaining a Business Partner

In the following sections, we'll create the following business partner roles:

- 000000: General
- FLV001: Vendor FI
- ZHVPV01: High-value purchases vendors (a copy of the standard business partner FLVN01)

Further, we'll cover the master data steps required for creating an organization as a business partner as well as create the associated business partner roles.

6.5.1   Business Partner General Data

Use Transaction BP to access the screen shown in Figure 6.22. The top menu bar provides options for creating an organization, a group, or a person as a business partner. The left hand side of the screen offers search functions, while the **Business Partner** field is available to display or change an existing business partner. To change or display another business partner, click the open icon 🗁. In the popup that appears, enter the business partner number. To hide the left-hand **Find** function to display in fullscreen mode, click the close icon ⊠. To switch between displaying and changing a business partner, click the change/display icon ✎. Finally, to check the completeness and correctness of business partner data, click the check icon 🔍.

Figure 6.22 Business Partner: Initial Screen

Note

You will *not* find Transaction BP in the MM node of your SAP system. Instead, follow the menu path **Logistics • SCM Extended Warehouse Management • Extended Warehouse Management • Master Data • Maintain Business Partner**.

Also, even in the SAP S/4HANA MM node, you'll still see some standard SAP ERP transaction codes, such as Transactions XK01 or MK01 for vendors. But clicking or entering any of these transactions into the command bar will direct you to Transaction BP instead.

To create a new organization as a business partner, click **Create Organization**.

> **Note**
>
> The business partner screen consists of several tabs as well as a lot of fields, check-boxes, and dropdown menus and frequently requires scrolling down. Not all the available options in each tab are shown with screenshots in this chapter. Instead, we've covered the maximum information available in a given tab. For example, in the **Address** tab, only limited information is displayed in Figure 6.23. Scrolling down will reveal more fields and options than we've covered in this chapter.
>
> Similarly, if a function of any field or a checkbox has already been explained, we won't repeat the information.

As shown in Figure 6.23, choose the **Grouping HVPV** from the dropdown menu we configured in the previous section. While creating a new business partner, the **Create in BP role** automatically selects the business partner role **000000 Business Partner (Gen.)**, but still do check and ensure to select it at the time of creating a new business partner. The general business partner information maintained will then be replicated in all subsequent business partner roles that are created.

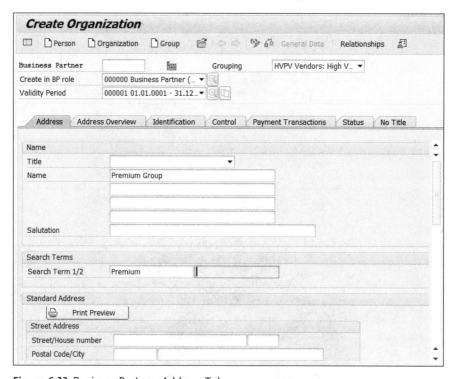

Figure 6.23 Business Partner: Address Tab

Some of the fields on multiple screens and tabs, shown in Figure 6.23, include the following:

Address

The information to be entered includes the business partner's **Name** and address and communications data, including **Telephone**, **Fax**, and **Email**.

Title

This field is the title for the vendor. If the vendor is a company, then select the **Company** option; otherwise, select the appropriate salutation.

Name

The **Name** of the vendor should be consistent to avoid duplicate vendor entries. The purchasing department should create a template to follow so that vendor names always appear the same way as entered into the vendor master. This consistency will benefit purchasing users when searching for specific vendors.

Search Terms

The search term is used to find vendors. The entry of data into the **Search term 1/2** field can be structured so that purchasing users can easily remember the criteria for this type of search. Your company's policy may require entering a search term that includes the first five characters of the vendor name plus the two-letter country code for the vendor's country location. For example, the search term for Smith Brothers of London, England, is "SMITHGB," and the code for Lakshmi Machine of Coimbatore, India, is "LAKSHIN." This field is not case sensitive.

Street Address

The **Street/House Number** field is the address of the vendor. The **Country**, **Region**, and **Postal Code/City** fields are used to calculate the tax jurisdiction code. If connected to an external tax system, such as Vertex or Taxware, the system may validate the address information that you enter to ensure that a valid tax jurisdiction code is obtained.

PO Box Address

Many companies use post office boxes, and these fields allow that information to be added to the vendor master.

Communication

The **Communication** fields should be kept up to date, especially because fax numbers and email addresses regularly change.

Customer

This **Customer** field allows a purchasing user to enter a customer number for the vendor, if the vendor is both a vendor and a customer of the company. For example, a paper pulp company may be a vendor for paper products to a particleboard manufacturer but also may be a customer of the particleboard manufacturer, from whom it purchases scrap particleboard to create pulp.

Trading Partner

If a vendor is part of an independent company that has been designated in FI for consolidation purposes, then you can enter that company in this field as a trading partner. These companies are configured as internal trading partners in FI by following the navigation path **Enterprise Structure • Definition • Financial Accounting • Define Company**.

Corporate Group

The **Corporate Group** key is used to combine vendors to enhance the search capability. A group key is a 10-character string and isn't configured. Therefore, a policy for entering group keys must be established before any vendor entry commences.

For example, you might create a group key policy based on characters that have meaning, for example:

- Characters 1 and 2: Country of vendor
- Characters 3 and 4: Industry code
- Characters 5 through 7: Minority indicator
- Character 8: ABC indicator
- Characters 9 and 10: Shipping conditions

Tax Number 1 and 2

These fields allow an accounting user to enter the tax identification number, or numbers, of a vendor. In the United States, this number is an Employer Identification Number (EIN) or a Social Security Number (SSN), if the vendor is an individual. In France, this field is the SIRET number; in Spain, the NIF number.

Control

As shown in Figure 6.24, assign the **BP Type** ZHVP, which we previously configured on the screen shown earlier in Figure 6.20. You can also control access to business partner data creation or change functions by assigning relevant codes from the **Authorization Group** dropdown list.

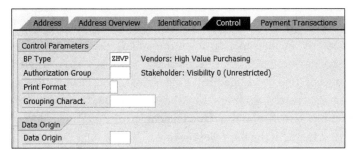

Figure 6.24 Business Partner: Control Tab

Payment Transactions

Figure 6.25 shows the **Payment Transactions** tab with options for maintaining the bank and payment details of a vendor. Let's review some of the available fields and options.

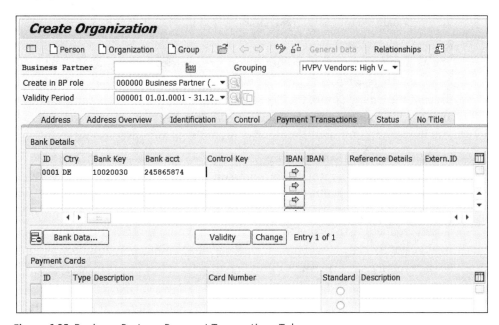

Figure 6.25 Business Partner: Payment Transactions Tab

Bank Details

The **Bank Details** section allows the entry of vendor bank details. More than one bank account can be added for each vendor:

- **Ctry (country)**
  Enter the country where the vendor's bank is located.

- **Bank Key**
  The bank key can be selected from the matchcode with the country code entered. The bank key can be entered as the bank routing number (US), the bank sort code (GB), or other country-specific bank identification. The bank key isn't entered through configuration but can be created in FI via Transaction FI01, where all details for the bank can be created. After entering the **Bank Key** in the **Create Vendor: Payment transactions** screen, you'll see the relevant bank details by clicking on the **Bank Data** button beneath the **Bank Details** table.

- **Bank Account**
  This field allows an accounting user to enter a bank account number for the vendor at the bank. The **Bank Account** field can be up to 18 characters long.

- **Acct holder**
  If the bank account isn't in the name of the vendor or the vendor company, then the account holder of the bank account can be entered in this field. This field can accommodate a name of up to 60 characters long.

- **AK (bank control key)**
  The **AK** field is specific to each country. Some countries involve no information to enter; in others, such as France, Spain, Japan, and the United States, this field is used. In the United States, the field's value should be "01" for checking accounts and "02" for savings accounts. Check with your accounting department to ensure that the correct information is entered into the field for a given country.

- **IBAN (International Bank Account Number)**
  IBAN was designed to meet growing pressure for improved efficiency with respect to cost, speed, and quality in cross-border payments in Europe. These improvements required easier validation of foreign bank account numbers. IBAN provides a standard method to enable the cross-border account number formats to be recognized and validated. An IBAN is additional information put in front of a national account number format, which differs by country:

  - Check digits and a single simple algorithm perform validation. The algorithm covers the whole IBAN and ensures that individual digits aren't transposed.

- Recognition is in two parts. The IBAN commences with an ISO 3166 two-letter country code. Therefore, the country in which the account is held can be easily recognized. Within the national account identifier part of the IBAN, the ISO standard requires that the bank be unambiguously identified.

- The length of the IBAN isn't standard across countries. The length can range from 28 characters in Hungary and Cyprus to only 15 characters in Norway.

- **BnkT (partner bank type)**
  If a vendor has more than one bank account, then this field allows an accounting user to specify in what sequence the accounts are used by entering a value in this key field. This value can then be used for line item payments.

- **Reference details (reference specifications for bank details)**
  This field can be used in countries where additional information or authorization is needed. This information is normally required in Norway and the United Kingdom.

- **Debit Auth.**
  This field denotes the code of the debiting authority.

- **Name of bank**
  This field enables users to maintain the name of the bank involved in the payment.

Payment Transactions

The **Payment transactions** tab contains the following fields:

- **Alternative payee**
  This field can be used to enter another vendor number to whom the automatic payments are made. An alternative payee may be needed if the vendor's bank accounts have been frozen.

- **DME Indicator**
  This key is only used for data medium exchange (DME) in Germany. The DME engine enables a company to define file formats to meet requirements set by their financial institution. No standard has been set: Each country can have different formats, and the DME allows SAP to read an incoming file that isn't in the correct country format.

- **Instruction key**
  For DME, this field controls which statements are given to the banks during the payment order. This functionality is used in Germany, Spain, Norway, Japan, and other countries, as well as for the SWIFT format.

> **SWIFT**
>
> The Society for Worldwide Interbank Financial Telecommunication (SWIFT) is a financial industry-owned cooperative that supplies secure, standardized messaging services and interface software to more than 7,800 financial institutions in more than 200 countries. Many institutions use the MT-103 Single Customer Credit Transfer customer transfer format for one-off credit transfers and repetitive payments, such as lease payments.

- **ISR Number**

  The ISR number is a special payment procedure of the Swiss Postal Service that is only relevant within Switzerland. A payment slip with an ISR reference number uses an electronic debtor service that allows open invoices to be billed in Swiss Francs (CHF) and Euros (EUR) in a simple way and to quickly post incoming payments.

Status

Figure 6.26 shows the **Status** tab, including options for blocking or locking a vendor.

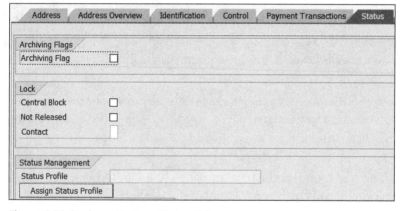

Figure 6.26 Business Partner: Status Tab

Vendors can be blocked for a variety of reasons as required. Often, a vendor is blocked due to poor adherence to delivery dates, unsatisfactory material quality, or outside market events. You can block a vendor master account, which can stop any future purchase orders (POs) from being placed with the vendor until the vendor master record has been unblocked.

Tips & Tricks

A vendor master record can also be blocked by using Transaction MK05 or by following the navigation path **Logistics • Materials Management • Purchasing • Master Data • Vendor • Purchasing • Block**.

Transaction MK05 is used for blocking vendors via purchasing. The initial screen of the transaction allows a purchasing user to enter the vendor number and the purchasing organization.

The second screen shows the fields relevant to blocking the vendor. The first indicator determines whether the block should be for the vendor in **All purchasing organizations** or just in the **Selected Purchasing Organization**.

After maintaining the necessary details for a business partner, save your entries, and the system will create a business partner by assigning it a number. In our example, our newly created business partner 20000012 conforms to the number range we configured previously, which starts with 200XXXXX.

Tips & Tricks

Creating a business partner or changing its details, such as a change in payment terms, has financial implications that often involve a company's finance department. To confirm updates or changes to important fields in a business partner, use Transaction FK08 (often used by the finance department). Not confirming changes to a business partner will repeatedly bring up popup messages to remind the user what needs to be done.

Now that the general data of a business partner is maintained, and the system has assigned an internal number to the business partner (which in our example is 20000012), let's *extend* the same business partner role as an FI vendor so we can maintain its financial details.

6.5.2 Extending Business Partner as FI Vendors

As shown in Figure 6.27, you're now in change mode. Choose the standard business partner role **FIVN00 FI Vendor (New)** available from the **Change in BP role** dropdown list.

Now, the system will display, not just the existing and general data already maintained for the business partner, but will bring up additional fields and tabs. Choose **Company Code**.

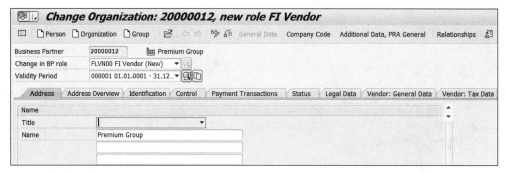

Figure 6.27 Business Partner Role FLVN00

As shown in Figure 6.28, first click the **Company Codes** button so that the screen shown in Figure 6.29 appears. Also maintain the **Reconciliation acct** field for the vendor, which is mandatory.

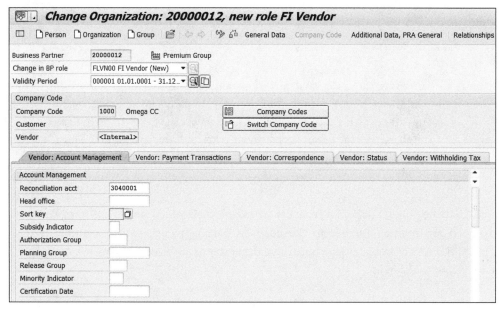

Figure 6.28 Business Partner: Account Management Tab

As shown in Figure 6.29, first click **Create** and then enter "1000" in the **Company code** field, which is the same company code we've been using since Chapter 2. Next, click **Adopt** to maintain the business partner data for company code 1000. You can also delete an incorrectly assigned company code or a business partner that no longer needs to be associated with the company code.

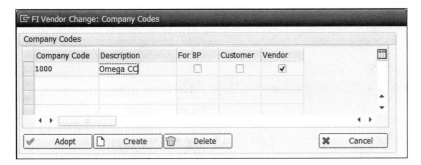

Figure 6.29 Company Codes

As shown in Figure 6.30, not only has company code 1000 been assigned to the business partner, but if you save the new business partner role at this time, the system will assign the same number (20000012) as the **Vendor** to business partner 20000012. (As shown earlier in Figure 6.28, the **Vendor** field is marked as **<Internal>**.) This vendor number range conforms to the FI vendor number ranges we maintained earlier in the configuration settings.

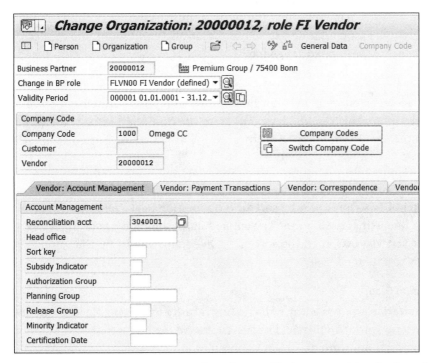

Figure 6.30 Assigning a Company Code and Reconciliation Account to a Business Partner

In the following sections, we'll look at the most important settings on each tab on this page.

Vendor: Account Management

Let's discuss some of the fields available in the **Vendor: Account Management** tab.

Reconciliation Account

The reconciliation account (**Reconciliation acct**) is an individual general ledger (G/L) account. A reconciliation account is recorded in line item detail in the subledger and summarized in the G/L. The detailed information entered into the reconciliation account is all line item data from the vendor account. These reconciliation accounts in the subledger are important and must be maintained for vendors, for customers, and for asset accounts.

Reconciliation in the G/L occurs at the summary level and is used to reconcile against the vendor account at the total level. However, the subledger can be used to identify line item data if necessary.

A reconciliation account can be created using Transaction FS01. When creating a reconciliation account, remember that the account must be a balance sheet account. Also, the account group must be selected as a reconciliation account, and the **Recon. account** field must be entered as vendor.

Head Office

This field allows an entry of a vendor number, which represents the head office or master account for this vendor. Payments are made from the head office account, whereas purchase orders (POs), deliveries, or invoices may be posted to branch accounts.

Sort Key

The **Sort key** allows you to select a sort for the allocation field. The system sorts the document line items based on the key entered in the allocation field. Therefore, if you select **Sort key 008**, then the sort of the line items will be by allocation 008, which is by cost center.

Authorization Group

The **Authorization** group is a way of increasing security on certain objects. Entering an authorization group in this field restricts access to the object to those users who have this authorization group in their SAP profiles.

Cash Management Group

In the Cash Management functionality, vendors can be allocated to a planning group. This planning group provides the cash management department better information for producing or planning the company's cash forecast.

Release Group

A release approval group can be defined and configured to allow only those in the group to be able to be released for payment. The **Release group** can be configured by following the navigation path **Financial Accounting • Accounts Receivable and Accounts Payable • Business Transactions • Release for Payment • Define Release Approval Groups for Release for Payment**.

Minority Indicator

The **Minority indic.** field is only relevant for implementations in the United States. Federal and local officials may request information on the number of minority vendors supplying material to a company. Configuration is required to enter the relevant information because the fields are not predefined. Virginia Polytechnic Institute's Purchasing Guidelines (2004) describes a minority vendor as:

> A minority vendor is a business that is owned and controlled by one or more socially and economically disadvantaged persons. Such disadvantage may arise from cultural, racial, chronic economic circumstances or background, or other similar cause. A minority-owned business is at least 51% owned and controlled by one or more such disadvantaged persons. Additionally, the management and daily business operations must be controlled by one or more such individuals. Minority means any African American, Hispanic American, Native American, or Alaskan American, Asian, or a person of Pacific Island descent who is either a citizen of the United States or a permanent resident.

To configure the **Minority indic.** field, follow the navigation path **Financial Accounting • Accounts Receivable and Accounts Payable • Vendor Accounts • Master Data • Preparations for Creating Vendor Master Data • Define Minority Indicators**.

Certification Date for Minority Vendors

The certification expiration date for the minority vendor field is only relevant for implementations in the United States. The certification for a minority vendor has an expiration date, which is required to be entered for the US government.

Interest Calculation Indicator

If this account is suitable for automatic interest, then an interest calculation indicator must be selected. These interest calculations can be configured by an accounting user by following the navigation path **Financial Accounting • Accounts Receivable and Accounts Payable • Business Transactions • Interest Calculation • Interest Calculation Global Setting • Define Interest Calculation Types**.

Interest Cycle

This field allows an accounting user to select a period that specifies when the interest calculation is run for this vendor. The period can range from monthly to yearly.

Vendor: Payment Transactions

Let's discuss some of the fields available in the **Vendor: Payment Transactions** tab, as shown in Figure 6.30.

Payment Terms

Payment terms are defined to allow the vendor to offer cash discounts and favorable payment periods to the company. In many accounts payable departments, before ecommerce came along, the rule was to pay the vendor as close as possible to the last day of the agreed payment period to maximize the day's payables and keep the cash within the company. However, over the past ten years, vendors have been offering incentives to companies for fast payment, and purchasing departments have responded by implementing best practices for paying vendors as soon as the invoice arrives or even before.

The **Payt Terms** on the vendor master record are maintained by the accounting department and are configured if the payment terms aren't found on the system. The payment terms can be configured by following the navigation path **Financial Accounting (New) • Accounts Receivable and Accounts Payable • Business Transactions • Incoming Invoices/Credit Memos • Maintain Terms of Payment**, as shown in Figure 6.31.

Tolerance Group

A tolerance is a percentage or a value that represents the limit to which an event can deviate. For example, a tolerance of 10% on a line item that is expected deliver 100 units will allow a delivery of 109, which is under the 10% tolerance. A delivery of 111 won't be allowed because this value is over the 10% tolerance limit. A tolerance group is a set of tolerances that can be configured and assigned to a specific vendor, if necessary. Each tolerance group is defined for a unique company code. Refer to Chapter 23 in which we cover tolerance groups in greater detail.

```
┌─────────────────────────────────────────────────────────────────────┐
│  Change View "Terms of Payment": Details                              │
│  ▧  New Entries  ▤ ▣ ◫ ▨ ▣ ▦                                          │
│                                                                        │
│  Payment terms  │0002│  Sales text      │14 days 2%, 30 net    │  ▧   │
│  Day Limit      │ 0 │   Own Explanation  │                      │      │
│  ┌─Account type──────────┐  ┌─Baseline date calculation───────┐       │
│  │ ☑ Customer            │  │ Fixed Day              │   │     │       │
│  │ ☑ Vendor              │  │ Additional Months      │   │     │       │
│  └───────────────────────┘  └─────────────────────────────────┘       │
│                                                                        │
│  ┌─Pmnt block/pmnt method default─┐ ┌─Default for baseline date──────┐ │
│  │ Block Key          │  │ ☐      │ │ ○ No Default    ○ Posting Date │ │
│  │ Payment Method     │  │ ☐      │ │ ⦿ Document Date ○ Entry Date   │ │
│  └────────────────────────────────┘ └────────────────────────────────┘ │
│                                                                        │
│  ┌─Payment terms─────────────────────────────────────────────────────┐│
│  │ ☐ Installment Payments      ☐ Rec. Entries: Supplement fm Master  ││
│  │ Term   Percentage  No. of Days  /  Fixed Day   Additional Months  ││
│  │ 1.      2.000 %      14                                            ││
│  │ 2.            %      30                                            ││
│  │ 3.                                                                 ││
│  └───────────────────────────────────────────────────────────────────┘│
│                                                                        │
│  ┌─Explanations──────────────────────────────────────────────────────┐│
│  │ within 14 days 2 % cash discount  │ within 30 days Due net         ││
│  │                                   │                                ││
│  └───────────────────────────────────────────────────────────────────┘│
└─────────────────────────────────────────────────────────────────────┘
```

Figure 6.31 Payment Terms

The **Tolerance group** can be configured using Transaction OBA3 or by following the navigation path **Financial Accounting (New) • Accounts Receivable and Accounts Payable • Business Transactions • Open Item Clearing • Clearing Differences • Define Tolerances for Customers/Vendors**.

Check Flag for Double Invoices

This indicator should be set if the accounting department wants the system to check for double or duplicate invoices when they are entered.

Check Cashing Time

The value of the check cashing time is used in Cash Management to calculate cash outflows. An entry in this field can be calculated by an analysis of the issue-to-cash date and the average used.

Payment Methods

The payment method entered in this field is used if no payment method has been entered in the line item. The options for this field can be configured by following the navigation path **Financial Accounting (New) • Accounts Receivable and Accounts Payable • Business Transactions • Outgoing Payments • Automatic Outgoing Payments • Payment Method • Set Up Payment Methods per Country for Payment Transactions**.

Payment Block

The accounting department can enter a **Payment block** on the vendor master, which will prevent any open items from being paid. Payment block keys are defined in configuration using Transaction OB27 or by following the navigation path **Financial Accounting (New) • Accounts Receivable and Accounts Payable • Business Transactions • Outgoing Payments • Outgoing Payments Global Settings • Payment Block Reasons • Define Payment Block Reasons**.

House Bank

A **House Bank** can be entered if the same bank is always used. This field negates the configuration on the bank selection screen. The house bank is defined as a business partner that represents a bank through which a company can process its own internal transactions.

Individual Payment Indicator

If this indicator is set, then every item is paid individually rather than combining items into one payment. Some vendors require items be individually paid and not combined with other line items on the invoice.

Bill of Exchange Limit

A *bill of exchange* is a contract entitling an exporter to receive immediate payment for goods that will be shipped elsewhere in the local currency. Time elapses between payment in one currency and repayment in another, so the interest rate will also be brought into the transaction. The accounting department will determine whether the vendor requires a bill of exchange limit.

Payment Advice by EDI

If this indicator is set, then all payment advices to this vendor should be sent via electronic data interchange (EDI).

Vendor: Correspondence

Let's discuss some of the fields available in the **Vendor: Correspondence** tab, as shown in Figure 6.30.

Dunning Procedure

Normally, dunning involves sending reminder letters to customers for payment. However, in this case, dunning relates to reminding vendors to deliver the material from POs.

The **Dunn.Procedure** field can be selected to reflect how dunning should be carried out for this vendor. The dunning procedure can be configured using Transaction FBMP or by following the navigation path **Financial Accounting (New) • Accounts Receivable and Accounts Payable • Business Transactions • Dunning • Dunning Procedure • Define Dunning Procedures**.

Dunning Block

If a **Dunning block** is selected, then the vendor isn't selected for the dunning run. The **Dunning block** can be entered at any time. The **Dunning block** can be defined by following the navigation path **Financial Accounting (New) • Accounts Receivable and Accounts Payable • Business Transactions • Dunning • Basic Settings for Dunning • Define Dunning Block Reasons**.

Dunning Recipient

This field should be completed if the vendor isn't the recipient of the dunning notices. If instead the correspondence should go to a central office or production site, then that vendor number should be entered.

Legal Dunning Procedure

If the dunning procedure undertaken against a vendor hasn't been successful, then legal dunning is an option. Attorneys carry this process out, and documents can be produced through the SAP system. A separate form should be identified for the legal dunning procedure.

The **Legal dunn.proc.** field can be maintained with the date when legal dunning procedures began.

Last Dunned

This date is simply the date on which the vendor was last sent a dunning document.

Dunning Level

This field indicates how many times a vendor has been dunned. This field is updated whenever a new dunning notice is sent.

Dunning Clerk

A dunning clerk is the person in the accounting department who is responsible for the dunning of this vendor. A two-character field identifies the dunning clerk. This field is configured by following the navigation path **Financial Accounting (New) • Accounts Receivable and Accounts Payable • Vendor Accounts • Master Data • Preparations for Creating Vendor Master Data • Define Accounting Clerks**.

Account Statement Indicator

This indicator allows the accounting department to define when the vendor will receive periodic statements. The vendor may receive them weekly, monthly, or yearly.

Accounting Clerk

The **Acctg clerk** field uses the same lookup table as the dunning clerk. The accounting clerk doesn't necessarily have to be the same as the dunning clerk. However, if the **Dunning clerk** field is blank, then the dunning clerk is assumed to be the same as the accounting clerk.

Account with Vendor

If known, the account number that the vendor uses to identify the company should be entered in this field. This number is often found on the vendor's invoice.

Vendor Clerk Information

The last fields on this screen relate to information concerning the person at the vendor who manages the day-to-day operations between the vendor and your company.

Vendor: Withholding Tax

Let's discuss some of the fields available in the **Vendor: Withholding Tax** tab, as shown in Figure 6.30.

Withholding Tax Code

Withholding tax generally refers to income tax on foreign vendors from country B and applies to vendors that don't reside in country A but do derive incomes from profits, interest, rentals, royalties, and other incomes from sources in country A. The company in country A is the withholding agent. An income tax of a certain percentage will be withheld on incomes by the company from country A, which should turn the amount of taxes on each payment over to the local state treasury and submit a withholding income tax return to the local tax authority.

Withholding Tax Country Key

This additional country key is used in countries that require the calculation and/or reporting on withholding tax.

Vendor Recipient Type

In the United States, Form 1042 is the annual taxable return used by withholding agents to report tax withheld on US source income paid to certain nonresident individuals and corporations. The withholding agent issues a Form 1042S, "Foreign Person's US Source Income Subject to Withholding." The 1042S requires that a recipient type be entered. That two-digit code can be configured into SAP. Some examples of this code are 01 (individuals), 02 (corporations), 06 (foreign governments), 11 (US branch treated as a US person), and so on.

The **Recipient type** field is also used in Spain for similar reporting. The **Recipient type** field can be configured by following the navigation path **Financial Accounting (New) • Accounts Receivable and Accounts Payable • Vendor Accounts • Master Data • Preparations for Creating Vendor Master Data • Check Settings for Withholding Tax • Maintain Types of Recipient**.

Exemption Number

If a vendor is exempt from withholding tax and has an exemption certificate, then that number should be entered on the vendor master record.

Validity Date for Exemption

The exemption certificate has an expiration date that should be entered in the **Valid until** field. Often, the certificate is extended, so the date of expiry should be updated when necessary.

Exemption Authority

On IRS Form 1042S, a code is required for explaining why no withholding tax has been calculated. This code can be configured in SAP and entered on the vendor master. Examples of this code are 01 (income effectively connected with a US trade or business), 03 (income isn't from US sources), and 07 (withholding foreign partnership).

Previous Account Number

This field can be used if the vendor master has been renumbered, or you want to store the legacy vendor number.

Personnel Number

If a vendor is also an employee, then this field will accommodate the employee's personnel number. Figure 6.32 shows the **Vendor: Tax Data** tab.

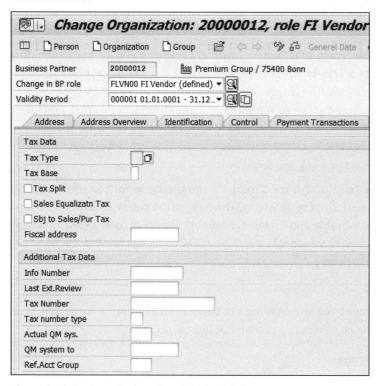

Figure 6.32 Business Partner Tax Details Maintenance

Tax Type

The **Tax type** can be assigned to the vendor to identify its responsibility over sales tax and use tax.

Jurisdiction Code

The tax jurisdiction code is either determined in SAP by the information entered in the **Address** field or referenced from an external tax package, such as Vertex or Taxware. The tax jurisdiction code is valid only to vendors in the United States.

Country-Specific Tax Fields

Some of the fields on the vendor master control screen are specific to certain countries:

- **Tax number type**
  Specific to Argentina

- **Equalizatn tax**
  Specific to Spain

- **Sole Proprietr**
  Specific to 11 countries, including Italy, Peru, and Mexico

- **Sales/pur. tax**
  Specific to countries that levy value-added tax (VAT)

- **VAT Reg. No.**
  The VAT number for the vendor, which is important in EU countries

- **Fiscal address**
  Specific to Italy

Global Location Number

In the **Create Vendor: Control** screen, you can optionally enter the 13-digit global location number (GLN) of the vendor. In SAP, this number is divided into three fields in the **Reference Data** section: **Location no. 1, Location no. 2,** and **Check digit.** A GLN is issued to a company to identify a legal, functional, or physical location within a business or organizational entity. GLNs are governed by strict rules to guarantee that each is unique worldwide. The identification of locations by GLN is required for the efficient flow of goods and information between trading partners through EDI messages, payment slips, and so on. A GLN is often found as a barcode on documents.

Industry Key

The **Industry** key is another grouping that allows similar vendors to be grouped by industry. This field can also be found in customer master records. The **Industry** key can be configured by following the navigation path **Sales and Distribution • Business Partners • Marketing • Define Industry Sector for Customers**.

Standard Carrier Alpha Code

The National Motor Freight Traffic Association (NMFTA) in the United States maintains the Standard Carrier Alpha Code (SCAC). The NMFTA is a nonprofit membership organization with more than 1,000 shipping carrier members, regulated by the US

Department of Transportation's Surface Transportation Board and various state and federal agencies.

The **SCAC** code is a four-letter string that uniquely identifies a shipping carrier. SCAC codes are frequently used in EDI; on the 856 Advance Ship Notice; the 850 Purchase Order; and all motor, rail, and water-carrier transactions where carrier identification is required. SCAC codes are mandatory when doing business with US government agencies.

Certain groups of SCAC codes are reserved for specific purposes:

- Codes ending with the letter U are reserved for the identification of freight containers.

- Codes ending with the letter X are reserved for the identification of privately owned railroad cars.

- Codes ending with the letter Z are reserved for the identification of truck chassis and trailers used in intermodal service.

Forwarding Agent Freight Group

The forward agent freight group key, identified in the **Car.freight grp** field, can be assigned to the forwarding agent to group together similar forwarding agents. For example, your company's transportation department may decide to group its freight forwarders by mode of transport. Therefore, transportation staff could configure three freight groups: rail, road, and shipping. The freight groups are part of the determination of freight costs. The configuration for freight groups can be found by following the navigation path **Logistics Execution • Transportation • Basic Transportation Functions • Maintain Freight Code Sets and Freight Codes • Define Forwarding Agent – Freight Groups**.

Service-Agent Procedure Group

Freight costs can be calculated as part of the pricing procedure. To calculate the correct freight costs, the service-agent procedure group (**ServAgntProcGrp**) can have a range of forwarding agents assigned to it. The service-agent procedure group is then assigned to a pricing procedure to calculate freight costs. The group can be configured by following the navigation path **Logistics Execution • Transportation • Shipping Costs • Pricing • Pricing Control • Define and Assign Pricing Procedures • Define Service Agent Procedure Group**.

Vendor's Quality Management System

Many government agencies require that a vendor's quality management (QM) systems meet certain levels of verification. These verifications check the level of certification of the system, for example, ISO 9001, ISO 9002, and so on. Verification levels can be configured using Transaction OQB7 or by following the navigation path **Quality Management • QM in Logistics • QM in Procurement • Define QM Systems**.

QM System Valid-To Date

The **QM system to** date field is the expiration date for the certification of the vendor's QM system. For example, a company that has an ISO 9001:2000 certification has to renew the certification every three years according to ISO regulations.

External Manufacturer Code Name or Number

This field can be used to hold a number or reference for a vendor that isn't the vendor number. For example, this field could be for a nickname for a vendor; "SCT" may be entered as a shortened version of Southwark Clapton and Thomas. This field allows up to 10 characters.

Save your entries. Now, as a final step to the business partner master data creation process, let's now extend the business partner role of the business partner 20000012 to the specific business partner role ZHVP01 we previously configured in Section 6.2.2.

6.5.3 Extending Business Partners for Purchasing

While in change mode, as shown in Figure 6.33, choose the newly configured business partner role **ZHVP01 Vendor-High Value (New)** available from the **Change in BP role** dropdown list. Now, the system will not just display the existing and general data already maintained for the business partner, but will bring up additional fields and tabs. Click **Purchasing**.

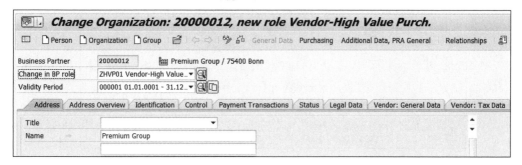

Figure 6.33 Business Partner Role ZHVP01

Purchasing-related options, including their associated tabs, are now available to maintain. Click the **Purchasing Organizations** button so that the screen shown in Figure 6.35 appears.

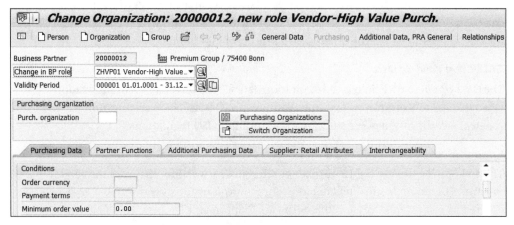

Figure 6.34 Business Partner: Purchasing Data Tab

Like the company code data we previously maintained, this time we'll maintain the purchasing organizations by first clicking on **Create** and entering "1000" and "6000" followed by choosing **Transfer**, as seen in Figure 6.35.

Recall from Chapter 2 that we defined purchasing organization 1000 as a reference organization to the purchasing organization 6000. Thus, maintaining purchasing organization 1000 is required to ensure the procurement process runs even only purchasing organization 6000 is involved. If no reference purchasing organization exists in the SAP system, then maintaining its data isn't necessary either.

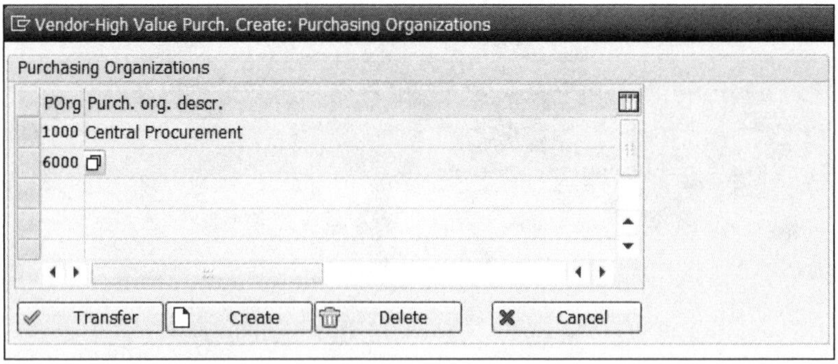

Figure 6.35 Purchasing Organization

As shown in Figure 6.36, maintain the relevant data for purchasing organization 6000 including the **Order currency** (a mandatory field). Repeat the same data maintenance for the reference purchasing organization 1000.

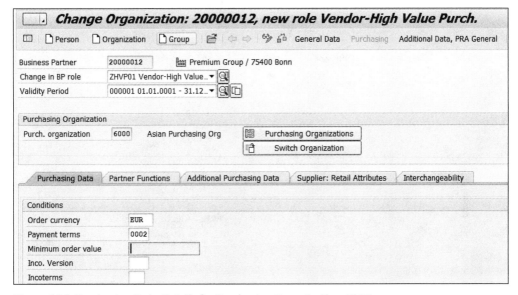

Figure 6.36 Purchasing Data Details for Purchasing Organization 6000

Let's discuss some of the fields shown in Figure 6.36.

Order Currency

The **Order currency** to be used on POs with this vendor can be entered in this field. The currency is usually that of the vendor's country or that of the purchasing department.

Incoterms

Incoterms facilitate international trade by helping vendors and customers in different countries understand each other. Incoterms are standard trade definitions used in international contracts and devised by the International Chamber of Commerce (ICC), based in Paris, France. The latest version is Incoterms 2018, which has been translated into 31 languages.

The 11 Incoterms, as shown in Table 6.2, are divided into two groups:

- Any mode of transport for arrival or departure (group 1)
- Sea and inland waterway transport only (group 2)

Group	Incoterm	Long Name	Location
1	EXW	Ex Works	Named place
1	DAP	Delivered at Place	Destination
1	DAT	Delivered at Terminal	Destination
1	DDP	Delivery Duty Paid	Destination
1	CIP	Carriage, Insurance Paid	Destination
1	CPT	Carriage Paid To	Destination
1	FCA	Free Carrier	Named place
2	CFR	Cost and Freight	Port of destination
2	CIF	Cost, Insurance, Freight	Port of destination
2	FAS	Free Alongside Ship	Port of destination
2	FOB	Free on Board	Port of destination

Table 6.2 Incoterms 2018

Supplier Schema Group

The calculation schema maintained in the **Schema Grp Supp** field is used to determine the pricing procedure for the vendor with relation to purchasing documents. The schema group can be configured by following the navigation path **Materials Management • Purchasing • Conditions • Define Price Determination Process • Define Schema Group**.

Pricing Date Control

The **Pricing Date Control** is used to determine the date on which the pricing determination will take place. For example, if the purchasing department decided to select the PO date, then the new price is calculated when the PO is created with the vendor.

Order Optimum Restrictions

This field allows a user to enter a key for PO-based load building. This field identifies whether a vendor is included in optimized load building or whether target values should be taken into account in optimized load building.

Goods Receipt-Based Invoice Verification

Setting the **GR-Based Inv. Verif.** indicator allows the system to perform invoice verification based on goods receipt amounts. Invoice verification involves three-way matching among the PO, the goods receipt, and the invoice to ensure that the totals are correct and that the invoice can be paid.

Automatic Evaluated Receipt Settlement

The Evaluated Receipt Settlement (ERS) agreement (**AutoEvalGRSetmt Del.**) is created between the vendor and the purchasing department. This agreement allows the purchasing department to send payments for the goods received at the time those materials are posted into stock. In this scenario, the vendor doesn't send an invoice for the material sent. This method of ERS, sometimes called a two-way match, is designated a best practice by many purchasing experts.

Acknowledgement Required

This indicator determines whether a vendor is supposed to send an acknowledgement that your order has been received. This acknowledgement can be sent via EDI.

Automatic Purchase Order

If a purchase requisition has been created and assigned to this vendor, then an automatic PO can be created if this indicator is set, which reduces work for the purchasing department. Chapter 13 covers this functionality.

Subsequent Settlement

A vendor may offer some kind of incentive to the purchasing department to purchase more material. This incentive may take two forms. One may be an instant reduction in price—a promotional price—for a given period. The second incentive may take the form of a subsequent settlement, which is an agreement between the vendor and the purchasing department under which, depending on how much material is purchased, a rebate is offered at the end of an agreed period.

For example, let's say an office supply vendor agrees to give a 10% rebate for the total amount of purchases over a 3-month period. This agreement may have a provision that the total amount of purchases must be more than 50% greater than for the same period in the previous year. If the purchases are in excess of the 50%, then the subsequent settlement with the vendor takes place at the end of the period. The vendor then gives a 10% rebate on all of the purchases over that period.

Business-Volume Comparison/Agreement Necessary

If the **B.vol.comp./ag.nec** indicator is set, data must be compared between the vendor and the purchasing department before any subsequent settlement is posted. In our example involving our office supply vendor, the agreement may depend on the comparison of files from both parties.

Document Index Active

The document index is a way of automatically adjusting purchasing documents if conditions change.

Service-Based Invoice Verification

Some vendors provide services, and the work performed is entered using service entry sheets. If the **Srv.-Based Inv. Ver.** indicator is set, acceptance is carried out at the level of the service entry sheet.

ABC Indicator

The ABC indicator is used for many objects in SAP. The ABC indicator for vendors relates to the amount of sales the vendor does with the company. The ABC indicator is manually entered.

Mode of Transport for Foreign Trade

The **ModeOfTrnsprt-Border** indicator is used if a vendor is involved in foreign trade. The mode of transport is defined for each country; this field determines how the vendor transports material. The field can be configured by following the navigation path **Materials Management • Purchasing • Foreign Trade/Customs • Transportation Data • Define Modes of Transport**.

Office of Entry

The **Office of entry** field defines where the material purchased from this vendor will enter the country or leave in the case of a return. The office of entry is the customs office, which is configured by following the navigation path **Materials Management • Purchasing • Foreign Trade/Customs • Transportation Data • Define Customs Offices**.

Sort Criterion

This field allows the purchasing department to sort delivery items from a vendor in a specific manner. The default is by vendor subrange (VSR), but the sort can be by material number, material group, or EAN.

Grant Discount in Kind

A vendor is labeled as granting a discount in kind when that vendor offers materials to the purchasing department free of charge as an incentive to purchase.

Relevant for Price Determination for Vendor Hierarchy

If the vendor master record represents a node in a customer hierarchy, the pricing indicator determines whether the node is relevant for pricing. If you're maintaining the vendor master record for a customer hierarchy node and want to create pricing condition records for the node, this indicator must be set.

Purchasing Group

The purchasing group that most often deals with this vendor can be entered. The purchasing group can be associated with one or more vendors.

Planned Delivery Time

This field represents the average time it takes for a material to be delivered from this vendor. If a vendor supplies many materials, then this field may not be useful if delivery times differ for each material supplied by the vendor. In this case, maintaining planned delivery times in a purchasing information record makes sense, which we'll cover in Chapter 7.

Confirmation Control Key

A confirmation control key can be entered to determine which confirmation categories are expected from a PO item. The confirmation control key defines the confirmation sequence expected from a vendor. The confirmation sequence specifies the order in which the individual confirmations defined in a confirmation control key are expected and which confirmation categories are to be automatically monitored. For example, the confirmation control key 0001 can be configured to expect an order acknowledgement and a shipping notification. Chapter 13 covers this topic in detail.

The confirmation control key is configured in the IMG by following the navigation path **Materials Management • Purchasing • Confirmations • Set Up Confirmation Control**.

Unit of Measure Group

The **Unit of measure grp** defines the allowed units of measure (UoM)s, which defined as part of a unit of measure group. This information should be entered when a rounding profile is used.

The unit of measure group is configured in the IMG by following the navigation path **Materials Management • Purchasing • Order Optimizing • Quantity Optimizing and Allowed Logistics Units of Measure • Unit of Measure Groups**.

Rounding Profile

A rounding profile determines how a material quantity is rounded to optimize an order. The rounding profile reviews and rounds the quantity depending on the threshold value in the profile.

Rounding profiles are configured in the IMG by following the navigation path **Materials Management • Purchasing • Order Optimizing • Quantity Optimizing and Allowed Logistics Units of Measure • Unit of Measure Rounding Rules**.

The **Service data** section describes a number of fields related to retail companies and load building.

Price Marking Agreement

Let's say the vendor and customer enter into a price marking agreement. The vendor will apply price labels to the materials prior to shipping to the customer.

Rack-Jobbing Service Agreement

Retail companies use this field. If the indicator is set, then the vendor will be responsible for stock planning/replenishment and for filling the shelves at the retail outlet.

Order Entry by Vendor

When this indicator is set, the vendor is responsible for entering the PO. The order can be created in the background via an EDI order confirmation received from the vendor.

Vendor Service Level

This field is used for automatic PO-based load building. If the service level drops below the desired value, SAP will try to order an entire load of goods from this vendor.

Figure 6.37 shows the various partner functions, such as the supplier and invoicing party, which were previously configured and are now assigned automatically. Save the business partner.

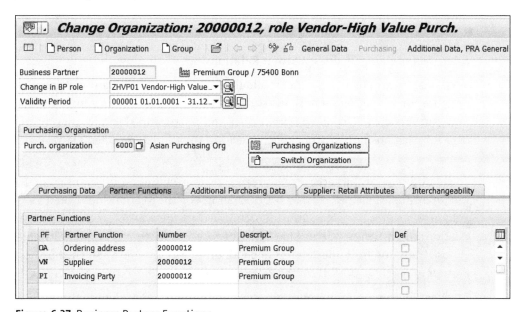

Figure 6.37 Business Partner Functions

6.5.4   Sales Data

The **Sales data** refers to the sales department person at the vendor who deals with your company. Most vendors will have a contract person whose information should be entered into this section.

Salesperson

This field is for the name of the person at the vendor who is the contact for purchases from your company. This person can either a salesperson or a sales clerk.

Telephone

This field is for the vendor's telephone contact number and is used when a PO is created.

Account with Vendor

This field is for the customer number that the vendor uses for your company. This number can be found on documentation from the vendor.

The control data for the vendor is made up of a number of indicators that are used in the procurement functionality.

6.5.5   Maintaining Business Partner Relationships

Relationships are created to connect and link different business partner roles of an organization with different business partners. Maintaining relationships with business partners entails having different roles and separate business partner master data for each business partner role, which are then interconnected via relationships.

To create a relationship, access the screen shown in Figure 6.38 via Transaction BP for our example business partner 20000012. Click on the relationships icon. To create a new business partner relationship, choose from the available business partner relationships from the **Relationship Cat.** (category) dropdown list. For our example, choose **FCRHM04** from the **Relationship Cat.** dropdown list and enter the business partner number "20000011" in the **Relationship to BP** field. Next, click on **Create**.

As shown in Figure 6.38, the business partner 20000011 has a bill-to-party relationship to business partner 20000012. To create this relationship, create another business partner relationship of the business partner 20000012 with the same business partner 20000011, but this time, choose **Invoicing Party** from the **Relationship Cat.** dropdown list.

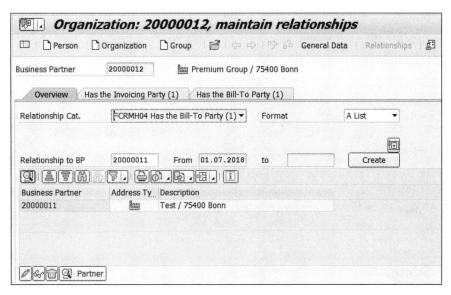

Figure 6.38 Business Partner Relationships Maintenance

Figure 6.39 shows the **Overview** tab, which displays two business partner relationships of business partner 20000012 with the business partner 20000011. Details about the individual relationships are shown in their respective tabs.

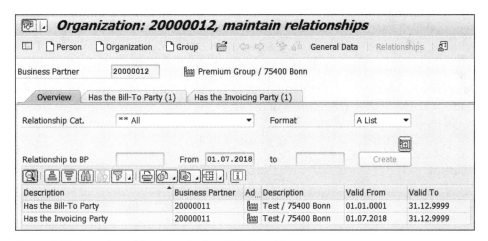

Figure 6.39 Overview of Business Partner Relationships

With configuration and master data of business partner in place, you can now check to see whether the system can successfully run the associated transactions or business processes.

> **Note**
>
> To access a business partner's or vendor's report, use Transaction MKVZ or follow the menu path **Logistics • Materials Management • Purchasing • Master Data • Vendor • List Display • Purchasing List**.
>
> On the initial screen that appears, enter the account group, for example, "HVPV," which we configured earlier, and click **Execute**. The resulting report will list the vendors belonging to the account group HVPV and other relevant details.

6.6   Summary

In this chapter, we thoroughly discussed the business partner function introduced in SAP S/4HANA. Different ways exist to enter vendor data, and both the purchasing department and the accounting department play a role in this important task. Having the correct vendor information entered is important when material needs to be ordered quickly and correctly. Any errors in the vendor master can be costly if a material can't be sourced in a timely fashion and shipments are delayed to customers. In this chapter, we provided you all of the tools you'll need to work with the purchasing department and meet their needs when SAP is implemented.

Chapter 7 examines purchasing information data as it relates to specific information available for a vendor and a material. Contracts with vendors may have special provisions, for example, in the number of delivery days or pricing conditions for certain materials.

Chapter 7
Purchasing Information Record

The documented relationship between a vendor and a material is important for the purchasing department. To reduce the length of the procurement process, a purchase order (PO) can be generated from the information in a purchasing information record, thus reducing manual data input.

The information found on a purchasing information record (info record, for short) is data specific to that vendor and that has been negotiated in a verbal or written agreement. The information supplied by the vendor or from the contract is entered into the purchasing information record. A normal purchase information record exists between a vendor and you, as the customer, for a specific material. However, a vendor can also supply a service defined by a material group rather than a specific material, and this information can be entered into a purchasing information record.

In vendor and material master records, you'll maintain vendor- and material-specific information. In purchasing information records, you'll maintain information about the relationships between vendors and their materials. For example, each vendor may have specific terms and conditions of purchase for each material—this information is stored in purchasing information records. In other words, a purchasing information record has a one-to-one relationship between a vendor and a material. If one vendor supplies three different materials, then the system will create three information records. Similarly, if three vendors supply the same material, even then the system will create three different information records.

In this chapter, we'll help you understand the data in a purchase information record. You'll learn about different types of records and how they can be used by purchasing departments.

7.1   Purchasing General Data

Information from an information record is defaulted (copied) during the purchase order creation process. You can maintain the following data in purchasing information records:

- Current and future prices and conditions (gross price, freight, and discounts)
- Delivery data (planned delivery time and tolerances)
- Vendor data (vendor material number, vendor material group, etc.)
- Text

Information records can be maintained at different organizational levels, as shown in Figure 7.1. Examples include the client level, the purchasing organization level, and the plant level. Purchasing information records have general data, purchasing organization data, and plant data. When you create a PO, the system searches for a valid information record for the purchasing organization/plant combination. If no such information record exists, the system searches for the purchasing organization only.

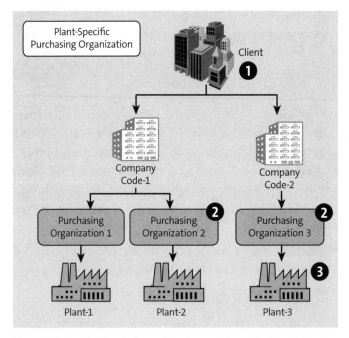

Figure 7.1 Purchasing Information Record Organizational Levels

An information record contains the following:

❶ General data: vendor's material number, reminder data, order unit, etc.

❷ Purchasing organization data: delivery time, minimum quantity, gross price, freight, discounts, price history, and text

❸ Purchasing organization/plant data: delivery time, minimum quantity, gross price, freight, discounts, price history, and text

Your first step in this process will be to create a purchasing information record. We'll start by showing you the general process, before moving on to creating information records with a material number and without a material number.

7.1.1   Creating a Purchasing Information Record

To create a purchasing information record, use Transaction ME11 or follow the navigation path is **Logistics • Materials Management • Master Data • Info Record • Create**. Figure 7.2 shows the initial data entry screen for creating a purchasing information record.

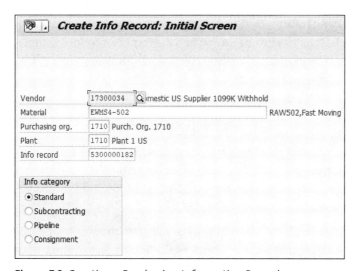

Figure 7.2 Creating a Purchasing Information Record

At the initial purchasing information screen, as shown in Figure 7.2, a purchasing user can decide what data to enter to create one of the four types of records:

- **Standard purchasing information record**
  The **Standard** type of purchasing information record contains information supplied by the vendor for a specific material, service, or group of materials or services.

- **Subcontracting purchasing information record**
  The **Subcontracting** purchasing information record can be used when the order is a subcontracting order. In manufacturing plants, a material being produced may require some outside service, such as enameling or partial assembly. The work may be performed by a subcontractor, and the price that the subcontractor charges for the work is included in a subcontracting purchasing information record.

- **Pipeline purchasing information record**
  Pipeline materials, such as electricity, water, and oil, are supplied by utility vendors and are used by the customer through pipeline withdrawals. The **Pipeline** purchasing information record reflects the information for this vendor/material combination. With pipeline materials, the system assumes that material will always be available, and the company will only pay for what it consumes.

- **Consignment purchasing information record**
  When a vendor supplies material to be stored at a customer's site for customer withdrawal, the purchasing department can create a **Consignment** purchasing information record for that material.

7.1.2 Creating a Purchasing Information Record with a Material Number

A purchasing information record can be created for a specific material by entering the supplying **Vendor**. A record can be created with or without a purchasing organization. If no **Purchasing Org.** is entered, then the purchasing information record will only be created with general data, as shown in Figure 7.3.

If a **Purchasing Org.** is entered with the **Material** and **Vendor**, then the purchasing data screen will be available for a purchasing user to enter specific data that relates to that purchasing organization.

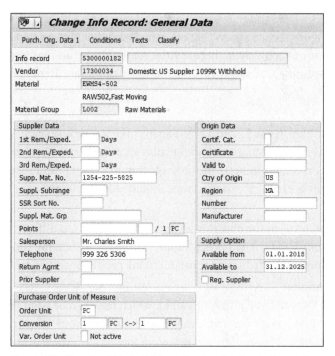

Figure 7.3 Standard Material/Vendor Purchasing Information Record

7.1.3 Creating a Purchasing Information Record without a Material Number

Simply entering a **Vendor** in the initial data screen can create a purchasing information record. This purchasing information record will be valid for the vendor and a **Material Group**, which is a mandatory entry on the **General Data** screen. Entering a description for the purchasing information record that describes the material group entered in the purchasing information record is also mandatory. This description isn't required if a **Material** is entered because the material already has a description attached. The description allows a purchasing user to describe the service that the vendor will provide for the materials in the entered material group. This type of record can be created with or without a purchasing organization. If no purchasing organization is entered, then the purchasing information record will only be created with general data.

7.1.4 General Data Screen

The **General Data** screen is valid for either a material/vendor purchasing information record or for a material group/vendor purchasing information record. Figure 7.3

shows that, for a material group/vendor record, the information record must be given a valid description. Figure 7.3 also shows that only the **Order Unit** is shown and not the other unit of measure (UoM) fields because the materials in the material group may have varying ordering units of measure. The most important items on this screen are as follows:

- **Reminder fields**

  The reminder fields—**1st Rem./Exped.**, **2nd Rem./Exped.**, and **3rd Rem./Exped.**— contain the number of days that urging letters or emails can be sent to the vendor for this material. Negative numbers indicate the message should be sent prior to the delivery date; positive numbers indicate the message should be sent after the date.

- **Vendor subrange**

  The **Vendor Subrange** can be used to subdivide a vendor's products into different ranges. For example, if our vendor is an office supply company, its vendor sub-ranges (VSRs) could be computer media, paper products, ink products, and so on.

- **Vendor subrange sort number**

  The **VSR Sort No.** allows VSRs to have different values, which can then be used to create sort sequences. When a PO is created, the VSR sort number from the purchasing information record will be used to sequence the materials in the PO. For example, if computer media has a sort number of 40, and the sort number for ink products is 24, then the ink products will be sequenced before the computer media products in the PO.

- **Points**

  The points system can be used when the purchasing department has negotiated a subsequent settlement or rebate arrangement with a vendor. The **Points** field in the purchasing information record allows a purchasing user to enter the number of points recorded each time a certain value of the material is ordered. The numbers of points is recorded for the amount ordered rather than the total value ordered. At the end of the rebate period, the number of points accumulated determines the value of the rebate from the vendor.

- **Return agreement**

  The **Return Agmt** field determines what arrangement the company has with the vendor for the return of material. The **Return Agmt** field can be configured so that unique return agreements can be defined. The return agreement is usually used for retail implementations and can be configured by following the navigation path **Logistics – General • Material Master • Retail-Specific Settings • Settings for Key Fields • Return Agreement**.

- **Regular vendor**
  The regular vendor is used by the system during source determination. This vendor is who you regularly buy a particular material from. You can set the **Regular Vendor** indicator in the general data of a purchasing information record. Only one purchasing information record for each material can be designated as the regular vendor. If the use of a regular vendor is permitted and configured for a specific plant in Customizing, the regular vendor will always be suggested during source determination.

In the next section, we'll discuss the more specific data required by the purchasing organization.

7.2   Purchasing Organization Data

After the general data has been entered, the next screen is for the purchasing organization data. The data fields shown in Figure 7.4 are also found in the vendor master and the material master. However, the information entered into the purchasing information record will be specific to the vendor/material combination and will be used in purchasing documents.

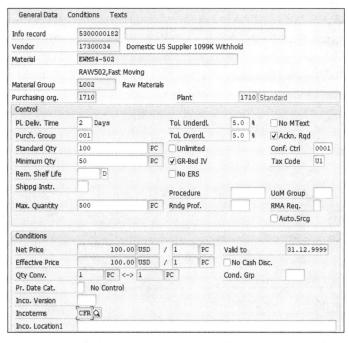

Figure 7.4 Purchasing Organization Screen for the Purchase Information Record

Depending on the agreement with the vendor, the purchasing department will enter information regarding under- or overdelivery tolerances, delivery times, quantities, and net prices. Setting up confirmation control (**Conf. Ctrl**) as well assigning the **Tax code** applicable to a vendor-material combination is all possible on this screen.

In the following sections, we'll discuss conditions, such as discounts and surcharges, as well as different options for maintaining purchasing texts.

Configuration Tip

As with most procurement screens, such as contracts, purchase orders, or purchase requisitions, you can control which fields are mandatory, optional, or for display only. For controlling fields on the information record, follow the menu path **Materials Management • Purchasing • Purchasing Info Record • Define Screen Layout**.

7.2.1   Conditions

The purchasing information record contains data that defines the conditions for the material/vendor. The **Condition** screen is shown in Figure 7.5. The screen shows that, from the date **01.05.2018** (May 01, 2018), the **Gross Price**, indicated by condition type (**CnTy**) **PPR0**, for **Material** EWMS4-502 from **Vendor** 17300034 was 100.00 USD per piece. Apart from the gross price, further pricing details can be maintained such as discounts or surcharges based on fixed values, percentages, or quantities. Figure 7.5 shows condition type **DRV1** with a fixed amount (surcharge) of 50.00 USD, condition type **FQU1** of 2.00 USD per 1 PC, and a discount (condition type **DCD1**) of 5%.

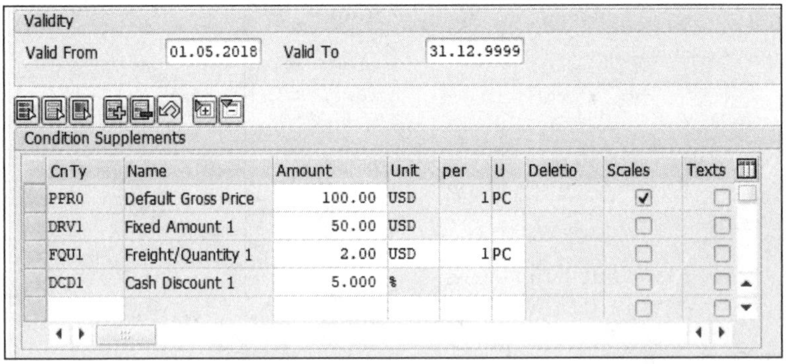

Validity		
Valid From 01.05.2018	Valid To	31.12.9999

Condition Supplements

CnTy	Name	Amount	Unit	per	U	Deletio	Scales	Texts
PPR0	Default Gross Price	100.00	USD		1 PC		✔	☐
DRV1	Fixed Amount 1	50.00	USD				☐	☐
FQU1	Freight/Quantity 1	2.00	USD		1 PC		☐	☐
DCD1	Cash Discount 1	5.000	%				☐	☐
							☐	☐

Figure 7.5 Condition Screen for Purchasing Information Record

7.2.2 Validity

The conditions entered in a purchasing information record are valid for a certain time period. For instance, if an agreement with the vendor is valid for three months, then the **Valid to** date should reflect that, as shown in Figure 7.5. If the information is for future agreements, validity dates can be entered to reflect this situation.

As shown in Figure 7.5, select the condition type **PPRO** and click the scales icon ![icon].

Validity			Control		
Valid From	01.05.2018		ScaleBasis	C	Quantity scale
Valid To	31.12.9999		Check		None

Scales

Scale Type	Scale quantity	U	Amount		Unit	per	UoM	PricActive
From	100	PC	100.00		USD	1	PC	○
	101		95.00					○
	500		90.00					○
	1,000		88.00					○
								○

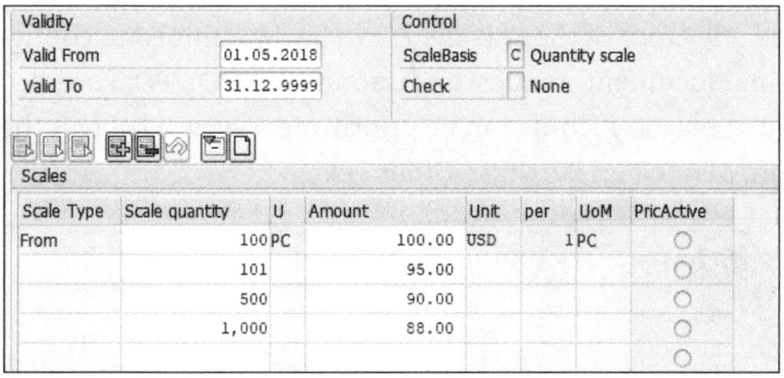

Figure 7.6 Maintaining Scales

The **Scales** fields allow a purchasing user to enter information on the condition type if valid for scaling. *Scaling* is when a discount from a vendor isn't a blanket 4% but is changes depending on the amount ordered. A vendor can give discounts for a specific material with increasing discounts the more the company purchases. For example, if a PO is for a quantity up to 30 units, the vendor could give the company a 1% discount; for 31 to 60 units, the discount could be 2%; from 61 to 120 units, the discount could be 4%; and for over 121 units, the discount could be 6%.

Configuration Tip

You can define how prices are stored in purchasing information records for each plant by following the menu path **Materials Management • Purchasing • Conditions • Define Condition Control at Plant Level**. For each plant, you can select one of the following options:

- **Conditions Allowed with and without Plant**
  You can create purchasing information records either at the plant level or at the purchasing organization level.

- **Only Plant-Related Conditions Allowed**
  You must create purchasing information records and contract items at the plant level. Therefore, centrally agreed contracts can't be created.

- **No Plant-Related Conditions Allowed**
  You may not create any purchasing information records or contract items at the plant level.

7.2.3   Text Screen

Texts fields can be used to enter specific information regarding a particular purchasing information record. The relevance of the text fields can be determined in configuration. For each purchasing document, request for quotation (RFQ), PO, contract, and so on, the texts defined in master records can be prioritized. Figure 7.7 shows the two available text fields: **Info Memo** and **Purchase Order Text**.

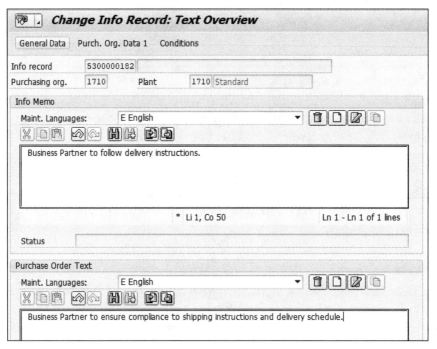

Figure 7.7 Text Input Screen for a Purchasing Information Record

The screen displays a few text lines of up to 40 characters. However, selecting the **More text** indicator displays a freeform text input screen similar to a normal word processing program. You can include additional text if significant information must be included in the purchasing information record. To the far right of the text box, the

Status field is displayed when text has been entered. (In this example, the **Status** field isn't shown.) This field indicates how the text can be used:

- Text should be used as is, with only changes to the original text allowed.
- Text should be used, and changes to the text are allowed, which will be reflected in the original text, but the modified text will be adopted.
- Text should be displayed but not printed or changed.

> **Configuration Tip**
>
> The text entered on a purchasing information record should be relevant to a PO line item. In configuration, you can define the priority against other text fields. This transaction can be accessed by following the navigation path **Materials Management • Purchasing • Messages • Text for Messages • Define Texts for Purchase Order**.
>
> The configuration for the PO texts can be further subdivided into header, line item, supplement, and headings texts. The purchasing information record text is most relevant to the document item.

7.2.4   Statistical Data

Within a purchasing information record, statistical information is recorded and can be reviewed. The statistical screens can be accessed from within the **General Data** screen by selecting **Extras • Statistics**.

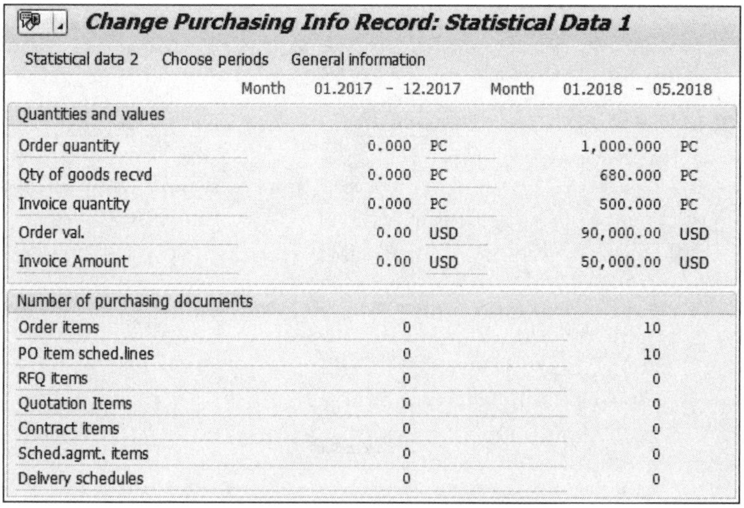

Change Purchasing Info Record: Statistical Data 1

Statistical data 2   Choose periods   General information

	Month 01.2017 – 12.2017		Month 01.2018 – 05.2018	
Quantities and values				
Order quantity	0.000	PC	1,000.000	PC
Qty of goods recvd	0.000	PC	680.000	PC
Invoice quantity	0.000	PC	500.000	PC
Order val.	0.00	USD	90,000.00	USD
Invoice Amount	0.00	USD	50,000.00	USD
Number of purchasing documents				
Order items	0		10	
PO item sched.lines	0		10	
RFQ items	0		0	
Quotation Items	0		0	
Contract items	0		0	
Sched.agmt. items	0		0	
Delivery schedules	0		0	

Figure 7.8 Statistical Data for a Purchasing Information Record

The **Statistical Data** screens shown in Figure 7.8 can be controlled to allow a comparison between two different time periods. The statistical data reflects information on the following:

- Order quantity and invoice value
- Number of purchasing documents
- Delivery time information
- Delivery reliability information
- Quantity reliability information

Saving the information record in this example will create information record 5300000182.

Access the screen shown in Figure 7.9 via Transaction ME21N (Create Purchase Order), and after you enter basic details, such as the vendor (or supplier) and material, the system will automatically copy as much detail from information record 53000000182 as possible (as shown in the **Info. rec.** field on the right-hand side of Figure 7.9). The **Conditions** tab also incorporates all the conditions types maintained in the information record. Click on the **Texts** tab shown in Figure 7.9, which will make the screen shown in Figure 7.10 appear.

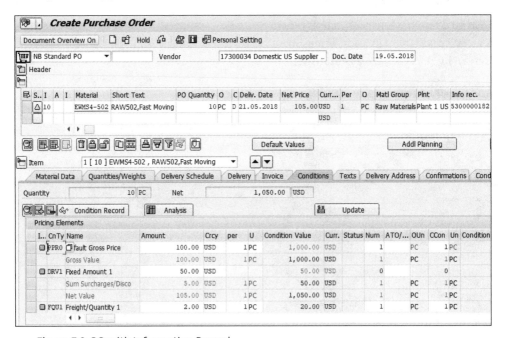

Figure 7.9 PO with Information Record

Figure 7.10 shows how data has been automatically copied the information record to the line item of the PO. The two green checkmarks on the left-hand side denotes that texts are maintained for this item.

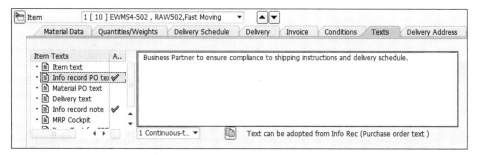

Figure 7.10 Texts Copied from an Information Record

7.3 Summary

In this chapter, we discussed the functionality behind purchasing information records. A purchasing information record contains specific data relevant to the purchasing department as it describes the relationship between a vendor and a material that the purchasing department procures. However, understanding that the information may vary by purchasing organization is important. When purchasing departments negotiate with vendors, the information from the final contract is entered into the purchasing information records. This data drives the purchasing of materials and services within a business. Accurate data reduces unnecessary delays in receiving material, which in turn reduces production problems and improves overall customer satisfaction. Accurate purchasing data, stored in records such as the purchasing information record, can help reduce purchasing costs for a company.

In Chapter 8, we'll examine the batch management functionality for describing quantities of the same material and help you understand the transactions used to create, change, and delete batch records in SAP. The chapter will also discuss batch determinations, how a specific batch is selected, and how batch management integrates with warehouse management (WM) and sales and distribution (SD) functionalities.

Chapter 8
Batch Management Data

Batch management is an important part of a company's ability to produce, store, and sell material. A batch defines a quantity of material by characteristics unique to that batch. These characteristics determine how the material in that batch is used, sold, or moved.

Certain materials can be defined in SAP as being batch managed. A *batch* is a quantity of material that represents a homogeneous unit with unique specifications. A batch can be defined in many ways. A batch of material may refer to a quantity of chemical that is produced in one process or a quantity of bottles of water filled at a certain filling line from a specific tank. In SAP, a batch can be used to identify units of material as they move through the system. A batch can have specific characteristics that enable it to be identified and used within the materials management (MM) functionality. In this chapter, we'll describe the process behind creating and changing batches and the process behind batch determination. In the first section, we'll provide an overview of batches and how they're used in various industries.

We'll start out this chapter by covering the configurations settings you'll need to maintain before using the batch management functionality in an SAP system. After configuration, we'll cover the requisite master data for batch management, followed by a discussion of the business processes associated with batch management, such as manually creating a batch master. We'll also describe how the system automatically creates a batch master during various business transactions. We'll then cover specialized but important batch management topics, such as automatic batch determination, batch derivation, and shelf life. This chapter will conclude with some important batch management reports, including the Batch Information Cockpit.

8.1 Batch Management Overview

The definition of a batch differs among companies, industries, and countries. For example, in the pharmaceuticals industry, strict guidelines and regulations determine what a batch is. These regulations governing batches and batch control include the ANSI/ISA-88 standard and the Food and Drug Administration's (FDA) 21 CFR Part 11 specifications in the United States.

Although no one definition of a batch covers all situations, the following definition from ExxonMobil Aviation may help:

A batch is the specific quantity of a material produced in a single manufacturing process, i.e., under the same conditions, thus featuring identical properties. Each batch of material is given a batch number. Each batch of a material is tested with regard to relevant characteristics to ensure it meets the values or within the range for those characteristics.

A second definition of a batch is from the Marathon Oil Company, which significantly differs from other definitions:

A batch is a shipment of a single product that is handled through the pipeline without mixing with preceding or following shipments.

Let's look at a third definition of a batch from the Hawaiian Coffee Association:

A batch refers to a quantity of coffee coming to the roaster. Quantities of the same coffee arriving at different times would be viewed as separate batches. Changes from batch to batch—even of the same variety of bean—must be detected by the roaster if he is to produce coffees that are consistently the same.

Whatever the definition, a batch must be identified by a batch record. This requirement may involve simply identifying bags of coffee beans as they arrive at the plant or may be more complex, such as identifying a batch by numerous qualifying characteristics to ensure quality and safety.

A batch of material can either be purchased from a vendor or produced internally. If you need to manage materials in batches, however, in SAP, the material must be identified as one that is batch-relevant.

The identification of a batch record is especially important for the pharmaceutical industry to comply with FDA regulations in the United States and other regulatory bodies across the world, such as the Drugs Controller General of India (DCGI), the Bundesgesundheitsamt (BGA) in Germany, Health Canada, and the Medicines and Healthcare Products Regulatory Agency (MHRA) in the United Kingdom.

These regulatory bodies are primarily interested in public safety. Regulations such as the FDA's 21 CFR Part 11 in the United States are aimed at improving the efficiency of quality control and quality assurance processes. Each batch produced must be quality tested, and the results of testing stored electronically against the batch number.

The most critical use of batch numbers in the pharmaceutical industry is for product recalls. A batch number also can be used as the tracking device for companies in case of subsequent errors or contamination. Manufacturers publish product recalls every day, but for the pharmaceutical industry, product recalls save lives.

A pharmaceutical company can voluntarily recall a product. If the company finds that a result from a test on a batch was incorrect and that puts the batch out of tolerance, then the product made from that batch could be hazardous.

The errors could go all of the way back to the vendor, if any of the material was purchased. If a vendor informs the company that a batch of purchased material was out of tolerance, then this batch must be traced through the production process to find all finished goods batches that may contain the faulty batch.

In the United States, the FDA has the power to compel a company to initiate a recall when it believes a drug violates the Food, Drug and Cosmetic Act (FDCA). A recall will be requested when the FDA concludes the following:

- A drug that has been distributed presents a risk of illness or injury or gross consumer deception.
- The manufacturer or distributor hasn't recalled the drug voluntarily.
- FDA action is necessary to protect public health.

In a recall, the manufacturer will inform the retailer, the wholesaler, or even the consumer directly about how to identify the batch number on the recalled product and which batch numbers are part of the recall.

Let's begin with the basic configuration steps for batch management.

8.2 Batch Level and Batch Status Management

In the following sections, we'll follow a step-by-step approach to the configuration steps required to set up batch management in an SAP system.

8.2.1 Defining the Batch Level

A batch level can be defined at the different levels but, by default, is defined at the plant level. At the beginning of an SAP implementation project, an MM consultant should help your company decide the appropriate batch level for monitoring and reporting.

Use the following guidelines to ensure that batch numbers are unique at the following three levels:

- **Plant and material combination level**

  At this level, the plant and material combination have unique batch numbers. Different materials in the same plant can be assigned the same batch number, and the same material in different plants can also be assigned the same batch number. In this context, the material is transferable from one plant to another, and although the batch number is the same, the specification of the destination batch will remain unchanged.

- **Material number level**

  If batch numbers are created at the material level, the same batch numbers can be used for other materials as well. After you set the batch level as the material in the system, the following can happen: A material can have the same batch number even though the materials are in different plants with the same specifications. The same batch number can be reassigned for other materials with a different specification.

- **Client level**

  The batch level is set at the client level, which is the highest level. The same batch number can't be used for different material or different plants. The batch number assigned is rather unique and can be assigned only once; thus, every material will always have a new or different batch number.

The system's default setting is the plant level, but the level can be customized as needed. However, you'll need to keep in mind that, while switching to a higher level is always possible, lowering the level is only possible from the client level to the material level. This limitation exists because batch data is organized in such a way that it has to be converted when switching to another batch level.

To define a batch level, follow the menu path **Logistics - General • Batch Management • Specify Batch Level and Activate Status Management**. Choose the **Batch level** (client, plant, or material level) and then save.

In the second step, choose **Batch status management** to activate the batch management status in the client, select the **Active** checkbox, and then save.

In the third step, choose **Plants with batch status management** and set the **Batch status management** indicator in the resulting list for those plants where batch status management should be active. Select the relevant checkboxes and save.

In the fourth step, choose the **Initial status of a new batch**, specify which initial new batches should be assigned for each *material type* and select the **Initial Status** checkbox for each material type that will be batch managed.

8.2.2 Batch Number Assignment

In this step, you'll define and assign batch number ranges by following the menu path **Logistics – General • Batch Management • Batch Number Assignment • Activate Internal Batch Number Assignment**.

In the resulting screen, select the **Active** radio button to activate internal batch number assignment. You can also define whether internal batch number assignment is allowed for goods receipts that have an account assignment by following the menu path **Logistics – General • Batch Management • Batch Number Assignment • Internal Batch Number Assignment for Assigned Goods Receipt**.

In the next step, you'll define the number ranges for internal batch number assignment. Follow the menu path **Logistics – General • Batch Management • Batch Number Assignment • Maintain Internal Batch Number Assignment Range**.

In a standard SAP system, you can set the number range object BATCH_CLT, and the number range 01 from 0000000001 to 9999999999 has been defined.

Similar to an internal batch number assignment, you can assign a number range for external number assignment. Follow the menu path **Logistics – General • Batch Management • Batch Number Assignment • Maintain Number Range for External Batch Number Assignment**.

You can maintain the external number range by clicking on the **Number Ranges** button and then the change **Intervals** button. Next, you can use the already-defined number range, and you can create a new number range by clicking on the **Insert Interval** button. Enter the number (**No.**), **From number**, and **To number**, and then click **Save**.

> **Note**
>
> SAP enhancement SAPLNOIZ can be used for internal batch number assignment. This enhancement comprises two function module exits to define number ranges or templates for batch numbers:
>
> - EXI_SAPLV01Z_001: This exit is used to replace the proposed number range object and/or interval with your own number range object by the system and/or interval. This exit is also used to stop the system from assigning an internal number

based on the material or plant. This exit can be used to stop the dialog box from appearing.

- EXIT_SAPLV01Z_002: This exit helps you assign your own number or even change the number assigned by the system.

8.2.3   Creating New Batches in the Production Process

In this step, you'll configure how the system creates new batches for process/production orders.

To define the new batch creation for process/production orders, follow the menu path **Logistics – General • Batch Management • Creation of New Batches • Define Batch Creation for Production Order/Process Order**.

You can make specific settings in batch management for existing production control profiles. Choose the production control profile for which you want to make settings and select the required option, as shown in Figure 8.1, for automatic batch creation:

- Automatic batch creation at order creation
- Automatic batch creation at order release
- No automatic batch creation in production/process order

Next, select the batch classification option in the **Batch Classification** field and select the **Extended Classification** checkbox so that more batch-specific functionalities are available.

The production scheduling profile (**PS Profile**), which in this example is **SFG**, is then assigned in the **Work Scheduling** tab of the material master.

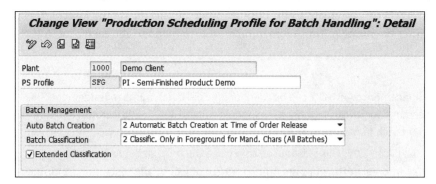

Figure 8.1 Batch Management in the Production Process

8.2.4   Batch Creation for Goods Movement

You can also define the new batch creation settings for movement types. Follow the menu path **Logistics – General** • **Batch Management** • **Creation of New Batches** • **Define Batch Creation for Goods Movements**.

For instance, when batch numbers aren't determined by the system automatically, you may want to manually assign a batch number for goods receipt on a purchase order (movement type 101). To achieve this, choose the **Automatic/manual without check** option for movement 101, as shown in Figure 8.2.

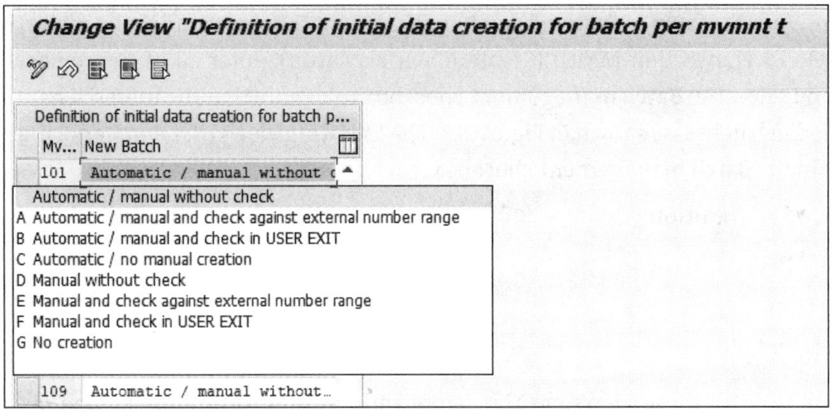

Figure 8.2 Batch Management with Movement Type

For each material type, you can also define whether a new batch can be created via the batch master creation transaction (Transaction MSC1N) or by following the menu path **Logistics – General** • **Batch Management** • **Creation of New Batches** • **Define Initial Creation of Data for Batch Master Transactions**. If you only want batch numbers to be assigned automatically by the system and don't want the option of manual assignment, for example, for finished products, then choose the **C: Automatic/No manual creation** option for material type FERT.

At this point, we've covered the basic configuration settings you'll need for batch management. In the next section, we'll cover how to set up master data for batch management.

8.3   Master Data in Batch Management

A first step when working with batch management is to identify the material that needs to be batch managed and then update the material master record by setting the batch management requirement. Let's go over the different master data management processes and steps specific to batch management in the following sections.

8.3.1   Activating Batch Management in the Material Master

In an SAP system, batch master records always depend on material master records. Therefore, your first step is to define batch management requirements in the material master. Go to Transaction MM01 (Create Material Master), enter all of the required details, and select the **Batch management** checkbox to denote that the material has to be handled in batches, as shown in Figure 8.3. The following views of the material master contain the **Batch management** checkbox:

- Sales and distribution
- General plant data
- Purchasing
- Work scheduling

In this context, all these views are the same, and any change/update to one view appears in all views.

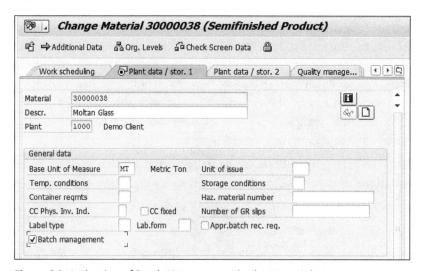

Figure 8.3 Activation of Batch Management in the Material Master

Tips & Tricks

The indicator for the material can be changed from "batch managed" to "non-batch managed" only if no stock exists for the current period and the previous period. This limitation allows for transactions posting of batch-managed materials in any previous period.

In an SAP system, batches are posted *for* a material, so batch master records are always dependent on material master records. If a mismatch exists between a material and a batch requirement, all stocks need to be posted from the previous fiscal year, the previous period, and the current period. In this case, you'll reset the indicator for batch requirements and repost the stock in batches into the system.

Similarly, you can cancel batch requirements for any material you don't want to be batch managed. If you must reorganize batch master records, you must reset the indicator to blank, post the required batch requirement, and then post the stock back into the SAP system using Transaction MIGO.

8.3.2   Batch Classification

To differentiate between batches of material depending on their individual properties, you can use characteristics to define batch properties. For example, the paint industry uses color, coverage, and viscosity as characteristics to classify different batches. The cold-roll coil (CRC) steel industry uses finish, thickness, and quality to classify different batches.

These characteristics are created in the SAP system and assigned to materials. The same concepts behind materials classification is applied in batch classification. (See Chapter 25 on classification for more information.)

A company that deals with various types of paints will want to capture characteristics of the paint: coverage, color, and viscosity. A class must be created with characteristics for coverage, color, and viscosity wavelength. This class will be assigned to a material. Every time a new batch is created for the material, these characteristic values will be entered. Let's briefly define characteristics and their assignment to a class specific to batch management.

Defining Characteristics

First, you'll create the various characteristics for your materials, such as thickness, viscosity, density and so on. We'll discuss the characteristics and classes in detail later in Chapter 24, so we won't go into great detail here.

To create characteristics, use Transaction CT04 or follow the menu path **Cross-Application Components • Classification System • Master Data • Characteristics**.

In the resulting screen, enter the **Characteristic** name and click on **Create**. Enter a **Description**, as shown in Figure 8.4. In the **Status** field, you'll have three options: **In Preparation**, **Locked**, and **Released**. A **Released** status means that the characteristic can be used; a status of **In Preparation** or **Locked** means that the characteristic can't be used.

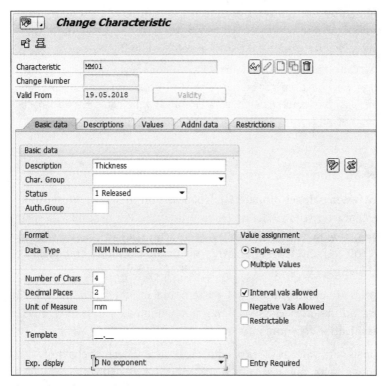

Figure 8.4 Characteristics

In the **Value assignment** section, select either **Single-value** or **Multiple Values**. The **Single-value** radio button specifies that only one value can be assigned to this characteristic; the **Multiple Values** radio button is used when more than one value is possible.

Select the **Values** tab and enter the possible values for this characteristic, as shown in Figure 8.5.

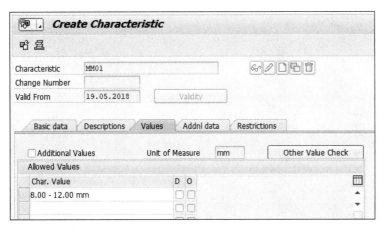

Figure 8.5 Characteristics: Values

The **Additional Values** indicator allows you to enter characteristic values that aren't defined. After you've defined these values, you can save the characteristic. In this example, we've taken the characteristic **Thickness** and specified that the value of thickness can range from 8.00 mm to 12.00 mm.

Now that you've created a characteristic, you'll need to assign the characteristics to the class, which we'll explain next.

Defining Classes and Assigning Characteristics

A class represents a group of characteristics. Classes are defined based on the material classification, such as a garment, oil and grease, or metals. To define a class, use Transaction CL02 or follow the menu path **Cross-Application Components • Classification System • Master Data • Classes**. Enter "023" (batch class) as the **Class type** and fill in the appropriate **Class** name, which in our example is "ZTGDEMOPP." Then, click on **New**. Enter a description and set the **Status** to **Released**. Enter the validity dates. On the **Char.** tab, assign the characteristics to the class, as shown in Figure 8.6. In this case, we've assigned three characteristics: **ZCLS (Product Class)**, **ZPD (Date of Manufacture)**, and **MM01 (Thickness)**.

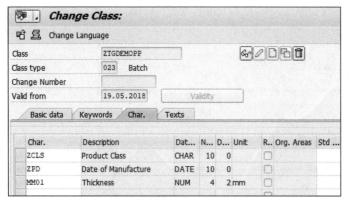

Figure 8.6 Assigning Characteristics to a Class

8.3.3   Assigning Classification in the Material Master

After you've defined a class, you'll need to assign it to the material master via Transaction MM01. Choose the **Classification** view for the **Material** 30000038 and select the **Class Type 023** to assign the previously created class ZTGDEMOPP. The assignment will automatically bring up all three characteristics assigned to the class, as shown in Figure 8.7.

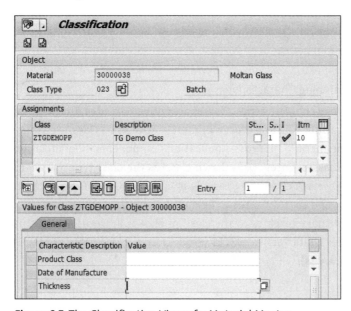

Figure 8.7 The Classification View of a Material Master

Now, you can maintain specific values for the characteristics pertaining to this material. Since this step is a master data step, note that the characteristic values you assign on this screen are for the material master only and *not* for batches of a material.

With the requisite master data created for batch management, in the next section, we'll discuss the business processes associated with batch management.

8.4 Business Processes of Batch Management

In the following sections, we'll cover the business processes of batch management in the SAP system. Some of these business processes are manual or automatic creation of a batch, changing or deleting a batch, the classification function in batch, and attaching documents to a batch.

8.4.1 Creating the Batch Master Manually

A batch master record for a material can be created manually or automatically in the background by the system when you receive goods for the first time. A manually created batch of a material can then be assigned during stock postings, such as for a goods receipt of a material from procurement or production processes.

To create batch master records manually, use Transaction MSC1N or follow the menu path **SAP Menu • Logistics • Central Functions • Batch Management • Batch • Create**, as shown in Figure 8.8.

Enter a material, a plant, and a storage location for which you want to create a batch master record. If you've defined an internal number range, the system will automatically create the batch number after you press Enter. In general, the data in a material master applies for all the batches assigned to this master record. By contrast, a batch master record contains data that uniquely identifies the corresponding batch and characterizes the unit as one that can't be reproduced.

Various types of information are stored in the batch master record. Some can be updated manually, and some can be updated automatically. We'll discuss some of the relevant information in different tabs in the following sections.

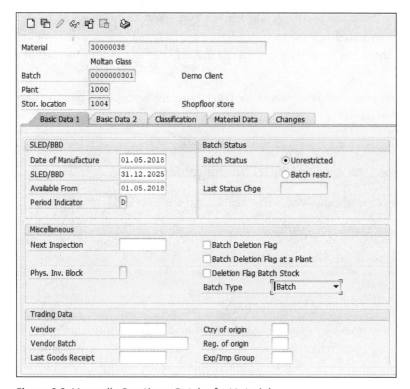

Figure 8.8 Manually Creating a Batch of a Material

Basic Data 1

Important fields and indicators of **Basic Data 1** tab, shown in Figure 8.8, are as follows:

- **Date of manufacture**

  The date when a batch was produced can be entered into this field. In some indus-tries, this field is also used as the date a material was tested or retested. If a material is found to be still within tolerance after the shelf-life expiration date (SLED) has passed, the material can be retested, and the date of the retest is entered into this field, in addition to a new **Shelf Life Exp. Date.** Check with the relevant depart-ments to determine they need to use this field.

- **Shelf-life expiration date**

  The **SLED/BBD** field is the date on which the shelf life of this batch will expire. The shelf life of a product can vary between plants. This date can be used in the sales process, since customers require a specific acceptable number of days of shelf life remaining. Some companies use this field to indicate the date on which a batch needs to be retested. If your company has implemented quality management (QM) in SAP S/4HANA, then the system uses this field to see if the material's batch expiration date is approaching so that the system can create a quality inspection lot for retesting the material.

- Available from

  The **Available From** field indicates when a batch will be available. For example, if a material must remain in the quality inspection process for a certain number of days after testing, then the quality department can enter a date to inform other departments about when the batch is expected to be available.

- Batch status

  The **Batch Status** indicator allows a batch to be classified as having restricted or unrestricted use. If the **Unrestricted** indicator is set, then the batch has no restriction placed on its use. If the **Batch restr.** indicator is set, the batch is treated like blocked stock in planning but can be selected by batch determination if the search includes restricted-use batches.

  The **Batch Status** can be set to restricted from unrestricted by changing the indicator in the batch record. A material document will be posted that shows the movement of stock between the two statuses.

- Next inspection

  The **Next Inspection** date field allows the quality department to enter the date of the next quality inspection of the batch, if applicable to this material. This field is helpful when a company must retest a material's batch after every predefined period. This material retesting process is known as *recurring inspection*.

- Vendor batch

  If a material is purchased, then the batch number assigned by the vendor can be added to the batch record. This vendor batch number is important for tracking any product recall procedure initiated by the vendor. The **Vendor Batch** field allows a 15-character string to be entered.

Basic Data 2

In this tab, you can maintain the **Texts** and **Freely definable date** fields. The six date fields (**Date 1**, **Date 2**, and so on) are optional and only necessary if you want to use these dates somewhere in the process. These fields don't have any standard functionality. The six date fields can be used for whatever purpose is defined by the company. For example, these fields could contain the dates on which a material was inspected by the quality department.

Classification

In this tab, you can use the class that was assigned to a material during material master classification. You can enter values for characteristics by clicking on the **New** button. After you click on the **New** button, you can enter values for all of the characteristics listed on the material class, as shown in Figure 8.9.

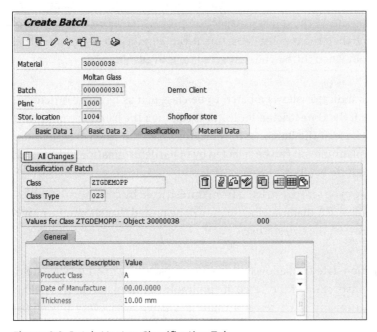

Figure 8.9 Batch Master: Classification Tab

Material Data

In this tab, you can change the information from the material master record. If you click **Changes**, all of the change history is updated and displayed in this tab. This tab won't appear when you're creating a batch for the first time, but you can see it when changing or displaying a transaction.

Configuration Tip

If you want to link documents to a batch, then a configuration step must be completed. Use Transaction ODOC or follow the navigation path **Logistics – General • Batch Management • Batch Master • Activate Document Management for Batches**.

The configuration step in Transaction ODOC is to simply select an indicator to allow document management for batches. The options are active and inactive. Chapter 26 covers SAP's Document Management System (DMS).

8.4.2   Changing a Batch

After a batch has been created, sometimes you may need to amend the batch record, either to modify a characteristic or to add a new linked document. To change a batch record, use Transaction MSC2N or follow the menu path **Logistics • Materials Management • Material Master • Batch • Change**.

You can make changes to the batch record, but these changes are recorded and are available for review before being committed. The **Change Batch** screen has an extra tab in the change mode. This tab accesses a screen to view all changes made to the batch record. The **Changes** tab (refer to Figure 8.8) shows the changes made to the batch record. The information recorded includes the users who created and changed the record, as well as what fields have been changed, including their values. This information is important to some companies because a strict audit record may be needed to show compliance with federal or local regulations. In the pharmaceutical industry, for instance, companies that manufacture items that will be consumed are under strict regulations from the FDA. Companies should at all times ensure that their record keeping is compliant with regulations.

8.4.3   Deleting a Batch

No transaction exists solely for deleting a batch, but you can delete a batch through Transaction MSC2N.

Figure 8.8 shows the initial screen of the change batch transaction, which has a **Batch Deletion Flag** indicator. Select this checkbox if the batch is to be deleted. However, setting the deletion flag doesn't immediately delete the batch. The indicator simply allows the batch to be processed by an archiving program, which will determine whether the batch can be deleted. If the batch can't be deleted, the deletion flag will remain until either the archiving program determines that the batch can be deleted or until the deletion flag is removed.

8.4.4   Automatic Creation of a Batch in Goods Movement

You can define the automatic creation of batch numbers in the SAP system, whether for movement types or production and process orders. For instance, you can customize the system to automatically create unique batch numbers whenever goods are delivered by a particular vendor against a PO with movement type 101, depending on your business requirements. Thus, every time goods with movement type 101 are received, a unique batch number for the material received is created by the system automatically.

Let's look at an example of the system automatically creating a batch master on goods receipt without reference to a PO (movement type 501).

To receive goods without a PO via movement type 501, go to Transaction MIGO. As shown in Figure 8.10, enter the material master 30000038 and in the item details, you'll see one more tab: the **Batch** tab. Notice that the system has already automatically created batch 302.

Click on the **Classification** button in the **Batch** tab, as shown in Figure 8.10, to enter values for the characteristics, as shown in Figure 8.11.

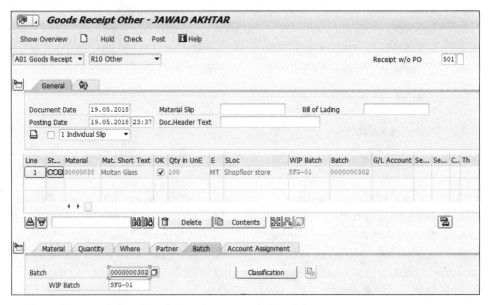

Figure 8.10 Goods Receipt of a Batch-Managed Material

As shown in Figure 8.11, you can maintain characteristic values, such as values for **Product Class** and for **Thickness**.

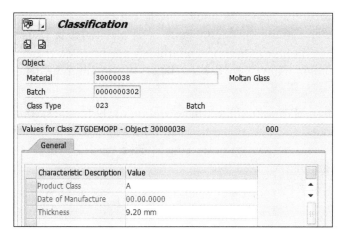

Figure 8.11 Classification View of a Batch during Goods Receipt

8.4.5   Stock Overview

The stock overview report shows how stock is kept in different batches. Go to Transaction MMBE, enter the plant code and material number, and execute the report. You'll see the stock overview report with batch numbers, such as batch number 302, which we received in the previous step. Figure 8.12 shows batch 302 of material 30000038 with quantity 100 MT.

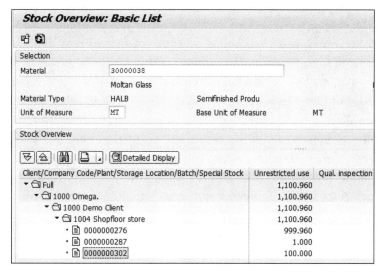

Figure 8.12 Stock Overview

To issue a material, if multiple batches of the same material exists in stock, the system automatically lets you choose the batch number from the material to be issued. If you want to assign a batch number based on some strategy, the batch determination strategy should be configured. We'll cover batch determination in more detail later in Section 8.5.

You can use batch usage transactions to track batches and for analysis. Transaction MB56 will give you the details of a batch where-used list. SAP also provides the Batch Information Cockpit, which is a central tool for tracking batches. We'll also cover the Batch Information Cockpit in more detail in Section 8.9.

8.5   Batch Determination

The batch determination process isn't unique to MM. The process is important in sales and distribution (SD), production planning (PP), and warehouse management (WM) as well. Batch determination uses strategy types, search strategies, and search procedures for a batch to be identified in the relevant area.

In a real-world scenario, you'll be receiving one material in a number of batches, and this material will be kept in storage location stock or in warehouse storage bins. When you want to issue a material to production, you'll need a strategy to choose the batch. You can define a strategy in the system, which the system will use to determine the right batch to pick. This process is called *batch determination*. Batch determination uses the condition technique. Strategy records from the relevant applications, such as MM, PP, SD, or WM, determine batch determination. Different strategy records in the system must be created for different purposes, such as goods issue to production, goods issue to customer, and so on. Batch determination can be used in the goods movement, production/process order, sales order/delivery, cost center, and transfer order functions.

Customizations for each application such as inventory, production, sales, and stock transfers are stored in search procedures, which run the batch determination. While the batch determination procedure is running, the system automatically accesses the corresponding entry of the application, which further locates the relevant entries in Customizing.

Figure 8.13 shows how the system searches for batch numbers using the batch determination procedure. In any transaction, the system will first determine the application area—production planning (PP) and production planning process industry (PP-PI), materials management (MM), warehouse management (WM), or sales and distribution (SD)—and then determine the search procedures, which are assigned based on different combinations (❶, ❷). In the case of a PP and PP-PI combination, the system will determine the order type and plant from the transaction and then find a search procedure (❸, ❹). For MM, the system will find a search procedure based on movement type. In case of SD, the search procedure will be based on sales organization, distribution channel, division, and sales document type.

The search procedure helps the system determine the search type (❺). The search type identifies the condition type and condition tables (❻). The system will find the appropriate batch number based on the access sequence system.

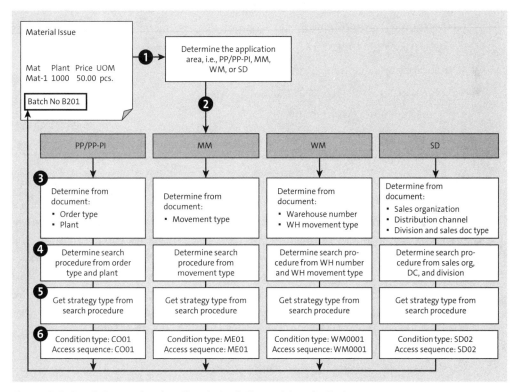

Figure 8.13 Batch Determination Flow in Logistics and Supply Chain

In the following section, we'll start out with the necessary configuration steps required to set up automatic batch determination in the inventory management (IM) business processes of MM. However, you can also use this same logic and these steps to set up automatic batch determination in other applications, such as PP, PP-PI, SD, and WM, as well. These configuration steps are then followed by covering the necessary master data required for batch determination. Finally, we'll also show you how to configure and set up the master data to reflect in the business process of batch determination.

Next, let's perform the seven steps in the logical and sequential order.

8.5.1   Defining Condition Tables

The batch determination condition table consists of a number of fields available for selection and to be used to record and assign values.

Five options exist for condition table creation, depending on which business process the batch determination is for:

- Inventory management (Transaction OMA1)
- Process order (Transaction OPLB)
- Production order (Transaction OPLB)
- SD (Transaction V/C7)
- WM (Transaction OMK4)

To define a condition table of inventory management, follow the menu path **Logistics – General • Batch Management • Batch Determination and Batch Check • Condition Tables**. You'll find options for defining condition tables for each application area, that is, inventory management, production order, process order, sales and distribution, and warehouse management. In the SAP menu, click on the **Define Inventory Management Condition Table** option. You'll get a new screen with **Create, Change**, and **Display** options. To create a new condition table, click on the **Create Condition Table for Batch Determination (IM)**, enter the condition table number, and choose fields from the field catalog. You can also edit the already created tables by choosing the **Change Condition Table for Batch Determination (IM)** option. You'll see a screen with only a **Condition** table field; enter the condition table and press ⌈Enter⌋. The screen shown in Figure 8.14 will appear where you can select the fields for the condition table from the **Field** catalog. You can define condition tables for each application area in the same way.

The standard delivery contains the following condition tables for batch determination in inventory management:

- 020: Movement type
- 021: Movement type/plant
- 022: Movement type/material
- 023: Plant/material
- 024: Movement type/plant/material
- 025: Plant

As shown in Figure 8.14, in our example, we created a new **Table 501** by copying the standard condition table 024. By copying this standard condition table, we'll have the option of using the batch determination procedure that will be specific to the material-plant-movement type combination.

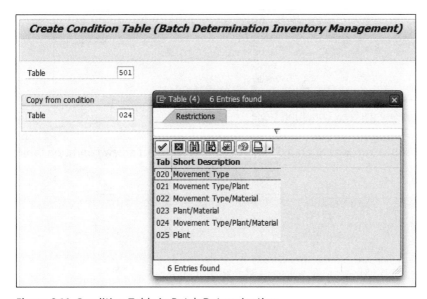

Figure 8.14 Condition Table in Batch Determination

Figure 8.15 shows the newly created condition table 501 in which the three selected fields are **Movement type**, **Plant**, and **Material** shown on the left-hand side of the figure. You can choose additional fields from the catalog on the right-hand side of the same figure so they too are available for selection during the batch determination procedure. For example, you can the place the cursor in the **Storage location** from the field catalog and click on **Select field** button, and then during the batch determination, the system will only suggest batches of materials available in specific storage locations.

Click on the **Generate** button, and the system will create the condition table, as shown in Figure 8.16.

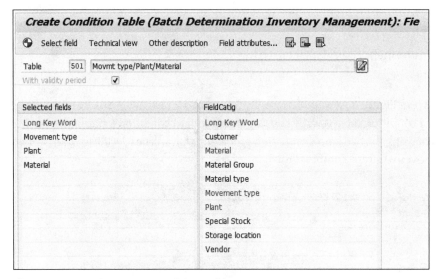

Figure 8.15 Creating a New Condition Table

Figure 8.16 shows the log generated on successful creation of a new condition table, 501.

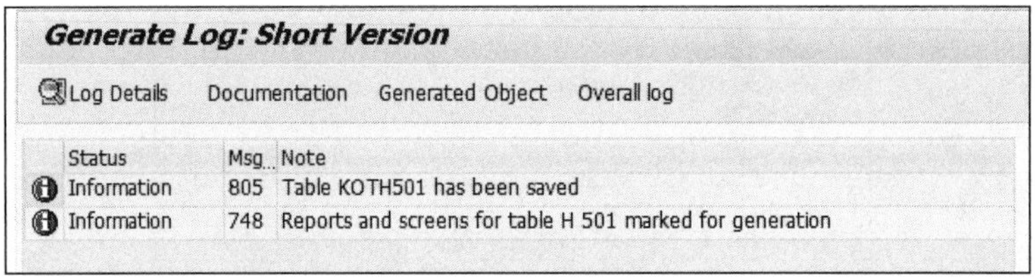

Figure 8.16 Log after Condition Table Creation

8.5.2   Defining the Access Sequence

Each batch strategy type has a batch determination access sequence. This access sequence allows the batch strategy type to access the condition tables in the correct sequence. To define an access sequence for each application area follow the menu path **Logistics – General • Batch Management • Batch Determination and Batch Check • Access Sequences • Define Inventory Management Access Sequences**.

Figure 8.17 shows the access sequence for inventory management. Select the access sequence and click on the **Edit** button. You can define the sequence of tables you want the system to follow. For example, as shown in Figure 8.17, the system will first search the movement type/plant/material combination, then the plant/material combination, and so on.

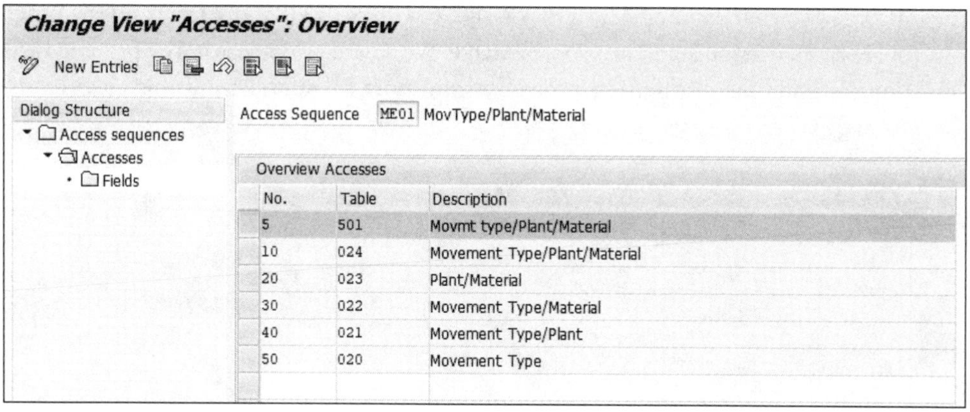

Figure 8.17 Access Sequence in Batch Determination

In a standard SAP system for inventory management, access sequences ME01 and ME02 are defined. In a standard system for production orders, access sequences CO01 and CO02 are defined, and in the standard system for sales and distribution, access sequences SD01, SD02, and SD03 are defined. We recommend making a copy of the standard access sequence available and then making changes in the condition table sequences to meet your unique requirements.

Next, we'll place the newly created condition table **501** at the top position (**5**) so that the system accesses this condition table for batch determination before any other condition table.

8.5.3   Defining Strategy Types

A batch strategy type is a specification that tells the system what type of criteria to use during the batch determination process. A batch strategy can be defined in the five areas mentioned earlier. Define the strategy types for each application area by following the menu path **Logistics – General • Batch Management • Batch Determination and Batch Check • Strategy Types • Define Inventory Management Strategy Types**. Click on the **New** button or copy the standard strategy type provided by SAP. We recommend copying the standard strategy type, then making the required changes, and saving the new strategy type. Figure 8.18 shows the strategy types for batch determination in inventory management.

In the standard SAP system for inventory management, strategy types MEO1 and MEO2 are defined.

Also, as shown in Figure 8.18, we can assign the **Class 023 (Batch Class)** and the previously created associated **Class ZTGDEMOPP**. We created this class in the previous section for batch determination processes, and now we're assigning this class to the strategy type.

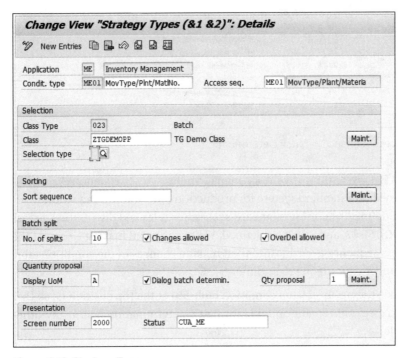

Figure 8.18 Strategy Type

In the **Selection** area, you have the option of defining the values of certain characteristics within a class. The values can be maintained by clicking on the **Maint.** button. Additionally, you'll need the following information:

- The **Selection type** field allows you to determine how the batches should be selected at the commencement of the batch selection. If the **Selection type** is left blank, then the system will display batches that meet the selection criteria.

- The **Sort sequence** field allows you to choose a sort to define how the batches are sorted if selected. The **Sort sequence** can be maintained on this screen if desired. Later in this section, we'll also cover how to create a sort sequence and assign it to a condition record.

- The **Batch split** section contains the **No. of splits** field, which defines the number of batch splits allowed during the batch determination.

8.5.4   Defining the Batch Search Procedure

In this IMG activity, you'll define search procedures for batch determination in inventory management. Follow the menu path **Logistics – General • Batch Management • Batch Determination and Batch Check • Batch Search Procedure Definition • Define Inventory Management Search Procedure**, as shown in Figure 8.19.

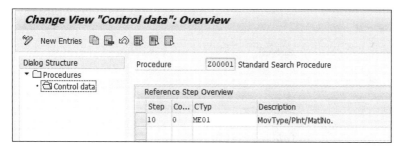

Figure 8.19 Batch Search Procedure

Click on the **New** button to define the search procedure or define it by copying an SAP-provided search procedure. We recommend copying a standard procedure (so that you don't miss any required settings), then make the required changes, and save the entries.

All strategy types used for a particular goods movement are included in a search procedure. The standard SAP system contains search procedure ME0001.

As shown in Figure 8.19, we created a new batch search procedure **Z00001** by copying the standard procedure ME0001 and assigning the condition type (**CTyp**) **ME01**.

8.5.5   Batch Search Procedure Allocation

In this step, you'll allocate the search procedure to different combinations for each application area. Follow the menu path **Logistics – General • Batch Management •**

Batch Determination and Batch Check • Batch Search Procedure Allocation and Check Activation.

For MM, you'll need to assign a search strategy to a movement type, as shown in Figure 8.20. So, for a particular movement type, this search strategy will help find the relevant batches using the batch determination procedure. For example, goods issues to cost centers have the movement type 201, and search strategy Z00001 can be assigned to this movement type on the screen shown in Figure 8.20. We'll soon show how the cost center, movement type (201), and plant combination enables automatic batch determination.

As shown in Figure 8.20, we assigned the previously configured batch search procedure **Z00001** to movement type **201**. Make sure you select the **Check Batch** checkbox for the relevant movement type so that the system can trigger automatic batch determination while issuing out the material against the cost center for movement type 201.

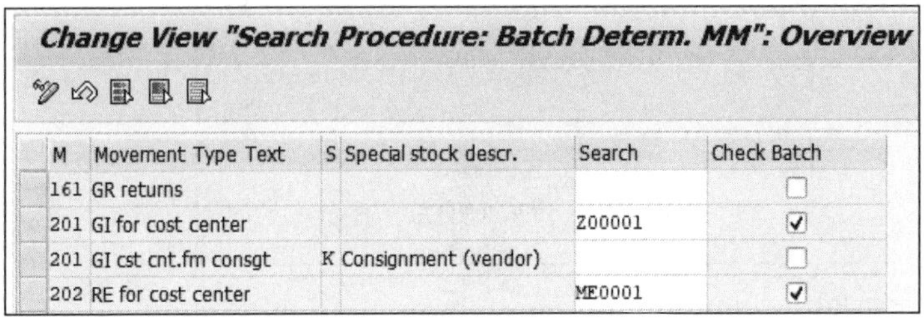

M	Movement Type Text	S	Special stock descr.	Search	Check Batch
161	GR returns				☐
201	GI for cost center			Z00001	☑
201	GI cst cnt.fm consgt	K	Consignment (vendor)		☐
202	RE for cost center			ME0001	☑

Change View "Search Procedure: Batch Determ. MM": Overview

Figure 8.20 Assigning Batch Search Procedure to Movement Type 201

With these steps, the necessary configuration required for batch determination is complete. The next two steps are master data management steps required for setting up automatic batch determination.

8.5.6   Creating a Sort Sequence

A sort sequence enables the system to choose batches that meet user-defined sort criteria for characteristics. For example, batches of a material *expiring first* are prime candidates to be sorted in ascending order so they can be consumed at the earliest possible date. This sort strategy is known as first expiration first out (FEFO). Other sort strategies can be first in first out (FIFO) and last in first out (LIFO).

Access the screen shown in Figure 8.21 using Transaction CU71 or by following the menu path **Logistics • Central Functions • Batch Management • Batch Determination • Sort Rule • Create**.

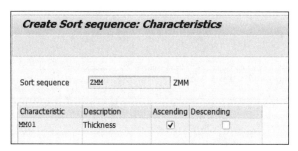

Create Sort sequence: Characteristics

Sort sequence	ZMM	ZMM	

Characteristic	Description	Ascending	Descending
MM01	Thickness	☑	☐

Figure 8.21 Creating a Sort Sequence for Batch Determination

Create a new **Sort sequence ZMM**, assign the previously created characteristic **MM01**, and select the **Ascending** checkbox. As a result, the system will suggest batches of material with values in ascending order during the batch determination process. For example, let's say four batches have the thicknesses characteristic (MM01) as 0.6 mm, 0.5 mm, 0.9 mm, and 0.35 mm, respectively. The system will first suggest batches of material with 0.35 mm thickness followed by batches having a thickness of 0.5 mm and so on to adhere to ascending order of thickness during the batch determination procedure.

8.5.7 Maintaining Condition Records

As a last step to automatic batch determination, you'll need to maintain condition records. These condition records are then picked up by the system.

To maintain a condition record, use Transaction MBC1 or follow the menu path **Logistics • Central Functions • Batch Management • Batch Determination • Batch Search Strategy • For Inventory Management • Create**.

Select the strategy that we defined in the earlier configuration steps (in this case, **ME01**) and select the movement type (**201** – goods issuance against cost center) and plant (**1000**) combination. Enter "30000038" in the **Material**, "201" in the **Movement type** field, and "100" in the **Plant** field, as shown in Figure 8.22. Select the first line item and then click the **Sort** button, which will open the screen shown in Figure 8.23.

Create MovType/Plnt/MatlNo. (ME01) : Fast Entry
Selection criteria
Sort
Movement type
201
GI for cost center
Plant
1000
Demo Client
Valid From
20.05.2018
Valid to
31.12.9999
Movmt type/Plant/Material
Material
Description
No. batch splits
Changes allo
Dialog batch determin.
DisplayUoM
Quantity proposal
Ov...
Selection type
S...
S...
D...
30000038
Moltan Glass
10
A
1

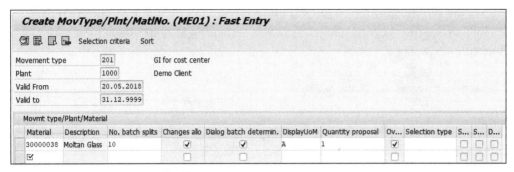

Figure 8.22 Batch Search Strategy

Figure 8.23 shows the complete details of the condition record, including our previously created **Sort rule** ZMM.

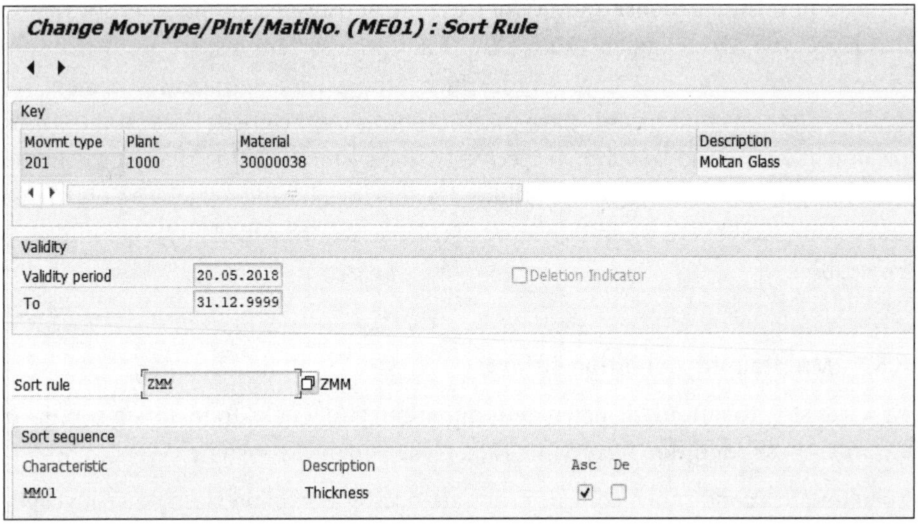

Change MovType/Plnt/MatlNo. (ME01) : Sort Rule
Key
Movmt type
Plant
Material
Description
201
1000
30000038
Moltan Glass
Validity
Validity period
20.05.2018
Deletion Indicator
To
31.12.9999
Sort rule
ZMM
ZMM
Sort sequence
Characteristic
Description
Asc
De
MM01
Thickness

Figure 8.23 Assigning a Sort Sequence in a Batch Search Strategy

Now, the configuration and master data setup required for the batch determination procedure is complete. Let's run a business process, which entails issuing out material 30000038 in plant 1000 against the movement type 201 (GI for cost center).

8.5.8 Business Process of Batch Determination

Access the screen shown in Figure 8.24 via the Transaction MIGO and enter the material 30000038 in plant 1000 and against the movement type 201 (GI for cost center). Enter a quantity of "55 MT" and click on the stock determination for all icon ; the screen shown in Figure 8.25 will appear.

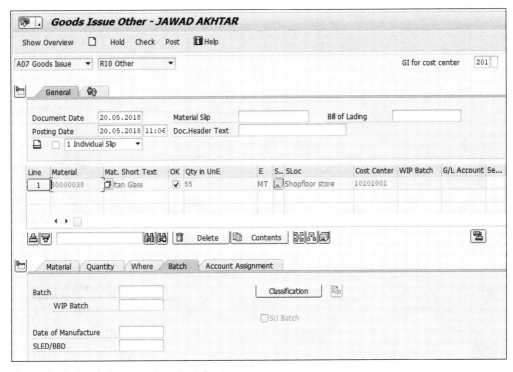

Figure 8.24 Goods Issuance to a Cost Center

Figure 8.25 shows the automatic batch determination of the required quantity split into three batches. Since we defined the **Characteristic sort.** as ascending order, the system selected batch 302, with characteristic value (thickness) of 9.2 mm, and all its available quantity of 30 MT. But the quantity of 30 MT is not enough to meet the required total quantity of 55 MT; therefore, the system will select the next batch (batch 287) having 1 MT in stock, which has the next highest characteristic value (thickness) of 10.00 mm. Finally, the system will select the third batch (batch 276) to suggest the remaining quantity of 24 MT, which has the third highest characteristic value of 12.00 mm.

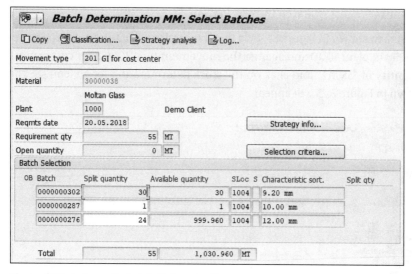

Figure 8.25 Automatic Batch Determination

Choose the **Copy** button, which will open the screen shown in Figure 8.26.

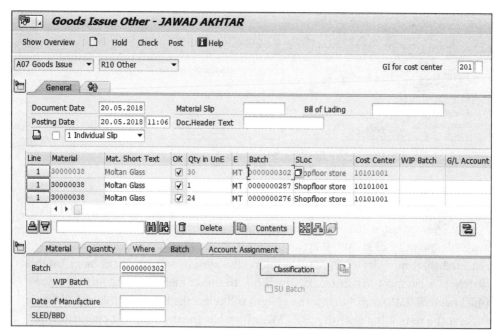

Figure 8.26 Batches Split According to the Batch Determination Procedure

Figure 8.26 shows the total required quantity of 55 MT of material 30000038 being split into three batches in ascending order by the characteristic value, in this case, thickness.

8.6   Recurring Inspection and Expiration Dates

The ability to inspect batch-managed goods, whether procured raw materials or produced semifinished or finished goods, before their expiration dates ensures sufficient time and flexibility to respond to any unforeseen situations.

Recurring inspection (also called repeat inspection) at regular intervals allows business users to take advantage of standard functionality to automatically create inspection lots when expiration dates of batch-managed goods approach. The shelf life-related details of materials are managed in individual batches. These inspection lots then go through quality control checks, as well as subsequent results recording and usage decisions, to decide whether the material can still be used. This functionality offers time and cost savings by enabling your business to act proactively and, thus, optimizes the entire logistics and supply chain operations for the company.

A significant challenge for any organization is to keep track of batch-managed materials with shelf-life expiration dates (SLEDs). This challenge is especially the case in process-based industries for materials that are slow-moving or have a short shelf life. Tracking this information ensures that those materials are consumed first, in the case of raw materials, or sold first, in the case of finished goods. This preference minimizes the material and financial costs associated with the need to destroy and scrap goods or materials.

At the time of producing goods, the system can calculate and suggest a best-before date (BBD). Similarly, on procurement of goods, the system can calculate and suggest a SLED. Therefore, ensuring that recurring inspection takes place *before* the goods are about to expire makes sense.

> **Note**
>
> Although this example illustrates the integration between MM and QM components of the SAP system, you can still use several batch-specific functions even if QM is not yet implemented in your company.

> We recommend that you engage a QM consultant to ensure end-to-end integration between MM and QM functionalities for the batch-managed business processes covered in this section.

This section outlined the important master data you'll need to set up recurring inspection. Next, we'll show you how to manually create an inspection lot that triggers the recurring inspection program and also touch upon an automatic trigger option. We'll also cover BBD and SLED in detail.

8.6.1   Quality Management Master Data Checklist

For recurring inspection to work correctly, you'll need to set up the following QM master data:

- Activation of inspection type 09 (Recurring Inspection) in the material master (inspection type 09)
- Inspection plan usage as 9 (material check) and the status set to 4 (released)

Activation of Inspection Type Recurring Inspection in the Material Master

Although a material may have been already previously created, you'll still need to activate its QM view. If the QM view is already activated, you'll need to activate the new inspection type for recurring inspection at the organizational level (plant). To activate the inspection type for a recurring type, use Transaction MM01 or follow the menu path **Logistics • Materials Management • Material Master • Material • Create (General) • Immediately**.

Enter the material and choose the **Select view(s)** button. In this example, we'll use material CH-3000. Select the **Quality Management** view and then choose **Organizational levels**. Enter "3000" for the **Plant** and choose **Continue**. The **Quality management** tab of the material master will open.

Next, maintain an **Inspection interval** of 10 days to denote that material inspection is due every 10 days. With recurring inspection, the system refers to the information maintained in this field to calculate the next inspection date. Choose **Insp. Setup**, and in the ensuing popup, maintain the **Inspection Type 09** recurring inspection. Make sure to select the **Active** checkbox to activate this inspection type.

Back in the **Quality management** tab, this time, click the **Plant data/Stor. 1** tab, and the screen shown in Figure 8.27 will appear.

Figure 8.27 shows the **Shelf life data** area where we'll maintain shelf life data, including the minimum, maximum, and total shelf life of a material. While calculating or updating the SLED, the system looks for the date of manufacturing against the production/process order or the date of goods receipt against a purchase order and adds up the period, such as days or weeks, from the **Total Shelf Life,** to calculate the SLED/BBD. In this example, the system adds 20 days from the field **Total Shelf Life** to the date of manufacture to suggest a SLED/BBD. For SLED/BBD calculations, the system considers calendar days.

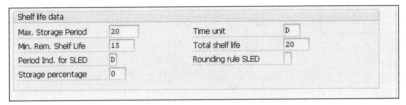

Figure 8.27 Shelf-Life Data in Plant/Stor. 1 Tab of the Material Maser

> **Tips & Tricks**
>
> The maximum storage period of a material should have the longest duration in terms of period. The total shelf life of a material must be greater than its minimum remaining shelf life. Further, using inspection intervals that are less than the total shelf life makes sense. Refer to Figure 8.31, which shows how the system uses the **Max. Storage Period** data to calculate SLED/BBD in the production process.

Batch Master

Let's look at some details about a material's batch that is about to expire. When materials are batch managed, the batch—not the individual material—expires. To change the batch, use Transaction MSC2N or follow the menu path **Logistics • Materials Management • Material Master • Batch • Change.** Enter "CH-3000" for the material (**Material**), "3000" for the plant (**Plant**), "001" for the storage location where the batch is stored (**Stor. Location**), and "0000000479" for the material batch number (**Batch**). Press Enter, and the screen shown in Figure 8.28 will appear.

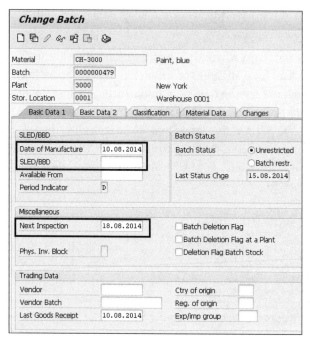

Figure 8.28 Shelf-Life Expiration Date and the Next Inspection Date

The **Next Inspection** field is of paramount importance for recurring inspection. Together with the inspection interval that we created earlier (in the QM view of the material master), the system calculates the next inspection date whenever a business user records the usage decision of an inspection. In our example, the next inspection date is August 18, 2014 (18.08.2014), and another inspection should occur every 10 days. On executing the recurring inspection program, which we'll cover next, the system adds another 10 days to this date (18.08.2014) to arrive at 26.08.2014. In reality, the system comes up with a date that is one day earlier than the date maintained in the **Next inspection** field. In this way, the quality inspector is able to inspect the material, record its results, and decide on its usage (the usage decision) at least a day before the product will expire.

The **Date of Manufacture** field in this case is 10.08.2014 (August 10, 2014). For in-house production of finished or semifinished goods, this date is when a user records a goods receipt against a process or production order. If this batch contains material (such as raw material) received against a procurement process, then at the time of recording its goods receipt, the system prompts the warehouse person to enter the date of manufacturing, which should be included in the vendor's accompanying quality certificate or other supporting documents, such as a packing list. On executing a recurring inspection program, the system looks for the data maintained on shelf-life expiration to come up with a new SLED/BBD. As you've maintained a shelf life of 20 days, the system adds this up to the manufacturing date, which is 10.08.2014 (August 10, 2014) to arrive at 30.08.2014.

> **Note**
>
> For unique business needs, the SAP system also provides user exit QEVA0003 to define a different logic for calculating the next inspection date in a recurring inspection. You'll need to engage the ABAP resource for this activity.

8.6.2   Business Processes

To set the initial parameters for recurring inspection, use Transaction QA07 or follow the menu path **Logistics • Quality Management • Quality Inspection • Worklist • Inspection Lot Creation • Deadline Monitoring • Trigger Manually**. As shown in Figure 8.29, enter "CH-3000" for the material, "3000" for the plant, and "479" for the batch. You can define other parameters as needed.

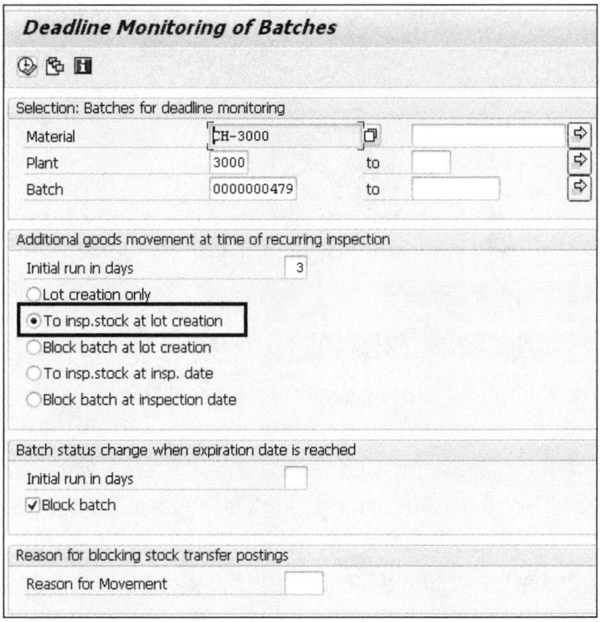

Figure 8.29 Deadline Monitoring (Recurring Inspection)

In this example, we'll enter "3" in the **Initial run in days** field and specify that the material should transfer to quality inspection stock at the time of inspection lot creation by the recurring inspection program. Therefore, all materials whose inspection dates fall in the next three days (from today's date or the date on which you run the transaction) are considered during the deadline monitoring program run. Once such materials are identified, the system not only creates inspection lots for them, but also moves the stock from unrestricted stock to quality inspection through the transfer posting process. Refer to Table 8.1 for information about the various fields and functions, which you can eventually map with your company's business processes.

Field	Function/Description
Initial run in days	The number of days ahead in the next inspection date for the system to consider for recurring inspection purposes. If you've maintained three days, and if today is August 15, 2014, then the system looks for all the material batches whose next inspection date is on or before August 18, 2014.
Lot creation only	The system only creates an inspection lot, but the batch is still in unrestricted-use stock.
To insp. stock at lot creation	The system creates an inspection lot and transfers the batch to quality inspection stock. The status of the batch changes to restricted.
Block batch at lot creation	An inspection lot is created, and the batch is blocked for any usage until the usage decision is taken.
To insp. stock at inspection date	The system transfers the batch to inspection stock on the date when a user needs to perform a quality inspection.
Block batch at inspection date	The system transfers the batch to blocked stock on the date when a user needs to perform an inspection.

Table 8.1 Details of Fields and Functions in a Recurring Inspection Manual Run

Click **Execute** to see the detailed log shown in Figure 8.30. The system creates an inspection lot, and the material's batch is transfer-posted from unrestricted-use stock to quality stock. The system also displays the inspection lot number and transfer posting document from unrestricted to quality inspection stock.

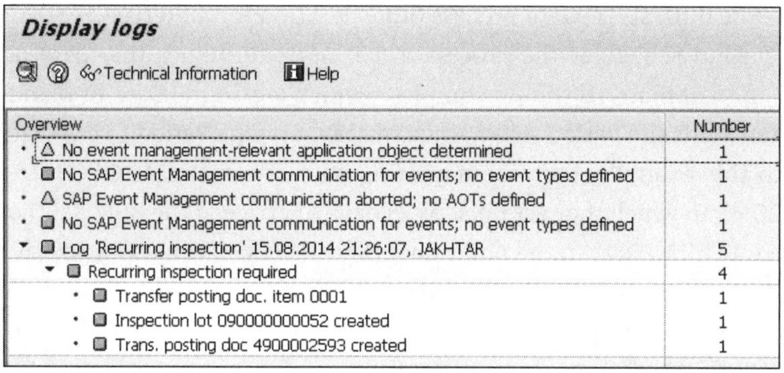

Overview	Number
• △ No event management-relevant application object determined	1
• ☐ No SAP Event Management communication for events; no event types defined	1
• △ SAP Event Management communication aborted; no AOTs defined	1
• ☐ No SAP Event Management communication for events; no event types defined	1
▼ ☐ Log 'Recurring inspection' 15.08.2014 21:26:07, JAKHTAR	5
▼ ☐ Recurring inspection required	4
• ☐ Transfer posting doc. item 0001	1
• ☐ Inspection lot 090000000052 created	1
• ☐ Trans. posting doc 4900002593 created	1

Figure 8.30 The Log Display of Deadline Monitoring

Tips & Tricks

For organizational efficiency and optimization, you can automate and schedule the recurring inspection process via scheduling jobs at regular intervals using Transaction QA06. First, you'll need to define a variant. The next step is to maintain the frequency with which the system should run the scheduled program for recurring inspections. We recommend scheduling these programs during slow working hours (such as weekends or overnight) to conserve system resources.

The remaining steps in recurring inspection consist of the standard processing of results and usage decision recording. In the usage decision, the system automatically updates the SLED/BBD, and on saving the usage decision, the system correspondingly updates the information on the material's batch.

The system automatically updates the **Next Inspection** date and SLED/BBD, based on the data that you have maintained in the relevant views of the material master.

Tips & Tricks

You can use Transaction MB5M, which is the shelf-life list, to gain a comprehensive view of materials whose shelf lives have ended or are about to end.

Finally, let's take a look at how the system uses the **Max. Storage Period** information that you maintained in the **Plant/Stor. 1** tab of the material master (as shown earlier in Figure 8.27) to calculate the BBD/SLED.

Figure 8.31 shows the **BBD/SLED** tab of process order creation for material CH-3000. As soon as the system schedules the process order and determines that date on which the production of material should complete (which is also the **Date of Manufacture**), the system adds the period maintained in **Max. Storage Period** to calculate the BBD/SLED. In this example, the manufacturing date of material is 04.09.2014 (September 04, 2014), to which the system adds 25 days to arrive at the BBD/SLED of 29.09.2014 (September 29, 2014). In the **Additional Days** field, you can add a positive number of days to increase the BBD/SLED or a negative number of days to reduce the BBD/SLED. With the right configuration in place, the system can automatically recalculate the BBD/SLED based on a rescheduled date of manufacturing.

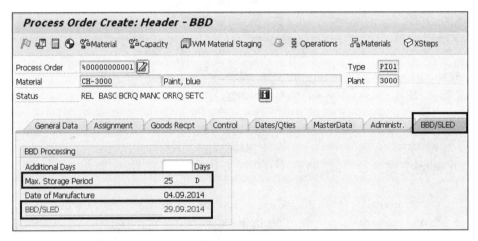

Figure 8.31 BBD/SLED in a Process Order

Tips & Tricks

To activate the BBD/SLED for a process order, use Transaction CORY and follow these steps:

1. Choose the relevant **Plant** and the **Production Scheduling Profile**.

2. Select both the **Copy BBD/SLED to Batch Master** and **Recalc. BBD when Rescheduling** checkboxes.

3. Assign the **Production Scheduling Profile** in the **Work Scheduling** tab of material and plant with Transaction MM02.

8.7 Batch Derivation

With batch derivation, you can efficiently and automatically transfer a batch's characteristic values from the sender material's batches to the receiver material's batches, thereby saving you time, data entry effort, and costs. Batch derivation enables you to maintain one-to-one, one-to-many, and many-to-one relationships between a sender's and a receiver's materials to enjoy complete visibility of information and data.

Whenever a batch-managed material is processed in the production process, its characteristics change, and the batch-managed material acquires different physical and chemical attributes. These changed attributes are maintained as characteristic values of the batch-managed materials. With batch derivation, you can control how the system manages the characteristic values flowing from the parent material to a child material.

In this section, we'll cover the basic configuration settings you'll need to activate batch derivation. Next, we'll move on the master data that you'll need to set up, including settings in the material master, classification, and batch derivation–specific settings. Finally, we'll cover the end-to-end business process to illustrate how the settings made for master data reflect in the batch derivation process. For our example, the sender material is CH-4100, whereas the receiver material is CH-3000.

Let's start with the basics of configuring batch derivation.

8.7.1 Configuration Basics: Batch Derivation

Activate batch derivation in the configuration settings using Transaction DVSP or following the menu path **Logistics – General** • **Batch Management** • **Derivation of Batch Data** • **Activate Batch Derivation**. On the screen that appears, select the **Derivation Active** radio button and save your settings.

8.7.2 Classification in the Material Master

In the material master of the sender material and receiver material, you'll need to maintain the classification view, where you can incorporate class type 023, which is specific to batch-managed materials. To maintain the classification view or make changes to the already maintained classification view in the material master, follow the menu path **Logistics** • **Materials Management** • **Material Master** • **Change** • **Immediately** or use Transaction MM02, as shown in Figure 8.32.

Figure 8.32 incorporates class O23_MM of class type O23 (Batch) and has two characteristics whose descriptions are given as **Volume of 100cc Bottle** and **Date of last
goods receipt**, respectively. On this screen, you'll only need to assign an already created class, which in this example is **O23_MM**. After you assign a class, the system will
automatically assign the characteristics associated with that class. You don't have to
assign any specific values to these characteristics (in the value column) because
you'll add these values during the transactional data entry.

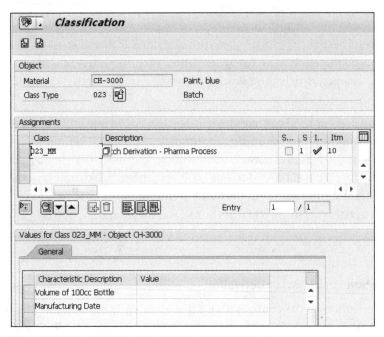

Figure 8.32 Classification View in the Material Master

Note

The classification settings that you make for the sender material also apply to the
receiver material, especially the common characteristics whose values you want the
system to transfer during batch derivation. Although our example shows classification details of the receiver material CH-3000, we've made similar classification settings for the sender material CH-4100. Refer to Chapter 24 on classification for more
information.

In the following sections, we'll cover the end-to-end business process of first setting up batch derivation master data, which entails setting up details about sender and receiver materials in a batch's data. We'll then show you, through an example, how the sender material's batch data automatically flows into a receiving material's batch data through the batch derivation process.

Classification: Class with Characteristics

Understanding how class and characteristics are linked together is important. To view the structure of class O23_MM and the characteristics associated with it, use Transaction CL02 or follow the menu path **Cross-Application Components • Classification • Master Data • Classes**. In the initial screen that appears, enter "O23_MM" as the class and "023" as the class type as (for batch) and click **Change**.

Figure 8.33 shows two characteristics, whose descriptions appeared or were visible on the screen shown in Figure 8.32: VOL001 and D010. We'll refer to several instances when the system interchangeably displays the characteristics or their descriptions. The data type of the first characteristic, VOL001, is numeric and consists of five characteristics and two decimal places, whereas the second characteristic, D010, has a data type of date.

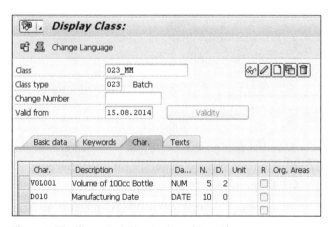

Figure 8.33 Characteristics Assigned in a Class

Batch Derivation: Sender Material

For batch derivation settings for the sender material, including its characteristics, use Transaction DVS1 or follow the menu path **Logistics • Central Functions • Batch**

Management • Batch Derivation • Sender Condition Records • Create. On the initial screen, in which the standard **Strategy type** option is available, the available key combinations offer options to choose only the sender material number radio button or receiver material and sending material radio button. This key combination enables you to maintain not just the sender material's information, but also the receiver's material information. Place your cursor in the **Strategy type** field, press F4 to see the dropdown list, and select condition type BDS1. After you select **BDS1** and press Enter, the system opens a popup with radio buttons so you can select a combination of both receiving and sending material information on the same screen, and only sender material number information. For this example, we selected the first radio button (**Receiving material + sending material**). Choose **Continue**.

As shown in Figure 8.34, enter "CH-3000" in the **Receiver Material** field and validity dates in the **Valid From** and **Valid to** fields. If you don't enter validity dates, the system automatically selects the date the condition record was created until December 31, 9999 (infinity). If you wish to use a different validity date than what the system proposes, use the validity (not shown).

Figure 8.34 Defining the Sender-Receiver Relationship

Enter "CH-4100" in the **Sender Material** field in the lower half of the screen. In this section of the screen, you can enter multiple sender materials for one receiver material. Select the **Sender material CH-4100** and choose **Details**.

Figure 8.35 shows details about both sender material CH-4100 and receiver material CH-3000. Enter the characteristics "VOL001" and "D010" in the lower half of the screen, which tells the system to send the characteristic values of these two characteristics from material CH-4100 (the sender material) to CH-3000 (the receiver material). These characteristics are the same characteristics that you previously maintained in the **Classification** view of material masters CH-4100 and CH-3000 (as shown earlier in Figure 8.32).

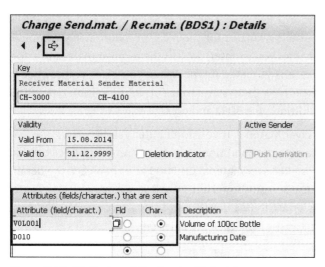

Figure 8.35 Attributes of the Sender Material

The next step is to define the event or instance when the system performs batch derivation for the receiver material. Automatic batch derivation is possible at the time of usage decision, the release of a production or process order, a goods receipt for a production or process order, a goods receipt of a purchase order, or a transfer posting between two batches of different materials with some common characteristics. You can also perform manual batch derivation, if needed. Choose **Condition usage** or press F7.

Click on **Event 100** once to highlight it to enable the system to perform batch derivation on usage decision. Choose **Continue**, and save your settings.

So far, we've covered batch derivation for the sender material while also associating the sender material with the receiver material. However, the settings for the receiver material are significantly more detailed than the setting for the sender material, especially with regard to how the system responds if it can't perform batch derivation on the receiver material or if one of the characteristic values derived from batch derivation is missing.

8.7.3 Batch Derivation: Receiver Material

For batch derivation settings for receiver material, including its characteristics, use Transaction DVR1 or follow the menu path **Logistics • Central Functions • Batch**

Management • Batch Derivation • Recipient Condition Records • Create. On initial screen, the **Strategy type** option is available for the receiver material key combination. This key combination enables you to enter, not just the receiver material's information, but also that of the receiving material type. When you place your cursor in the **Strategy type** field and press F4 , the system brings up the **Condition types BDR1** and **BDR2** to select. Select **Condition type BDR2** and press Enter .

Enter "CH-3000" for the **Receiver Material**. If you don't enter validity dates, the system automatically selects the date the condition record was created until December 31, 9999 (infinity). Next, choose **Receiver material CH-3000** and then click the details icon (magnifying glass), and the screen shown in Figure 8.36 will appear. Now, enter the same two characteristics or attributes VOL001 and D010 of the class O23_MM. Next, select both these characteristics and click the **Rules** tab.

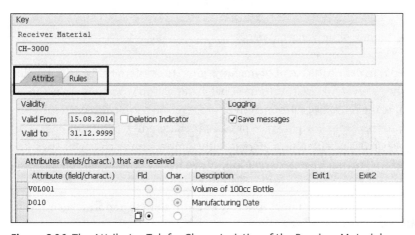

Figure 8.36 The Attributes Tab for Characteristics of the Receiver Material

As shown in Figure 8.37, you can define the rules (for every individual characteristic) that the system must follow if it can't perform a batch derivation. In this example, we'll set the rules for the first characteristic VOL001, in which we'll set the control level to create warning if the system finds the sender field empty. An empty sender field means that no characteristic value exists in the sender material's classification, and therefore, nothing transfers to the receiver material during batch derivation. You can also turn these warning messages into error messages to ensure that users handle batch derivation-related issues as soon as an error message appears. The second control setting for the same characteristic VOL001 stipulates how the system reacts if it finds an already-entered value in the characteristic. You can indicate whether the system should overwrite the characteristic with a warning message or brings up an error message that does not allow overwriting.

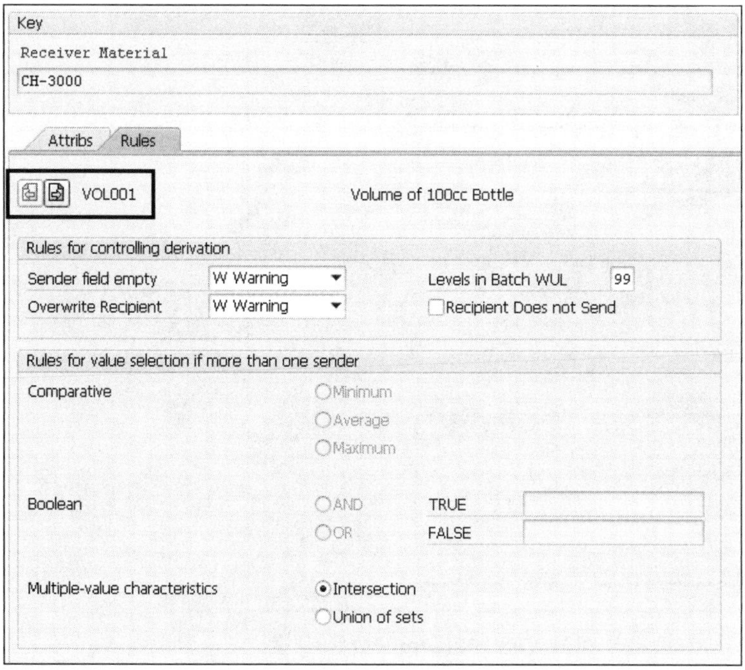

Figure 8.37 The Rules Tab for Characteristics of the Receiver Material

Choose **Next characteristic** and set both of these control functions for the characteristic VOL001 and D010 as warnings. Choose **Condition usage** or press F7, and select **Event 100** on the next screen so that the system can perform batch derivation on usage decision. Choose **Continue** and save your settings.

8.7.4   Business Processes in Batch Derivation

You'll perform a goods receipt for the sender material and enter the values of a batch's characteristics, which are eventually sent forward to the receiver material during batch derivation. Although various ways exist to post a material receipt in the system, such as posting a goods receipt against a purchase order or against another process order, the objective of this step is to increase the sender material's inventory and at the same time manually incorporate the characteristic values that are then used with batch derivation. For this example, we'll use the batch number of the sender material (CH-4100) whose characteristic values we maintained earlier as a component in the process order of the receiver material (CH-3000), as shown in Figure 8.38.

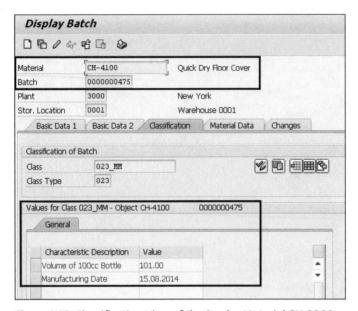

Figure 8.38 Classification View of the Sender Material CH-3000

8.7.5 Process Order and Sender Material Assignment

The next step is to create a process order for the receiver material CH-3000 (the finished good) in which the system automatically assigns the sender material CH-4100 (the raw material) as its component. Assign the specific batch number 475 of the material CH-4100.

To create a process order, use Transaction COR1 or follow the menu path **Logistics •
Production—Process • Process Order • Process Order • Create • Create with Material**.
Enter the "CH-3000" for the receiver material (**Material**), "3000" for the plant (**plant**),
and ""PI01" for the order type (**type**) and press ⌈Enter⌋.

Figure 8.39 shows the header data screen to create a process order. Enter the process order quantity of "100" in the **Total Qty** (total quantity) field and select the **Current date** from the list of options in the **Type** field in the **Scheduling** section. The system incorporates the date the process order was created (today's date). Release the process order by clicking **Release** (the green flag).

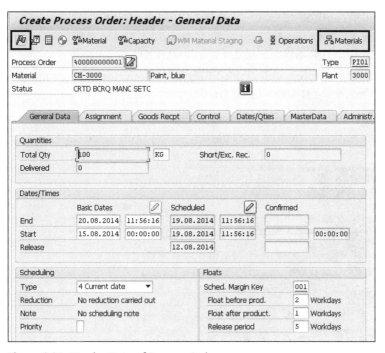

Figure 8.39 Header Data of Process Order

In the material list view of the process order, as shown in Figure 8.40, the system has read the bill of materials (BOM) for material CH-3000 and automatically incorporated the component CH-4100. In this screen, enter "475," the batch number that was previously available. Thus, the system refers to the characteristic values of sender material CH-4100 during batch derivation to receiver material CH-3000. Save the process order, and the system will generate a process order number, which in our example is 70001008.

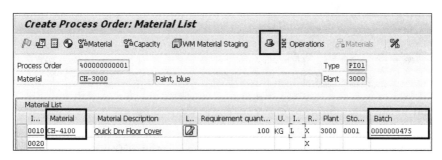

Figure 8.40 The Component View of a Process Order

The remaining business process steps for batch derivation are as follows:

1. Goods issuance against process order 70001008, which includes batch number 475 of sender material CH-4100, using Transaction MIGO.

2. Goods receipt against process order 70001008; the system creates batch number 478 of receiver material CH-3000, using Transaction MIGO.

3. Record inspection results, using Transaction QE01.

4. Perform usage decision, including stock posting, using Transaction QA11.

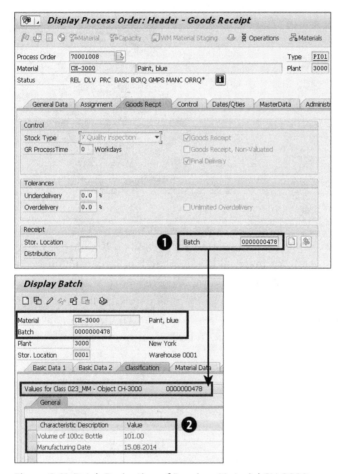

Figure 8.41 Batch Derivation of Receiver Material CH-3000

Figure 8.41 ❶ shows the goods receipt tab of process order 70001008. The system updates batch number 478, which it created on goods receipt for the process order.

Since the results recording and the usage decision are also against the same batch (478), the system performs batch derivation of the receiver material (CH-3000) upon saving the usage decision ❷. Figure 8.41 ❷ shows batch 478, which can be accessed using Transaction MSC3N.

8.7.6   Reporting of Batch Derivation

Transaction DVMO creates the Batch Derivation Monitoring Report, which shows the status of batch derivations of different materials, see Figure 8.42. Statuses indicated with different traffic lights (red, yellow, and green) denote the current batch derivation status of various batches of sender and receiver materials.

🗐	Material	Description	Batch	Sta	Description Status	Deriv. no.	Sequenz derivation	Event	Derivation event description	Order	Purchasing Doc.	Created On	Created At	Mes	Att	Status
	30000120	SFG	0000000026	⊡	Derivation o.k.	1000000069	1000000069_000001	300	Batch Record	200000183		17.01.2018	23:41:52	🟢	🟢	0
		SFG		⊡	Derivation o.k.	1000000046	1000000046_000001	200	Release Process/Production Order	200000183		17.01.2018	22:17:36	🟢	🟢	
		SFG		△	Carried out with warning	1000000047	1000000047_000001	100	Usage Decision	200000183		17.01.2018	23:12:20	🟡	🟡	1
		SFG	ZEBR_00001	△	Carried out with warning	1000000036	1000000036_000001	200	Release Process/Production Order	200000182		16.01.2018	16:53:53	🟡	🟡	
		SFG		⊠	Terminated with error	1000000040	1000000040_000001	300	Batch Record			16.01.2018	17:56:09	🔺	🔺	2
		SFG		⊠	Terminated with error	1000000038	1000000038_000001	100	Usage Decision			16.01.2018	17:30:01	🔺	🔺	
	30000037	Demo SFG	0000000034	△	Carried out with warning	1000000070	1000000070_000001	200	Release Process/Production Order	200000188		20.01.2018	18:13:10	🟡	🟡	1
		Demo SFG	0000000037	△	Carried out with warning	1000000072	1000000072_000001	200	Release Process/Production Order	200000189		20.01.2018	19:31:19	🟡	🟡	
		Demo SFG	0000000137	⊠	Terminated with error	1000000075	1000000075_000001	200	Release Process/Production Order	200000242		18.04.2018	11:06:17	🔺	🔺	2
		Demo SFG	4700000000	⊡	Derivation o.k.	1000000000	1000000000_000001	500	Goods Receipt for Subcontract Order		4700000000	13.10.2016	00:00:00	🟢		0
		Demo SFG	AI-001	△	Carried out with warning	1000000027	1000000027_000001	200	Release Process/Production Order	200000120		05.12.2017	17:12:56	🟡	🟡	1
		Demo SFG	CCRR_011	⊡	Derivation o.k.	1000000030	1000000030_000001	200	Release Process/Production Order	200000160		02.01.2018	11:12:09	🟢		0
		Demo SFG	PRNT_001	⊡	Derivation o.k.	1000000028	1000000028_000001	200	Release Process/Production Order	200000140		09.12.2017	23:15:33	🟢		
		Demo SFG	S4_HANA	⊡	Derivation o.k.	1000000031	1000000031_000001	200	Release Process/Production Order	200000000		02.01.2018	16:29:19	🟢	🟢	
		Demo SFG		⊡	Derivation o.k.		1000000031_000001	200	Release Process/Production Order	200000161		02.01.2018	16:29:19	🟢	🟢	
		Demo SFG		⊠	Terminated with error	1000000035	1000000035_000001	300	Batch Record	200000000		16.01.2018	15:34:43	🔺	🔺	2
		Demo SFG	TAB_BATCH	⊡	Derivation o.k.	1000000015	1000000015_000001	200	Release Process/Production Order	200000020		05.02.2017	19:03:28	🟢		0

Figure 8.42 Batch Derivation Monitor

8.8   Batch Traceability of Work in Process Batches

Batch traceability is a key functionality used not only in the chemical and food industries but also in almost all industries, including in discrete manufacturing. SAP delivers the batch where-used list (Transaction MB56) in the SAP system. This where-used list enables business users to trace a batch from the finished product to the raw material (top-down) or from the raw material to the finished product (bottom-up). The work in progress (WIP) batch is used to keep the batch traceability on a production order when several batches of raw material are consumed and several batches of a finished product are generated.

Transaction MB56 works well in most cases. However, a limitation exists on production orders with N:N batches. In a standard production order, no link exists between the raw material batch consumed and the finished product's batch received in the warehouse; therefore, the batch where-used list determines all the batches of raw material for each batch of the finished product.

Let's say, for example, that a problem was detected in one of our raw material batches after production. In this case, identifying exactly which batch of finished product was produced with this problematic batch of raw material isn't possible. In previous releases, the only solution for this scenario was to create separate production orders for each raw material batch, but this process required more data entry, inefficient business processes, and a significant amount of manual work.

In this example, we'll focus on the WIP batch functionality available for production and process orders in SAP S/4HANA and even in SAP ERP EHP 4 and later releases. More specifically, we'll explain how to enhance the batch where-used list to show links between each raw material batch consumed and the relevant finished product batch produced on a production order. Our example involves a simple production order with two operations and a single component.

In the following sections, we'll start with the necessary configuration that you'll need to set up WIP batches, followed by the required master data setup. Next, we'll transition to the business processes involved in WIP batches and finally conclude by using the Batch Information Cockpit reporting tool to trace WIP batches.

8.8.1   Configuration Settings

You'll need to perform the following configuration steps before creating the confirmation profile.

Activating Work in Process Batches Business Functions

You'll need to activate two business functions related to the WIP batch functionality using the Transaction SFW5: LOG_PP_WIP_BATCH and LOG_PP_WIP_BATCH_02. For the basic use of WIP batches and for our example scenario, you'll only need to activate the first business function. However, you should activate the second business function as well, which brings additional functionalities for the WIP batch, such as inventory valuation, use with documentary batches, and use on an order split.

To activate the business function using the Switch Framework (Transaction SFW5), select the business function and choose **Activate Changes** button.

> **Warning**
>
> You can't deactivate these business functions after they are activated.

Activate Work in Process Batch

After the business function activation, you'll need to activate the WIP batch function-ality in configuration. To complete this step, use Transaction OMCWB, choose the **Active** radio button, and then save.

> **Warning**
>
> Once activated, this configuration setting also can't be reversed, In other words, when you allow the use of the WIP batch functionality in your SAP system, you won't be able to go back to the original state in which WIP batches can't be used.

Activating the Original Batch

You must also activate **Original Batch Reference Material**. To complete this step, use Transaction OMTO. In the initial screen that appears, as shown in Figure 8.43, select the **Original Batch Reference Material** indicator and save. Now, the system can use this functionality in the master data.

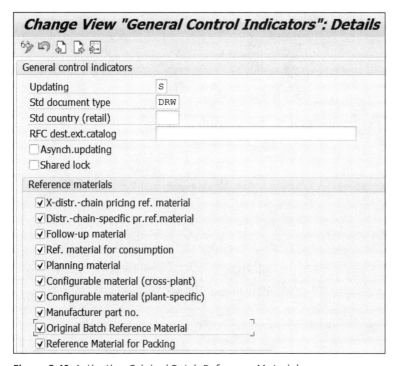

Figure 8.43 Activating Original Batch Reference Material

Confirmation

Now that you've activated WIP batch and original batch management functionalities, you'll need to create a new confirmation profile. Because the WIP batch information must be posted during production order confirmation, your confirmation profile will include the WIP batch-specific subscreens.

For the necessary configuration settings for the confirmation profile, use Transaction OPK0. On the screen that appears, copy the standard confirmation profile SAP001 by selecting it and choosing **Copy**. In the next screen, as shown in Figure 8.44, you'll need to add **Areas 8285 WIP Batch: Goods Receipts**, **8290 WIP Batch: Goods Issues**, and **8295 WIP Batch: WIP Batch Entry** to the newly created **Profile WIP-BATCH01**.

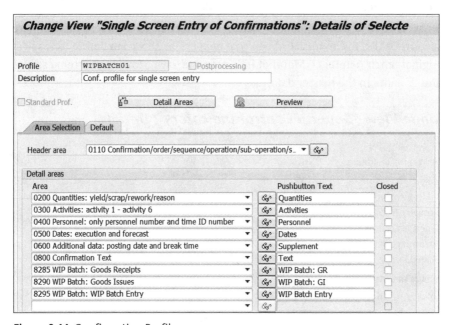

Figure 8.44 Confirmation Profile

Since WIP batches are part of the production process, we recommend you engage a PP consultant to perform the necessary configuration covered in this section.

8.8.2   Master Data Setup

Let's now delve into the requisite master data that you'll need to set up for WIP batches.

Confirmation Profile in the User Profile

To set the confirmation profile created in the previous step to default while posting a confirmation using Transaction CO11N, you'll need to select the **Standard Prof.** (standard profile) checkbox on the initial screen of Transaction OPKO.

However, because the WIP batch is a very specific functionality not relevant to all scenarios, an alternative exists. For each business user who posts a confirmation using a WIP batch, you can add this confirmation profile to the user parameters. User parameters store user-specific settings. To add a new user parameter, use Transaction SU3, enter "CORUPROF" as the **Set/Get parameter ID**, and enter the previously created confirmation profile ("WIPBATCH01") as the **Parameter value**, as shown in Figure 8.45. You can either do this step yourself or ask an SAP NetWeaver team member for help.

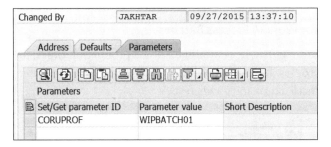

Figure 8.45 Confirmation Profile in the User Profile

Original Batch in the Material Master

As explained earlier in Section 8.8.1, activating the **Original Batch Reference Material** indicator in configuration activates the **OB Management** (original batch management) field in the material master's **Work scheduling** tab, as shown in Figure 8.46. The value of the **OB Management** field must be set to **1** (**Allowed**) for the finished product, but you don't need to set any value for the raw material. Note also that the **BatchManagement** checkbox has been selected.

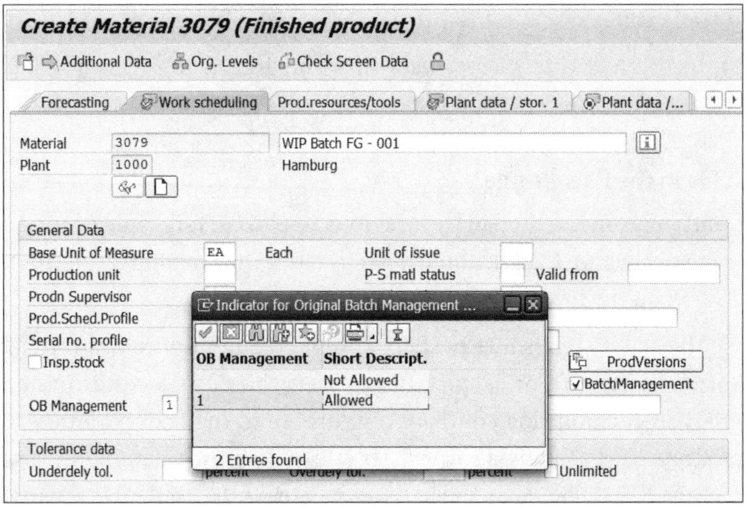

Figure 8.46 Allowing Original Batch Management in the Material Master

Let's now move to the business processes of using WIP batches.

8.8.3   Business Processes for Work in Process Batches

The business process for using WIP batches entails creating a production order, followed by the confirmation process in which you create the WIP batches. The system automatically posts the goods issuance and goods receipt.

Production Order

Consider the example, shown in Figure 8.47, of a regular production order that appears after executing Transaction CO02. This screen shows two operations in the **Operation Overv.** (operation overview) section and a single component in the **Objects** section.

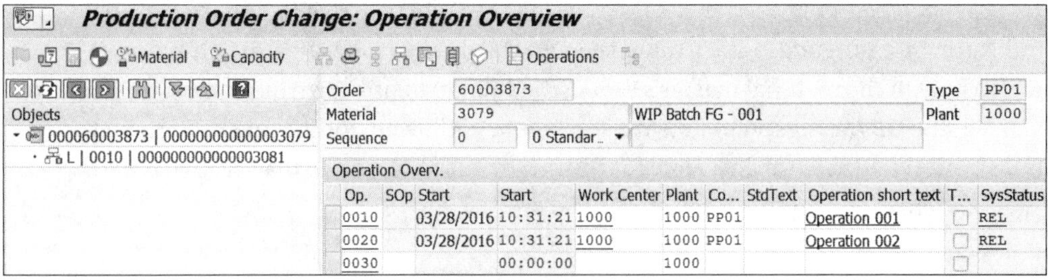

Figure 8.47 Production Order with Component and Operations

To post the confirmation using WIP batches, you'll need to create a link between the raw material and the finished product. Changes on the production order header or components aren't necessary. You can go directly to the order confirmation.

Confirmation and Goods Issuance

When posting a confirmation using the WIP batch confirmation profile, notice some of the following details:

- The button to display the **Goods movements** overview isn't displayed.
- The goods receipt goods movement is always proposed, even if automatic goods receipt isn't set for the production order.
- The goods issues goods movements is always proposed, even if the **Backflush** indicator isn't set for the components.
- All the goods movements are proposed without quantities.

Access the screen shown in Figure 8.48 using Transaction CO11N and enter the "60003873" in the **Order** field and its first operation "0010" in the **Operation** field. Scroll down the screen to evaluate the information provided.

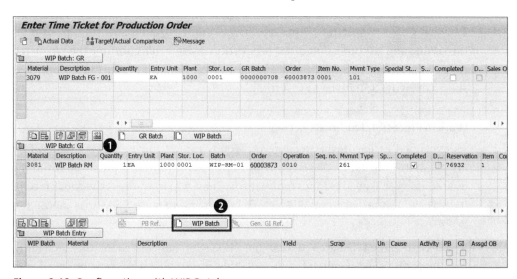

Figure 8.48 Confirmation with WIP Batches

The same three areas—**WIP Batch: GR**, **WIP Batch: GI**, and **WIP Batch Entry**—that were set up in the confirmation profile are displayed. In the **WIP Batch: GI** area ❶, the system proposes the raw **Material 3081** together with its **Batch WIP-RM-01** for consumption (using **Mvmt Type 261**). Select this line item and then choose the **WIP Batch** button ❷.

In the popup that appears, enter the name of your WIP batch in the **WIP Batch** field (e.g., "WIP_B_001"). With this step, you've created a link between the raw material batch consumed and the WIP batch. Click the continue icon (green checkmark).

The screen that appears shows the **WIP Batch WIP_B_001**, as shown in Figure 8.49, for which you'll have to manually enter the **Yield, Scrap,** or any **Rework** (scroll to the right to see the **Rework** field). Save your confirmation for operation 0010.

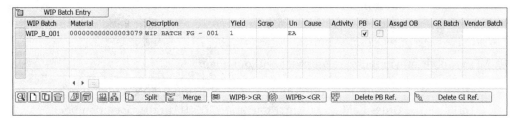

Figure 8.49 Yield Entry for the WIP Batch

The next step is to post a confirmation for operation 0020. Because this operation is the second and last operation of the production order, you'll consume the WIP batch created previously and post a goods receipt of the finished product batch, which is shown in Figure 8.50 in the next section.

Work in Process Batch Goods Receipt

As explained earlier in this section, the goods receipt movement is proposed by default in the **WIP Batch: GR** section; however, this movement is proposed without a quantity, so you'll need to input the quantity. Then, you must select the goods receipt item ❶ and the respective **WIP Batch** ❷, as shown in Figure 8.50. Now choose the **WIPB->GR** button ❸.

Notice that, in the **WIP Batch: GR** section, the system has created the **GR Batch** number **708** for finished good **Material 3079**. This confirmation can now be saved, and because the WIP batch was already linked to the raw material, you now have a link between the raw material and the finished product.

The following summarizes how the system links up a raw material's batch to a WIP batch and then to a finished good's batch for the production order 60003873:

Raw Material 3081 (batch number WIP_RM_01): WIP Batch (WIP_B_001): Finished Good 3079 (batch number 708).

You'll use the same link for reporting, which we cover in Section 8.8.4.

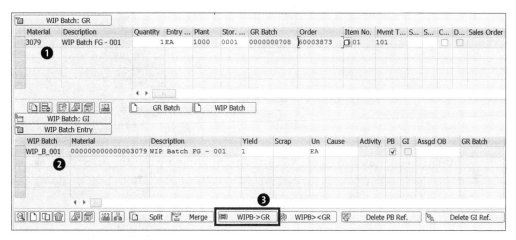

Figure 8.50 WIP Batch Goods Receipt

Note

Now that you have a basic understanding of WIP batches and how they work, we suggest you explore several additional features and functionality available to handle all business processes.

For example, in Figure 8.50 ❸, we show how to link up **WIPB->GR** (linking WIP batch with goods receipt), but what if you mistakenly created an incorrect link? To undo this linkage, click the **WIPB><GR** button to correct the error.

8.8.4   Work in Progress Batch Reporting

Access the **Batch Information Cockpit** screen, as shown in Figure 8.51, using Transaction BMBC to see the report on WIP batches. Enter the **Material** "3079," which is the finished good, and click **Execute** or press F8.

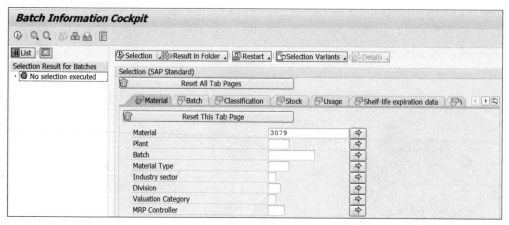

Figure 8.51 Batch Information Cockpit

On the screen shown in Figure 8.52, the system brings up the one batch (**708**) ❶ that meets the selection criteria for material **3079**. Click on batch **708**, click **Execute** ❷, and then select **Usage** from the **Details** dropdown menu ❸.

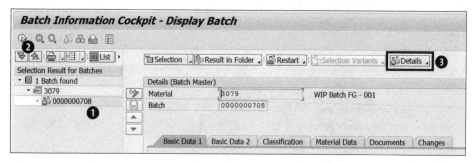

Figure 8.52 Batch Usage

For batch **708** ❶ for the finished good **3079**, Figure 8.53 shows the **Top-Down** view ❷ of the production order **60003873**, the raw material **3079**, and its associated batch **WIP-RM-01**. However, these screen details still don't show the associated WIP batch that was created during confirmation.

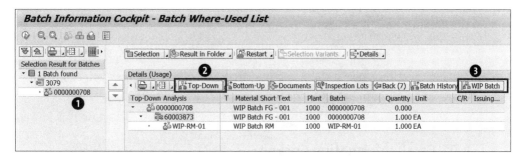

Figure 8.53 Top-Down Analysis

To view the details of the WIP batch, click on production order **60003873** and then choose **WIP Batch ❸**.

> **Tips & Tricks**
>
> **WIP Batch ❸** won't be immediately visible in Figure 8.53. You'll have to scroll to the right of the menu bar to get to this icon.

The screen shown in Figure 8.54 displays the same WIP batch's linkage that we previously covered:

```
Raw Material 3081 (batch number WIP_RM_01): WIP Batch (WIP_B_001): Finished Good
3079 (batch number 708)
```

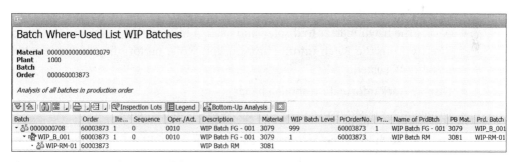

Figure 8.54 WIP Batches Traceability

> **Note**
>
> See Chapter 24 for more information on classification or refer to SAP Note 1473025, which answers frequently asked questions about WIP batches.

Transaction BMOBPRO is a report to show original batches in production. Transaction BMOBPUR is a report to trace original batches in procurement.

The next section looks at the Batch Information Cockpit and how you can use it to analyze and monitor batches.

8.9   Batch Information Cockpit

In process industries such as food and pharmaceuticals, traceability of ingredients or components within a production or procurement process is of paramount importance. Batch traceability across all logistics and supply chain processes is also a legal requirement in many industries, and according to Good Manufacturing Practice (GMP), keeping in mind that batch recall may arise. Companies often develop complex custom reports to view and analyze the batch traceability when the Batch Information Cockpit can serve the same purpose. With the Batch Information Cockpit, you can do the following:

- Perform top-down and bottom-up traceability analysis. With top-down traceability analysis, a finished good traces all the raw materials, packaging, and semi-finished materials that were used in making the finished product's batch. With bottom-up traceability analysis, you gain traceability in the ingredients or raw materials and can trace all the finished goods that were made using these ingredient or raw material batches.

- Access the batch master to display and change information related to the batch directly from the Batch Information Cockpit while performing the traceability analysis of a batch.

- Display stock information about a batch.

- Display stock position of a material and its associated batches.

Access the Batch Information Cockpit using Transaction BMBC or follow the menu path **Logistics • Central Functions • Batch Management • Batch Information Cockpit**. Figure 8.55 shows the initial screen to configure the parameters that the system will consider when bringing up relevant batches of materials. Notice the various tabs available on the right-hand side, which you can use to enter specific information. The left-hand side of the screen provides search functionality.

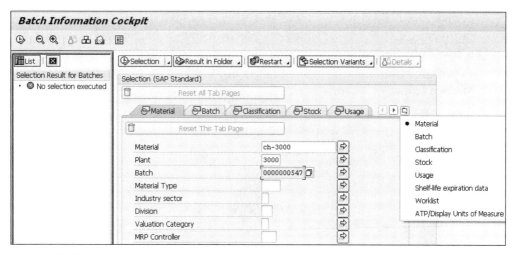

Figure 8.55 Batch Information Cockpit

For our example, enter "CH-3000" for the material (**Material**), "3000" for the plant (**Plant**), and "547" for the batch (**Batch**). Click **Selection** and then **Execute**, which will bring up the screen shown in Figure 8.56. The left-hand side shows that the system can find the relevant material–plant–batch combination. The right-hand side appears when you select **Usage** from the **Details** dropdown menu.

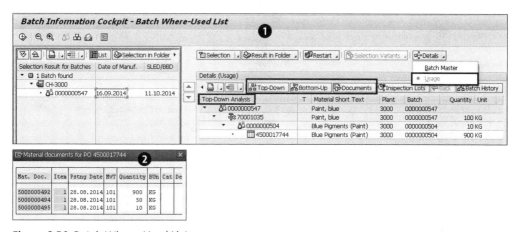

Figure 8.56 Batch Where-Used List

Figure 8.56 ❶ shows the top-down analysis for the batch 547 of material CH-3000 in plant 3000. This batch was produced from the process order 70001035. The process order 70001035, in turn, consumed batch 504 of material CH-4100. Batch 504 of material CH-4100 was procured via purchase order number 4500017744. If you choose this purchase order and then choose **Documents**, ❷ appears. In ❷, the system shows three material document numbers against which the company received goods from a vendor.

> **Note**
>
> We suggest that you explore several features and functionalities of Batch Information Cockpit so you can take advantage of the large amount of available information.
>
> For example, as shown in Figure 8.55, in the **Usage** tab, you can choose whether the system should bring up a top-down list or bottom-up list. Similarly, you can gain comprehensive visibility of all batches that have expired or with approaching expiration dates.

As shown in Figure 8.57, the Batch Information Cockpit has been run, and several batches have been selected. The relevant materials are shown, and the matches can be displayed by highlighting the material. The information regarding the batch is then displayed in a main screen. The tabs represent a number of different screens with information on this batch.

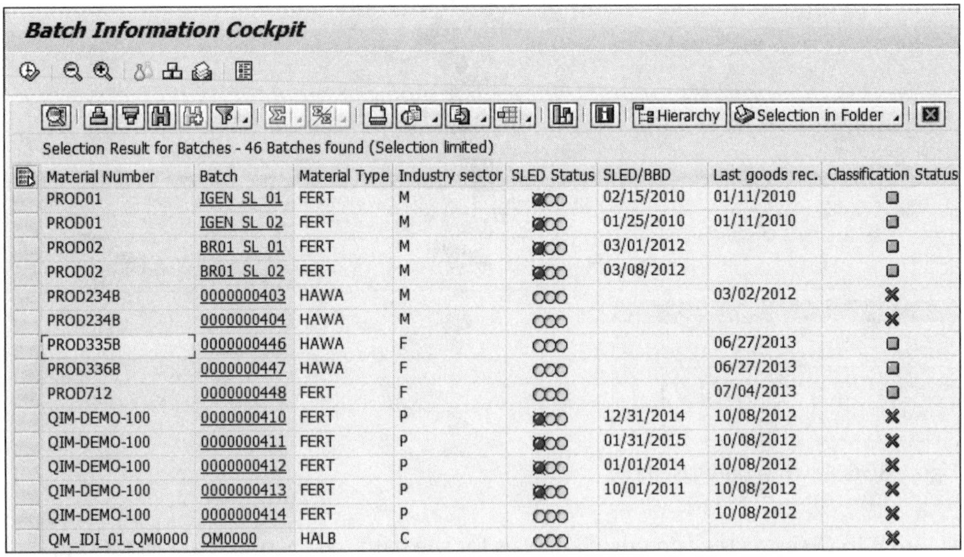

Material Number	Batch	Material Type	Industry sector	SLED Status	SLED/BBD	Last goods rec.	Classification Status
PROD01	IGEN_SL_01	FERT	M		02/15/2010	01/11/2010	
PROD01	IGEN_SL_02	FERT	M		01/25/2010	01/11/2010	
PROD02	BR01_SL_01	FERT	M		03/01/2012		
PROD02	BR01_SL_02	FERT	M		03/08/2012		
PROD234B	0000000403	HAWA	M			03/02/2012	
PROD234B	0000000404	HAWA	M				
PROD335B	0000000446	HAWA	F			06/27/2013	
PROD336B	0000000447	HAWA	F			06/27/2013	
PROD712	0000000448	FERT	F			07/04/2013	
QIM-DEMO-100	0000000410	FERT	P		12/31/2014	10/08/2012	
QIM-DEMO-100	0000000411	FERT	P		01/31/2015	10/08/2012	
QIM-DEMO-100	0000000412	FERT	P		01/01/2014	10/08/2012	
QIM-DEMO-100	0000000413	FERT	P		10/01/2011	10/08/2012	
QIM-DEMO-100	0000000414	FERT	P			10/08/2012	
QM_IDI_01_QM0000	QM0000	HALB	C				

Figure 8.57 Central Area of the Batch Information Cockpit

8.10   Electronic Batch Record

In highly regulated industries such as pharmaceuticals, companies are often legally required to maintain a complete audit trail and record of all the batches used in the entire logistics and supply chain to manufacture a product. Often, legal requirements demand, not just the batches received from the procurement process or batches consumed in the production process, which are important for recordkeeping, but also demand a complete record of various quality inspections that took place during the manufacturing process. An electronic batch record (EBR), or batch record for short, captures these inspection details.

Access the screen shown in Figure 8.58 using Transaction COEBR or by following the menu path **Logistics • Central Functions • Batch Management • Tools • Batch Record**.

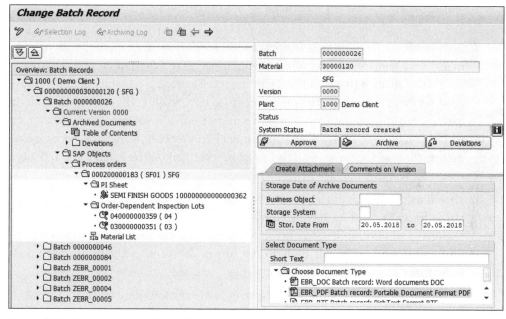

Figure 8.58 Electronic Batch Record

On the left-hand side, you'll see the complete trail of material 30000120 and its associated batch 26. As you drill down in the same node, you'll see the process orders, the two types of quality inspections (04 – for finished goods inspections, 03 – for in-process inspections) as well as the material list (or bill of materials [BOM]) used in the production process.

On the right-hand side of the same screen, you can only **Approve** an EBR for archiving if the statuses of its various elements (such as process order, inspection lots, etc.) are set as required for electronic archiving. The system will also guide you through fulfilling all the prerequisites for EBR. After **Approval**, an EBR can be archived by clicking on the **Archive** button.

> **Note**
>
> We recommend engaging a SAP NetWeaver consultant to ensure the necessary authorizations required for archiving electronic batch records are granted. The SAP NetWeaver consultant can also ensure that the document repository required to store the EBRs is set up correctly.
>
> Additionally, engaging a PP consultant will also ensure the necessary configuration and master data settings are in place for EBR to work properly.

In some industries, such as consumer products or automotive suppliers, legal requirements may demand storing where-used data of materials used for production and materials delivered to customers. Enabling recall actions is a mandatory and critical issue for these industries. Data can be recorded by managing all relevant materials in batches, but this method has a negative impact on data volume. When turning on batch management, entering a batch number becomes obligatory for all goods movements. Then, all inventory postings must be executed on the batch level, and labor costs for inventory management will increase.

With the documentary batch record, you must ensure that a partial stock of a material is traceable without having to maintain a batch's data. As a result, the effort required and the complexities involved in maintaining batch data. is reduced The documentary batch record finds heavy use in automotive and consumer goods industries but is unsuitable for use in dangerous goods.

Documentary batch processing can be achieved in the following ways:

- Documentary batches can be entered during goods movements.
- In a production order, entering documentary batches is only possible at backflush.
- In warehouse management (WM), entering documentary batches must be enabled during transport order confirmation.

In this section, we described the transactions that you'll use to create, change, and delete a batch record. The next section examines how the batch records are used to perform batch determination.

8.11   Summary

Batch management is an important topic to a growing number of industries, developing from simply the identification of a group of items to a process that allows companies to product recalls, selecting and selling by batch characteristics, and identifying expiring stock. As the drive for competitive advantage continues, companies will further investigate how batch management can lower production time and hasten material to the customer.

In Chapter 9, we'll provide an overview of purchasing processes and describe the various purchasing elements available in SAP S/4HANA.

8

Chapter 9

Purchasing Overview

Technology has brought the purchasing department into the front line of cost efficiency with tools and procedures that allow them to negotiate larger savings, better quality, and more secure supply, resulting in a smooth supply chain.

Every company that operates a business purchases materials whether raw materials, office supplies, consumables, services, and other items. The science of purchasing has become an important part of making today's business operations efficient. The purchasing department can research and negotiate significant savings for a company through policies and technology.

Today's purchasing department has access to a plethora of information from associations, purchasing think tanks, and specialist purchasing consultants. Companies can introduce best practices along with specialized technology to ensure that the best information is available to the purchasing professional for negotiating and managing contracts.

In this chapter, we'll begin by covering the main procurement components that include purchase requisitions, requests for quotation (RFQs), maintaining quotations, and purchase orders (POs). We'll also briefly cover source lists and source determination. A *source list* is a list of procurement sources, such as vendors from which companies buy materials. Next, we'll cover conditions in purchasing including discounts and surcharges. The last section of the chapter will briefly introduce serial numbers and quota arrangements.

9.1 Purchase Requisitions

A *purchase requisition* is the procedure by which general users and departments can request the purchase of goods or services that require processing by the purchasing department. Companies can allow only certain authorized users to enter purchase requisitions directly into the SAP S/4HANA, but in situations involving a particular dollar value or type of goods or services, your company may require another method of notifying the purchasing department of a purchasing requisition, such as fax or email. A purchase requisition is a company's internal document that business users create manually, or if the right settings are made, the system can create it automatically. Printouts of purchase requisitions are often neither required nor desired as most companies prefer going digital and adopting as many paperless business processes as possible.

Many companies have implemented an Internet frontend, such as SAP Fiori, for purchase requisitions, and authorized users can use the relevant SAP Fiori app to enter the materials or services they need.

After a being created, a purchase requisition can be converted to a PO, a quantity or a value contract, or a scheduling agreement. A purchase requisition can also be used as the basis for an RFQ, which we'll describe next.

9.2   Requests for Quotation

After the purchasing department has received and processed a purchase requisition, the company may require that the purchasing department issue out a request for quotation (RFQ). Some reasons for this requirement include the following:

- The material hadn't been previously used at the company.
- The previous material now has no identified vendor.
- A new vendor is required due to termination of a contract, such as for quality issues.
- A new vendor is required due to the bankruptcy of a vendor.
- A new vendor is required due to government regulations.
- A new vendor is required due to logistical issues.

When selecting which vendors invite to submit quotations, the purchasing department will use a number of inputs:

- Vendor suggestions from the requisitioner, especially for a new material
- Research on vendors, using professional associations and buying groups
- Trusted vendors with whom the company has contracts

The format or the layout of an RFQ can be customized as per business requirements. An RFQ can be sent to vendors via mail, fax, or electronically via email or electronic data interchange (EDI).

With today's level of company spending, the purchasing department must evaluate each vendor's capacity, on-time performance, quality performance, and understanding of the company's business long before the RFQ is sent.

For their part, vendors have become more aware of companies' needs to reduce purchasing costs and prepare for RFQs in a more strategic way. Many vendors are using technology to calculate the threshold of what a purchasing department is willing to pay based on quality and logistical factors. Vendors know that being the lowest bidder won't necessarily win the bid, but they also know that submitting a low bid is important.

After the RFQ is sent to vendors, each vendor who decides to bid will send back a quotation, as described in the next section.

9.3   Quotations

A vendor sends a quotation to the purchasing department that posted the RFQ. The response from the vendor should follow the stipulations set down in the RFQ. Many vendors fail to read and understand RFQs before submitting quotes. If a vendor fails to follow the instructions in the RFQ, you can disqualify the quotation from the vendor.

The purchasing department maintains the received quotations in the SAP S/4HANA system, performs a price comparison of the quotations sent by the bidders or suppliers, and then chooses one. The other quotations are rejected. While the system offers price comparison capabilities to enable a purchasing user to decide the lowest bidder, the lowest bid can also be rejected. For example, perhaps your company has an urgent need for a material, and therefore, the bid ultimately chosen costs more, or offers less favorable payment terms, but takes less time for the vendor to deliver.

The vendor that supplied the winning bid will then be offered a PO, which is described in the next section. If the RFQ was for long-term supply or requires a specific delivery schedule, then company can issue a quantity contract, a value contract, or a scheduling agreement.

A *quantity contract* is a contract with a vendor where the company commits to buy agreed-upon quantities of materials and services from a vendor over a specified period of time. A *value contract* stipulates a company's commitment to procure materials or services of agreed-upon value from a supplier over a given period of time. Even when contracts with the vendors are in place, the company still needs issue out contract release orders with reference to the contract each time the company is ready to purchase material or services from the vendor. The contract release step ensures effective control is in place over the procurement process by verifying, for example, that the contract is still valid at the time of a contract release order or that the quantity being procured doesn't exceed the quantity (or value) stipulated in the contract. The scheduling agreement's validity is of particular importance as well to check the vendor's compliance to the communicated schedule to deliver the ordered goods.

9.4   Purchase Orders

A *purchase order* (PO) is a commercial document issued by a purchasing department (the buyer) to a supplier (the seller), indicating the materials, quantities, and negotiated prices for materials or services that the seller will provide to the buyer. A PO can be created with reference to the quote of the winning bidder.

A PO usually contains the following:

- PO number
- Date of the PO
- Billing address of the buyer
- Ship-to address of the buyer
- Special terms or instructions
- List of items with quantities
- Payment terms agreed with the vendor
- Negotiated price of each item

Companies use POs for many reasons. POs allow purchasing departments to clearly communicate their intentions to vendors, and they protect vendors in the event if a dispute arises over the items, quantities, or price. A PO is also a component in a three-way match, which matches a PO to a goods receipt document and a vendor invoice against which the payment to the vendor is made.

POs can be printed out and sent to a vendor, faxed, or emailed to a vendor. A vendor can be assigned when the PO is created via a source list or via a process called source determination. We'll discuss both of these topics in the next section.

9.5   Source Lists and Source Determination

For a purchasing decision to be made, a buyer will look at the *source list*, which contains contracted or certified vendors for a particular material. In the following sections, we'll discuss the use of a single source and of multisourcing for materials as well as how to generate a source list and use source determination.

9.5.1   Single Sourcing

Many companies are trying to implement single sourcing for their materials. A *single source* for a material means that, for each material that is purchased, only one vendor is used. Many companies spend a great deal of effort to negotiate single-source contracts to reduce the cost of items they purchase.

For example, your purchasing department may have purchased photocopiers from three different companies: Canon, HP, and Panasonic. But with single sourcing, the purchasing department can negotiate a lower price with one supplier of photocopiers, Canon, and will only use that vendor for a specified period. Single sourcing can cut costs substantially if a company also gives vendors the chance to single-source a range of products, but it can also leave the buyer in a problematic situation if that source experiences a disruption.

Many requisitioners ask their purchasing departments to single-source a particular item. The purchasing department will ask the requisitioner to justify this purchase in a document called a *sole source justification*, often used by government and state authorities.

A requisitioner may have a valid reason to purchase a particular material, which was purchased previously, if no other vendor can supply the requisitioner with a compatible material. For example, a request for information (RFI) may have found that no other vendors can supply the material in question.

If the requisitioner needs to justifying using a sole source, then he or she will need to describe what equipment is involved and explain why no other solution exists except to purchase from the vendor who originally supplied the product. In many research situations, identical materials are needed to replicate experiments, and materials from an alternative vendor may not be acceptable for verifying results. For example, in quality inspection labs, tests that use certain chemicals may require that the chemical be purchased from the same vendor used for all previous tests. This requirement may violate the purchasing department's sourcing policy, but the lab can provide a sole source justification to use the same vendor as previously.

The purchasing department will usually require some verification that an extensive search has been made and that the parts couldn't be located at a lower price from a wholesaler or an alternative source. The larger the unit price of the material, the more investigation will be required. If the cost is high enough, then the purchasing department may suggest using the RFQ process to ensure that the correct procedures have been followed.

Requisitioners can use economic justifications to suggest a single source for a material. Opting for the lowest price isn't always the most economical way of purchasing a material. Other factors, such as performance, the cost of incidentals, or even the time it takes a vendor to deliver a product, should be taken into account.

A common example can be found in the PC printer market. The prices of printers have fallen substantially, but to create a cheaper printer, manufacturers have produced printers that can cost less than the ink or toner refills. When looking at the cheapest printer in economic terms, a requisitioner will need to look at the number of prints per refill, the cost of the machines, and the cost of refill. Therefore, the requisitioner can submit a sole supplier justification based on economic reasons.

In the absence of any contract or agreement with a vendor, when a purchaser creates a purchase order for a vendor that contains individual materials to be purchased, the system creates a *purchasing information record* (info record). An info record has a one-to-one procurement relationship between a vendor and the material. If three vendors supply the same materials, then the system will create three info records. Similarly, if the same vendor supplies three materials, again, the system will create three info records. We'll cover info records in Section 9.7.

9.5.2   Multisourcing

Purchasing departments commonly use more than one vendor as the supplier of a material. Although best practices lean toward single sourcing with a trusted vendor, many companies want to reduce the risk of failure in the supply of a material and thus will have more than one vendor qualified to supply the material.

In an SAP system, each vendor can be entered into the source list for a certain material for a particular plant and/or purchasing organization. You can maintain source lists in the system using Transaction ME01 or by following the navigation path **Logistics • Materials Management • Purchasing • Master Data • Source List • Maintain**.

On the initial screen, a purchasing user must enter the **Material** and the **Plant** for which the source list is being maintained. Different plants may have different vendors for the same material, due to logistical issues or the costs of transportation. Other reasons may include the fact that the vendor has different regional outlets with different vendor numbers. The screen shown in Figure 9.1 includes the following fields that are relevant to maintaining the source list:

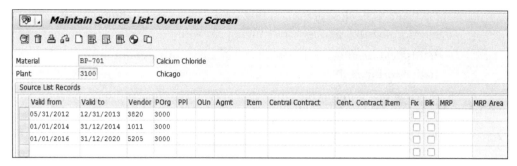

Figure 9.1 Maintenance Screen for the Source List of a Material

- **Valid to/valid from**

  These fields allow a purchasing user to provide a validity range detailing when a vendor will be allowed to be the source for the specified material at the specified plant.

- **Agreement/item**

  These fields can be completed if an outline agreement between the vendor and the company exists. This outline agreement can be either a contract or a scheduling agreement. The **Item** field is the item number of the material in the outline agreement.

- **Fixed source**

  The **Fix** indicator should be set if this vendor is the preferred source of supply for the material at this plant. The system uses this indicator to select the fixed source in the source determination process.

- **Blocked source**

  The **Blk** indicator can be set if the vendor is blocked from supplying the material for a specified time, based on the validity period. The blocked source indicator doesn't allow POs to be created with this material/vendor/plant combination.

> **Note**
>
> You can't select both the blocked and fixed indicators at the same time. Only one of these indicators can be set, or neither.

- **Material requirements planning field**

  A source list can be used in the material requirements planning (MRP) process to determine the vendor for requisitions and creating schedule lines from scheduling agreements. The **MRP** column on this screen allows the planning department to determine how this source vendor influences MRP:

- If this field is left blank, the vendor isn't taken into account in source determination within MRP.
- If you enter "1" in this field, this vendor is taken into account as the source for purchase requisitions generated in MRP.
- If you enter "2" in this field, then this vendor is identified as the source for the scheduling agreement, and delivery schedule lines can be created if a scheduling agreement is in place.

Tips & Tricks

Click on the generate records icon ⊙, and the system will bring up all the available procurement elements, such as the info record, the quantity or value contract, and the scheduling agreement, all of which are relevant for the source list.

9.5.3   Generate a Source List

A purchasing user can generate a source list for a single material or for a range of materials, rather than manually creating these lists. Use Transaction ME05 or follow the navigation path **Logistics • Materials Management • Purchasing • Master Data • Source List • Follow-on Functions • Generate**.

The screen shown in Figure 9.2 allows you to generate a source list based on the selection of a **Material** range and a **Plant** range. This capability is useful if no source lists have been created because a mass maintenance program is a fast way to generate the lists.

In the **Generate** section of the screen, you can choose to include, exclude, or only allow outline agreements. Most companies will include all material or vendor scenarios when initially creating a source list.

The other selection fields are similar to those that can be created in Transaction ME01, including validity dates and MRP relevance. You also have the option of deleting all existing source list records or allowing them to remain. Finally, the **Test Run** indicator allows a purchasing user to run the program without actually creating the source lists. We advise running this program with the **Test Run** indicator set because changes in the selection parameters are often required.

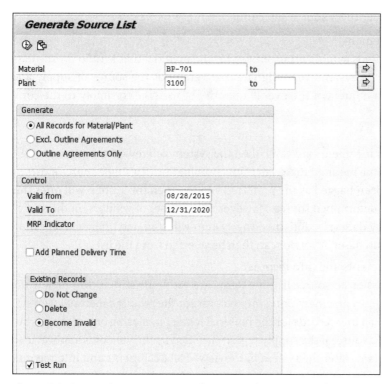

Figure 9.2 Generating a Source List of a Material or a Group of Materials

9.5.4   Source Determination

Source determination allows a buyer to find the most suitable source of supply for a purchasing need, based on various sourcing information. This information doesn't necessarily have to come directly from the source list. Sourcing information can found in other places.

Outline agreements can offer the buyer information about current contracts in place with regard to a specific vendor/material combination. An agreement such as a quota arrangement can influence sourcing by informing buyers of the level of commitment the vendors have contracted to for a given time period. Other source determination information can be found from the purchasing info record and plant information. The system includes a source determination procedure for determining the best source of supply for the buyer's need.

The order of relevance for source determination is as follows:

1. **Quota arrangement**

   If the system finds a quota arrangement for the material that is valid for the date needed, then the system will designate that vendor as the source of supply and assigns a certain quota of the overall quantity of material to supply to the company.

2. **Source list**

   If no quota arrangements are valid, then the system will review the entries on the source list for the required material/plant combination. If a single source exists or a source has been flagged as the preferred vendor, then the system will offer this vendor as the determined source. However, if a number of vendors on the source list are valid by date selection, then the system will stop and offer several candidates to the purchaser. A vendor can then be selected from the list.

3. **Outline agreements and info records**

   If no source list or no source list line items are valid, the system will review the contracts, outline agreements, and info records for the required material. The system will check all info records for the material for all purchasing organizations but will only offer a source if the supply region specified by the vendor is applicable to the relevant plant. After the system has reviewed all documents and info records, a selection will be available to the buyer, providing that the system has determined any valid vendors.

9.6   Conditions in Purchasing

Condition procedures are more commonly associated with sales and distribution (SD) functionality; however, the same condition processes are also used in purchasing. In the following sections, we'll discuss conditions in purchasing such as discounts, surcharges, taxes, and delivery costs.

9.6.1   Condition Processing

A *condition procedure* in purchasing is used to calculate the purchase price by processing all relevant pricing factors. By using defined conditions, the purchasing process arrives at a determined price for purchasing transactions, such as POs.

Condition processing is made up of four distinct areas: calculation schemas, condition types, access sequences, and condition tables.

Condition types represent the pricing dynamics in the system. The system allows condition types for absolute and percentage discounts, freight costs, duty, and taxes. Through the condition type, the buyer can see how the price is calculated in the purchasing document. Some examples of condition types include the following:

- PB00: Gross Price
- RB00: Absolute Discount
- ZB00: Absolute Surcharge
- FRB1: Absolute Freight Cost
- ZOA1: Percentage Duty
- SKTO: Cash Discount
- NAVS: Nondeductible Input Tax

9.6.2   Pricing Conditions

Pricing conditions allow a purchasing user to enter details into the system about the pricing agreements negotiated with the vendor. These contractual agreements can include discounts, surcharges, agreed freight costs, and other pricing arrangements. The buyer can enter any of these conditions in a purchasing document, such as a quotation, an outline agreement, or a purchasing info record. These conditions are then used in POs to determine prices.

Time-Dependent Conditions

This type of condition is mostly used for scheduling agreements and quotations. Time-dependent conditions allow a purchasing user to introduce limits and scales into the condition record. A pricing scale is based on quantity, meaning that the more a buyer orders of a particular product, the lower the price.

A purchasing user can also create condition records with graduated scales. A pricing scale can be created using the following criteria: quantity, value, gross or net weight, and volume. The purchasing department can create a rate for each level of the scale. For example, if a buyer orders up to 100 units, the price may be $10.00 per unit; if the buyer orders between 101 units and 150 units, the price may fall to $9.45. Above 151 units, the price may fall again to $9.12 per unit. This unit price will apply to all units purchased.

In a graduated pricing scale, the unit price changes at a certain level, but the price of the unit isn't applicable to all of the units sold. For example, using the regular pricing scale, a purchase of 155 units means the total cost is 155 multiplied by the unit cost of $9.12, which is equal to $1,413.60. Using a graduated price scale, the calculation for 155 units is 100 units at $10.00, 50 units at $9.45, and 5 units at $9.12, for a total of $1,518.10.

Time-dependent conditions are always used in purchasing info records and contracts.

Time-Independent Conditions

Time-independent conditions don't include any pricing scales or validity periods. POs contains only time-independent conditions. Quotations and scheduling agreements can include both types of conditions.

9.6.3   Taxes

Tax information can be calculated during the price determination process using tax conditions. The tax rate is coded into the **Tax** field in the PO item. The tax calculations are determined by the tax conditions described in the PO.

9.6.4   Delivery Costs

Delivery costs can be determined via conditions in the PO. The planned delivery costs are entered in the PO for each order item. These costs have been negotiated with the vendor or the freight company. Planned delivery costs usually include the actual freight charges, any relevant duty payments, a quality-dependent cost, and a volume cost.

In this section, we looked at the use of conditions in purchasing to determine things like pricing. In the next section, we'll cover the purchasing information record.

9.7   Purchasing Information Records

A purchasing information record allows additional information to be held on a specific material purchased from a specific vendor. This information can then be further specified for a particular purchasing organization.

Purchasing information records are used in purchase orders (POs), where information from the record is defaulted into the PO. Information such as purchasing group, net price, invoice verification indicators, and delivery tolerances all can be entered into the purchasing information record.

Four categories of purchasing information records can be created:

- Standard
- Pipeline
- Consignment
- Subcontracting

Identifying the correct category before creating a purchasing information record is important so that the system can automatically bring up the relevant information when a business user performs specific business transactions.

In the following sections, we'll discuss the purchasing information record for non-stock materials, the number ranges for purchasing information records, and the layout of the purchasing information record screen.

9.7.1   Purchasing Information Record for a Nonstock Material

A purchasing information record usually applies to a specific vendor and a specific material that it supplies. However, a vendor occasionally may be supplying a service to a nonstock material. For example, an operation may exist in a production order where material is sent out for a treatment. At this point, no material number for the material exists in the production order, but instead, a purchase information record is available for a group of materials, that is, a specific material group such as certain raw materials or semifinished nonstock items. In the system, you can create a purchasing information record for a vendor and a material group. This info record would contain the same information that a vendor/material purchasing information record would have.

9.7.2   Purchasing Information Record Numbering

The fact that there are different types of purchase information records makes number ranges necessary. Number ranges for the purchase information record can be assigned either externally or internally.

Number ranges for purchasing information records can be predefined in the SAP system, and SAP recommends that you accept the provided number ranges. The system does allow the number ranges to be changed if required. To define purchasing information record number ranges, use Transaction OMEO or follow the navigation path **Materials Management • Purchasing • Purchasing Information Record • Define Number Ranges**.

The predefined number ranges for the purchase information records are the following:

- Stock material, internally assigned: 5300000000 to 5399999999
- Stock material, externally assigned: 5400000000 to 5499999999
- Nonstock material, internally assigned: 5500000000 to 5599999999
- Nonstock material, externally assigned: 5600000000 to 5699999999

9.7.3   Purchasing Information Record Screen Layout

The screens in purchasing information record transactions can be modified to allow field changes. Follow the navigation path **Materials Management • Purchasing • Purchasing Information Record • Define Screen Layout**.

On the screen that appears, choose the modifications for each transaction. To select a transaction, double-clicking on the transaction will take you to a screen where you can modify the screen layout. You then can select one of the field selection groups to modify the individual fields. Figure 9.3 shows the individual fields of the **Quantities** field selection group.

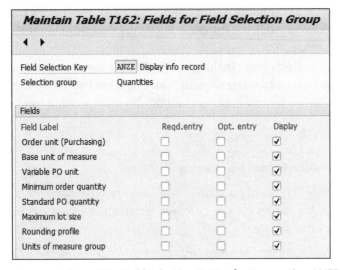

Figure 9.3 Quantities Field Selection Group for Transaction ANZE

9.8   Serial Numbers

To uniquely identify a single unit of material, then the unit must be identified by a serial number. A serial number is given to a unique item to identify and record information about the item. A serial number is different from a batch number because a batch number is given to a number of items, whereas a serial number is unique to one item. Serial numbers are most often found on equipment, such as motors, lathes, drills, or vacuums. For the SAP customer, many areas may require serial numbers. If you produce items that should be uniquely defined, then serial numbers may be used. If using machines in production, your company may regularly purchase maintenance items that are serialized. The plant maintenance (PM) functionality in SAP frequently uses serial numbers because the functionality includes use data for equipment, which is most often serialized.

In this section, we'll cover how to define and then assign a serial number profile to an object, such as a material master or a piece of equipment.

9.8.1   Serial Number Profiles

A serial number profile is created to define attributes for serial numbers. A serial number profile is a four-character alphanumeric field defined by using Transaction OIS2 or by following the navigation path **Plant Maintenance and Customer Service • Master Data in Plant Maintenance and Customer Service • Technical Objects • Serial Number Management • Define Serial Number Profiles • Serial Number Profile**.

The fields shown in Figure 9.4 are needed for configuring serial number profiles. The first field is the profile (**Profl.**), a four-character field, followed by a profile description (**Prof. text**). The **ExistReq.** indicator, when not set, allows users to create the serial number master record during a business transaction. If the indicator is set, the serial number master record must exist before the transaction can take place.

The **Cat** field is for the equipment category, a PM item, which defines the type of equipment for which this serial number profile is used. For example, A is for machines, while S is for customer equipment.

The **StkCk** field indicates whether the system should perform a stock check when the serial number is assigned.

The configuration of serial number profiles should be performed with a PM consultant to ensure that your PM requirements are taken into account. The serial number profile is then assigned in the **Plant data/Stor. 2** tab of the material master.

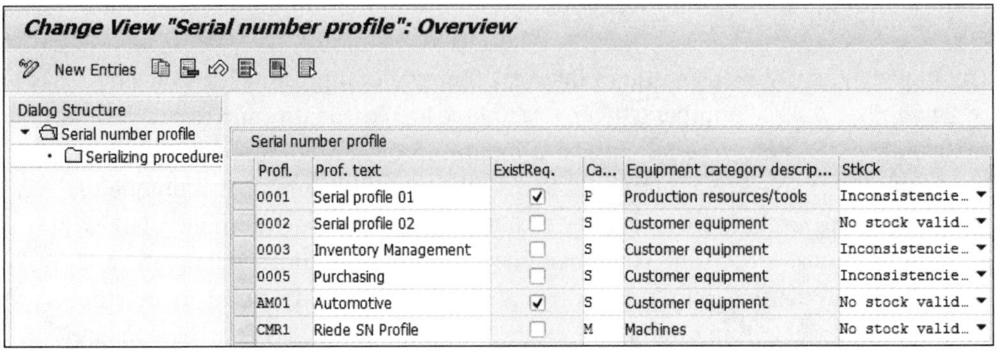

Figure 9.4 Configuration Screen for Serial Number Profiles

9.8.2   Serializing Procedures

Serial numbers are used in many areas of SAP. Using Transaction OIS2, you can define whether a serial number is optional, required, or automatic for a number of serializing procedures. Follow the navigation path **Plant Maintenance and Customer Service • Master Data in Plant Maintenance and Customer Service • Technical Objects • Serial Number management • Define Serial Number Profiles • Serializing Procedures**.

As shown in Figure 9.5, the serial number profile 0001 has been assigned a number of procedures. For each of these procedures, configuration items for serial number usage are available. The **SerUsage** field can be configured to be none, optional, obligatory, and automatic. The **EqReq** field enables serial numbers to be allowed with or without PM equipment.

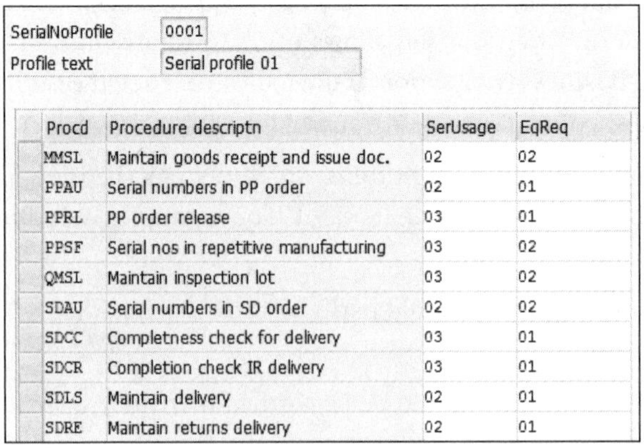

SerialNoProfile	0001		
Profile text	Serial profile 01		

Procd	Procedure descriptn	SerUsage	EqReq
MMSL	Maintain goods receipt and issue doc.	02	02
PPAU	Serial numbers in PP order	02	01
PPRL	PP order release	03	01
PPSF	Serial nos in repetitive manufacturing	03	02
QMSL	Maintain inspection lot	03	02
SDAU	Serial numbers in SD order	02	02
SDCC	Completness check for delivery	03	01
SDCR	Completion check IR delivery	03	01
SDLS	Maintain delivery	02	01
SDRE	Maintain returns delivery	02	01

Figure 9.5 Serializing Procedures for Serial Number Profile 0001

The procedures that can be assigned to each serial number profile are defined in SAP. Table 9.1 identifies procedures and their business meanings as related to serial numbers.

Procedure	Business Meaning
HUSL	Enables serial numbers to be assigned in handling unit management (HUM)
MMSL	Enables serial numbers to be assigned in goods receipts, goods issues, stock transfers, and stock transport orders and during physical inventory
PPAU	Enables serial numbers to be assigned in production and refurbishment orders
PPRL	Enables serial numbers to be assigned in production and refurbishment orders when orders are released
QMSL	Enables serial numbers to be assigned when entering the original value in a quality management (QM) inspection lot
SDAU	Enables serial numbers to be assigned in sales orders, inquiries, and quotations
SDCC	Enables serial numbers to be assigned when performing completeness checks for deliveries
SDCR	Enables serial numbers to be assigned when performing completeness checks for return deliveries
SDLS	Enables serial numbers to be assigned for deliveries
SDRE	Enables serial numbers to be assigned for return deliveries

Table 9.1 Business Procedures and Meanings for Serial Number Profiles

9.9 Quota Arrangements

At some point, a materials planner may face a nightmare situation where one or more suppliers cannot meet the company's materials demand, which can lead to significant production slowdown or even a complete stoppage. To avoid this problem, a materials planner must diversify material supply sources by bringing more suppliers on board. Quota arrangements can help materials planner with better, more organized planning.

A *quota arrangement* is a planner-defined division or split of the total required material quantity and greatly helps to distribute total material requirements among multiple suppliers. Quota arrangements not only work well for externally procured material but also for material produced internally by a company at multiple manufacturing sites.

A materials planner also can enter the base or the minimum quantity the system must consider before splitting a material's total requirement among multiple suppliers. A base quantity is the minimum quantity the system considers before activating a quota arrangement. For example, if the planner enters a base quantity of 800 pounds, but the purchase requisition is for 1,000 pounds, the system will allocate 800 pounds to the first supplier before allocating the remaining 200 pounds to the second supplier. If, for example, the second supplier requires a minimum order quantity, such as 500 pounds, the materials planner can maintain this information in the quota arrangement, and the second supplier will receive a PO for 500 pounds instead of 200 pounds.

Similar to the procurement example discussed earlier for managing procurement from two different vendors, quota arrangements in production let materials planners split the total production quantity of a material into various production or manufacturing units. All quota arrangement functions in production are the same as in procurement; the only difference is that a supplier's quota split is replaced with manufacturing units.

Quota arrangements also integrate with MRP, a system that materials planners frequently use to plan which material and in what quantity to procure or produce to ensure smooth and uninterrupted supply chain operations.

To set up quota arrangements, use Transaction MEQ1 or follow the menu path **Logistics • Materials Management • Purchasing • Master Data • Quota Arrangement • Maintain**.

Figure 9.6 shows the quota arrangement maintenance screen where you'll maintain the validity (**Valid to**) as well as the minimum quantity (**Minimum Qty**) of the material-plant combination that the system should consider for a quota split. On the detailed screen, you can maintain quotas for different vendors as well as specify minimum and maximum lot sizes that each vendor can deliver.

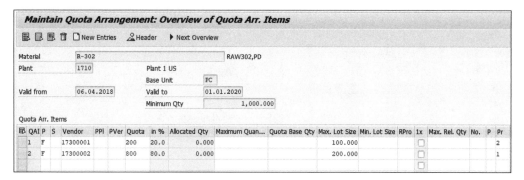

Figure 9.6 Quota Arrangement Maintenance Screen

9.10   Summary

In this chapter, we discussed the purchasing functionality in SAP S/4HANA. The purchasing of materials and services is often a large part of a company's business function. Selecting vendors and obtaining the best price and service for a material are keys to producing products at competitive retail prices while maximizing company profits.

Chapter 10 will examine the purchase requisition process. A purchase requisition can be manually created or can be created by other functionality such as production. We'll also discuss creating, modifying, and processing purchase requisitions.

Chapter 10
Purchase Requisitions

A purchase requisition is the procedural method by which users or departments can request the purchase of goods and services. A purchase requisition can be entered manually by a user or can be generated automatically as a result of a demand from materials requirements planning (MRP).

A purchase requisition is the first step in the demand for material either entered by the requisitioner or generated out of a requirements system such as MRP. A requisition contains the material or services to be procured, a required date of delivery, and a quantity. The purchase requisition doesn't contain a vendor and is generally not printed out because it's an internal company document.

In this chapter, we'll begin by covering the configuration basics for creating a new document type of a purchase requisition and assigning a newly defined number range. The configured purchase requisition document type is then put to the test in the associated business processes, including creating purchase requisitions with a material and without a material. Next, the chapter covers the purchase requisition approval process (known as the *release procedure*). Both types of release procedures—with and without classification—are covered, including configuration basics, master data, and business processes.

10.1 Configuring a New Purchase Requisition Document Type

You can configure document types for purchase orders (POs), purchase requisitions, requests for quotations (RFQs), quantity or value contracts, and scheduling agreements. The configuration steps for these documents are all quite similar; therefore, we'll focus only on the process for purchase requisitions. You'll follow these same steps to define document types for the other document categories.

In the following sections, we'll provide a step-by-step approach to defining a new number range for the purchase requisition, configuring a new purchase requisition document type, and then assigning the newly defined number range to the purchase requisition. We'll also show you how to create a purchase requisition with the newly configured purchase requisition document type.

10.1.1 Defining a Number Range

Every purchasing document type must have a number range, which can be internal, external, or both. To define the number range, follow the menu path **Purchasing • Purchase Requisition • Define Number Ranges**. Click on the **Change Intervals** button. You'll see a list of existing number ranges. Add a new number range by clicking on the **Insert Line** button, as shown in Figure 10.1.

Enter a number range key in the **No** column and then make entries in the **From No.** and **To Number** fields. To make a number range external, select the **External Number Ranges** checkbox; to make a number range internal, leave this checkbox unselected, as shown in Figure 10.2.

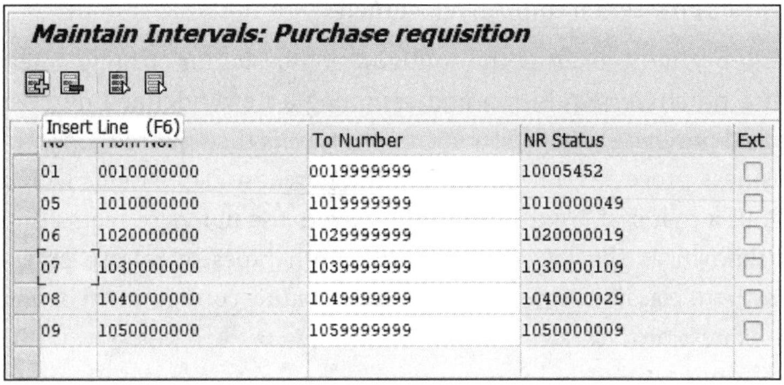

Maintain Intervals: Purchase requisition

Insert Line   (F6)

No	From No.	To Number	NR Status	Ext
01	0010000000	0019999999	10005452	☐
05	1010000000	1019999999	1010000049	☐
06	1020000000	1029999999	1020000019	☐
07	1030000000	1039999999	1030000109	☐
08	1040000000	1049999999	1040000029	☐
09	1050000000	1059999999	1050000009	☐

Figure 10.1 Interval Maintenance of a Purchase Requisition

Note

Number range intervals can't overlap each other, and number ranges are year-independent in MM.

Figure 10.2 shows the number range key **02** in the **No** column, which starts **From number 2000000000** and **To number 2999999999**. Save your entries.

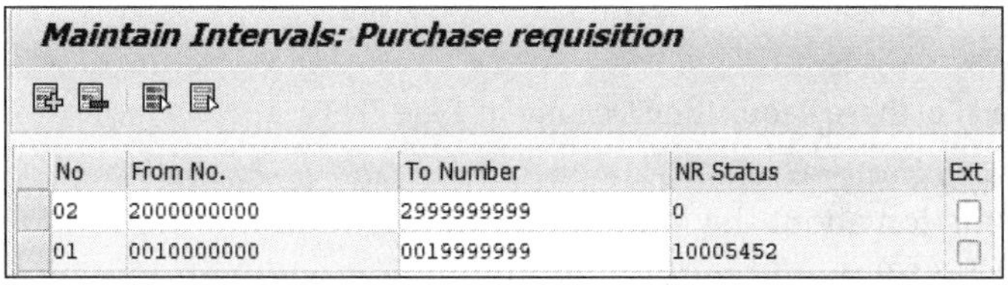

Maintain Intervals: Purchase requisition				
No	From No.	To Number	NR Status	Ext
02	2000000000	2999999999	0	☐
01	0010000000	0019999999	10005452	☐

Figure 10.2 New Interval of a Purchase Requisition

10.1.2   Defining Document Types

To configure a document type for purchase requisitions, follow the navigation path **Materials Management • Purchasing • Purchase Requisition • Define Document Types**. Figure 10.3 shows the different purchase requisitions that have been already configured. A standard purchase requisition has the **Type NB**. The configuration allows internal (**NoRgeInt**) and external (**NoRge Ext**) number ranges to be defined for each requisition type.

To create a new purchase requisition document type, select the standard purchase requisition document **Type NB**, as shown in Figure 10.3, and choose **Copy as**.

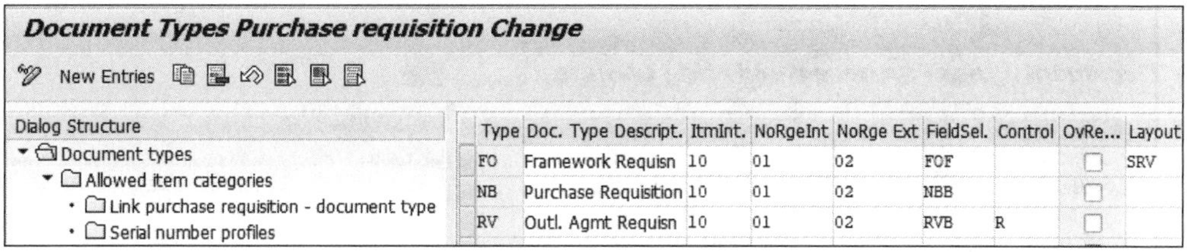

Document Types Purchase requisition Change										
✎ New Entries			Type	Doc. Type Descript.	ItmInt.	NoRgeInt	NoRge Ext	FieldSel.	Control	OvRe...	Layout
Dialog Structure			FO	Framework Requisn	10	01	02	FOF		☐	SRV
▼ ☐ Document types			NB	Purchase Requisition	10	01	02	NBB		☐	
▼ ☐ Allowed item categories			RV	Outl. Agmt Requisn	10	01	02	RVB	R	☐	
• ☐ Link purchase requisition - document type											
• ☐ Serial number profiles											

Figure 10.3 Available Document Types of Purchase Requisition

As shown in Figure 10.4, maintain the new purchase requisition document type **ZNB** and maintain the previously configured internal number range (**NoRegInt**) as **02**. Also, maintain a short description of the new purchase requisition document type (**Doc. Type Descript.**). When you press ⌅Enter⌅, the **Specify object to be copied** popup will appear. In this window, you'll choose whether you want to copy all dependent entries of the reference document type NB into newly configured document type ZNB or not. Choose **copy all**, and the screen shown Figure 10.5 will appear.

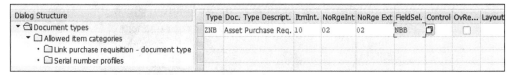

Figure 10.4 Newly Created Purchase Requisition Document Type ZNB

Figure 10.5 shows information about the number of dependent entries in purchase requisition document type NB that have been copied to our newly configured purchase requisition document type ZNB, which in this example is 170 entries.

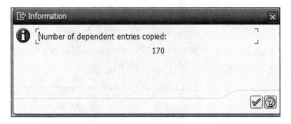

Figure 10.5 Number of Dependent Entries Copied

The screen shown in Figure 10.6 will appear where you can make changes, as needed. Select the line item **ZNB** and then double-click on **Allowed item categories** on the left-hand side.

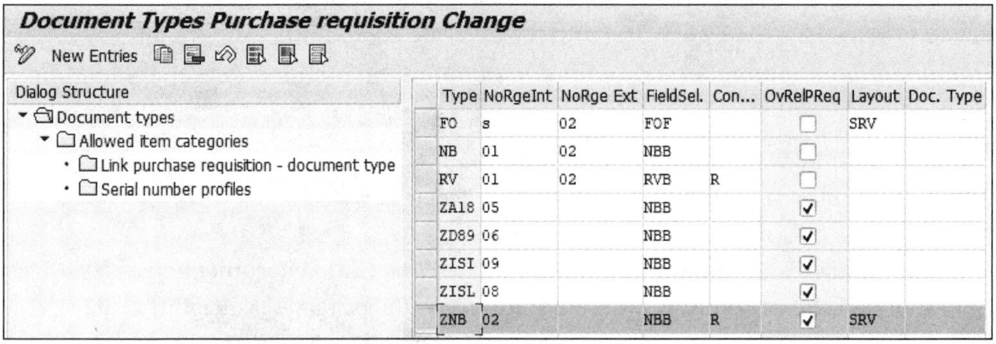

Document Types Purchase requisition Change

New Entries

Dialog Structure		Type	NoRgeInt	NoRge Ext	FieldSel.	Con...	OvRelPReq	Layout	Doc. Type
▼ Document types		FO	s	02	FOF		☐	SRV	
▼ Allowed item categories		NB	01	02	NBB		☐		
• Link purchase requisition - document type		RV	01	02	RVB	R	☐		
• Serial number profiles		ZA18	05		NBB		☑		
		ZD89	06		NBB		☑		
		ZISI	09		NBB		☑		
		ZISL	08		NBB		☑		
		ZNB	02		NBB	R	☑	SRV	

Figure 10.6 Newly Configured Purchase Requisition Document Type ZNB

Figure 10.7 shows the list of item categories that were copied directly from the purchase requisition document type **NB**. On this screen, you can eliminate or add item categories allowed for the purchase requisition document type **ZNB**.

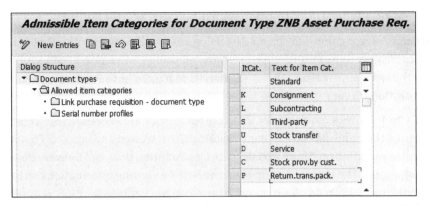

Figure 10.7 Allowed Item Categories of Purchase Requisition Document Type ZNB

Access the screen shown in Figure 10.8 by choosing **Serial number profiles** and make purchase requisitions of document type ZNB required or optional to a serial number for equipment when creating a purchase requisition.

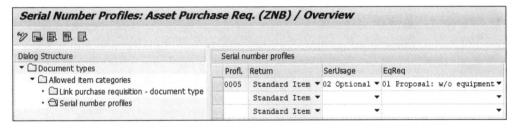

Figure 10.8 Serial Number Profile for Purchase Requisitions

With these configuration steps complete, let's now test whether the SAP system can successfully create a newly configured purchase requisition of document type ZNB with the new number range starting with 200000000.

> **Note**
>
> During the course of an SAP implementation project, the MM consultant and the client should agree on all the purchasing document numbers and associated number ranges to be configured to meet various business scenarios. Our example covered creating purchase requisition document type ZNB, which business users need to use when requesting (in the form of a purchase requisition) the purchase of an asset.

10.1.3   Creating a Purchase Requisition with a Material Master Record

Requisitions are most commonly created by using an item or service with a material master record. A purchase requisition can be created using Transaction ME51N via by following the navigation path **Logistics • Materials Management • Purchasing • Purchase Requisition • Create**.

This transaction allows a requisitioner to define what fields are visible on the screen when entering the requisition data. Many fields can be reviewed and entered. Figure 10.9 shows the **Material,** the **Short Text** description, **Quantity, Unit**, and **Delivery Date** fields. In addition to the fields shown in Figure 10.9, the following information can be entered in the requisition line item: material group, plant, storage location, requisitioner, purchasing organization, manufacturer's part number, purchasing information record, desired vendor, and requirement tracking number.

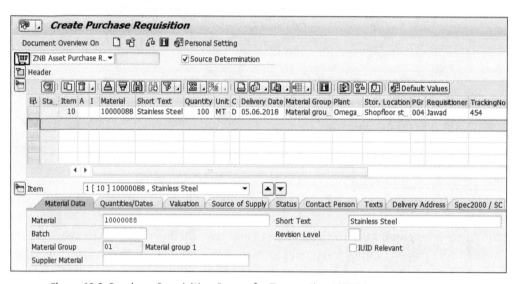

Figure 10.9 Purchase Requisition Screen for Transaction ME51N

A requisition for materials that have a material master record requires the requisitioner to enter the following information:

- Material number of item or service
- Quantity to be procured
- Unit of measure
- Date of delivery of the material

The requisition process will populate default information into the **Purchase Requisition** screen. Examples of this information include the material group and purchasing group. In the following sections, we'll evaluate some of the important fields for purchase requisitions.

Document Type

The document type for a purchase requisition is important because it defines the internal and external number ranges used for requisitions and because it defines the valid item categories and follow-on functions. For our example, we'll use our newly configured purchase requisition document type ZNB.

Purchase Requisition Number

A purchase requisition number can be defined as an internal or an external number. In our example, the internal number range (**NoRgeInt**) has been configured with range number **02**.

Item Category

Refer to Figure 10.9, which shows the item category field (**I**), another control field that allows a purchase requisition to follow the correct path for that category of purchase requisition. The SAP system includes a set of predelivered item categories:

- **Blank**: Standard
- **K**: Consignment
- **L**: Subcontracting
- **S**: Third party
- **D**: Service
- **U**: Stock transfer

The item category allows for the selective display of certain fields and not others. For example, if a purchase requisition item has an item category **K** for consignment, then invoice receipts won't be allowed.

Account Assignment Category

An account assignment category field (**A**) determines what type of accounting assignment data is required for purchase requisitions. Examples of account assignments are cost centers, cost objects, SAP General Ledger (SAP G/L) accounts, and assets.

The account assignment categories can be configured in the IMG. You can create a new account assignment category by following the navigation path **Materials Management • Purchasing • Account Assignment • Maintain Account Assignment Categories**, as shown in Figure 10.10.

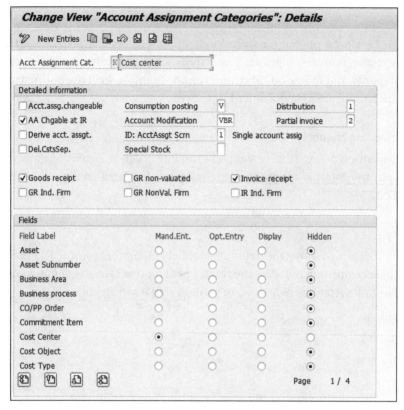

Figure 10.10 Fields Control of Account Assignment Category

A purchasing user can create a new account assignment category and configure its fields. For example, some companies may not want certain fields to appear or to be changeable when using particular account assignments. The configuration allows the fields, such as **Asset**, **Business Area**, and **Cost Object**, to be mandatory entries (**Mand.Ent.**), optional entries (**Opt.Entry**), display-only fields (**Display**), or **Hidden.** The accounting department is primarily involved in creating new account assignment categories.

Required account assignment data is needed for specific account assignments, as follows:

- **Asset (A)**
  Asset number and subnumber
- **Production order (F)**
  Production order number
- **Cost center (K)**
  Cost center and G/L account number
- **Sales order (C)**
  Sales order and G/L account number
- **Project (P)**
  Project number and G/L account number
- **Unknown (U)**
  None

The next four fields can be entered on the line item of the purchase requisition, as shown earlier in Figure 10.9.

Plant/Storage Location

The plant and storage location fields can be entered if the location where the material must be shipped is known. If only one receiving dock exists for the whole plant, then this dock can be defaulted.

Purchasing Group

A purchasing group number is a number for the buyer (or buyers) of a material. If a purchasing group is entered at the order level, then this group will be defaulted for each of the purchase requisition line items.

Requirement Tracking Number

This requirement tracking number (RTN) doesn't represent the requisition or the requisitioner but is a free-form field in which a tracking number can be entered. This field can be used by the person entering the RFQ to uniquely identify specific POs. For example, if purchasing agents are entering a number of POs for a project, they may want to enter a unique RTN so that the POs can be located together instead of having to know each individual PO number.

Requisitioner

This field is another free-form field where a purchasing user can add the requisitioner's name to search and order the purchase requisitions. For example, if one person is tasked with entering all purchase requisitions for a department, that person can enter the name of the person who actually wrote the requisition in the **Requisitioner** field.

Figure 10.11 shows the item details of a purchase requisition. The **Closed** indicator can be set if the purchase requisition no longer needs to be converted into a PO. Selecting the **Fixed ID** checkbox will prevent automatic changes to the purchase requisition during an MRP run. The data on planned delivery time (**Pl. Deliv. Time**) and the goods receipt processing time (**GR proc. time**) are taken from the material master if these details are maintained in the material master.

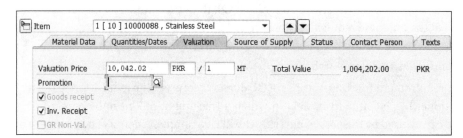

Figure 10.11 Quantities/Dates Details in a Purchase Requisition

Figure 10.12 shows the **Valuation** tab of a purchase requisition. The **Valuation Price** is taken directly from the material master if the material had previously been procured. The valuation price at the item level also forms the basis of triggering a release (approval) procedure.

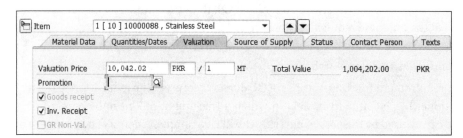

Figure 10.12 Purchase Requisition: Valuation Tab

Figure 10.13 shows a procurement planner to assign sources of supply to the purchase requisition. This step can be performed manually by clicking on the **Assign Source of Supply** button or can be done automatically, as we'll discuss later in this section.

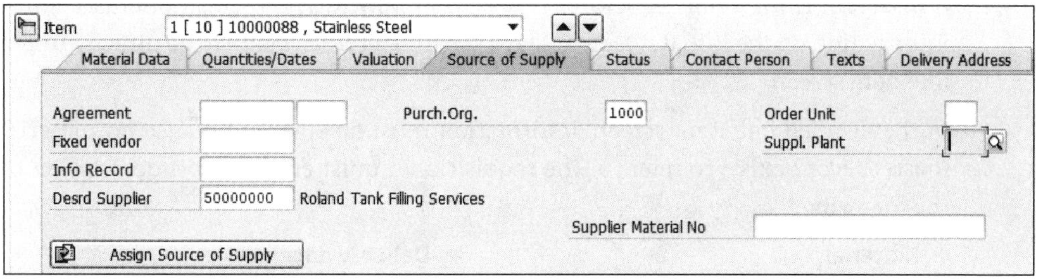

Figure 10.13 Purchase Requisition: Source of Supply Tab

Figure 10.14 shows the **Status** tab in which information is continually updated when more business processes are performed, such as releasing purchase requisitions or creating POs. You can also block a purchase requisition from further processing to ensure the purchase requisition isn't mistakenly converted into an RFQ, an agreement, or a PO.

Figure 10.14 Purchase Requisition: Status Tab

Save the purchase requisition in the newly configured document type ZNB, and the system will show an information message displaying the newly defined internal number range is correctly configured and assigned to the newly configured purchase requisition document type ZNB.

10.1.4   Creating a Purchase Requisition without a Material Master Record

When creating a purchase requisition without a material master record for the item, then the purchase requisition must have an account assignment to direct costs to a specific account.

The account assignment categories described in the previous section allow a requisitioner to allocate the costs of the purchase to the correct accounts.

To enter a purchase requisition for an item without a material master record, the transaction is the same as before: Transaction ME51N. The requisitioner can enter information on the initial screen or leave the initial screen blank to go directly to the line item screen.

In the detailed line item screen, information must be entered because no material master record exists to refer to. The requisitioner must enter a short description of the following:

- Material
- Account assignment category
- Quantity to be supplied
- Unit of measure

- Delivery date
- Plant
- Purchasing group
- Material group

The required information will correspond to the account assignment category was entered in the line item. Figure 10.15 shows the required account information.

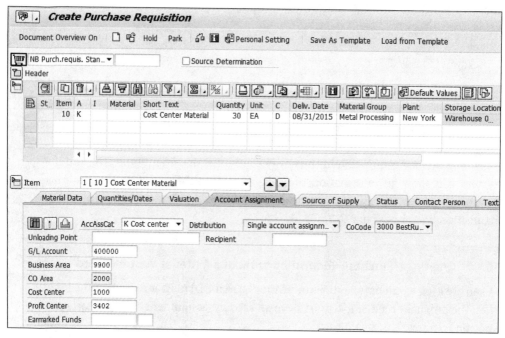

Figure 10.15 Purchase Requisition Line Item with No Material Master Record

10.2   Processing a Purchase Requisition

After a purchase requisition has been created, it can be further amended using the change process, which we'll discuss next. This section also discusses the methods for displaying purchase requisitions.

10.2.1   Changing a Purchase Requisition

A purchase requisition can be changed as part of the material planning process, that is, by an MRP controller or by a requisitioner prior to being processed by the purchasing department. A purchasing requisition can be changed using Transaction ME52N or by following the navigation path **Logistics • Materials Management • Purchasing • Purchase Requisition • Change**.

10.2.2   Displaying a Purchase Requisition

A number of methods to display purchase requisitions are available, which we'll describe next.

Purchase Requisition: Display

A purchase requisition can be displayed using Transaction ME54N or by following the navigation path **Logistics • Materials Management • Purchasing • Purchase Requisition • Display**.

Purchase Requisition: List Display

To show a list of purchase requisitions, use Transaction ME5A (Display Purchase Requisitions) or follow the navigation path **Logistics • Materials Management • Purchasing • Purchase Requisition • List Displays • General**.

Transaction ME5A allows a requisitioner to enter a wide range of selection criteria to display the valid requisitions. Some common examples of selection criteria include **Purchase requisition, Document Type, Material, Requirement tracking number,** and **Delivery Date.** Enter the newly configured **Document type** "ZNB" and **Plant** "1000" and execute. The screen shown in Figure 10.16 will appear.

Figure 10.16 shows a list of newly configured purchase requisitions of document type ZNB in detail.

List Display of Purchase Requisitions

Rel	Item	S	Delet.ind.	I	A	Material	Short Text	Quantity	Unit	C	Delv. Date	Matl Group	Plant	SLoc	PGr	Requisitioner	TrackingNo	Vendor	Fixed vend
Purchase Requisition 2000000000																			
	10	N	☐			10000088	Stainless Steel	100	MT	D	20180605	01	1000	1004	004	Jawad	454	50000000	
Purchase Requisition 2000000001																			
	10	N	☐			10000088	Stainless Steel	100	MT	D	20180605	01	1000	1004	004	Jawad	454		
Purchase Requisition 2000000002																			
	10	N	☐			10000088	Stainless Steel	100	MT	D	20180605	01	1000	1004	004	Jawad	454	50000000	
Purchase Requisition 2000000003																			
	10	N	☐			10000088	Stainless Steel	10	MT	D	20180602	01	1000	1004	004				
Purchase Requisition 2000000004																			
	10	N	☐			10000088	Stainless Steel	100	MT	D	20180604	01	1000	1004	004	Jawad			
Purchase Requisition 2000000005																			
	10	N	☐			10000088	Stainless Steel	10	MT	D	20180604	0004	1000	1004	004				
Purchase Requisition 2000000006																			
	10	N	☐			10000088	Stainless Steel	10	MT	D	20180602	0004	1000	1004	004	Jawad	545		50000000
Purchase Requisition 2000000007																			
	10	N	☐			10000088	Stainless Steel	15	MT	D	20180602	0004	1000		004	Jawad	725		
Purchase Requisition 2000000008																			
	10	N	☐			10000088	Stainless Steel	10	MT	D	20180604	0004	1000		004				50000000
Purchase Requisition 2000000009																			
	10	N	☐			10000088	Stainless Steel	10	MT	D	20180602	0004	1000	1004	004				
Purchase Requisition 2000000010																			
	10	N	☐			10000088	Stainless Steel	10	MT	D	20180602	0004	1000	1004	004	Jawad			

Figure 10.16 List of Purchase Requisitions

Purchase Requisitions by Tracking Number

Transaction MELB can be used to select purchase requisitions by their RTNs. This number doesn't represent the requisitioner but instead can be a tracking number entered by the requisitioner to identify a particular person's purchase requisitions.

This transaction can be found using the navigation path **Logistics • Materials Management • Purchasing • Purchase Requisition • List Displays • By Account Assignment • Transactions per Tracking Number**.

10.2.3 Closing a Purchase Requisition

A purchase requisition can be closed if an indicator is set within the item detail screen. Normally, the purchase requisition is closed when the amount requested on the line item of the purchase requisition is equal to the amount that has been purchased via a PO.

To close a line item on a purchase requisition, the requisitioner needs to access Transaction ME52N (Change Purchase Requisition). The line item to be flagged for deletion must be selected, and the requisitioner should select **Delete**. The **Delete** indicator on the line item will be checked, as shown in Figure 10.17.

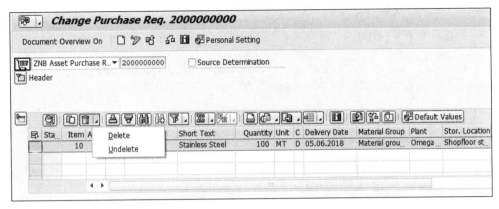

Figure 10.17 Deleting a Purchase Requisition

10.2.4   Follow-On Functions

As the purchase requisition is processed, follow-on functions can be carried out before the purchase requisition is converted to a PO.

Transaction ME56 allows a purchasing user to select a range of purchase requisitions to assign a source. The purchase requisitions can be selected via a large range of selection criteria, including material group, item category, delivery date, cost center, and so on.

Transaction ME56 can be found by following the navigation path **Logistics • Materials Management • Purchasing • Purchase Requisition • Follow-on Functions • Assign**.

The initial screen allows entry of a large selection of variables to create a list of purchase requisitions for vendor assignment.

After the selection criteria have been entered into the initial screen of Transaction ME56, the transaction will return a number of relevant purchase requisitions based on that search criteria.

Figure 10.18 shows the purchase requisitions that were returned as a result of the selection criteria entered. You can select the purchase requisitions that will be assigned a vendor.

After selecting purchase requisitions, you can choose to have the vendor assigned automatically to the purchase requisitions by selecting the **Assign Source of Supply** option from the green document icon, as shown at the bottom of Figure 10.18. The results are shown in Figure 10.19.

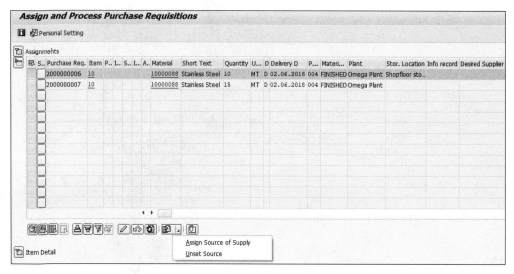

Figure 10.18 Assigning a Source of Supply to a Purchase Requisition

Figure 10.19 shows the assignment of not just the **Fixed Supplier 5000000** but also the associated **Info Record 5300000358** as seen on the right-hand side of the screen for purchase requisition **2000000006**.

Figure 10.19 Assigning a Source of Supply to Purchase Requisitions

10.3   Indirectly Created Requisitions

A purchase requisition may be created if some business process needs materials or services. An indirectly created purchase requisition is usually created when a user performs another business function, such as creating a production order or a maintenance order.

10.3.1   Purchase Requisition Created by Production Order

In a production order, two elements determine how operations take place. The *routing* is the sequence of the operations that should take place, and the *bill of materials (BOM)* is the recipe used to produce the final material.

A purchase requisition can be generated automatically when the routing in a production order involves an operation where material needs to be sent out for external processing, for example, in subcontracting work.

Another way a purchase requisition can be produced is when a BOM calls for a material that is a nonstock item. This situation may occur when a special item is required for a production order or if the material is no longer purchased by the company. For example, a company that produces furnaces may need to incorporate a special filter for furnaces made for customers based in California. The clean air laws in California may require a special part to be ordered and fitted during the production process. This triggers a purchase requisition for the special part and possibly a purchase requisition for a subcontractor to fit the part.

10.3.2   Purchase Requisition Created by Plant Maintenance Order

This type of order produces purchase requisitions that are similar to the production order. The maintenance order is created for plant maintenance (PM) operations on a technical object (in other words, equipment) at the plant. Similar to a production order, a maintenance order has a list of operations that must be performed. The operations give the maintenance user a step-by-step list of what needs to be performed and the materials and equipment needed for each step.

In the operation, a certain nonstock material may be needed, which may cause a purchase requisition to be created. A maintenance order may also have an operation that requires an external operation be performed by a subcontractor, which will also cause an indirect purchase requisition to be created.

10.3.3   Purchase Requisition Created by Project System

The project system (PS) functionality in SAP S/4HANA uses objects called *networks*, a set of instructions that tell users what tasks need to be performed, in what order, and by what date.

A network has two options for creating material requirements. The network can create purchase requisitions for nonstock materials and external services, similar to the

379

production and maintenance orders. The network can also be configured to allow the creation of purchase requisitions as soon as the network is released.

10.3.4   Purchase Requisition Created by Materials Planning

Consumption-based planning or the material requirements planning (MRP) functionality can create purchase requisitions based on its calculations. When creating POs, MRP calculates quantities and delivery dates. The planning run can also produce planned orders for in-house production, but these orders can be converted to purchase requisitions.

A purchase requisition is an internal purchasing suggestion that can be modified before being converted into a PO. After the MRP controller has determined the accuracy of the external purchasing requirements, the controller can convert some planned orders to purchase requisitions and perhaps convert some purchase requisitions to POs. The level of interaction between the planning department and the purchasing department will determine what procedures are in place to allow the MRP controller to create purchase requisitions and POs.

In this section, we covered purchase requisitions. The next section covers the approval process for purchasing documents, known as release procedures.

10.4   Release Procedures

Release procedures are approval procedures for purchasing documents such as purchase requisitions and purchase orders (POs). The manner in which these procedures are configured is called a *release strategy*. A release strategy involves a process whereby an approver verifies document data (such as material, quantity, and value) and then authorizes the purchase. The process takes place online, which saves time and is more efficient than previous manual approval processes.

The SAP system provides two different types of release procedures:

- **Release procedure without classification**
  A release procedure without classification can be configured only for item level releases in purchase requisitions. Therefore, this release procedure can only be used for internal documents (such as purchase requisitions). This limitation arises because external documents (such as POs) must be sent to vendors and therefore can't be partially approved. In a release procedure without classification, you can set the release based on the following four criteria:

- Plant
- Value
- Material group
- Account assignment category

- **Release procedure with classification**

  A release procedure with classification offers many more criteria to define the release strategy. You can use either of these procedures (with or without classification) for purchase requisitions. But, for POs and RFQs, you must use a release procedure with classification. Before getting into the release procedure configuration steps, let's define the key terms used in release procedures, as follows:

  - Release strategy: Defines the entire approval process and consists of release conditions, release codes, and release prerequisites.
  - Release conditions/criteria: Determines which release strategy applies for a particular purchasing document. For example, if the value of a requisition item is $100, a certain strategy may be required; if the value of the item is $10,000, a different strategy may be required. If purchasing documents fulfill release conditions, they must be approved before they can be processed further.
  - Release code/point: A two-character key that represents an individual or department responsible for giving approval. Each person involved in the release procedure signifies an approver in a release transaction using his/her the release code.
  - Release prerequisite: Sets the order in which approval must take place. For example, a manager must approve a document before the vice president approves it.
  - Release status/indicator: Represents the current status of the item or document such as blocked and released. For example, if the document isn't fully approved, it may have been blocked.

Now that you have an understanding of the basic concepts behind release strategies, let's move on to the configuration steps involved. We'll discuss both types of configuration: without classification and with classification.

10.4.1   Release Procedures without Classification

To configure release procedures without classification, follow the menu path **Materials Management • Purchasing • Purchase Requisition • Release Procedure • Set Up Procedure Without Classification**. This SAP system will display five activities, as shown in Figure 10.20.

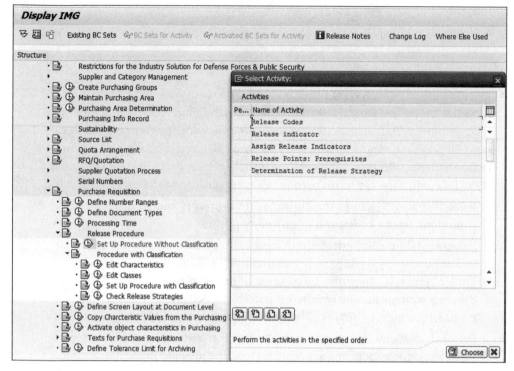

Figure 10.20 Setting Up a Release Procedure without Classification

You'll need to select and perform each activity, one by one, as discussed in the following sections.

Selecting Release Codes

A *release code* is used to approve the document and are references to specific users. Click on **New Entries** and enter a two-digit **Release code** key and **Description**, as shown in Figure 10.21. The release code can be either a numeric or an alphanumeric entry.

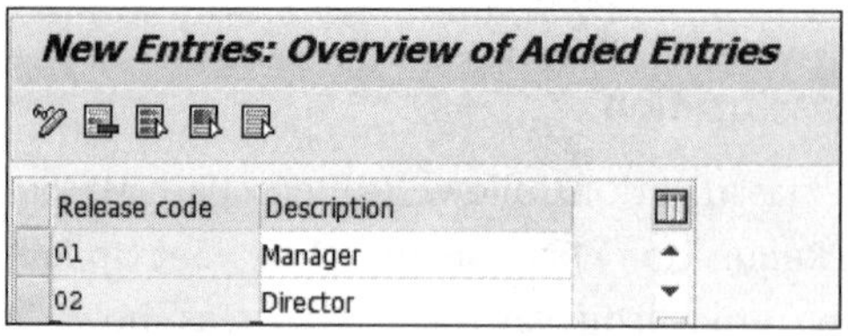

Release code	Description	
01	Manager	
02	Director	

New Entries: Overview of Added Entries

Figure 10.21 Release Codes

Selecting the Release Indicator

The *release indicator* specifies the release status of the purchase requisition, which can define the release indicator, as shown in Figure 10.22. Click on **New Entries** and enter the following:

- **Fixed for MRP**
  If you select this checkbox, the purchase requisition can't be changed by material requirements planning (MRP).

- **Released for quot.**
  This indicator specifies that quotations and RFQs may be processed with reference to purchase requisitions. If you select this checkbox, the purchase requisition is available for RFQ and quotation processing.

- **Rel. for ordering**
  This indicator specifies whether POs can be generated with reference to purchase requisitions.

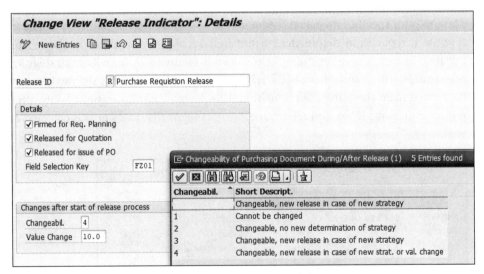

Figure 10.22 Release Indicator in a Release Procedure without Classification

- **Field selection key**
  When setting up a release strategy and release indicators, you can use the field selection key to determine whether certain fields in a purchase requisition may or may not be changed with approval. For example, let's say you need to prevent changes to the requested quantity in a purchase requisition after the release

indicator has been set in the purchase requisition. For this requirement, you would configure the order quantity field as **Display only** in the field selection key.

- **Changeabil.**
  This field defines how the system reacts if a purchasing document is changed after the start of the release procedure, as shown in Figure 10.22.

- **Value chgs.**
  This field specifies the percentage by which the value of the purchase requisition can be changed after the release procedure has started. If the requisition is changed by more than the specified limit entered in this field, the requisitions will be subjected again to the release procedure.

Assigning Release Indicators

In this step, you'll assign the release indicators to a release strategy, as shown in Figure 10.23. Click the **New Entries** button, enter the release strategy code, select the release indicator, and save.

This indicator specifies the release sequence, that is, which release point(s) must have a released requisition before the current individual or department is allowed to release that requisition. For example, as shown in Figure 10.23, for release strategy **R1**, release indicators **1** and **2** have been defined. If release indicator 1 is set, the RFQ can be created from the purchase requisition. Release indicator 2 can be set only after release indicator 1 is set, and release indicator 2 means that RFQs or POs can be created.

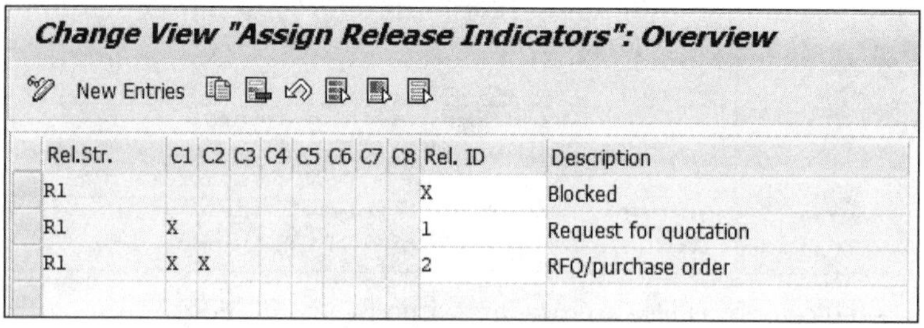

Rel.Str.	C1	C2	C3	C4	C5	C6	C7	C8	Rel. ID	Description
R1									X	Blocked
R1	X								1	Request for quotation
R1	X	X							2	RFQ/purchase order

Change View "Assign Release Indicators": Overview — New Entries

Figure 10.23 Assigning a Release Indicator to a Release Strategy

Selecting Release Points as Prerequisites

In this step, you'll configure the sequence of release codes and the prerequisites purchase requisitions must fulfill before they can be released. As shown in Figure 10.24, for this release strategy, we have two release codes: R1 and R2. Release code R1 has no prerequisite, which means it can approve the purchase requisition. Release code R2, however, does have a prerequisite: The purchase requisition must be approved by release code R1 before it can be approved by release code R2. (Remember, release codes are references to specific people.) Test the sequence and its prerequisites by clicking on the **Simulate release** button. A popup window will appear where you can test the release strategy.

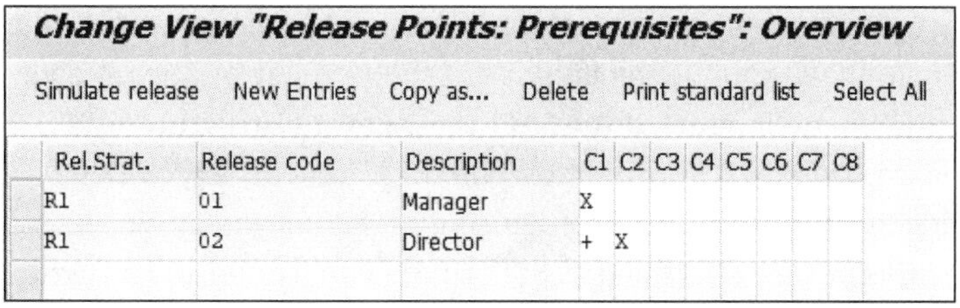

Change View "Release Points: Prerequisites": Overview

Simulate release	New Entries	Copy as...	Delete	Print standard list	Select All						

Rel.Strat.	Release code	Description	C1	C2	C3	C4	C5	C6	C7	C8
R1	01	Manager	X							
R1	02	Director	+	X						

Figure 10.24 Prerequisites of Release Points

Determining When to Apply a Specific Release Strategy

In this step, you'll define when a purchase requisition should be considered for a release procedure and which release strategy is applicable. As mentioned earlier, a release strategy without classification can be configured with only four criteria: account assignment category, material group, plant, and value. As shown in Figure 10.25, for account assignment category **K** (cost center), material group **004**, plant **1000**, and value **1,000.00 PKR**, the release strategy R1 is applicable. When a purchase requisition is created with these attributes, the system will automatically assign release strategy R1 and will follow the approval process configured in this strategy.

Change View "Determination of Release Strategy": Overview

New Entries

AcctAssCat	Mat. Grp	Plnt	Value of purch. req.	Crcy	Release strategy	
K	0004	1000	1,000.00	PKR	R1	

Figure 10.25 Release Strategy Determination

In this section, we covered release procedures without classification. The next section delves into release procedures with classification.

10.4.2   Release Procedures with Classification

A release procedure with classification can be defined for internal documents (purchase requisitions) and external documents (POs, RFQs, contracts, and scheduling agreements). You'll need to define both characteristics and classes for release procedures with classification. We'll discuss these steps next.

Before you start configuring release strategies with classification in the SAP system, we'll need to identity and define the combination of parameters that will trigger the release. PO-triggering criteria can be a combination of document type, plant, and purchasing organization along with value depending on the number of release codes assigned when the document is created. In SAP, the relevant structure—CEKKO (Communication Release Strategy Determination Purch. Document)—provides a list of all the possible fields that can be used for configuring a release strategy. To view all the fields in structure CEKKO, use Transaction SE12 where you'll enter the structure name and then click on the **Display** button. Figure 10.26 shows the various fields available for configuring release strategies for a PO.

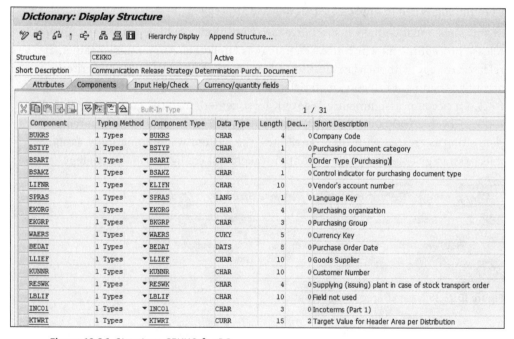

Figure 10.26 Structure CEKKO for PO

> **Note**
>
> While our example in this section covers release procedures with classification for purchase orders, you can use the same concepts and logic when configuring release procedure for purchase requisitions.
>
> The structure for purchase requisitions is CEBAN, the field BSART is used for the order type, and GNETW is used for the total order value. Later in this section, we'll also show you how the newly configured purchase requisition document type ZNB has a release procedure activated at the item level of a purchase requisition using these two fields (BSART and GNETW).

Master Data Setup

In this example, let's assume that we want to configure a release strategy based on the combination of two fields: **Document Type** (CEKKO-BSART) and **Purchase order total value** (CEKKO-GNETW).

We'll need to create individual characteristics for each field and then group these characteristics into a release class. To create a characteristic, use Transaction CT04 or follow the configuration menu path **Materials Management • Purchasing • Purchase Order • Release Procedure for Purchase Orders • Edit Characteristic**, as shown in Figure 10.27.

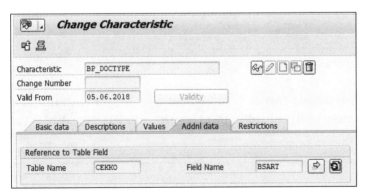

Figure 10.27 Table Field for Structure (Table Name) CEKKO

Provide the characteristic name **BP_DOCTYPE** and then click on **Create** button to create the characteristic. Now, we'll refer to the fields from structure CEKKO by providing the reference to this structure (**CEKKO**) and corresponding field (**BSART** for document type). Since this characteristic is created for a document type, specify the structure and field name given in Figure 10.27. Once you enter the structure name and field name, the system will generate a warning message: "Format data taken from Data Dictionary (press enter)." This warning message indicates that the data type of the characteristic will be taken from the data dictionary of this structure in SAP.

In the **Basic Data** tab of the characteristic screen, as shown in Figure 10.28, provide an appropriate description. If you want to configure the release strategy for a single document type, you'll need to select **Single Value** radio button in the **Value Assignment** block. If multiple document types are required, then select the **Multiple Values** radio button.

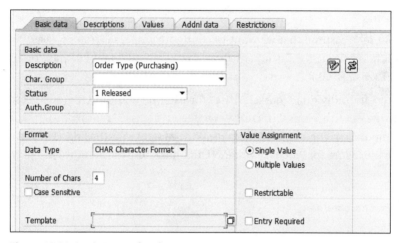

Figure 10.28 Basic Data of a Characteristic

Now, navigate to **Values** tab and provide the document types required in this release strategy. For our example, we'll use PO document type **NB**, which is a standard PO, as shown in Figure 10.29.

> **Note**
>
> The values shown in Figure 10.29 are not available as a F4 selections or in drop-down lists. Be sure these values are typed in correctly and exactly match with the procurement document types.

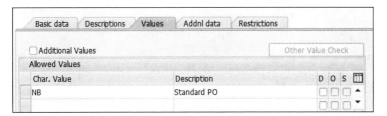

Figure 10.29 Characteristic Values

To ensure that these characteristics are used only in classes made for purchase order releases, we'll need to provide a restriction in the characteristic by entering class type **032** in the **Restrictions** tab. Save the characteristic.

Using the same method, let's create another characteristic **BP_NETVAL**, which is for **Purchase order Net value**, as shown in Figure 10.30.

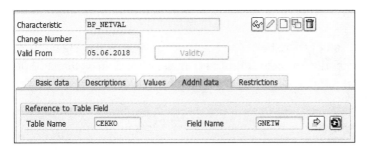

Figure 10.30 Table CEKKO and Its Associated Field Name GNETW

When entering the structure name **CEKKO** and field **GNETW** for the purchase order net value, the system will ask for a currency since this field is related to numbers and the net value of a purchase order. Maintain the local currency, which in this example is PKR (Pakistani Rupees), for the characteristic, as shown in Figure 10.31. If you have multiple criteria for different ranges of values, these criteria must be provided in the **Values** tab with the **Multiple Values** radio button selected in the **Basic Data** tab. Since there will be intervals in the purchase order values, you'll have to configure the characteristic to allow the values in intervals by selecting the **Interval vals allowed** checkbox under the **Value assignment** block in **Basic data** tab.

389

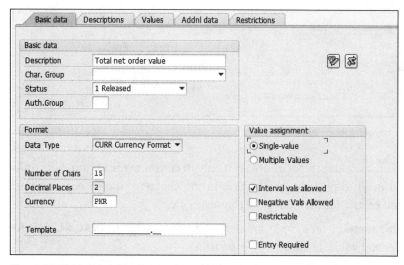

Figure 10.31 Maintaining Currency and Value Assignments in a Characteristic

For this characteristic, values are to be defined in intervals, as shown in Figure 10.32. This first interval denotes that the net value of a PO must be less than (<) than 100.00 PKR, while the second interval denotes PO values of more than or equal (>=) to 101.00 PKR.

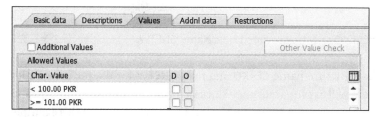

Figure 10.32 Allowed Interval of Characteristic Value

Once we have all the characteristics ready, we'll need to group them into a class.

Creating Classes and Assigning Characteristics

To create a class, use Transaction CL02 or follow the configuration menu path **Materials Management • Purchasing • Purchase Order • Release Procedure for Purchase Orders • Edit Class**.

In the main screen of Transaction CL02, provide an appropriate **Class Name (BP_ RELPO)** and click the **Create** button. Make sure that the **Class type** is **032 (Release**

Strategy). In the detailed screen, provide an appropriate description. Assign the two characteristics we created earlier to this class, as shown in Figure 10.33.

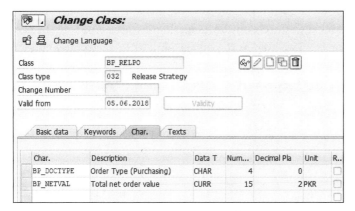

Figure 10.33 Assigning Characteristics to a Class

> **Note**
>
> Classes and characteristics are treated as master data in the SAP system. As a result, classes and characteristics aren't transported from development systems to quality and production systems through transport requests. Instead, you must manually create them in each client or automatically upload them via Application Linking and Enabling (ALE), provided by SAP. Transactions BD91, BD92, and BD93 can be used to transfer classes and characteristics via ALE. You can manually assign classes and characteristics to release strategies in each client by using Transaction CL24N. See Chapter 24 on the classification system for more information.

Configuration Basics of Release Procedure

After creating a class, the next step is to configure the elements required in the release strategy. To configure release procedure for PO, follow the configuration menu path **Materials Management • Purchasing • Purchase Order • Release Procedure for Purchase Orders • Define Release Procedure for Purchase Orders**.

The following elements are required:

- **Release Groups**
- **Release Codes**
- **Release Indicator**
- **Release Strategies**
- **Workflow**

To begin, follow these steps:

1. Select **Release Group** and click the **Choose** button. Click on the **New Entries** button to create a new release group. In the new record, provide an appropriate name such as "BP" in the **Rel.Grp** field and, in the **Class** field, maintain the class name "BP_RELPO," which we created in the previous step, as shown in Figure 10.34. Save your entries.

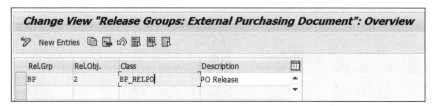

Figure 10.34 Release Group

2. Select release codes and click the **Choose** button. As shown in Figure 10.35, click on the **New Entries** button to create release codes for the release strategy. The number of release codes depends on number of approval levels. In our example, we'll only create two release codes: **10** and **20** for **Buyer** and **Manager**, respectively. Ensure you create these release codes under the same release group (**Grp**) **BP** that was configured in the previous step.

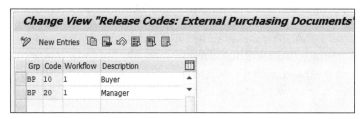

Figure 10.35 Release Codes

3. Select a release indicator, as shown in Figure 10.36 This screen indicates the **Release ID** for initial and released statuses. Release **ID 0** indicates a **Blocked** status, and release **ID 1** indicates a **Released** status. The **Chgable** field contains the parameter that will define how the system reacts if a purchasing document is changed after the start of the release procedure. In other words, once an order is released, we can still change the values in the purchase order, which will trigger a new release status. If the field is allowed to change, we can define the % of change allowed, which in this example is 10.0%.

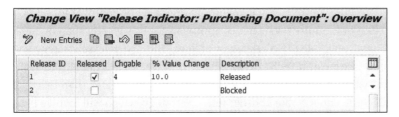

Figure 10.36 Release Indicator

4. Select release strategies, click on **New Entries** button, and enter the previously configured release group **BP**. After entering the release group, provide an appropriate release strategy (in our case, **BP**) and a short description, as shown in Figure 10.37. Double-click the **Release group BP** so that the screen shown in Figure 10.38 appears.

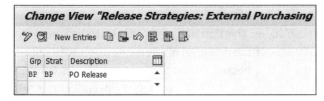

Figure 10.37 Release Strategy

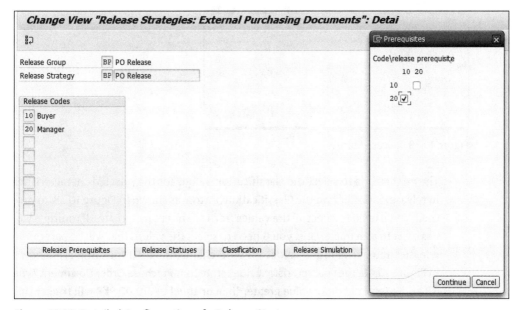

Figure 10.38 Detailed Configuration of a Release Strategy

On this screen, in our example, you'll keep only one level of approval for all POs below 100.00 PKR but require two levels of approvals for POs greater than or equal to 100 PKR. Thus, you'll need two release strategies. The first release strategy will have only one release code and will only be triggered for values less than 100.00 PKR in the characteristic BP_NETVAL. For purchase orders with greater than or equal value to 100.00 PKR, you'll create another release strategy, which will involve both the release codes and the two levels of approvals needed in this case. The following steps demonstrate how to create this second release strategy (with two approvals):

– Maintain release codes **10** and **20**. Now click on the **Release prerequisites** button, shown in Figure 10.38, and select prerequisites for each release code. Figure 10.38 shows that no prerequisites exist for release code **10**, but for release code **20**, release code **10** must first be released. This prerequisite is achieved by selecting the checkbox from column **10** and next to the row **ID 20**. Save these settings.

– The next step is to click **Release statuses**, as shown in Figure 10.38, which will open the screen shown in Figure 10.39. The first stage of the release indicator will always show a **Blocked** status. After the first level of release by a user with release code 10, the overall status is still **Blocked**. When a document is released by a higher-level user having release code **20**, the document's overall status will be **Released**.

Figure 10.39 Release Statuses

– The next step is to select the classification values for the selected characteristics in release class. Click on the **Classification** button, as shown in Figure 10.38, to proceed. You'll need to select all the values from all the characteristics. If multiple values exist in a characteristic, you'll need to select the values that will be part of the release strategy. Maintain values for both characteristics; for example, as shown in Figure 10.40, the characteristic values state that **Purchase Order Document Type NB** and a **Total net order value greater than or equal to 100.00 PKR** will trigger this release strategy.

> **Note**
>
> You can also directly maintain the values provided in the **Additional Values** option while creating the characteristics. Refer to Figure 10.32.

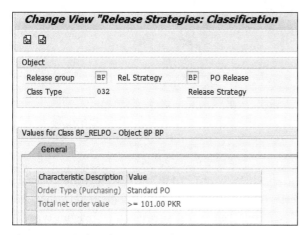

Figure 10.40 Classification in Release Strategy

5. You can simulate the entire release strategy to ensure all steps are correctly configured by choosing **Release simulation**, as shown in Figure 10.38. Place your cursor on release codes **10 20**, as shown in Figure 10.41, and click on **Simulate Release**, which will open the screen shown in Figure 10.42.

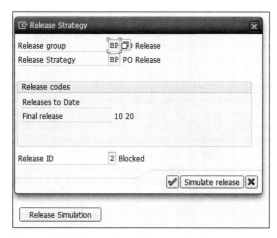

Figure 10.41 Simulating a Release Strategy

Figure 10.42 shows that releases are possible for both release codes **10** and **20**. First, place your cursor over release code **10** and click on **Set/reset release**. Repeat the same steps for release code **10**. If performed correctly, the **Release Options** will change to **Release already effected**, and the status will changed to **Released**.

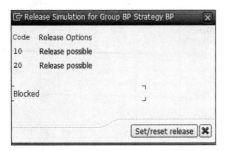

Figure 10.42 Release Simulation

6. As a last step, select **Workflow**, as shown in Figure 10.43. Choose **New Entries** to create records for involved users. Specify the release group, the appropriate release codes, and the user ID in the **Agent ID** column. The user IDs specified with agent type **US** indicates that the agent name is an SAP user ID. Create a line for each user involved in the release process and maintain an appropriate release code.

Grp	Code	Description	OT	Agent ID
BP	10	Buyer	US	JAKHTAR
BP	20	Manager	US	AMAQBOOL

Change View "Assignment of Role to Release Code: Ext. Purchasing Docs.

New Entries

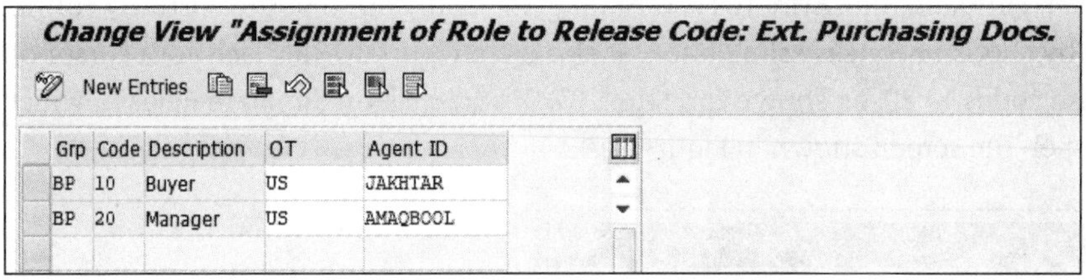

Figure 10.43 Configuring a Workflow

We've come to the end of release strategy configuration. Let's now create a purchase order to test for completeness and correctness in the configured release strategy. If a purchase order is not released, then buyers will not be able to print out the purchase order. Also, in goods receipts, the message "ME 390 – Purchasing document XXXXXXX not yet released" may arise.

Business Processes of Release Strategy: Individual Release

Create a purchase order using Transaction ME21N with document type NB and make the value of purchase order greater than 100 PKR to trigger the configured release strategy. Save the PO. In this example, the system has created PO number 4500000204.

To release the PO, access the screen shown in Figure 10.44 via Transaction ME29N. Notice the purchase order **Release Strategy** tab at the end of the PO header. The PO has all the details correctly configured and can now be released simply by clicking the release icon in the **Release options** column next to the release code.

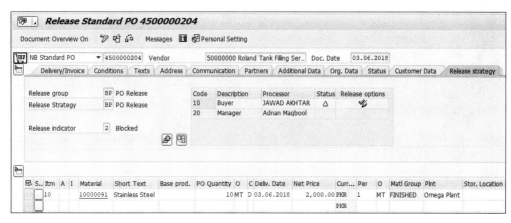

Figure 10.44 Purchase Order with Release Strategy

Collective Release

Access the screen shown in Figure 10.45 via Transaction ME28 for the release of individual POs. On the initial screen, enter the **Release Code** and any other relevant parameters so that the system only brings up relevant POs for release, which will open the screen shown in Figure 10.46.

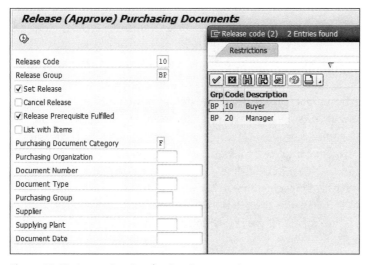

Figure 10.45 Approving Purchasing Documents

Figure 10.46 shows that PO 4500000204 with PO **Type NB** of **Net price 2,000 PKR** (which has a value greater than the 100 PKR required for a PO release strategy to work) can be released.

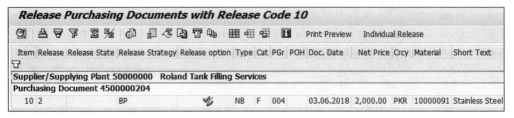

Figure 10.46 PO Release

Release Strategy for Purchase Requisition

Now that you know the end-to-end configuration, master data, and business processes for release strategy for POs, you can replicate these steps for purchase requisitions.

For practice, and as an example, set up a release strategy for a purchase requisition by maintaining the purchase requisition document type to be the newly configured on **ZNB** and maintaining a purchase requisition value at the item level to be greater than 100.00 PKR (or local currency).

Access the screen shown in Figure 10.47 via Transaction ME54N for an individual release of a purchase requisition. Notice the details at the item level of the purchase requisition. For a collective release of purchase requisitions, use Transaction ME55.

> **Note**
>
> Releasing each line item separately is called an *item-level release*. A purchase requisition may contain one or more line items. With item-level release, a particular line item can be released while other line items may be pending for approval or rejection.
>
> You cannot perform item-level release procedures using a release procedure with classification for external documents because external documents (such as POs, RFQs, scheduling agreements, quantity or value contracts) are always released or blocked as whole documents. However, for internal documents, you can configure line item level approval or complete document approval using a release procedure with classification. To configure item-level release for a purchase requisition, follow the menu path **Materials Management • Purchasing • Purchase Requisition • Define Document Types**. As shown earlier in Figure 10.6, select the **OverReqRel** checkbox to enable the overall release of a purchase requisition. If you want item-level approval, don't select this checkbox.

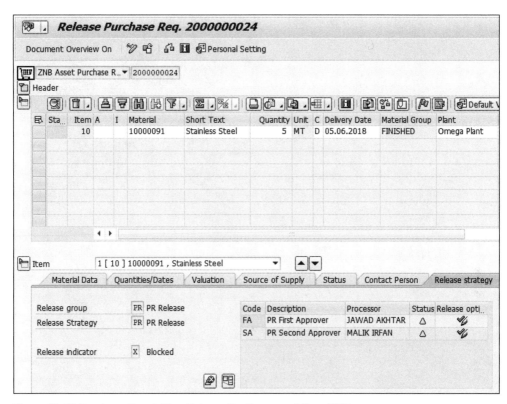

Figure 10.47 Purchase Requisition Release for Document Type ZNB

10.5   Summary

In this chapter, we examined the purchase requisition process. Most companies use a purchase requisition process to identify what material is needed and to allow the purchasing department to review and create the optimum POs for each vendor by taking into account the volume discounts and favorable terms offered by the vendor. Without purchase requisitions purchasing decisions would be made by end users and not by the purchasing department.

Chapter 11 follows up from the creation and processing of purchase requisitions to discuss the creation of RFQs. RFQs aren't universally used and may not be part of your company's purchasing policy. However, an RFQ can be an important purchasing tool, and you should understand how to create and process RFQs.

Chapter 11
Requests for Quotation

After the purchasing department has received and processed a purchase requisition, a line item may require the purchasing department to send out a request for quotation (RFQ) to certified vendors for that material needed at a particular plant.

In some cases, the purchasing department can't process purchase requisition items by simply selecting a vendor or issuing a purchase order (PO) to a single-source vendor. In cases where the company has never used the material before or when a new vendor is required due to vendor bankruptcy or decertification, the purchasing department issues a request for quotation (RFQ).

In this chapter, we'll begin by discussing the business processes involved in creating RFQs, including maintaining quotation validity and specific material delivery schedules. Next, we'll cover how RFQs must be released or approved using a release strategy. A *release strategy* is a set of rules maintained in the system that must conform to company's approval (release) process. Finally, we'll cover how to maintain quotations, perform a price comparison among quotations, and reject losing quotations.

11.1 Creating a Request for Quotation

An RFQ can be created using Transaction ME41, shown in Figure 11.1, or by following the navigation path **Logistics • Materials Management • Purchasing • RFQ/Quotation • Request for Quotation • Create**. In this section, we'll lead you through the important steps and fields necessary to create an RFQ.

> **Tips & Tricks**
> You can also create an RFQ with reference to a purchase requisition or an outline agreement (a quantity or value contract) or even copy an existing RFQ into a new one. These options are all available in the top menu of the screen shown in Figure 11.1.

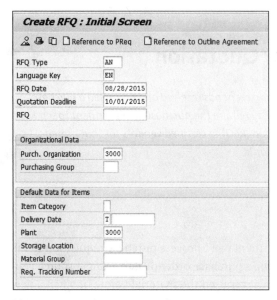

Figure 11.1 Initial Entry Screen for Transaction ME41: Create RFQ

11.1.1   Request for Quotation Type

The **RFQ Type** can be defined in the configuration and allows a company to distinguish between types of RFQs that it may send out. The predefined RFQ type is **AN**, which doesn't need any configuration changes if the company has simple RFQ needs. If you need to distinguish between several types of RFQs, you'll need to create more RFQ types in the IMG.

The configuration transaction can be found by following the navigation path **Materials Management • Purchasing • RFQ/Quotation • Define Document Types**.

Figure 11.2 shows the configuration for an RFQ document type. The two-character field defines the document type; you'll need to enter a description and number ranges for internal and external assignment.

The other field to note is the **GP bid** field, which is set if the RFQ is for a global percentage (GP) bid. The standard RFQ type for a GP bid is supplied with standard SAP, which is the document type **AB**.

A GP bid is used by purchasing to send suppliers a price that purchasing is willing to pay for a service, rather than having the supplier send in a bid. In this case, the supplier will send back a percentage, either positive or negative, to indicate the level below or above the bid amount sent by the purchasing department that it can accept. Although uncommon, this method is less complicated than the normal RFQ procedure.

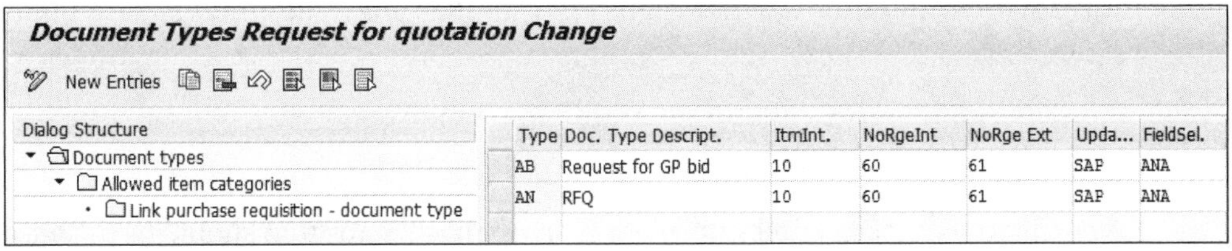

Figure 11.2 Configuration for RFQ Document Types

Tips & Tricks

In this configuration step, shown in Figure 11.2, you can also map and connect an RFQ document type with purchase requisition types. As a result, only purchase requisitions of specified document types are correctly converted into RFQs of the specified document type. Select the RFQ document type (such as **AN**) and then double-click on **Link Purchase requisition – document type** on the left-hand side. Then, you can add or remove specific document types of purchase requisitions allowed for the RFQ document type AN.

11.1.2   Request for Quotation Date

The **RFQ Date** field, shown earlier in Figure 11.1, defaults to the date of entry but can be overwritten with an appropriate date.

11.1.3   Quotation Deadline

The date entered in the **Quotation Deadline** field is the date by which the suppliers must reply to the RFQ with a quotation. This field is mandatory and should be clearly identified to suppliers on the RFQ print or fax document.

11.1.4   Request for Quotation Document Number

The RFQ document number, in the **RFQ** field shown earlier in Figure 11.1, is determined either externally or internally assigned. This configuration setting was defined in the configuration shown earlier in Figure 11.2. The field should be maintained if the number assignment is external.

11.1.5   Organizational Data

The **Purch. Organization** and **Purchasing Group** should be maintained for the RFQ. The **Purch. Organization** is a four-character field, and the **Purchasing Group** is a three-character field.

11.1.6   Default Data for Items

A purchasing user can enter information pertinent to items that should be included in the RFQ. The fields that can be defaulted include **Item Category**, **Delivery Date**, **Plant**, **Storage Location**, **Material Group**, and **Req. Tracking Number**:

- **Item category**
  The following categories can be entered in the **Item Category** field:
  - **L**: Subcontracting
  - **S**: Third party
  - **D**: Service
  - (blank): Standard item category

- **Delivery date**
  This date is the **Delivery Date** for the item to be delivered or the service to be performed by the supplier.

- **Plant/storage location**
  These are the company's locations where the item should be delivered or the service should be performed. These locations are the default plant and storage locations for deliveries.

- **Material group**
  The **Material Group** can be used in lieu of a material number or service (if these aren't known). The material group is assigned to each material when it's created. This configured field groups together materials of similar characteristics. For example, if material group 017789 represents HD DVD players, then this material group can be entered in the RFQ if the actual material isn't known at the time, but the RFQ is for an HD DVD player.

- **Requirement tracking number**
  The requirement tracking number (RTN) can be traced back to the original requisition if the RTN was entered at that level. The person entering the RFQ can use the **Req. Tracking Number** field to uniquely identify specific POs.

  For example, if purchasing agents are entering a number of POs for a project, they may want to enter a unique RTN so that the POs can be located together instead of having to know each individual PO number.

The header details for an RFQ are shown in Figure 11.3, which we'll describe in detail next. The data entered at the top of the initial screen are defaulted, and further information can be added in the **Administrative Fields** section.

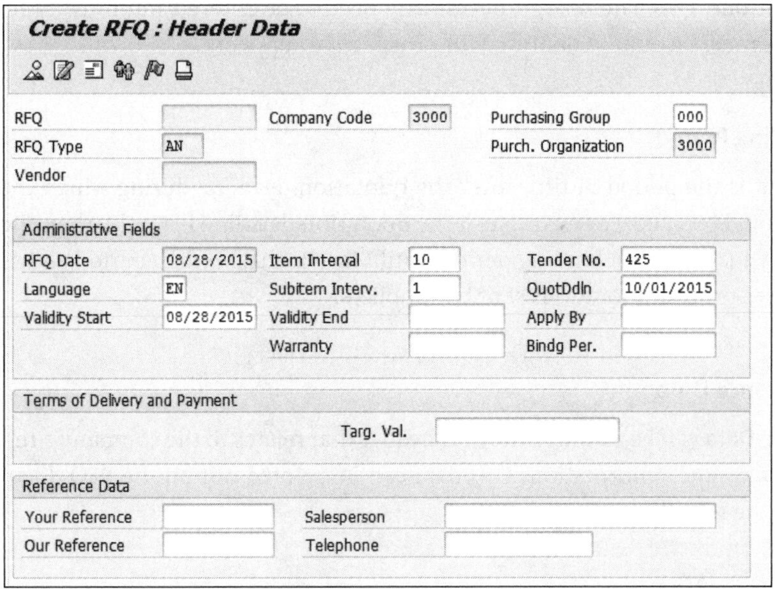

Figure 11.3 RFQ Header Details Screen

11.1.7   Collective Number

Companies that send out RFQs for a collective bid can use a collective number (**Coll. no.**). For example, when creating a new product, you may need dozens of new materials as well as new services. To collectively identify the many RFQs involved, you can use a collective number to ensure that individual RFQs are tied to a single project. The collective number can be used to search purposes, and finding RFQs with a collective number is easier than finding them individually. Transaction ME4S allows you to display RFQs by collective number.

11.1.8   Validity Start/Validity End

The **Validity Start/Validity End** fields are defined as the dates during which the material or services should be delivered or performed.

11.1.9   Apply By

The **Apply By** date field is different from the quotation deadline date. The application date is the date by which the suppliers need to inform the company that they will submit quotations. This date doesn't necessarily need to be entered, but if required, then this date must be clearly identified for prospective suppliers.

11.1.10   Binding Period

The **Bindg Per.** is the period of time after the quotation deadline during which the quotation should be valid. For example, if the quotation deadline is April 1, then the company may insist upon a binding period until May 31. This binding period allows the company to process quotations sent by suppliers.

11.1.11   Reference Data

The **Reference Data** can be added to the RFQ header that relates to the company's reference and its contact information. This data can be printed out on the RFQ document sent to the supplier.

11.1.12   Request for Quotation Item Detail

The line item details include the **Item** category, the **Material** number, a description (**Short text**), the **RFQ Quantity**, the **Deliv. date**, and the material group (**Mat Grp**).

Figure 11.4 shows the item detail, which allows purchasing users to add the materials or services that require the creation of RFQs. For this example, **material 3003** was entered with **RFQ quantity** of **1,000** each.

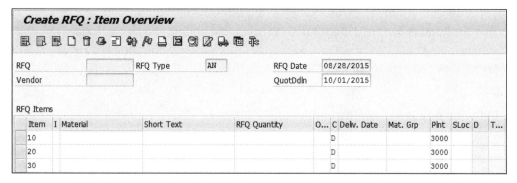

Figure 11.4 RFQ Item Detail Screen

11.1.13   Request for Quotation Delivery Schedule

After the item detail information has been added, additional information can be entered if relevant. For example, if an RFQ requires that the supplier deliver the material to the plant in a certain sequence on certain dates, this requirement can be entered in the **Create RFQ: Delivery Schedule** screen, shown in Figure 11.5. To access the **Create RFQ: Delivery Schedule** screen, select **Item • Delivery Schedule** or press [Shift] + [F5].

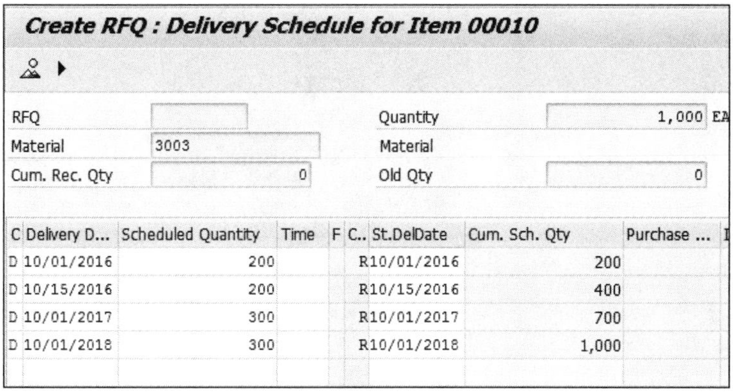

| | | *Create RFQ : Delivery Schedule for Item 00010* | | | | | | |

RFQ				Quantity			1,000 EA	
Material	3003			Material				
Cum. Rec. Qty		0		Old Qty			0	

C	Delivery D...	Scheduled Quantity	Time	F	C..	St.DelDate	Cum. Sch. Qty	Purchase ...	I
D	10/01/2016	200			R	10/01/2016	200		
D	10/15/2016	200			R	10/15/2016	400		
D	10/01/2017	300			R	10/01/2017	700		
D	10/01/2018	300			R	10/01/2018	1,000		

Figure 11.5 Delivery Schedule Screen for the RFQ Item

In the **Create RFQ: Delivery Schedule** screen, a purchasing user can enter the date, time, and the amount required on that date. Any number of delivery schedule lines can be entered for the amount of material specified in the line item.

11.1.14   Additional Data

To enter any further data for the line item, a purchasing user can access the additional data screen by selecting **Item • More Functions • Additional Data** or by pressing [Ctrl] + [F1].

Figure 11.6 shows the data that can be added, including the planned delivery time and the reason for the order. The **Reason for Ord.** field is configurable and can be used by the purchasing department for statistical data collection. You can define the field in configuration by following the navigation path **Materials Management • Purchasing • Purchase Order • Define Reasons for Ordering**.

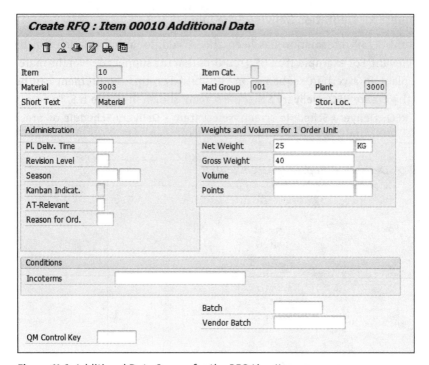

Figure 11.6 Additional Data Screen for the RFQ Line Item

Figure 11.7 shows ordering reason codes that have already been configured. The reason code (**OrRsn**) is a three-character field, and a short **Description** can be added as appropriate for the company.

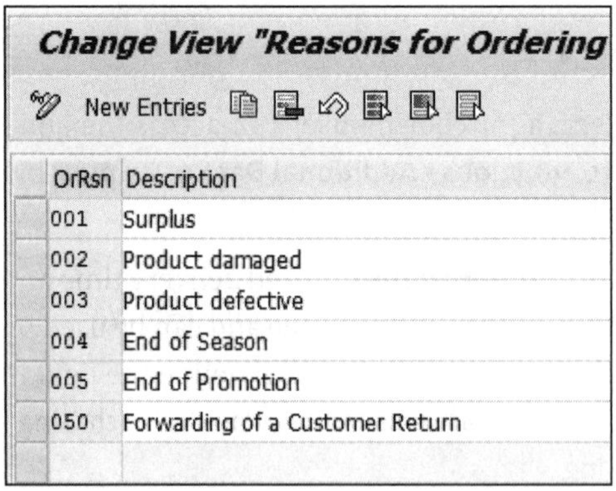

Change View "Reasons for Ordering

✎ New Entries 🗋 🗐 ⬀ 🗒 🗒 🗒

OrRsn	Description
001	Surplus
002	Product damaged
003	Product defective
004	End of Season
005	End of Promotion
050	Forwarding of a Customer Return

Figure 11.7 Reason for Order Field Configuration

11.1.15 Vendor Selection

After the material details have been entered with any additional data, an RFQ requires that a vendor (or vendors) be selected to receive the RFQ. The vendor can be selected by using the menu selection **Header • Vendor Address** or by pressing ⌊F7⌋.

The **Create RFQ: Vendor Address** screen, shown in Figure 11.8, allows a purchasing user to select a vendor for the RFQ. After the vendor is entered, save the RFQ. The screen is refreshed, and the RFQ number appears on the status line at the bottom of the screen.

The screen shown in Figure 11.8 allows another vendor to be entered. If the RFQ should be sent out to more than one vendor, more vendor numbers can be entered, and saving after each addition creates a number of RFQ documents for the same item details.

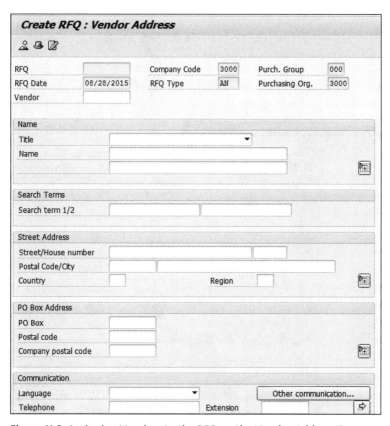

Figure 11.8 Assigning Vendors to the RFQ on the Vendor Address Screen

Now that we've examined how to create an RFQ, let's look at the process to change an RFQ after it's been created.

11.2   Changing a Request for Quotation

RFQs can be changed using Transaction ME42 or by following the navigation path **Logistics • Materials Management • Purchasing • RFQ/Quotation • Request for Quotation • Change**.

If a purchasing user doesn't know the RFQ number to be changed, then a matchcode can be selected. Figure 11.9 shows the valid matchcodes that can be used to find the RFQ. Note that, in Figure 11.9, two matchcodes can be used if the relevant data was added to the RFQ:

- **Purchasing Documents per Requirement Tracking Number**
- **Purchasing Documents per Collective Number**

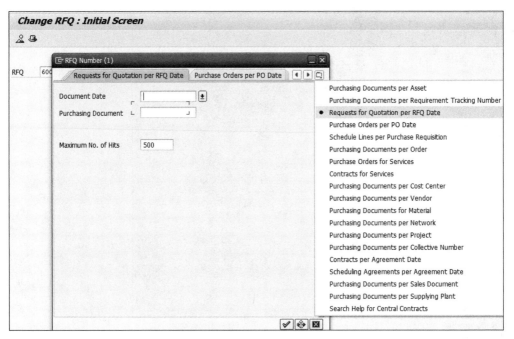

Figure 11.9 Initial RFQ Change Screen with Valid Matchcodes Available to Find an RFQ

After the correct RFQ number has been entered or selected via a matchcode, the RFQ line item detail is displayed, and certain fields become available for editing.

A number of fields can be edited, including the RFQ material quantity (**RFQ Qty**), the quotation deadline (**QuotDdln**), and the required delivery date (**Deliv. date**). Note that, if the RFQ has already been sent to the vendor, any changes to these dates must be communicated to the vendor associated with the RFQ. Figure 11.10 shows the options for the line item. If a line item has been entered incorrectly, or if the RFQ is no longer needed, the line item can be deleted in Transaction ME42. To delete the line item, first select the line item and then set the delete indicator by choosing **Edit •**
Delete or by pressing ⎡Shift⎤ + ⎡F2⎤. The deletion indicator can be removed by choosing **Edit • Reset Deletion Ind**. from the menu bar.

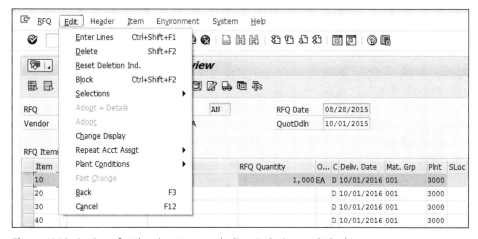

Figure 11.10 Options for the Line Item, Including Deletion and Blocking

If a line item doesn't need to be deleted, but the status of the RFQ is in doubt, the line item can be blocked using Transaction ME42 as well. To block a line item, select it and then set the blocking indicator by choosing **Edit • Block** or by pressing ⎡Ctrl⎤ +
⎡Shift⎤ + ⎡F2⎤. The blocking indicator can be removed by choosing **Edit • Reset Deletion Ind**.

In this section, we described how to change RFQs. The next section discusses the methods by which an RFQ can be released.

11.3   Releasing a Request for Quotation

After the RFQ has been completed, the document can be subject to release. The release procedure is more often associated with purchase requisitions or POs but can be relevant for RFQs, depending on your needs.

The release procedure for RFQs only allows an RFQ to be released at the header level and not at the line item level. Therefore, the RFQ as a whole is released or not released.

Figure 11.11 shows the screen in Transaction ME45 where a purchasing user will enter information to release RFQs. You can also use the same transaction (Transaction ME45) to release all types of purchasing documents, such as purchase requisitions, POs, and quantity or value contracts by choosing the relevant scope of the list.

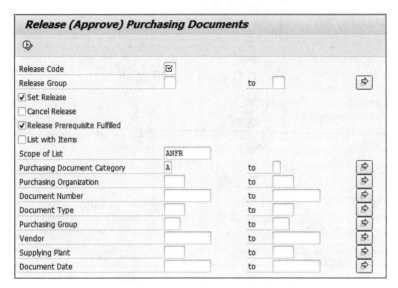

Figure 11.11 Release Request for Quotations in Transaction ME45

The important fields and indicators on this screen are as follows:

- **Release code/release group/release strategy**
  The **Release Code** is the code that has been configured for a position in the company, such as manager, supervisor, and so on. A release code is associated with a release group. The **Release Group** contains a number of release strategies that are defined in configuration. The release strategy is configured using classification characteristics. A characteristic can be defined to allow ranges of values for the RFQ. Below a certain value, the RFQ won't be subject to the release strategy; above a certain amount, it will be. The release can be made using Transaction ME45.

- **Set release/cancel release**
  These indicators can be set to allow a purchasing user to release the relevant RFQs or to cancel their release.

- **Release prerequisite fulfilled**

  This indicator, when set, allows a purchasing user to view only those RFQs ready to be released. If the indicator isn't set, all RFQs are released, even if they haven't fulfilled all prerequisites.

- **List with items**

  If this indicator is set, then the RFQs will be shown with all line item information shown. If the indicator isn't set, then only the header information for the RFQ is shown.

- **Scope of list**

  The **Scope of List** field is a variable that shows different information based on the selected value. The default value for Transaction ME45 is **ANFR**, which in this case represents RFQs with collective numbers. Pressing ⌷F4⌷ causes a scope of list selection to appear, from which a different choice can be made.

- **Purchasing document category**

  The **Purchasing Document Category** for RFQs is a single character, for example, **A** for RFQs. Other document categories are **F** for POs, **K** for contracts, and **L** for scheduling agreements.

- **Other selection criteria**

  A number of other selection criteria fields can further narrow down the search for RFQs to be released in Transaction ME45. These criteria include **Purchasing Organization, Purchasing Group, Vendor, Document Number,** and **Document Date**.

After an RFQ has been released for sending to a number of vendors, the RFQ still must be issued to those vendors. The next section describes the mechanisms for issuing the RFQ.

11.4   Issuing a Request for Quotation to a Vendor

After an RFQ has been entered into the system, the purchasing department must decide to fax or otherwise send a copy to the particular vendor. An RFQ document can be printed using Transaction ME9A or by following the navigation path **Logistics • Materials Management • Purchasing • RFQ/Quotation • Request for Quotation • Messages • Print/Transmit**.

Figure 11.12 shows that RFQs can be selected by a number of criteria. If the **Document Number** isn't known, the document can be found by entering the **Vendor, Purchasing**

Organization, **Purchasing Group**, or **Document Date**, which is the date the RFQ was created.

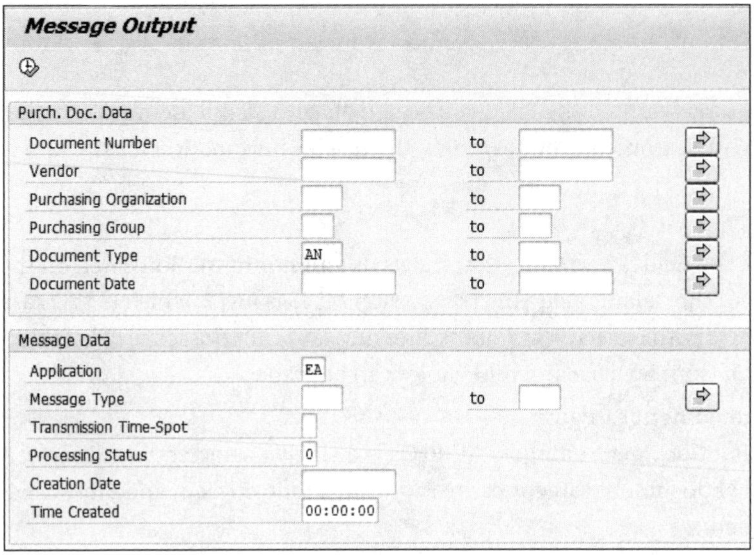

Figure 11.12 Message Output Screen for Printing or Transmitting the RFQ

After selection criteria have been entered and Transaction ME9A is executed, the results for the selection criteria are shown if any RFQs are found.

From the results, shown in Figure 11.13, the appropriate RFQ can be selected and then printed or transmitted. The resulting RFQ printout can be modified to reflect your company's requirements by using ABAP, SAPscript, or a tool such as Adobe Form Designer.

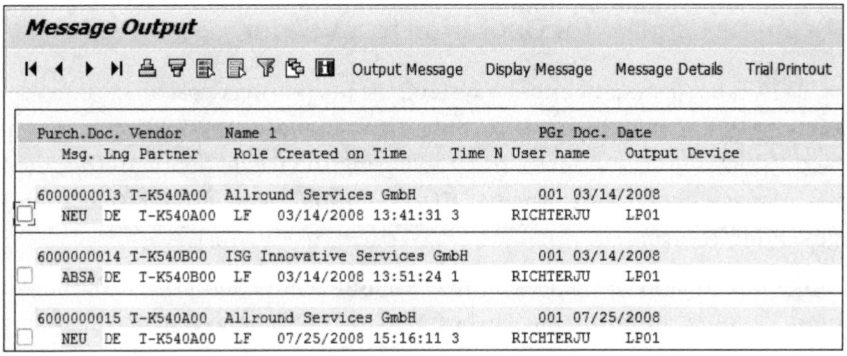

Figure 11.13 Result for the Selection Criteria of Transaction ME9A

After the purchasing department has received responses from the selected vendors that received then RFQ, the quotations can be entered into the system, comparisons made, and the most appropriate vendor bid accepted. In the next sections, we'll cover these quotation-related tasks.

11.5   Maintaining Quotations

A quotation that has been returned by the vendor should be entered into the SAP system in a timely manner due to the deadline set within each RFQ. The quotation can be entered into the system by using Transaction ME47 or by following the navigation path **Logistics • Materials Management • Purchasing • RFQ/Quotation • Quotation • Maintain**. The initial screen of Transaction ME47 requires a purchasing user to enter a single RFQ number.

The vendor's bid includes details for the line items that need to be entered into the screen. As shown in Figure 11.14, a vendor has entered a bid for 125,000 USD per item on the RFQ. For each vendor quotation submitted, the appropriate RFQ is updated with the quotation.

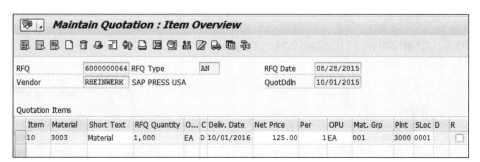

Figure 11.14 Line Item Screen for the Quotation Maintenance

The price quotation can be entered as a single figure in the **Net Price** field. If discounts, taxes, or other conditions are offered, these conditions can be added into the system using the **Conditions** screen.

Figure 11.15 shows that an entry was made for a quotation of **125,000 USD** per item. In the condition record, a further entry has been made using the condition for a discount (**RA00**) of 4%. A further entry has been made for the freight (**FRB1**) to be charged by the vendor for the items to be delivered, which in this case is 4,000 USD. On this **Change Quotation: Item – Conditions** screen, any tax details that may be relevant for the purchase or further discounts and freight costs can be added. The actual price on this quotation is then determined to be 120,000 USD.

Change Quotation: Item - Conditions

Item	10			Material	3003								
View	1 Pricing Elements: Table			Quantity		1,000 EA	Net		120,000.00 USD				

Pricing Elements

N..	CnTy	Name	Amount	Crcy	per	U...	Condition value	Curr.	Status	Num...	OUn	CCon...	Un	Stat	Condition value	CdCur
☑	PBXX	Gross Price	125.00	USD		1 EA	125,000.00	USD			1 EA		1 EA	☐	0.00	
☑	RA00	Discount % on Net	4.000-	%			5,000.00-	USD			0		0	☐	0.00	
		Net incl. disc.	120.00	USD		1 EA	120,000.00	USD			1 EA		1 EA	☐	0.00	
		Net incl. tax	120.00	USD		1 EA	120,000.00	USD			1 EA		1 EA	☐	0.00	
☑	FRB1	Freight (Value)	4,000.00	USD			4,000.00	USD			0		0	☑	0.00	
☑	SKTO	Cash Discount	0.000	%			0.00	USD			0		0	☑	0.00	
		Actual Price	124.00	USD		1 EA	124,000.00	USD			1 EA		1 EA	☐	0.00	
														☐		

Figure 11.15 Quotation Price Entered into the Conditions Screen

After the quotation has been entered, quotations must be compared to select the vendor who will be offered the purchase order (PO). This next section examines how quotations are compared.

11.6   Comparing Quotations

After the quotations have been entered for the RFQs sent to vendors, then the purchasing department reviews them and decides on the vendor for the material or service that won the bid.

One element of the quotation process is reviewing the bids on a price comparison basis. This comparison is the most basic analysis and may not necessarily be the deciding factor. Each purchasing department will have to develop a procedure for selecting vendors based on RFQs/quotation responses.

11.6.1   Price Comparison Factor in Quotations

Price comparisons can be performed using Transaction ME49 or by following the navigation path **Logistics • Materials Management • Purchasing • RFQ/Quotation • Quotation • Price Comparison**.

Price comparison can be performed between several quotations, as shown in Figure 11.16, and these quotations can be selected using a number of selection criteria, such as **Purchasing Organization**, **Vendor**, **Material**, or **Collective RFQ** number. The collective number is the most useful field when sending a number of RFQs to different vendors and can be used to easily make comparisons. The other criteria in Transaction ME49 include the following comparison value criteria:

- **Reference Quotation**
  This criteria is the quotation against which all others are compared. If no **Reference Quotation** is entered, then the quotations are compared against each other.

- **Mean Value Quotation**
  If this indicator is set, then the comparisons are made against the average price of the quotations. All the quotations are averaged, and the average quote is ranked at 100%. The quotes then reflect a percentage that shows whether it's above or below the average. Thus, a lower-than-average quote will show a percentage below 100%; a higher-than-average quote will show a percentage of greater than 100%.

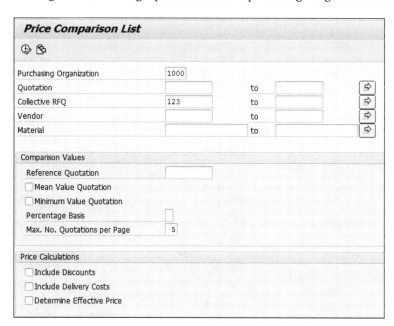

Figure 11.16 Price Comparison Selection Screen for Transaction ME49

- **Minimum Value Quotation**
  If this indicator is set, then the comparisons are made against the lowest price quotation. As a result, the first rank, or the best price quote, is a 100% rank. All other more expensive quotes will show a percentage that is calculated from the lowest bid, that is, 124%, 136%, and so on.

- **Percentage Basis**

  The **Percentage Basis** allows a purchasing user to specify which value will be used as the 100% basis. The user can choose the mean price, the maximum price, or the minimum price, which alters how the rank percentage is shown in the quotations.

In addition to the value comparison criteria, the following price comparison criteria indicators can be set:

- **Include Discounts**

  If this indicator is set, the quotation comparison will include any price discounts that the vendor has applied. If the indicator isn't set, then the discounts won't be used in the comparison.

- **Include Delivery Costs**

  If the indicator is set, then the delivery costs will be included in the price on the quotation and therefore used in the quotation comparison. Delivery costs can include the freight costs, duties levied, or other procurement costs such as packing, insurance, and handling.

- **Determine Effective Price**

  This indicator is set if cash discounts and delivery costs should be included in the price comparison.

After the selection criteria have been entered, you'll obtain the price comparison.

Figure 11.17 shows a price comparison for collective RFQ number 6, featuring the quotations from four vendors, or bidders, for a quantity (**Qty**) of **Material 110873**. The price comparison has been used with the **Mean Value Quotation** indicator set. In other words, the average price has been set as 100%, and bids will be a lower percentage or a higher percentage. Notice that one vendor (**1005**) did not submit the quotation **6000000060**, and thus, all its details are empty.

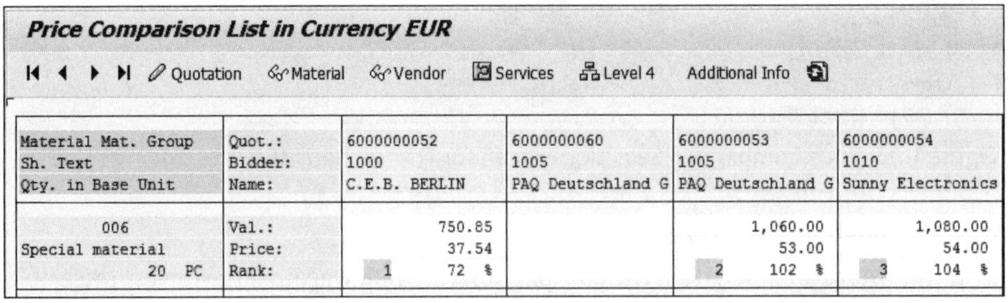

Price Comparison List in Currency EUR

|◀◀ ◀ ▶ ▶▶   ✎ Quotation   ⟲ Material   ⟲ Vendor   ☒ Services   ⬚ Level 4   Additional Info ⬚|

Material Mat. Group	Quot.:	6000000052	6000000060	6000000053	6000000054
Sh. Text	Bidder:	1000	1005	1005	1010
Qty. in Base Unit	Name:	C.E.B. BERLIN	PAQ Deutschland G	PAQ Deutschland G	Sunny Electronics
006	Val.:	750.85		1,060.00	1,080.00
Special material	Price:	37.54		53.00	54.00
20 PC	Rank:	1 72 %		2 102 %	3 104 %

Figure 11.17 Price Comparison among Four Quotations

11.6.2   Other Qualitative Factors in Quotations

The price comparison report provides a clear indication to the purchasing department about which bidder is offering the company the best price for a material. However, the best price may only be one of several factors that the purchasing department wants to take into account. Many purchasing organizations believe that choosing vendors based only on the lowest bid dollar amount results in purchasing lower-quality goods. Successful bids are more often awarded on a comparative evaluation of price, quality, performance capability, and other qualitative factors that will prove the most advantageous to your company.

Other qualitative factors that may be identified by a purchasing department include the following:

- **Previous relationship with client**
  If the bidder has a successful relationship with the company, this relationship history may be taken into account in any final decision on the winner of the bid.

- **Compliance with the Equal Employment Opportunity Act (US)**
  Many companies insist that vendors must be in compliance with the Equal Employment Opportunity Act (EEOA). For example, the EEOA can be violated if a company discriminates by a number of factors, including age, disability, national origin, race, or religion.

- **Strategic alliances**
  A company may have a number of strategic alliances with vendors or trading partners, which may influence the decision to award a bid. For example, a company may have put an RFQ out to vendors for a new UNIX server, and the lowest bidder by price was HP. However, if the company had a strategic relationship with IBM, the bid may be placed with IBM despite the lower bid from HP.

- **Minority-owned and women-owned businesses (US)**
  Some companies may prefer minority-owned or women-owned businesses for certain contracts or POs. If the RFQ falls into an area where the company has indicated a preference for this type of vendor, then this factor may have more weight in the award decision than the price.

- **Warranty and return policies**
  The warranty period of an item or the return policy offered by the bidder can be quite important to the purchaser. For example, if the RFQ is for PCs, the purchaser may be more inclined to accept a bidder with a higher price per unit if the warranty is for two years, than to select a bidder offering only a six-month warranty. The

11

same is true for return policies. The easier the return procedure, the more attractive a bid from a supplier becomes.

- **Creative pricing**
  Often, a bidder may not offer the best price in response to an RFQ but may offer a creative pricing schedule. Purchasing departments are often looking for ways to reduce cost outlays and often welcome vendors who can offer the company ways of purchasing material with delayed payments or payments on performance.

- **Technical evaluation**
  While a vendor may submit a quotation with competitive price, the offered product must still meet the technical criteria and specifications laid out by the purchaser.

In the next section, we'll look at the process of rejecting quotations that haven't been selected and communicating with these vendors.

11.7   Rejecting Quotations

After the purchasing department has compared quotations from bidders, as described in the previous section, the vendors whose quotations were rejected must be informed. In the system, these quotations also need to be flagged as rejected, so that a purchasing user doesn't accidentally convert a rejected quotation into a PO.

11.7.1   Flagging the Quotation as Rejected

Unsuccessful quotations can be flagged as rejected in the system using Transaction ME47 or by following the navigation path **Logistics • Materials Management • Purchasing • RFQ/Quotation • Quotation • Maintain**.

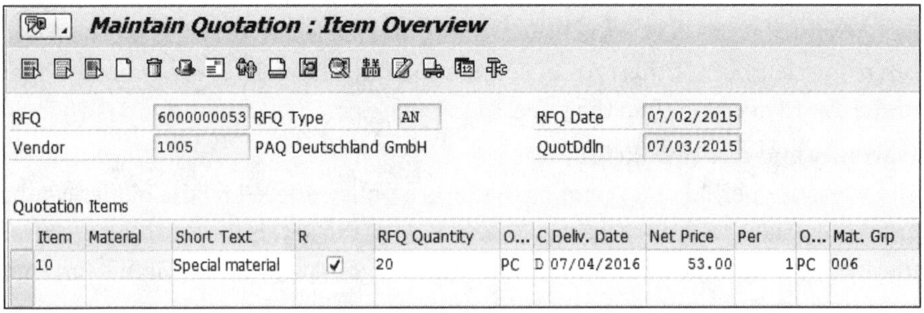

Item	Material	Short Text	R	RFQ Quantity	O...	C	Delv. Date	Net Price	Per	O...	Mat. Grp
10		Special material	✓	20	PC	D	07/04/2016	53.00	1 PC		006

Figure 11.18 Quotation Flagged as Rejected

In this process, a purchasing user enters the **RFQ** number for the quotation to be rejected, as shown in Figure 11.18. The line item should be flagged by selecting the checkbox in the rejected column (**R**) to reflect that the quotation has been rejected.

11.7.2 Printing the Quotation Rejection

If appropriate, all unsuccessful vendors in the RFQ process will be notified by the client representative, often the purchasing department, in writing. Notifications should be made as quickly as possible following the award of the contract, or when it has been determined that the vendor won't be asked to continue in the RFQ process.

A rejection letter can be printed out from the system using Transaction ME9A or by following the navigation path **Logistics • Materials Management • Purchasing • RFQ/ Quotation • Request for Quotation • Messages • Print/Transmit**.

For each rejected quotation, a rejection notice can be printed based on the **RFQ** number, as shown in Figure 11.19. The purchasing user enters the correct **Message Type** rejection quotation, which in our case is **ABSA**. The company can modify the standard rejection notice with SAPscript or with tools such as Adobe Form Designer.

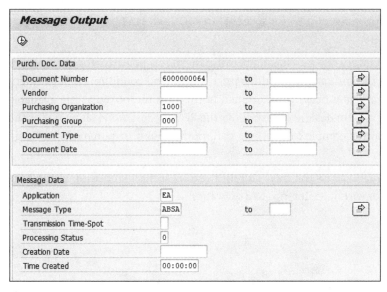

Figure 11.19 Printing Rejection Notes Using a Message Type

11.7.3   Advising Unsuccessful Bidders

Sometimes, a rejection notice isn't the most appropriate manner to reject a vendor's quotation submission. If the RFQ is for a particular project or of large monetary value, the company may decide that all unsuccessful vendors should be given, or may request, a debriefing session with respect to their submissions. These sessions should concentrate on the strengths and weaknesses of the individual vendor's response.

How quotations are rejected should be part of your company's overall purchasing policy. Check with individual purchasing departments for the correct method to use.

11.8   Summary

In this chapter, we described the receiving and processing of quotations from vendors in response to an RFQ. A quotation allows the purchasing department to review the price and terms offered by each vendor and to make the best decision for the company based on the replies given by vendors. The acceptance of a quotation and the issuing of a PO will reflect that a specific vendor has the right to supply the material to the customer for a period of time. Purchasing departments periodically seek quotations from other vendors to ensure that the material can't be procured at a better price elsewhere.

RFQs are important for the purchasing because they are a powerful tool with which the department can influence a vendor's price, terms, and conditions in a competitive bid situation. The process we examined in this chapter looked at the available tools in the SAP system designed to simplify the RFQ process while allowing for the flexibility crucial for complex situations commonly found in purchases for large projects.

In Chapter 12, we'll discuss the next step in the RFQ scenario: creating a purchase order (PO) with or without reference to a quotation.

Chapter 12
Purchase Orders

A purchase order (PO) is a document that shows the buyer's intention to buy a certain quantity of a product at a certain price from a specific supplier. By accepting a PO, a supplier agrees to supply the quantity of a product to the buyer on or before the required delivery date.

A *purchase order* (PO) is an external document issued by a purchasing department to send to a supplier. The PO contains the required products, the quantities of the products needed, and the price agreed to by the client and the supplier. In addition to the products, quantity, and price, the PO usually contains the PO number, order date, delivery address, and terms.

POs are used to communicate requests to suppliers and to give suppliers a written confirmation of requests. Depending on the legal jurisdiction involved, a PO can be considered a legally binding document.

In some cases, a PO doesn't specify the specific item number but rather gives a detailed description of the item. This scenario occurs if a material number doesn't exist or isn't known.

In this chapter, we'll begin by covering how to create and maintain a purchase order when the supplier is known. The chapter moves on to cover more functions of a PO, such as blocking or cancelling. Then we'll cover creating a PO from a reference purchasing document, how to automatically create a PO, and tracking the progress of POs. Next, we'll cover outline agreements, such as scheduling agreements or quantity and value contracts. The chapter then moves on to cover supplier confirmation followed by a step-by-step approach to messages and output. The chapter ends with final more topics: pricing procedure, supplier evaluation, and serial numbers in purchasing.

Release Procedures, Messages and Output, Document Types Configuration

We covered configuring document types step-by-step in Chapter 10. The same steps apply when configuring new purchasing document types for purchase orders, scheduling agreements, or quantity or value contracts. Therefore, we won't cover these topics in detail in this chapter.

Similarly, Chapter 10 also covered how to set up a release procedure for a PO in detail. The same steps and logic apply when setting up release procedures for purchase requisitions, requests for quotation (RFQs), scheduling agreements, quantity or value contracts, or service entry sheets for services procurement. Therefore, we won't cover these topics in detail this chapter.

Finally, since we'll cover messages and output in this chapter, the same steps and procedures will apply when setting up messages and output for RFQs, scheduling agreements, or quantity or value contracts.

12.1   Creating and Maintaining a Purchase Order

A PO can be created without any other specific purchase-related documents being created. A PO can be created from a purchase requisition. Depending on the complexity of purchasing activities, you may not want to implement purchase requisitions and may instead allow POs to be created directly. Once created, a purchase order can also be maintained.

12.1.1   Purchase Order Creation

To create a PO without reference to a purchase requisition but with a known supplier, use Transaction ME21N, as shown in Figure 12.1, or follow the menu path **Logistics • Materials Management • Purchasing • Purchase Order • Create • Vendor Known**.

As with most purchasing documents, this screen has three parts: **Header**, **Item Overview**, and **Item Detail**.

On this screen, select the PO document type **NB Standard PO** (or any other relevant PO document type) then enter the **Vendor**, which in our example is "50000000." All details maintained in the supplier master, such as the payment terms or currency will automatically be copied to the PO. Enter "10000091" for the **Material** and maintain the **PO Quantity** and **Plant** fields for which the material is being procured.

In the **Delivery/Invoice** tab, the already maintained **Exchange Rate** between the local currency and the currency of the PO (which in this case is **USD**) is automatically copied in the PO. Selecting the **Fixed Exch. Rate** checkbox will prevent any change from being made at the time of invoice verification (Transaction MIRO). This option is helpful in import purchases when the exchange rate with the bank is booked or locked in advance (known as *forward booking*).

The middle part of screen is the **Item Overview**, which contains purchase information record 5300000359 (**Info. rec.**). An info record has a one-to-one relationship between a supplier and a material in the SAP system (see Chapter 7 for more information on info records).

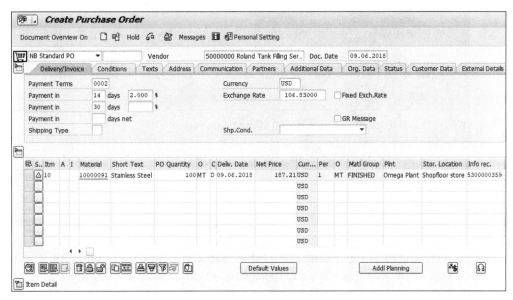

Figure 12.1 Initial Screen of a Purchase Order

> **Tips & Tricks**
>
> To minimize data entry, especially where entries are repeated, maintain the relevant values by clicking the **Personal Settings** and the **Default Values** buttons.

Let's explore some of the header tabs found in a PO.

Figure 12.2 shows the **Conditions** tab for conditions at the header level (applicable to the entire PO). All discounts or surcharges maintained at the header level will be automatically and proportionately divided to the line item level of the PO. For example, the **Insurance charges** of **200.00 USD** will automatically be divided at the item level to all the items maintained in the PO.

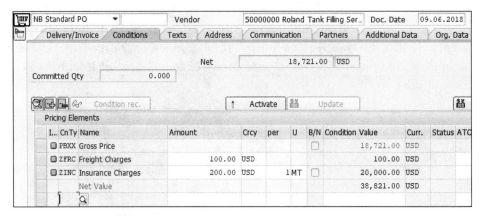

Figure 12.2 The Conditions Tab of a PO at the Header Level

Some other tabs at the header level are:

- **Texts**
  Several options are available to maintain texts for specific purposes such as text for header, deadlines, terms of delivery, warranties, penalties for breach of contract, and guarantees. The texts maintained in this tab are not only helpful for recording more details about the PO but can also be fetched by an ABAP consultant when designing company-specific layouts for POs.

- **Address**
  Address details are fetched directly from the supplier master but can be changed or more details added if necessary.

- **Communication**
  Under this tab, the purchaser can maintain the company's internal reference as well as the supplier reference, which makes searching for POs easier.

- **Partners**
  The default supplier function entails that the supplier itself is the goods supplier as well as the invoicing party. However, if these parties differ, that is, one partner functions as the supplier, another as the invoicing party, then these details can be maintained in this tab.

- **Additional Data**

  Under this tab, the single field, **Collective No.** is often used as an external reference to track and trace POs in various standard SAP reports. For example, when an SAP S/4HANA project goes live, a purchasing user can use this field to maintain a reference to the open legacy POs that need to be entered in the SAP system.

- **Organization Data**

  This tab contains details about the purchasing organization, purchasing group, and company code. As already covered, the values in these fields can be configured with default values to reduce data entry.

- **Release Strategy**

  If the release (approval) strategy is set at the PO level, then these details are available in this tab.

Note

We covered how to configure release strategies for POs in Chapter 10.

Figure 12.3 shows the **Status** tab of a PO and provides the latest status such as the quantity delivered, invoiced, or still to be delivered and indicates whether the PO has been printed out or not.

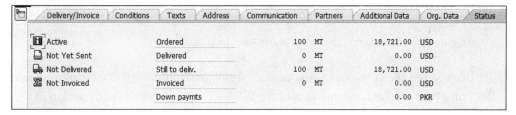

Figure 12.3 The Status Tab of a PO at the Header Level

Let's now focus on the tabs available at the item level.

Figure 12.4 shows the **Delivery** tab of the item detail for the material **10000091**. If specific details aren't maintained in the material master or in the purchasing information record, details like over- or underdelivery tolerances of the delivery material, the shipping instructions, or the planned delivery time, then these details can be maintained at the PO level. To remind supplier to send the material on time, the reminder/expeditor functionality can be used. A negative number (for example, –3 days) will enable the system to send a reminder to supplier three days *before* the expected delivery of the material. Up to three levels of reminders can be set in the procurement process.

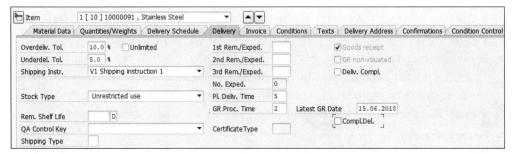

Figure 12.4 The Delivery Tab of a PO at the Item Detail Level

Figure 12.5 shows the **Invoice** tab where how a specific item needs to be invoiced and the applicable **Tax code** are maintained.

Figure 12.5 The Invoice Tab of a PO at the Item Detail Level

Figure 12.6 shows the **Confirmations** tab, which controls how the SAP system should monitor supplier confirmations of the PO. We'll cover supplier confirmation in Section 12.7.

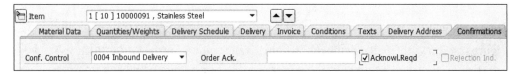

Figure 12.6 The Confirmations Tab of a PO at the Item Detail Level

Briefly, some other tabs at the item level are as follows:

- **Master data**
  Much of the information in this tab is copied from purchasing info records, but

you can maintain additional details such as a **Supplier Batch** (if already known) or even create your company's own internal batch number.

- **Quantities/Weights**

  Much of the information in this tab is copied from the material master, but you can maintain additional details provided by the supplier. In this tab, the system also converts the base unit of measure (UoM), which is the smallest unit of measure in which the inventory is maintained, with the order unit of measure. For example, if the base unit of measure is KG but orders are placed in packs, then the system shows the conversion between KGs and packs.

- **Delivery Schedule**

  If the same ordered item has multiple delivery lines, then you'll maintain that delivery schedule in this tab. Further, if several purchase requisitions for the same materials are converted into a single PO, then the delivery schedules of individual purchase requisitions are all copied into this tab. We'll be describing this feature in more detail in Section 12.3.

- **Texts**

  Like at the header level, several options are available to maintain texts for specific purposes, such as texts for items, info record PO texts, delivery texts, and info record notes. Texts maintained in this tab are not just helpful for recording more details about the PO but can also be fetched by an ABAP consultant when designing company-specific layouts for POs.

- **Delivery Address**

  Specific item-level addresses for deliveries of individual materials can be maintained in this tab if these addresses are different from the plant for which the material is being purchased.

- **Confirmations**

  This tab provides options for maintaining supplier confirmations including rough goods receipt and inbound delivery. We'll cover supplier confirmations in detail in Section 12.7.

12.1.2   Purchase Order Maintenance

After a PO has been created, the purchasing department may need to modify the PO due to a change in supplier, a change in the material quantity required, or the removal of a line item altogether.

To change a PO, use Transaction ME22N or follow the navigation path **Logistics • Materials Management • Purchasing • Purchase Order • Change**.

Apart from changes to a line item, a PO line can be added for another material, and line items can be deleted.

After the change, the PO should be resent to the supplier. A PO should be forwarded to the supplier by whatever method is appropriate: fax, email, electronic data interchange (EDI), and so on. However, if the supplier has already delivered the material against a PO, the purchasing department won't be able to reduce the ordered quantity below that which the supplier has already delivered.

If the supplier's invoice has been received, then any changes to the PO won't be valid.

Now that we've reviewed the maintenance of POs, the next section will examine blocking and canceling POs.

12.2   Blocking and Canceling a Purchase Order

POs are often blocked and canceled for a variety of reasons. This section describes the functionality evoked for blocking and canceling POs.

12.2.1   Blocking a Purchase Order Line Item

A PO may need to be blocked after it has been created. A block stops any goods receipts for the relevant line item. A block may be placed on the line item for many reasons, including quality issues with the material already received at the plant.

You can block a PO line item by using Transaction ME22N (Change Purchase Order). Select the relevant line item and click on the **Block** icon, as shown in Figure 12.7.

Tips & Tricks

To unblock or undelete a line item, simply select it and click on the **Unblock** icon.

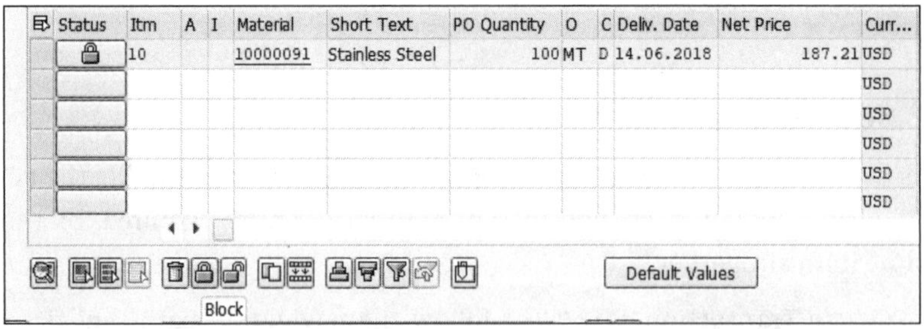

Figure 12.7 Blocking a PO

Tips & Tricks

Using the business function LOG_MM_CI_3, you can save the reasons for blocking a PO item in the PO.

Activate the business function LOG_MM_CI_3 via Transaction SFW5. After activation, you'll see new menu nodes in customization. To customize the blocking reasons, follow the menu path **SAP IMG • Materials Management • Purchasing • Purchase Order • Define Blocking Reason**. Define all the possible blocking reasons applicable in a company's procurement process with two-digit reason codes and **Descriptions**.

To use the blocking reasons functionality, go to Transaction ME22N to change a PO and enter the item details. Click on the **Block** icon, and in the line item details on the **Purchase Order History** tab, you'll see the blocking reasons.

12.2.2   Canceling a Purchase Order Line Item

At times, you may need to cancel a line item, rather than just block it. Issues may exist with the supplier, or the material may no longer be required. You can cancel the material by using Transaction ME22N (Change Purchase Order). You can then choose the **Delete** icon for the selected line item.

If the PO line item has already been subject to a partial goods receipt, the line item can't be fully deleted because of the delivery. If the line item doesn't show any delivery, then the PO can be set to zero to cancel out the line item.

After the line item has been canceled, as shown in Figure 12.8, the purchasing department needs to inform the supplier of the change in the PO. This communication can be performed by whatever method has been agreed upon between the purchasing department and the supplier.

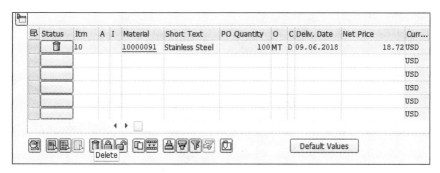

Figure 12.8 Cancelling or Deleting a PO

Figure 12.9 shows the menu bar available at the item overview level, which offers more functionalities, such as copying a line item of one PO to another or even making mass changes to items in a PO.

Figure 12.9 Functions Bar for Item Overview

12.3   Creating a Purchase Order with Reference to Purchasing Documents

Often, creating a PO with reference to another purchasing document is both necessary and quite effective and efficient. Reference documents can be purchase requisitions, RFQs, quantity or value contracts (outline agreements), or even other POs.

Let's see how to do it not just for the PO but also for purchase requisitions, which we covered in Chapter 10.

Access the screen shown in Figure 12.10 via Transaction ME21N (Create Purchase Order) and, in the top left side, click on **Document Overview On**, which will bring up the dropdown list, as shown in Figure 12.10. Choose the reference purchasing document you'd like to copy into a PO. For our example, choose **Purchase Requisitions**, and the screen shown in Figure 12.11 will appear.

Figure 12.10 Document Overview in a PO

Figure 12.11 offers several selection parameters to choose the purchase requisitions that you want to convert into a PO. To limit the selection, select options such as the **Open only** checkbox to display only open purchase requisitions. **Released only** will display only those already released purchase requisitions. For our example, choose the previously configured purchase requisition **Document Type ZNB** and click **Execute**.

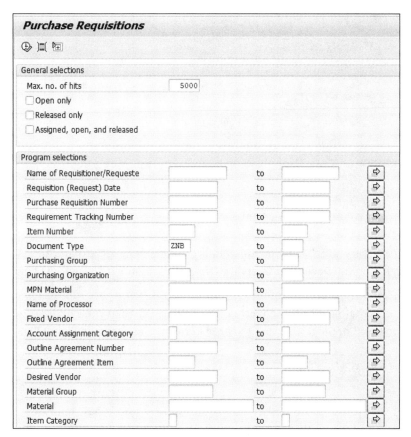

Figure 12.11 Selection Screen from the Document Overview

The left-hand side of Figure 12.12 shows a long list of purchase requisitions of the document type **ZNB** and the associated item numbers of each purchase requisition. To covert a purchase requisition into a PO, simply select the line item (which in this example is the radio button **10** of purchase requisition **2000000020**) and then click the copy icon located on the left-hand side of the same screen.

Tips & Tricks

You can even drag and drop purchase requisitions into the shopping cart icon located both at the header and item level. Notice this icon next to the PO **Document Type NB – Standard PO**.

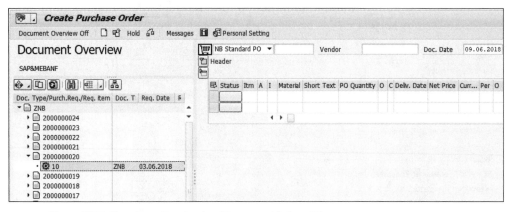

Figure 12.12 Copying a Purchasing Document into a PO

After all the necessary purchasing documents are copied, you can expand the PO screen by clicking on the **Document Overview Off** button, as shown in Figure 12.12.

Figure 12.13 shows the **Delivery** tab of the item level of a PO. If you have multiple purchase requisitions that need to be converted into a single PO, then you can drag and drop them into the shopping cart icon at the item level, as shown in Figure 12.13.

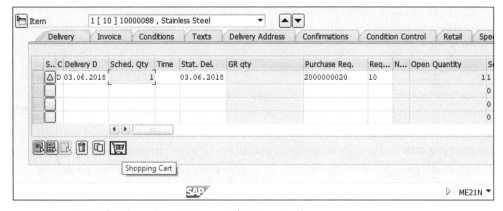

Figure 12.13 The Shopping Cart Icon at the Item Level

> **Note**
>
> By using the shopping cart icon at the header level, the system will create individual line items for each copied purchasing document in the item overview of the PO. Using the shopping cart icon at the item level will keep a single line item of the material at the item overview level but will allow creation of multiple line items in the item details screen. For example, as shown in Figure 12.12, you can have one material (10000088) in the item overview but still add multiple purchase requisitions in the item details screen.

12.4   Account Assignment in a Purchase Order

A line item in a PO can be assigned to an account (or a number of accounts), which will be charged when an invoice for PO items is posted. You can assign a single account code or a number of account codes to a PO. Assigning account information describes how the purchased material is being used, such as fulfilling a sales order or consumption by a cost center.

In the following sections, we'll cover different types of account assignment categories as well as show you how to automatically convert purchase requisitions into POs.

12.4.1   Account Assignment Categories

A number of account assignment categories can be used in a PO. On the initial screen of Transaction ME21N (Create Purchase Order), a purchasing user can enter an account assignment, as shown in Figure 12.14.

The account assignment category determines what account assignment details are required for the item. So if **AcctAssgntCateg K** is selected, then the transaction will, depending on the specific configuration, require a general ledger (G/L) account and cost center to be entered.

The different account assignments can be configured in the IMG. The configuration allows a new account assignment to be added and the fields modified to be required, optional, or hidden. The transaction can be found by following the navigation path **Materials Management • Purchasing • Account Assignment • Maintain Account Assignment Categories**.

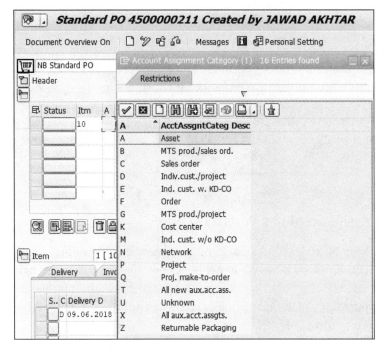

Figure 12.14 Account Assignment Categories in a PO

After creation, a new account assignment must be made to an item category in configuration. The transaction to complete this assignment is found by following the navigation path **Materials Management • Purchasing • Account Assignment • Define Combination of Item Category/Account Assignment Categories**.

A purchasing user can decide which item category is relevant for the new account assignment.

12.4.2 Single Account Assignment

A single account assignment is the most common account assignment for POs. Single account assignment simply means that one account is assigned. This account assignment can be made in Transaction ME21N (Create Purchase Order). After the line item has been entered into the transaction, a purchasing user can navigate to **Item • Account Assignments** to access the **Account Assignment** dialog box.

12.4.3   Multiple Account Assignment

Multiple account assignment allows a number of accounts to be assigned to one PO line. This scenario might occur if a line item is for a material or service that is used by three laboratories and the total cost is split between the three. You can divide the amount of the material into that used by each lab or decide to split the charge by a percentage.

To assign multiple accounts, access the multiple account assignment screen from the **Account Assignment** dialog box, as shown in Figure 12.15. A purchasing user accesses the dialog box as if entering one account and then accesses the multiple account screen by clicking on the multiple account assignment icon . If multiple accounts are already maintained, the single account assignment icon will be grayed out.

In the multiple account assignment screen, as shown in Figure 12.15, the **Distribution** field can be changed to **1** for a quantity assignment or **2** for a percentage assignment. Any number of accounts can be added for the line item, as long as the total percentage doesn't exceed 100% or as long as the total quantity doesn't exceed the quantity entered in the line item.

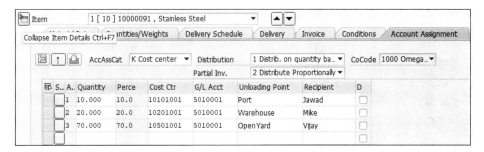

Figure 12.15 Multiple Account Assignments in a PO

12.4.4   Automatically Create POs from Purchase Requisitions

When the source of supply is already known and maintained in a purchase requisition, the system can automatically create POs from purchase requisitions to save time and effort.

To automatically convert purchase requisitions into POs, follow these steps:

1. Select the **Auto. PO** checkbox in the **Purchasing** tab of the material master.

2. Select the **Automatic PO** checkbox in the **Purchasing organization** data of supplier master (Transaction BP), as shown later in Figure 12.32.

3. Maintain a source of supply in the purchase requisition.

4. To automatically create POs from purchase requisitions, using Transaction ME59N or by following the menu path **Logistics • Materials Management • Purchasing • Purchase Requisition • Follow-On Functions • Create Purchase Order • Automatically via Purchase Requisitions**.

On the screen that appears, enter relevant selection parameters such as plant, purchasing group, fixed vendor, or purchasing organization. You can even perform a test run before actually converting purchase requisitions into POs.

Figure 12.16 shows a successful creation of the PO 4500000223 for purchase requisition 10005448.

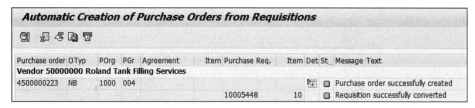

Purchase order	OTyp	POrg	PGr	Agreement	Item	Purchase Req.	Item	Det	St	Message Text
Vendor 50000000 Roland Tank Filling Services										
4500000223	NB	1000	004							Purchase order successfully created
						10005448	10			Requisition successfully converted

Figure 12.16 Automatic Creation of a Purchase Requisition into a PO

Note

Using a similar process for automatically creating POs from purchase requisitions, you can also create POs **Via Assignment Lists** by using the Transaction ME58. Refer to Chapter 10 for more information on this topic.

12.5   Progress Tracking

The progress tracking functionality in the SAP system tracks all purchasing activities related to purchase orders in materials management (MM) and network components in the project system (PS). Progress tracking serves the business need to monitor the progress or statuses of purchase orders that aren't otherwise possible or available. For example, in the imports business process, several sequential steps need to be followed. These steps include opening letters of credit (LCs) with the bank, sending letters of credit details to suppliers, monitoring delivery dates from suppliers against letters of credit expiration dates, and finally submitting the letters of credit clearing documents to the opening bank. All these events and scenarios can be captured using the progress tracking functionality.

Let's quickly review the terms used in the progress tracking functionality:

- **Event**
  A unique activity in the continuous process. For example, in the procurement process, creating a purchase order, sending the PO to a vendor, receiving an acknowledgement, and doing goods receipts are all events.

- **Event scenario**
  Collection of sequence of events for a process.

- **Progress tracking profile**
  The high-level object definition, for example, material purchases tracking, services procurement tracking, and network tracking in PS.

Two steps are involved when using the progress tracking functionality:

1. **Progress tracking**
   In this step, you'll maintain the basic details of a PO such as the baseline date (discussed in more detail in Section 12.5.2) and the actual dates of events so that the system can calculate variances between the baseline date (or the planned dates) with actual dates of events.

2. **Progress evaluation**
   To monitor progress of POs, a progress evaluation is a report that provides a holistic view of the statuses of various events of different POs.

In the following sections, we'll cover the configuration basics for progress tracking followed by a description of its business process. Finally, we'll discuss progress evaluation's output, a report tracking progress.

12.5.1   Configuration Basics

Perform the following configuration steps to set up progress tracking:

1. **Defining standard events**
   In this step, you'll define all the possible events for the procurement process that require tracking or monitoring, such as opening an LC with the bank, sending LC details to supplier, receiving acknowledgement from the supplier for the LC received etc. Each event is assigned to the particular rank (step). To set up standard events, follow the menu path **Materials Management • Purchasing • Purchase Order • Progress Tracking • Define Standard Events**.

2. **Defining event scenarios**

   In this step, you'll define event scenarios for the purchase order as well as assign a factory calendar to event scenarios. An event scenario is a high-level definition in progress tracking. To define event scenarios, follow the menu path **Materials Management • Purchasing • Purchase Order • Progress Tracking • Define Event Scenarios**.

3. **Maintaining relationships between events in a scenario**

   In this step, you'll assign an event scenario to all the possible events. In order words, you'll group all the possible events into an event scenario. Predecessor and successor relationships are defined for the scenario along with scheduling and relative offset in days between each predecessor and successor event. To maintain relationships between events in a scenario, follow the menu path **Materials Management • Purchasing • Purchase Order • Progress Tracking • Maintain Relationships Between Events in a Scenario**.

4. **Assigning default scenario to material group**

   In this step, a default scenario is assigned to a material group. You can also manually assign scenarios through enhancement. To assign a default scenario to a material group, follow the menu path **Materials Management • Purchasing • Purchase Order • Progress Tracking • Assign Default Scenario to Material Group**.

5. **Maintaining priorities for an event**

   In this step, you'll maintain the sequence of priorities or the order in which the system will display the progress tracking of POs. To set up maintenance of priorities for an event, follow the menu path **Materials Management • Purchasing • Purchase Order • Progress Tracking • Maintain Priorities for an Event**.

6. **Defining a progress tracking profile**

   The tracking profile is used to track the progress of all the events. Profile is mandatory while tracking the progress. To set up a progress tracking profile, follow the menu path **Materials Management • Purchasing • Purchase Order • Progress Tracking • Define Progress Tracking Profile**.

7. **Defining status info types**

   In this step, you'll define status info types, which are used to analyze whether a particular purchase document is complete or not. To setup configure status info types, follow the menu path **Materials Management • Purchasing • Purchase Order • Progress Tracking • Define Status Info Types**.

8. **Maintaining number range status information**

   Although SAP delivers a standard number range for status information, you can maintain it by following the menu path **Materials Management • Purchasing • Purchase Order • Progress Tracking • Number Range Status Information**.

9. **Using BAdIs**

   Standard BAdIs (Business Add-Ins) are available to populate all the relevant field values, status, and priorities automatically. To configure BAdIs, follow the menu path **Materials Management • Purchasing • Purchase Order • Progress Tracking • BAdI: Display Progress Tracking Data in Purchase Order**.

With the configuration settings in place, the following section covers the business process of progress tracking.

12.5.2   Business Processes

Create a new PO of the material belonging to the material group to which a default scenario has already been assigned (see step 4 in the previous section).

To maintain the date-related data in a PO in progress monitoring, use Transaction EXPD or follow the menu path **Logistics • Purchasing • Purchase Order • Follow-On Functions • Progress Tracking**.

On the initial screen, enter the previously configured **Profile** in the **Progress Tracking Profile** area and select from the available parameters, such as the PO number, the material, the supplier, or the events.

On executing the transaction, the screen shown in Figure 12.17 will appear. From this screen, further navigation is possible. For example, a PO can be displayed or changed from the overview, or items can be displayed. To track a purchase order, select a complete line item with the **Change** or **Display** icons.

Once you select a PO, you'll see two sections:

- Schedule lines/Items
- Events

The schedule lines overview contains the purchase order number, the name of the scenario, item details, and an event overview. The screen layout can be changed as per business requirements. In this first section on the screen, additional functionalities include status notes, subitems, date-related mass changes, and sending messages to requesters. In addition, the scenarios mass change functionality is also available. If needed, the scenario can also be displayed in fullscreen mode.

Based on configuration settings, the events assigned to the scenario will be displayed. All the date fields correspond to events, and variance, priority, and ranking of events

12

are displayed. In addition, event scenario, schedule, copy dates, and refresh facilities are possible. Each activity is assigned an icon.

Figure 12.17 shows the tracking of a purchase order after all the events are complete. The baseline date is defined as the base date for all the subsequent calculation (plan and forecast), and in absence of plan dates, the baseline date is compared with the actual date to calculate variances. Once the baseline date is populated, the **Baseline set** indicator will be set automatically. This process also applies for planned dates. The indicator will be set after planned dates are calculated. Planned dates are calculated from the baseline date and the relative offset days specified in the configuration setting of the event scenario.

Similarly, the same purchase order is modified with additional line items. As shown in Figure 12.17, all the events that deviate from the planned dates are variances and are indicated with red and yellow marks.

Baseline dates, actual dates, forecast dates, priorities, and indicator sets can also be triggered through BAdIs. The list of standard BAdIs are available for progress tracking. While tracking the purchase order, each event will be tracked with the help of the baseline date, the plan date, and the actual date. Any deviation will be addressed immediately. Scenarios completed within the event planned time frame will show variances with green and yellow marks.

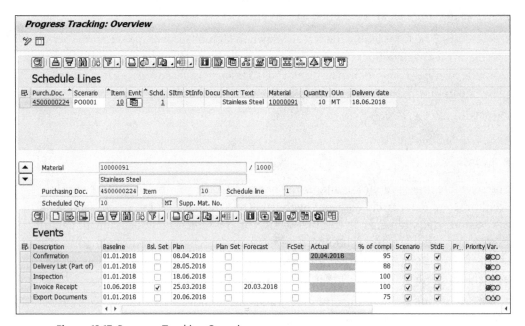

Figure 12.17 Progress Tracking Overview

12.5.3   Evaluation

To evaluate that status of purchase orders using the progress tracking feature, use Transaction AXPD or follow the menu path **Logistics • Purchasing • Purchase Order • Reporting • Progress Tracking Evaluations**.

Similar to progress tracking, the **Profile** plays a key role in evaluation too. For evaluations, the input parameter can be a purchase order or a vendor number. Once the transaction is executed, the screen shown in Figure 12.18 will appear, and the variances for each event can be evaluated.

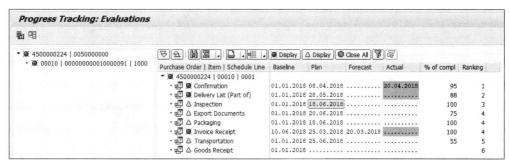

Figure 12.18 Progress Tracking Evaluation

12.6   Outline Purchase Agreements

An outline purchase agreement is often referred to as a *blanket PO* or an *umbrella PO*. An outline purchase agreement is basically a long-term agreement between the purchasing department and a supplier for materials or services for a defined period of time. The purchasing department negotiates with the supplier a set of terms and conditions that are fixed for the period of the agreement. The two types of outline purchase agreements are contracts and scheduling agreements:

- A *contract* is an outline purchase agreement against which release orders can be issued for materials or services when the customer requires them.

- A *scheduling agreement* is an outline purchase agreement whereby the purchasing department has arranged to procure materials based on a schedule agreed upon between the purchasing department and the supplier. This type of outline purchase agreement is useful for customers who operate repetitive manufacturing, where production consumes the same materials each month, and can plan accordingly.

In the following sections, we'll discuss each of these agreements in turn.

12.6.1   Scheduling Agreements

A scheduling agreement can be created manually or can be copied with reference to purchase requisitions, quotations, and centrally agreed contracts.

Before creating a scheduling agreement, a purchasing user must define the account assignment, purchasing organization, and purchasing group. A scheduling agreement can also be created for subcontracting, consignments, and stock transfers.

Creating a Scheduling Agreement Manually

Creating a scheduling agreement manually requires a purchasing user to enter details rather than referencing a quotation, purchase requisition, or contract. To create the scheduling agreement, use Transaction ME31L or follow the navigation path **Logistics • Materials Management • Purchasing • Outline Agreement • Scheduling Agreement • Create • Vendor Known**.

As shown in Figure 12.19, you can enter an **Agreement Type,** which can be either **LP** for a scheduling agreement or **LU** for a stock transport scheduling agreement. You can also enter a scheduling agreement number (**Agreement**) if an external number has been assigned.

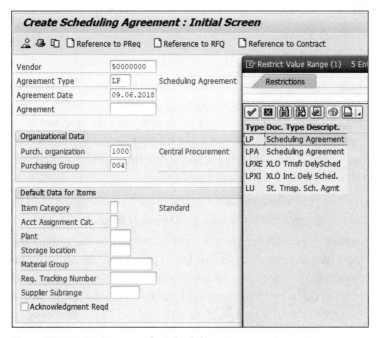

Figure 12.19 Initial Screen of a Scheduling Agreement

Figure 12.20 shows the validity dates of the scheduling agreement and the terms of delivery that have been agreed upon between the purchasing department and the supplier. The purchasing department may have agreed on a target dollar amount for the contract, which can be entered into the scheduling agreement.

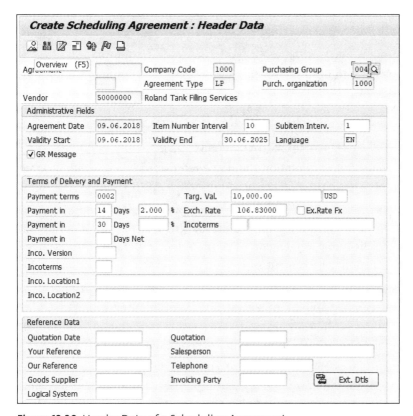

Figure 12.20 Header Data of a Scheduling Agreement

After the header information has been entered, the line items can be entered for the scheduling agreement. Each line item requires that a target quantity be entered, as shown in Figure 12.21. The **Targ. Qty** is the quantity that was agreed upon by the purchasing department and the supplier.

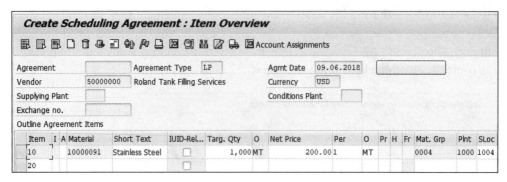

Figure 12.21 Item Overview of a Scheduling Agreement

Creating a Scheduling Agreement with a Reference

If a purchase requisition or quotation should be referenced in a scheduling agreement, the document can be identified when Transaction ME31L is run.

Other documents can also be referenced in Transaction ME31L. After choosing a purchase requisition, the details from the requisition are available for adoption and inclusion in the scheduling agreement. Click the **Adopt + Details** button to copy details into the scheduling agreement.

After the purchase requisition lines are copied into the scheduling agreement, you can enter the agreed price, and the system posts the scheduling agreement.

Manually Maintaining a Delivery Schedule in a Scheduling Agreement

To manually maintain a delivery schedule of a material in a scheduling agreement, use Transaction ME38 or follow the menu path **Logistics • Materials Management • Purchasing • Outline Agreement • Scheduling Agreement • Delivery Schedule • Maintain**.

As shown in Figure 12.22, maintain the delivery schedule of the scheduling agreement **6200000002**. You can maintain scheduling in date, week, or month formats.

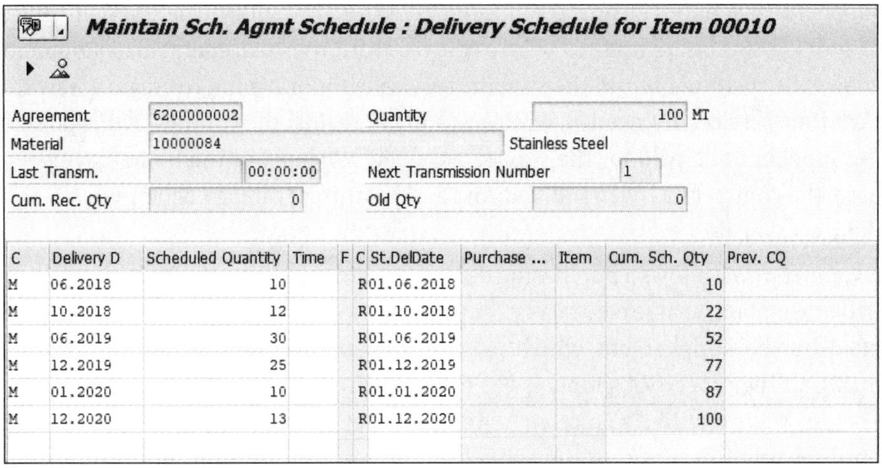

Figure 12.22 Maintaining a Schedule in a Scheduling Agreement

Automatically Maintaining Delivery Schedule in a Scheduling Agreement

After a material requirements planning (MRP) run, if you want the system to automatically assign delivery schedules to a material in a scheduling agreement, then you'll need to create a source list. In the source list of a material, maintain the scheduling agreement and also make sure the **2-Record relevant to MRP. Sched. lines generated** checkbox has been selected in the **MRP** column. Refer to Chapter 9 for more information on source list maintenance.

In the next section, we'll review both the quantity contract and the value contract, including how a contract is entered.

12.6.2 Contracts

A contract is an agreement between the supplier and the customer for the supplier to supply material to the customer at an agreed price over a specified period of time. In this section, we'll provide you with an overview of how contracts are used and then dive into their creation process. Unlike a scheduling agreement, a contract is based on releases to the contract, or the *contract release order*, as it's often called. These contracts can be either based on the total quantity or the total value:

- **Quantity contract**
  A *quantity contract* allows the purchasing department to agree with the supplier on a contract for a set quantity of material or services. A typical example involves a

supplier that supplies technical support for desktop computers. The supplier agrees to provide 480 hours under a yearly contract with the customer. This agreement allows the customer to use the support service without having to create a new PO each time services are needed. A release is made against the contract, which allows the supplier to be paid for the service provided. When all of the hours have been used, the contract has been fulfilled, and a new contract can be negotiated.

- **Value contract**

  A *value contract* allows a purchasing department to cap the spending with one particular supplier. A value contract isn't concerned with the quantity of material supplied by the supplier but with the total spending with the supplier for that material. The process of supply is the same as with the quantity contract because release orders are used to receive material. However, release orders are only valid until the total spending for the value contract reaches the total agreed to. In this way, the purchasing department can limit spending at suppliers to allow other suppliers to supply material.

Creating a Contract

A contract is created in a similar way to a scheduling agreement. A purchasing user can use Transaction ME31K or follow the navigation path **Logistics • Materials Management • Purchasing • Outline Agreement • Contract • Create**.

The initial screen, as shown in Figure 12.23, is similar to the initial screen for creating a scheduling agreement.

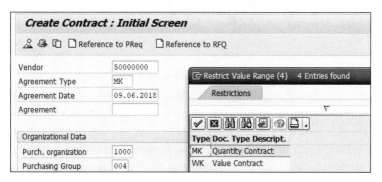

Figure 12.23 Initial Screen of a Quantity Contract

The **Agreement Type** field, shown in Figure 12.23, should be maintained to determine what type of contract is being created. The options are as follows:

- **WK**: Value contract
- **MK**: Quantity contract

After the initial information has been entered, the transaction displays the header information that needs to be completed, as shown in Figure 12.24. The value contract requires a target value (**Targ. Val.**) for the contract.

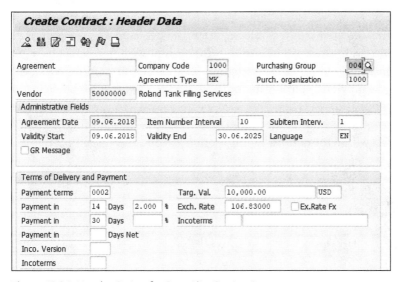

Figure 12.24 Header Data of a Quantity Contract

The line items that must be added to the detail screen are shown in Figure 12.25. A purchasing user must add a target for the line item.

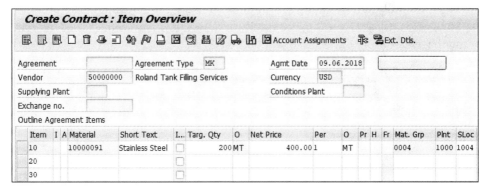

Figure 12.25 Item Overview of a Quantity Contract

Releasing an Order against a Contract

After the contract is in place, material can be requested from the supplier by using a release order against the contract. This release order can be created via the **Create Purchase Order** screen in Transaction ME21N.

As shown in Figure 12.26, choose the **Document Overview On** button and then choose the selection variant icon ![icon]. From the dropdown menu, choose **Contracts**. On the screen that appears, enter selection parameters, such as the contract number against which you want to create a contract release order. The left-hand side of Figure 12.26 shows the previously created contract 46000000019 that we'll now adopt as a PO. Enter the PO quantity, which in this example is "20 MT." In other words, out of the total quantity (the previously created quantity contract for 200 MT), as shown in Figure 12.25, a quantity of 20 MT is being released (or created) as a contract release order or a PO. Thus, another 180 MT of the material can still be released against the same quantity contract within the defined validity period. Save your entries.

Figure 12.26 Creating a Contract Release Order

Access the screen shown in Figure 12.27 via Transaction ME32K (Change Contract) and enter the quantity contract number (or agreement), in this case, "46000000019." The **Target Quantity** is **200.00MT**, which is the total agreed quantity, out of which **180.00MT** is still an **Open Target Quantity** because **20MT** has been released by creating the release order or the PO (**4500000214**).

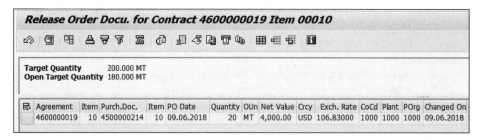

Figure 12.27 Contract Release Order in a Quantity Contract

12.7   Supplier Confirmation

Companies often require suppliers to communicate in advance the details of an impending delivery to help plan their logistics and supply chain accordingly. Alternately, many suppliers keep their customers informed about upcoming deliveries that contain delivery-specific details, such as packing lists, ports of shipment, or dates of shipment arrival at port. Inbound delivery for supplier confirmation facilitates the maintenance of this information. In fact, if needed, supplier confirmation can act as a control function between issuing a purchase order to a supplier and its delivery. An inbound delivery is alternately known as a *rough GR* (goods receipt).

A supplier confirmation occurs when the supplier communicates to the customer regarding a PO or inbound delivery. In this section, we'll provide an overview of supplier confirmation and then provide the steps for this task.

12.7.1   Supplier Confirmation Overview

Supplier communications to the purchaser can be in the form of a fax, email, or EDI. The communication can be for the following:

- Order acknowledgement
- Transport confirmation
- Advance ship notification (ASN)
- Inbound delivery

Supplier confirmations are manually entered into the SAP system. Confirmations are only loaded automatically when the confirmation is sent from a supplier using EDI.

Supplier confirmations are important because they provide updated information on the delivery of goods. As a result, you won't have to rely solely on the delivery dates agreed to by the supplier at the time the PO was created, or even before. Thus, the planning department can adjust the production schedule based on the supplier's information.

In the following sections, we'll cover configuration details, master data, and business processes and reporting monitoring for supplier confirmations.

12.7.2   Confirmation Configuration

Confirmation categories can be configured in the IMG for external or internal confirmations. External categories are defined for manual entries of supplier confirmations, whereas internal categories are for supplier confirmations using EDI.

External Confirmations

External confirmation categories can be configured using a transaction found by following the navigation path **Materials Management • Purchasing • Confirmations • Define External Confirmation Categories**.

You can also add new categories for confirmations, as shown in Figure 12.28, depending on your requirements.

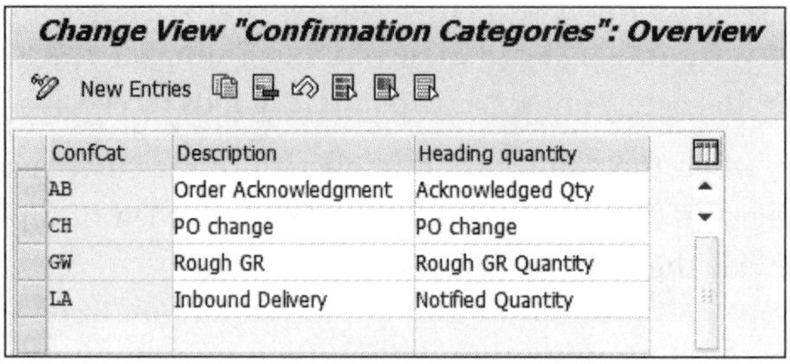

Change View "Confirmation Categories": Overview

%⁄   New Entries

ConfCat	Description	Heading quantity
AB	Order Acknowledgment	Acknowledged Qty
CH	PO change	PO change
GW	Rough GR	Rough GR Quantity
LA	Inbound Delivery	Notified Quantity

Figure 12.28 External Confirmation Categories

Internal Confirmations

Three internal confirmation categories for EDI-based communications are supplied in the standard system:

- **Category 1**
  Used for order acknowledgments

- **Category 2**
  Used for ASNs or inbound deliveries

- **Category 3**
  Used for rough goods receipts

An external confirmation category can be assigned to each internal confirmation category, as shown in Figure 12.29. As a result, purchasing documents can be automatically updated with data from the relevant confirmation. External confirmation categories can be configured using a transaction by following the navigation path **Materials Management • Purchasing • Confirmations • Define Internal Confirmation Categories**.

As Figure 12.30 shows, you can even control the sequence in which the system allows various types of confirmation to take place to meet business needs.

Change View "Internal Confirmation Categories": Overview

Internal Confirmation Categories

I		CC	Description	DlvTy	Ret. Del. ...	DlTy.Intra	
1 Order Acknowledgment ▼		AB	Order Acknowledgment		☐		▲
2 Shipping Notificati... ▼		LA	Inbound Delivery	EL	☐	ELR	▼
3 Rough Goods Receipt ▼		GW	Rough GR	EG	☐		
4 Purchase order chan... ▼		CH	PO change		☐		

Figure 12.29 Internal Confirmation Categories

Change View "Confirmation control keys": Overview

New Entries

Dialog Structure
▼ ⬚ Confirmation control keys
  • ⬚ Confirmation sequence

Confirmation control keys

Co...	Description	Create Inb. Deli...	POD-Rel.	Tracking active
0001	Confirmations	☐	Not POD relevant ▼	☐
0002	Rough GR	☐	Not POD relevant ▼	☐
0003	Inb. Deliv./Rough GR	☐	Not POD relevant ▼	☐
0004	Inbound Delivery	☑	A Always POD rel... ▼	☑

Figure 12.30 Confirmation Control Keys

Figure 12.31 shows the detailed screen of **Confirmation control 0004** for the **Confirmation category LA (Inbound Delivery)**. On this screen, you can control whether recording an inbound delivery in the SAP system is considered during an MRP run for materials planning or whether an inbound delivery is **GR-Relevant**, which cancels out when the actual goods receipt of a material takes place. You can even control whether this confirmation category is subject to reminders and how soon or late a supplier can send a confirmation from the date of a material's delivery.

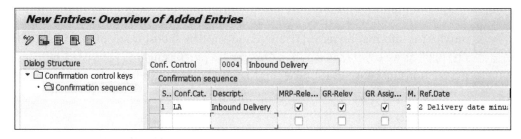

New Entries: Overview of Added Entries

Dialog Structure
▼ ⬚ Confirmation control keys
  • ⬚ Confirmation sequence

Conf. Control 0004 Inbound Delivery

Confirmation sequence

S..	Conf.Cat.	Descript.	MRP-Rele...	GR-Relev	GR Assig...	M.	Ref.Date
1	LA	Inbound Delivery	☑	☑	☑	2	2 Delivery date minu:
			☐	☐	☐		

Figure 12.31 Details of a Confirmation Control Key

At this point, we've completed configuration details for supplier confirmations. In the next section, we'll show you how to assign the configured confirmation control to master data.

12.7.3   Master Data Maintenance of Confirmation Control

You can maintain the confirmation control (**Conf. Control**) in the **Purchasing Data** tab of the supplier master or business partner (Transaction BP). This control would be applicable to all purchases from the specific supplier, as shown in Figure 12.32.

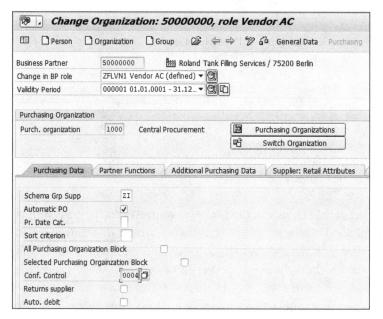

Figure 12.32 Assigning a Confirmation Control Key in a Business Partner

The option of confirmation control is also available in the purchase data view of the purchasing information record (Transaction ME11) by choosing an option in the **Conf. Ctrl** field. As we covered in detail in Chapter 7, a purchasing info record is a purchasing relationship between a supplier and a material, as shown in Figure 12.33.

Tips & Tricks

If you want a supplier to always send confirmations, then set the confirmation control in the business partner function (Transaction BP). However, if you want a supplier to send confirmations on shipment of specific materials only, then select the

---

option of assigning a confirmation category in relevant purchasing information records (Transaction ME11).

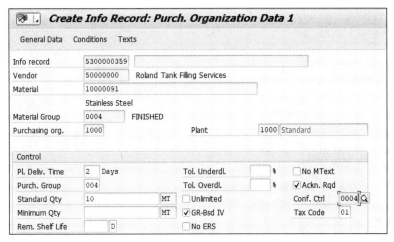

Figure 12.33 Assigning a Confirmation Control Key in a Purchasing Info Record

Let's now cover the business processes of supplier confirmations.

12.7.4 Business Processes of Supplier Confirmation

Figure 12.34 shows the PO (Transaction ME21N). In the **Confirmations** tab at the item level, choose the **Conf. Control 0004 Inbound Delivery** to manually enter the confirmation details received from the supplier.

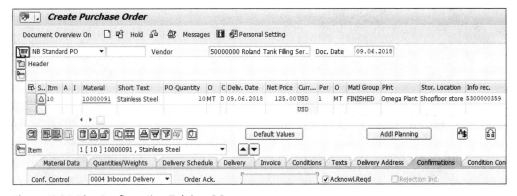

Figure 12.34 The Confirmation Tab in a PO

As shown in Figure 12.35, maintain the confirmation details received from the supplier, which in our example is 25 MT. At any time, you can change or even delete the confirmation details maintained on this screen.

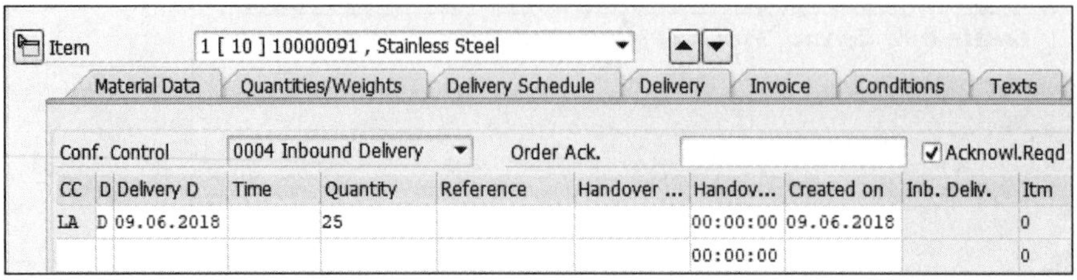

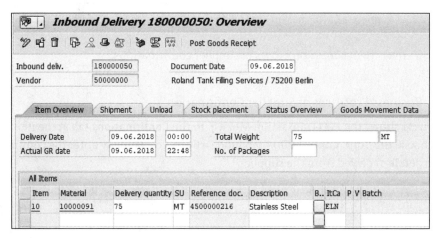

Figure 12.35 Manually Maintaining the Confirmation Details in a PO

Another way to maintain a supplier confirmation is to create an inbound delivery for purchase order 4500000216 using Transaction VL31N, as shown in Figure 12.36. Maintain the confirmation details, which in our example is the tentative delivery of 75 MT. Save your entries.

Figure 12.36 Inbound Delivery

Tips & Tricks

To delete a confirmation made via an inbound delivery, use Transaction VL32N (refer to Figure 12.36 again). Further, you can even directly post a goods receipt with reference to an inbound delivery from the same screen, as shown in Figure 12.36.

Once again, Figure 12.37 shows the PO 4500000216 for which the reference of inbound delivery 180000050 for 75MT of material recorded in the previous step is now part of the PO's confirmation details.

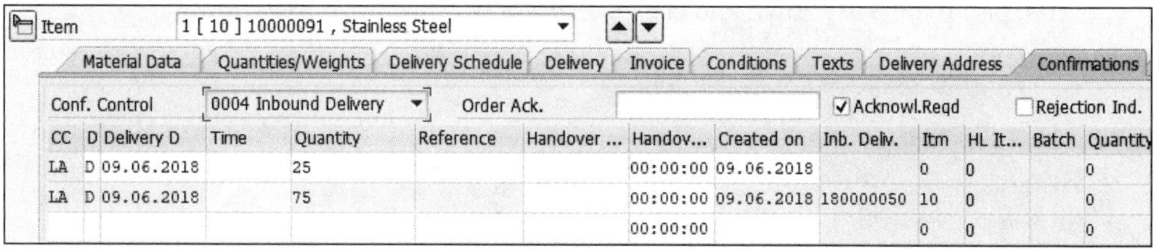

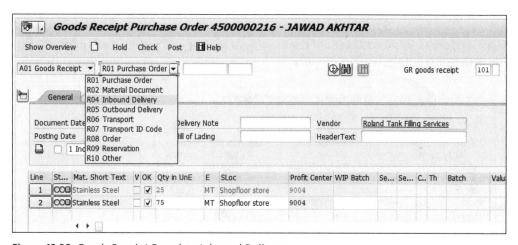

Figure 12.37 Updated Confirmation Details in a PO

Access the screen shown in Figure 12.38 via Transaction MIGO where you'll choose **Inbound Delivery** from the dropdown list to receive goods against the PO 4500000216 from the supplier with reference to inbound delivery numbers.

Figure 12.38 Goods Receipt Based on Inbound Delivery

At this point, the business process for supplier confirmations is at an end. In the next section, we'll cover the reporting or monitoring of supplier confirmations.

12.7.5   Monitoring Supplier Confirmations

Access the screen shown in Figure 12.39 using Transaction ME2A or by following the menu path **Logistics • Purchasing • Reporting • Monitor Confirmations**. Enter the initial parameters as shown and click **Execute**.

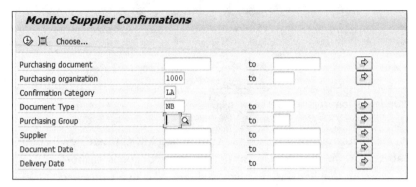

Figure 12.39 Initial Screen of a Supplier Confirmations Monitoring

Figure 12.40 shows the list of confirmations against various purchase orders that are still pending from your suppliers.

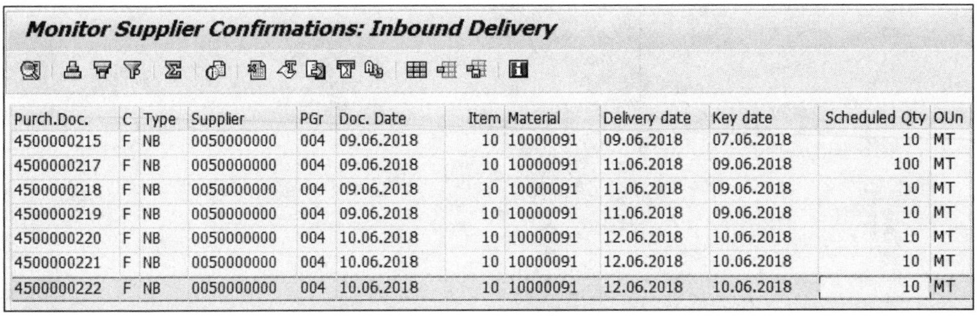

Monitor Supplier Confirmations: Inbound Delivery

Purch.Doc.	C	Type	Supplier	PGr	Doc. Date	Item	Material	Delivery date	Key date	Scheduled Qty	OUn
4500000215	F	NB	0050000000	004	09.06.2018	10	10000091	09.06.2018	07.06.2018	10	MT
4500000217	F	NB	0050000000	004	09.06.2018	10	10000091	11.06.2018	09.06.2018	100	MT
4500000218	F	NB	0050000000	004	09.06.2018	10	10000091	11.06.2018	09.06.2018	10	MT
4500000219	F	NB	0050000000	004	09.06.2018	10	10000091	11.06.2018	09.06.2018	10	MT
4500000220	F	NB	0050000000	004	10.06.2018	10	10000091	12.06.2018	10.06.2018	10	MT
4500000221	F	NB	0050000000	004	10.06.2018	10	10000091	12.06.2018	10.06.2018	10	MT
4500000222	F	NB	0050000000	004	10.06.2018	10	10000091	12.06.2018	10.06.2018	10	MT

Figure 12.40 Supplier Confirmations Monitoring

> **Note**
>
> To monitor reminders in an SAP system, use Transaction ME91F. To monitor order acknowledgements, that is, acknowledgment that the supplier has received a PO, use Transaction ME92F.

In this section, we reviewed how, in supplier confirmation, a supplier can acknowledge the receipt of a PO. The next section reviews the messages and outputs associated with POs.

12.8   Messages and Output

External purchasing documents generate outputs—in other words, messages. These messages contain information sent to a supplier using a variety of media such as mail, EDI, fax, or email. The variety of media will depend on each supplier; some may prefer faxes whereas others may prefer email, and so on. While generating output for a supplier, the user may not remember the type of media acceptable for the supplier. For this reason, the SAP system provides the message determination functionality where you'll define the output media for each supplier. The system then automatically proposes the appropriate output media during document creation.

For example, let's say your company wants the system to output messages when purchasing documents such as POs, contracts, and so on are created or changed. For each purchasing transaction, you can define whether the system should use message determination. When not using message determination, the system will generate an output according to SAP-defined messages, such as message NEU for POs. However, you can change their proposed parameters in the individual documents. For messages that need to be printed out, the system must determine the printer.

For messages with message determination, the SAP system uses condition techniques. Messages are determined based on predefined criteria, such as document type and supplier.

In the following sections, we'll adopt a step-by-step approach to show you how to set up the message determination functionality to create a specific kind of message output, such as a PO printout.

12.8.1   How Message Determination Works

Let's look at how the system determines messages through an example. Let's say a PO is created with supplier ABC, purchasing organization 1000, and purchasing document type NB. Let's see how the message is determined for this PO:

1. **Determining the message schema**

   The system determines the schema from the document category. In this example,

12

the document category is PO, and the schema is RMBEF1. For each document category, the schema is defined in the system in Customizing (IMG).

2. **Determining the condition type**
The schema consists of various condition types listed in a sequence. In this example, condition type NEU has been determined.

3. **Determining the access sequence and condition table**
The system determines the access sequence (0001) assigned to the condition type (NEU).

4. **Determining the condition record**
The system determines the condition tables assigned to access sequence 0001. A *condition table* consists of condition records in a sequence that defines priorities. In our example, the system first determines condition table 27 and searches for a valid condition record in this table. Because the system doesn't find the condition record, it moves to the next condition table, which is condition table 25.

5. **Determining the next condition record**
Condition table 25 consists of condition records for the combination of document type, purchase organization, and supplier. In this example, the system determines the condition record for document type NB, purchase organization 1000, and supplier ABC. The condition record consists of medium, partner function, and partner. Medium 1 (printout) is used in this example. The partner is blank in the condition record; therefore, the output partner will be the PO supplier.

6. **Copying message details into the document**
The system copies all of the details, such as the medium, the partner, and the printer, into the document. If required, you can change the print parameters for specific documents.

Let's now cover the confirmation steps involving message determination and output.

12.8.2   Configuration Steps

In this section, we'll discuss message determination configuration for POs, as follows:

> **Note**
> You can use the same configuration steps for all other external purchasing documents such as scheduling agreements, RFQs, and quantity or value contracts.

1. **Define the condition table**

   In a condition table, you'll define the combination of fields for which message records should be created. To define new condition tables or to check existing condition tables, follow the menu path **Materials Management • Purchasing • Messages • Output Control • Condition Table • Define Condition Table for Purchase Order**.

   You can define a new table by copying an existing condition table. For example, condition table O25 has three fields assigned to it, as shown in Figure 12.41: **Purchasing Doc. Type**, **Purch. Organization**, and **Vendor**. A condition record is maintained for the combination of these selected fields.

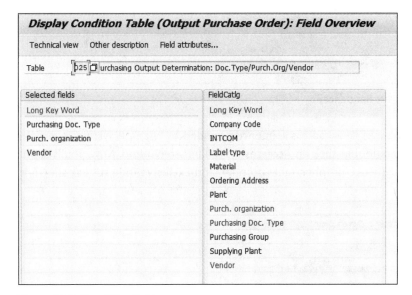

Figure 12.41 Condition Table

> **Warning**
>
> The condition tables included in a standard SAP system shouldn't be changed. To make changes, you should create new condition tables by copying a similar, existing condition table and then making the necessary changes. New condition tables can be created with table numbers ranging from 501 to 999.

2. **Define the access sequence**

   In this step, you'll define the access sequence, which is a search strategy by which the SAP system searches for valid message records. We recommend using the access sequence provided by the SAP system. To define the access sequence, follow the menu path **Materials Management • Purchasing • Messages • Output Control • Access Sequence • Define Access Sequence for Purchase Order**.

You can define an access sequence by clicking on the **New Entries** button or by copying an SAP-provided access sequence, as shown in Figure 12.42.

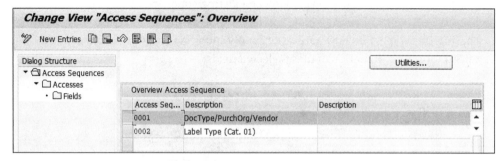

Figure 12.42 Access Sequences

To make changes to an access sequence provided by the SAP system, select the sequence and double-click on **Accesses** on the left tree menu. Now, you'll define the access sequence number, table number, and **Exclusive** indicator, as shown in Figure 12.43.

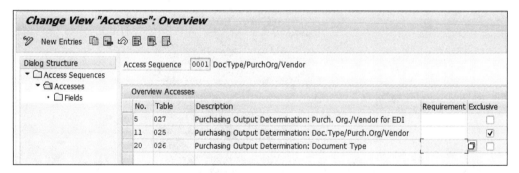

Figure 12.43 Accesses of Access Sequence 0001

3. **Define the message type**

In this step, you'll define the message types relevant to a PO. To define a message type, follow the menu path **Materials Management • Purchasing • Messages • Output Control • Message Types • Define Message Types for Purchase Order**. You can define a message type by clicking on the **New Entries** button or by copying a standard message type provided by the SAP system, as shown in Figure 12.44.

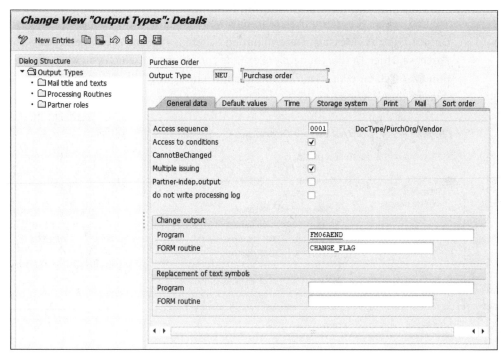

Figure 12.44 Output Types

An access sequence is assigned to a message type, and you can define the processing routines. For different output mediums, you can define the **Form** and **FORM routine**, as shown in Figure 12.45. Existing forms can be realigned per customer requirements, or you can create new forms.

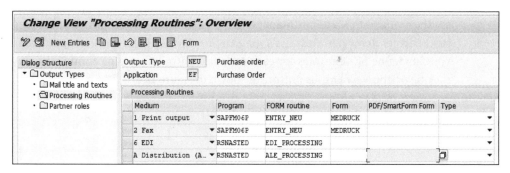

Figure 12.45 Processing Routines

4. **Define the message schema**

   In this step, you'll define the message schema for purchasing documents. The allowed message types are stored in the message schema. To define a message schema, follow the menu path **Materials Management • Purchasing • Messages • Output Control • Message Determination Schemas • Define Message Schema for Purchase Order**. Define the sequence of the conditions for which you want the system to search for condition records, as shown in Figure 12.46. The defined schema needs to be assigned to a PO.

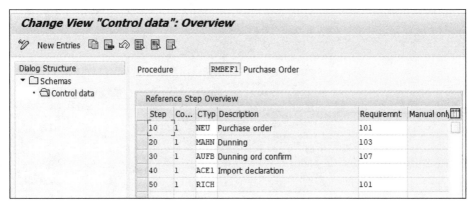

Figure 12.46 Message Schema

Note

Only one schema and one message type can be assigned to each purchasing document.

---

5. **Define partner roles**

   In this step, you'll define the allowed partner roles for the message types by following the menu path **Materials Management • Purchasing • Messages • Output Control • Partner Roles per Message Type • Define Partner Roles for Purchase Order**. You can define partner roles for each output type/medium type combination by clicking on the **New Entries** button, as shown in Figure 12.47.

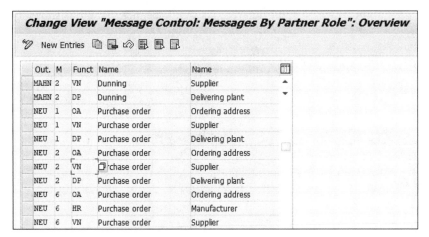

Figure 12.47 Message Schema by Partner Function

6. **Assign output devices to purchasing groups**

   In this step, you'll assign output devices to purchasing groups by following the menu path **Materials Management • Purchasing • Messages • Assign Output Devices to Purchasing Groups**. Assign the output device (such as a printer) to the purchasing group, as shown in Figure 12.48.

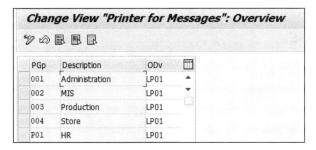

Figure 12.48 Assigning Output Devices to Purchasing Groups

At this point, we've completed necessary configuration settings. In the next section, we'll cover the business processes of message determination and output.

12.8.3   Maintaining Condition Records

Condition records must be maintained for the condition tables configured for message determination. To define condition records, use Transaction MN04 and select the key combination for which condition records should be maintained, as shown in Figure 12.49.

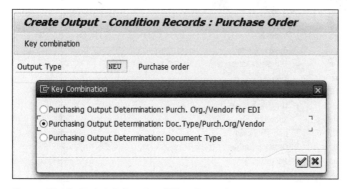

Figure 12.49 Maintaining Condition Records

For the selected key combination, enter a condition record, as shown in Figure 12.50. Fill in the **Vendor** (number), **Partner** function, **Medium**, and **Date/Time** fields. If the **Partner** field is left blank, the system will assign the ordering supplier to the output partner in the purchasing document. After you've maintained the condition records, the system will automatically determine the message condition in POs. Choose **Communication** and assign the **Output device** (the printer). (Printers are generally configured by your company's SAP NetWeaver team in the SAP system.) Save your settings.

Communication						
Purchasing Doc. Type	NB	Purchase Requisition				
Purch. organization	1000	Central Procurement				

Condition Recs.						
Vendor	Name	Funct	Partner	Medium	Date/Time	Lan...
50000000	Roland Tank Filling...	VN	0050000000	1	4	EN
☑						

Figure 12.50 Condition Record

12.8.4   Creating a Purchase Order

Create a PO via Transaction ME21N. Enter the supplier, purchasing organization, purchasing group, company code, and line item details. When you click on the **Message** button, you'll see the message determined by the system, as shown in Figure 12.51. The printer is determined from the purchase group. Changes to the print parameters can be made in a document. You can even get a repeat output (a reprint) of the purchase order after the original PO has been printed.

Change Pur. Order :: Output
Communication method
Processing log
Further data
Repeat output
Change output
Pur. Order.......... 4500000221
Output
Status Outp... Description Medium Fu... Partner La... C... Processing... Time
MAHN Dunning 1 Print out... VN 50000000 EN 00:00:
NEU Purchase ord... 1 Print out... VN 50000000 EN 10.06.2018 01:57:

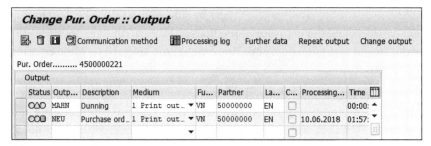

Figure 12.51 Output Details in a PO

The message that you've created can be viewed. If the message can be processed, its status is green. By selecting the **Processing log** button, a purchasing user can view any error or warning messages that prevent the document from being processed. The print preview and the PO layout is based on a standard SAP-delivered script.

> **Tips & Tricks**
>
> You can also use the Transaction SPAD to process or reprocess your own spool (print) jobs.

Access the screen shown in Figure 12.52 via Transaction ME9A and, on the initial screen that appears, enter the relevant output parameters such as purchase order document numbers, plants, purchasing organizations, and suppliers and click **Execute**. Figure 12.52 shows more options to print or reprint an output message.

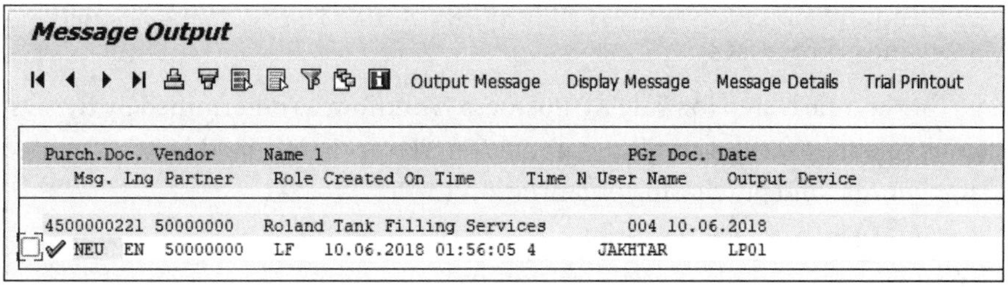

Message Output
Output Message
Display Message
Message Details
Trial Printout
Purch.Doc. Vendor Name 1 PGr Doc. Date
Msg. Lng Partner Role Created On Time Time N User Name Output Device
4500000221 50000000 Roland Tank Filling Services 004 10.06.2018
NEU EN 50000000 LF 10.06.2018 01:56:05 4 JAKHTAR LP01

Figure 12.52 Messages Output List

At this point, we've completed all the steps for messages and output determination. The next section covers pricing procedures.

12.9   Pricing Procedures

A *pricing procedure* determines the price of a material in a PO. The net price of a material depends on discounts, surcharges, taxes, freight, and so on. The purchasing department can calculate the net price of the materials based on its gross price, discounts, taxes, freight charges, and so on. These values are referred to while creating POs and contracts.

In the SAP system, the price, discounts, surcharges, freight costs, and so on are represented in the form of *condition types*. Condition types are used to determine net and effective prices in POs. Each condition type contains condition records (i.e., values), and these records are defined in condition tables. The sequence in which condition records are referred to is defined in the access sequence, and this sequence is assigned to condition types.

Various condition types are grouped in a sequence in a *calculation schema*. A calculation schema is assigned for a combination of supplier schema groups and purchasing organization schema groups.

> **Note**
>
> Conditions can be time-dependent or time-independent. Time-dependent conditions are defined for a certain validity period; time-independent conditions don't have a validity period. Conditions in info records and contracts are always time-dependent conditions. Conditions in POs are always time-independent.

In the following sections, we'll discuss how to configure pricing procedures and the business processes for using pricing procedures.

12.9.1   Business Processes

We'll go through each step for the SAP Business Workflow, as determined by the system, and explain how the price for material MAT-1 was determined in a PO created with supplier ABC and purchasing organization 1000.

1. **Determining the supplier schema group and the purchasing organization schema group**
   The system determines this information based on the supplier master record and the purchasing organization. Our example involves **Supplier Schema Group 01** and **Purchasing Organization Schema Group 01**.

2. **Determining the calculation schema**

   The system determines the relevant calculation schema based on a combination of the supplier schema group and the purchasing organization schema group. In this example, the calculation schema is **RM0000**.

3. **Determining the condition type**

   The calculation schema consists of various condition types listed in a sequence. Here, **Condition Type PB00** is defined for the material price.

4. **Determining the access sequence**

   The system uses the calculation schema to determine the access sequence (in this example, **0002**) assigned to the condition type (in this example, **PB00**).

5. **Determining the condition tables**

   The system determines the condition tables assigned to the access sequence (in this example, **0002**).

6. **Determining the condition record (Part I)**

   The condition table of access sequence 0002 consists of many condition records of which the contract item has the highest priority. A system search yields no value for this condition record.

7. **Determining the condition record (Part II)**

   In the previous step, the system search yielded no result for the highest priority condition record, which is the contract item. Therefore, the system moves to the next condition record, which is the plant info record.

8. **Determining the material price**

   The system search yields a value of $50.00 for plant info record. This value for **Condition Type PB00** is assigned to the material as the price in the PO.

9. **Copying the material price to the PO**

   Once the system finds the value for the condition type, the value is assigned to the PO.

> **Note**
>
> Material-specific discounts and surcharges are supplementary conditions linked to the gross price (condition type PB00). No access sequence is assigned to supplementary conditions, and no separate price determination is carried out for them. Supplementary conditions are found using condition records for the gross price. To maintain material-specific conditions, such as prices, discounts, and surcharges, follow the menu path **Logistics • Materials Management • Purchasing • Master Data • Conditions**.

Settings made in Customizing determine the details of these pricing elements and how the price is computed.

12.9.2   Configuration Basics

In the following sections, we'll cover the steps involved in configuring a pricing procedure.

Defining Condition Types

Condition types are used to represent pricing elements such as prices, discounts, surcharges, taxes, or delivery costs in the SAP system. For example, condition type is PB00 for gross price. These types are stored in the system in the form of condition records. Condition types have control parameters and are differentiated by condition classes. For condition types for which you want to maintain records with their own validity period, you must specify an access sequence. An access sequence is used to search valid condition records.

To configure condition types, follow the menu path **Materials Management • Purchasing • Conditions • Define Price Determination Process • Define Condition Types**.

On this screen, shown in Figure 12.53, you'll see a list of condition types provided by the SAP system. You can create new condition types by clicking on the **New Entries** button or by copying from existing SAP-provided condition types.

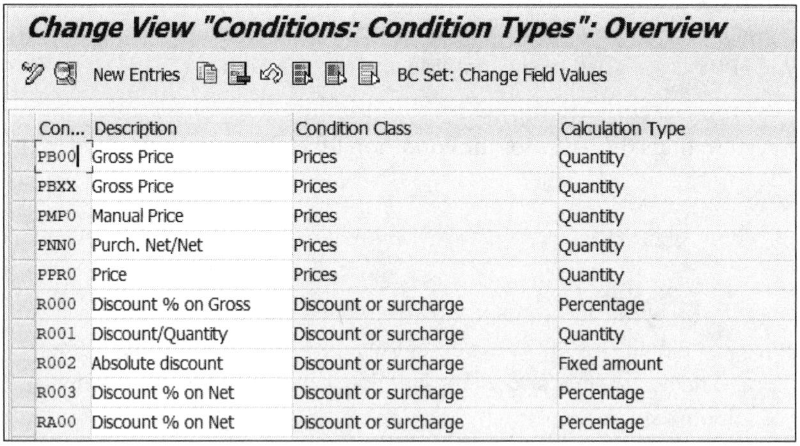

Change View "Conditions: Condition Types": Overview

New Entries   BC Set: Change Field Values

Con...	Description	Condition Class	Calculation Type
PB00	Gross Price	Prices	Quantity
PBXX	Gross Price	Prices	Quantity
PMP0	Manual Price	Prices	Quantity
PNN0	Purch. Net/Net	Prices	Quantity
PPR0	Price	Prices	Quantity
R000	Discount % on Gross	Discount or surcharge	Percentage
R001	Discount/Quantity	Discount or surcharge	Quantity
R002	Absolute discount	Discount or surcharge	Fixed amount
R003	Discount % on Net	Discount or surcharge	Percentage
RA00	Discount % on Net	Discount or surcharge	Percentage

Figure 12.53 Condition Types

> **Note**
>
> If you define your own condition types, the key should begin with the letter "Z" because SAP reserves these name slots in the standard system. You shouldn't change the condition types included in the standard SAP system. Figure 12.54 shows the details of the condition types. In the **Control data 1** section, you'll see the **Cond. class, Calculat.type, Cond. category, Rounding rule**, and **Plus/minus** fields.

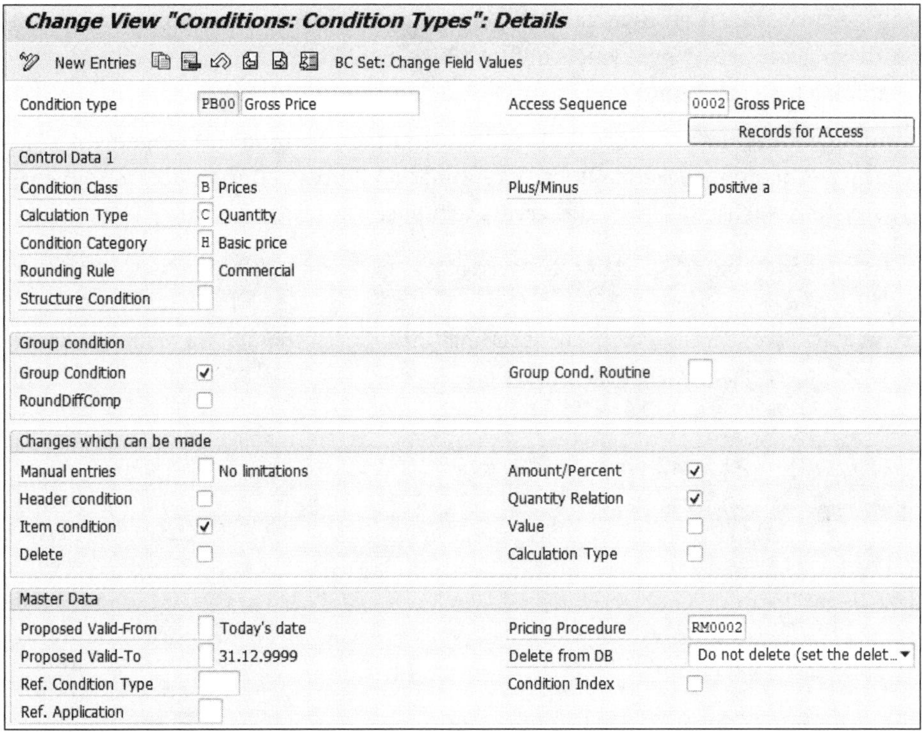

Change View "Conditions: Condition Types": Details

New Entries   BC Set: Change Field Values

Condition type	PB00 Gross Price	Access Sequence	0002 Gross Price
			Records for Access

Control Data 1

Condition Class	B Prices	Plus/Minus	positive a
Calculation Type	C Quantity		
Condition Category	H Basic price		
Rounding Rule	Commercial		
Structure Condition			

Group condition

Group Condition	✓	Group Cond. Routine	
RoundDiffComp	☐		

Changes which can be made

Manual entries	No limitations	Amount/Percent	✓
Header condition	☐	Quantity Relation	✓
Item condition	✓	Value	☐
Delete	☐	Calculation Type	☐

Master Data

Proposed Valid-From	Today's date	Pricing Procedure	RM0002
Proposed Valid-To	31.12.9999	Delete from DB	Do not delete (set the delet... ▼
Ref. Condition Type		Condition Index	☐
Ref. Application			

Figure 12.54 Details of Condition Type PB00

A *condition class* is used for grouping similar condition types; for example, condition class A is used for discounts and surcharges, and condition class B is used for prices. The **Calculation Type** determines how the condition value should be calculated, that is, whether it's based on quantity, weight, or volume. The **Plus/Minus** controls whether the condition results in a negative amount (a discount), positive (a surcharge), or whether both positive and negative amounts are possible.

Based on your requirements, you'll need to define all of the control data for the condition type you want to create.

Defining an Access Sequence

An access sequence is a search strategy that the SAP system uses to search for valid condition records of a certain condition type. For example, when supplying a price, you can stipulate that the SAP system first looks for the price for a specific plant and then for a generally applicable price. For condition types for which you want to maintain records with their own validity periods, you must assign an access sequence. With an access sequence, you'll define which fields the SAP system checks when searching for a valid condition record.

To define an access sequence, follow the menu path **Materials Management • Purchasing • Conditions • Define Price Determination Process • Define Access Sequence**. The system will list SAP-provided access sequences, as shown in Figure 12.55.

> **Note**
>
> An access sequence is a cross-client setting; that is, each change you make will have an effect on all other clients in the system.

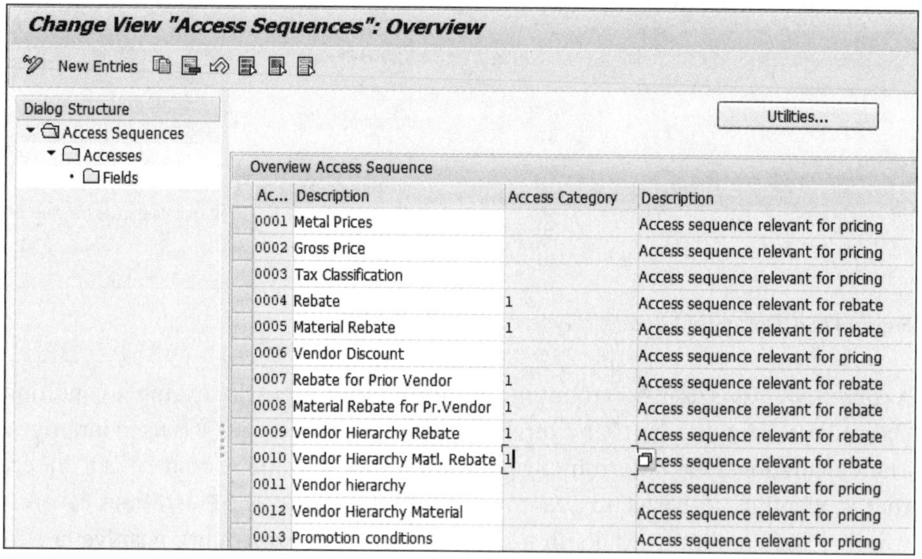

Figure 12.55 Access Sequence

> **Note**
>
> If you define your own access sequence, the key should begin with the letter "Z" because SAP reserves these name slots in the standard system. You shouldn't change the access sequences included in the standard SAP system.

For example, if you've defined access sequence 0002 for the gross price condition PBOO, the system will search for the valid condition record in this sequence. The system will pick the lowest number table first and search for the condition record. If not found, the system will search in the next table, and so on. The **Exclusive** checkbox, as shown in Figure 12.56, controls whether the system stops searching for a record after a successful result has been obtained.

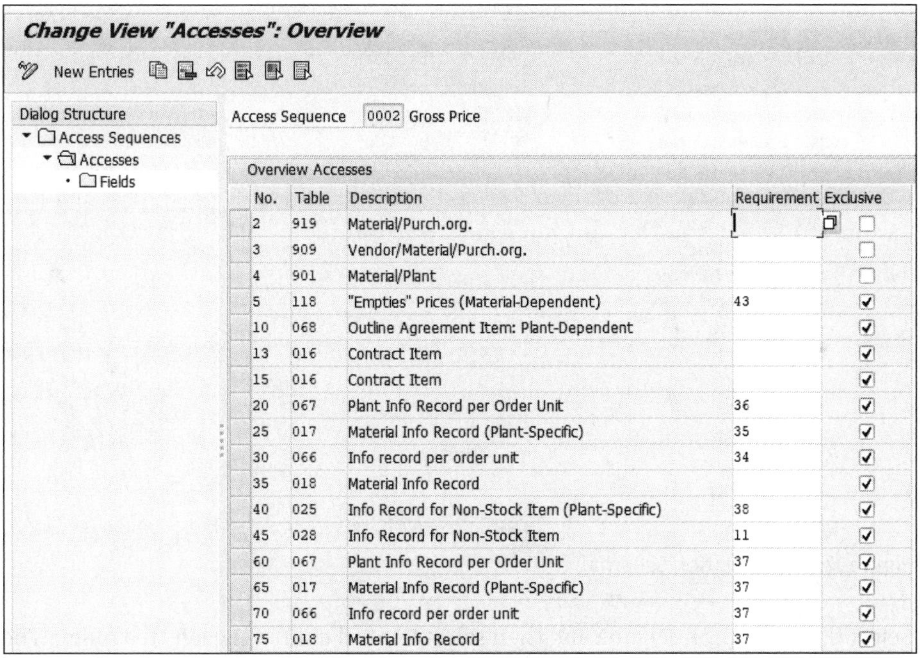

Change View "Accesses": Overview

New Entries

Dialog Structure
▾ ☐ Access Sequences
  ▾ ☐ Accesses
    • ☐ Fields

Access Sequence   0002   Gross Price

Overview Accesses

No.	Table	Description	Requirement	Exclusive
2	919	Material/Purch.org.		☐
3	909	Vendor/Material/Purch.org.		☐
4	901	Material/Plant		☐
5	118	"Empties" Prices (Material-Dependent)	43	☑
10	068	Outline Agreement Item: Plant-Dependent		☑
13	016	Contract Item		☑
15	016	Contract Item		☑
20	067	Plant Info Record per Order Unit	36	☑
25	017	Material Info Record (Plant-Specific)	35	☑
30	066	Info record per order unit	34	☑
35	018	Material Info Record		☑
40	025	Info Record for Non-Stock Item (Plant-Specific)	38	☑
45	028	Info Record for Non-Stock Item	11	☑
60	067	Plant Info Record per Order Unit	37	☑
65	017	Material Info Record (Plant-Specific)	37	☑
70	066	Info record per order unit	37	☑
75	018	Material Info Record	37	☑

Figure 12.56 Accesses within an Access Sequence

Defining the Calculation Schema or the Pricing Procedure

In a *calculation schema*, you'll define the complete structure of different price components (i.e., conditions) with a sequence and control parameters. When creating a PO, the system looks for a calculation schema and, based on the schema system, finds the value of each condition defined in that schema. For example, you might have a scenario where you have the gross price of a material and additional freight charges and handling charges. You may also have discounts. You'll need to define all of these conditions in the schema.

To define a calculation schema, follow the menu path **Materials Management • Purchasing • Conditions • Define Price Determination Process • Define Calculation Schema**. An SAP-provided calculation schema can be used, or you can create your own. To create your own, click on **New Entries** or copy an existing calculation schema, as shown in Figure 12.57.

Step	Co...	Co...	Description	From...	To...	Manual	Req...	Statis...	Print	Subtotal	Requi...	CalTy	Ba...	Accou...	A
1	1	PB00	Gross Price			☐	☐	☐		9					
5	1	GAU1	Orignl Price of Gold			☐	☐	☑							
10	1	RB00	Absolute discount			☐	☐	☐							
10	2	ZB00	Surcharge (Value)			☐	☐	☐							
10	3	RA00	Discount % on Net			☐	☐	☐							
10	4	ZA00	Surcharge % on Net			☐	☐	☐							
10	5	RA01	Discount % on Gross	1		☐	☐	☐							
10	6	ZA01	Surcharge % on Gross	1		☐	☐	☐							
10	7	RC00	Discount/Quantity			☐	☐	☐							
10	8	ZC00	Surcharge/Quantity			☐	☐	☐							
31	6	RUC1	Neutral Accruals/Qty			☐	☐	☑						FRE	RU
31	7	ZOA1	Customs %	20		☐	☐	☑						FRE	FF
31	8	ZOB1	Customs (Value)			☐	☐	☑						FRE	FF
31	9	ZOC1	Customs/Quantity			☐	☐	☑						FRE	FF
31	10	FRA2	Freight %	20		☐	☐	☑						FRE	FF
31	11	FRB2	Freight (Value)			☐	☐	☑						FRE	FF
31	12	FRC2	Freight/Quantity			☐	☐	☑						FRE	FF
40	0		Actual price	20	39	☐	☐	☐		S					

Figure 12.57 Calculation Schema

Select the calculation schema and then select **Control data** in the left tree menu. The system will display the screen shown in Figure 12.57. The following list provides an explanation of the different controlling fields in calculation schemas:

- **Step**
  Determines the sequence of the condition types.

- **Counter**
  The access number of the conditions within a step in the pricing procedure.

- **CType**
  Defines the condition type you want to include in the pricing procedure.

- **From/To**
  Calculates the number of condition types based on which the amount should be calculated for that condition. For example, to calculate a surcharge on the gross price, you'll need to define the sequence number of the gross price in the **From** field. The system will then calculate the surcharge based on the gross price.

- **Manually**
  Defines manually entered conditions.

- **Required**
  Defines mandatory conditions.

- **Statistical**
  Sets a condition as required for some calculation other than price. The value of this condition isn't directly included in the pricing.

Defining the Schema Group

A company may use multiple calculation schemas on a purchasing organization or a supplier. Defining a *schema group* helps you keep track of these schemas by grouping together the purchasing organizations or suppliers that use the same calculation schemas. For example, if you have a group of suppliers for whom the same pricing schema is applicable, you'll create a supplier schema group and assign those suppliers to the group. Similarly, the same calculation schema can be applicable for more than one purchasing organization; in this case, you'll assign the all these purchasing organizations to a purchasing organization schema group.

To define a schema group, you'll need to do the following:

- Define a supplier schema group.
- Define a purchasing organization schema group.
- Assign a purchasing organization schema group to the purchasing organization.
- Assign a supplier schema group in the supplier master record.

To define a supplier schema group, follow the menu path **Materials Management • Purchasing • Conditions • Define Price Determination Process • Define Schema Group • Schema Group: Supplier**, as shown in Figure 12.58.

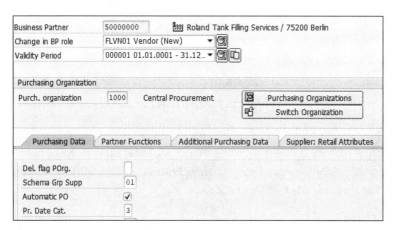

Change View "Schema Groups for Suppliers": Overview

New Entries

Sch.Grp Supp	Description
	Standard schema vendor
01	Schema Supplier 01
02	Schema Supplier 02
09	Schema Grp Interchangeable Mtl

Figure 12.58 Schema Groups for Suppliers

To define a purchasing organization schema group, follow the menu path **Materials Management • Purchasing • Conditions • Define Price Determination Process • Define Schema Group • Schema Groups for Purchasing Organizations**, as shown in Figure 12.59.

Change View "Schema Groups for Purchasing Organizations": Overview

New Entries

Schema GrpPOrg	Description
	Standard Schema
0001	Schema 0001
1000	Demo Schema

Figure 12.59 Schema Groups Purchasing Organizations

When creating a supplier master record, assign the schema group to that supplier in the **Purchasing Data** tab via Transaction BP, as shown in Figure 12.60.

Business Partner	50000000	Roland Tank Filling Services / 75200 Berlin
Change in BP role	FLVN01 Vendor (New)	
Validity Period	000001 01.01.0001 - 31.12...	

Purchasing Organization

Purch. organization	1000	Central Procurement	Purchasing Organizations
			Switch Organization

Purchasing Data | Partner Functions | Additional Purchasing Data | Supplier: Retail Attributes

Del. flag POrg.	
Schema Grp Supp	01
Automatic PO	✓
Pr. Date Cat.	3

Figure 12.60 Assigning a Schema Group to a Business Partner or a Supplier

Defining the Schema Determination

To define the schema determination, follow the menu path **Materials Management •
Purchasing • Conditions • Define Price Determination Process • Define Schema Determination • Determine Calculation Schema for Standard Purchase Orders**. Define the
calculation schema determination for standard POs and stock transport orders, as
follows:

- **Standard POs**

    Click on **Determine Calculation Schema for Standard Purchase Orders**. Now, you'll
    need to define the calculation schema for each purchasing organization schema
    group and supplier schema group combination, as shown in Figure 12.61. Click on
    the **New Entries** button, enter the purchasing organization schema group and sup-
    plier schema group, select the calculation schema group from the dropdown
    menu, and save.

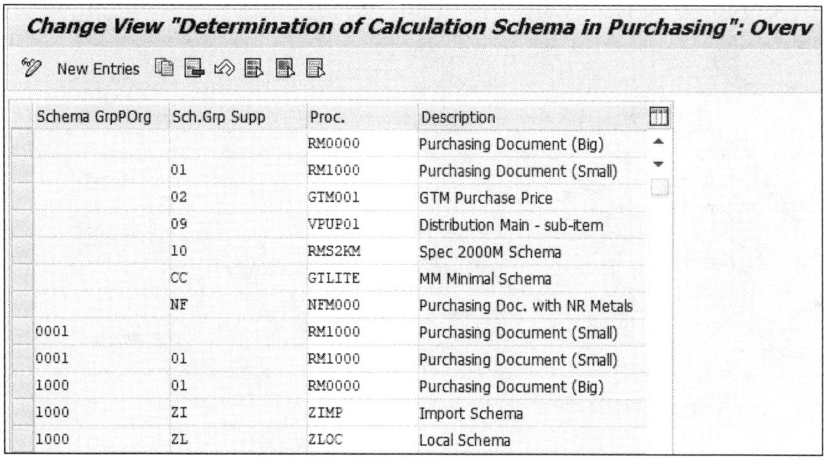

Change View "Determination of Calculation Schema in Purchasing": Overv

New Entries

Schema GrpPOrg	Sch.Grp Supp	Proc.	Description
		RM0000	Purchasing Document (Big)
	01	RM1000	Purchasing Document (Small)
	02	GTM001	GTM Purchase Price
	09	VPUP01	Distribution Main - sub-item
	10	RMS2KM	Spec 2000M Schema
	CC	GTLITE	MM Minimal Schema
	NF	NFM000	Purchasing Doc. with NR Metals
0001		RM1000	Purchasing Document (Small)
0001	01	RM1000	Purchasing Document (Small)
1000	01	RM0000	Purchasing Document (Big)
1000	ZI	ZIMP	Import Schema
1000	ZL	ZLOC	Local Schema

Figure 12.61 Determination of a Calculation Schema in Purchasing

- **Stock transport orders**

    Define the calculation schema for stock transport orders by following the menu
    path **Materials Management • Purchasing • Conditions • Define Price Determina-
    tion Process • Define Schema Determination • Determine Calculation Schema for
    Standard Purchase Orders**. Click on the **New Entries** button, enter the purchasing
    organization schema group and document type, select the calculation schema,
    and save these entries. You can also define a supplying plant-specific calculation

schema (if you have any) by selecting the supplying plant, or you can leave this field blank. If left blank, the calculation schema will be applicable for all plants.

Figure 12.62 shows the PO (Transaction ME21N), and in the **Conditions** tab, you'll see the condition type **PB00** (gross price), the condition type **SKTO** (cash discount), etc. You can explore more details and activities related to pricing by clicking on the **Analysis**, **Condition rec.**, or **Update** buttons.

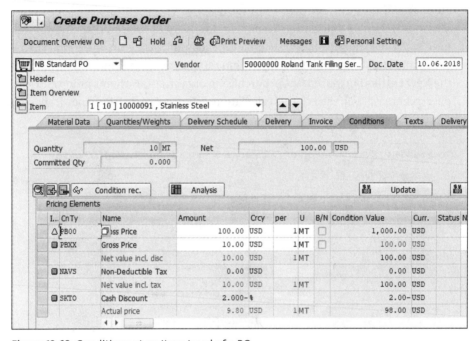

Figure 12.62 Conditions at an Item Level of a PO

12.10   Supplier Evaluation

Supplier evaluations facilitate procurement and quality management (QM) functions to pursue business objectives by providing clear and comprehensible key figures. These objectives include the following:

- Determining the current status of a supply relationship
- Determining and communicating the extent to which the requirements of the purchaser are met by a supplier
- Creating a basis for supplier selection or supplier exclusion

- Determining support after an RFQ to extend the supply relationship
- Determining support for higher weighting for goods receipt inspection and inspection planning
- Providing background information to conclude a quality assurance agreement

In a supplier evaluation, you'll use main criteria and subcriteria to establish key figures to enable the evaluation of individual criteria and the creation of rankings with overall scores. Based on these key figures, you can initiate corrective measures and improvements in a targeted and focused way. A meaningful supplier evaluation is not restricted to determining a supplier's current status; instead, this information can serve as the starting point for ongoing quality improvements.

The SAP system provides flexible tools to evaluate your suppliers. All of these tools meet the standard requirements, and you can easily adapt them to meet the specific business needs of your company. While you'll learn all the important steps involved in supplier evaluations, the focus of this section will remain primarily on price as a critical criterion for evaluating suppliers.

Supplier evaluation takes an intermediate position between procurement and QM by incorporating information and criteria from both a commerce- and quality-related point of view. In SAP systems, you find in the supplier evaluation in MM is evaluated from a commercial point of view, while the supplier is evaluated in the procurement domain. In addition, using master and transaction data from MM, such as material, supplier, and purchasing information records, the system can evaluate suppliers at the purchasing organization level. A purchasing organization is assigned to one or more plants.

> **Note**
>
> During an SAP system implementation project, both procurement (MM) and quality (QM) teams should deliberate and agree on the percentages and weighting of the criteria and subcriteria that influence supplier evaluation.

Supplier evaluation enables the evaluation of each supplier using a quality score (QS). A QS is a combination of all evaluation criteria so that the system can create a hit list (a ranking) of suppliers. You can also consider each criterion in isolation. Supplier evaluation is not limited to the evaluation of suppliers of materials but also suppliers of services, such as maintenance services, cleaning services, and crafts.

In the next section, you'll learn how to configure criteria and subcriteria, including weighting and percentages for each criterion and subcriterion. Then, you'll maintain the master data required for supplier evaluation, followed by running end-to-end business processes. In the end, you'll see how automatic supplier evaluation continuously updates the QS of suppliers.

12.10.1   Configuration Basics

In this section, you'll learn how to make necessary configuration settings to enable supplier evaluations.

Weighting Keys

The weighting key is the basic identification to denote the equal, different, or unequal weighting of criteria. A criterion is a benchmark, such as price, quality, or on-time delivery, which you'll use to evaluate a supplier's compliance to the company's business needs.

To navigate to the weighting keys, follow the menu path **Materials Management • Purchasing • Supplier Evaluation • Define Weighting Keys**. On the screen that appears, the **Weighting key** 01 denotes **Equal weighting**, whereas **Weighting key** 02 denotes **Unequal weighting**.

Defining Criteria

To evaluate suppliers, the system provides five main criteria and additional subcriteria. The main criteria are the following:

- Price
- Delivery
- External service provision
- Service
- Quality

To navigate to criteria, follow the menu path **Materials Management • Purchasing • Supplier Evaluation • Define Criteria**. As shown in Figure 12.63, choose the **Eval. Crit. Price** and then choose **Subcriteria** on the left-hand side, and the screen shown in Figure 12.64 will appear.

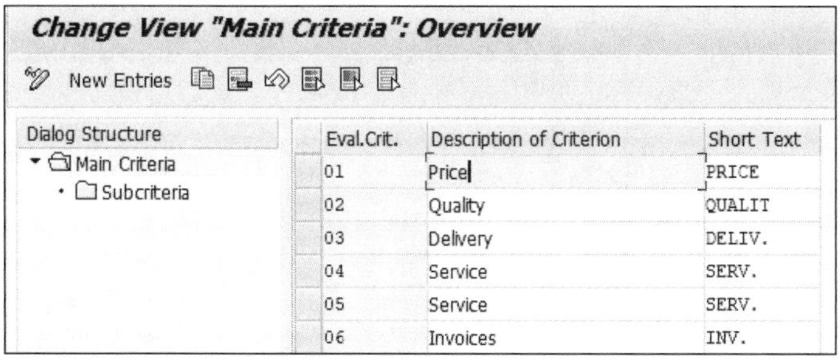

Figure 12.63 Main Criteria of a Supplier Evaluation

Figure 12.64 shows the main criterion 01 (**Price**) with the following subcriteria:

- **Price level**
  The function of the price level subcriterion is to compare a vendor's price with the market price at specified times. A vendor will receive a high score if its price is lower than the market price, while a low score is given when a vendor's price is higher than the market price. This function helps flag potentially high costs that you can investigate to remove cost drivers.

- **Price history**
  The price history subcriterion, on the other hand, compares the buildup of a vendor's price with changes in market price over a certain period. If vendor prices decrease, the vendor gets a high score, but if vendor prices increase above the market price, the vendor gets a low score. This function also helps flag potentially hidden costs that you can investigate and address.

Figure 12.64 shows several scoring methods available for each subcriteria. Since our focus is on the pricing aspects of supplier evaluation, **Scoring Methods** 4 and 5 apply to price level and price behavior/history, respectively. Other scoring methods apply to quantity reliability, quality, adherence to communicated shipping instructions, or timeliness of service delivery.

> **Tips & Tricks**
>
> If you don't want to use a specific subcriterion for the criteria **Quality**, you can simply leave the **Scoring Method** field blank (which means **No Automatic Determination**) from the dropdown list shown in Figure 12.64.

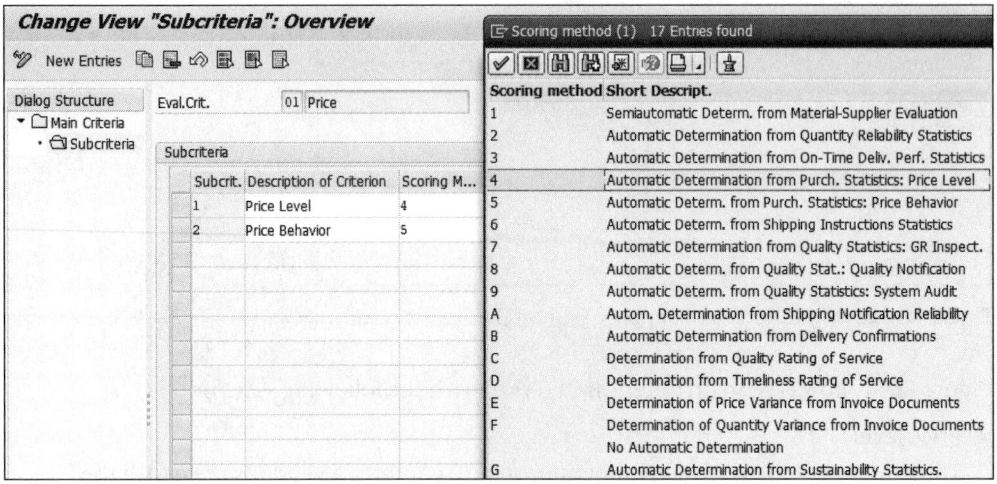

Figure 12.64 Subcriteria of the Main Criteria Price in Supplier Evaluation

Figure 12.65 shows the four subcriteria of the main criteria **Delivery**, which includes on-time delivery performance, quantity reliability (that is, ordered quantity versus delivered quantity), adherence to shipping instructions, and timely delivery confirmations before the actual delivery of goods.

Figure 12.65 Subcriteria of the Main Criteria Delivery

Tips & Tricks

You can always amend the standard settings to meet your company's specific business needs by adding or removing main criteria or subcriteria as deemed necessary. In total, up to 99 main criteria and 20 subcriteria per main criterion are possible.

Purchasing Organization Data for Supplier Evaluation

In this step, you'll maintain supplier evaluation settings that apply to the entire purchasing organization of a company. To maintain supplier evaluation data for a purchasing organization, follow the menu path **Materials Management • Purchasing • Supplier Evaluation • Define Purchasing Organization Data for Supplier Evaluation**.

Figure 12.66 shows the purchasing organization details for **Purchasing Organization 1000**. The **Best Score** that a supplier can have is 100. The system divides the screen into various areas that apply to different criteria in supplier evaluation.

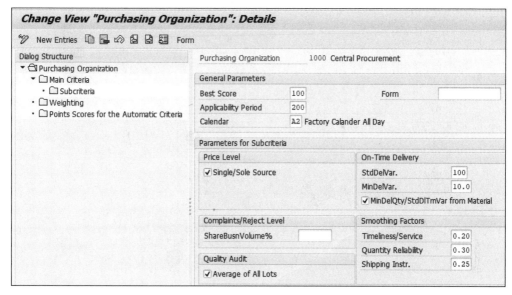

Figure 12.66 Maintaining Supplier Evaluation Details at a Purchasing Organization Level

Let's evaluate the parameters that are important from a price perspective. In the **On-Time Delivery** area, you can control the percentage of a supplier's on-time delivery or deviation from this value (**StdDelVar.**), which impacts a supplier's scores during supplier evaluation. The higher the percentage defined in this field, the higher the QS of the supplier during supplier evaluation. In the **Price Level** area, if you select the **Single/Sole Source** checkbox, then the system takes into account whether the supplier is the only source for this material *and* whether market price has been maintained for the material. Set this indicator if the company prefers to work with only few/selected suppliers due to quality reasons.

Choose **Main Criteria** on the left-hand side to see the screen shown in Figure 12.66. You'll see the four criteria—**Price, Quality, Delivery,** and **Service**—which will be used in the supplier evaluation for **Purchasing Organization** 1000. Selecting the **Manual Maint.** (maintenance) checkbox enables you to manually maintain the QS of a supplier. This checkbox is also available for subcriteria, which may be necessary in service scenarios, where how well the supplier has performed in providing the requisite services in a timely fashion is subjective, as shown in Figure 12.67.

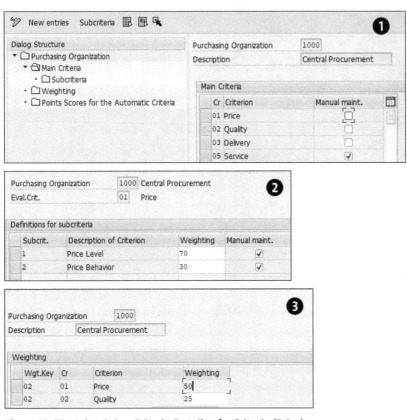

Figure 12.67 Maintaining Criteria Details of a Criteria (Price)

Choose **Price** ❶, as shown in Figure 12.67, and then choose **Subcriteria**, so that ❷ appears. In ❷, you can define the weighting for each of the two subcriteria—that is, for **Price Level** and **Price Behavior**. In our example, the weightings are 70 and 30, respectively. The screen ❸ appears when you choose **Weighting** in ❶, where the **Weighting Key** is 02 (for unequal weighting), with **Price** weighted at 50%, **Quality** at 25% and **Quantity** at 25% (not shown).

The QS calculation is established from the bottom up, which means that subcriteria are evaluated first. You'll determine the QS of the corresponding main criterion by combining the subcriteria according to the weighting. Finally, the system will reflect the main criteria in the corresponding weighting in the overall score.

> **Warning**
>
> Our objective in this section is to show you the maximum range of business scenarios where price or quality, as criteria, can influence a supplier's evaluation. In reality, don't select too many main criteria and subcriteria! A small number of criteria will increase the level of acceptance and understanding among users.

In real-life situations, you may find that calculating an overall score based on the main criterion isn't critically important. Although an overall score does allow for a ranking (hit list) of your suppliers, you may also need to focus on negative ratings, which, in turn, prompts you to ask which main criteria or subcriteria are required for negative evaluations. In our experience, the monitoring of negative criteria can often be of far greater business value.

12.10.2   Master Data Maintenance

To maintain the weighting key for supplier evaluations, use Transaction ME61 or follow the menu path **Logistics • Materials Management • Purchasing • Master Data • Supplier Evaluation • Maintain**. In the initial screen that appears, specify the number of the **Purchasing Organization** by entering "1000" and **Supplier** for which you want to create a supplier evaluation by entering "50000000." The screen shown in Figure 12.68 will appear.

Initially, for a supplier who hasn't been evaluated yet, the system won't populate the fields for the main criteria, indicating that the QS hasn't yet been determined. Enter "02" (unequal weighting) for the **Weighting key** field and save. Notice that, when you enter this weighting key, the system brings up the numbers in the **Weighting** column that you just configured.

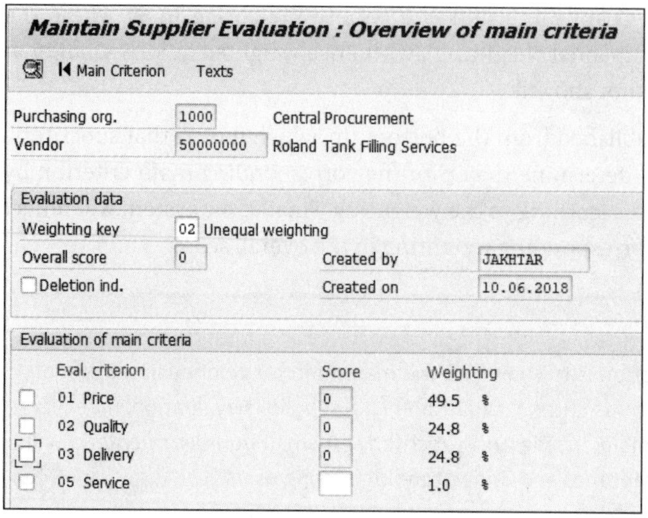

Figure 12.68 Maintaining Supplier Evaluation

Tips & Tricks

While you'll use a different transaction for supplier evaluation, you can also navigate to **Edit • Auto. New Evaluation** in Figure 12.68 (not shown). The system will recalculate all subcriteria and thus all main criteria, as well as recalculate the overall score based on current data. After performing the automatic reevaluation, the system will populate the fields for the overall scores, as well as the main criteria and subcriteria with the current QS.

Tips & Tricks

You can use Transaction ME6E for suppliers whose weighting key isn't maintained yet.

12.10.3   Business Processes

As your business processes, such as creating purchase orders, receiving goods, or maintaining confirmations, continue as normal, the system will keep updating the QS.

Once some or all of these tasks are completed, you can then proceed with supplier evaluations.

12.10.4 Calculating Scores

For automatic new evaluation for supplier Morris, use Transaction ME63 or follow the menu path **Logistics • Materials Management • Purchasing • Master Data • Supplier Evaluation • Automatic New Evaluation**.

Enter the "50000000" for the supplier and the "1000" for the purchasing organization. Optionally, you can specify that scores should be calculated only for suppliers that haven't been evaluated since a specific date (**Not Evaluated Since...**). Choose **Execute**, and the screen shown in Figure 12.69 will appear. The system shows the results of the automatic new evaluation. This log provides a comparison of the scores between the last evaluation and the current evaluation with regard to the overall score, as well as the main criteria and subcriteria.

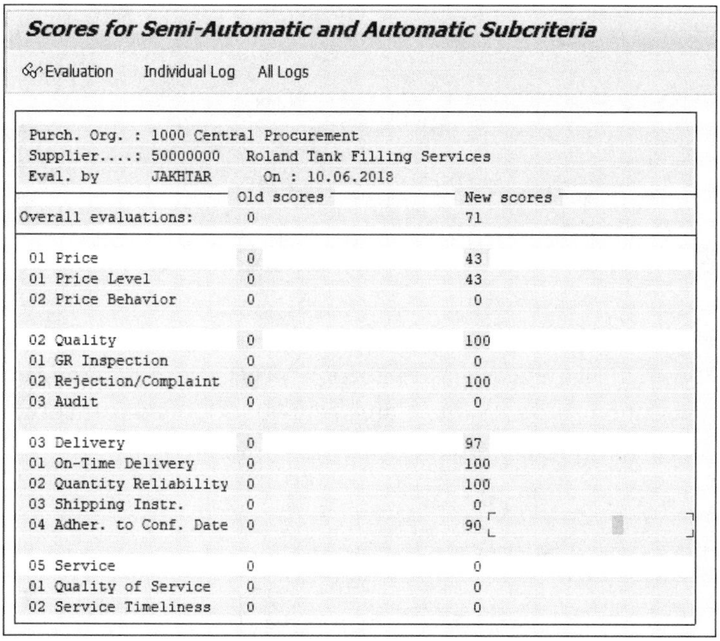

Scores for Semi-Automatic and Automatic Subcriteria

Evaluation   Individual Log   All Logs

Purch. Org. : 1000 Central Procurement
Supplier....: 50000000 Roland Tank Filling Services
Eval. by JAKHTAR On : 10.06.2018

	Old scores	New scores
Overall evaluations:	0	71
01 Price	0	43
01 Price Level	0	43
02 Price Behavior	0	0
02 Quality	0	100
01 GR Inspection	0	0
02 Rejection/Complaint	0	100
03 Audit	0	0
03 Delivery	0	97
01 On-Time Delivery	0	100
02 Quantity Reliability	0	100
03 Shipping Instr.	0	0
04 Adher. to Conf. Date	0	90
05 Service	0	0
01 Quality of Service	0	0
02 Service Timeliness	0	0

Figure 12.69 Scores Calculation from Automatic Supplier Evaluation

Place your cursor in the **New scores** of **43** for the criteria **Price** and choose **All logs**, which will open the screen shown in Figure 12.70.

Figure 12.70 shows the individual-level details of how the system calculated the **QS** of **43** for the criteria **Price**.

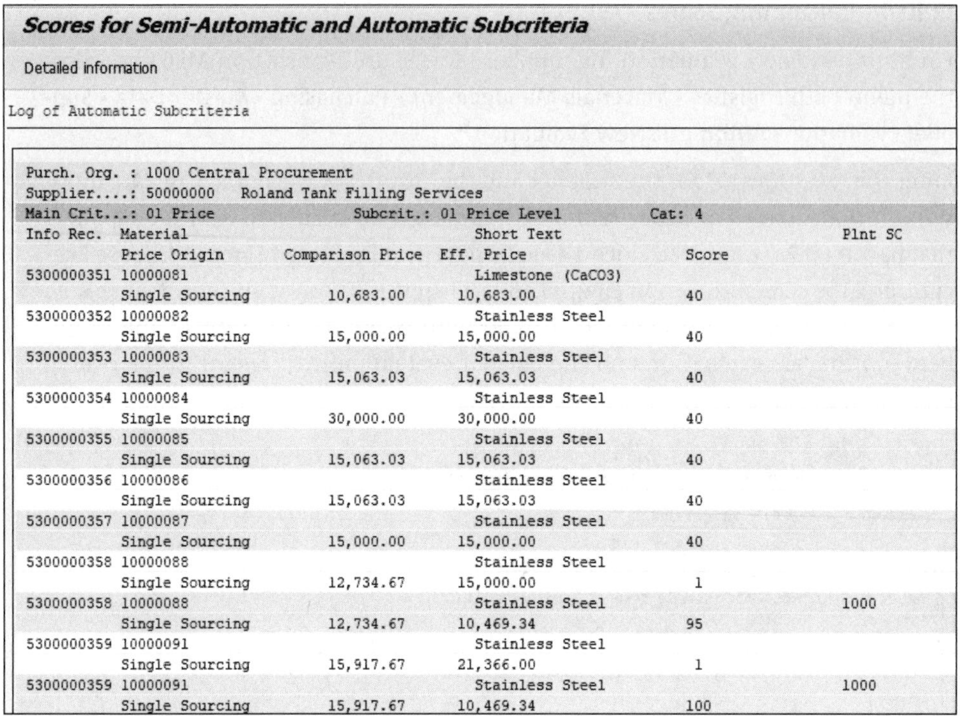

Scores for Semi-Automatic and Automatic Subcriteria

Detailed information

Log of Automatic Subcriteria

```
Purch. Org. : 1000 Central Procurement
Supplier....: 50000000   Roland Tank Filling Services
Main Crit...: 01 Price            Subcrit.: 01 Price Level           Cat: 4
Info Rec.  Material                           Short Text                        Plnt SC
           Price Origin     Comparison Price  Eff. Price          Score
5300000351 10000081                           Limestone (CaCO3)
           Single Sourcing         10,683.00  10,683.00           40
5300000352 10000082                           Stainless Steel
           Single Sourcing         15,000.00  15,000.00           40
5300000353 10000083                           Stainless Steel
           Single Sourcing         15,063.03  15,063.03           40
5300000354 10000084                           Stainless Steel
           Single Sourcing         30,000.00  30,000.00           40
5300000355 10000085                           Stainless Steel
           Single Sourcing         15,063.03  15,063.03           40
5300000356 10000086                           Stainless Steel
           Single Sourcing         15,063.03  15,063.03           40
5300000357 10000087                           Stainless Steel
           Single Sourcing         15,000.00  15,000.00           40
5300000358 10000088                           Stainless Steel
           Single Sourcing         12,734.67  15,000.00           1
5300000358 10000088                           Stainless Steel                   1000
           Single Sourcing         12,734.67  10,469.34           95
5300000359 10000091                           Stainless Steel
           Single Sourcing         15,917.67  21,366.00           1
5300000359 10000091                           Stainless Steel                   1000
           Single Sourcing         15,917.67  10,469.34           100
```

Figure 12.70 Details of Supplier Evaluation

Access the screen shown in Figure 12.71 via Transaction ME6H, which is a standard analysis of vendor evaluation. In our example, supplier 50000000 did particularly well in terms of quantity and on-time delivery.

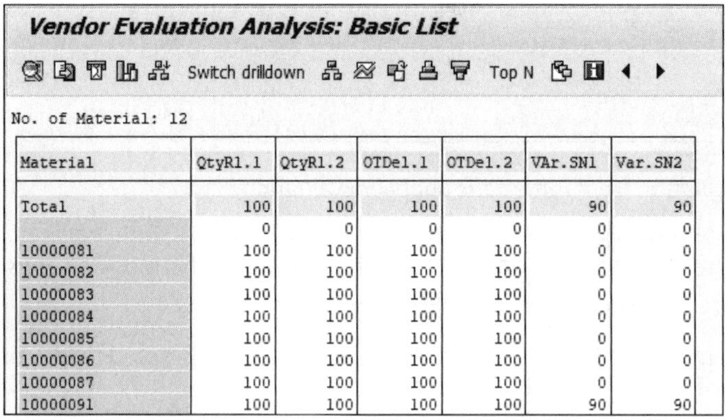

Vendor Evaluation Analysis: Basic List

Switch drilldown Top N

No. of Material: 12

Material	QtyRl.1	QtyRl.2	OTDel.1	OTDel.2	VAr.SN1	Var.SN2
Total	100	100	100	100	90	90
	0	0	0	0	0	0
10000081	100	100	100	100	0	0
10000082	100	100	100	100	0	0
10000083	100	100	100	100	0	0
10000084	100	100	100	100	0	0
10000085	100	100	100	100	0	0
10000086	100	100	100	100	0	0
10000087	100	100	100	100	0	0
10000091	100	100	100	100	90	90

Figure 12.71 Supplier Evaluation Analysis

12.11 Serial Numbers in Purchasing

While some materials are grouped and managed in batches, sometimes you'll need to identify single units of a material uniquely. Thus, individual units must be identified by individual serial numbers. In this section, we'll cover how to define and then assign a serial number profile to an object, such as material master or a piece of equipment.

A serial number is assigned to a unique item to identify and record information about the item. A serial number is different from a batch number because a batch number is given to a number of items, whereas a serial number is unique to each item. Serial numbers are most often found to refer to equipment, such as motors, lathes, drills, or vacuums. For your company, many areas may require using serial numbers to meet the company's business, tracking, and monitoring needs. If your company produces items that should be uniquely defined, then serial numbers may be used. If your company uses machines in production, maintenance items may be regularly purchased and then serialized. Apart from MM, plant maintenance (PM) frequently uses serial numbers because the functionality includes use data for equipment, which is most often serialized.

You can use the serial number functionality in purchasing. You can define serial numbers when creating purchase requisitions and purchase order (POs). For example, an industrial-grade air conditioner manufacturing company in South Korea procures preassembled kits, known as complete knockdown (CKD) kits, which are then used in the manufacturing process. For each CKD kit, the company needs unique serial numbers. Unique serial numbering also helps the company track potential future issues with specific air conditioning units.

The following serial number features are available:

- **Serial number transfer**
  When you create a sales order for third-party processing and assign serial numbers to its items, the created purchase requisition will contain these serial numbers. This purchase requisition is created in the background. When you create a PO with reference to a purchase requisition, the serial numbers are transferred automatically from the purchase requisition to the PO.

- **Schedule lines**
  You can have more than one serial number per schedule line. If a PO has several schedule lines, the serialized numbers must be assigned manually to the correct schedule line or must be created by the system.

- **Base units of measure**

    When serializing base units of measure (e.g., piece), the conversion of an order unit of measure (e.g., kg) must result in a whole number at the schedule line level for POs and at the item level for purchase requisitions. For example, if the base unit of measure was 3 pieces, and the order unit was 2kg, each unit would be 0.66, which you can't serialize.

You can't change the configuration of a purchase requisition or a PO item if you're working with already configured objects to which serial numbers have already been assigned and the original configuration in the material serial number isn't linked to these objects.

In the following sections, we'll show you the necessary configuration steps for setting up serial number profiles in the SAP system. We'll also assign a newly configured serial number profile in the material master and walk you through the associated business processes.

12.11.1   Configuration Steps

Now, let's discuss the step-by-step procedure for configuring serial numbers for purchasing.

Determining the Serial Number Profile

In this step, you'll need to maintain the serial number profile. Follow the menu path **Materials Management • Purchasing • Serial Numbers • Determine Serial Number Profiles**, as shown in Figure 12.72.

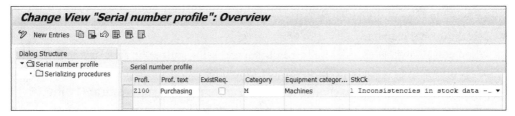

Figure 12.72 Setting Up the Serial Number Profile

You can control the following in the serial number profile:

- The serialization transactions for the profile define the transactions for which serialization is possible.

- Serial number usage defines whether serialization is mandatory or optional.
- The equipment required function specifies whether a piece of equipment is required.
- The serial number profile can be allocated to different transactions with different parameters.
- The equipment category distinguishes individual pieces of equipment according to their usage.

Click on **New Entries** or use the copy function to copy an existing profile. Enter the serial number profile code, which in this example is "Z100"; maintain a short text; and then select the equipment category. You can create a new category by clicking on the **Create** button in the list option. Select the appropriate option (such as **No Stock Check**, **Stock Check with warning**, or **error**) in **Stock Check for Serial Numbers**. The **Stock Check** indicator states whether the system should perform a stock check during serial number assignment. If required, this indicator also establishes what type of notification (warning or error) about stock inconsistencies with inventory management the system will react to.

Selecting the **ExistReq.** checkbox will require business users to *first create* serial numbers for material or equipment (via Transaction IQ01) beforehand these numbers can be *assigned* at the time a purchase requisition or a PO is created.

After entering these details, click on **Serializing procedures** on the left side. You'll need to select the procedure (**Procd**), usage (**SerUsage**), and equipment requirement (**EqReq**), as shown in Figure 12.73.

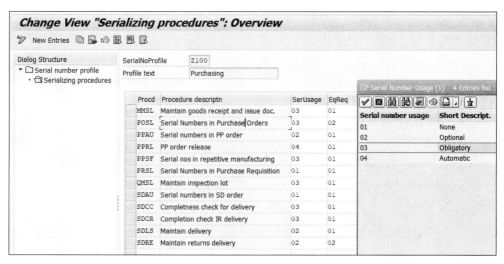

Figure 12.73 Control Settings of a Serial Number Profile

The procedures that can be assigned to each serial number profile are defined in SAP. Table 12.1 identifies the procedure and its business meaning with relation to serial numbers.

Procedure	Business Meaning
HUSL	Enables serial numbers to be assigned in handling unit management (HUM)
MMSL	Enables serial numbers to be assigned in goods receipts, goods issues, stock transfers, stock transport orders, and physical inventory
PPAU	Enables serial numbers to be assigned in production and refurbishment orders
PPRL	Enables serial numbers to be assigned in production and refurbishment orders when they are released
QMSL	Enables serial numbers to be assigned when entering the original value in a QM inspection lot
SDAU	Enables serial numbers to be assigned in sales orders, inquiries, and quotations
SDCC	Enables serial numbers to be assigned when performing completeness checks for deliveries
SDCR	Enables serial numbers to be assigned when performing completeness checks for return deliveries
SDLS	Enables serial numbers to be assigned for deliveries
SDRE	Enables serial numbers to be assigned for return deliveries

Table 12.1 Business Procedures and Meanings for Serial Number Profiles

For purchase requisitions, the serializing procedure is PPRL; for POs, use serializing procedure POSL. Let's now consider the significance usage indicators and equipment requirements:

- **SerUsage**
  Determines one of the following for a business transaction:
  - No serial numbers are assigned.
  - Serial numbers can be assigned.
  - Serial numbers must be assigned.
  - Serial numbers are assigned automatically.

- **EqReq**

  Determines whether or not an equipment master record should be created for each serial number. If you choose the **Default: Without Equipment** option, a user can later decide whether an equipment master record should still be created when they're assigning serial numbers in the dialog box. If you choose the indicator **With equipment**, an equipment master record is required. The indicator can't be reset.

Defining the Serial Number in Purchasing Document Types

In this step, you'll define the serial numbers for a purchasing document type (i.e., purchase requisition document types and PO document types). To define the serial number in a PO, follow the menu path **Materials Management • Purchasing • Purchase Order • Define Document Types**, as shown in Figure 12.74.

To define serial number in a purchase requisition, follow the menu path **Materials Management • Purchasing • Purchase Requisition • Define Document Types**.

Select the document type and, from the left-hand menu, click on **Serial Number Profiles**, as shown in Figure 12.74. Now, you'll need to select the serial number profile Z100 we created in the previous step and then save.

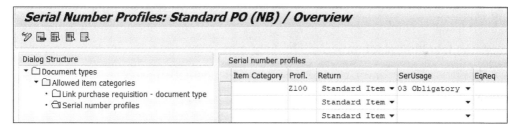

Figure 12.74 Assigning a Serial Number Profile in a Purchase Order Document Type NB

Assigning a Serial Number in a Material Master

You also need to assign a serial number profile in the material master of a material managed in serial numbers. Access the screen shown in Figure 12.75 via Transaction MM01. In the **Plant data/stor. 2** tab, assign the previously configured serial number profile Z100 and save.

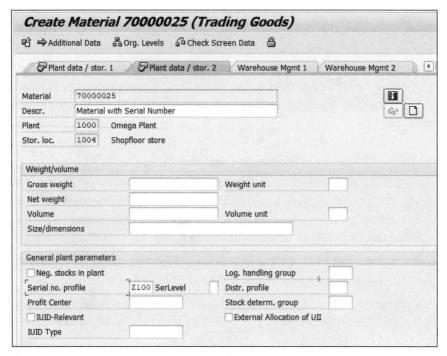

Figure 12.75 Assigning a Serial Number Profile in the Material Master

12.11.2   Business Processes

Let's discuss how you can use serial numbers in purchasing next.

Creating a Purchase Requisition

Create a purchase order by using Transaction ME51N and then enter the material number, vendor, and all other required fields. Click on the **Material Data** tab. Click on the **Assign Serial Numbers** button and enter the serial number for the material. After entering the details, click **OK** and save the document. You can also choose an option to create serial numbers automatically; in this case, the system will automatically create serial numbers for the material.

Creating a Purchase Order

You can either directly create a purchase order via Transaction ME21N or create a PO with reference to the purchase requisition. After entering the details, you'll see the

Create serial number automatically button in the PO screen, as shown in Figure 12.76. If you're creating a PO directly without reference to a purchase requisition, you can maintain a serial number in the PO. To enter a serial number in a PO, go to the item details **Delivery Schedule** tab, click on the **Serial Number** button, and enter the serial number, as shown in Figure 12.76. Either assign the serial numbers manually or click on the **Create serial number automatically** button to have the system assign serial numbers automatically.

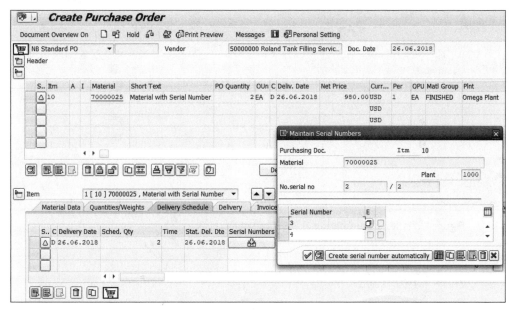

Figure 12.76 Serial Numbers in a Purchase Order

Posting a Goods Receipt

To post a goods receipt, go to Transaction MIGO and enter the PO number that you created earlier. In the item details, you'll see a new tab called **Serial Numbers**, as shown in Figure 12.77.

> **Tips & Tricks**
>
> To see the details about serial numbers, use Transaction IQ03.

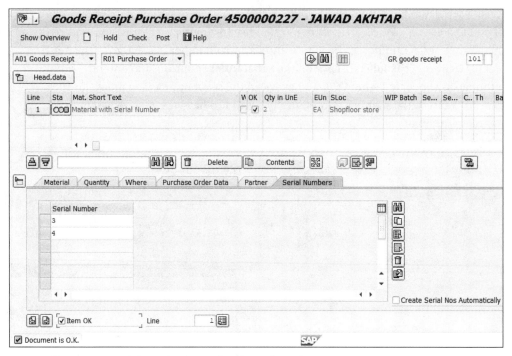

Figure 12.77 Serial Numbering at the Time of Goods Receipt

12.12   Summary

The PO is probably the most familiar process in MM. Importantly, the PO provides material to the production process or to a requestor in a timely fashion, at the best available price, and with the best terms. For an MM user, especially for a purchasing user, all aspects of creating and maintaining a PO should be studied. MM users must understand links with finance, for example, account assignments. Two topics discussed in this chapter, message output and price determination, often create issues for purchasing users. If POs can't be printed out, delays may arise in receiving material, and understanding the process of printing out purchasing output is quite important.

In Chapter 13, we'll examine the external services management (ESM) functionality, including key points such as the service master record and the standard service catalog (SSC).

Chapter 13
External Services Management

Companies purchase services in the same way that they purchase materials. A vendor just supplies a service, rather than a material. When that service has been received, a service entry sheet is maintained in the SAP system. The invoice is matched against the PO and a goods receipt document, like a time sheet.

External services management (ESM) incorporates functionality that is relevant to the procurement and execution of services at a company. A service master record is the document that contains the information on a service. The service specifications are listed services that can make up a particular task or project that your company needs to procure.

Services can be planned using a service master record, or they can be unplanned, which means that, instead of referencing a service master, they reference a monetary limit for the services performed. A service received from a service provider can be entered using a service entry sheet, whereby documented hours or specific details about the contracted and delivered services can be approved and authorization can be given for payment.

Figure 13.1 shows an end-to-end services procurement process. First, a user creates a purchase requisition for the services required. Assuming that the requisite services are procured from a regular service provider, you won't be seeking quotations. The purchase requisition is then converted into a purchase order. The service provider performs or delivers services, and these services delivery are maintained in service entry sheets. Invoice verification takes place against the service entry sheets maintained in the SAP system.

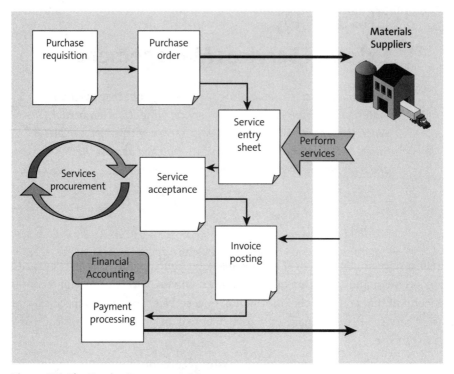

Figure 13.1 The Service Procurement Process

In the first section of this chapter, we'll describe the document that contains the basic information of a service: the service master record. We'll then outline the steps required to maintain a service catalog. Next, we'll cover the business processes involved in procuring services. Finally, we'll cover blanket purchase orders.

13.1   Service Master Record

A service master record is a document that contains the basic information about a service, similar to a material master record.

A service master record can be entered using Transaction AC03, as shown in Figure 13.2, or by following the menu path **Logistics • Materials Management • Service Master • Service • Service Master**.

Figure 13.2 shows a service described as "Oil Tank Filling Services." In addition, **SERV Service: purchasing** has been selected as the **Service Category**. The third entry for the service master record is the **Base Unit of Measure**, which in this case is **M3** (cubic meter). This unit of measure (UoM) is the basis on which a delivered service is measured and can be, for example, the measurement of labor in hours or square feet for new flooring or paint. The **Mat/Srv.Grp** (material/services group) is maintained as **0005** (for services), and the **Valuation class** is maintained as **3200** (services).

In the **Formula** field, the formula **VOL01** is used so that the service entry sheet is maintained, in our example, on the basis of the volume of the oil tank that the contractor is contracted out to fill. Saving the **Service** will create an **Activity number** 3000141.

> **Note**
>
> The service number and the activity number are the same thing.

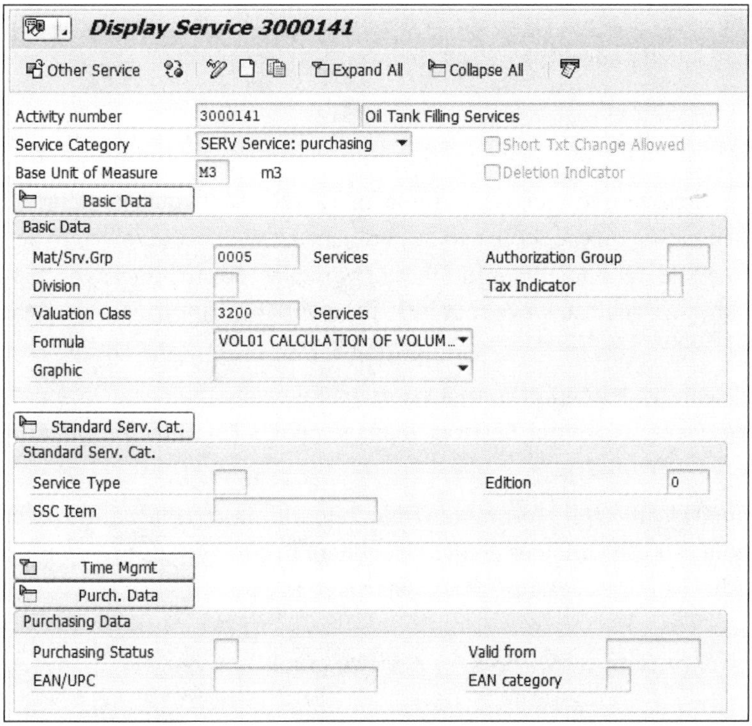

Figure 13.2 Entry Screen for Creating the Service Master Record

Some of the important fields shown in Figure 13.2 will be discussed in the following sections.

13.1.1   Material/Service Group

The material/service group (**Mat/Srv.Grp**) field allows a material group to be selected for grouping purposes. This selection is the same for a service master as for a material master.

13.1.2   Tax Indicator

The **Tax Indicator** for a service master allows a purchasing user to enter a not-taxed code if the service isn't taxed, or the user can enter a tax code for taxable services.

13.1.3   Valuation Class

The **Valuation Class** for the service master is the same field that is used in the material master. Using the valuation class, the system can find the general ledger (G/L) accounts associated with a specific service's financial postings.

13.1.4   Formula

The **Formula** field allows you to choose a formula for a service that you'll predefine in configuration. Depending on the service to be performed, the effort involved in performing a task may be definable by a number of variables. For instance, you may have a formula for lawn maintenance that includes a variable capturing size of the area to be mown.

The **Formula** field can be defined in configuration by following the navigation path **Materials Management • External Services Management • Formula for Quantity Determination • Define Formulas**.

A formula is defined by entering a formula key and then adding variable names to the formula. A formula can use variables defined elsewhere in configuration. A formula must also have a base unit of measure, as shown in Figure 13.3.

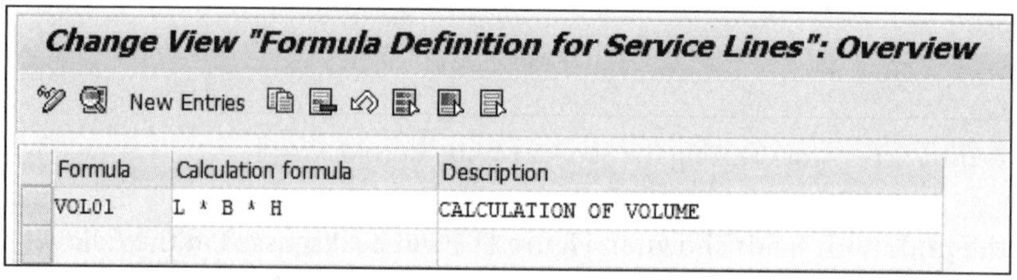

Formula	Calculation formula	Description
VOL01	L ^ B ^ H	CALCULATION OF VOLUME

Figure 13.3 Formula for Calculating Volume

Variables can be defined by following the navigation path **Materials Management •
External Services Management • Formula for Quantity Determination • Specify Names
of Formula Variables**.

Figure 13.4 shows three formula variables: **B**, **H**, and **L**. These three variables are used
in the calculation formula VOL01, shown earlier in Figure 13.3. Double-click on **Variable B**, and the screen shown in Figure 13.5 will appear.

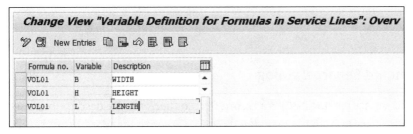

Figure 13.4 Variables for Calculating Volume

Figure 13.5 shows **Variable B** with a **Base UoM** (unit of measure) as **M** (meter) and a
short description.

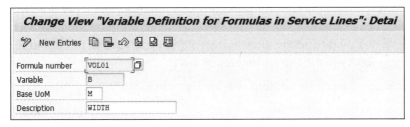

Figure 13.5 Details of Each Formula Variable

13.1.5   Graphic

The service master includes a **Graphic** field, where a purchasing user can select a picture or graphic to aid the supplier of the service. For example, the service may be to
polish a finished good, and the company may have a specific way to complete the
task. Thus, a graphic could be included with the purchase order (PO) or the request for
quotation (RFQ) to ensure that the service is performed correctly.

In the next section, we'll discuss the standard service catalog (SSC), which is a list of
the service descriptions that can be used by the purchasing use to reduce the number
of entries required.

> **Tips & Tricks**
>
> You can also maintain a *model service specification*, which lists out all the services or activities a contractor needs to perform. Use Transaction ML10 to create a model service specification and, on the detailed screen, maintain individual and previously created services (which we covered in Section 13.1). The model service specification will then be available for selection while creating a service PO or even while maintaining a service entry sheet for a service PO.

13.2   Standard Service Catalog

The standard service catalog (SSC) is a record that contains service descriptions used when a service master hasn't been created. The SSC keeps a standard list of service descriptions to eliminate the need for descriptions to be created each time a nonservice master record is entered, which avoids a great deal of data duplication.

An SSC entry can be created by using Transaction ML01 or by following the navigation path **Logistics • Materials Management • Service Master • Standard Service Catalog • Create**. On the initial **Create Standard Service Catalog** screen, enter a **Service Type** number and an **Edition** or version number. The detailed information for a service type includes a validity period, shown as **Valid from** and **Valid to** fields, and the **Service category** field, which has been entered as **SRV1**.

The next section reviews the conditions that are found in ESM.

13.3   Conditions in External Services Management

Conditions are found in ESM similar to those found in normal purchasing. Conditions apply to services such as discounts, surcharges, and taxes. One method of entering a condition for a service is to enter a total price condition using Transaction ML45 or by following the navigation path **Logistics • Materials Management • Service Master • Service • Service Conditions • For Service • Add**. This transaction allows a purchasing user to enter a condition, which provides an overall estimate of the service to be performed over a certain time period.

In our example shown in Figure 13.6, the service has been given a total price condition (**Amount**) of $100 per m^3 of work. The total price condition can also be defined as a scale by pressing the ⌊F2⌋ function key or by choosing **Goto • Scales.** Figure 13.6 shows the **Validity** as **01.01.2018** until **30.12.2025.**

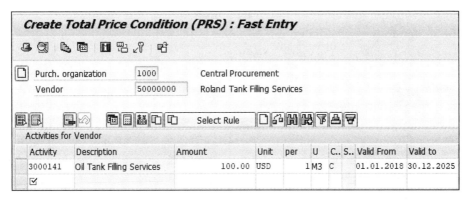

Figure 13.6 Maintaining the Pricing Condition of an Activity

The **Control** section shows that the **Scale Basis** is set to **C**, which defines a quantity scale.

The **Scale Type** shows that the scale is from one **Scale quantity** to another. For example, a scale can be maintained that, from 100 m³ (cubic meter) to 500 m³ of tank filling services, the **Amount** is $100 per m³. From 501 m³ to 1,000 m³, the amount is $90 per m³. The scaling continues until the upper limit is reached at 2,000 m³, at which point any m³ above this amount will be charged at a rate of $85 per m³.

The next section describes the actual procurement of services.

13.4   Procurement of Services

Services can be purchased using Transaction ME21N (Create Purchase Order). In addition to the maintaining the **Vendor, Purch. Organization, Purchasing Group**, and **Delivery date**, the **Account Assignment** needs to be maintained as **K** (for cost center), and **Item Category** needs to be set as **D** (for services), as shown in Figure 13.7. The **Short Text** field can be maintained for an overall description of the services being procured.

Figure 13.7 shows the data entry screen for the service specification. A number of items can be entered on this screen. In the item details, the service number **3000141** can be manually entered or can be selected by clicking the **Service Sel**. button. This number is the same service number we created in the previous step.

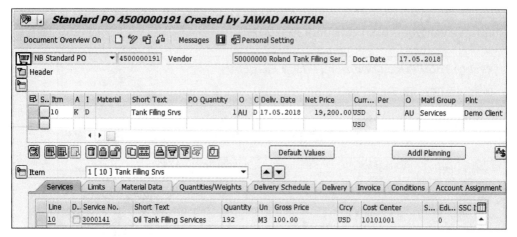

Figure 13.7 Services Purchase Order

Figure 13.8 shows the popup window where a business user will need to enter the volume details of the tank filling services required. In our example, the **Length** is maintained as **4M** (meter), the **Width** as **6M**, and the **Height** as **8M**. Thus, the total volume can be calculated as:

Volume = 4 m × 6 m × 8 m = 192 m3

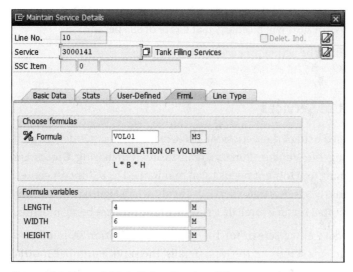

Figure 13.8 Formula Details in a Services PO

Figure 13.9 shows the popup for maintaining the G/L account (a G/L account is automatically selected if a valuation class is maintained for the service). Enter the cost center to which the services will be charged.

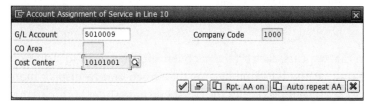

Figure 13.9 G/L Account and Cost Center Details

As many services as required can be added to the PO. The **Service number** is entered with a quantity (**Qty**) and price per UoM (**Un**). After information is entered for individual services, the PO can be completed after the header information, shown in Figure 13.7, has been verified.

Since we maintained a price of \$100 per m^3 in service number 3000141 and since, according to the PO, the quantity or the volume of tank filling is calculated as 192 m^3, therefore, the total value of the PO is \$19,200 (192 m^3 × \$100/m^3 = 19,200). On saving, the system will create a PO, in our example PO number 4500000191.

In the next section, we'll review how to enter services that have been performed.

13.5   Entry of Services

When a supplier has completed a service, or even partially performed a service, this information can be entered into the SAP system. Delivered or performed services are recorded on the service entry sheet, which can accommodate both planned and unplanned services.

In a service entry sheet, data is entered with respect to the service ordered via a PO. A service entry sheet can be found using Transaction ML81N or by following the path **Logistics • Materials Management • Service Entry Sheet • Maintain**, as shown in Figure 13.10.

13

> **Note**
>
> While maintaining a service entry sheet in SAP S/4HANA, if you encounter the error message, "SE 729 Customizing incorrectly maintained," then you'll need to follow the steps described in SAP Note 1382685.

On the initial screen that appears, click on the overview off/on icon 🕭 to switch off the overview appearing on the left-hand side of the screen and to display more details on the service entry sheet. Next, click the **Other Purchase Order** button so that the screen shown in Figure 13.11 appears.

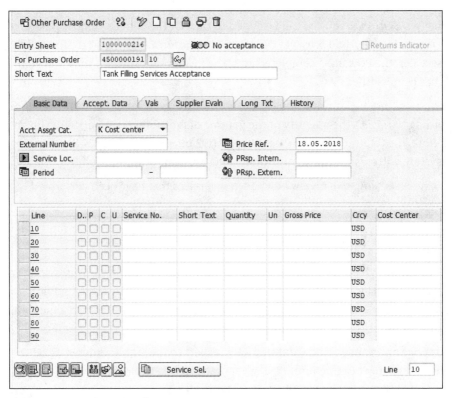

Figure 13.10 Service Entry Sheet

As shown in Figure 13.11, enter the PO number and its line item number (in our example "10") and select the **Adopt full quantity** checkbox so that the full quantity is maintained in the PO.

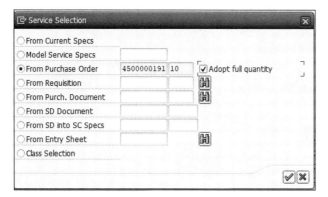

Figure 13.11 Service Selection

Next, click on the new sheet icon ⬜, as shown in Figure 13.10, and the system creates service entry sheet number 1000000216. At the bottom of Figure 13.10, click the **Service Sel.** button, and the screen shown in Figure 13.12 will appear. Select line item 10 and then click the **Copy Services** icon. The system will automatically copy all service details from activity 3000141 (**Service No.**) from the PO. The screen shown in Figure 13.13 will appear.

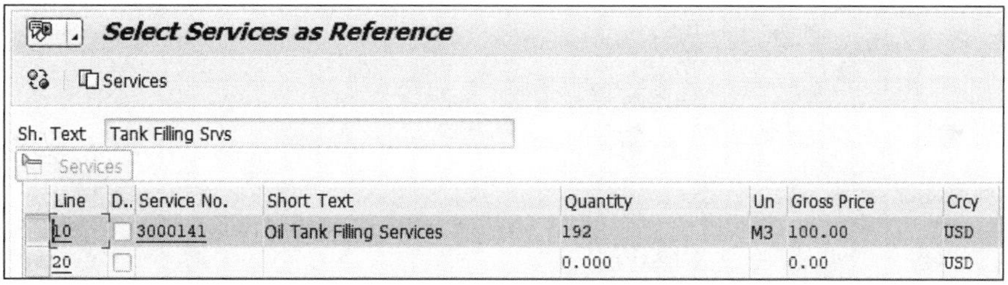

Figure 13.12 Available Services for Selection

After the data has been entered, the data sheet can be accepted by clicking the accept ⓟ icon. After being entered, the service entry sheet will appear as accepted (green light) or ready for acceptance (yellow light) on Transaction ML81N's initial screen, shown in Figure 13.13, with a traffic light indicator at top.

Subsequently, an invoice can also be posted (via Transaction MIRO) with reference to the PO or the service entry sheet. Figure 13.14 shows the complete PO history of the PO 4500000191, which includes the service entry sheet 1000000216 as well as the invoice number 5105600977.

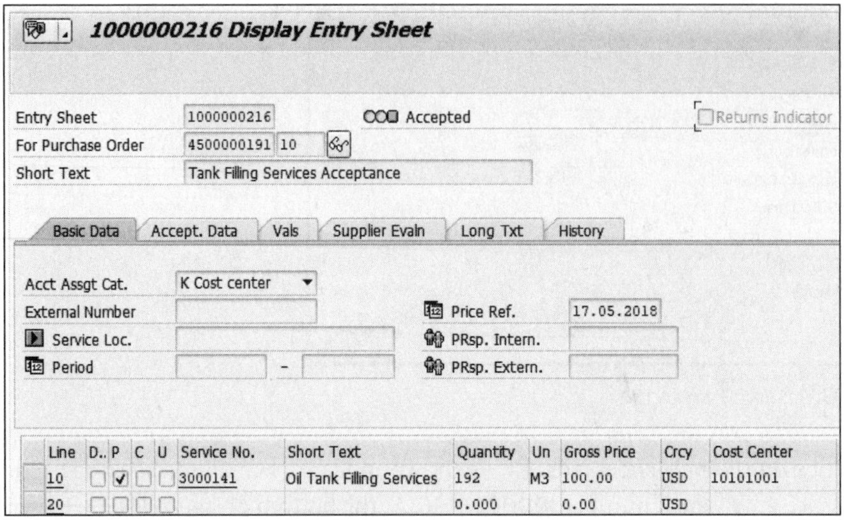

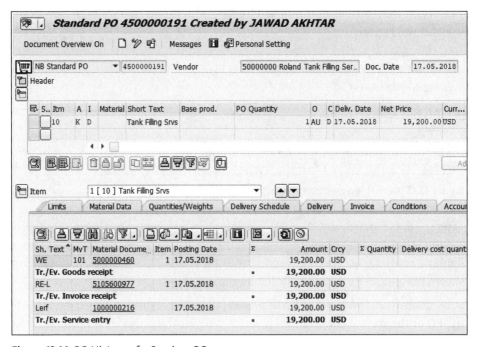

Figure 13.13 An Accepted Service Entry Sheet

Figure 13.14 PO History of a Services PO

When no more service entry sheets will be entered against the PO, you can set the final entry indicator by choosing **Entry Sheet • Set Status • Final Entry**. You also have options to block or delete a service entry sheet, as shown earlier in Figure 13.11.

Tips & Tricks

To view reporting about services, such as planned versus actual services delivered, use Transaction ME2S. Another important and services-specific standard report for service entry sheets can be accessed using Transaction MSRV6.

The next section reviews blanket POs, which many companies use to purchase services.

13.6   Blanket Purchase Orders

A blanket PO is used when a company needs to purchase low-value services or materials at minimal cost. By reducing the effort needed by the purchasing department, you can more economically monitor the transaction. For example, let's say your company supplies its offices with general cleaning and janitorial supplies, ordered on a biweekly or monthly basis. This company should use a blanket PO rather than creating a separate PO each time they need supplies. When the material is consumed or services are performed, an invoice is posted in the system with reference to the PO, and no goods receipts or service entry sheets are posted in the system. You can directly post invoices for the materials procured, as shown in Figure 13.15.

The blanket PO process has several business advantages that result in lower transaction costs, as follows:

- Blanket POs are valid for the long term; therefore, you don't need to create them every time you reorder supplies.
- A goods receipt or service entry sheet maintenance isn't required.
- Material master records aren't required.

A blanket PO is created via Transaction ME21N (Create Purchase Order), as shown in Figure 13.16.

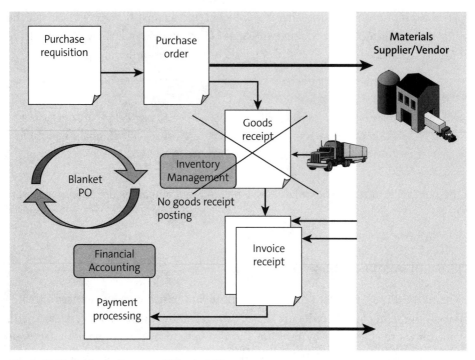

Figure 13.15 Business Process of Blanket PO

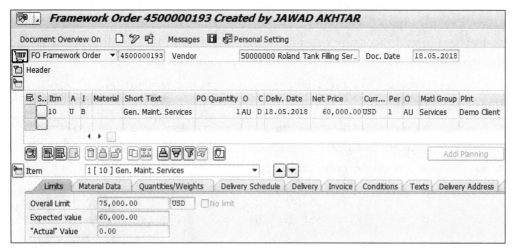

Figure 13.16 Detail Information for a Blanket Purchase Order

The most important fields in this area are:

- **Document type**

  The **Document Type** for a blanket order is **FO** rather than the normal document type for POs, which is usually **NB**. When creating a blanket PO, make sure you select the correct document type.

- **Item category**

  The item category in a blanket order is **B** for a limit order. As a result, the PO will be created with a limit value and not a line item, as shown under the **Limits** tab in the lower half of the screen.

- **Validity period**

  Using a blanket PO requires that the value limit be contained within a period of time. Therefore, the vendor has a limited period in which to submit invoices up to the value limit entered within the blanket order. The validity period is shown in two fields, **Validity Start** and **Validity End** in the header of a PO.

- **Vendor invoicing**

  The vendor will send invoices to the purchasing department with reference to the PO. The accounts payable (AP) department will process invoices that fall within the validity period of the blanket PO. These invoices will also only be processed if the total amount of the combined invoices from the vendor doesn't exceed the **Overall limit** in the blanket PO. However, if **no limit** should exist on the value amount of the invoices sent for the PO, the **No limit** indicator should be selected.

- **Overall limit**

  An **Overall Limit** can be entered for all unplanned services on the PO. This limit can't be exceeded.

- **Expected value**

  An **Expected value** of unplanned services can be entered. This value doesn't necessarily need to be equal to the overall limit, and the expected value can be exceeded unlike the overall limit. The expected value is the figure that will be used if an appropriate release strategy is in place.

- **"Actual" value**

  This field is calculated by the system and is updated continually from service sheet entries or from goods receipt transactions.

- **Contract**

  A service PO can allow a purchasing user to add one or more purchase **Contracts**. A limit to the services purchased against the contract can be added.

Figure 13.17 shows the blanket PO for which an invoice of 25,000 USD has been posted via Transaction MIRO. In Transaction MIRO, click the **Account Assignment** button and, in the popup that appears, enter details such as the G/L account and the cost center to which these materials or services should be charged.

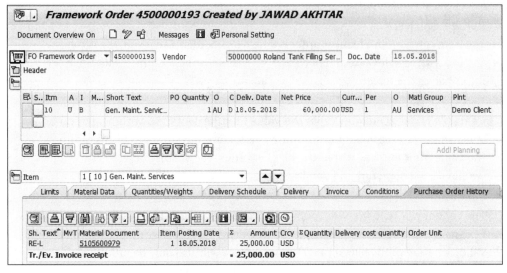

Figure 13.17 PO History of a Blanket PO

Configuration Tip

When creating a blanket PO, the account assignment will be initially maintained as unknown (**U**), as shown in Figure 13.17. Therefore, you'll need to maintain the account assignment details when posting an invoice for the blanket PO. To maintain account assignment details in invoice verifications (Transaction MIRO), use configuration Transaction OME9 and choose **Account Assignment U**. In the detailed screen, select the **AA Chgable at IR** checkbox.

13.7   Configuration Basics of External Services Management

Let's now briefly cover some important configuration steps for ESM. To view all the configuration options for ESM in one node, use Transaction OLMSRV. Follow these configuration steps:

1. **Defining activity numbers**

   An **Activity Number** is similar to the material number, and this field can be defined for external or internal numbering. The number ranges can be defined in configuration using Transaction ACNR or by following the navigation path **Materials Management • External Services Management • Service Master • Define Number Ranges**.

2. **Defining organizational statuses for service categories**

   The SAP system enables you to assign service master records, administered in your company, to different groups according to their usage. These groups are called *service categories*. In this step, you'll maintain the organizational status of the service categories. To characterize service categories in more detail, you'll assign them an organizational status. An **organizational status** indicates the areas in which a service master record is used. Examples include basic data, controlling (CO) or cost accounting data, purchasing data, and sales data.

   To define organizational statuses for service categories, follow the menu path **Materials Management • External Services Management • Service Master • Define Organizational Status for Service Categories**. The following organizational statuses can be maintained for service categories:

   - **BDS** (basic data status): Select this indicator to store basic data in the service master record.
   - **CnSt** (controlling status): Select this indicator to store controlling/cost accounting data in the service master record.
   - **PuSt** (purchasing data status): Select this indicator to store purchasing data in the service master record.
   - **SDSt** (sales and distribution status): Select this indicator to store sales and distribution (SD) data in the service master record.

3. **Defining a service category**

   The **Service Category** differentiates between different types of services, similar to what a material type does for materials. A service category, as shown in Figure 13.18, can be configured in the SAP IMG by following the navigation path **Materials Management • External Services Management • Service Master • Define Service Category**.

To define a new service category, click **New Entries** and enter the service category code in the **Serv. cat** column. Next, select the organization status service category (**OrgSrvCat.**) and account category reference (**ARef**), as shown in Figure 13.18. The account category reference is used for valuation classes, and each account category reference has a set of valuation classes assigned to it.

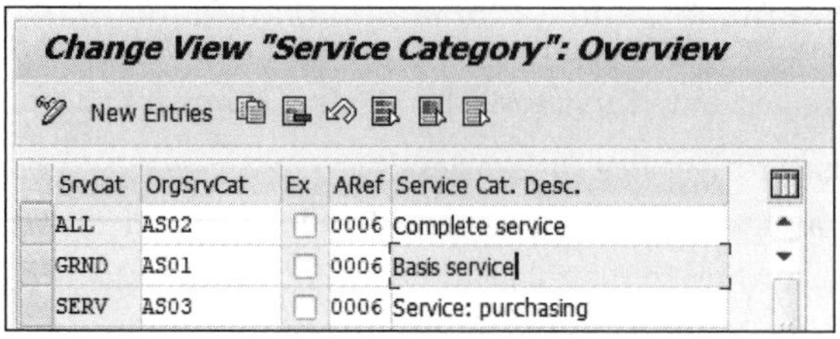
Change View "Service Category": Overview

New Entries

SrvCat	OrgSrvCat	Ex	ARef	Service Cat. Desc.
ALL	AS02	☐	0006	Complete service
GRND	AS01	☐	0006	Basis service
SERV	AS03	☐	0006	Service: purchasing

Figure 13.18 Configuration of a Service Category

13.8 Summary

In this chapter, we discussed the ESM functionality. Since most companies purchase services as well as materials, ESM allows a purchasing department influence how services are purchased and monitor the consumption of those services. As more companies use SAP systems to purchase and record service usage, purchasing personnel must become fully familiar with this functionality. The topics we covered in this chapter should help you understand more fully the process of procuring services. This chapter also covers the basics concepts you'll need to know for using blanket POs.

In the next chapter, we'll cover special procurement types used in the MM processes.

Chapter 14

Special Procurement Types

SAP S/4HANA provides special procurement types that you can use to attend to unique business scenarios, for example, for the production, assembly, and procurement of components that are nontraditional in nature and involve complex and diverse logistics processes.

The traditional production process involves procuring components from suppliers and vendors, producing them in-house, and eventually selling them to customers. However, in an integrated and truly globalized economy, both companies with small manufacturing bases and companies with giant production setups spread out across many countries and locations must deal with diverse, challenging, and complex logistics and supply chain processes. These processes also need to be mapped in SAP S/4HANA for effective planning of procurement, inventory management, and production processes.

Consider the following business processes and the complexities involved:

- You outsource some operations of your production to specialized vendors for value-adding processes.

- You need to procure some components used in assembly from your company's other plant, in a distant location.

- You have a vendor who keeps its material stock in your warehouse, but you only pay the vendor when your company actually consumes the material.

- Your utility company provides you with a utility, such as water or natural gas in a pipeline, which is always available. However, you only pay the utility company for the quantity of utility consumed.

These business scenarios and more are accommodated with *special procurement types* in SAP S/4HANA. These business processes vary from subcontracting to inter-plant transfers, from consignment to direct procurement.

When special procurement is involved, you must ensure that the relevant special procurement type key has been assigned, either in the **MRP 2** tab of the material master or in the detailed view of the component in the material bill of materials (BOM). In this chapter, we'll first provide an overview of available special procurement types in SAP S/4HANA, and then we'll discuss each type of special procurement, as follows:

- Direct procurement
- Stock transfers (interplant transfers)
- Withdrawals from an alternate plant
- Subcontracting
- Consignment
- Pipeline material

14.1   Overview

A *special procurement type key* is the control function that the system looks for when planning a material to calculate the relevant results (after planning) for immediate execution. The special procurement type key is plant-specific, and you can assign this key at two levels, depending on the business processes:

- Material master (in the **MRP 2** tab)
- BOM in the detailed view of the component

Figure 14.1 shows the **MRP 2** tab of **Material P-100** and **Plant 3000**. In the **Special Procurement** field, you'll assign the special procurement type key. Place your cursor in the **Special Procurement** field and press F4 or click the dropdown menu, which will open a popup window containing a list of procurement types delivered by SAP S/4HANA in its standard offering, as well as additional special procurement types created to fulfill specific business needs.

You can configure special procurement type keys by following the menu path **Materials Management · Consumption-Based Planning · Master Data · Define Special Procurement Types**, as shown in Figure 14.2.

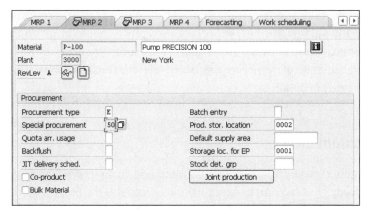

Figure 14.1 Special Procurement Type Field in the Material Master

Change View "Special Procurement": Overview

New Entries

Plnt	Name 1	Sp.Pr.Type	Special procurement type description
3000	New York	10	Consignment
3000	New York	30	Subcontracting
3000	New York	40	Stock transfer (proc.from alter.plant)
3000	New York	42	Stock transfer (proc.from plant 3200)
3000	New York	45	Stock transfer (proc.from plant 1000)
3000	New York	50	Phantom assembly
3000	New York	52	Direct production/Collective order
3000	New York	60	Planned independent requirements
3000	New York	70	Reservation from alternate plant
3000	New York	72	Reservation from alternate plant 3200
3000	New York	80	Production in alternate plant
3000	New York	82	Production in alternate plant (3200)

Figure 14.2 Configuration of the Special Procurement Type Key for Plant 3000

Tips & Tricks

In a non-production SAP S/4HANA system, whenever you assign a special procurement type key in the **MRP 2** tab of the material master or to a component in a BOM and then perform the necessary business transaction (e.g., creating a production order or purchase requisition), you can always run material requirements planning (MRP) on that material/component (Transactions MD02 or MD01N) to test how the system reflects the planning results of that specific special procurement type key. The same testing logic applies when you create a new special procurement key to fulfill a business requirement.

At this point, you should have a general understanding of special procurement processes. In your company's actual business processes, preference should be given to making better and effective use of MRP results, so that predecessor-successor relationships along the entire chain of events are available. Now let's consider each of the special procurement types in detail.

14.2   Direct Procurement

The special procurement type key for direct procurement is 51. In *direct procurement*, the system automatically creates a purchase requisition or initiates the procurement process the moment a production order is created manually. If you use the MRP run's results, the system can correctly reflect the material for direct procurement, as long as the relevant special procurement type key 51 has been assigned to the component. In the configuration screen for **Direct Procurement** for a specific plant, ensure that the **Direct procurement** checkbox has been selected.

> **Note**
>
> You can use the default values for direct procurement to control whether requirement coverage elements are generated through dependent requirements of the planned orders (in the corresponding MRP run) or by the requirements that result from production orders. Refer to Figure 14.2 to see such default values; you can maintain these default values using Transaction OPPB or by following the Customizing menu path **Production • Material Requirements Planning • Planning • Direct Procurement • Settings for Direct Procurement**.

On the initial screen to maintain direct procurement settings, as shown in Figure 14.3, click **Plant** to open the screen, which in our example will show three options ❶ available for plant 3000. Selecting option **3** in the **Direct procurement/production** field enables the system to automatically trigger direct procurement planning during the MRP run. Save these settings and click **Back**, which brings you back to the initial screen. This time, choose **MRP group** to see the group information ❷. On this screen, you can make relevant settings specific to the MRP group. This option helps when different MRP controllers want the system to generate direct procurement proposals according to their specific business needs.

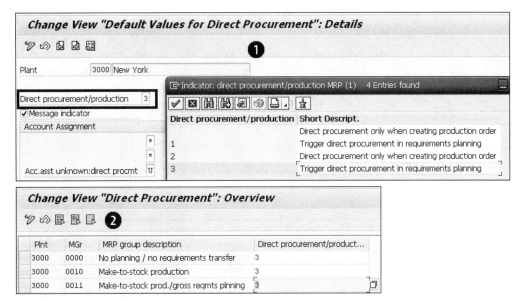

Figure 14.3 Configuration Settings for Direct Procurement

In our example, as shown in Figure 14.4, the special procurement type key 51 has been assigned to the material masters undergoing direct procurement as displayed in the **Component Overview** screen of the production order for **Material P-100**. Notice that the **Component 100-300** is the direct procurement material, as indicated by the assignment of **1** in the **Direct procurement** column, which stands for **External procurement**, in the dropdown list shown.

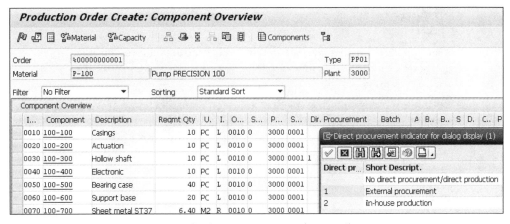

Figure 14.4 Component 100-300 with Direct Procurement (External)

Figure 14.5 shows the planning results when a user runs MRP for the **Material 100-300** and **Plant 3000**. The system considered the existing stock of 5 PC, calculated the requirement quantity for the component 100-300 as 5 PC, and created planned order 37074. The next step would be to convert these results into a purchase requisition, so the system generates a purchase requisition number.

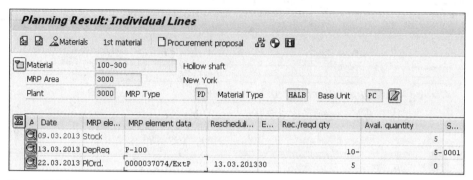

Figure 14.5 MRP Results of Material 100-300 for Direct Procurement

Let's look back at the production order containing the direct procurement's component 100-300. Figure 14.6 shows the detailed component view of the **Material 100-300** and the corresponding purchase requisition number **10013837** ❶. Click the **Purchase Requ.** button ❶ to open the **Display Purchase Req. 10013837** screen ❷. On this screen, all procurement details are automatically copied into the purchase requisition. Also note that the account assignment category **F** (column **A**) denotes that this order is a production order.

Tips & Tricks

If a component is generally not a part of direct procurement, you have the option of assigning a special procurement key for direct procurement directly in the BOM item, not in the **MRP 2** tab of the material master. In this way, you can maintain better control of the material, which is only specific to certain production processes by virtue of its direct procurement status.

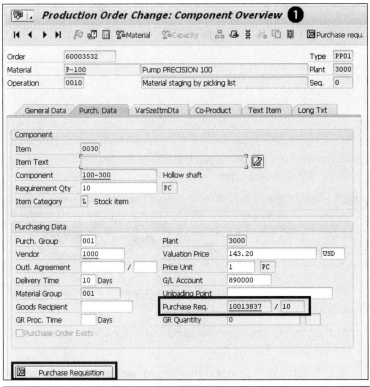

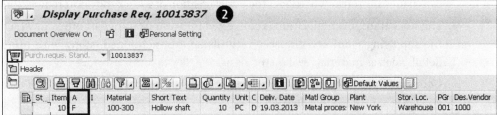

Figure 14.6 Purchase Requisition with Direct Procurement

14.3   Stock Transfers (Interplant Transfers)

The special procurement type key for stock transfer is 40 and is characterized as an *interplant transfer*. For example, components produced in one plant may be required for the assembly in another plant, which requires a stock transfer of components. The special procurement type key requires that a supplying plant also be defined in the special procurement type key and plant (which becomes the receiving plant) combination. Additionally, **Special Procurement U** is assigned to the special procurement type key.

Tips & Tricks

Since a one-to-one relationship exists between a supplying plant and a receiving plant in the interplant transfer business process, you'll need to create individual special procurement keys for every such combination. The quickest way to do this is to make a copy of special procurement type 40 and then make the required changes in the newly created special procurement type.

This method of copying the standard and available special procurement types can be put to use for all such special procurement scenarios where the existing standard special procurement types aren't enough to meet your business needs and you need to create new keys for special procurement types.

Depending on the configuration and master data settings made, the sequence of steps involved is usually as follows:

1. After the MRP run, the system creates a planned order for an interplant stock transfer.

2. The planned order is converted into a stock transport requisition. Alternatively, you can change the settings to trigger the direct creation of a stock transport requisition.

3. The stock transport requisition is converted into a stock transport order, in which the supplying plant and the receiving plants are mentioned, along with other details such as materials and quantities.

4. Goods are issued from the supplying plant against the stock transport order. These goods are shown as stock in transit.

5. Goods are received at the receiving plant against the same stock transport order, and the business process of interplant transfer ends.

Use Transaction ME21N to open the initial screen for the stock transport order (for interplant transfer), as shown in Figure 14.7. Select **Stock Transp. Order** from the drop-down list on the top-left side of the screen. Assign the **Supplying Plant** as "1100 Berlin" and then enter the item category (column I) as "U," the **Material** as "400-300," the **PO Quantity** as "2," and the receiving plant (**Plnt**) as "Stuttgart" (1400). Save the stock transport order. The next step is to issue the material from the supplying plant against the same stock transport order number.

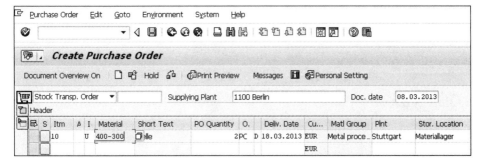

Figure 14.7 Stock Transport Order

Access the screen shown in Figure 14.8 via Transaction MIGO and select **Goods Issue** and then **Purchase Order** from the dropdown lists at the top. Enter the PO number (stock transport order). The movement type for issuance against a stock transport order is **351**, which is shown on the top-right corner of the screen. Save the entries, and the stock will appear as in transit.

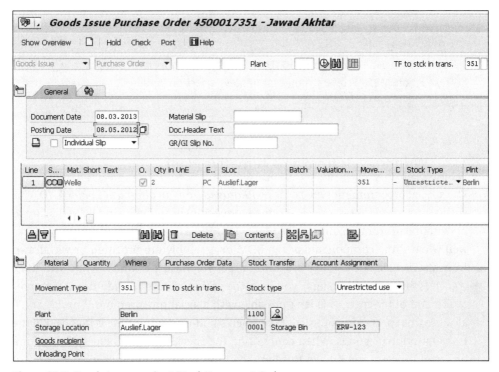

Figure 14.8 Goods Issue against Stock Transport Order

Transaction MB5T takes you to the screen shown in Figure 14.9 after you've entered the initial parameters such as **Supplying plant**, **Issuing plant**, and so on.

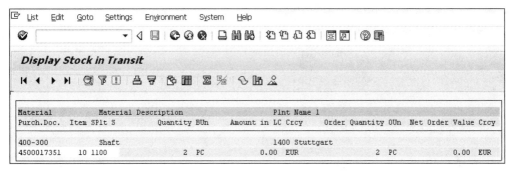

Figure 14.9 Stock in Transit

The stock remains in transit until the receiving plant receives goods against the same stock transport order. The relevant movement type for receiving the stock-transported material at the receiving plant is 101.

> **Tips & Tricks**
>
> You can also use Transaction MB5TD to view stock in transit on a key date, whereas Transaction MB5SIT offers more parameters selection options as well as greater detail about the stock in transit.

14.4   Withdrawals from an Alternative Plant

The special procurement type key for *withdrawal from an alternative plant* is 70. This special procurement type key is assigned to specific components in a BOM that are to be withdrawn from an alternative plant. This special procurement type key works well when some components of the BOM or assembly are procured or withdrawn from another plant that is in close physical/geographical proximity. While with stock transfers (interplant transfers), you have the option of entering additional transportation and other costs, this isn't possible with special procurement type 70. You'll also use this special procurement type when significantly less time is involved in the transportation of goods. When configuring the special procurement type key for a business process, you'll have to select the **Withdr. Alter. Plant** checkbox and also assign the **Issuing Plant**.

When a production order is created for an assembly at one plant, the system automatically suggests alternative plants for issuance of the component.

With special procurement type key 70 assigned to the component, Figure 14.10 shows the **Component Overview** screen of the production order, in which the **Component 400-500** shows the issuance **Plant** (withdrawal plant) as **3100**, compared to **Plant 3000** for all of the remaining components.

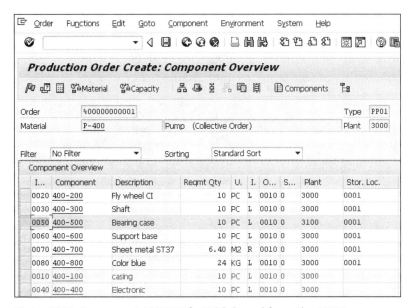

Figure 14.10 Component 400-500 for Withdrawal from Plant 3100

14.5   Subcontracting

The special procurement type key for subcontracting is 30. The *subcontracting* process begins when your company hands over (issues out) components to a subcontractor, who is usually a vendor, against a subcontracting PO, either to assemble or to add value to the product. Your company would take the components inventory out of its books, and the components would be reflected in the vendor's inventory. When the vendor has done what it's contracted to do, your company receives the goods against the same subcontracting PO from the vendor. The vendor invoices the company for the services rendered and receives payment.

For the subcontracting process to work effectively, the following prerequisites in the system must be met:

1. The material master of the assembly must have the special procurement type key assigned as 30.

2. A subcontracting BOM must exist in the system.

3. The purchasing view of the material master must be maintained.

4. A *purchasing information record* (info record) is needed between the material and vendor to reflect the source of supply.

5. In SAP S/4HANA, a production version must also exist. (See Sections 14.5.1 and 14.5.2 on how to create and mass manage production versions.)

> **Note**
>
> A *purchasing info record* is the purchasing relationship between a material and a vendor. When creating an info record, be sure to choose the **Subcontracting** option on the initial screen.

14.5.1   Production Version

Creating *production versions* is now mandatory in SAP S/4HANA for subcontracting BOMs to work. To facilitate production version creation, a new report called CS_BOM_PRODVER_MIGRATION is available. To execute the report/worklist, use Transaction SE38. On the screen that appears, enter "CS_BOM_PRODVER_MIGRATION" and click **Execute** or press F8.

On the screen that appears, you can choose to enter materials and the associated plants or simply enter a plant to bring up all the materials whose BOMs exist. To simulate the creation of new production versions, select the **Run in Simulation Mode** radio button and then click **Execute**. To create production versions after testing, select the **Run in Actual Mode** radio button.

As shown in Figure 14.11, you can choose to approve individual, selective, or all production versions being created. For our example, we chose material 3000000 and then clicked on **Approve**. A message will appear to confirm the creation of production versions. In the next section, we'll show you how to set up the automatic creation of production versions as well as perform mass processing on production versions.

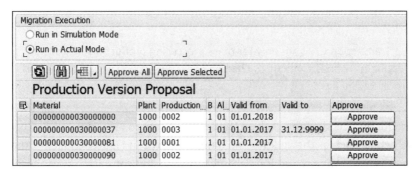

Figure 14.11 Creating Production Versions

14.5.2   Production Version: Mass Processing

Since MRP always reads production versions to determine a valid BOM, a new option for locking is available in the production version. As shown in Figure 14.12, you can also define whether a production version is locked for automatic sourcing only (Section 14.8 on automatic sourcing, also called simplified sourcing). With this locking option, you can avoid the production version selected by MRP, but the production version can still be used to create production orders or even for costing.

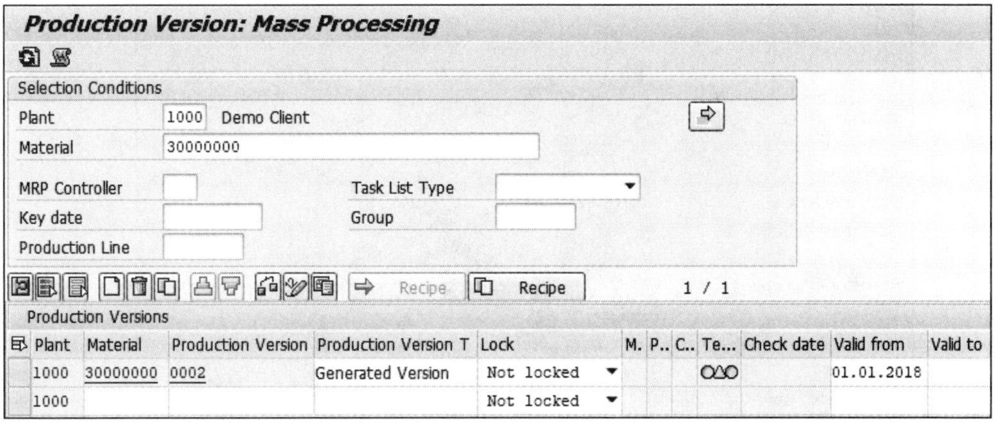

	Plant	Material	Production Version	Production Version T	Lock		M.	P..	C..	Te...	Check date	Valid from	Valid to
	1000	30000000	0002	Generated Version	Not locked	▼				ᴑᴧᴑ		01.01.2018	
	1000				Not locked	▼							

Figure 14.12 Mass Processing of Production Version

Access the screen shown in Figure 14.12 via Transaction C223, enter material 3000000 and plant 3000, and press (Enter). The automatically created production version from the previous step appears. Since the Transaction C223 also offers a mass processing option, you can make changes to production versions too.

> **Tips & Tricks**
>
> You can use Transaction C223 not only for mass processing production versions but also for creating new ones. Options to change, copy, delete, and check production versions are also available.

Select the production version and click on the detail icon  to view and/or to incorporate more details such as the validity end date, as shown in Figure 14.13. Click the **Check** button to ensure the production version is correct and complete. After checking is complete, each production version will have a traffic light indicator—red for error, yellow for a warning, and green for completeness and correctness.

Figure 14.13 Detailed Screen of a Production Version

In SAP S/4HANA, you now have also the option of locking a production version from simplified sourcing. This option is helpful if your company no longer wants to use a specific production version; MRP will also not consider a locked production version during automatic sourcing. The option to lock a production version is available from the **Lock** dropdown list, as shown in Figure 14.13.

14.5.3   Business Processes in Subcontracting

Figure 14.14 shows the **Create Purchase Order** screen (Transaction ME21N), where you'll assign the **Vendor** as **1000 C. E. B. Berlin** and assign item category : in column **I** to denote that the PO is a subcontracting order. Also, enter the assembly **Material** code as "103-100," set the **PO Quantity** as **1 PC**, enter the **Net Price** as "100.00" **USD**, and enter the plant (**Plnt**) as "New York" (3000).

At the bottom of the screen, click the **Components** button to open the **Component Overview** screen.

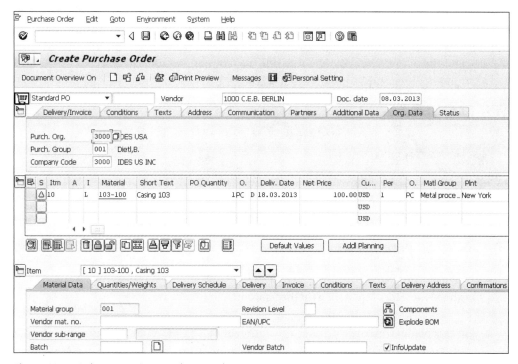

Figure 14.14 Subcontracting Purchase Order

In the **Component Overview** of the subcontracting PO, shown in Figure 14.15, issue the component **100-120** in quantity of **1 PC** to the vendor, so that the vendor returns with the assembled item 103-100. Save the subcontracting PO. The next step is to issue the component 100-120.

Figure 14.15 Component Overview of the Subcontracting Purchase Order

After you enter "1000" as the vendor on the initial parameters selection screen for the subcontracting order for the vendor (Transaction ME2O), the screen shown in Figure 14.16 will appear. You'll see the component you need to issue to the vendor against the subcontracting order, which in our example is material 100-120 with a quantity of 1 PC. Select the checkbox next to component **100-120** and click on the **Post Goods Issue** button. A popup window will appear.

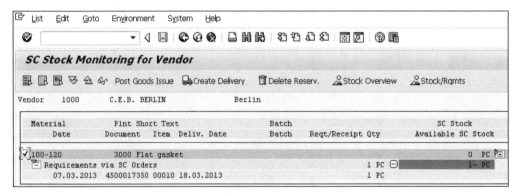

Figure 14.16 Stock Monitoring for the Subcontracting Purchase Order

In this popup window, you have the option of issuing **Material 100-120** to the **Vendor 1000** in **Quantity** of **1 PC** and from **Stor. location 0001**. Also note that the **Movement Type** for issuance to subcontract stock is **541**. You have the option of issuing excess components, if required for specific business needs.

> **Tips & Tricks**
>
> You can use Transaction MIGO for transfer posting in-house stock to the vendor's subcontracting stock with reference to a PO and using the same movement type 541. In Transaction MIGO, choose **Transfer Posting** from the first dropdown list and then choose **Purchase Order** from the second dropdown list. Ensure that the movement type on the right-hand side of the screen is set to **541 (GI whse to subc.stck)**.
>
> Transaction ME2ON opens the Subcontracting Cockpit to perform the subcontracting business process.

Figure 14.17 shows the stock overview for **Material 100-120** (Transaction MMBE); the system shows the **Stock Provided to Vendor** as a separate line item. In this example, this line item is for 923 PCS.

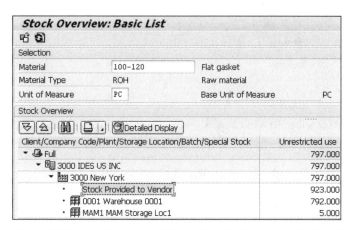

Figure 14.17 Stock Overview of Stock Provided to Vendor (Subcontractor)

> **Tips & Tricks**
>
> At any time, you can view the stock provided to or available with a vendor via Transaction MBLB.

The last step is to receive the goods against the subcontracting order. Figure 14.18 shows the initial screen to receive goods against the subcontracting PO (Transaction MIGO). Notice that not only can you receive the assembly material with **Movement Type 101**, but you can also record the actual consumption of components by the vendor with **Movement Type 543 O**, for goods issuance against the subcontracted stock.

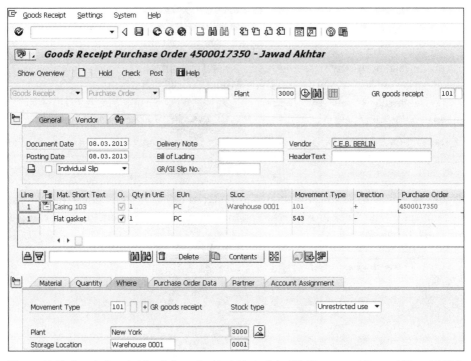

Figure 14.18 Goods Receipt for Subcontracted Material with Movement Types 101 and 543 O

14.6   Consignment

The special procurement type key for consignment is 10. In *consignment*, a vendor provides you with material that isn't billed until you remove the material from the consignment store. For example, a vendor places its goods on your premises for you to consume. When you record consumption of this consigned material against a production order or even a cost center, you become liable to pay the vendor. For the consignment process to work effectively, the following prerequisites in the system must be met:

- The material master must have the special procurement type key 10 assigned.

- The purchasing view of the material master must be maintained, including selecting the **Source list** checkbox. You'll also need to maintain the source list for the material.

- The vendor must already exist in the system.

- A *purchasing information record* is needed between the material and the vendor to reflect the source of supply. When creating an info record, be sure to choose the **Consignment** option on the initial screen.
- The source list of the material and plant combination must be maintained.

Special procurement key 10 is assigned to the material master, as shown in Figure 14.19, which presents the **Component Overview** screen of the production order for **Material AS-100** ❶. The component **AS-400** is a consignment material, which is denoted by the value **K** (material provided by customer) in the **Mat. Prov. Ind.** field shown further down the screen ❷.

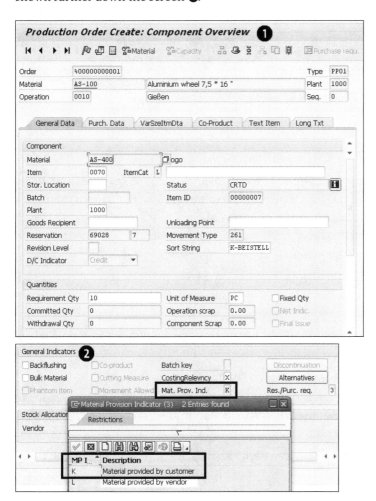

Figure 14.19 Consignment Component AS-400 Provided by the Customer

Save the production order and run MRP (using Transaction MD02) on component AS-400 and plant 3000.

After the MRP is run and results are saved, you can view the stock/requirements list (Transaction MD04) for material AS-400 and plant 3000. Figure 14.20 shows the purchase requisition for the same **Material AS-400** and **Plant 3000**, with the relevant item category **K** (in column I).

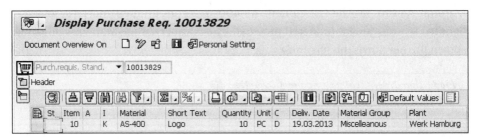

Figure 14.20 Purchase Requisition for Consignment

14.7   Pipeline Material

Pipeline material doesn't require any special procurement type key. *Pipeline material* denotes that the material is in a pipeline and is always available. Customers only pay for the pipeline material consumed. Examples of pipeline material are natural gas or heavy water, supplied by various vendors. You'll need to set up the following data in the system for pipeline material:

- The material type of the material master is pipeline material and has purchasing views activated, in addition to other views such as basic data and accounting/costing views.

- The purchasing view of the material master must be maintained, including selecting the **Source list** checkbox.

- The vendor must already exist in the system.

- A *purchasing information record* is needed between the material and vendor to reflect the source of supply. When creating an info record, choose the **Pipeline** option on the initial screen.

- The source list of the pipeline material and plant combination must be maintained.

14.8   Simplified Sourcing

In SAP S/4HANA simplified sourcing, the source list is no longer required for material planning through MRP, which reduces the effort to maintain master data. From the point of view of external procurement, since the source list is no longer relevant to MRP, the main benefit is that you have one less master data to create and maintain. No functionality is lost because the quota arrangement replaces the source list functionality.

We'll soon cover how MRP considers the validity dates of different source determination elements, such as info record, scheduling agreements, or contracts.

While a source list is no longer required, the creation of a production version is now mandatory for internal procurement. Extra effort may be required to create production versions during an SAP S/4HANA implementation project, but a report is provided to create such production versions to avoid delays. To manage source determination for external procurement in SAP S/4HANA, the following sequence of steps is executed:

- If the system finds a quota arrangement, then MRP creates replenishment proposals according to the percentages defined in the quota arrangement.
- If the system finds a valid scheduling agreement, then a delivery schedule will be created for the vendor assigned to the schedule agreement.
- If the system finds a valid quantity or value contract, then purchase requisitions will be created with reference to this contract.
- If the system finds a valid info record, purchase requisitions for the respective vendor are created.

While running MRP Live (Transaction MD01N), you don't need to inform the system whether MRP should generate planned orders, purchase requisitions, or delivery schedules. MRP decides automatically which kind of replenishment proposals to generate, depending on the source of supply selected during source determination.

14.8.1   Source of Supply without a Source List

The simplest way to activate the source determination for MRP is to create an info record. To define a source of supply as relevant for MRP, a new field called **Auto. Srcg** (automatic sourcing) is available in the info record when being created using Transaction ME11. If you select the automatic sourcing field, the source of supply will be considered by MRP.

14

The validity check of source list in SAP S/4HANA are also much simpler with source determination using an info record. When creating a new info record, no start validity date is entered, and the info record will be valid until December 31, 9999 (infinity). As a result, no problems should arise related to the info record's validity check.

An additional feature is that the info record provides fields where you can define maximum and minimum quantities and makes those limits relevant to source determination. For example, if a maximum quantity of 200 EA was defined on the info record, this vendor will not be selected by MRP to create purchase requisitions that require more than 200 EA.

14.8.2   Simplified Sourcing with Quota Arrangement

With MRP Live, using quota arrangements no longer causes any kind of performance problem. This quota arrangement setting, originating from the material master, is no longer checked by MRP. As a result, if a quota arrangement exists for a material, it will be considered by MRP.

A quota arrangement can be used to replace the source list functionality and prioritize a certain source of supply over a specific period. For example, you can use a quota arrangement to allocate 100 percent of the quota to the supplier PLANT_0001 between 01.01.2019 and 31.12.2019.

14.8.3   Simplified Sourcing with a Scheduling Agreement or a Contract

Both contracts and scheduling agreements can be created using Transaction ME31 and can be changed using Transaction ME32. The basic difference between a scheduling agreement and a contract is the document type. Scheduling agreements are created with document type LP (or a similar document type created in Customizing), whereas contracts are created with document types MK or WK (or a similar document type created in Customizing).

With simplified sourcing, you'll only need to create the contract or the scheduling agreement in order for MRP to consider them. You won't even need to set the **Auto.Srcg** indicator on the info record to have these sources of supply selected.

For source determination with scheduling agreements or contracts, make sure that the validity dates are still relevant so that these items can be selected by MRP.

14.8.4 Simplified Sourcing for Internal Procurement

With simplified sourcing for internal procurement, BOMs for planned orders created by MRP are selected. The BOM will only be selected by MRP if a valid production version exists for the material, which means that production versions must be created for the BOM selection. Refer to Section 14.5.1 where we covered how to create production versions.

14.9 Summary

In addition to traditional and routine procurement processes, SAP S/4HANA offers a large number of options for managing complex and diverse business processes throughout the entire supply chain and across logistics functions. Some of these processes include subcontracting, stock transfers, withdrawals from alternative plants, and consignment materials. If correctly configured and implemented, these processes can be greatly improved and optimized for planning, procurement, and production needs.

In the next chapter, we'll cover material requirements planning (MRP) in SAP S/4HANA.

14

Chapter 15
Material Requirements Planning

Material requirements planning (MRP) is an integral part of materials management (MM) and production planning (PP). In this chapter, you'll learn how to use MRP to optimize your logistics and supply chain planning processes.

Material requirements planning (MRP) is a highly versatile and intuitive planning tool for generating procurement proposals to fulfill external procurement and in-house production demands to help procurement and production planners optimize business processes. Furthermore, MRP can generate these procurement proposals for all levels of production-based materials and can also take lead times, scrap quantities, external procurements, special procurements, planning cycles, planning calendars, and lot sizes into account. MRP isn't limited to calculating quantities—while including scrap and stock considerations, MRP also provides in-depth scheduling solutions.

To effectively use MRP and its results, you'll need to ensure complete, correct, and comprehensive master data is always available. To facilitate this initiative, the system also offers several helpful tools: planned delivery time calculation, for external procurement; statistical analyses, for in-house production times or external procurement times; forecasting tools; automatic calculation of safety stock; and re-order point planning. As you gain more experience and as your data becomes more reliable over time, you can continue to update the planning data (the MRP view with its four different MRP tabs in a material master) and continue refining and optimizing the process.

In this chapter, we'll provide an overview of the MRP process, including the important role of MRP in all supply chain planning. We'll cover three types of MRP—consumption-based planning, forecast-based planning, and MRP—and their variants. We'll cover important MRP elements that the system will consider when calculating reliable planning results. Some of these MRP elements include lot sizes, MRP types, scheduling, net requirements calculation logic, and stocks. Wherever applicable,

15

we'll also cover the necessary configuration steps to get MRP up and running in your system.

Next, we'll cover the types of planning available in MRP. Then, we'll move on to cover the steps involved in running MRP Live, SAP S/4HANA's materials planning tool, and analyzing planning results in detail. We'll then follow step-by-step the process of converting MRP results into a procurement process for externally procurement materials and into a production process for internally produced materials. The chapter concludes with detailed coverage of two important topics in materials planning: MRP areas and the planning calendar.

15.1   Process Overview

Figure 15.1 shows an overview of MRP's role in the planning and production areas of the SAP system. The planning process starts with requirements coming from sales and distribution (SD) or from a material forecast and becomes a part of demand management. The system also takes customer requirements and *planned independent requirements (PIRs)* into account. A PIR with an active version consists of quantities of the material on which you want to run MRP. The system runs the MRP based on the details given in the demand program, and the outcome of the MRP run is the creation of *procurement proposals*. These procurement proposals can be planned orders (order proposals), purchase requisitions for external procurement, or delivery schedules for scheduling agreements with vendors. Procurement proposals can be distinguished into two separate yet interlinked areas: procurement for externally procured materials and production for in-house produced materials.

> **Note**
>
> Since using the MRP tool involves deeply integrated MM and PP processes, we recommend both teams to work together on the implementation project to ensure success.

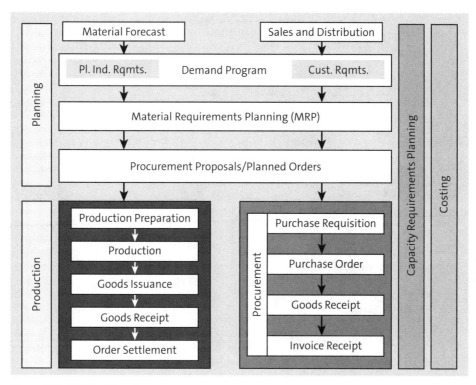

Figure 15.1 MRP in Planning

Figure 15.2 shows how MRP can be categorized into two major subareas:

- **Material requirements planning**
  For in-house produced material of high value (type A), you would use MRP. In this case, the system explodes the bill of materials (BOM) and routing (or master recipe) and plans materials at all assembly and subassembly levels. MRP will calculate basic dates and even lead time scheduling, as well as capacity requirements.

- **Consumption-based planning**
  For B- and C-type materials, you would categorize the materials as consumption-based and plan them accordingly. Reorder point planning can be either automatic or manual and is often used when planning for B- and C-type materials.

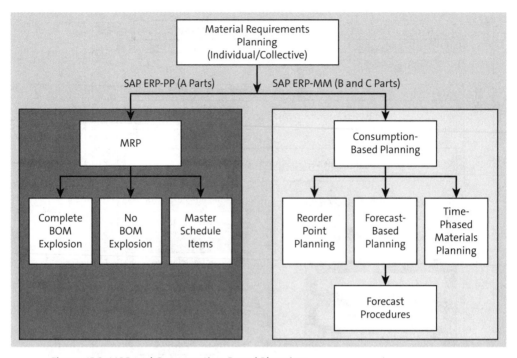

Figure 15.2 MRP and Consumption-Based Planning

Generally, MRP consists of the following steps, as shown in Figure 15.3:

❶ Check the planning file to avoid planning materials that aren't needed.

❷ Determine the material shortage quantity (or surplus quantity) by carrying out a net requirements calculation.

❸ Calculate the procurement quantity to include lot sizes for planned orders or purchase requisitions.

❹ Schedule basic dates or lead time (for in-house production only).

❺ Select the source of supply by determining the procurement proposals.

❻ Determine the required subordinate parts on the basis of the BOM explosion by carrying out a dependent requirements determination.

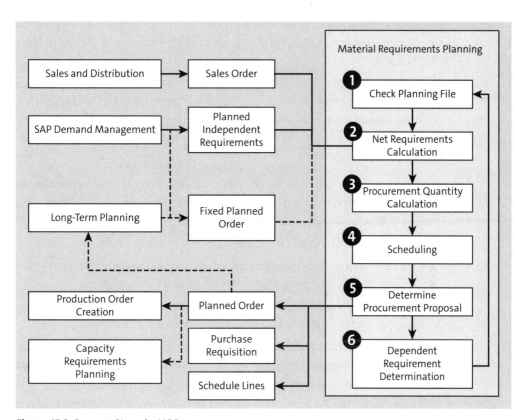

Figure 15.3 Process Steps in MRP

During an SAP system implementation project, or even later when you want to start taking advantage of planning tools such as MRP, you'll need to ensure that you follow a step-by-step approach to identify materials to be planned with MRP. You can plan just about any kind of material with MRP. Broadly, you should consider the following factors and/or take the following steps:

1. To begin, prepare a comprehensive list of all materials in, for example, a Microsoft Excel file. This Excel file may be a template that your SAP system consultant makes available for you. Materials can be finished goods, components, assemblies, raw materials, packing materials, consumables, or maintenance spares. You can also plan materials with special procurement types, such as subcontracting materials, phantom assemblies, pipeline materials, withdrawals from another plant, production in another plant, stock transport orders (interplant transfers), and so on. (For more information on special procurement types, see Chapter 14.)

2. Segregate the materials that you want to plan from those that aren't worth the time, effort, or cost involved in planning and then eliminate these materials from the Excel file.

3. For materials that you want to plan, segregate them further by classifying them as A, B, or C types. Type A materials are high value and generally cover finished goods, semifinished/assemblies, raw materials, packaging materials, and so on. Type B and C are medium- to low-value materials such as consumables, routine maintenance spares, and so on.

For all materials, you should individually evaluate each and every important factor involved in MRP to see how these fit in the planning to get the desired results. For example, ask yourself questions such as the following:

- What should the safety stock of this material be?

- How many days in a planning window do I need so that the system doesn't make any automatic changes to my procurement (or production) plan?

- When a material is required, how much should I plan (exact quantity, minimum order quantity, replenish to the maximum stock level, etc.)?

- How much raw material or packing material scrap (as a percentage) does the production of a material generate for a product or subassembly, so I can incorporate scrap in procurement and production planning?

- Should I also first forecast material requirements by using a forecasting tool and adjusting forecast values before proceeding with material planning?

You'll need to ask these (and many more) questions for each material and correspondingly enter or update the information in the Excel file. In this chapter, you'll find some factors that MRP will consider to come up with the planning results.

For raw materials or packaging materials, and because these materials are externally procured, you'll need to know the answers to questions, such as the following:

- What is the planned delivery time of this material?

- What is the goods receipt processing time including in-house quality inspection time?

- How much underdelivery and overdelivery of a material is allowed?

- Is there a scheduling agreement or a contract (quantity or value) with a vendor for a material?

- Is there a quota arrangement in place, in case of multiple vendors for the same material?

We suggest that you involve your production personnel to help you answer these (and many more) questions because they'll have the firsthand knowledge and production experience to complement your knowledge of procurement and inventory management.

For B- and C-type materials, consider using consumption-based planning. With consumption-based planning, you can choose whether to use reorder-based planning, which can manually or automatically suggest reorder points for each material based on historical consumption data. For manual reorder point planning, you'll enter a reorder point quantity, which may be based on your past experience or from consumption figures available in another planning program (not necessarily in the SAP system). Further, you can also take advantage of the forecasting tool to help you plan your future consumption using the historical consumption data available in the system.

Because planning is a continuously evolving and ongoing process, you can continue to fine-tune the planning parameters of materials to help the system come up with planning results to use in your procurement and production processes almost immediately (and without the need for significant adjustments). For example, when first entered, the planned delivery time of a material may have been five days, but as the system built up a significant database of this information (planned delivery times) in the past year, the average delivery time may turn out to be seven days. You'll need to update this information in the MRP view of the material master so that future planning results from MRP are more reflective of this reality. The system also offers a tool (Transaction WPDTC) that compares the information that you've entered in the material master and the actual planned delivery time that the system recorded for each delivery. Several such reports and tools for analysis are available.

15.2   Material Requirements Planning Elements

Whether you use MRP or consumption-based planning, you'll define a large number of factors in the four different MRP views of the material master to influence planning results. In fact, the system refers to the detailed information found in the MRP views to come up with procurement proposals. Some of these factors include how the system performs the net requirements calculations, what percentage of safety stock to consider in planning, the lot-sizing procedures to use, whether forecasting is a necessary perquisite to planning, and how special procurement types should be managed. In the following sections, we'll cover the important factors and parameters that

15

you'll need to set up to achieve the desired planning results from MRP, which you can subsequently use in your procurement and production activities.

15.2.1   Material Requirements Planning Types

When you decide to plan a material using MRP, one of the first parameters that you'll define in the material master is the MRP type. An MRP type is a control function used to control several subsequent steps. For example, if you define the MRP type as "ND" for no planning, the system won't plan the material at all. If you use an MRP type that starts with P* (e.g., PD, P1, P2, etc.), you can control how the system takes net requirements calculations into account and how it firms the procurement proposals for MRP during MRP runs. The net requirements calculation takes the plant stock and all receipts into account and then subtracts the required quantities from this sum. If the net requirements calculation comes up with a shortage or deficit quantities, the system creates procurement proposals during the MRP run. If the calculation determines that no shortage will arise, then the system won't create procurement proposals.

In the following sections, we'll detail some of the most commonly used MRP types and end with a summary of when to use each type.

MRP Type PD

This type of planning is carried out for the quantities planned in PIRs or quantities planned in incoming sales orders (MTO or MTS), dependent requirements, and stock transfer requirements—that is, any requirement that is MRP relevant. In this type of net requirements calculation and its planning, the following statements apply:

- The system doesn't consider nor ask for any forecast information or historical consumption values. Material planning is ensured only on the basis of absolute requirements or demands at hand.
- The system determines the available stock in the planning run, which is required to meet the demands, with the following logic:

  Plant stock + scheduled receipts from production and purchase – all of the demands (for example, from sales order, material reservations, and PIRs)

If the available stock is unable to fulfill the demand, then depending on the settings of the planning run, planned orders for in-house production may be created as well as purchase requisitions, delivery schedules/scheduling lines, or purchase requisitions for external procurement.

You can maintain the planning time fence in the **MRP 1** tab of the material master or in Customizing. The system firms the procurement proposals to protect them from any changes. However, as an MRP planner, you'll still have the flexibility to make last-minute changes manually, if needed. Firming of the procurement proposals (planned orders, purchase requisitions, delivery schedules) that fall within the planning time fence prevents these proposals from being adapted in the next planning run.

Furthermore, you can define the planning time fence in the configuration settings of the **MRP Group** because assigning this MRP group to the material master is easier. There two firming options for procurement proposals are automatic firming and manual firming.

Let's consider an example of firming type P1 to explain how firming works. In firming type P1, the system automatically firms the existing procurement proposals as long as these proposals are within the defined planning time fence. Additionally, new order proposals are created when the system determines that a shortage of material will occur within the planning time fence. However, the system pushes the new procurement proposals outside the planning time fence to ensure that the production plan isn't disturbed. When the newly created procurement proposals begin to fall within the planning time fence, the system automatically firms them and makes them a part of the production plan.

> **Note**
>
> You can configure MRP type in Transaction SPRO by following the menu path **Production • Material Requirements Planning • Master Data • Check MRP Types**.

MRP Type VB: Manual Reorder Point Planning

MRP type VB is the simplest and most manual of reorder point MRP type. When using MRP type VB, you'll have to calculate and set the reorder point and the safety stock manually. When using this MRP type, you'll have to maintain the **Reorder Point** field in the material master manually, and what you enter may be based on historical consumption values or may even be just a best guess. We recommend looking at the past consumption of the material in question and derive an estimated, future daily consumption quantity from that amount. You can then multiply this quantity by the number of working days (days when your company consumes the material) within the total replenishment lead time (TRLT). This lead time should be maintained in the **MRP 2** tab of the material master record (**Planned Delivery Time** + **GR Proc.Time** + **Purchasing Time** fields). The product of future daily consumption with lead time gives you an inventory point that, if reached, will require reordering so that you don't run out of a material before the next receipt comes in. Depending on the variability you've set in your estimated consumption or lead time, you should raise the reorder point by a safety stock when that shift underneath.

Many methods are available for calculate and estimating future daily consumption. One way is to use Transaction MC.9, for example, to view historical consumption data. However, when looking at tables of key figures and characteristics, you may only see monthly totals. You could divide these monthly totals by the number of working days in that month, but you can't be sure that consumption was consistent day by day. However, by displaying the consumption graphic in the logistic information system (LIS), you can apply a number of helpful tools to get the information you need. With LIS, you'll see whether consumption has been consistent over time and can figure out how much inventory you'll need to get you through the lead time without any stockouts. Then, you can add safety stock and put this value into the material master's MRP 2 tab. Subsequently, you'll maintain MRP type VB and fill in the **Reorder point** field in the **MRP 1** tab.

Thus, the reorder point quantity is your estimated consumption within the TRLT plus the safety stock quantity. You actually aren't required to maintain a safety stock setting at all in the **MRP 2** tab, but we do recommend having one readily available. As an added incentive, you'll get exception message 96 every time you dip into that range, allowing you to tell over time whether the reorder point is too low or whether you have the opportunity to lower it (and with it, the overall average stock holding of this material). The more often you see exception message 96, the more likely your reorder point is too low. However, if you do see exception message 96 but only rarely, we recommend considering lowering the reorder point.

> **Note**
>
> We'll demonstrate how to use reorder point planning with an example in Section 15.4.

In reorder point planning, you would normally maintain a safety stock, which you would enter in the **MRP 1** tab of the material master, although this step is not mandatory. Safety stock accounts for any additional unplanned consumption during the replenishment lead time. You can also have the system calculate the safety stock automatically by selecting the relevant checkbox in the configuration of the MRP type. Maintaining accurate reorder lead times can greatly help planners.

For reorder point planning, the system doesn't take incoming demand into account, unless you configure the reorder point planning with external requirements. In fact, demand generally plays no role in planning or creating procurement proposals. The system creates a procurement proposal for a quantity equal to the reorder point or equal to a fixed lot size, if the lot size is maintained in the material master. If procurement proposals already exist for a material with quantities greater than the required quantity, the system won't create a new procurement proposal.

As shown in Figure 15.4, you can control the MRP procedure that the system uses in the MRP type. Place your cursor in the **MRP Procedure** field and click on the drop-down option or press F4.

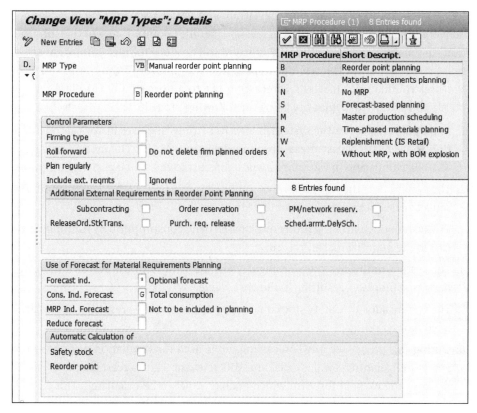

Figure 15.4 Reorder Point Planning

MRP Type VM: Automatic Reorder Point Planning

To achieve more automation and more accuracy in reorder point planning, you can use MRP type VM. MRP type VM takes the guesswork out and lets the system do the calculations. But the system can only calculate reliable and authentic values if the underlying data, specifically historical consumption data, is accurate. This procedure requires timely and accurate goods receipt and goods issue postings because the system uses that data to calculate the mean absolute deviation (MAD). Therefore, consistency in consumption, lead time deviation, and various settings such as planned delivery time and service level are relevant to reorder points. If any of this information isn't maintained correctly, MRP type VM will produce reorder points that either cause stockouts or drive inventory to potentially high levels. In any case, MRP type VM uses the material master's **Forecasting** tab to automatically calculate reorder points and safety stock quantity using the following procedure:

1. In the **Forecasting** tab, the system follows its settings and uses historical consumption to calculate a past mean absolute deviation (MAD). The system calculates MAD by comparing the so-called *ex-post forecast* to the actual past consumption.

2. The system uses the service level maintained in the **MRP 2** tab and a standard formula to calculate a safety stock quantity.

3. The system calculates the future anticipated daily consumption by running a forecast in the material master record.

4. The system multiplies the working days in the TRLT with the future anticipated daily consumption, resulting in the *basic value*.

5. The system adds the safety stock quantity to the basic value, resulting in the calculated reorder point.

6. During this procedure, the **Forecasting** tab is used for simulation purposes only. Forecasted quantities will not become MRP relevant. The forecast is simply used to perform the ex-post forecast, which enables MAD to be calculated. This MAD is then used to determine the degree of variability for the calculation of reorder point and safety stock.

Regarding this procedure, consider the following:

1. The higher the degree of variation (MAD), the higher the safety stock requirement and the higher the reorder point will be.

2. The longer the replenishment lead time, the higher the reorder point must be to get through the replenishment lead time.

3. The longer the replenishment lead time, the greater the chance of unforeseen consumption. This increasing variability increases the variability of safety stock requirements and, thus, the reorder point.

4. The higher the service level percent maintained in the **MRP 2** tab, the higher the safety stock requirement and, thus, the reorder point.

5. The higher the daily consumption, the higher the reorder point. At the same time, the forecast is obligatory and uses total consumption.

MRP Type V1: Manual Reorder Point with External Requirements

MRP type V1 acts exactly like MRP type VB, except that MRP type V1 takes external requirements into consideration. The safety stock and reorder point must be calculated manually for this procedure. You can determine what those external requirements are in a Customizing table.

In MRP type V1, the system uses order reservations, released stock transport orders, and released purchase requisitions for external demand. If a sales order reservation exists within the replenishment lead time (**Include ext. reqmts** "2"), then the order is triggered early because the amount of demand from the reservation is taken into account when determining at what point the reorder point will be broken. For this procedure, a lot-sizing procedure may be helpful for adding those external requirements within the lead time to the ordering quantity. Because these demands are already known, adding them to the order size makes sense, so that at the time of receipt, the consumption can be replenished in full. Therefore, MRP type V1 offers advantages over both MRP type VB and MRP type VM by not being purely driven by past data. MRP type V1 is a little more proactive by including future requirements in the planning process.

MRP Type V2: Automatic Reorder Point with External Requirements

MRP type V2 provides the most sophisticated and advanced reorder point procedure so far. Not only does this MRP type include external requirements, it also calculates safety stock and reorder points automatically using the **Forecasting** tab in the material master record. Again, just as in the case of MRP type VM, be mindful of

15

basic data quality and be wary of too much automation, unless the procedure is fully understood.

MRP type V2 automatically calculates a reorder point based on the length of the lead time, variability in the consumption, and the service level you've set. Thus, MRP type V2 combines the automatic calculation of planning parameters with considerations of external demand. This procedure is grounded on a simple reorder point philosophy that is sophisticated enough to automate the planning process and optimize your inventory holdings.

MRP Type VV: Forecast-Based Planning

With MRP type VV, a forecast is carried out at an individual material level. In fact, each material can have its own **Forecasting** tab activated in the material master. MRP type VV is particularly relevant for finished goods. MRP type VV is a consumption-based replenishment strategy; in other words, the system maintains inventory in anticipation of actual demand. The inventory is replenished to a forecast, which is based on the material's own consumption history (hence, the name *material forecast*). Using MRP type VV is a good strategy when demand is predictable, but the lead time to replenish is long. But by putting an "artificial" demand in the mix via a forecast, MRP can generate all supply elements way ahead of time. All you'll need to do is turn the requisition into an order on the date the system tells you to do so.

> **Warning**
>
> MRP type VV doesn't take demand spikes into consideration. Any changes in demand will flow into the consumption pattern and eventually be picked up by the forecast module. The system might increase or decrease the forecast or tell that the current underlying model isn't applicable anymore. So, like all the other strategies, use the MRP type VV if it meets your business needs.

Forecasting means anticipating consumption. Safety consumption from the previous year will usually exist. However, in materials planning, we are always concerned about that possibility. If planners find themselves to investigating huge spikes in demand, then the logical choice is to resort to a time buffer or to expedite orders manually. If spikes occur constantly, the material doesn't qualify for MRP type VV replenishment anyway.

For MRP type VV to function, you'll maintain all the parameters in the **Forecasting** tab of SAP system. Identify the periodicity by which to run the forecast to create demand with the **Period Indicator** in the **Forecasting** tab of the material master. This setting will eventually determine with what frequency the forecast is run automatically for the material in question. The options are listed here:

- **Daily (D)**
  Results in daily demand records for every working day visible in Transaction MD04 and relevant to the MRP run. Be aware, however, that a daily forecast will also result in daily replenishment and may unnecessarily consume system resources.

- **Weekly (W)**
  Weekly is the most often used periodicity and allows for relatively low average inventory holding because doing so brings in less inventory than in a monthly periodicity. This periodicity is also flexible and quick to detect both spikes and drops in consumption.

- **Monthly (M)**
  Monthly is used for less important or less expensive items because doing so bring in large quantities with few orders.

- **Posting period (P)**
  This option allows a freely definable period maintained in financials (FI). After the **Period Indicator** is set, you can decide how many periods from the past you want included in the forecast calculation. You can also set aside a number of periods for an ex-post forecast, and you can identify the number of periods for which the forecast run generates demand.

The **Splitting** indicator contains the number of periods to be considered as well as the number of days and/or weeks for which the splitting is to be carried out. You can maintain the **Splitting indicator** in configuration (Transaction SPRO) by following the menu path **Production • Requirements Planning • Forecast • Define Splitting of Forecast Requirements for MRP**.

MRP Types R1 and R2: Time-Phased Planning

Materials replenished using a time-phased planning method are scheduled so that the MRP run considers them for planning only at specific dates in the week. This is determined by the planning cycle in which the MRP run is only triggered on specific days of a week. Time-phased planning can be carried out with consumption-based (stochastic) procedures or with deterministic ones. If you use time-phased planning in MRP type Px, creating a new MRP type (PT) for deterministic, time-phased planning with

MRP may make sense. MRP type R1 simply plans for an MRP run on the days scheduled by the planning cycle, which might lead to stockouts when large consumption happens on a day not included in the planning cycle. In this case, MRP type R2 is a better choice because it calculates a reorder point automatically and triggers the planning run whenever a reorder point is broken.

Which MRP Type to Use in Materials Planning?

Table 15.1 provides a summary of MRP types and when to use them for materials planning.

MRP Type	Description	When to Use
VB	Sets the reorder point manually	When consumption is regular (X items) and lead time is short
VM	Calculates the reorder point automatically	When you must update many materials on a periodic basis, and the consumption is less regular (Y items)
V1	Considers external requirements when calculating the reorder point	When you want to include external requirements that consume inventory within the replenishment lead time
V2	Considers external requirements when calculating the reorder point	For items that need to be updated frequently
VV	Material forecast	When consumption is regular and lead time to replenish is long
PD	Plan on demand	When there is irregular demand and valuable materials
P1, P2, P3	Plan on demand with a time fence	When you need to protect a frozen zone from too much "noise"
M0	Master planning	When you have A items that have a large value contribution
R1	Time-phased planning	When you want to limit the amount of planning runs
R2	Time-phased planning with automatic reorder point	When you want to minimize stockouts occurring with MRP type R1

Table 15.1 Summary of MRP Types and When to Use Them

15.2.2   Lot-Sizing Procedures

When the system determines a material shortage after performing a net requirements calculation, lot-sizing information maintained in the **MRP 1** tab of the material master will be looked up next. Lot sizing specifies the quantity that the system should propose when a quantity shortage of a material may occur. For the system to create the correct lot size in a procurement proposal, other information will be considered as well, such as safety stock, maximum/minimum lot sizes, dynamic safety stock, scrap percentage, and rounding values.

Three different lot-sizing procedures are available in the SAP system, which we'll discuss in the following subsections:

- Static lot-sizing procedures
- Periodic lot-sizing procedures
- Optimum lot-sizing procedures

Static Lot-Sizing Procedures

Static lot-sizing procedures can further be categorized as exact lot sizing, fixed lot sizing, fixed lot sizing with splitting, and replenish to maximum stock level, as follows:

- **Exact lot sizing (EX)**
  The system creates planned orders or procurement proposals to cover the exact shortage requirement only. For example, if a net requirement quantity of a material is 110 units, the system creates a procurement proposal for exactly 110 units.

- **Fixed lot sizing (FX)**
  The system proposes the total requirement in multiples of fixed lots. For example, if the lot size is fixed as 60 units, and the shortage quantity is 240, then the system creates 4 planned orders to cover the shortage.

- **Fixed lot sizing with splitting (FS)**
  The system proposes the total requirement in multiples of fixed lots with overlap. This lot sizing is generally preferred if you can't procure a large quantity at once and thus must split the quantity with overlap. With this lot-sizing procedure, you'll have to assign a fixed lot quantity together with a rounding value. The rounding value must be a multiple of the fixed lot quantity. For example, if the lot size is fixed as 100 units, and the rounding value is 20 units, then the system creates 5 planned orders to cover the shortages.

- **Replenish to maximum stock level (HB)**
  The system creates planned orders to fill inventory to the maximum stock level.

15

You'll have to define the maximum stock level in the relevant field of the **MRP 1** tab in the material master. For example, if the maximum stock level is 300 units, and the demand quantity is 50 units, the system creates a planned order of 350. This order first ensures that that the 300 units of stock fill up and then that the demand quantity has been added.

Periodic Lot-Sizing Procedures

Periodic lot-sizing procedures are further categorized into daily lot sizing, weekly lot sizing, and monthly lot sizing. If the lot-sizing procedure is daily, then the system considers demand with all of the receipts for that day and creates a daily shortage proposal in case a shortage exists. If weekly, then the system combines all of the requirements for a week and comes up with one procurement proposal.

The lot-sizing procedure is assigned in the **MRP 1** tab of the material master (Transaction MM02). In our example, shown in Figure 15.5, we selected **EX: Lot-for-lot order quantity** as the **Lot size**.

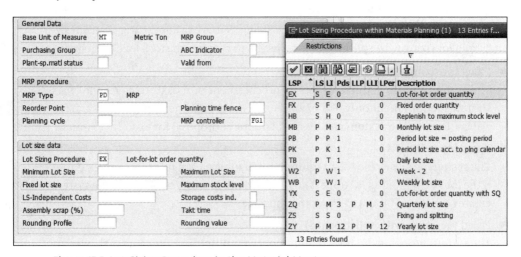

Figure 15.5 Lot-Sizing Procedure in the Material Master

> **Note**
>
> You can configure the MRP lot size using Transaction OMI4 or by following the menu path **Logistics • Production • Material Requirements Planning • Planning • Lot-Size Calculation • Check Lot-Sizing Procedures**, as shown in Figure 15.6.

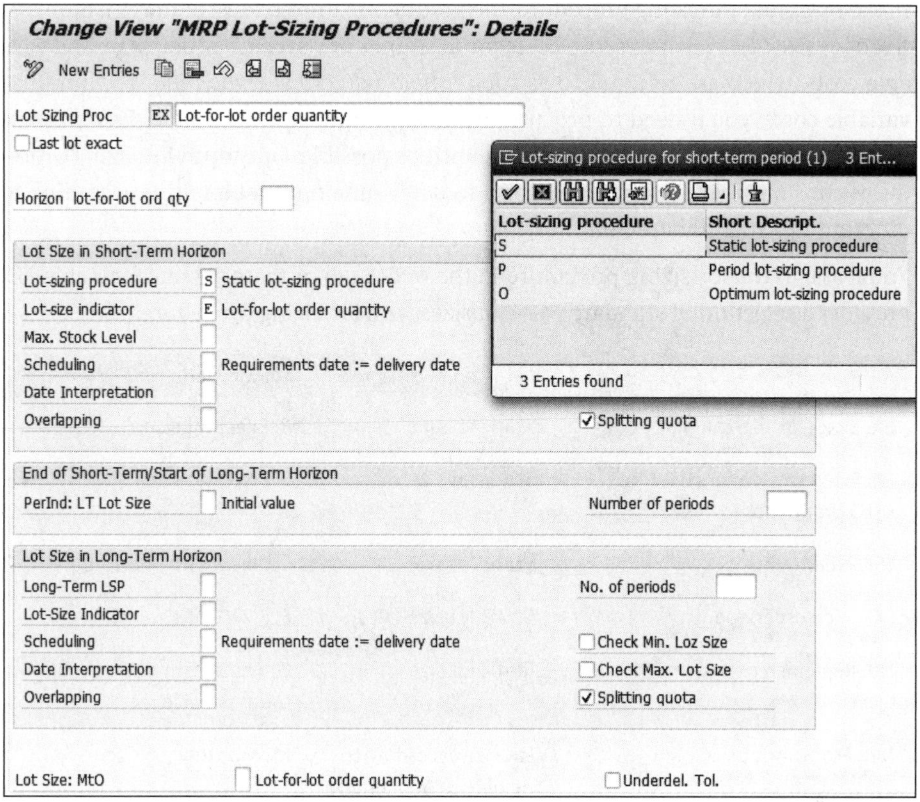

Figure 15.6 Lot Size Configuration

Note

Configure the MRP lot size by using Transaction OMI4 or by following the menu path **Logistics • Production • Material Requirements Planning • Planning • Lot-Size Calculation • Check Lot-Sizing Procedures**.

Optimum Lot-Sizing Procedures

Optimum lot-sizing procedures attend to economical lot-sizing requirements of the company and include the Groff lot-sizing method and part-period balancing. In these kinds of procedures, the system takes into account the costs of the procurement as a well as storage costs.

In the optimum lot-sizing procedure, the production or purchase of materials entails fixed lot size costs such as setup costs for machines or purchase order costs and variable costs, which are referred to as *capital tie-up due to stockholding*. To minimize variable costs, you'll need to procure the smallest quantities possible. To minimize fixed costs, you'll procure the largest quantities possible. Optimum lot-sizing procedures consider variable and fixed costs to determine optimal lot sizes according to different procedures based on these costs.

You'll assign the lot-sizing procedure in the **MRP 1** tab of material master. Table 15.2 provides a selection of standard MRP lot sizes with lot-sizing procedures.

MRP Lot Size	Lot-Sizing Procedure	Lot Size Indicator
EX: Exact lot size calculation	Static lot size	E: Exact lot size
FK: Fixed lot size for customer MTO production	Static lot size	F: Fixed lot size
FS: Fixed/splitting	Static lot size	S: Fixed with splitting
FX: Fixed order quantity	Static lot size	F: Fixed lot size
HB: Replenish to maximum stock level	Static lot size	H: Replenishment to maximum stock level
MB: Monthly lot size	Lot size according to flexible period length	M: Monthly lot size
PK: Lot size according to flexible period length and planning calendar	Lot size according to flexible period	K: Period based on planning calendar
TB: Daily lot size	Lot size according to flexible period length	T: Daily lot size
WB: Weekly lot size	Lot size according to flexible period length	W: Weekly lot size
WI: Least unit cost procedure	Optimization lot size	W: Least unit cost procedure
DY: Dynamic lot size creation	Optimization lot size	D: Dynamic planning

Table 15.2 Selection of MRP Lot Sizes and Lot-Sizing Procedures

Some lot sizes require additional information that must be maintained in the material master, as listed in Table 15.3.

MRP Lot Size	Fields
HB: Replenish to maximum stock level	**Maximum stock level**
FS: Fixed/splitting	**Fixed lot size, Rounding value, Takt time**
FX: Fixed order quantity	**Fixed lot size**
GR: Groff lot-sizing procedure	**Ordering costs, Storage costs ind.**
DY: Dynamic lot size creation	**Ordering costs, Storage costs ind.**
SP: Part-period balancing	**Ordering costs, Storage costs ind.**
WI: Least unit cost procedure	**Ordering costs, Storage costs ind.**

Table 15.3 Required Data in Fields Based on MRP Lot Size Selection

Although the standard lot sizes available in the SAP system are generally sufficient to fulfill most business needs, you can configure your own MRP lot sizes to accommodate any specific business process.

Example

Phosphoric acid is the main component used in the production of a specialized fertilizer, di-ammonium phosphate (DAP). Let's say your company wants to replenish to maximum its stock of phosphoric acid when placing new orders. However, supplier requirements exist regarding minimum and maximum order limits for shipment. To cater to this business need, you'll create a new MRP lot size (which may be a copy of MRP lot size HB: Replenish to maximum stock level) and select the **Check Min. (minimum) lot size** and **Check Max (maximum) lot size** checkboxes. You'll then assign this custom MRP lot size to the **MRP 1** tab of the material master. Now, the system will prompt you to enter the minimum and maximum acceptable lot sizes of the material. Not only will the system now ensure that material is replenished to the maximum stock level, but it will also take the vendor's minimum and maximum lot size requirements into account while creating procurement proposals.

Let's take this example further, the capacity of your storage tank capacity for phosphoric acid is 40,000 MT, while the vendor's minimum lot size is 20,000 MT and its maximum is 25,000 MT. Currently, the stock in the storage tank has dropped to 10,000 MT. In this situation, the system will create one planned order for 25,000 MT, which ensures that adheres to the vendor's maximum lot size limit while still remaining within the maximum storage tank capacity of 40,000 MT. If minimum or

15

> maximum lot sizes hadn't been defined, the system would have created a planned order of 30,000 MT to replenish the existing stock of 10,000 MT to the maximum of 40,000 MT.

You can also set different lot-sizing parameters applicable for short-term and long-term horizons. Procurement/production always takes place with lot sizes determined with a short-term horizon in mind. Using a long-term horizon enables the forecast function (mostly aggregated, e.g., via monthly periodic lot size). Long-term horizons are often useful for reducing the number of requirement coverage elements, especially if fixed lot sizes are used that are smaller than the average requirement quantity. Typically, a period-based lot size is used for long-term horizons.

15.2.3   Scrap

Companies are often faced with problems relating to materials they can't use, known as scrap, whether from producing defective finished goods, excess consumption of raw material due to wastage in the production process, or operational inefficiency. The SAP system offers several options to enter scrap or waste details at every level—at the assembly or the component (raw material) level—so that procurement and production planning are closely synchronized with actual and practical situations.

Based on historical data or practical experience, you can maintain assembly and component scrap as master data, which subsequently facilitates procurement and production processes. Scrap is treated differently in the SAP system. Scrap in real life can be available or even sold but isn't treated as inventory in the SAP system.

The two types of scrap can be used:

- **Assembly scrap**
  Completely unusable finished or semifinished product for which raw material was issued in accordance with a BOM. Assembly scrap is different from co-products or by-products, which are treated as inventory managed in the SAP system.

- **Component scrap**
  Allows the system to increase the issuance quantity of a component, such as raw material or packing material, against a production order by a defined percentage to account for scrap or wastage during production.

Successfully assigning assembly and component scrap in master data enables the SAP system to consider scrap during procurement planning. During the MRP run, the system takes scrap percentages into account, which is reflected in the planning proposals generated.

To enter details about assembly or component scrap in the MRP view of the material master, use Transaction MM02 or follow the menu path **Logistics • Materials Management • Material Master • Material • Change • Immediately**.

In the following sections, we'll provide additional details on the different types of scrap and also explain how to configure different uses for scrap.

Assembly Scrap

You can enter assembly scrap in the **MRP 1** tab of the material master. Enter the assembly scrap in the form of a percentage in the **Assembly scrap (%)** field. If this material is used in an assembly, the system considers this percentage during scrap calculation by correspondingly increasing the production order quantity. For example, let's say you've defined an assembly scrap of 10% for the material. When you create a production order, say of quantity 100 PC, the system automatically increases the production order quantity to 110 PC to account for the 10% scrap. At the same time, the system will also issue an information message. Because the production order quantity increased to 110 PC, the system accordingly increases the components' quantities also, based on the material's BOM, and multiplies the production order quantity, which in this case is now 110 PC with the components' quantities.

Component Scrap

You can enter component scrap in the **MRP 4** tab of the material master in the form of a percentage. If this material is used as a component in a BOM, the system considers this percentage during scrap calculation. For example, entering 10% scrap for 100 kg of component material increases the component issuance quantity in the production order to 110 kg.

15.2.4   Safety Stock

The system offers two types of safety stocks: absolute safety stock and safety days' supply. The *absolute safety stock* enables the system to subtract the safety stock from the material availability calculation (net requirements calculation) because safety stock must always be available to cover for unforeseen material shortages or unexpected high demand.

For *days' supply/safety time*, the system plans the goods receipt in advance by the period specified as safety time. Thus, the planned days' supply of the stock, in fact, corresponds to the number of days specified as safety time. The system shifts backs the date of the receipts by the number of working days and also takes the factory calendar into account.

You make the relevant entries in the **MRP 2** tab of the material master. The system refers to the planning of a safety days' supply as safety time. To consider safety time, you'll need to set the **Safety time ind.** to "1" (for independent requirements) or "2" (for all requirements) and then also provide a **Safety time/act. cov.** in days. Further, you can define deviations from constant safety time using a safety time period profile (**STime period profile** field).

In the following sections, we'll cover how safety stock availability is used in net requirements calculation and also the selection method that the system uses for receipts.

To avoid the unnecessary creation of planned orders for small quantities, which can otherwise be covered by the safety stock, you can define the percentage (share) of safety stock that the system can use in such business scenarios. For example, let's say, during an MRP run, the system assesses a shortage of 2 PC of a material. You have, however, maintained a safety stock of 40 PC for this material, which the system doesn't consider in the MRP run. If you specify that 10% of the safety stock can be used to account for small shortages (in this example, 4 PC are needed from safety stock), then the system can cater to this small requirement or shortage of 2 PC from the 4 PC available from safety stock. A procurement proposal won't be created.

To define the safety stock parameters, use Transaction SPRO or follow the menu path **Logistics • Production • Material Requirements Planning • Planning • MRP Calculation • Stocks • Define Safety Stock Availability**. In the **MRP group 0010** for net requirements calculation, maintain the requisite details. You'll eventually assign the MRP group in the **MRP 1** tab of the material master.

15.2.5   Scheduling

For the system to automatically schedule procurement proposals during the MRP run, you'll need to enter the requisite information in the MRP views of the material master, as shown in Figure 15.7. The required master data are include the following:

- Planned delivery time (applicable for external procurement)
- Planned goods receipt times (optional)
- Schedule margin keys for float times (optional)

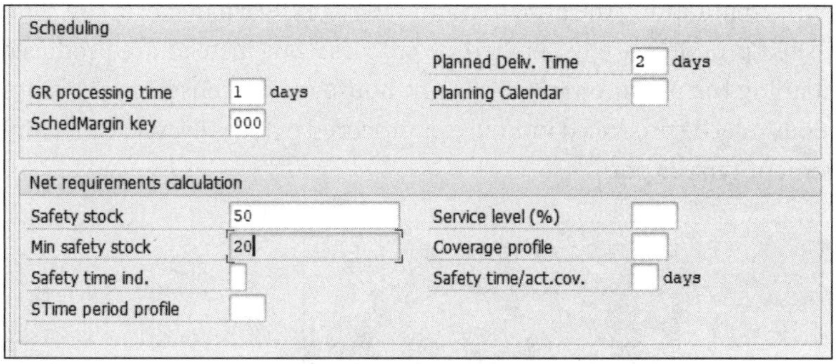

Figure 15.7 Scheduling and Net Requirements Calculation

In reorder point planning, dates are defined by means of forward scheduling. If a reorder point has fallen short during the planning run, you'll need to initiate procurement activities. The availability date of the materials is determined based on the date of the material shortage.

15.2.6   Net Requirements Calculation Logic

In net requirements planning, the system checks for each requirement date to determine whether the plant stock or incoming goods receipts can cover the requirement. If not, then the system calculates the material shortage quantity. The lot size calculation determines the quantity of the goods that the system must receive by the given date to fulfill the requirement. In net requirements calculation, the system determines the available stock based on the following formula:

Plant stock – safety stock + open order quantity (purchase orders, production orders, fixed procurement proposals) – requirement quantity (PIRs, customer requirements, material reservations, forecast requirements for unplanned additional requirements) = Available stock

15.2.7   Procurement Proposals

When you run MRP in the system, the system looks for procurement type information to decide if the ensuing procurement proposals entail in-house production, external procurement, or both. The **Procurement Type** in the **MRP 2** tab of the material master defines which alternative applies to the material in the plant, as shown in Figure 15.8. If both in-house production and external procurement are allowed, MRP assumes in-house production by default. Since raw material is generally not sold or produced in-house, maintaining the procurement type as external makes sense. Similarly, since finished products are generally not procured but instead are produced in-house, maintaining the procurement type as in-house makes sense. Finally, since semifinished goods may be produced in-house or procured externally, you can maintain the procurement type as both.

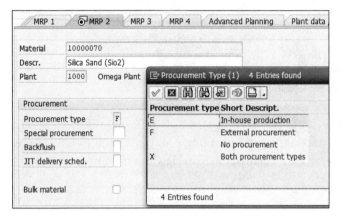

Figure 15.8 Procurement Type in the Material Master

In the planning run, the system creates planned orders. These planned orders are converted into a production order (or process order) for in-house production. For external procurement, the planned order can be converted into a purchase requisition, which in turn is converted into purchase order item.

Now that we've covered basic concepts behind MRP, the next section covers MRP procedures.

15.3   Material Requirements Planning Procedures

When you decide to implement MRP in your company on a specific set of materials (whether finished goods, raw materials, assemblies, consumables, packing materials, or spare parts), you'll have to determine the MRP procedures will be followed. For example, perhaps you don't want to plan a few materials at all because these materials aren't worth the time, effort, and resources involved in planning them. Similarly, for some critical components of the supply chain, you may want to accord them a much higher priority than the normally planned materials. Further, to bring logic and stability to your procurement plans, you'll want a time horizon in which the system won't make any changes to the procurement proposals between the various MRP runs.

In the following sections, we'll discuss consumption-based and forecast-based planning procedures and then move on to cover the different types of planning runs available in an SAP system. Next, we'll show you how to run MRP Live, SAP S/4HANA's materials planning tool, and discuss material planning results created by the system running MRP Live. We'll then show you how to convert MRP-generated order proposals, such as planned orders or purchase requisitions, into purchase orders for an external procurement process. For in-house production, planned orders can be converted into production or process orders.

15.3.1   Consumption-Based Planning

In consumption-based planning, replenishment is triggered by the consumption of stock. The system uses past consumption history, and by taking advantage of the forecasting functionality, the system can predict and suggest both the reorder level and safety stock level. A good example of consumption-based planning is reorder point planning, in which the planning of a material is triggered when stock falls below a reorder point. On the other hand, forecast-based planning can be carried out based on forecasted figures (based on historical data) for a material.

> **Note**
>
> For consumption-based planning, you'll need to ensure that your company has a well-functioning and integrated inventory management functionality. Further, consumption-based planning requires a constant replenishment lead time (RLT) and more or less constant (stable) consumption of the material under consideration.

The MRP procedures for consumption-based planning are primarily used in areas without in-house production, for planning B and C parts, or for planning operating supplies in manufacturing organizations. The type of procurement proposal automatically generated during MRP depends on the procurement type of the material. For external procurement, the MRP controller can choose between creating a planned order and a purchase requisition. If the MRP controller wants a planned order, the planned order must be converted into a purchase requisition and then into a purchase order.

The available planning types in consumption-based planning include the following:

- Reorder point planning
- Forecast-based consumption planning (Section 15.3.2)
- Time-phased materials planning (Section 15.2.1)

In reorder point planning, the system compares the available stock at the plant level with the reorder point. The reorder point is made up of the safety stock and the average material required during the RLT. Reorder point stock ensures that sufficient stock is available to cover the demand during the period required for replenishing the stock. Accordingly, when defining a reorder point, you'll need to take into account the safety stock, the historical consumption, or the future requirements and RLT. Safety stock must cover the additional material consumption that occurs during the RLT itself as well as additional requirements if delivery is delayed. Manual reorder point planning requires you define the reorder point and safety stock by yourself and store these parameters in the corresponding material master record. In automatic reorder point planning, the reorder point and safety stock are determined by the integrated forecast program.

Using historical material consumption values, the program determines future requirements. Depending on the service level defined by the MRP controller and on the RLT of the material, the reorder level and the safety stock are then calculated and transferred to the relevant material master record. If the forecast program is run at regular intervals, the reorder point and safety stock are adapted to the current consumption and delivery situation and thus help to reduce the stock level.

15.3.2 Forecast-Based Consumption Planning

Some consumption-based MRP procedures require that you execute and save the forecast before the system can carry out MRP. In such cases, the **Forecasting** indicator in the relevant MRP type is marked as mandatory/obligatory, rather than optional. When you execute a forecast on a material, the system looks for the forecasting parameters you maintained in the forecasting view of the material master, such as forecasting model and historical or forecast (future) periods. Further, depending on the model that you've selected, the system may also consider smoothing factors (alpha, beta, or gamma factors). In forecasting, the system considers the planned and unplanned consumption quantities of the material for the periods under evaluation and comes up with forecast (future) figures. When forecast results are saved, the MRP for forecast-based consumption planning uses these forecast figures to create procurement proposals after the MRP run. This type of planning is generally applicable for materials where consumption is unpredictable and varies greatly, in which case the company must rely on past consumption figures to arrive at realistic future consumption figures.

> **Note**
>
> Refer to Chapter 16 on forecasting for more information.

15.3.3   Types of Planning Runs

Depending on the business process, you can use one of several types of planning runs available in the SAP system. A planning run denotes the level and mode at which you want to run MRP. For example, you may want to run MRP on an individual plant or a group of plants, an individual material or a group of materials (product group), or in online mode or in background mode.

Some of the planning runs include the following:

- Single-item, single-level
- Single-item, multilevel
- Total planning online
- Total planning background
- Single-item planning, sales order
- Single-item planning, project

We'll discuss each of these planning runs in the following subsections to explain the options available. However, we highly recommend using MRP Live, available in SAP S/4HANA and even in SAP ERP (with EHP 7 and later), to take full advantage of materials planning capabilities. We'll cover MRP Live in SAP S/4HANA in Section 15.3.4.

Single-Item, Single-Level

You can use this type of planning run for a single material at the plant level, when you only want to plan a single material without disturbing the planning situation of all other dependent materials (no BOM explosion). You'll use Transaction MD03 for a single-item, single-level planning run and its BOM explosion. For example, let's say sudden changes in the production plan of a single material have occurred. You would run MRP to account for the changed planning situation and enable the system to create

15

new procurement proposals. Because the components for this material (the material BOM) are already available in stock, you wouldn't want to disturb their planning, so you'll plan only the single item at the single level.

Single-Item, Multilevel

This type of planning run is used when you want to plan a single material, including its BOM. Because assemblies in the BOM may also contain additional assemblies and components, these subitems are also planned.

For single-item, multilevel planning runs, use Transaction MD02. The system will plan the single material (at a plant) that you provided on the initial parameters selection screen.

When using this planning run option, the **Display Planning Results before they are saved** option allows you to check the planning results before saving. During the planning run, the system stops at each breaking point, which allows you to save the planning results created so far and move to the next breaking point. Alternatively, you enable the system to continue planning without stopping at each breaking point.

You can also select the **Display Material List** option, and the system displays the following information at the conclusion of the planning run:

- Number of materials that have been planned
- Planning parameters that have been used in the selection screen
- Number of materials that have been planned, with exceptions
- Number of planned orders created
- List of materials that were planned
- Start time of the planning run
- End time of the planning run

Total Planning Online

In this type of planning run, the system carries out a multilevel planning run, in other words, for all the materials in a plant, for all the materials in multiple plants, or for MRP, as defined through **Scope of Planning**, which is available in the selection screen. Total planning online is carried out using Transaction MD01.

Total Planning Background

With the total planning background method, planning will take place in the background instead of in the foreground or online. Using Transaction MDBT, you can create a variant of the Transaction MD01 screen and schedule it to run in the background on a periodic basis. The program name for Transaction MDBT is RMMRP000. Use Transaction SE38, enter the program name "RMMRP000," and define the variant to execute the MRP in the background.

Single-Item Planning, Sales Order

For make-to-order (MTO) production, you can use single-item planning for a sales order. You'll need to enter the sales order number with the line item of the sales order and use Transaction MD50 to execute the planning. The system not only creates a procurement element or receipt with the sales order reference for the finished good but also plans all of the components defined in the BOM of the finished good.

Single-Item Planning, Project

You can also execute separate planning for engineer-to-order (ETO) materials. If the material—whether finished good or a spare part of a raw material—is assigned to a work breakdown structure (WBS) element, then you can use Transaction MD51 to execute planning.

15.3.4   MRP Live

MRP Live is the new version of MRP, developed to achieve a maximum performance when using an SAP HANA database. In MRP Live, the entire MRP logic is carried out directly in SAP HANA, including database selection. As a result, all of the MRP steps, from net requirements calculation to the creation of the replenishment proposal are carried out in SAP HANA.

Let's first look at how MRP Live differs from the classic MRP transactions, comparing especially the main differences in terms of functionalities, restrictions, and transactions.

The new Transaction MD01N was created specifically to run MRP Live. In classic MRP, different transactions were required to execute a total MRP run (Transaction MD01); a single-item, multilevel MRP (Transaction MD02); and a single-item, single-level MRP (Transaction MD03). Transaction MD01N replaces all of those classic MRP transactions, while providing more flexible selection criteria, with more fields and options for selection, as shown in Figure 15.9.

However, you cannot replace multilevel, make-to-order planning (Transaction MD50) or individual project planning (Transaction MD51) with MRP Live. For these

15

business scenarios, you should still use the classic MRP transactions. Alternatively, header material could be planned within MRP Live, with the **BOM Components** indicator set so that all of the components are also included.

Transaction MD01N was also designed with simplification in mind. Therefore, when compared with the classic MRP transactions, some notable changes include:

- The creation indicator for purchase requisitions and schedule lines does not exist in Transaction MD01N. As a result, MRP Live directly creates purchase requisitions for materials procured externally or according to the schedule list.

- The creation indicator for MRP lists is also not available in MRP Live for performance reasons. As a result, MRP lists are not created by MRP Live. If you need to create MRP lists, the material should be planned with the classic MRP transactions (such as Transaction MD01, shown in Figure 15.24). Otherwise, you can use the stock/requirements list (Transaction MD04) to analyze the MRP results.

- The scope of planning is no longer necessary, since you can now select one or more plants in Transaction MD01N. MRP Live can also automatically determine the sequence of plants for planning, so the scope of planning becomes obsolete with MRP Live.

- Processing key NETPL (Net Change in the Planning Horizon) is not available in Transaction MD01N. This processing key was created to restrict the MRP run on the planning horizon for faster MRP runs. Since performance is much better with MRP Live, this processing key and the planning horizon concept are obsolete.

- The flag to determine whether parallel processing should be used is not available in MRP Live; parallel processing is automatically triggered by the system. You also won't need to define the destinations for parallel processing in Transaction OMIQ, since these destinations will be determined automatically based on the server group.

- The user exit key and user exit parameter fields are not available. In classic MRP transactions, user exits SAPLM61C_001 and EXIT_SAPMM61X_ 001 allow users to select which materials would be planned by MRP. Most commonly, all the materials of a specific MRP controller would be planned. In Transaction MD01N, the MRP controller is available as a selection criterion. If a different selection criterion is necessary, you can use the product group or the material multiple selection as a selection criterion.

Besides changes related to the transaction design, some changes to the MRP process must be considered:

- **Total requirements are not supported on MRP Live**
  Just like the classic MRP transactions, total dependent requirements and sales requirements are not supported on MRP Live.

- **Subcontracting on MRP Live is only supported with MRP areas**
  In classic MRP transactions, a separate planning segment is created for each vendor in a subcontracting scenario. In MRP Live, however, this functionality is no longer available. As a result, subcontracting scenarios must be mapped with MRP areas. Therefore, you'll need to create an MRP area for each vendor in Customizing and then assign MRP areas to materials used in the subcontracting scenario. For more information, Section 15.4, where we'll cover MRP areas in more detail.

- **Reusability of the replenishment proposals**
  In classic MRP transactions, unfirmed planned orders and purchase requisitions were not necessarily changed during the MRP run when quantities or dated changed. Now, in MRP Live, if a date or quantity in a replenishment proposal must be changed by MRP, the replenishment proposal is deleted, and a new proposal is created. Basically, the number of existing planned orders and purchase requisitions may change more frequently in MRP Live than in the classic MRP.

> **Note**
>
> As MRP Live is a new materials planning tool, some specific settings have not yet been implemented; a complete overview of these restrictions can be found in SAP Note 1914010.

- In specific scenarios, the number of replenishment proposals generated by MRP Live can differ from the number of replenishment proposals generated by classic MRP. This discrepancy happens, for example, when using a reorder point MRP type with external requirements (such as MRP type V1) or a safety stock. This discrepancy happens because, in classic MRP, the safety stock (or reorder point) quantity is added to the replenishment proposal created to cover the first requirement, while in MRP Live, a separated replenishment proposal is created to cover the safety stock. Although more replenishment proposals will exist in MRP Live, the total quantity among the replenishment proposals generated should be the same as the total quantity on classic MRP. We'll explore this issue more with an example later in Section 15.4.

To access MRP Live, use Transaction MD01N or follow the menu path **Production • MRP • Planning • MRP Live**, as shown in Figure 15.9.

15

Notice that far more materials planning options are available in MRP Live, such as selecting a specific group of materials and saving this group as a variant. Planning via **Product Group**, via **MRP Controller**, and even choosing **Material Scope** to make MRP Live run on MPS (master production schedule) materials only, MRP materials only, or both. **BOM Components** can also be planned. Enter the parameters shown in Figure 15.9 and click **Execute**.

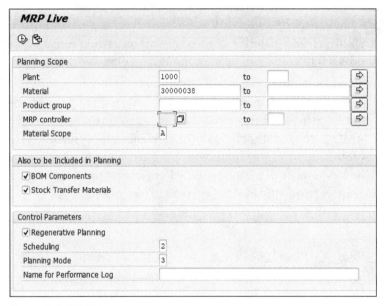

Figure 15.9 MRP Live

Whenever MRP Live finds a setting that is not supported, it will automatically change to the classic MRP logic. The material will be planned without further problems using the classic MRP logic. However, this approach is not always the best for achieving optimal performance with MRP Live. We can identify which materials were unsupported and instead execute classic MRP by analyzing the MRP Live results in Transaction MD01N. On the MRP Live results screen, the system will display how many materials were planned directly in SAP HANA and how many were planned using the classic MRP logic. By clicking the **Materials with messages** button on the results screen, as shown in Figure 15.10, you can see exactly which materials could not be planned with MRP Live and because of which restriction it was necessary to plan them using the classic MRP logic.

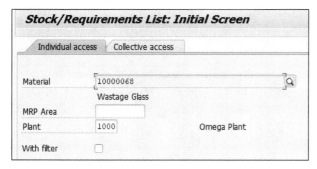

MRP Live

| MRP Level | Stock/Requirements list | Materials with messages | | | | | | | | | | | | | | | | | | All Steps | | |

Name for Performance Log	MRP Start Date	Start Time	MRP End Date	End Time	Tot.PlgTme	Alert	User	Matls Planned	Mat.Failed	ClassicMRP	MRPon Hana
JAKHTAR 17.06.2018 15:16:41	17.06.2018	15:16:41	17.06.2018	15:16:45	00:00:04		JAKHTAR	9	0	9	0

Figure 15.10 Planning Results from MRP Live

Figure 15.11 shows materials with messages after the MRP Live execution. Clicking on the **Solve Issue** button will redirect you to the master data where the restriction was found (generally the material master), so that you can change your settings and avoid this restriction and ensure future planning with MRP Live.

Info and Settings for Materials in MRP on HANA: Display

Solve Issue   Info Details

Material	MRPCn	Plant	Last Planned In...	Restrictn	Information from Last MRP Live on HANA Run	Date	Time
30000038	SF1	1000	Classic MRP	✓	Splitting quota arrangements not supported in MRP Live on HANA	17.06.2018	15:16:41
10000076	RM1		Classic MRP	✓	Splitting quota arrangements not supported in MRP Live on HANA	17.06.2018	15:16:43
10000075	RM1		Classic MRP	✓	Splitting quota arrangements not supported in MRP Live on HANA	17.06.2018	15:16:43
10000073	RM1		Classic MRP	✓	Splitting quota arrangements not supported in MRP Live on HANA	17.06.2018	15:16:43
10000072	RM1		Classic MRP	✓	Splitting quota arrangements not supported in MRP Live on HANA	17.06.2018	15:16:43
10000071	RM1		Classic MRP	✓	Splitting quota arrangements not supported in MRP Live on HANA	17.06.2018	15:16:43

Figure 15.11 Materials with Messages from MRP Live

15

Once the MRP has run, the stock/requirements can be examined by the materials planner can spend more time evaluating the supply-demand situation of material and taking actions as required.

15.3.5   Stock/Requirements List

Figure 15.12 shows the initial screen of stock/requirements list (Transaction MDO4).

Stock/Requirements List: Initial Screen

| Individual access | Collective access |

Material	10000068
	Wastage Glass
MRP Area	
Plant	1000 Omega Plant
With filter	☐

Figure 15.12 Initial Screen of the Stock/Requirements List: Individual Access

The stock/requirements list describes all MRP-relevant elements for a material within a plant, including the stock, customer requirements, and PIRs, dependent demands, planned orders, and production orders. In addition, you see parameters relevant to MRP, such as the safety stock or the planning time fence. For all elements, details can be displayed and changed, if permitted. Usually, the system will display the availability date of a goods receipt. But you can also display the goods receipt date instead, for example, to plan actions in case of delays as well as navigate to different elements of the stock/requirements list as follows:

- Display of exception messages
- Jump into the detail view
- Jump into the order report
- Display goods receipt date or availability date
- Show the RLT (replenishment lead time)
- Change the MRP elements

Figure 15.13 shows that, when you're in the stock/requirements list, you can click on the **Header Data** icon to find all of the parameters used by the system in planning the material. In other words, you no longer have to separately view the MRP parameters in the material master but can do so while remaining in the stock/requirements list.

Let's evaluate some of the details shown in Figure 15.13. On **17.06.2018** (June 17, 2018), the opening **Stock** of material **10000068** in the **Available quantity** column was zero (**0.000**). An order reservation (**OrdRes**) of material **10000068** for the quantity **191.625** exists and is required on **14.05.2018** (this date is already past at the time MRP Live is run) from the material **30000038** (the same material on which we just run MRP via the MRP Live transaction shown earlier in Figure 15.9). Thus, the system shows a deficit quantity of **-191.625** in the **Available quantity** column. To meet this deficit quantity of **191.625**, the system creates **MRP element 10005731**, which is a purchase requisition (**PurRqs**).

Click on the element details icon (magnifying glass) next to **MRP element 10005732**, as shown in Figure 15.13, and the popup window shown in Figure 15.14 will appear.

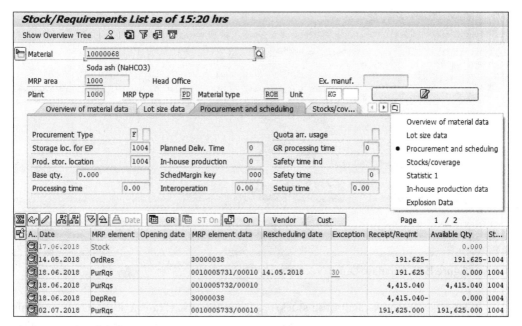

Figure 15.13 Stock/Requirements List

Figure 15.14 shows more details about the system-generated (automatic) purchase requisition 10005732 for the quantity **4,415.040**. Not only can an MRP controller display this purchase requisition, but this user can also make any manual changes as needed. Further, this purchase requisition can be converted into a purchase order by clicking on **-> Purchase order**. The screen shown in Figure 15.15 will appear.

Figure 15.14 Converting a Purchase Requisition into a Purchase Order

As shown in Figure 15.15, which is a purchase order, notice the automatically assigned purchase requisition number **10005732** in the lower half of the screen. Save the PO, and the system will create a PO number, which in our example is **4500000225**.

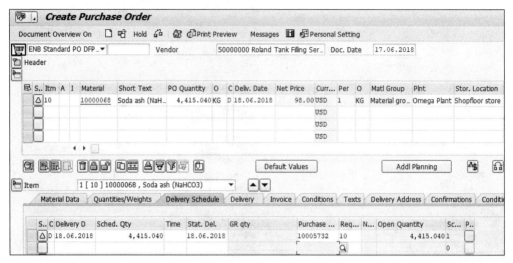

Figure 15.15 Purchase Order Created via MRP Live

Figure 15.16 shows again the stock/requirements list (Transaction MD04), and this time after converting purchase requisition **10005732** into a PO, the PO **4500000225** will be displayed.

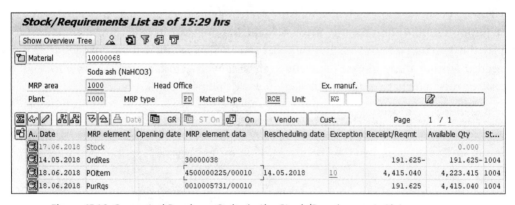

Figure 15.16 Converted Purchase Order in the Stock/Requirements List

Referring again to the initial screen for Transaction MD04, as shown earlier in Figure 15.12, this time click on the **Collective access** and enter any selection parameters, such as **MRP controller RM1**. You can also use Transaction MD07 for collective access of the stock/requirements list.

Figure 15.17 shows traffic light indicators for each material assigned to the MRP controller RM1.

Light	Val...	Material	MRP Area	Material description	A	StckDS	1st RDS	2nd R	1	2	3	4	5	6	7	8	Plant stock	B	Safety...	Reorder ...	M
◉○○		10000207	1000	Silico Manganese		1.0-	1.0-	1.0-	1								325.000	KG	0.000	0.000	ROI
◉○○		10000266	1000	RE		1.0-	1.0-	1.0-							92		114.730	KG	0.000	0.000	ROI
◉○○		10000208	1000	Ferro Manganese		0.9-	0.9-	0.9-	1								887.500	KG	0.000	0.000	ROI
◉○○		10000212	1000	Rice Husk		0.7-	0.7-	0.7-	1								952.000	KG	0.000	0.000	ROI
◉○○		10000204	1000	RAW SCRAP SHREDDED..		0.6-	0.6-	0.6-	1								964.250	MT	0	0	ROI
◉○○		10000265	1000	RA		0.6-	999.9	999.9							17		472.909	KG	0.000	0.000	ROI
◉○○		10000209	1000	Ferro Silicon		0.5-	0.5-	0.5-	1								975.000	KG	0.000	0.000	ROI
◉○○		10000216	1000	Thermal GBC(Granulate..		0.5-	0.5-	0.5-	1								975.000	KG	0.000	0.000	ROI
◉○○		10000211	1000	Thermocouple Tips wit..		0.4-	0.4-	0.4-	1								980	EA	0	0	ROI
◉○○		10000210	1000	Pet Coke		0.2-	0.2-	0.2-	1								995.000	KG	0.000	0.000	ROI
○○◨		10000073	1000	Sodium Oxide		12.9	12.9	12.9									2,252.000	KG	0.000	0.000	ROI
○○◨		10000075	1000	Calcium Oxide		38.5	38.5	38.5									2,124.250	KG	0.000	0.000	ROI
○○◨		10000001	1000	RA II		999.9	999.9	999.9									94.000	KG	0.000	0.000	ROI
○○◨		10000002	1000	RAW SCRAP SHREDDED.		999.9	999.9	999.9								2	10	MT	0	0	ROI

Stock/Requirements List: Material List

Selected Stock/Requirements Lists   Define Traffic Light   Exception Groups

Plant   1000   Omega Plant
MRP controller RM1   Raw Material Reqm

Figure 15.17 Stock/Requirements List: Collective Access

Traffic Lights for Days' Supply and Receipt Days' Supply

The red, yellow, and green traffic light indicators in both Transaction MD06 and Transaction MD07, as shown in Figure 15.17, provide a quick indication in a list view about potential overstocking or understocking situations. A red light will appear if a demand in the past is still unfulfilled. How far in the past this demand element lies is specified by the negative days of supply value shown in a column in the list display. Be aware that a green light doesn't mean everything is in order. In fact, a green light may indicate that more stock exists than needed to fulfill future requirements. Green lights, therefore, can alert that too much inventory is being held. Yellow lights are assigned to materials where demand and supply is in perfect balance. SAP allows changes to the traffic light settings to customize what is being alerted by each color and what range is acceptable for an item to be have balanced demand and supply.

For example, you can develop a traffic light system that provides relevant and useful information. For example, consider setting up the lights so that items are sorted from most urgent materials handling down to long-term opportunities. One such scenario can be setting the monitor so that materials with stock days of supply below safety levels have a red light (and not only after they are overdue). Anything with

15

receipts coming in to cover demand within an acceptable time frame can get a yellow light, and anything that has too many receipts coming too early—and therefore needs to be expedited out—can get a green light.

You can also use the traffic light indicators for exception messages so that the exception groups considered more important are sorted above the ones that aren't so urgent, combined with the ranges of cover.

In the stock/requirement list or in the MRP list, the system calculates the number of days on a time axis to indicate when the existing stock of material can fulfill the requirements.

Receipt days' supply indicates how long the current stock and the expected receipts can cover the requirements. The system offers two different types of receipt days' supply:

- Receipt days' supply 1
- Receipt days' supply 2

You can select the receipt elements for both types of receipt days' supplies by following the configuration (Transaction SPRO) menu path **Production • Material Requirements Planning • Evaluation • Define Receipt Elements for Receipt Days' Supply**. In the configuration, select which procurement elements the system should consider or exclude in its calculation for days' supply.

Exception Messages

The system generates exception messages in MRP when alerts arise during the planning run. The system displays exception messages for each relevant procurement element in the stock/requirements list (refer to the column **Exception** shown earlier in Figure 15.13). You can also view exception elements by choosing **Edit • Find in the List**.

The main elements of an exception message are its priority, its group assignment, whether it is suppressed, whether it creates an MRP list, and its text.

Exception messages are displayed primarily in four transactions:

- Transaction MD04 displays dynamically created stock requirements situations for an individual material.
- Transaction MD05 displays the MRP list, a snapshot from when the MRP run last planned the material.

- Transaction MD06 displays a collective list of materials with their respective MRP lists.

- Transaction MD07 displays a collective list of materials with their respective stock/requirements situations.

> **Tips & Tricks**
>
> You can change the text of exception messages to denote the importance of an exception. For example, changing a text to "Warning: stock fallen below safety stock level" can help you quickly segregate exception messages with warnings from exception messages with information. To make limited changes to the existing exception message, follow the configuration (Transaction SPRO) menu path **Production • Material Requirements Planning • Evaluation • Exception Messages • Define and Group Exception Messages**.

Referring to Figure 15.17 again, Table 15.4 provides a comprehensive list of selected exception messages, including their importance to a smoother logistics and supply chain and information about how to address these exception messages.

No.	Message Description	Recommended Remedies and Actions	Importance
03	**New, and start date in the past**	The requisition is scheduled to start in the past. Expedite this order or requisition to ensure you meet the demand on time.	Critical
04	**New, and finish date in the past**	The requisition is scheduled to finish in the past. Expedite this order or requisition to ensure you meet the demand on time.	Critical
06	**Start date in the past**	The order or requisition is scheduled to start in the past. Expedite this order or requisition to ensure you meet the demand on time.	Critical
07	**Finish date in the past**	The order or requisition is scheduled to finish in the past. Expedite this order or requisition to ensure you meet the demand on time.	Critical

Table 15.4 A Summary of Exception Messages

No.	Message Description	Recommended Remedies and Actions	Importance
10	**Bring process forward**	Order or requisition is too late to cover requirements. Review the supply and demand and reschedule appropriately.	Important
15	**Postpone process**	Order or requisition is too early based on requirements. Review and reschedule appropriately.	Important
20	**Cancel process**	Supply exists beyond total demand in the system, and therefore, the stock is no longer required! Review and replan appropriately.	Critical
26	**Shortage in individual segment**	A material has been "provided to vendor" for the subcontracting process. Remove the material using the Transaction MIGO and run MRP manually.	Critical
52	**No BOM selected**	The system couldn't find a valid BOM for the item. Check the BOM, production version, and selection method.	Error
53	**No BOM explosion due to missing config.**	Plant set up incorrect. Contact your SAP functional consultant to address this issue.	Error
58	**Uncovered reqmt after effective-out date**	System is unable to find replacement material. Review the run-out strategy and adjust master data appropriately. Once resolved, run MRP manually.	Critical
59	**Receipt after effective-out date**	Receipt of discontinued material planned. Review the run-out strategy and adjust orders appropriately. Run MRP manually once resolved.	Critical
62	**Scheduling: Master data inconsistent**	Recheck master data. Remove **In House Processing Time** in the **MRP 2** tab of the material master. Ensure that the production version and routing are correct. Run MPS/MRP manually once corrected.	Error

Table 15.4 A Summary of Exception Messages (Cont.)

No.	Message Description	Recommended Remedies and Actions	Importance
82	Item is blocked	The requisition has been manually blocked and therefore can't be converted. Remove the block from the requisition or delete the requisition and run Transaction MD02 to regenerate new planning data for the material.	Critical
96	Stock fallen below safety stock level	Supply plan insufficient to cover safety stock requirement. Review and adjust as appropriate.	Informative

Table 15.4 A Summary of Exception Messages (Cont.)

When dealing with exception messages, some ways to prioritize the handling of them include the following:

1. Group 8 is the most important group, so look at the abnormal ends first where the planning run aborts. Address these materials first.

2. Next, look at group 5. These messages concern structural problems, and the planning run can't even come up with a date or quantity because the demand doesn't get exploded down to the lower level.

3. Then, check out group 3. Not only is a date to firm a receipt missing, it's already after when the receipt was supposed to come in to fulfill the demand.

4. After that, address group 2 problems where dates were missed when proposal needed to be firmed, so that you can receive the quantity after the regular lead time. If a date is missed, rescheduling and manual expediting is your only option.

5. Group 1 exceptions are only relevant while using the opening horizon for an additional check where external procurement is triggered first by a planned order and then by a purchase requisition.

6. Therefore, group 7 messages should be tackled next. These messages require expediting and may take much more time to get through, but at least create a list at this point. This list can be addressed later (by calling vendors, checking with purchasing, looking at the warehouse for inventory, etc.).

7. Next, deal with group 6. Inventory excess or shortages usually require a change in strategy. Again, make a list and see how you can reduce these exceptions over time

15

by, for example, applying a different MRP type, changing the lot-sizing procedure, looking at safety stock levels, and more.

8. Last but not least, you'll look at the general messages in group 4 to see why a new proposal has been created or an existing proposal changed. These messages are for information only and don't necessarily require action.

While trying to address exceptions, all kinds of problems in the process, the master data setup, the system setup, or with human behavior will need to be identified. A worthwhile exercise is to learn about all exception messages and their purposes.

> **Note**
>
> We encourage you to explore the several other features and functionalities in the stock/requirements lists by clicking on the different icons and choosing from the menu options.

15.4   Planning Areas

Apart from running MRP at a single plant level, at a material level, or at a product group level, you can activate MRP areas if you want to run MRP on the following:

- A single storage location or a group of storage locations
- A subcontractor

The advantage of setting up MRP areas is that you can plan material at the storage location level, which allows you to plan material differently from the MRP planning of the material at the plant level. For example, if you have a consumable material stored at several storage locations in a plant, then you can select MRP type ND (no planning) for this material. However, for two specific storage locations that feature high consumption of this consumable material, you can use MRP type VB (reorder point planning) to ensure that the system initiates the replenishment of this material as soon as its level drops below the reorder point level. MRP areas make this scenario possible.

In this section, we'll show you how to configure and activate MRP areas in the material master, including defining important planning parameters, running the MRP for MRP areas, and finally evaluating planning run results.

> **Warning!**
>
> After you activate MRP areas in an SAP system, you can't deactivate them. Hence, you'll need to extensively consider how MRP areas will be used before implementing them.

15.4.1 Configuration

The main configuration steps involved in setting up MRP areas include the following:

1. Select the **MRP area active** checkbox.

2. Define the MRP areas.

For our example, we'll show you how to set up MRP areas for a storage location.

In the first step, to activate MRP areas, follow the SAP configuration (Transaction SPRO) menu path **Production • Material Requirements Planning • Master Data • MRP Areas • Activate MRP for MRP Areas**. Select the **MRP area active** checkbox and save.

In the second step, to define MRP areas, follow the SAP configuration (Transaction SPRO) menu path **Production • Material Requirements Planning • Master Data • MRP Areas • Define MRP Areas**. Click **New Entries**, enter "1000-1004" as the **MRP Area**, and provide a description. For **MRP Area Type**, select **02** from the dropdown menu, which indicates we're setting up storage location MRP. Enter "1000" as the **Plant** and press ⌷Enter⌷. Next, on the right-hand side of the screen, double-click on **Assign storage locations,** and the screen shown in Figure 15.18 will appear.

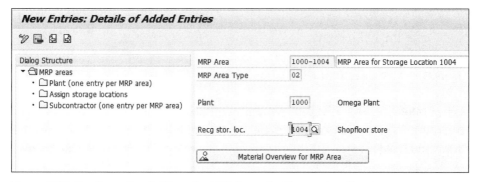

Figure 15.18 Configuration Settings for MRP Areas for Storage Location

> **Note**
>
> MRP area type 02 is the standard type for defining additional MRP areas at the storage location level. MRP area type 01 is for plant-level MRP areas and is created automatically by converting the planning file for MRP areas. MRP area type 03 is for subcontracting, specifically if you maintain your company's stock at the vendor's premises.

Enter "1004" as the **Stor. Loc.** (storage location) for **Plant** "1000" and save the entry. For our example, we'll use a single storage location for the plant, but you can also group several storage locations under one MRP area. This storage location (or group of locations) will be planned separately and independently from planning at the plant level. Additionally, you can define subcontracting MRP areas within a plant to enable the planning of material availability at the subcontractor (vendor) level.

15.4.2   Setting Up in the Material Master

With the necessary configuration settings for MRP areas in place, you can now activate storage location MRP for the material 10000070 for plant 1000 and for storage location 1004.

Using Transaction MM02 to change the material master, enter "10000070" as the **Material**, "1000" as the **Plant**, and "1004" as the **Stor. Loc.** and then select the **MRP 1** tab. As shown in Figure 15.19, click on the **MRP areas** button so that the screen shown in Figure 15.20 appears. Select the configured **MRP Area 1000-1004**.

Figure 15.19 MRP Areas in the Material Master

Assign MRP type VB for manual reorder point planning at the MRP area level and enter "200" as the **Reorder Point**. Assign other parameters such as **MRP Controller** "RM1" and **Fixed Lot Size** of "100" as shown in Figure 15.20. Click on the MRP 2 tab.

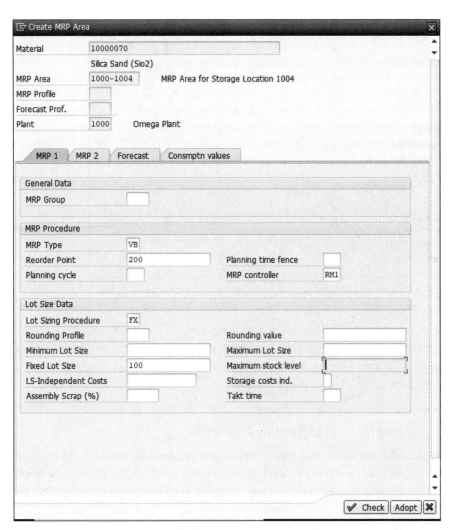

Figure 15.20 MRP Area Settings for the Storage Location in the Material Master

In the **MRP 2** tab, more planning options are available at the material level, such as defining a **Safety stock** (in our case, "70.000") at the MRP area level. Enter a **Planned delivery time** of "5" days and click on the **Forecast** tab as shown in Figure 15.21.

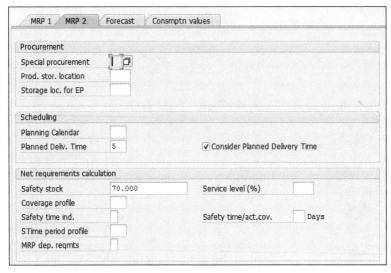

Figure 15.21 MRP 2 Tab of MRP Area 1000-1004

The **Forecast** tab enables you to enter forecast parameters and also execute a forecast of the material. Finally, click on the **Consmptn values** tab. You can enter the planned and unplanned consumption values in this tab. Click on the **Adopt** icon in MRP areas, and save the settings of the material master.

15.4.3   Running MRP at the Planning Area Level

To run the MRP for MRP areas interactively, use Transaction MD01N (MRP Live in S/4HANA) and enter parameters, such as the material 10000070. On executing the MRP Live transaction, the screen shown in Figure 15.22 will appear. Notice that the material 10000070 belongs to the **MRP Area 1000-1004**. Click on the **Selected Stock/Requirements Lists** button to go to screen shown in Figure 15.23.

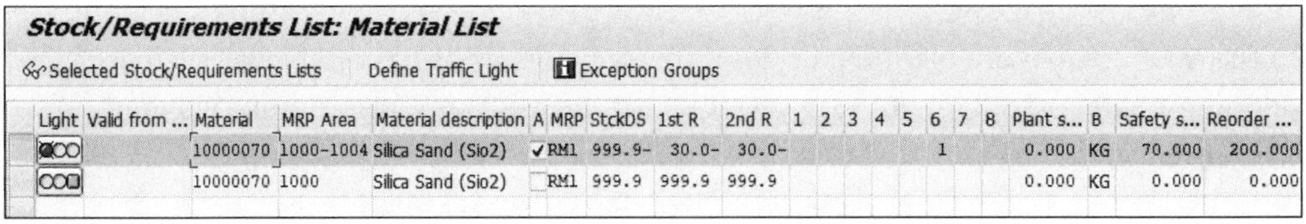

Light	Valid from ...	Material	MRP Area	Material description	A	MRP	StckDS	1st R	2nd R	1	2	3	4	5	6	7	8	Plant s...	B	Safety s...	Reorder ...
●○○		10000070	1000-1004	Silica Sand (Sio2)	✓	RM1	999.9-	30.0-	30.0-							1		0.000	KG	70.000	200.000
○○□		10000070	1000	Silica Sand (Sio2)		RM1	999.9	999.9	999.9									0.000	KG	0.000	0.000

Stock/Requirements List: Material List
&⟲ Selected Stock/Requirements Lists   Define Traffic Light   ℹ Exception Groups

Figure 15.22 Planning Results from MRP Live Using MRP Areas

15.4.4   Planning Results

Figure 15.23 shows the planning results of **Material 10000070** in **MRP Area 1000-1004**. Since no opening **Stock** existed and since the stock has fallen below the safety stock in the warehouse (storage location of the MRP areas), the system created planned orders 56894 and 56895 for a fixed quantity of 100 each. (We had defined a fixed lot size earlier, as shown in Figure 15.20.) Notice **Exception 96** (message details in the lower half of the screen) to indicate that the **Stock fallen below safety stock level**. Also, since this material is externally procured, therefore, the planned orders can be converted into purchase requisitions.

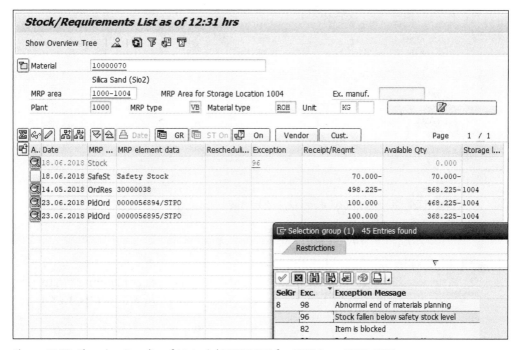

Figure 15.23 Planning Results of Material 10000070 for MRP Area 1000-1004

15.5   Classic MRP

Now that we've covered MRP Live and its associated business processes, let's also briefly cover the basics of classic MRP and some of its important functionality. Access the screen shown in Figure 15.24 via Transaction MD02 to run MRP on a single material at an MRP area level 1000-1004.

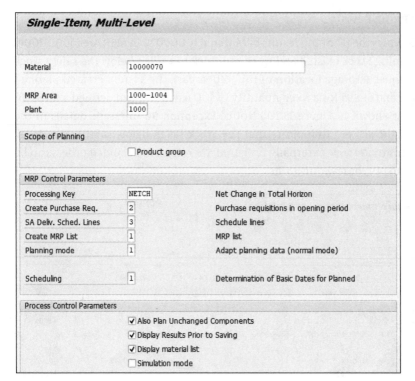

Figure 15.24 Single-Item, Multilevel MRP (Initial Screen)

The following are some important selection parameters for classic MRP:

- **Processing key**
  The processing key enables the system to decide the type of planning run to carry out for the material. The options for the planning run are **NETCH**, **NETPL**, and **NEUPL**.

- **Purchase requisition key**
  If external procurement is implied, the system considers this setting during the planning run. If the necessary settings are in place, then the system can directly create purchase requisitions for all externally procured materials. Alternatively, the system can create planned orders that you can convert into purchase requisitions.

- **Delivery schedules**
  If you've maintained a source list for the material and have incorporated scheduling agreements with vendors in the source list, the system can create schedule lines.

- **Creation of material requirements planning list**
  The system includes the results of the planning run in the MRP list after the planning run. An MRP list is a static or frozen list of stock/requirements situations with the date and time immediately after the planning run. This indicator controls how the system should create the MRP list. The available options are for the system to create an MRP list for all planned orders, to create an MRP list for planned orders with exceptions, or to not create any MRP list at all. Exceptions are alerts in the system that planners will need to keep an eye on.

- **Planning mode**
  During the planning run, the system plans various procurement elements, such as the unfirmed planned orders, purchase requisitions, and scheduling agreements, once again in the next planning run. You can control how the system should proceed with the planning data that already exists (i.e., from the latest planning run or due to the MRP planner's recent activities). Three options are available:

  - **Adopt Planning data**
    If any changes occur in required quantities, dates, or lot-sizing procedures in unfirmed planned orders (or other procurement elements), the system re-explodes the BOM for the new quantities in the MRP run.

  - **Re-explode BOM and routing**
    The system re-explodes the BOM and routing if a change occurs in the BOM master data, routing, production versions, or BOM explosion numbers. This option ensures that the system re-explodes the BOM for existing, unfirmed planned orders. Procurement proposals created in the previous planning run aren't deleted but are adjusted to take the changes into account.

  - **Delete and Recreate Planning data**
    The system deletes the existing procurement proposals (i.e., the entire planning data of the previous planning run), unless they are firmed, and re-explodes the BOM and routing, thereby creating completely new procurement proposals.

15

- **Scheduling types**
  For in-house produced materials, the system offers two types of scheduling options:
  - Basic date scheduling
  - Lead time scheduling

  After you enter the parameters on the initial screen of Transaction MD02, press [Enter] twice (first to confirm the MRP parameters causing the entered parameters to turn red and then to execute the MRP). The system will open a screen displaying the planning result of a large number of materials. These results not only include finished or semifinished goods (10000070) planned but also all of the components of the BOM. You can view the planning results of a material by double-clicking the material.

15.6   Configuration Settings

In the following subsections, we'll show you the configuration settings that you'll need to make to run MRP at the plant level:

- MRP activation
- Scope of planning configuration
- Plant parameters configuration
- MRP group configuration

15.6.1   Material Requirements Planning Activation

In this configuration step, you'll choose the plant for which you want to activate MRP. Use Transaction OMDU or follow the configuration menu path **Logistics • Production • MRP • Planning File Entry • Activate MRP and Set Up Planning File**.

15.6.2   Plant Parameters Configuration

You can configure MRP up to the following three levels:

- Plant parameters
- MRP groups
- Material master (MRP views)

Material master settings have a higher priority than MRP group parameters, which in turn have a higher priority than plant parameters. No setting can be found on all three levels, but may be on up to two of them. Therefore, plant parameters are usually used to set defaults, which can be overruled if necessary. The plant parameters of MRP contain a view of numerous configuration settings relevant to MRP. The plant parameters screen shows whether certain configuration settings have been maintained or whether they are still in their initial statuses. Using this screen enables you to navigate directly to the relevant configuration area.

In the plant parameter configuration step, the following are some of the possible configurations:

- Reference Plant
- Number ranges
- Direct Procurement
- Available Stock
- Rescheduling
- External Procurement
- Conversion of planned orders
- Dependent Requirements availability
- Floats (Schedule Margin Keys)
- BOM Explosion
- BOM/Routing Selection

To configure plant parameters, use Transaction OPPQ or follow the configuration menu path **Logistics • Production • Material Requirements Planning • Plant Parameters**. Click on the **Maintain** button. A popup window appears in which you enter the **Plant** as "3000" and then click on the **Maintain** icon. You'll then see a detailed screen where you can maintain the individual plant parameters.

15.6.3   Material Requirements Planning Group Configuration

You can group materials using MRP groups and then assign the MRP group in the **MRP 1** tab of the material master. Each MRP group can have its own set of MRP parameters. When you work with an MRP group, you'll have the following options, which are specific to a material or group of materials:

591

- Strategy group
- Settlement type and horizon
- Rescheduling horizon and planning horizon
- Production storage location selection
- Conversion order types of planned orders
- Planning horizon
- Planning time fence and roll-forward periods
- BOM and task list selection IDs
- Direct procurement parameters
- Planned order scheduling parameters
- Start number of days allowed in the past
- Availability checking groups
- Period split for distributing the independent requirement
- Maximum MRP intervals
- Availability of safety stock for MRP
- BOM explosion
- Direct procurement of nonstock items
- Creation indicators for purchase requisitions
- Scheduling of external procurement according to the info record
- Checking rule for dependent demand

To configure MRP groups, use Transaction OPPR or follow the configuration menu path **Logistics • Production • Material Requirements Planning • MRP Groups • Carry Out Overall Maintenance of MRP Groups**. In the **Material Requirements Group (MRP) Group** initial screen, enter the **Plant** as "1000" and click on the **Maintain** button. In the popup window that appears, enter "0040" as the **MRP group** and click on the **Maintain** button. The detailed screen appears for maintaining individual parameters of MRP group.

When you've configured the MRP group, save the group and assign the group in the **MRP 1** tab of the material master.

> **Note**
> While this example covers the maintenance of an existing MRP group, you can also create new MRP groups, delete MRP groups, or copy an MRP group from an existing

one. You can also assign the MRP group to a material type by following the configuration menu path **Logistics • Production • Material Requirements Planning • MRP Groups • Define MRP Group for Each Material Type**.

15.7   Planning Calendar

In some instances, your company may receive goods on specific days of the week or the vendor supplies goods only during specific days of the week. In other words, the planning of material differs from the factory calendar of the company. For example, agricultural products used in the production process for finished edible products may only be produced during specific periods of the year. The company must procure and store these materials to ensure their availability for consumption during the production process. For example, red chilies, an agricultural product, are only produced from January to April. The company can use the planning calendar to ensure the system creates procurement proposals of this raw material (red chilies) within the four-month time period.

You can also specify a planning date in the planning run. This option is useful because you can bring the planning run forward to an earlier date. If the planning run is set for Monday, for example, you can perform this planning run on Friday.

You can assign a planning calendar in the **MRP 2** tab of the material master (Transaction MM02).

To create a new planning calendar, use Transaction MD25 or follow the configuration menu path **Production • Material Requirements Planning • Master Data • Maintain Planning Calendar**.

As shown in Figure 15.25 ❶, after entering "0001" as the **Planning calendar** and "3000" as the **Plant**, select the **Following working day** radio button if the period start date isn't a working day. You can also define the minimum number of periods that the system must generate in the planning calendar. When you press ⌨Enter, a popup window appears ❷, in which you'll select weekdays, workweek, workdays, work months, and so on. Click on the **Generate Periods** icon, and the **New Dates** popup window appears ❸, in which you'll enter the start and end dates of the planning calendar. Click **Continue**.

As shown in Figure 15.26, notice that all period planning starts from Tuesday, which is the same as defined in the lower half of the first screen shown in Figure 15.25 ❶.

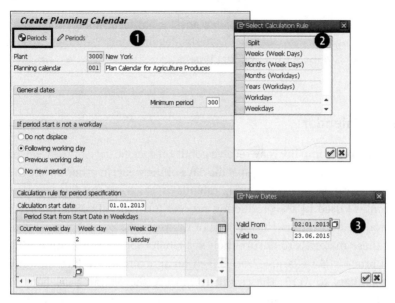

Figure 15.25 Creation of the Planning Calendar

Create Planning Calendar: Periods

Plant   3000 New York
Plng calendar   001   Plan Calendar for Agriculture Produces

▶ | 🔏 ▾ | 🔍 Check | 📑 📑 | Firm/Fix | Unfreeze

From date	Period to	Period	Year	Firmed
22.01.2013	04.02.2013	1	2013	☐
05.02.2013	18.02.2013	2	2013	☐
19.02.2013	04.03.2013	3	2013	☐
05.03.2013	18.03.2013	4	2013	☐
19.03.2013	01.04.2013	5	2013	☐
02.04.2013	15.04.2013	6	2013	☐
16.04.2013	29.04.2013	7	2013	☐
30.04.2013	13.05.2013	8	2013	☐
14.05.2013	27.05.2013	9	2013	☐
28.05.2013	10.06.2013	10	2013	☐
11.06.2013	24.06.2013	11	2013	☐
25.06.2013	08.07.2013	12	2013	☐
09.07.2013	22.07.2013	13	2013	☐
23.07.2013	05.08.2013	14	2013	☐
06.08.2013	19.08.2013	15	2013	☐
20.08.2013	02.09.2013	16	2013	☐
03.09.2013	16.09.2013	17	2013	☐
17.09.2013	30.09.2013	18	2013	☐
01.10.2013	14.10.2013	19	2013	☐
15.10.2013	28.10.2013	20	2013	☐
29.10.2013	11.11.2013	21	2013	☐
12.11.2013	25.11.2013	22	2013	☐
26.11.2013	09.12.2013	23	2013	☐

Figure 15.26 Planning Calendar Created

15.8 Summary

You can take enormous advantage of the MRP functionality in SAP to help improve and optimize your business processes. You can plan all types of materials, including high-, medium-, and low-value materials, as well as materials with special procurement types. The planning calendar can help you plan materials that are specific to particular calendars only. Further, you can give individual attention to a material if it has specific or unique business needs. You can also use MRP area level planning to independently plan materials that are specific to a storage location (or a group of storage locations) or at the subcontractor level.

In the next chapter, we'll cover forecasting in SAP.

15

Chapter 16
Forecasting

Business decisions are based on forecasts. Decisions using material requirements planning (MRP) are based on forecasts of future conditions. Forecasts are needed continually, and, over time, the impact of a forecast on actual results can be measured, initial forecasts can be updated, and decisions can be modified.

Forecasting is a prediction of what will occur in the future and, therefore, is an uncertain process. Because of uncertainty, the accuracy of a forecast is as important as the outcome predicted by the forecast. Despite using the best forecasting tools, all forecasts will have a degree of error to account for deviations (the mean average deviation, or MAD) between forecast figures and the confidence in these figures. Forecasts usually start out wrong, and they are riddled with errors that only increase with time. Forecasts are also more inaccurate when made at the individual stock-keeping unit (SKU) level. Despite all these limitations, forecasting is still an invaluable tool to put to use in today's volatile, uncertain, complex, and ambiguous (VUCA) world of logistics and supply chain.

In this chapter, we'll focus on the key forecasting functions available in SAP S/4HANA, including the forecast models, parameters used in forecasting, and the various forecasting options. Forecast-based planning, or forecasting, also part of consumption-based planning, is a procedure where you'll actually run a material-based forecast to generate planned demand for which you can order and plan future inventory. In fact, each material can have its own forecasting screen activated in the material master. Forecasting can be used for finished goods as well as for any material whose consumption values can provide greater insight into its future demand.

Forecasting is a consumption-based replenishment strategy that entails maintaining inventory in anticipation of actual demand. Inventory is replenished to a forecast, which is based on the material's own consumption history, hence the name *material forecast*. Forecasting works well when you have demand that is predictable, but the lead time to replenish is long. Because you're using an "artificial" demand by using a forecast, MRP can generate all supply elements way ahead of time. As a materials planner, all you would need to do is turn the planned orders (or order proposals) into orders on the date the system tells you to do so. However, forecast-based planning doesn't take demand spikes into consideration. Any changes in demand will flow into the consumption pattern and eventually be picked up by the forecast module. The system might increase or decrease the forecast or tell you that the current underlying model isn't applicable anymore.

Let's discuss some of the more frequently used forecast models before delving into how they work in SAP S/4HANA.

16.1   Forecast Models

Forecast modeling is designed to aid in forecasting particular events. The forecast model is designed around factors that you may believe are important in influencing the future use of a material. You can also use past consumption of a material to determine its future use. Both of these methods should produce a reliable forecast. A number of forecast models are available in the forecasting functionality within SAP S/4HANA, as shown in Figure 16.1.

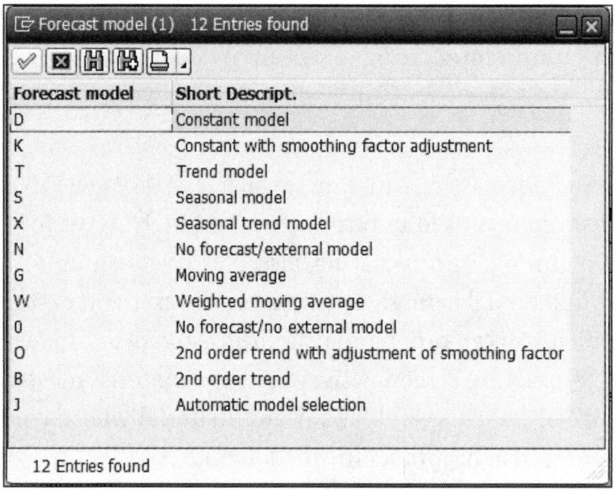

Forecast model	Short Descript.
D	Constant model
K	Constant with smoothing factor adjustment
T	Trend model
S	Seasonal model
X	Seasonal trend model
N	No forecast/external model
G	Moving average
W	Weighted moving average
0	No forecast/no external model
O	2nd order trend with adjustment of smoothing factor
B	2nd order trend
J	Automatic model selection

12 Entries found

Figure 16.1 Available Forecast Models

In this section, we'll discuss four forecast modeling types: the constant model, the trend model, the seasonal model, and the seasonal trend model.

16.1.1 Constant Model

The constant model assumes that the use of a material is constant. Being constant doesn't mean that the use of material is the same each month, but rather that variation in material usage fluctuates a little, and a constant mean value can be calculated. This forecast model can apply, for example, to electricity consumption in an office. Although summer months raise electricity consumption due to increased air conditioning use, consumption doesn't vary a great deal from the mean value over a longer period of time, such as a year.

16.1.2 Trend Model

The trend model is used when an identifiable increase or decrease of material exists over a period of time. The trend may include areas of movement away from the trend, but the overall movement follows the trend. For example, a downward trend over time may represent the use of printer cartridges for top-selling printers that become obsolete over a short period of time, perhaps only 12 to 18 months. As the purchase and use of the printer becomes decreases, the cartridges used in that printer will also decrease.

16.1.3 Seasonal Model

The seasonal model affects many businesses due to the weather, holidays, or vacations. The seasonal model is defined as a pattern that repeats for each period. For example, the annual seasonal pattern has a cycle that is 12 periods long, if the periods are months. A seasonal model may be applicable to a company that makes patio furniture, which experiences greater demand from May through September, and this pattern is repeated each year.

16.1.4 Seasonal Trend Model

The seasonal trend model is similar to the seasonal model, except that instead of the same pattern occurring each period, the pattern is moving further away from the mean value, either positive or negative. For example, California sparkling wine manufacturers can see a positive seasonal trend. Demand for their products follows a seasonal pattern, and for them, the seasonal pattern has a positive trend, as sales have continued to rise. A negative seasonal trend can be shown in beer manufacturers who have a seasonal market, but the overall trend continues to be negative as sales slow each year.

16

> **Tips & Tricks**
>
> If your company hasn't developed forecast models in the past or don't know which forecast model fits best, you can have the SAP system analyze the historical data and determine an appropriate forecast model to use. The forecast model J (automatic model selection) is available in SAP S/4HANA. After the model has been selected, you can use this model as a starting point and make modifications in the future. However, equally important is revisiting the system-proposed and selected forecast model to ensure the forecast closely matches consumption trends.

16.2   Forecasting Master Data

In addition to maintaining the forecasting data that we'll cover in this section, you'll need to maintain the planning data in the MRP views of the material master, which is equally necessary. Such MRP-specific data can be using the MRP type VV (forecast-based planning) and other stock and scheduling parameters. Stock parameters can maintain the safety stock of the material. The period split is also maintained in the **MRP 3** tab of the material master. Chapter 15 covered MRP in detail.

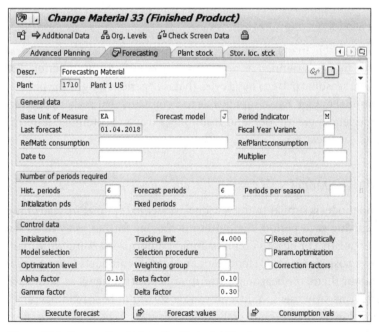

Figure 16.2 Forecasting Tab in the Material Master

Figure 16.2 shows the **Forecasting** tab of material master, which can be accessed via Transactions MM01 or MM02. Table 16.1 explains these fields in detail.

Field	Description
Forecast model	Indicates your chosen forecast model. For example, entering forecast model "N" (no forecast/external model) enables the SAP system to create forecasts from external sources such as an MS Excel file or even a legacy system. We'll cover this topic in more detail in Section 16.4.3.
Period indicator	The periods in which the consumption values and the forecast values are managed.
Fiscal year variant	The fiscal year in which the consumption values and the forecast values are managed.
RefMat: Consumption	The consumption data a material that the system uses to forecast values of new material. If two or more materials have a similar consumption history, then one material can become the reference material for other, and a multiplier can still apply to an individual material to account for any increase or decrease in consumption values and forecast values (see the definition of **Multiplier** below).
Date to	Date up to which the system will use the consumption values of the reference material to calculate new material forecast values.
RefPlant: Consumption	The plant of the reference material.
Multiplier	The multiplication factor that the system uses for a reference material's historical values to calculate new material forecast values.
Hist. periods	Indicates the number of historical values the system uses for a material forecast.
Forecast periods	Indicates the number of period splits for which the forecast values should be created.
Periods per season	Indicates the number of periods that belong to a season. Use this option only if the forecast model is a seasonal forecast model.

Table 16.1 Parameters Details of the Forecasting Screen in the Material Master

16

Field	Description
Initialization pds.	Number of periods used for initialization. Initializing is resetting the system's settings can be automatically or manually enabled. Initialization takes place when a material is forecast for the first time or when structural changes to a material's time series have occurred, such as a change in a materials' forecast model or a change in historical or forecast values.
Fixed periods	Number of periods the system will not recalculate the forecast values in the next forecast. This option is helpful for avoiding fluctuations in a forecast's calculation or for giving production more time to react to changed planning figures within the planning horizon.
Model selection	Specifies whether the system should check the values for one or more trends or seasonal fluctuations. Set this indicator if the system should help in automatic forecast model selection.
Optimization level	Specifies the increment by which the system optimizes (rough, middle, finer) the forecast parameters.
Alpha factor	Specifies the smoothing factor for updating the basic values. If left blank, the default value is 0.2.
Gamma factor	Specifies the smoothing factor for updating the seasonal index. If left blank, the default value is 0.3.
Tracking limit	Specifies the amount (or number of times) by which forecast values may deviate from the actual values. Every time a forecast runs, the system compares the tracking limit with the tracking signal. The tracking signal, which is calculated internally, is the quotient and the MAD (mean average deviation). The system uses the tracking signal to control the accuracy of the forecasts. If the tracking signal is greater than the tracking limit, the system issues exception message and asks you to (re)check the selected forecast model.
Selection procedure	Defines the procedure by which the system selects the optimum forecast model. By default, the two methods that the system uses are:

Table 16.1 Parameters Details of the Forecasting Screen in the Material Master (Cont.)

Field	Description
	■ Procedure 1: Uses a significant test to determine whether a trend or a seasonal pattern is present and then selects the forecast model based on the basis of these results. ■ Procedure 2: Uses more a precise and granular calculation than procedure 1 but consumes more system resources. This procedure carries out forecasting using all models, optimizes the parameters, and then selects the model with the smallest MAD.
Weighting group	Indicates how many historical values are used to calculate the forecast and what weighting is given to each historical value. We'll cover setting up weighting groups in more detail in Section 16.5.2.
Beta factor	Specifies the smoothing factor for the trend value. If left blank, then the default value is 0.1.
Delta factor	Specifies the smoothing factor for the MAD. If left blank, then the default value is 0.3.
Reset automatically	If selected, the system automatically resets the forecast model if the tracking limit is exceeded. Additionally, the system selects a new model during the next forecast run.
Param. Optimization	If selected, the system optimizes the smoothing factors needed by the given forecast model. When this indicator is set, parameter optimization is carried out both for the first forecast and for subsequent forecasts. The system calculates a number of different parameter combinations and selects the one that produces the lowest MAD.
Correction factors	If selected, the system calculates forecast values by taking into account correction factors as defined in Customizing.

Table 16.1 Parameters Details of the Forecasting Screen in the Material Master (Cont.)

Maintain the desired parameters details, as shown in Figure 16.2, and maintain the MRP parameters in the four MRP tabs of the material master. In our example, we maintained **MRP type** VV (forecast-based planning) in the **MRP 3** tab of material master and maintained the lot size as **EX** (lot-for-lot). We also maintained a **Safety stock** of 10.

Tips & Tricks

When SAP S/4HANA is implemented for the first time, historical consumption values won't be available in the system for forming the basis of forecasting. In these scenarios, you can manually enter the unplanned or the total consumption quantities of a material. If maintaining consumption values for a large number of materials, then creating an upload program is a more practical approach. As shown in Figure 16.3, total consumption values from the last six months are manually entered.

Access the screen shown in Figure 16.3 in the material master (Transaction MM02) by clicking on the **Additional Data** button followed by clicking the **Consumption** tab.

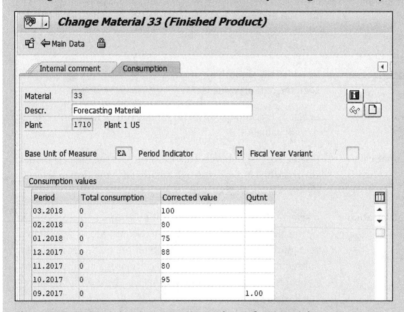

Figure 16.3 Maintaining Consumption Values of a Material

16.3   Forecast Profile

The parameters on the **Forecast** tab in the material master record can be predefined using a forecast profile. A forecast profile allows you to create a default set of parameter values to be copied directly into the material master record. A forecast profile for the forecast parameters can be created using Transaction MP80 or by following the navigation path **Logistics • Materials Management • Material Master • Profile • Forecast Profile • Create**.

On the initial screen of Transaction MP80, you can select which parameters to enter values for. In addition, you can determine whether a value should be defaulted into the material master, or whether the parameter is write-protected and can't be changed in the material master. Next, click on the **Data Screen** to maintain specific values in the forecast profile.

16.4   Business Processes in Forecasting

Business processes in forecasting entail first executing the forecast followed by executing the MRP. We'll cover both these steps in the following sections. We'll also briefly cover the steps required for using external data for forecasting a materials requirement that is then subsequently planned using MRP.

16.4.1   Executing Forecast

Before executing forecasting, ensure that you've maintained consumption values for the material. As shown in Figure 16.2, click on the **Execute forecast** button to bring up the screen shown in Figure 16.4. Click on the **Forecasting** button so that the screen shown in Figure 16.5 appears.

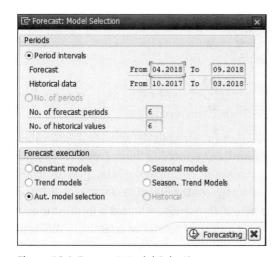

Figure 16.4 Forecast Model Selection

Figure 16.5 shows a screen for the materials planner to make any last-minute changes to any parameter before executing the forecast. Click on the **Forecasting**, which will open the screen shown in Figure 16.6.

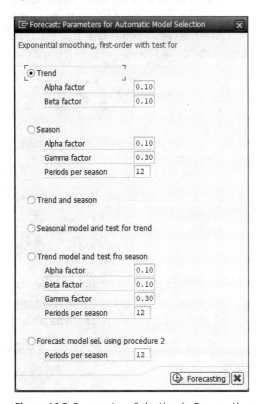

Figure 16.5 Parameters Selection in Forecasting

Figure 16.6 shows the forecast values of the next six months. (The forecast period was defined as 6 in the **Forecasting** tab of the material material.)

Now, the system will calculate the **MAD** (mean average deviation), the **Trend value**, and the **Error total** of the forecast values. **MAD** helps identify the degree of variability and helps planners make subsequent decisions on buffering strategies to avoid stockouts. The **Error total** of 44 is divided by the **MAD** value of 13 (44 ÷ 13 = 3.385) and is compared with the **Tracking limit** set at 4.000 to decide whether a forecast model is still applicable or warrants creating a new forecast model or selecting a different forecast model. An error total is the sum of all errors in the past consumption series.

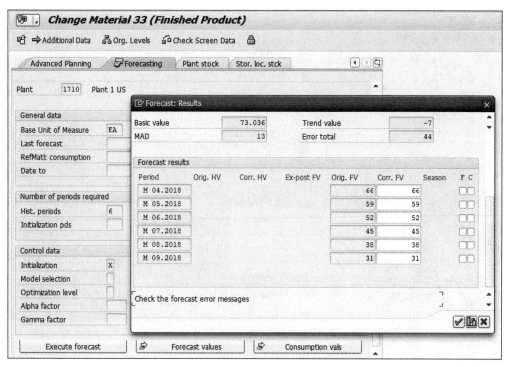

Figure 16.6 Forecast Values

> **Warning**
>
> Check out the forecast error messages shown in Figure 16.6 by double-clicking the messages and addressing them as appropriate.

Press F5, and the screen shown in Figure 16.7 will appear, which shows the following:

- In yellow, the details of the corrected historical consumption values
- In blue, the details of the original historical consumption values, if any
- In red, the original forecasting values
- In green, the corrected forecasting values, if any

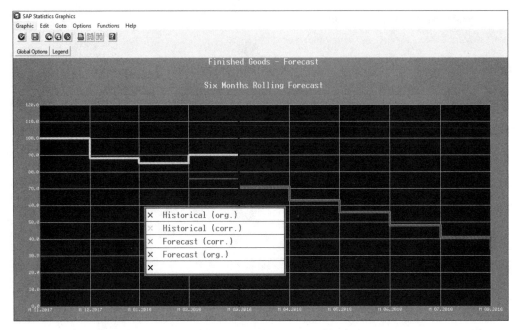

Figure 16.7 Consumption and Forecast Values: A Graphical View

> **Tips & Tricks**
>
> The forecast model is another important parameter that tells the system what to look for: a trend pattern, constant consumption from period to period, or seasonality, as shown in Figure 16.7. You can also choose to let the system perform a number of tests to automatically identify the right pattern and set it after the executing a forecast run.

Three different ways to perform forecasting on individual materials or a group of materials exist:

- At a single material and plant level, use Transaction MP30 or follow the menu path **Logistics • Materials Management • Material Requirements Planning (MRP) • Forecast • Individual forecast • Execute**.

- At the total materials and plant level, use Transaction MP38 or follow the menu path **Logistics • Materials Management • Material Requirements Planning (MRP) • Forecast • Total forecast • Execute**.

- At a single material and plant level, use Transaction MM02 or follow the menu path **Logistics • Materials Management • Material Master • Material • Change**.

Tips & Tricks

To view or to print the consumption values and the forecast values of individual materials or all materials in a plant, the relevant transaction codes and menu paths include the following:

- Individual material: use Transaction MP32 or follow the menu path **Logistics • Materials Management • Material Requirements Planning (MRP) • Materials Forecast • Forecast • Individual Forecast • Display.**
- Total forecast: use Transaction MPDR or follow the menu path **Logistics • Materials Management • Material Requirements Planning (MRP) • Materials Forecast • Forecast • Total forecast • Display.**

16.4.2 Executing Material Requirements Planning

To ensure that the forecast values are taken into account in materials planning you'll need to run a material requirements planning (MRP) program using Transaction MD01N (MRP Live).

Access the screen shown in Figure 16.8 via Transaction MD04 to view the planning results. As no opening or existing stock is available, the system first ensures the safety stock of 10 is filled by creating a planned order (**PldOrd**) for that quantity.

16

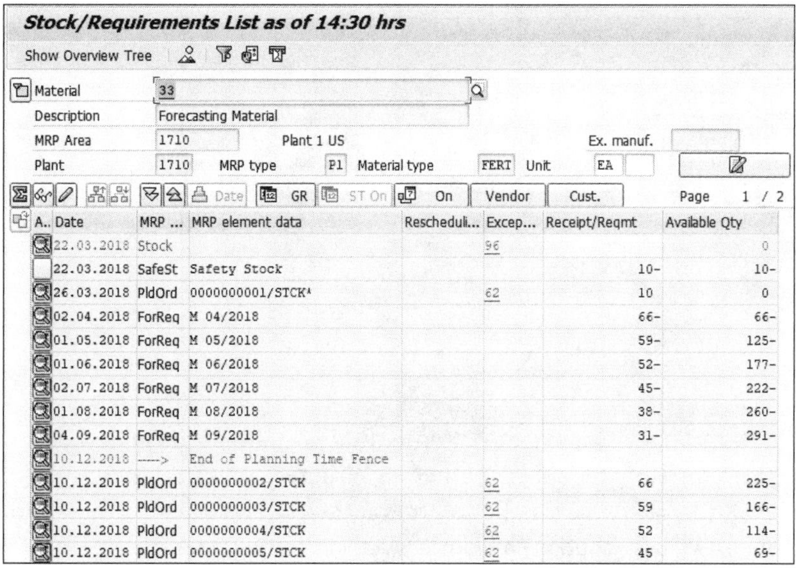
Stock/Requirements List as of 14:30 hrs
Show Overview Tree
Material 33
Description Forecasting Material
MRP Area 1710 Plant 1 US
Ex. manuf.
Plant 1710 MRP type P1 Material type FERT Unit EA
Date GR ST On On Vendor Cust. Page 1 / 2
A.. Date MRP ... MRP element data Rescheduli... Excep... Receipt/Reqmt Available Qty
22.03.2018 Stock 96 0
22.03.2018 SafeSt Safety Stock 10- 10-
26.03.2018 PldOrd 0000000001/STCK* 62 10 0
02.04.2018 ForReq M 04/2018 66- 66-
01.05.2018 ForReq M 05/2018 59- 125-
01.06.2018 ForReq M 06/2018 52- 177-
02.07.2018 ForReq M 07/2018 45- 222-
01.08.2018 ForReq M 08/2018 38- 260-
04.09.2018 ForReq M 09/2018 31- 291-
10.12.2018 ----> End of Planning Time Fence
10.12.2018 PldOrd 0000000002/STCK 62 66 225-
10.12.2018 PldOrd 0000000003/STCK 62 59 166-
10.12.2018 PldOrd 0000000004/STCK 62 52 114-
10.12.2018 PldOrd 0000000005/STCK 62 45 69-

Figure 16.8 Forecast Values and Planned Orders after an MRP Run

Thereafter, the system will consider the monthly forecast figures (**ForReq**) and accordingly create planned orders that can then be converted into production or process orders for in-house production or into purchase requisitions for external procurement.

16.4.3   Forecasting Using External Data

To incorporate forecasting results from an external system into SAP, follow the following steps:

1. You must specify, in the forecast view of the material master, the **Method** field as **N** (no forecast/external model).

2. Execute Transaction SE38 to run the standard program RMPR1001. User exits are available for program RMPR1001 to fulfill specific business requirements.

3. Two options are available when adopting an external forecast. You can use the option **T** to test the forecast results, but when you're ready to bring in external forecast data into SAP, use the option **U**, as shown in Figure 16.9.

4. The program searches for the material/plant combination defined for the external forecast.

5. Using the user exit EXIT_SAPLMPR1_002, you can set a filter on the materials to be forecast externally.

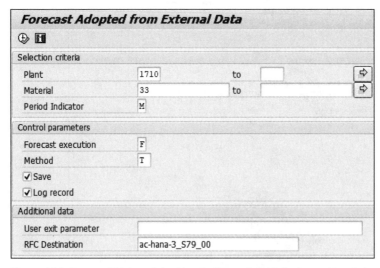

Figure 16.9 Forecast Values Adoption Program in SAP for Importing External Forecast Data of Materials

6. The program calls user exit EXIT_SAPLMPR1_001 and transfers information about the materials to be forecast.

7. The user exit must have the forecast values from the external system at its disposal.

8. After the user exit is run, the forecast values are posted into SAP system.

16.5   Configuration Settings for Forecasting

In this section, we'll cover the configuration settings necessary to set up and run forecasting in SAP S/4HANA.

16.5.1   MRP Types

An MRP type controls the type of material planning the SAP system will perform on individual materials.

Navigate to the MRP type's configuration settings using Transaction SPRO and by following the menu path **Materials Management • Consumption-Based Planning • Master Data • Check MRP Types**.

Figure 16.10 shows the configuration screen for MRP type VV (forecast-based planning). Like any MRP type, you can adjust the configuration parameters to meet specific business needs. Notice that using MRP type VV means the forecast must be executed (the parameter **Obligatory forecast**) first before the MRP run. If required, you can also have the system automatically calculate safety stock by selecting the **Safety Stock** checkbox. Further, you can also specify whether the system should consider total consumption or only unplanned consumption when forecasting the future demand for a material.

> **Note**
>
> Some versions of SAP S/4HANA may not have all MRP types available, as shown in Figure 16.11. These MRP types are basically the SAP Best Practices available for SAP S/4HANA. In this case, you would create a copy of an available standard MRP type and make relevant changes for forecast-based planning. Alternatively, you can adjust the settings of the available MRP types to meet your company's specific business needs.
>
> Preferably, you would execute forecasting as an individual step then use these forecast values for planned independent requirements (PIRs) in demand management (Transaction MD61). The system does offer the option of copying forecast values into PIRs, and these forecast values can then form the basis of MRP via Transaction MD01N.

16

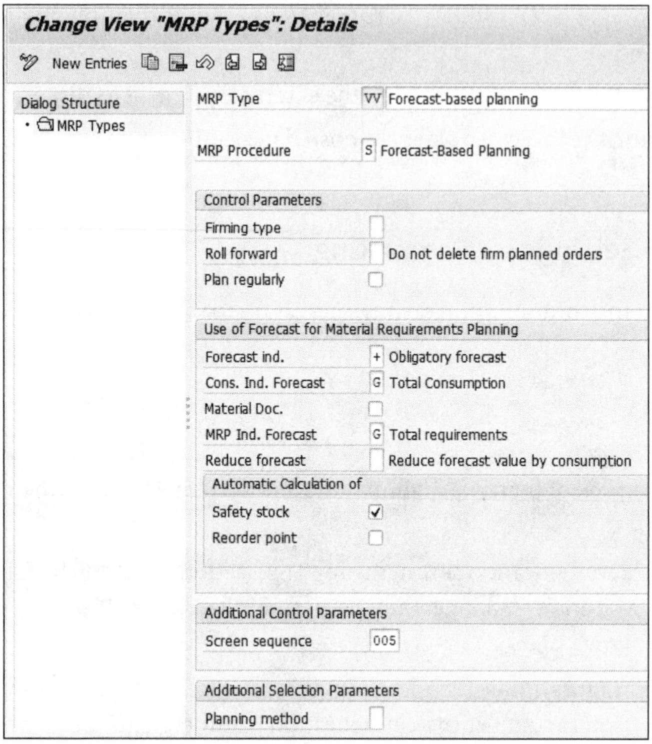

Figure 16.10 Configuration Settings of MRP Type VV

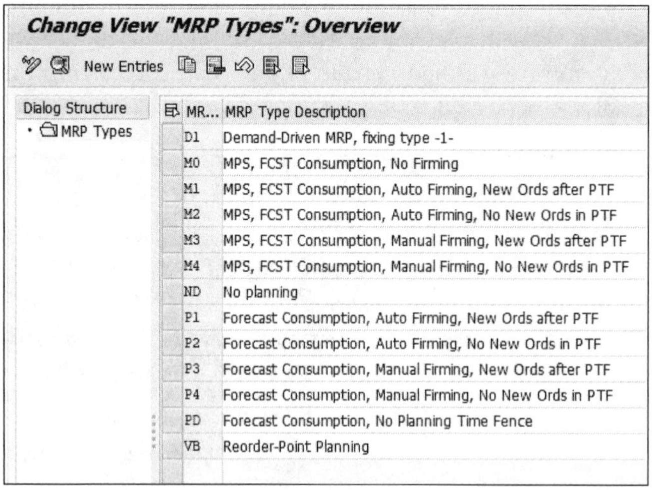

Figure 16.11 MRP Types Available in SAP Best Practices for SAP S/4HANA

16.5.2 Weighting Group

A weighting group defines how the system should take into account various consumption values during the forecast run, including a weight given to each value. Often, more recent consumption values will be weighed more heavily than the past values.

A weighting group works only for the weighted moving average forecast model or forecast model W. You can set the **Delta factor** to smooth out the forecast values using this forecast model. To set up a weighting group, follow the menu path **Materials Management • Forecast • Weighting Groups for Weighted Moving Average**, as shown in Figure 16.12.

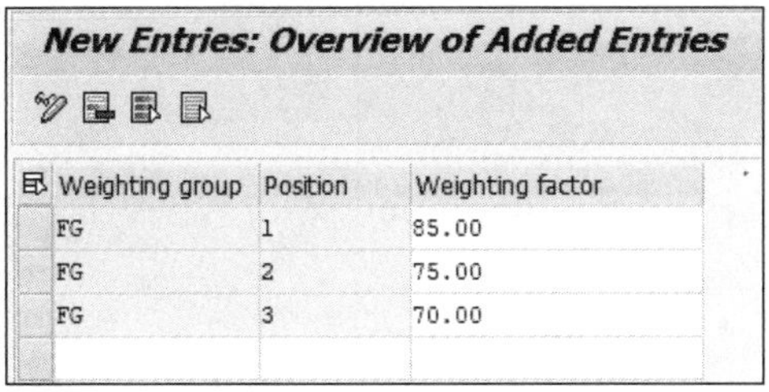

Weighting group	Position	Weighting factor	
FG	1	85.00	
FG	2	75.00	
FG	3	70.00	

Figure 16.12 Weighting Group for Forecast

16.5.3 Splitting Indicator

In forecast-based planning, you'll have to execute a material forecast first, and based on the results of the material forecast, the system can calculate and plan future consumption quantities. You can select the forecasting periods to be in days, weeks, or months or for the entire year. The system can consider safety stock when calculating net requirements. The system takes receipts into account to ensure the demand from the forecast can be met. If the demand can't be met, then the system will create procurement proposals.

You can specify the number of historical periods that the system uses in forecasting and also specify the future forecast horizon (periods) for each material. After the planning run, the system will make material available in the beginning of the period. You have the option of further dividing or splitting these material requirements into finer detail by using the **Splitting indicator** in the **MRP 3** tab of the material master.

The period pattern for the forecast (day, week, month, or posting period) and the number of prediction periods can be defined separately for each material. However, the period pattern of the forecast may not be detailed enough for MRP because it may not provide the required granularity. For this reason, you can use the **Splitting indicator** to define, for each material, how forecast requirement values may further be distributed to a more detailed period pattern for MRP purposes.

You can maintain the **Splitting indicator** in configuration by following the menu path **Materials Management • Consumption-Based Planing • Forecast • Define Splitting of Forecast Requirements for MRP**. The **Splitting indicator** contains the number of periods to be considered as well as the number of days and/or weeks for which the splitting is to be carried out, as shown in Figure 16.13.

Forecast requirements can be split in three possible ways as follows:

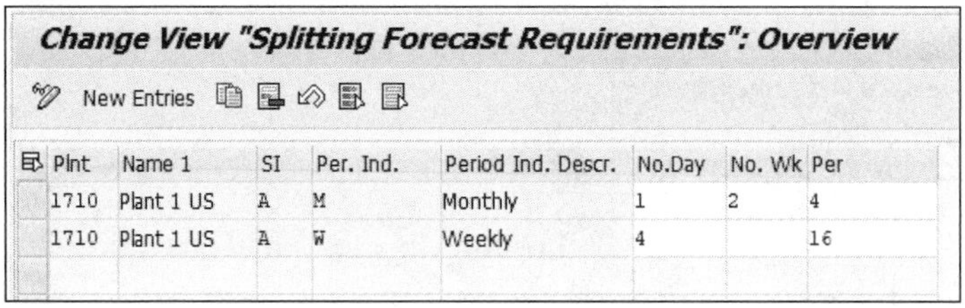

Change View "Splitting Forecast Requirements": Overview

New Entries

Plnt	Name 1	SI	Per. Ind.	Period Ind. Descr.	No.Day	No. Wk	Per
1710	Plant 1 US	A	M	Monthly	1	2	4
1710	Plant 1 US	A	W	Weekly	4		16

Figure 16.13 Splitting Forecast Requirements

- **No. of days**
  How many periods are to be calculated "to the day" in MRP.

- **No. of weeks**
  How many periods are to be calculated "to the week" in MRP.

- **No. of periods**
  How many periods—in addition to the periods to be split—the system will carry out the net requirements calculation in the planning run.

16.6 Summary

In this chapter, we discussed the forecasting methods available in SAP S/4HANA. Forecasting is important to a company because forecasting can determine how much material they produce, how much material they'll need, and when to market the product based on forecasts. However, for a forecast to be accurate, the forecast must be run with complete and verified data. A forecast model is used in companies to produce forecasts for their materials. Some companies spend a great deal of time creating forecasts to help calculate future production requirements. The food and beverage industry regularly uses forecasting to determine how much product is made avoid overproduction or underproduction. As an MM consultant, you must understand how the forecasting functionality works and how it integrates with other functionalities, such as production planning (PP) and sales and distribution (SD).

Chapter 17 introduces the inventory management functionality for SAP S/4HANA, including goods issues, goods receipts, physical inventory, returns, stock transfers, and reservations.

16

Chapter 17

Inventory Management Overview

The processes supported by the inventory management (IM) function-
ality in SAP S/4HANA allow a company to meet customer needs for the
availability of material, while maximizing the company's profits and
minimizing costs.

In a sales situation, management is always under constant pressure to reduce the time between a customer's order and delivery. Your customers will use order-to-delivery time as a factor in deciding on a vendor. Therefore, you must use effective inventory management (IM processes to reduce this time to a minimum. To reengineer the order-to-delivery process, improvements can be made in the following ways:

- Improving the electronic data interchange (EDI) process with customers and vendors
- Increasing the single sourcing of materials
- Increasing the level of just-in-time (JIT) inventory
- Reducing dependence on long-term forecasts for stocking levels
- Using real-time reports and inventory key performance indicators (KPIs)

IM within SAP offers an effective set of processes for all types of goods movement within the plant. Streamlining plant processes can help your company compress order-to-delivery time, decrease costs, reduce inventory, and improve customer service. In this chapter, we'll discuss the major IM processes, including goods movements, goods issues/goods receipts, physical inventory, returns, reservations, and stock transfers. We'll also cover how to configure new movement types to meet the specific business and reporting needs of your company.

Let's start with covering the basic concepts behind IM.

17.1 Goods Movements

The IM processes within SAP are, in essence, movements of materials inside a plant that can create a change in stock levels within the storage locations designated to that plant. The movement of stock can be inbound from a vendor, outbound to a customer, a transfer between plants, or an internal transfer within a plant, such as between two storage locations or transferring stock from one stock type to another. In other words, whenever a material moves—whether a goods issuance, consumption, a goods receipt, or a transfer of material from one location to another—the movement is represented by a unique identification known as a movement type. We'll cover movement types shortly.

For every goods movement, the SAP system can create two types of documents: a material document and an accounting document. An accounting document may have an associated financial document, such as a controlling document (CO) or a Material Ledger document. The SAP system follows the accounting principle that, for every material movement, a corresponding document provides details about that movement. In addition, an accounting document describes the financial aspects of the goods movement. However, the accounting document is only relevant if the material is valuated. For example, a goods issuance to a customer or a goods receipt from a vendor or from a manufacturing process will not only create a material document but also an accounting document. A transfer of material from one storage location to another storage location within the same plant will only create a material document but not a financial document.

In the following sections, we'll cover various inventory management reports that show the actual stock situation at the time the report is generated. Next, we'll discuss movement types, which serve not only as identifiers of the different types of inventory movements taking place in the system but also act as a control function in inventory management. Next, we'll show you the material and accounting documents that the SAP system creates each time an IM transaction takes place. Finally, we'll briefly discuss various types of goods issuances and goods receipts in the SAP system.

17.1.1   Stock Overview

The inventory in the plant is managed by quantity or value. Inventory movements are entered in real time, and a snapshot can be taken at any given moment to inform an inventory user of any material status. This snapshot, as shown in Figure 17.1, is called the *stock overview* (Transaction MMBE) and can be found by following the navigation path **Logistics • Materials Management • Inventory Management • Environment • Stock • Stock Overview**. On the screen that appears, enter selection parameters, such as the material, plant, and storage location, and then click **Execute** so that the screen shown in Figure 17.1 appears.

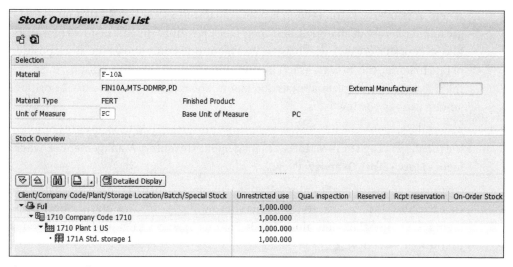

Figure 17.1 Stock Overview

Click on the **Detailed Display** button to see the complete stock details of a material. As shown in Figure 17.2, not only is the detail of unrestricted-use (free to consume) stock available but also stock placed in quality inspections or sales order stock.

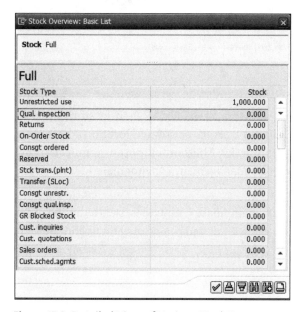

Figure 17.2 Detailed View of Various Stock Types

A new stock overview transaction is now available in SAP S/4HANA that provides far greater details about materials and their stock positions. In contrast to Transaction MMBE (Stock Overview), which as we just mentioned only shows the stock position of one material, this new transaction enables far greater selection options, including the selection of multiple materials and plants. You can also compare stock positions among various posting dates.

Access the screen shown in Figure 17.3 using Transaction J3RFLVMOBVEDH or follow the menu path **Logistics • Materials Management • Inventory Management • Environment • Stock • Stock Overview (New)**.

On the screen that appears, enter selection parameters, such as the posting dates, and click **Execute**. The stock overview of materials will appear. Click on the **Show Documents** of a material to view more details. Figure 17.3 shows a detailed stock overview for the material F-10A.

Stock overview documents

Start date	24.03.2018	End date	07.04.2018
Start Quantity	1,000	End Quantity	1,980
Start Value	1,000,000.00	End Value	1,980,000.00

Material	Plant	Stor.	Batch	S	Val.	Matl Group	Material description	Mo.	T...	Material Doc.	Mat...	Posting Date	Item	Quantity of Received Material	RecvdMat Qty	UoEntry	Value of Received Material
F-10A	1710	171A			1710	L004	FIN10A,MTS-DDMRP,PD	561	FO	4900000122	2018	07.04.2018	1	1,000	1,000		1,000,000.00
F-10A	1710	171A			1710	L004	FIN10A,MTS-DDMRP,PD	Z65	TO	4900000123	2018	07.04.2018	1	0	0		0.00
F-10A	1710	171A			1710	L004	FIN10A,MTS-DDMRP,PD	Z01	TO	4900000124	2018	07.04.2018	1	0	0		0.00

Figure 17.3 New Stock Overview in SAP S/4HANA

17.1.2   Warehouse Stock of Materials

Materials planners or warehouse supervisors often need to view the stock situation of materials across the same or different plants or storage locations. Access the screen shown in Figure 17.4 using Transaction MB52 or follow the menu path **Logistics • Materials Management • Inventory Management • Environment • Stock • Warehouse Stock**.

You can use several reporting and data manipulation functions, such as hiding or displaying fields, downloading the data to MS Excel, and performing totals and subtotals on key figures.

Display Warehouse Stocks of Material

Material	Material description	Plnt	SLoc	SL	Batch	BUn	Unrestricted	In Quality Insp.	Restricted-Use	Blocked
1000000000000…	Bypass Dust	1000	1001			MT	30	0	0	0
10000001	RA II	1000	1001		A1	KG	10.000	0.000	0.000	0.000
10000001	RA II	1000	1001		A2	KG	0.000	0.000	6.000	0.000
10000001	RA II	1000	1001		A3	KG	18.000	0.000	0.000	0.000
10000001	RA II	1000	1001		A4	KG	21.000	0.000	0.000	0.000
10000001	RA II	1000	1001		A5	KG	25.000	0.000	0.000	0.000
10000001	RA II	1000	1001		A6	KG	20.000	0.000	0.000	0.000
10000002	RAW SCRAP SHREDDED UNPROCESSED	1000	A001			MT	12	0	0	0
10000004	Shelf Life Testing	1000	1001		0000000087	KG	5.000	0.000	0.000	0.000
10000080	Demo RW	1000	1001		A10	EA	6	0	0	0
10000080	Demo RW	1000	1001		A20	EA	20	0	0	0
10000080	Demo RW	1000	1001		A30	EA	10	0	0	0
10000080	Demo RW	1000	1001		A40	EA	40	0	0	0
10000080	Demo RW	1000	1001		A50	EA	50	0	0	0
10000080	Demo RW	1000	1001		D1	EA	100	0	0	0
10000104	White crystalline powder	1000	1001			KG	1,038.000	0.000	0.000	0.000
10000104	White crystalline powder	1000	1003			KG	2.000	0.000	0.000	0.000
10000105	White crystalline	1000	1001			KG	10.000	0.000	0.000	0.000
10000138	Raw M AI	1000	1001		AI-002	KG	919.584	0.000	0.000	0.000

Figure 17.4 Warehouse Stock (Transaction MB52)

17.1.3 Material Document

A *material document* is produced for each movement and is an audit of the details of the material movement. A material document contains the date of the material movement, the material number, the quantity of the material moved, the location of the movement, the batch number if applicable, and the movement type.

The material document number is displayed after a material movement. Figure 17.5 shows the material document for the transfer of material **F-10A**. As part of an audit, the document can be checked to review the details of the movement. Review the material document using Transaction MIGO.

On the screen that appears, click **Display** and then **Material Document** and then enter the **Document number**. As previously mentioned, in addition to a material document, the system also create accounting documents where applicable.

Click on the **FI Documents** button, as shown in Figure 17.5, so that the popup window shown in Figure 17.6 appears.

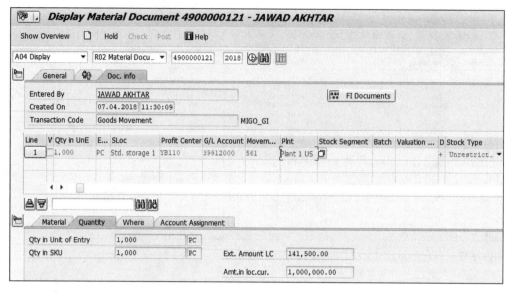

Figure 17.5 Material Document

Figure 17.6 shows three types of accounting documents have been created: the accounting document, the controlling document, and the Material Ledger document. Click on the **Accounting document** to view its details, as shown in Figure 17.7.

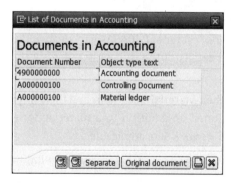

Figure 17.6 List of Documents in Accounting

Figure 17.7 shows the accounting details resulting from the creation of a material document.

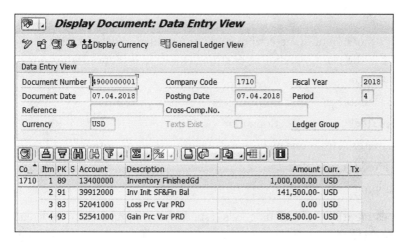

Figure 17.7 Accounting Document

Changes can't be made to a material document after it has been posted. If an error was made on the material movement, the material document can't be changed to alter the material movement. If an error was made, then the material movement must be reversed, and the movement must then be reentered correctly. Correcting errors this way produces a material document for the reversal process and also a new material document for the correct stock movement. To reverse or to make minor changes to a material document, such as adding or changing text fields, use Transaction MIGO.

17.1.4   Movement Types

A *movement type* is a three-character field used to describe the type of movement of a material that needs to be performed. The movement type is used for all type of movements: goods receipts, goods issuances, transfers, and reversals.

The SAP system is delivered with predefined movement types between 100 and 899. Movement types 900 and higher can be used for customized movement types.

> **Note**
>
> We'll cover how to configure a new movement type and perform its associated business functions in Section 17.7.
>
> Refer to Appendix A, which contains a list of the most important movement types for goods issuance, goods receipts, and transfer postings available in SAP.

17.1.5   Goods Issue

A *goods issue* is a movement of material that causes a reduction of stock; that is, the amount of stock in the plant, warehouse, or storage location is reduced when one of the following happens:

- Shipment to a customer
- Withdrawal of stock for a production order
- Transfer of a material from one plant or a storage location to another
- Material required for sampling
- Material scrapping

Movement types identify the various goods issues. Many scenarios can be called goods issues, such as goods issue to scrap or goods issue to sampling; these and other scenarios are discussed more fully in Chapter 19.

The other movement of materials, the opposite of a goods issue, is the goods receipt, which we'll examine in the next section.

17.1.6   Goods Receipt

The *goods receipt* process allows the receipt of material from a vendor or from the in-house production process. In addition, SAP allows other types of goods receipts, including initial stock creation. A goods receipt is an increase in stock that is triggered by one of the following:

- Receipt from a production order or a process order
- Receipt from a purchase order (PO)
- Initial entry of inventory at the time of SAP system go-live
- Receipt from subcontracted material

A number of different goods receipts exist, including a goods receipt for a PO and a goods receipt from a production order or a process order. These and other goods receipts are discussed more fully in Chapter 20.

In the next section, we'll examine how a business counts material in its plant, a business process is known as physical inventory.

17.2   Physical Inventory

Physical inventory is a process by which a company stops all goods movement trans-actions and physically counts the current inventory. A physical inventory may be required by financials (FI) rules or local tax regulations to determine an accurate value of the inventory. Other reasons for a physical inventory may include the need to establish inventory levels so materials can be restocked. Performing a physical inventory also ensures that differences between the actual inventory of materials and the inventory in the SAP system are reconciled to account for any unaccounted for theft or wastage.

When performing a physical inventory, the company is counting material at a loca-tion, whether a physical plant, a third-party warehouse, or a customer's site. A physi-cal inventory doesn't have to involve every material but can focus on a subset of the company's current stock.

Cycle counting is a type of physical inventory. Cycle counts have advantages in that they are less disruptive to operations, provide an ongoing measure of inventory accuracy, and can be configured to focus on higher-value materials or materials with frequent movement. Physical inventory has become an important topic for compa-nies as they work to keep their inventory counts as current and accurate as possible. The many important steps to perform a physical inventory are discussed more fully in Chapter 21.

In the next section, we'll discuss the subject of returns. Returns aren't just materials to be returned to a vendor but also related items, such as returnable packaging.

17.3   Returns

The returns process often varies among companies. Each plant can have a different policy and procedure for creating and processing returns. The process of returning material is sometimes referred to as *reverse logistics*. Returns cover activities related to returning materials, pallets, and containers. Companies may also return material to vendors for disposal or recycling. Returns to a vendor may also be related to a product recall notice. Returns could also involve returnable packaging. For example, an automotive parts distributor received inbound deliveries on wooden pallets. The pallets are either sent back to the supplier when the next delivery arrives or used in the warehouse.

Before any material can be returned to a vendor, an agreement between the customer and vendor with regards to returns should be examined. The agreement is either part of an overall agreement between the two companies or specifically for the individual material or group of materials.

The returns agreement usually determines the valid reasons for a material to be returned to a vendor, which may include obvious material defects, incorrect material received, overdelivery of material, and returnable packaging. The process may involve the customer obtaining a Return Material Authorization (RMA) number from the supplier, which allows the vendor and customer to successfully track the return.

Material to be returned to a vendor don't require a special status. Material returns can be from stock in quality inspection stock, blocked stock, goods receipt blocked stock, or even unrestricted stock.

In the next section, we'll show you how to create returns, including configuring reasons for returns.

17.3.1   Creating a Return

The returns process is the reverse of the goods receipt process. A return delivery is created by Transaction MIGO_GR, which is the same transaction for the goods receipt of materials. Transaction MIGO also serves the same purpose. A return delivery in SAP is always made with reference to the same material document against which the original material receipt was made.

Transaction MIGO_GR can be found by following the navigation path **Logistics • Materials Management • Inventory Management • Goods Movement • Goods Receipt • For Purchase Order • Good Receipt for Purchase Order**.

Figure 17.8 shows the information from the material document created from the original goods receipt for the PO. The information from the material document shows the **Vendor,** the vendor's **Delivery Note** number, and the item details. The line item details show the **Movement Type** for the return delivery, which is **122**, and the material status, which can either be **Unrestricted use, Quality inspection**, or **Blocked stock.**

After the reason for movement has been chosen and the return is posted, the SAP system will produce a material document to provide an audit trail of what happened.

The material document will show the material, quantity, and original PO for the material, as shown in Figure 17.8. The material document can be identified as a return to a vendor because movement type 122 is shown at the line item.

The material documents relevant for goods receipts and returns can be seen by selecting the relevant line item and selecting **Environment • Material Document for Material**.

An inventory user can alter the quantity of the material to be returned and also can enter a reason for the return, if configured. We'll cover how to configure reasons for return in Section 17.3.2.

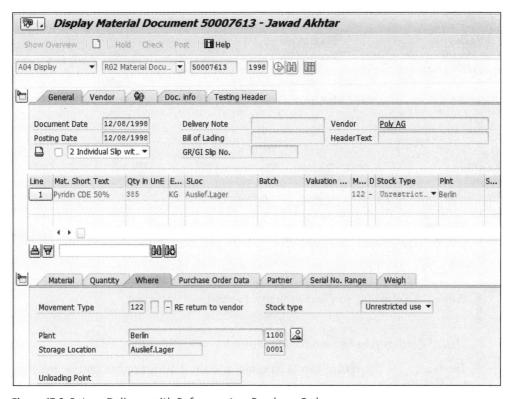

Figure 17.8 Return Delivery with Reference to a Purchase Order

Figure 17.9 shows that return delivery is also possible when excess material is issued against a production order or a cost center, and the remaining, excess, or unused material needs to be returned to the warehouse. In our example, a quantity of 4 PC is being returned to the warehouse with reference to the original material document number 4900000125.

For example, in the pharmaceutical industry, commonly more packing material than needed is used to account for wastages and to limit how often the warehouse is requested to issue packing material. When a batch of a pharma product is complete, the excess packing material is returned through the return delivery process.

Figure 17.9 Return Delivery with Reference to a Material Document

17.3.2   Configuring Reason for Movement

The reason for the return can be entered into the return process on the line item level. The reason can only be added if configured for that movement type, which in our previous example is for movement type 122 (return to vendor).

Transaction OMBS can be used to create and change the reasons for a movement and can be accessed by following the navigation path **Materials Management • Inventory Management and Physical Inventory • Movement Types • Record Reason for Goods Movements**.

Transaction OMBS allows a number of reasons to be added for each movement type. An inventory user can add a number of reasons for the return of goods, and the **Reason** field can be used to monitor returns to vendors, as shown in Figure 17.10. As a result, the purchasing department can identify issues with vendors or with materials.

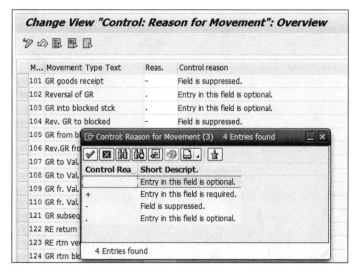

Figure 17.10 Configuring the Reasons for Goods Movements in Transaction OMBS

The reason for movement (**Reas.**) field can be configured to be suppressed, optional, or mandatory, as shown in Figure 17.11, in the same configuration as Transaction OMBS. Three options are available each movement type: A plus sign represents that the field is mandatory, a minus sign indicates that the field is suppressed, or a blank field indicate that entering a reason for movement is optional.

Change View "Control: Reason for Movement": Overview

M...	Movement Type Text	Reas.	Control reason
101	GR goods receipt	–	Field is suppressed.
102	Reversal of GR	.	Entry in this field is optional.
103	GR into blocked stck	.	Entry in this field is optional.
104	Rev. GR to blocked	–	Field is suppressed.
105	GR from b		
106	Rev.GR fro		
107	GR to Val.		
108	GR to Val.		
109	GR fr. Val.		
110	GR fr. Val.		
121	GR subseq		
122	RE return		
123	RE rtrn ve		
124	GR rtrn bl		

Control: Reason for Movement (3)   4 Entries found

Control Rea	Short Descript.
	Entry in this field is optional.
+	Entry in this field is required.
–	Field is suppressed.
.	Entry in this field is optional.

4 Entries found

Figure 17.11 Control of the Reason for Movement Field in Transaction OMBS

Existing movement types can be modified to restrict or allow certain functionalities. For example, certain movement types may require certain reasons, which require the configuration of the **Control Reason** field, as shown in Figure 17.11. The **Control Reason** field is defaulted as optional, but you can make this field a requirement for any movement type. Overall, the movement type is key to the IM process because it controls the updating of the stock quantity, determines what fields are displayed and required for entry, and also updates the correct account information.

17.4   Material Documents

Transaction MB51 consists of material documents with information on the material and vendor information carried over from the material documents. The detail screen of Transaction MB51 shows all material documents relevant for the material/vendor combination as well as other details.

In our case, as shown in Figure 17.12, several material documents appear under the heading **Material Doc.** consisting of goods receipts from the initial stock upload as shown by movement type 561.

```
Material Document List

K  ◀  ▶  ▶|    ▦ ▼ 🗐   ▥ ▼    ▣ ▦ ▣   Σ ‰   ▣ ⚇ ▦


Material                                    Material description              Plnt Name 1
SLoc MvT S Mat. Doc.  Item Pstng Date   Quantity in UnE EUn

F-10A                                       FIN10A,MTS-DDMRP,PD              1710 Plant 1 US
171A 561    4900000122   1 07.04.2018          1,000  PC
171A Z65    4900000123   1 07.04.2018             10- PC
171A Z01    4900000124   1 07.04.2018             10- PC
171A 561    4900000121   1 07.07.2016          1,000  PC

* Total
                                               1,980  PC
```

Figure 17.12 Material Document List

The returns process can be complex and require policies that vary from company to company and even from site to site within a company.

In the next section, we'll review the functionality for material reservations, including manual reservations and the link between reservations and material requirements planning (MRP).

17.5 Reservations

A *reservation* is a request to hold material in the plant or storage location before the process of material movement begins. For example, if a material is needed for a production order, then a reservation can automatically be created by the system for that material so that enough material allocated for production. You can also manually create a reservation. Automatic reservations are created by a process, such as a project or a production order, and a reservation for the material is created without manual intervention.

After a reservation has been created, the reserved amount can be viewed using Transaction MMBE (Stock Overview), which shows the reserved quantity for the material. However, the unrestricted stock total won't be reduced by the reserved stock amount. The reserved stock is still part of the unrestricted stock. The reservation is treated differently within MRP. The reservation of material lowers the MRP available stock in the stock/requirements list (Transaction MD04). Therefore, realizing the effect a reservation has on different parts of the system is important.

In this section, we'll cover how to create reservations as well as discuss the reporting tool available to monitor various statuses of reservations.

17.5.1 Creating a Manual Reservation

A manual reservation can be created using Transaction MB21 or by following the navigation path **Logistics • Materials Management • Inventory Management • Reservation • Create**, as shown in Figure 17.13.

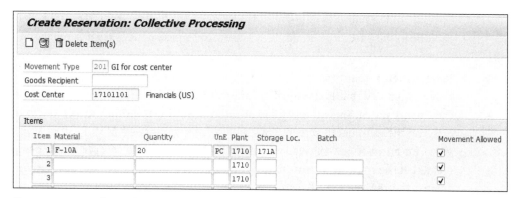

Figure 17.13 Detail Line for a Reservation Created Using Transaction MB21 for Movement Type 201

On the initial screen that appears, enter the basic details such as the date, the plant, and the movement type. A reservation is a planned movement, so the date of the reservation can't be in the past. Before creating a reservation, the movement type should be determined because, after a reservation is created, the movement type can't be changed. However, the reservation can be deleted and reentered if the movement type was initially entered incorrectly.

> **Tips & Tricks**
>
> To delete an incorrectly created reservation, use Transaction MB22 (Change Reservation) and enter the reservation number that needs to be deleted. Then, from the top menu, choose **Reservation • Delete**.

As shown in Figure 17.14, the most important fields and indicators are as follows:

- **Movement type**
  A number of movement types are available to choose from, as follows:
  - Consumption: This movement type includes consumption by a cost center, network, or sales order.
  - Transfer posting: This movement type includes plant to plant or storage location to storage location transfers.
  - Goods receipts: This movement type includes receipts from production, as by-products, or without POs.

  Double-click on a reservation item to view the details.

- **Requirements date**
  The date of the planned movement is entered into the **Requirem. Date**. This date can't be in the past and should be as accurate as possible because it is relevant to MRP.

- **Requirements quantity**
  Enter a quantity that is the most accurate at the time the reservation is made in the **Quantity** area. This quantity can be fixed by setting the **Quantity is fixed** indicator on the item detail screen. You can also use Transaction MMBE (Stock Overview) for an overview of available stock against which the reservation is being created. If the material is unrestricted stock, then this material can be issued out against the reservation. If restricted stock, then the system will create procurement proposals during the next MRP run.

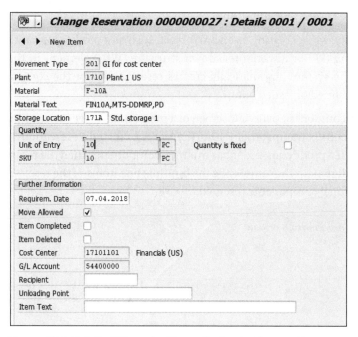

Figure 17.14 Detailed View of a Manually Created Reservation

- **Movement indicator**
  The movement indicator (**Mvt**) is defaulted to be always on, allowing a goods movement to take place for the entered reservation. However, if an inventory user wants to delay the goods movement until a future period, indicator can be unchecked, thus preventing any goods movement. Unchecking this indicator also helps if the reservation must go to through a review and approval process after being created.

- **Final issues indicator**
  The final issues indicator (**FIs**) is automatically set when a goods movement (or several goods movements) have fulfilled the reservation. If an inventory user decides that, after a partial goods movement, the reservation can't or shouldn't be completed, the user can set the **FIs** indicator.

- **Deletion indicator**
  The deletion indicator (**Del**) is used when the reservation line item is incorrect or no longer needed.

- **Debit/credit indicator**
  The **D/C** field shows whether a line item is a credit or debit. **H** indicates a credit; **S** indicates a debit.

17.5.2   Automatic Creation of Reservation

As discussed previously, while creating as an SAP object, such as a production order in production planning (PP) or a work breakdown structure (WBS) element in the project system (PS), the system automatically creates reservations for the components that will be consumed or issued out.

Figure 17.15 shows the component overview screen of a production order for material 33 and whose component is the material F-10A. The system created **Reservation 31** along with line item **1**. If a production order has multiple components, then the reservation number will still remain the same while the multiple line items of the reservation will denote individual components reserved.

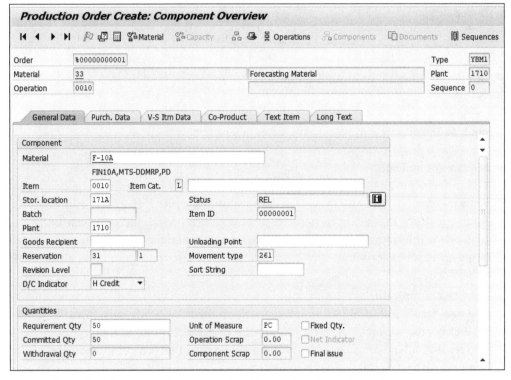

Figure 17.15 Automatic Reservation Creation on Creating a Production Order

17.5.3 Material Requirements Planning and Reservations

Reservations are relevant to MRP, and when MRP is run, reservations will appear on the MRP list for that material.

You can use Transaction MD04 to view the MRP list for a material or follow the navigation path **Logistics • Materials Management • Material Requirements Planning • MRP • Evaluations • Stock/Reqmts List**.

On the initial screen that appears, enter the material number and the plant to view the details of relevant reservations.

The line items shown in Figure 17.16 display manual reservations (**MltRes**) with their **Date** of expected delivery and the available quantity (**Available Qty**) on that date after material has been issued.

Figure 17.16 also shows a reservation for material 33 that the system automatically created when the production order was created. Click on the element details icon 🔲 so that the screen shown in Figure 17.17 appears.

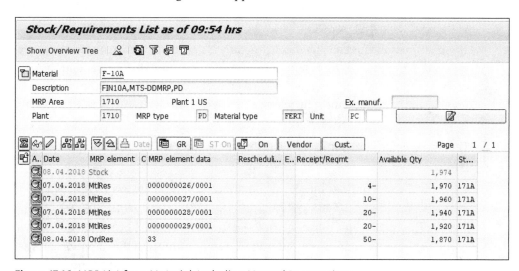

Figure 17.16 MRP List for a Material, Including Manual Reservations

Figure 17.17 shows that reservation number 31 is a pegged (or connected) requirement to the main material 33 of the production order (**ProdOrder**) 1000002.

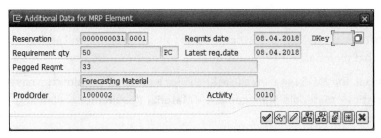

Figure 17.17 Details of Reservation 31 of Production Order 1000002

17.5.4   Reservations Management Program

Reservations that you create will need to be managed to control old and unnecessary reservations that were never eventually closed or deleted. Use Transaction MBVR (Management Program: Reservations) or follow the navigation path **Logistics • Materials Management • Inventory Management • Reservation • Administer**.

The reservation management program allows an inventory user to set the deletion indicator on the reservation file based on user-entered selection criteria.

The main reason this management program is needed is that many goods movements don't reference the reservation that was made for that movement. In such cases, the material has already been received or consumed, but the reservation remains in the system until the management program cleans up these unnecessary reservations.

The management program sets the deletion indicator for the following two scenarios:

- The final issues indicator (**FIs**) is set on reservations that have been satisfied.
- The requirement date of the reservation is prior to a date calculated by the system. The system calculates the date using the base date entered in Transaction MBVR, minus a set number of retention days. The usual number of the retention days set for this transaction is 30. However, this value can be changed to meet the customer's needs in configuration.

17.5.5   Configuration Settings of Reservations

To change the number of retention days for the reservation management program, changes need to be made in configuration. Transaction OMBN allows a user to change the retention days for the calculation, as shown in Figure 17.18.

Transaction OMBN can be found by following the navigation path **Materials Management • Inventory Management and Physical Inventory • Reservation • Define Default Values**.

An inventory user can change a number of defaults for the reservation based on the plant, as follows:

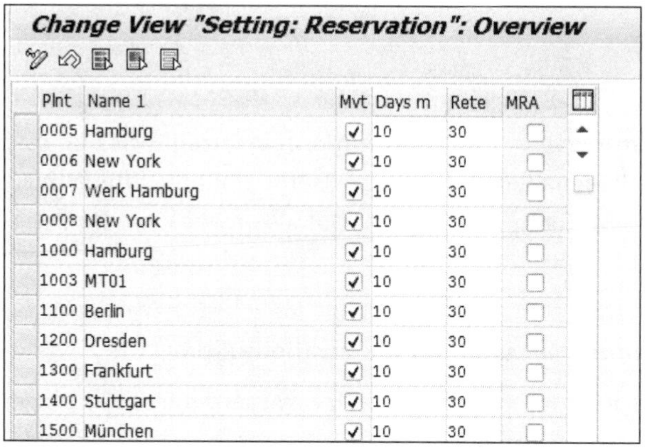

Change View "Setting: Reservation": Overview

Plnt	Name 1	Mvt	Days m	Rete	MRA
0005	Hamburg	✓	10	30	☐
0006	New York	✓	10	30	☐
0007	Werk Hamburg	✓	10	30	☐
0008	New York	✓	10	30	☐
1000	Hamburg	✓	10	30	☐
1003	MT01	✓	10	30	☐
1100	Berlin	✓	10	30	☐
1200	Dresden	✓	10	30	☐
1300	Frankfurt	✓	10	30	☐
1400	Stuttgart	✓	10	30	☐
1500	München	✓	10	30	☐

Figure 17.18 Configuration Transaction OMBN for Changing the Reservation Default Values

- **Movement indicator**
  If the movement indicator (**Mvt**) is set, goods movements are allowed for the reservation item. If the indicator isn't set, then this indicator must be set manually in each reservation line item before goods movements can take place.

- **Days for movement default value**
  The **Days m** field is used when the movement indicator (**Mvt**) isn't set in configuration. The reservation management program uses this value to set the indicator in the reservation line item, if not already manually set. If the requirement date of a reservation item is farther in the future than the number of days configured in this field, the goods movement indicator (**Mvt**) won't be set, and thus, no goods movements will be allowed for this item.

- **Retention period in days**
  An inventory user can enter a value for the retention period (**Rete**), which is the number of days that the reservation item resides in the system before being deleted by the reservation management program.

If the required date of a reservation item is older than the current date minus the number of retention days, the reservation management program sets the deletion indicator (**Del**) in the reservation item.

- **MRA indicator**
  If this indicator is set, storage location information is created automatically, based on the information from the reservation, when the goods movement is created.

17.5.6 Pick List

In manufacturing industries, reservation lists are commonly referred to as *pick lists*. SAP offers a standard pick list that enables a warehouse user to not only interactively manage stock issuances against different reservations but also make changes to reservations, as needed.

To access the pick list, use Transaction MB26 or follow the menu path **Logistics • Materials Management • Inventory Management • Reservation • Picking**.

On the initial screen, enter the selection parameters as individual values or as ranges of values. These selection parameters can be materials, requirement dates, cost centers, and production orders, among others.

Figure 17.19 shows a pick list with quantities of materials to be picked or issued out listed against different reservations (last column). You can also split a reserved quantity into multiple line items, for example, if you need to issue out the reserved quantity from multiple storage locations. Saving the worklist of the pick list will automatically issue out the reserved materials.

Pick List

Material	Description	Quantity	U...	Plant	RP	St...	Batch	Valuation	...	D...	M...	S..	Vendor	Customer	Compltd	Reservation
F-10A	FIN10A,MTS-DDMRP,PD	5 PC		1710	0	171A				H	201				☐	27
F-10A	FIN10A,MTS-DDMRP,PD	5 PC		1710	0	171A				H	201				☐	27
F-10A	FIN10A,MTS-DDMRP,PD	20 PC		1710	0	171A				H	201				☐	28

Figure 17.19 Pick List

17.6 Stock Transfers

A stock transfer can occur physically, for example, by moving material from one storage location to another or may occur logically, for example, by moving stock from a quality inspection status to unrestricted. The term *stock transfer* normally refers to a physical move, whereas *transfer posting* usually describes a logical move. A stock transfer occurs in three distinct ways:

- Storage location to storage location
- Plant to plant
- Company code to company code

A stock transfer can be performed by either a one-step or a two-step procedure. Transfer postings can also occur among various stock types, such as the following:

- From unrestricted-use stock to blocked stock
- From one sales order stock to another sales order stock
- From blocked stock to quality stock
- From quality stock to unrestricted-use stock

Transferring stock, either from storage location to storage location, or plant to plant, can be performed either using Transaction MIGO_TR or Transaction MIGO. In this section, we'll detail various stock transfer options. These options include plant-to-plant stock transfers, storage location-to-storage location stock transfers, and transfers between two company codes.

17.6.1   Transfer between Storage Locations

The movement of material between storage locations within a plant arises often because of normal everyday operations. Material may be moved due to storage limitations, future needs, reclassification of stock, and so on. The movement of material between storage locations doesn't create a financial record because the material's value doesn't change. The movement can be carried out by either a one-step or a two-step procedure.

One-Step Procedure

This straightforward procedure involves moving the material between storage locations in one step. The stock levels in the different storage locations are changed in relation to the amount entered in the transaction.

You can perform this one-step stock transfer using Transaction MIGO, which is found by following the navigation path **Logistics • Materials Management • Inventory Management • Goods Movement**.

17

In the initial screen, select the **Transfer Posting** from the first dropdown and then choose **Other** from the second dropdown. Enter "311" in the **Movement Type** field on the initial screen, which is the movement type for a one-step move between storage locations. However, if the material to be moved is special stock, then the **Special Stock** indicator must be selected as well as the **Movement Type**.

After a 311 movement, you can reverse this movement by using the reverse movement type 312, if an error has been made.

On the item detail screen for Transaction MIGO, the receiving storage location (**Rcvg SLoc**) and the **Material** to move should be maintained with the relevant **Quantity** and **Batch** number, if applicable.

Two-Step Procedure

The two-step transfer between storage locations is used when the materials are actually in transit, that is, not stored in a physical or logical location. This situation occurs in the plant where material must be moved out of a storage location, but where you can't store the material in the receiving storage location until a later time. However, the only material that can be moved using the two-step procedure is unrestricted stock.

The two-step procedure uses the same transaction as a one-step transfer: Transaction MIGO. In this case, two movements are made: a stock removal and a stock placement. The first movement is of movement type 313, which removes the material from one storage location, and then the second movement is of movement type 315, which places the material into the receiving storage location.

Because the movement of material between storage locations isn't instant, as with the one-step procedure, the materials are in different stock statuses as the movement progresses. The movement type 313 produces the following:

- The originating storage location unrestricted stock level is reduced.
- The receiving storage location stock in transit stock level is increased.
- The plant unrestricted stock level is reduced.
- The plant unrestricted stock in transit stock level is increased.

The movement type 315 produces the following:

- The receiving storage location stock in transit stock level is reduced.
- The receiving storage location unrestricted stock level is increased.
- The plant unrestricted stock level is increased.
- The plant unrestricted stock in transit stock level is reduced.

17.6.2   Transfer between Plants

The movement of material between plants occurs when material is moved to replenish stock levels, to deliver material from a production site to a distribution center, or to move obsolete or slow-moving stock, among other reasons.

Movements between plants can use a one-step or two-step procedure as with storage locations, but a financial element in this transaction makes this movement different from a movement between storage locations only. Either Transaction MIGO_TR or Transaction MIGO can be used for the plant-to-plant transfer of material.

One-Step Procedure

The one-step plant-to-plant transfer process is similar to the one-step storage location transfer with the movement type 301 used for plant transfers. However, in this case, the receiving plant and storage location are required by the transaction.

In the one-step transfer, the stock is reduced in the supplying plant and increased at the receiving plant simultaneously. Both material documents and accounting documents are produced by the system.

Two-Step Procedure

In the two-step procedure, the material is removed from the supplying plant and placed in the receiving plant. As with storage locations, two movement types are required: first, movement type 303 to remove the material from the supplying plant and, second, movement type 305 to place that material into the receiving plant.

When the movement type 303 is posted, the stock is reduced at the supplying plant and placed in the receiving plant's stock in transit. After the material is received and placed into stock at the receiving plant using movement type 305, the material moves from stock in transit to unrestricted stock.

17.6.3   Transfer between Storage Locations

Transferring from one storage location to another can also be executed by using Transaction MIGO_TR or even using Transaction MIGO. Transaction MIGO_TR can be found by following the navigation path **Logistics • Materials Management • Inventory Management • Goods Movement • Transfer Posting (MIGO_TR)**.

Figure 17.20 shows the transaction screen for Transaction MIGO_TR with material movement type **311** selected from the **TF tfr. within plant** dropdown list in the

17

upper-right corner. In this case, the one-step procedure has been chosen with no special stock. The information regarding the transfer posting, the material, the quantity, and storage locations involved in the move are available in the various tabs in the lower-half of the screen.

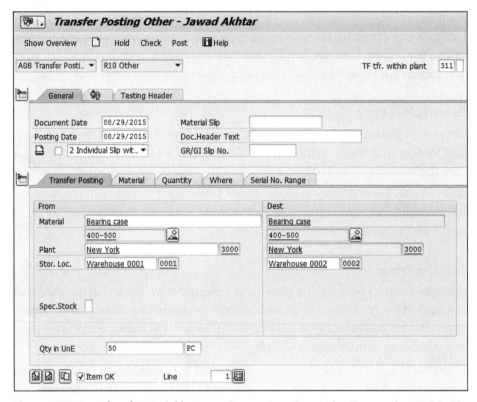

Figure 17.20 Transfer of Material between Storage Locations Using Transaction MIGO_TR

17.6.4   Transfer between Plants Using Transaction MIGO_TR

Plant-to-plant material transfers can also be executed by using Transaction MIGO_TR by following the navigation path **Logistics • Materials Management • Inventory Management • Goods Movement • Transfer Posting (MIGO)**.

Figure 17.21 shows the transfer of material between plants **3300** and **3350** using Transaction MIGO_TR. Further information is displayed in a number of tabs, such as **Transfer Posting**, **Material**, **Quantity**, and **Where**.

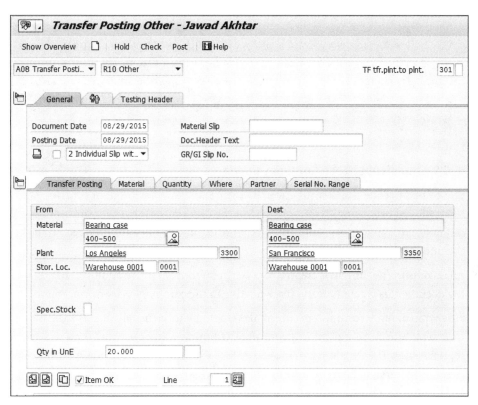

Figure 17.21 Transfer of Material between Plants Using Transaction MIGO_TR

Tips & Tricks

Often, companies want to build better business and audit controls by preventing the direct transfer of material from one plant to another (or from storage location to another) without first having an initiating request or a document for material transfer's request. In these scenarios, the requester can create a reservation (Transaction MB21) with the relevant movement types such as 301 (plant-to-plant transfer) or 311 (storage location-to-storage location transfer) to initiate the material transfer request. The warehouse person can then perform the transfer posting with reference to the reservation. To view all the goods movements possible via reservations, including goods issuance (consumption), transfer postings, or goods receipts, use Transaction MB21 and place your cursor in the **Movement Type** field to open its dropdown list.

Another option for plant-to-plant stock transfers is via a stock transport order (STO). This option is particularly attractive if your company engages a transporter or a transportation company to move its goods from one plant to another. Since the transporter charges a transportation fee, these fees can be incorporated into an STO and paid accordingly. We'll cover the STO process (interplant transfer) in Chapter 14, Section 14.3.

17.6.5   Transfer between Company Codes

The company code transfer functionally is similar to a plant-to-plant transfer. Material is moved between different plants, but the difference is that the plants belong to different company codes. Additional accounting documents are produced in either the one-step or two-step procedure.

An accounting document is created for each plant movement. In addition, an accounting document is created for the stock posting in the company's clearing accounts.

Stock transfers are common in companies where material usually needs to be moved from a manufacturing plant to a central distribution warehouse and then to smaller regional sites. The frequency of movements is thus increased when company policy requires material to be moved from site to site when necessary.

17.6.6   Additional Transfer Posting Scenarios

Let's look at some additional stock transfer scenarios and their relevant movement types and reversals to meet specific business and accounting needs.

Material-to-Material Transfers

A material-to-material transfer may be required when, due to physical, chemical, or other attributes, material A needs to be changed to material B. For example, in the textile industry, due to quality control issues, the material that was planned to be produced as an A (or a premium) quality product didn't happen. Instead, a B-quality material following a slightly lower manufacturing standard was produced. Therefore, using Transaction MIGO, a material-to-material stock transfer posting takes place through movement type 309. The reversal of movement type 309 is 310, which can be used if a material-to-material stock transfer using movement type 309 must be reversed because of error in transaction posting. In this stock transfer process, the system not only creates a material document but also creates associated financial accounting documents, such as an FI document, a CO document, and a Material Ledger document.

Batch-to-Batch Transfer of Material

A batch-to-batch stock transfer of a material may be required for materials when, for example, an incorrect batch number was allocated during a material's batch's production. Since you can no longer change a material's batch identification once created, the only option is to perform a transfer posting from one batch to another. During a batch-to-batch transfer of material, if the batch of the receiving material already exists, then the quantity from the material's sender batch will update the quantity of the material's receiver batch. If the receiver batch number of the material does not exist, then the system will automatically assign an internal number to the receiver batch (in case of an external batch numbering, the user can manually enter the batch number of the receiving material). Using Transaction MIGO, a batch-to-batch stock transfer of a material can take place by using movement type 309. The reversal of movement type 309 is 310.

Quality Stock with SAP QM Activated

It is common to have some materials in the quality stock, when the initial (or the cutover) stock balances are uploaded during an SAP S/4HANA implementation project. If the quality management (QM) is used in SAP S/4HANA, then the system will not allow stock transfers in quality stock. To address this scenario, you'll need to activate inspection type 0800, which will then allow stock transfer postings to take place. After inspection type activation, use Transaction QA08 to transfer post-quality stock into quality inspection stock, and the system will create an inspection lot for results recording and usage decision.

17.7   Configuration Basics in Inventory Management

In this section, we'll use an example from an actual SAP implementation project to demonstrate creating a new movement type. A new movement type creation needed to be created because a manufacturing unit needed to routinely issue out additional packing material during the production process of pharmaceutical products to account for an unusually high wastage of packing material during production. The company wanted visibility of how much excess issuance of packing material was made for each production order. To meet this business scenario, a customized movement type ZO1 for goods issuance was created by copying the standard movement type for goods issuance against the production order, which is movement type 261. The necessary changes to configuration were made to the customized movement type ZO1.

You can create a new movement type by copying an existing movement type and modifying it. A number to identify the new movement type is entered, and the fields from the existing movement type will be copied over, as shown in Figure 17.22.

To create a new movement type, use Transaction OMJJ or by following the navigation path **Materials Management · Inventory Management and Physical Inventory · Movement Types · Copy, Change Movement Types**.

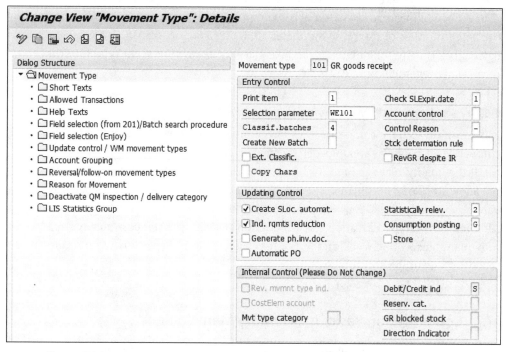

Figure 17.22 New Movement Type Creation by Copying from Existing Movement Type Using Transaction OMJJ

On the screen that appears, select the relevant checkboxes, such as the **Movement type**, **Account control**, or **Control Reason**. In the next popup window, enter specific parameters or their ranges. For example, if you select **Movement type** in the first popup, then in the second popup, you'll need to enter a movement type or a range of movement types, such as from movement types 261 to 315.

Enter not only the movement type 261 that you are going to copy from but also the new customized movement type Z01 that you plan to create, as shown in Figure 17.23.

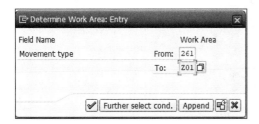

Figure 17.23 Using the Copy Function to Create a New Movement Type

Select movement type 261 and then click the copy icon , as shown in Figure 17.24. In the popup that appears, confirm that all dependent entries of the reference movement type 261 have also been copied to the newly created movement type Z01. Confirm your actions.

Change View "Movement Type": Overview

M...	Movement Type Text	Print	Auto.SLoc.	Acct	Reas.	Consumpt.postg
261	GI for order	1	☐	–	R	
262	RE for order	1	☐	–	R	
281	GI for network	1	☐	–	R	
282	RE for network	1	☐	–	R	
291	GI all acc. assigmts	1	☐	–	R	

Dialog Structure
- ▼ Movement Type
  - ☐ Short Texts
  - ☐ Allowed Transactions
  - ☐ Help Texts
  - ☐ Field selection (from 201)/Batch search procedure
  - ☐ Field selection (Enjoy)

Figure 17.24 Creating a New Movement Type Z01 Using Standard Movement Type 261

As shown in Figure 17.25, enter the new movement type Z01 as well as maintain or change any parameters to meet business needs.

Figure 17.26 shows the options for updating or maintaining parameters in the various areas available on the left side of the screen. In our example, we changed the short text in the **Short Texts** of the newly configured movement type.

Change View "Movement Type": Details of Selected Set

Movement type   Z01 GI for order

Entry Control

Print item	1	Check SLExpir.date
Selection parameter		Account control
Classif.batches		Control Reason	-
Create New Batch		Stck determation rule
☐ Ext. Classific.		☐ RevGR despite IR
☐ Copy Chars		

Updating Control

☐ Create SLoc. automat.		Statistically relev.	2
☑ Ind. rqmts reduction		Consumption posting	R
☐ Generate ph.inv.doc.		☐ Store
☐ Automatic PO		

Internal Control (Please Do Not Change)

☐ Rev. mvmnt type ind.		Debit/Credit ind	H
☐ CostElem account		Reserv. cat.	F
Mvt type category		GR blocked stock
		Direction Indicator

Figure 17.25 Detailed Screen of Movement Type Z01

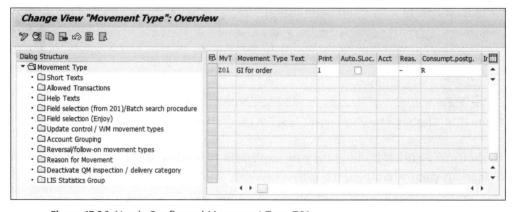

Figure 17.26 Newly Configured Movement Type Z01

Tips & Tricks

While configuring a new movement type, creating a new and customized movement type for the reversal process makes sense. For example, if we created movement type Z01 to manage unplanned goods issuances against process orders, then creating reversal movement type Z02 to reverse Z01 movements ensures a closed-circle approach. In our example, the reversal movement type can be a copy of the standard movement type 262, which is for the reversal of goods issuance against a production order.

The newly created and customized reversal movement type Z02 can then be assigned in the **Reversal/follow-up movement types**, as shown in Figure 17.26, to original customized movement type Z01.

This approach of linking newly created customized movement types to their reversal movement types follows the same approach as standard movement types and their reversals available in the SAP system. For example, if the original movement type for a goods receipt against a purchase order is 101, then its reversal movement type is 102. If the receipt of a by-product is denoted by movement type 531, then its reversal movement type is 532. If goods issuance for the scrap process is managed via movement type 551, then its reversal movement type is 552.

17.8 Summary

In this chapter, we introduced the IM functionality. Traditional goods movements, such as goods issues and goods receipts, will be discussed in detail in later chapters. However, MM users need to understand returns, reservations, and stock transfers. Returns are a part of everyday life at most companies. Often, material that can't be used by the company is delivered. Knowing your company's return process is important when decisions are being made concerning the material.

In addition to returns, reservations can be quite important to a manufacturing company, so you must understand how and when your company uses reservations. Stock transfers occur regularly, and the decision whether to use one-step or two-step transfers should be made early in the implementation project.

In Chapter 19, we'll discuss goods issues with an emphasis on how it's used in production and for other production-related operations.

Chapter 18
Goods Issue

When materials are issued, a goods issue decreases stock levels and makes a financial posting to reduce the quantity and the value of the stock. The goods issue process results in the creation of material and accounting documents in SAP.

Goods issues for material movements include issues for production orders, sampling, scrapping, and internal goods issues against cost centers. For each of these goods issues, the system will create both financial and material documents. Goods issues that most consultants find themselves reviewing are goods issues for production orders, for scrap, and for sampling processes.

You'll encounter many goods issue scenarios when working with materials management (MM). In manufacturing industries, the most common goods issues are for production orders or process orders. Other important goods issue scenarios include goods issue for scrap and for sampling processes. In this chapter, we'll discuss the mechanisms of these goods issues.

18.1 Goods Issue to a Production Order

The production order requires materials that are identified in the bill of materials (BOM) to complete the production of finished goods. The material requirements planning (MRP) process plans the order and ensures that the correct materials are available, and then the MM process supplies material to the order through a goods issue. Apart from the planned issue of material to a production order, material can be issued to a production order by an unplanned issue. An automatic goods issuance against the production process is known as *backflushing*.

18.1.1   Planned Goods Issue

In SAP, a goods issue can be created using Transaction MIGO or by following the navigation path **Logistics • Materials Management • Inventory Management • Goods Movement • Goods Issue (MIGO)**.

Figure 18.1 shows an overview of the Transaction MIGO's screen, including details of various fields, icons, tabs and input fields such as dates, or fields to maintain additional information in the form of text.

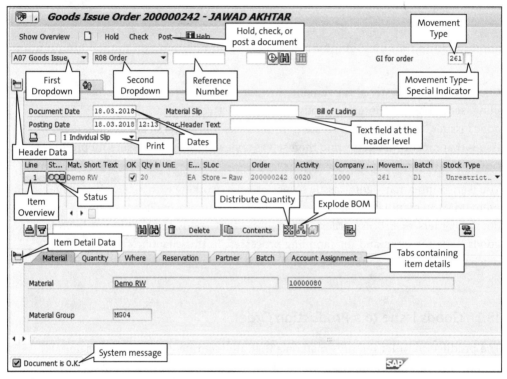

Figure 18.1 Overview of the Transaction MIGO_GI Screen

The initial screen for Transactions MIGO or MIGO_GI (Goods Issue), shown in Figure 18.2, requires that the correct type of goods issue be executed. For goods issues to a production order, **Goods Issue** and **Order** are chosen from the two dropdown menus followed by entering the production order number, in our case, "200000242"; the transaction will default to the correct movement type, in this case, **261**, as shown in the **GI for order** field.

> **Note**
>
> Refer to Appendix A for a selected list of movement types associated with goods issuance or consumption.

As shown in Figure 18.2, maintaining the correct **Posting date** as well as the correct **Document date** is important. A posting date must fall within the two financial periods (months) open in SAP. A document date can be the date on which the actual goods issuance took place. For example, if you're entering goods issuance data for the goods that were issued yesterday, then enter yesterday's date as the posting date makes sense. The document date can be the same date on which the document is posted in the system. Several SAP reports and analytic tools offer the option of entering a single posting date (or a range of posting dates) as a selection parameter. As a result, the inventory planner can have clear visibility on when a particular stock posting (goods issuance/consumption, transfer posting, or goods received) was made.

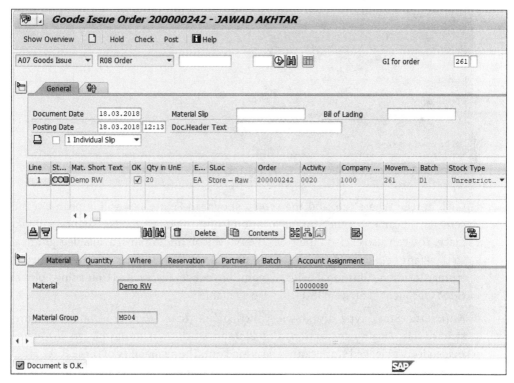

Figure 18.2 Initial Screen for Goods Issue Transaction MIGO_GI

18

After the order number is entered, the transaction adopts the materials from the production order; in this case, the material is **10000080**, and the quantity expected is **20 EA**.

Let's review the various tabs found in the item details. Click on the **Quantity** tab, and the screen shown in Figure 18.3 will appear. At this point, the quantity can be changed for the goods issue.

Tips & Tricks

Be sure to select the **Item OK** checkbox, shown in Figure 18.3, so that the system can consider the item for stock posting.

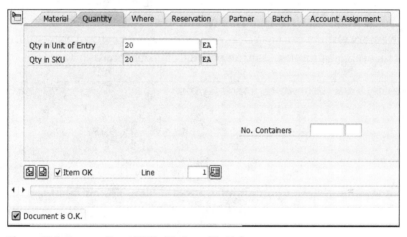

Figure 18.3 Transaction MIGO_GI: Quantity Tab

Click on the **Where** tab, and the screen shown in Figure 18.4 will appear. On this screen, you can enter the **Storage location** from which the goods issuance will take place. You can also click on the stock overview icon (mountains) available right next to the **Plant** field if you want to see the stock position of the material in a particular storage location. Additional fields to maintain text details, such as **Unloading Point** or **Goods recipient** at an item level are also available.

Notice the **Stock type** dropdown, which offers three stock type options—**Unrestricted-use**, **Quality Inspection**, and **Blocked** stock. A material placed in quality inspection or blocked stock cannot be issued out. The availability of these three stock type options is useful for companies that aren't using the quality management (QM) functionality in SAP S/4HANA but still want to maintain a limited degree of control on receiving goods from procurement or production. Material received in quality or blocked stock will need to be transfer-posted (Transaction MIGO) to bring their stock type to unrestricted-use stock.

> **Tips & Tricks**
>
> If a material quantity from multiple storage locations or from different batches needs to be issued out, then use the **Distribute qty** icon, shown earlier in Figure 18.1.

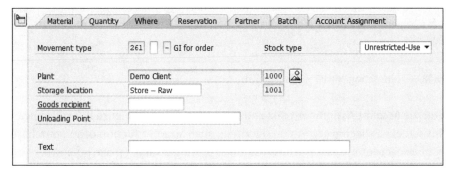

Figure 18.4 Transaction MIGO_GI: Where Tab

Click on the **Reservation** tab, and the screen shown in Figure 18.5 will appear. As we covered in Chapter 18, when a production order is created, the system also automatically creates a reservation of the required quantities of materials, in our example, the system-generated reservation number 8154. The field **Withdrawal quantity** is updated as soon as the goods issuance is posted. If a material quantity issued to a production order is less than the reservation quantity and no further issuance is expected, then selecting the **Final issue** checkbox will close the reservation, and no further goods issuance will be possible.

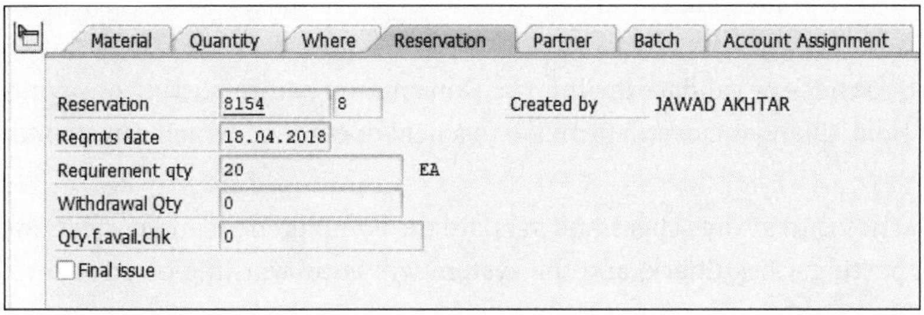

Figure 18.5 Transaction MIGO_GI: Reservation Tab

Click on the **Batch** tab, and the screen shown in Figure 18.6 will appear. On this screen, the system automatically calculates either the date of manufacturing of a material's batch, the shelf-life expiry date (**SLED**), or the best-before date (**BBD**). An inventory user can also enter these days manually.

Figure 18.6 Transaction MIGO_GI: Batch Tab

Click on the **Account Assignment** tab, and the screen shown in Figure 18.7 will appear. On this screen, a specific account assignment, such as a production order, purchase order, or a cost center, against which the stock posting is taking place is shown.

Figure 18.7 Transaction MIGO_GI: Account Assignment Tab

When you think all entered information is complete and correct, you can perform one of the following three functions:

- If you need to check or validate the information entered before posting or saving, then click **Hold**. Changes can still be made to a held document, which can eventually be posted.
- A good practice is to always check and validate the completeness and correctness of a stock posting. Click **Check**, and the system will issue warning or error messages, if any.
- You can post a transaction by clicking **Post**.

Figure 18.8 shows a message that appears after the goods issuance against the production order 200000242 has been posted. A material document is always created for any stock posting; in this case, the material document number is 4900000795.

☑ Material document 4900000795 posted

Figure 18.8 System Message Detailing the Material Document after a Document Is Successfully Posted

18.1.2   Unplanned Goods Issue

Often, you might need to issue additional material to a production order that is unplanned. For example, if a production order requires 100 kg of raw plastic pellets, a goods issue of 100 kg is performed. Then, if the production supervisor asks the inventory department for an additional 10 kg to be issued to that production order—an unplanned issue. Some reasons why an unplanned issue might occur include damage to the original material issued or problems with the production process. In such cases, additional material must be issued on an unplanned basis.

An inventory user can enter the header information as usual for a goods issue in the Transaction MIGO, but after the relevant movement type is entered, that is, 261, an inventory user then enters all the details previously noted in various tabs (shown from Figure 18.2 to Figure 18.7).

18.1.3   Backflushing

Backflushing is a process that occurs after production has taken place. Materials used in the production order aren't consumed in the system until the production is posted against the operation in the routing. The backflushing procedure then processes the production order using the sum of the finished products and scrap quantity to recalculate the materials required. An inventory user then issues all of the materials as one transaction, as the user would have done initially in a normal goods issue to a production order.

For example, let's say a saw manufacturer uses large coils of steel to produce its blades. The amount of steel varies depending on the size of the saw blade being produced. Although the amount of steel is known, the steel cannot be measured out before the production of the blades. Therefore, the production staff accurately measures the amount of steel used after the end of the production, enters this value into the production order, and then posts the order. The amount of steel used is then backflushed, removing the correct amount from inventory.

18

At this time, you can change individual material quantities and add individual scrap quantities to detail lines. Let's look at the production order from our earlier plastic pellets example, in Section 18.1.2, which requires 100 kg of raw plastic pellets. If the production order hadn't issued the 100 kg, but instead the quantity was backflushed, then the backflushing would have one issue of 110 kilograms, which includes the added scrap line item of 10 kilograms.

Backflushing occurs when either the material, the production work center, or the routing has been flagged as relevant for backflushing, and this designation is copied to the production order. A material can be flagged for backflushing by setting the **Backflush** indicator on the material master record. Figure 18.9 shows the decision tree through which the system decides if and when to backflush components.

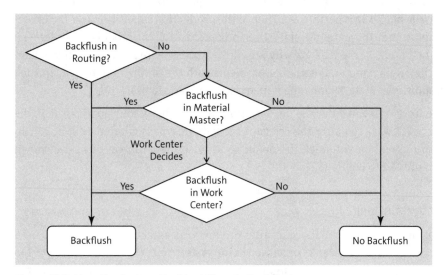

Figure 18.9 How the System Decides When to Backflush

The **Backflush** indicator can be found in the **MRP 2** tab of the material master record, as shown in Figure 18.10. Backflushing can be useful to production operations because it provides significant benefits over the normal goods issue procedure for certain production situations:

- If a production process has a long operation time, such as days or weeks, then moving the material out of stock and issuing it to a production order may not be beneficial because that material won't be recorded as consumed for a long period of time. With backflushing, this material will remain in stock until the operation is complete.

- When a production operation involves a lot of scrap material, a complicated issuing process may ensue where an inventory user won't know exactly how much material to issue. Using backflushing to calculate the used material on the basis of finished product plus scrap quantity is much simpler.

- Bulk materials make exact issuance difficult, and backflushing simplifies the process. Allowing the system to backflush the correct quantity after the operation is the easiest method.

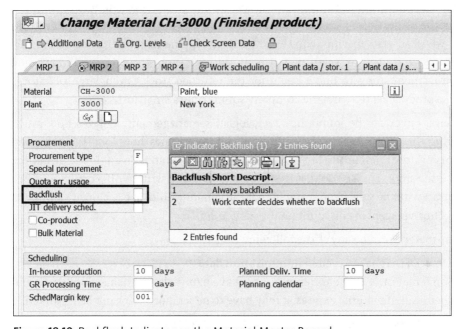

Figure 18.10 Backflush Indicator on the Material Master Record

A goods issue to a production order is the process most familiar to those working in MM; however, other goods issues scenarios need to be understood as well. In the next section, we'll look at goods issues to scrap.

18.2   Goods Issue to Scrap

Scrap material can be defined in any way that a company decides. A material that is scrap for one company may not be scrap for another. The most useful general definition of scrap is a material that is no longer of any use or value to the company.

When a material can't be used in the manufacturing process, due to quality issues or if finished goods have exceeded their best-before date, you can decide to scrap the material. The definition of scrap material will vary between companies and industries.

For example, let's say our saw manufacturer sold its products to tool manufacturers and home improvement stores. The company used coils of steel to fabricate the saw blades, and each blade is pressed from the steel using the minimum amount of waste possible. Even using the most complex fabrication machinery, a small percentage of scrap can't be avoided. However, on occasion, due to slight differences in the steel coils, the blades don't pass the quality checks undertaken by the company's customers, who had very specific requirements. Thus, shipments are returned to the saw manufacturer, whose sales department contacts other customers and home improvement stores to find a buyer for the returned stock. Often, large DIY stores take a product list this, and the company suffers only a small loss.

When a buyer can be found, however, logistics management analyzes how much storing the unwanted items would cost and determines how long the company wants to store them until a buyer was found. The sales staff is given this information, but if the shipment isn't sold, it has to be scrapped and written off. Fortunately, our contract with the steel vendor stated that the vendor would take scrapped shipments and offer a percentage discount on the next order.

Scrap material can be any of the following:

- **Material that has exceeded its expiration date**
  Some materials in the warehouse may have expiry dates, such as foodstuffs and chemicals. If material expires, it may have to be scrapped if it can't be reworked.

- **Material that is no longer in tolerance with respect to quality**
  Some chemicals may require periodic retesting because their characteristics may change over time. For example, if an ethanol-type material is tested and found to have a viscosity of 1.049 cP (centipoise), and the tolerance limits are between 1.065 and 1.083 cP, then the material is out of tolerance and may be scrapped.

- **Material that is unusable due to the production process**
  Some materials don't have expiry dates or quality tolerances but still may not be suitable for production. For example, if plastic beads to produce white plastic items have become discolored, they may no longer be suitable and need to be scrapped.

- **Material that is damaged in the warehouse**
  Material can easily be damaged as it moves around the warehouse. Damage from

forklifts often occurs as does damage by environmental factors, such as water or sunlight.

Material identified as scrap material must be removed from stock, and the value of the stock must be reduced. To perform the scrapping of material, an inventory user can perform a goods issue with the relevant movement type for scrapping: movement types 551 and 553.

Material to be scrapped can be in unrestricted stock, quality inspection stock, or blocked stock. Depending on the company and the scrapping procedure it uses, the material can be located in any of these three areas. The cost of scrapping a material is charged to a cost center.

Transaction MIGO_GI can be used for the goods issue with movement type 551, as shown in Figure 18.11, with the description **GI scrapping**. The **Cost Center** for the scrapping costs can be entered for the line item.

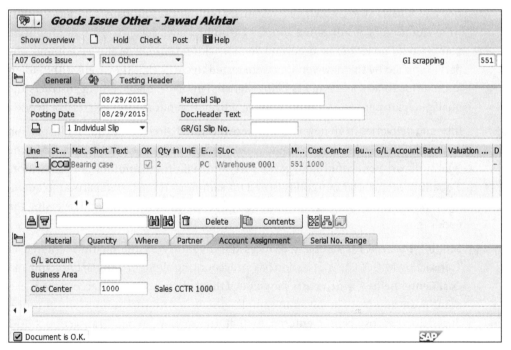

Figure 18.11 Item to Be Scrapped Using Transaction MIGO_GI

In the next section, we'll discuss another goods issue process: performing goods issues for sampling.

18.3   Goods Issue for Sampling

Companies take samples of material in conjunction with testing for quality. Chemical materials can be safe to use within a range of certain tolerances. If the material changes its chemical makeup over time, for example, the company needs to know about this change. To monitor a material, the company instructs its quality department to test the material in stock. In the majority of cases, a sample of the material is tested.

To test a sample, the sample quantity must be removed from stock. A goods issue is performed to issue some material for sampling. The sample can be taken from material in unrestricted, quality, or blocked stock. In this section, we'll use Transaction MIGO to perform the goods issue.

For example, let's say a manufacturer of household appliances has consolidated its manufacturing and administration in a central facility. Three manufacturing facilities and a parts store, which also originally housed the company's administration, were closed. As a result, some suppliers who had been local to the manufacturing plants would no longer be used, and vendors closer to the new site were found. The parts supplied by the new vendors were tested to check that they were within tolerances prior to any agreements being signed. However, management instructs the quality department to check the items sent by new vendors for the first 10 deliveries.

Inbound deliveries from new vendors were receipted directly into quality inspection so that the quality department could check them. Because the tests performed by the quality department could damage the parts and make them unusable for production, a quantity of material was goods issued for sampling. If the tested parts aren't damaged by the testing process, the parts can be returned to inventory by reversing the goods issue.

Sending material for sampling reduces the inventory by the quantity entered in Transaction MIGO. The transaction has an accounting element—the **G/L Account** and **Cost Center** fields—which posts the value of the stock to a sampling account. The element posts any costs involved in sampling, such as external testing labs or procedures, to the cost center entered in that transaction. While Transaction MIGO remains the same for goods issuance for sampling, the relevant movement type is 333 when samples are issued from unrestricted stock; movement type 331, from quality stock; and movement type 335, from blocked stock.

18.4 Goods Issue Postings

When a goods issue is posted, for example, to a production order, the system produces accounting and material documents, updates tables, and triggers events in other areas of SAP S/4HANA. In this section, we'll discuss the events that occur when a posting is made: creating material and accounting documents, printing the goods issue slip, changing stock levels, and updating the general ledger (G/L) account.

18.4.1 Material Documents

The material document is an audit document that describes the movements of the material entered in the goods issue. The material document is created during the posting of the goods issue and can be displayed using Transaction MIGO.

18.4.2 Accounting Documents

The accounting document is created in parallel with the material document during the posting of the goods issue. The accounting document describes the financial movements associated with the material issue. This document can be accessed from the material document by using Transaction MIGO and clicking the **Doc. Info** tab located at the header level. Clicking on the **FI Documents** icon will bring up all the accounting documents associated with the materials movement.

18.4.3 Goods Issue Slips

A *goods issue slip* is a printed document that can be used by the warehouse to find the material and provide a physical record that the material has been picked for goods issue. The goods issue slip can be considered an IM version of a warehouse management (WM) picking ticket. Three versions of goods issue slips can be selected in Transaction MIGO:

- **Individual slip**
  An individual goods issue slip is printed for each item in the material document.
- **Individual slip with inspection text**
  One goods issue slip is printed out per material document item but includes any quality inspection text contained in the material master record.
- **Collective slip**
  One goods issue slip contains all the items.

18

The goods issue slip has three printed versions defined within SAP system: WA01, WA02, and WA03. These versions can be modified to include the information relevant for the issuing procedure of each company.

18.4.4 Stock Changes

When a goods issue is posted, the relevant stock levels will change. The stock level will be reduced for a goods issueand increased for a goods issue reversal.

18.4.5 General Ledger Account Changes

During the goods issue process, the accounting software posts updates to the G/L material accounts. When a goods issue posts, the material is valuated at the current price, whether the material is valuated at a standard price or at a moving average price. Therefore, the goods issue process reduces the total value and the total quantity in relation to the price, but the price of the material doesn't change as a result.

In this section, we discussed the posting of goods issues, but in the next section, we'll cover how to deal with changes and how to execute a goods issue reversal.

18.5 Goods Issue Reversals

When material is issued to a production order, the material is issued as part of the BOM for the item that is being produced. A BOM is a list of materials with quantities that go into producing the finished item. Items on the BOM are goods issued to the production order.

A reversal can be entered with reference to the material document created on the initial goods issue. Figure 18.12 shows the cancelation of **Material Document 4900002888**. By canceling the material document, no movement type needs to be entered. This goods issue reversal method uses Transaction MIGO. The material document is entered, and the **Cancellation** option should be selected.

After the material document has been entered, the detail section is displayed, and the details of the material to be reversed are displayed with reference to the material document. Goods issue reversals are important transactions that may be required if mistakes are made. Some companies have strict policies on the use of reversal movement types, such as a goods issue reversal, so make sure that you follow the policy.

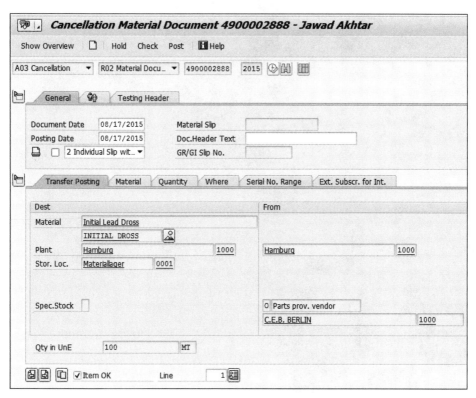

Figure 18.12 Goods Issue Reversal with Reference to a Material Document

18.6 Summary

Goods issues to production orders occur every day in a manufacturing plant, and PP elements such as backflushing should be understood by an MM user. The MM user should also closely examine the process of issuing materials to scrap. This process writes value from the company books; therefore, any movement of this kind requires a detailed procedure with checks at several levels. Issuing material to scrap is a simple transaction to perform in SAP, but the ramifications of the transaction can have a large financial effect.

Chapter 19 examines the processes that make up the goods receipt function and describes the necessary steps for successful goods receipt processing.

Chapter 19

Goods Receipt

A goods receipt is used to receive material from a purchase order or an in-house production order. The goods receipt process can be simple or complex depending on the nature of the material being received.

Goods receipts are mainly used for receiving stock from an external vendor via a purchase order (PO) or for receiving material from in-house production via a production or a process order. Goods receipts are also used for movements that initially create inventory in the system or for entering materials received without a PO. Goods receipts are important because they move the material into stock, updating the stock levels and allowing production to occur.

Every company has its own procedures for the receipt of material, and these procedures must be considered when using the goods receipt functionality in an SAP system. If a material is received into stock, either unrestricted or quality, the value of the material is posted to the plant accounts, meaning that the company has spent money to have that material in the plant. Minimizing the length of time that materials spend in the goods receipt process saves the company money.

This chapter will familiarize you with the goods receipt process and help you configure the steps required for successful goods receipt processing.

19.1 Goods Receipt for a Purchase Order

A *goods receipt* is a company's formal acceptance that materials were received from a vendor against a PO. After the material is received and the transaction is completed, the value of the material is posted to the general ledger (G/L). In this section, we'll cover goods receipts when the purchase order number is known and also when unknown. We'll also cover other types of goods receipts.

19.1.1   Goods Receipt with a Known Purchase Order Number

Transaction MIGO (Goods Receipt) can be used for the goods receipt whether the PO is known or unknown. The transaction can be accessed by following the navigation path **Logistics • Materials Management • Inventory Management • Goods Receipt • For Purchase Order • PO Number Known**.

The initial screen for Transactions MIGO or MIGO_GR (Goods Receipt), shown in Figure 19.1, requires that the correct type of goods receipt be executed. For goods receipts of materials in a PO, **Goods Receipt** and **Purchase Order** are chosen from the two dropdown lists followed by entering the PO number 4500000001; the transaction will default to the correct movement type, in this case, **101**, which is shown in the **GR Goods Receipt** field.

> **Note**
> Refer to Appendix A for a list of the most commonly used movement types.

As shown in Figure 19.1, maintaining the correct **Posting date** as well as the correct **Document date** is important. A posting date needs to fall within the two financial periods (months) open in SAP. A document date can be the date on which the actual goods receipt took place. For example, if you're entering goods receipt data for the goods that were received yesterday, then entering yesterday's date as the posting date makes sense. The document date can be the same date on which the document posted in the system. Several SAP reports and analytics offer the option of entering a single posting date (or a range of posting dates) as a selection parameter. Thus, the inventory planner can have clear visibility on when a particular stock posting (goods issuance/consumption, transfer posting, or goods received) was made.

After a PO is entered, the transaction adopts the materials from the PO; in this case, the material is **EWMS4-502**, and the quantity received is **100 PC**.

Let's review the various tabs in the item details (the lower half of the screen). Starting with the **Material** tab, the details shown in Figure 19.1 are taken either from the purchase order, the material master, or the purchasing information record. Since this goods receipt includes a reference to a purchase order, therefore, the system incorporates all the details from purchase, which are therefore not changeable. However, when goods are received without reference to a purchase order or for uploading initial stock balances upload (more on these topics in Section 19.1.2 and Section 19.3, respectively), the **Material** field is editable for input.

Figure 19.1 Transaction MIGO for Goods Receipt against Purchase Order

Click on the **Quantity** tab, and the screen shown in Figure 19.2 appears. At this point, the quantity can be changed to reflect the goods actually received. By default, the system proposes the quantity maintained in the purchase order that is expected to be received. For a partial receipt of goods against a purchase order, the system proposes the remaining quantity that still expected to be received from the supplier.

> **Tips & Tricks**
>
> Be sure to select the **Item OK** checkbox, as shown in Figure 19.2, so that the system can consider this item for stock posting.

19

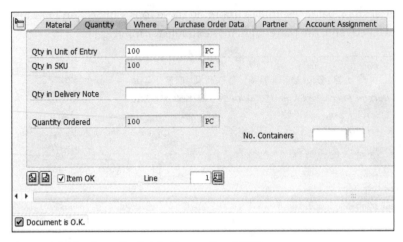

Figure 19.2 The Quantity Tab in Transaction MIGO

Click on the **Where** tab, and the screen shown in Figure 19.3 will appear. Enter the **Storage location** to which the goods receipt will take place. You can also click on the stock overview icon (mountains) available right next to the **Plant** field if you want to see the stock position of the material in a particular storage location. Additional fields to maintain text details, such as **Unloading Point** or **Goods recipient** at the item level are also available.

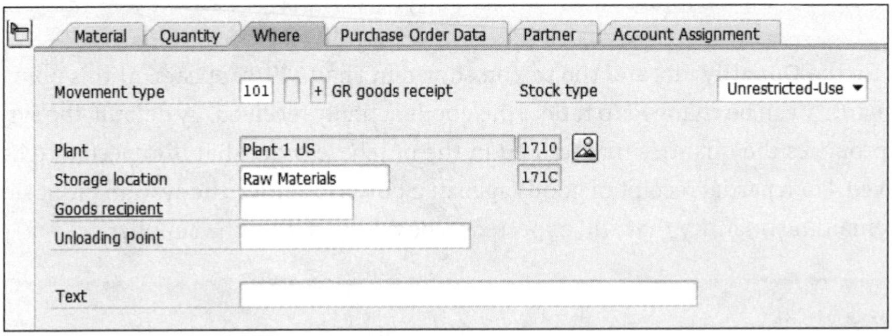

Figure 19.3 The Where Tab in the Transaction MIGO

Notice the **Stock type** dropdown list offers three stock type options—**Unrestricted-Use**, **Quality Inspection**, and **Blocked** stock. A material placed in quality inspection or blocked stock cannot be issued out. These three stock type options are useful for companies that haven't implemented the quality management (QM) component but still want to maintain some control on receiving goods from procurement or production. Material received in quality or blocked stock will need to be transfer-posted (Transaction MIGO) to change their stock type to unrestricted-use stock.

Notice the **Movement type** is **101**, which denotes a goods receipt for a purchase order. When goods are received without reference to a purchase order or for initial stock balance upload (more on these topics in Section 19.1.2 and Section 19.3, respectively), the **Movement type** field is editable for input.

> **Tip**
>
> If a material quantity needs to be received into multiple storage locations or into different batches, then use the **Distribute qty** icon shown earlier in Figure 19.1.

Figure 19.4 shows the **Purchase Order Data** tab, which contains the **Purchase order** number 4500000001 as well as the specific line item **10** within the purchase order. The **"Del.Completed" Ind.** dropdown list offers a few options for a warehouse user to choose from. For example, the system can automatically set the delivery completed indicator if and when a full quantity of a material is received against a PO. The delivery completed indicator can also be manually set if no further goods receipts are expected for the specific PO. The delivery completed indicator can stay unset even though the complete quantity against the PO is received.

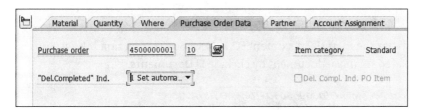

Figure 19.4 The Purchase Order Data Tab in Transaction MIGO

Figure 19.5 shows the **Partner** tab showing the brief details of the **Vendor** who delivered the goods. When goods are received without reference to a PO, the **Vendor** field is editable, and a warehouse user can enter the vendor code who delivered the goods.

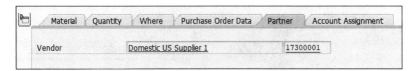

Figure 19.5 The Partner Tab in Transaction MIGO

Click on the **Account Assignment** tab, and the screen shown in Figure 19.6 will appear. A specific account assignment, such as the profit center against which the stock posting takes place, is shown.

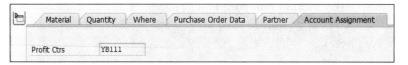

Figure 19.6 The Account Assignment Tab in Transaction MIGO

When you think all entered information is complete and correct, you can perform one of the following three functions:

- If you need to check or validate the information entered before posting or saving, then click **Hold**. Changes can still be made to a held document, which can eventually be posted.
- A good practice to always check and validate the completeness and correctness of a stock posting. Click **Check**, and the system will issue warning or error messages, if any.
- You can post a transaction by clicking **Post**.

Save the transaction, and a message reading "Material document 5000000050 posted" will appear. A material document is always created for any stock posting, and in this case, the material document number is 5000000050.

Figure 19.7 shows the material document 5000000050 (Transaction MIGO). You can see its associated financial document by clicking **FI Documents.**

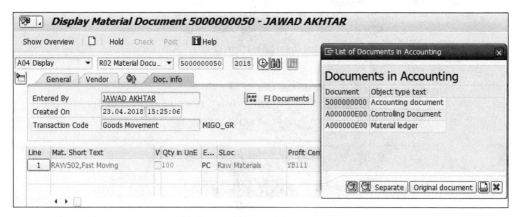

Figure 19.7 FI Documents in Transaction MIGO

19.1.2   Goods Receipt with an Unknown Purchase Order Number

On rare occasions, material arrives from a vendor with no PO with the documents from the vendor, and no suitable PO number can be found in SAP system. Perhaps a delay in entering the PO in SAP system occurred or the vendor mistakenly delivered material that was never ordered. In any case, your company will need a procedure for handling these instances.

Some companies won't accept material without a PO on the documents or for which no suitable PO can be found in SAP system. In this case, the material is refused, and the delivery isn't accepted. Other companies will accept the delivery and keep the material in quality or blocked stock until the situation is resolved. In this case, the material must be received using the correct movement type.

A goods receipt for receiving material without a PO number uses the same Transactions MIGO or MIGO_GR. The information required for this transaction is minimal because no details are available from a relevant PO. The material and quantity information should be entered manually as well as the plant and storage location information. The relevant movement type is 501 (receipt without purchase order into unrestricted-use stock).

After all relevant information has been entered, especially the material number and quantity, the goods receipt can be posted. The material will be part of the plant stock unless received into goods receipt blocked stock.

19.1.3   Goods Receipt Posting

After a goods receipt has been posted, a series of events are triggered, which we'll describe in this section.

Material Document

The material document is an audit document that describes the movements of the material entered in the goods receipt. The material document is created during the posting of the goods receipt and can be displayed using Transaction MIGO (as shown earlier in Figure 19.7).

Accounting Document

The accounting document is created in parallel with the material document during the posting of the goods receipt. The accounting document describes the financial movements associated with the material receipt and can be accessed from Transaction MIGO (Display Material Document), as shown earlier in Figure 19.7.

Goods Receipt Note

A goods receipt note is a printed document that the warehouse uses to store the material in the correct location.

Three versions of goods receipt notes can be selected in Transaction MIGO:

- **Individual GRN**
  An individual goods receipt note is printed for each item in the material document.

- **Individual GRN with inspection text**
  One goods receipt note is printed out per material document item but includes any quality inspection text contained in the material master record.

- **Collective slip**
  One goods receipt note is printed out containing all the items.

The goods receipt note has three printed versions defined within SAP system: WE01, WE02, and WE03. These versions can be modified to include the information relevant for the issuing procedure of each company.

Stock Changes

When a goods receipt is posted, the relevant stock levels change. The stock level will be increased for a goods receipt and decreased for a goods receipt reversal.

A goods receipt reversal may occur if the material was found to be defective or failed quality inspection. In this case, the inventory control department can reverse the goods receipt so the material will be deducted from the plant stock level. To reverse a goods receipt, use Transaction MIGO and choosing **Cancellation** from the first dropdown menu, **Material document** from the second dropdown menu. Then, enter the material document number and post or save the transaction. When canceling or changing a material document, only a little information can be amended.

Movement Types 107 and 109

Within the inventory management (IM) function, two underutilized movement types are available in SAP system:

- 107: Goods receipt to valuated GR blocked stock
- 109: Goods receipt from valuated GR blocked stock

In this section, we described in detail how material arriving at the plant is received using the goods receipt process for a PO. In the next section, we'll examine the goods receipt process for production orders.

19.2   Goods Receipt for a Production Order

If company is in the manufacturing industry, then you'll need to perform goods receipts for production orders to receive finished goods into stock for use or for sale.

A production order quantity can be received into stock using Transactions MIGO or MIGO_GO (Goods Receipt for Order) or by following the navigation path **Logistics • Materials Management • Inventory Management • Goods Receipt • GR for Order**.

Both transactions require the entry of the appropriate production order number in the **Order** number field. The production order number is usually found on the documents supplied from the production facility. The relevant movement type is 101.

> **Note**
>
> The fact that the movement type goods receipts against purchase orders is same as for goods receipts against production or process orders. In both cases, the movement type is 101. We'll show in Chapter 27 how reports such as the material document list (Transaction MB51) provide further filters, such as **Trans./Event Type** on the initial parameters selection screen, to differentiate between goods received from a production process from those received from a purchasing process (purchase order).

After the production order is entered, the material information is populated into the goods receipt. The quantity of the finished material can be entered into the goods receipt if different from the quantity on the production order.

After a goods receipt is posted, the production order assessed as fully delivered or partially delivered, provided that a partial quantity was delivered to the warehouse. The amount received is equal to the production order. The delivery completed indicator (**"Del.Completed" Ind.**) is set to automatic (as shown earlier in Figure 19.4) when the delivery quantity is equal to the production order quantity.

> **Note**
>
> If your company's manufacturing type is for process industries, replace the production order with a process order. All other business processes in goods receipt for process orders remains the same as in discrete manufacturing (production order).

In this section, we discussed goods receipts for production orders. In the next section, we'll move our focus from goods receipts to how inventory is initially entered into the SAP system.

19.3   Initial Entry of Inventory

When a new SAP system is brought into production, a number of tasks must be completed to make the transition from the legacy system to the new SAP system as seamless as possible. When replacing a legacy inventory system, the inventory on hand in the warehouse must be entered into the SAP system to reflect the current situation.

To enter inventory balances, primarily at the initial go-live of an SAP system, the goods receipt process uses specific movement types, depending on the status of the material.

The transaction requires the user to enter a **Movement Type.** Three movement types can be used for initial inventory loads:

- **561**
  Goods receipt for initial entry of stock balances into unrestricted stock

- **563**
  Goods receipt for initial entry of stock balances into quality inspection

- **565**
  Goods receipt for initial entry of stock balances into blocked stock

For example, an inventory controller can use Transaction MIGO and **Movement Type 563**, which represents the initial load of material balances into quality inspection. Movement type 561 is used if the material is unrestricted stock; movement type 565, if the stock will be placed in blocked stock.

Let's now demonstrate step-by-step how to use Transaction MIGO and movement type 561 to perform goods receipts for initial stock balances into unrestricted-use stock. As already mentioned, this activity will only be performed when a new SAP project is going live.

Access the screen shown in Figure 19.8 via Transaction MIGO and choose **Goods Receipt** from the first dropdown list followed by choosing **Other** from the second dropdown list. Ensure that movement type 561 is used for initial entry of stock balances, as shown on the right-hand side of the screen.

You can view a summarized view, shown in Figure 19.8, by clicking on the **Detail data** button located on the lower left-hand side of the screen. This view or the layout offers columns for data entry by hiding the detail view of an item and the associated tabs.

Click on the **Detail data** button so the tabs appear. Let's now quickly review the various tabs and the options available for entering the relevant information.

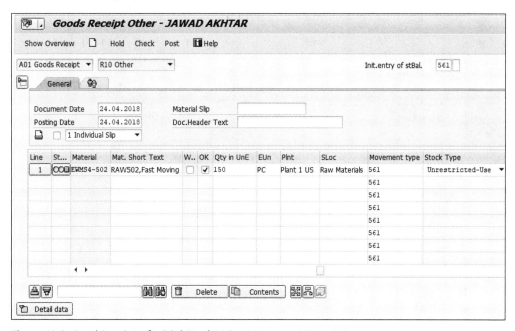

Figure 19.8 Good Receipt of Initial Stock Using Movement Type 561

Figure 19.9 shows the **Material** tab in which you'll need to enter a material number, which in our case is "EWMS4-502." Note that entering material EWMS4-502 in the editable field will automatically bring up a description of the material, which in this case is **RAW502,Fast Moving**.

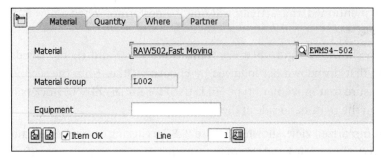

Figure 19.9 Entering the Material Number of the Initial Stock Balance Upload

Figure 19.10 shows the **Quantity** tab where you'll enter the quantity of the initial stock upload in the **Qty in Unit of Entry** field. Since each stock has a quantity as well as an associated financial value, the stock value (in local currency) is maintained in the **Ext. Amount LC** field.

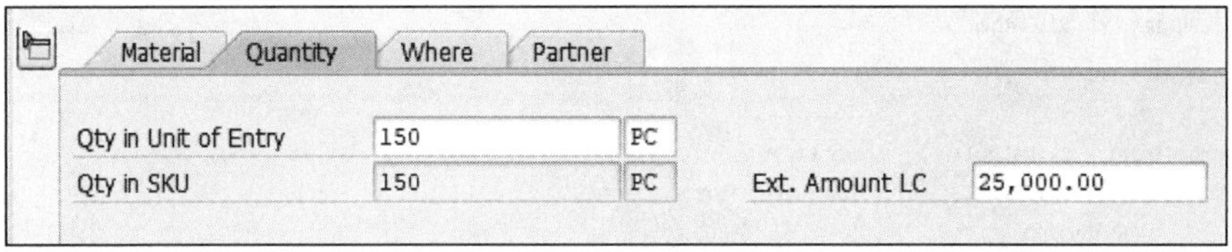

Material	Quantity	Where	Partner		
Qty in Unit of Entry		150	PC		
Qty in SKU		150	PC	Ext. Amount LC	25,000.00

Figure 19.10 Entering the Quantity of the Initial Stock Balance Upload

Figure 19.11 shows the **Where** tab where details of the **Plant (1710)** and **Storage Location (171C)** of the initial stock upload are maintained. Notice that you can make last-minute changes to the **Movement type** as well as the **Stock type** at the item level. The **+** sign next to the **Movement type** indicates an increase in stock at the plant-storage location combination.

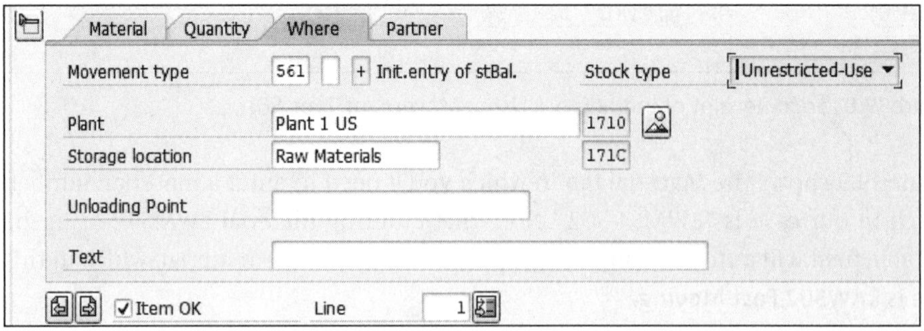

Material	Quantity	Where	Partner		
Movement type	561	+ Init.entry of stBal.	Stock type	Unrestricted-Use ▾	
Plant	Plant 1 US	1710			
Storage location	Raw Materials	171C			
Unloading Point					
Text					
☑ Item OK	Line	1			

Figure 19.11 Entering the Plant and Storage Location of the Initial Stock Balance Upload

Figure 19.12 shows the **Partner** tab where the information is only entered in goods receipt scenarios in which either a customer's or a vendor's stock is available with the company at the time of initial stock upload.

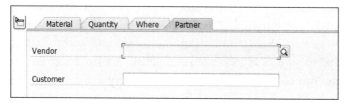

Figure 19.12 Entering Partner Details of the Initial Stock Balance Upload

On saving the transaction, you'll receive a confirmation, and the associated material document number **4900000134** will appear. Figure 19.13 shows the **Accounting document** directly associated with the material document number 4900000134 we just created in the previous step.

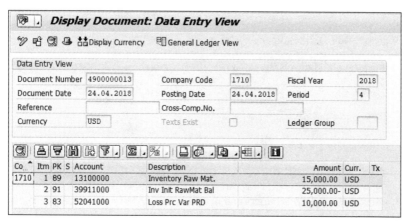

Figure 19.13 Accounting Document Display after Initial Stock Upload

In the following section, we'll describe some other, less familiar goods receipt processes that you may encounter.

19.4   Good Receipt of Co-Products or By-Products

A *by-product* is a secondary or incidental product created by the manufacturing process or from a chemical reaction in a manufacturing operation. A by-product is not the primary finished product being manufactured. In many cases, by-products can be captured, received into stock, and either used again in part of the manufacturing process or sold as a finished good.

An example of a by-product is lanolin from the processing of wool into textiles. As wool is processed into cloth, a by-product of that process is lanolin, also known as wool wax. Lanolin is sold as a finished good for skin ointments and waterproofing and also as a raw material for the production of shoe polish. A by-product can be received into stock using Transaction MIGO, and movement type 531 is used for receiving by-products.

A *co-product* is of significant financial value (by-products are of low financial value). Goods receipts for co-products are the same as normal goods receipts for production orders and use movement type 101. When receiving products against a production order, the warehouse person can also simultaneously receive co-products.

Table 19.1 lists some of the key differentiators of co-products and by-products.

Key Differentiator	Co-Product	By-Product
Significant financial value to the company	Yes	No
Can be planned in production processes	Yes	No
Ease of master data setup	No	Yes
Material master checkbox required	Yes	No
Bill of materials (BOM) checkbox required	Yes	No
Negative quantity in BOM	Yes	Yes

Table 19.1 Difference between Co-Products and By-Products

Note

Usually a company's product cost controlling (CO-PC) team declares a material as either a co-product or a by-product. The primary responsibility of implementing these materials falls to the production planning (PP) and materials management (MM) teams in coordination with the CO-PC team. Co-products and by-products are each handled differently in an SAP system.

In the following sections, we'll present side-by-side descriptions of co-products and by-products to show their similarities and differences so that you can see which option best suits your business requirements. Descriptions include details such as the required material master and BOM master data. We'll use example process orders to show the impact and behavior, including costing, when of co-products and by-products. Subsequent production transactions include confirmation and finally goods receipt for a process order. We'll also cover some of the standard material document information available in a process order, along with planned versus actual costs in analyses and itemized forms.

> **Note**
>
> While this chapter covers the production cycle of process industries, the same concepts and functionalities apply to discrete manufacturing.

Let's start with the master data that you'll need to set up for co-products and by-products in an SAP system.

19.4.1   Check in Material Master

To declare a material as a co-product, you'll set the **Co-product** flag in the material master of all materials to be designated as co-products, as well as in the BOM. All co-products include the main co-product (BOM header) and the co-products in the BOM items. There is no such requirement for a by-product.

Co-Product

To activate a co-product in the material master and to change the material master, use Transaction MM02 or follow the menu path **Logistics • Materials Management • Material Master • Material • Change • Immediately**. Then, follow these steps:

1. Enter the **Material** number and click the **Select view(s)** icon.

2. In the popup window, select the **Costing views** and click **Continue**.

3. Select the **Organizational levels** icon. Select the **Organizational level**, that is, plant. For our example, we'll enter plant "Z001."

4. Press ⌗Enter⌗ or click the **Enter** icon. The **Costing** tab of the material master will open, as shown in Figure 19.14. Select the **Co-product** checkbox to declare that the material is a co-product.

Figure 19.14 Costing View of the Material Master with the Co-Product Checkbox Selected

---

Tips & Tricks

You can activate co-products in either the **MRP 2** tab or the **Costing** tab. Whichever view is activated first causes will update the other view in the material master.

---

5. Click the **Joint production** button to open the screen shown in Figure 19.15, which is the cost apportionment structure for co-products. When a process order or a production order is created in an SAP system, the system generates an order item for each co-product. The actual costs for goods issues and confirmed internal activities are collected on the order header. Goods receipts for co-products are entered with reference to the order item. At the end of the period, the actual costs incurred for the order are distributed to the co-products as equivalence numbers or as percentages.

6. Enter "40" percent as the equivalence number (in the first column), followed by a short description ❶.

7. Enter the apportion structure (**Struc.**) as "PI", which is for a process order. Now, 40% of the total cost of production of material ZF01 will be allocated to material ZS11.

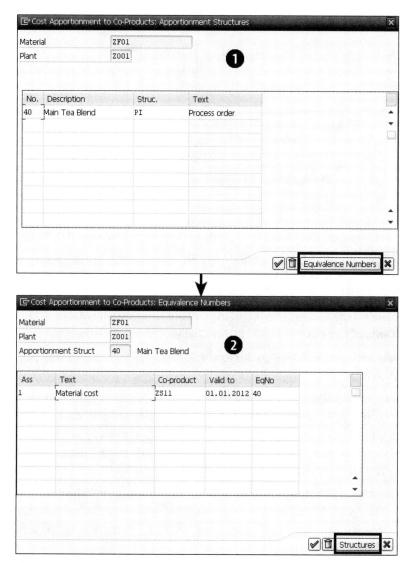

Figure 19.15 Cost Apportionment Structure to Co-Products and Equivalence Number

19

8. Keep the cursor in the first row of the table on the screen ❶ and click the **Equivalence Numbers** button. The screen that appears ❷ requires details about the assignment of the apportion structure, that is, the cost of the finished good (ZF01) that will be allocated to the co-product (ZS11), in our example, 40 percent.

9. Click **Continue** and save the material master by pressing [Ctrl] + [S].

By-Product

No checks or settings in the material master are needed for a by-product.

19.4.2   Bill of Materials

To declare a material as a co-product, you'll have to activate the relevant checkbox in the material BOM. To declare a material as a by-product, you don't need to select any checkbox in the material BOM. The quantity defined in the material BOM for both co-products and by-products is negative, for example, –2 units.

Co-Product

If a material is marked as a co-product, you must set the **Co-product** flag in the BOM of the product in which the co-product exists. Both the main product in the BOM header and co-products with negative quantities in the BOM will require the **Co-product** indicator set in the material master.

Use Transaction CS02 or follow the menu path **Logistics • Production • Master Data • Bill of Material • Bill of Material • Material BOM • Change**. Then, follow these steps:

1. Enter the **Material** number, "ZF01" in our example, together with the **Plant** "ZO01" and **Alternative BOM** usage ("1" for production).

2. Click the **Item** icon to open the **Change material BOM: General Item Overview** screen or press [Enter] to open the **Change material BOM: Item: All data** screen. You'll see the item overview of the BOM; enter a negative quantity for **Material ZS11**, which is a co-product. Other components such as ZP01 and ZP01 are defined in positive quantities and are consumed during production.

3. Select the line item **0010** and click the **Item** icon or press [F7], which opens the screen shown in Figure 19.16. Select the **Co-product** checkbox to declare material ZS11 as a co-product. Save the BOM by pressing [Ctrl] + [S] or clicking the **Save** icon.

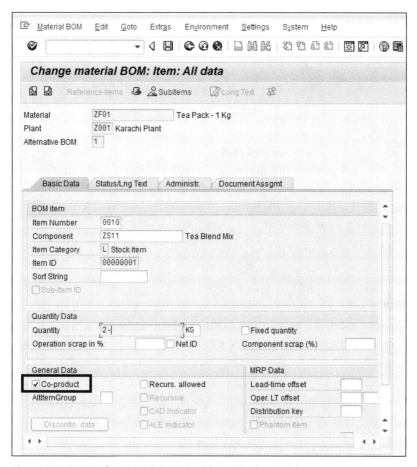

Figure 19.16 BOM for Material ZF01 with Co-Product ZS11

By-Product

For a by-product, simply entering a negative quantity is sufficient in a BOM, as shown earlier in Figure 19.16. The **Co-product** checkbox in the BOM should not be selected.

At this point, you've completed all the steps for setting up the relevant master data for both co-products and by-products. To reflect how co-products and by-products are handled in transactional data, we'll walk through the entire process in the following section.

19.4.3   Process Order

For transactional data, you'll first create a process order of the main material in which the co-product is also produced, followed by goods issuance, confirmation, and goods receipt. You'll then create another (new) process order of the main material in which the by-product is produced, and all subsequent steps are taken (such as goods issue, confirmation, and goods receipt).

In the following sections, you'll create separate process orders to show co-products and by-products.

Co-Product

To create a process order, use Transaction COR1 or follow the menu path **Logistics • Production – Process • Process Order • Process Order • Create • Create with Material**. Now follow these steps:

1. On the initial screen for creating a process order, as shown in Figure 19.17, enter the material number "ZF01," production plant "Z001," and process order type "TI01." Press Enter.

   Notice in the header data of the process order ❶ that, in addition to the main product ZF01, a co-product ZS01 is also being produced. Therefore, the system automatically selects the **Multiple items** indicator.

2. Click the **Materials** button to view the screen showing the material list view of the process order ❷. On this screen, the co-products are automatically reflected by the relevant checkboxes as well as by the fact that the quantities of both the product (main product = item 0000) and the co-product are shown in the negative. In a process order without a co-product, a main material isn't shown in the material list. The positive quantities are the consumption quantities of materials in the process order.

3. Click the **Release** icon ❸ and save by pressing Ctrl + S or clicking the **Save** icon. The system will generate a process order number.

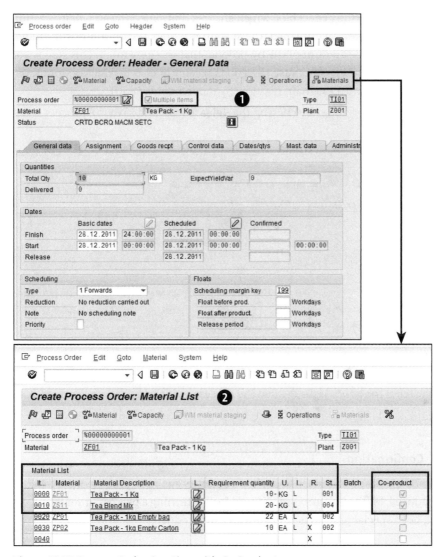

Figure 19.17 Process Order Creation with Co-Product

By-Product

For by-products, follow the same process to get to the screen shown in Figure 19.17. Then, follow these steps:

1. Click the **Materials** icon, shown in Figure 19.17 ❶, which takes you to the screen shown in Figure 19.18. For a by-product, the system shows just a negative quantity.

2. Select the **Backflushing** checkbox, which ensures that, when the actual production of the process order is confirmed, the system provides the option of simultaneously recording the amount of the by-product that was generated. This step is not required for co-products because the goods receipt of a co-product is simultaneously performed with the main material by movement type 101.

3. Release the process order by clicking the **Release** icon and save the process order by pressing $\boxed{\text{Ctrl}}$ + $\boxed{\text{S}}$.

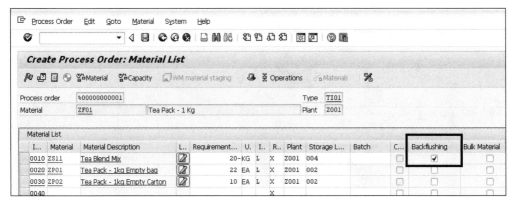

Figure 19.18 Material List with By-Product and Backflushing Selected

The next step is the goods issue against the process order, which we covered in Chapter 18.

19.4.4   Confirmation

Confirmation is the process used to declare a quantity against a process order that has been produced. No special process is needed for confirming a process order with a co-product, but a special process is needed with a by-product.

Co-Product

To confirm a process order of a main material with a co-product, use Transaction CORK or follow the menu path **Logistics • Production – Process • Process Order • Confirmation • Enter for Order**.

For a material with a co-product, the confirmation process is standard, as shown in Figure 19.19 ❶. For a main material with a by-product, the confirmation process is the same but, because we activated backflushing for the by-product, the details of the backflush entails recording the by-product quantity produced, which we'll cover in the next section.

In the initial screen for process order confirmation, enter the process order number ❶ and press Enter.

Figure 19.19 shows the process order confirmation screen in which you'll enter the quantity of goods produced ❷. For our example, enter a quantity of "10" to show that the yield or production quantity of the process order was 10 units. Save the confirmation by pressing Ctrl + S or clicking the **Save** icon.

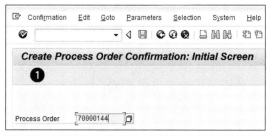

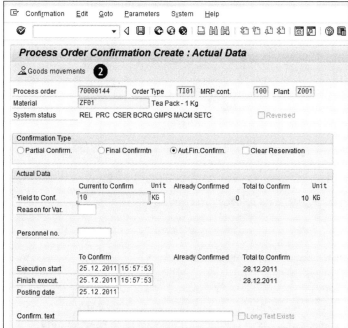

Figure 19.19 Confirmation of Process Order

By-Product

For a process order with a by-product, the process of confirmation is standard. Click the **Goods movements** icon, shown in Figure 19.20 ❶, to go to the **Goods movement** screen of the process order ❷, in which you can enter the quantity of the by-product generated. Also, notice that the by-product is denoted by **Movement Type 531**. Save the confirmation by pressing ⎡Ctrl⎤ + ⎡S⎤ or clicking the **Save** icon.

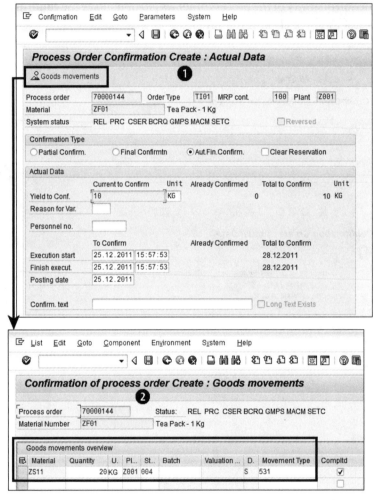

Figure 19.20 Goods Movement of a Process Order with the Backflush Functionality

The goods movement (a goods issue at this stage) is made possible by the backflush functionality. When a process order is confirmed, goods issues (through backflushing) are also performed simultaneously. For a by-product with movement type 531, during the actual confirmation process of the main material ZF01, we are declaring that 20kg of material ZS11 was produced as a by-product.

19.4.5   Goods Receipt

After the goods are produced for a process order, you can perform the goods receipt using Transaction MIGO or by following the menu path **Logistics • Materials Management • Inventory Management • Goods Movement • Goods Movement**, as shown in Figure 19.21. After this point, the process differs between the co-product and the by-product, which we'll discuss in the following sections.

Co-Product

For process orders with co-products, both the materials (the main material as well as the co-product) will be available for goods receipt. Just as with the main product, co-products are also received with movement type 101, as shown in Figure 19.21, whereas by-products are received via movement type 531, shown earlier in Figure 19.20.

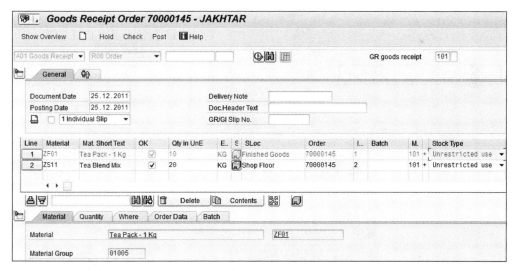

Figure 19.21 Goods Receipt for a Process Order with a Co-Product

Figure 19.21 shows the screen in which you'll perform the goods receipt for a process order. Enter the process order number and save by pressing $\boxed{\texttt{Ctrl}}$ + $\boxed{\texttt{S}}$ or clicking the **Save** icon.

By-Product

Earlier in Section 19.4.4, we showed you how to use the backflush functionality to record a by-product during the process order confirmation process. However, an alternative would be to record the by-product for a process order. You can use this option if you don't want to avoid the backflush functionality, or you realize some additional by-product quantity needs to be recorded for a process order.

You'll open the same screen shown in earlier Figure 19.21. As shown in Figure 19.22, select **Goods Receipt** and **Other** and then assign movement type 531. Now, you'll need to enter the component numbers along with quantities, which are declared as by-products, followed by the process order number. In this way, you can also receive by-products for a process order (if the backflush functionality in the process order confirmation isn't activated). Let's look at this process in detail, as an alternative option to declaring by-products as they are produced.

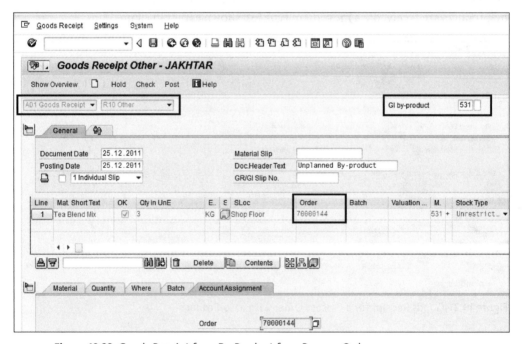

Figure 19.22 Goods Receipt for a By-Product for a Process Order

Save by pressing [Ctrl] + [S] or clicking the **Save** icon to generate a material document. A material document captures all of the details of the goods movement.

19.4.6   Documented Goods Movement

A documented goods movement against a process order is a list of all of the goods movements that have taken place, including goods issuance and goods receipts, along with any goods receipt of a co-product or a by-product.

Each goods movement is denoted by the material document number along with the quantity and value. To view the documented goods movement of a process order, use Transaction COR3 or follow the menu path **Logistics • Production – Process • Process Order • Process Order • Display**. Enter the process order number and press (Enter). On the **Display process order** screen, follow the menu path **Goto • Lists • Documented Goods Movement**, as shown in Figure 19.23 ❶.

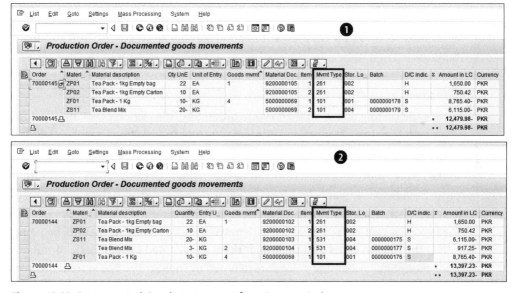

Figure 19.23 Documented Goods Movement for a Process Order

Co-Product

Figure 19.23 shows a list of quantities as well as the amount of goods receipt and goods issuance against a process order. The relevant movement types are also shown as well as whether the movement is a debit entry (S) or a credit entry (H).

By-Product

Figure 19.23 ❷ shows a list of documented goods movements in which a by-product was generated. A by-product received is denoted by movement type 531. The goods receipt of the finished good is denoted by movement type 101. The goods issuance of raw materials against a process order is denoted by movement type 261.

19.4.7 Cost Analysis

Now, let's look at how to perform an overall cost analysis either a co-product or a by-product in contrast to an itemized view of planned versus actual costs of a process order.

Because production planning (PP) completely integrates with product costing, all planned costs are calculated at the time of the process order is created and released, including the cost of a main material with a co-product or by-product. These planned costs are then updated with actual costs in the process order, when necessary transactional data such as goods issuance, confirmation, and goods receipts are entered. All planned versus actual costs are subsequently available for comparison and analysis purposes.

Co-Product

To view the costing details of the process order, use Transaction COR3 or follow the menu path **Logistics • Production – Process • Process Order • Process Order • Display**. Enter the process order number and press (Enter).

On the display process order screen, follow the menu path **Goto • Costs • Itemization**. Figure 19.24 ❶ shows quantities of the different elements found in the process orders. Activities such as machine or labor are denoted by **E**, while the goods receipt of a finished good (as well as its co-product) is denoted by **A**. Components that will be issued against the process order and their quantities are denoted by **M**. Finally, simulated goods receipt quantities and values are denoted by indicator **H**. The system includes an option to provide a financial value of simulated goods receipts (before actual goods receipt has taken place) with the indicator **H**. Thus, when the actual goods receipt (**A**) is undertaken, the values are automatically updated to reflect the difference between the simulated value and actual value.

Figure 19.24 ❷ shows a plan versus actual comparison of financial values against a process order. To view this comparison, follow menu path **Goto • Costs • Analysis** on the **Display Process Order** screen.

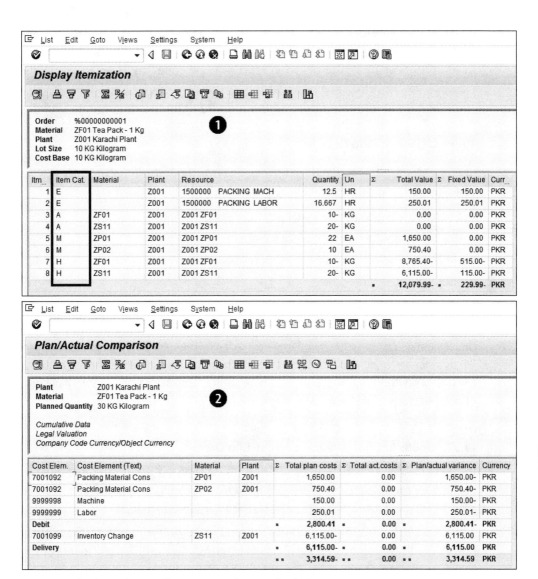

Figure 19.24 Planned Cost of a Process Order: Itemized View

By-Product

All details of planned versus actual values and quantities are automatically updated when you access a process order. You'll see a comparison of target versus actual values as well as quantities against a process order. On the display process order screen, follow menu path **Goto • Costs • Analysis**. The resulting screen shows that semifinished material **ZS11**, which is also the by-product, was generated in **23** units against the planned quantity of **20** units.

19.5   Other Goods Receipts

In some scenarios, a material can't be received by one of the normal procedures. These scenarios include the following:

- Goods with no production order
- Goods that are free (don't require payment)
- Goods receipts for returnable transport packaging
- Automatic goods receipts

In these cases, the goods receipt is treated slightly differently, and the company will have to decide whether and how these goods receipts take place. If a company decides that no goods receipt will take place without a PO, then goods that arrive without a PO number are rejected and not received. However, most companies need material that arrives without appropriate documentation at times, and you should have procedures in place to deal with these anomalies.

19.5.1   Goods Receipt without a Production Order

If your company or client hasn't implemented PP, then the goods receipt of finished goods from production can't reference a production order. In this case, the material must be received into stock using a miscellaneous goods receipt.

A goods receipt of finished goods without production orders uses the same transaction as the initial load of inventory—Transaction MIGO. The difference in this case is that the movement type isn't 561 but can be 521, 523, or 525.

A goods receipt without a production order requires one of the following three movement types:

- **521**

  Goods receipt for finished goods without a production order into unrestricted stock

- **523**

  Goods receipt for finished goods without a production order into quality inspection stock

- **525**

  Goods receipt for finished goods without a production order into blocked stock

19.5.2   Goods Receipt for Free Goods

Occasionally, a delivery from a vendor contains goods for which payment isn't required. These free goods may be promotional items or sample products. Although the materials are free of charge, their quantities and value will be posted to the G/L.

The purchasing department can create a PO for a zero value for free goods if the delivery from the vendor was planned. If a PO is entered into the system, then the goods receipt can be referenced to that PO. If no PO was created, then the goods receipt can be performed using Transaction MIGO but with movement type 511.

19.5.3   Goods Receipt for Returnable Transport Packaging

Packaging material can be very expensive for the vendor to produce, and as a result, the vendor may require packaging be returned for reuse. Returnable transport packaging (RTP) may be as simple as a drum or a tote but can be specific to an item and be costly to produce.

In these instances, packaging can be received into inventory using Transaction MIGO (Other Goods Receipts) but with movement type 511 and the special stock indicator M.

19.5.4   Automatic Goods Receipt

The automatic goods receipt functionality enables a production supervisor to perform goods receipts automatically on recording production confirmation. The automatic goods receipt functionality finds greater usage when several intermediate production steps are involved in the manufacturing process, such as in discrete manufacturing industries or when the business process requires intermediate storage of semifinished or finished goods. You'll need to engage a PP consultant for the necessary configuration required to maintain the control key of operations that allow the option of automatically receiving goods.

In this section, we dealt with a number of goods receipt processes that aren't as common as regular receipts for POs or production orders.

19

19.6   Summary

In this chapter, we discussed the goods receipt process that occurs in a normal manufacturing company. Receiving material is important for keeping the production line operational and to avoid stockouts. As companies move to just-in-time (JIT) operations, goods receipt must be achieved in a timely fashion to keep operations flowing. Understanding the goods receipt process for a PO or a production order is important for MM consultants because this process involves fundamental steps in the movement of materials. Other less common goods receipts are often found at plant sites and should be understood to successfully meet business needs.

Chapter 20 examines the physical inventory functionality. The regular counting of inventory, either by physical inventory or by cycle counting, has become a key element in helping companies ensure accurate and current inventory records.

Chapter 20

Physical Inventory

Regular physical inventories in the plant, combined with improvements in inventory accuracy, can be important goals for companies. Physical inventories can be customized to produce faster and more accurate results as well as lower inventory costs and improve customer service levels.

Performing a physical inventory entails counting what is currently in stock in the plant or storage location, comparing that count to what the SAP inventory system says is in stock, and making any necessary adjustments to make the counts in the system match the physical warehouse.

Some companies perform a full physical inventory only once a year, which is the traditional method. However, many companies need more accurate information more frequently. Many companies with fast-moving stock will perform *cycle counting*, which means that selected parts of the warehouse or specific products will be counted, usually on a more frequent basis.

Physical inventory in SAP system covers all aspects of counting material at the plant, including the yearly inventory, cycle counting, continuous inventory, and inventory sampling. Physical inventory can be performed on stock that is held in unrestricted, quality inspection or blocked stock. Physical inventory also can be performed on the company's own stock and special stocks, such as returnable packaging and consignment stock at customer locations.

Implementation Tip

In Chapter 19, we mentioned that, during an SAP implementation project's go-live phase, initial cutover stock balances are loaded into an SAP system using movement type 561. Sometimes, companies may only recognize *after* go-live that the uploaded stock balances were incorrect or that the initial stock details of some materials were not provided at all for the initial load of data into the SAP system. In both of these scenarios, instead of again uploading remaining stock balances using movement

> type 561, a better approach is to adjust the stock quantities using the physical inventory process. This method will also prevent internal and external audit objections that may arise because auditors expect to see initial stock uploads in the SAP system *only once.*

In the first section of this chapter, we'll discuss the preparatory steps required prior to the actual physical inventory process, before moving on to counting, recounts, and the physical inventory posting. This chapter ends by covering the end-to-end business process of cycle counting method for physical inventory.

20.1   Physical Inventory Methods

The four physical inventory methods available in the SAP system are the following:

- **Periodic inventory**
  All stocks in the company are physically counted on the balance sheet key date. Every material is counted, and the entire storage location is blocked for all types of materials movement and inventory postings during the counting.

- **Continuous inventory**
  Stocks are counted throughout the fiscal year. All materials must be counted at least once a year.

- **Cycle counting**
  Materials are physically counted at regular intervals throughout the fiscal year. Materials can be logically divided into various categories to separate high-value materials from other material and thus impose a more frequent inventory count. After this logical division, each material can be assigned a relevant category that the system then refers to during the physical inventory management process. As cycle counting is the more prevalent method used in most industries, we'll cover how to set up the cycle counting method in Section 20.5.

- **Inventory sampling**
  In this method, materials are selected on a random basis on the balance sheet key date for a physical count. If variances exist between the physical count and the book inventory balances (in the SAP system), the presumption is that the book inventory balances for other materials are also correct.

Figure 20.1 shows an overview of the physical inventory process in SAP system. The process begins by creating a physical inventory document. After physical counting, the inventory count and the differences are posted in the SAP system. As necessary, recounts can be initiated if, after a physical inventory count, the difference with the inventory in the system exceeds the company's defined tolerance. Posting difference transactions create a material and an accounting document.

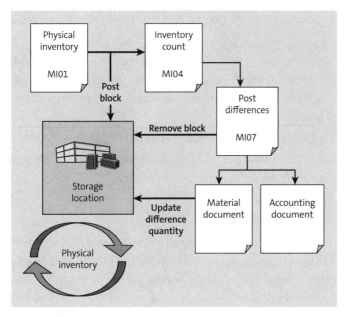

Figure 20.1 Physical Inventory Management Process: An Overview

20.2   Physical Inventory Preparation

Before physical inventory can begin, several operations must be performed to prepare for the count. In complex plants, companies may have to develop counting procedures that use different approaches to counting, such as one method for finished goods and another for raw materials. Deciding what to count is important because counting the wrong materials can waste time and effort.

Companies should weigh the effects of inventory inaccuracies to determine which materials or warehouse sections are more critical than others. Small variances in the stock levels of certain materials may have little or no effect on operations, whereas small inaccuracies in the inventory of critical materials may shut down production. Inventory inaccuracies in finished goods will have a negative effect on customer service if deliveries are delayed or canceled due to lack of inventory.

In the following sections, we'll describe the steps involved in preparing for the actual physical count. The first step is to prepare for the physical count.

20.2.1   Preparations for a Physical Inventory Count

The following procedures should be followed to complete the physical inventory process:

1. Process and post all transactions that will affect inventory counts, such as goods receipts, inventory adjustments, transfer postings, and sales orders that have been filled and shipped. These steps should be followed to keep the inventory transaction history sequenced properly.

2. Put away all the materials that are being counted in the warehouse.

3. Segregate the material stock that has been used to fill sales orders but that hasn't physically left the warehouse from the rest of the warehouse.

4. Stop all stock movements within the warehouse.

5. Stop all transactions in the warehouse.

6. Run a stock-on-hand report for the items you want to count. Transaction MB52 will show you the material in unrestricted, quality inspection, and block quantities for each storage location. This information is a record of the inventory's status before you start the physical inventory count.

20.2.2   Creating the Physical Inventory Count Document

You create physical inventory count sheets using Transaction MI01 or by following the navigation path **Logistics • Materials Management • Physical Inventory • Physical Inventory Document • Create**. In the following sections, we'll describe some of the important fields on the screen.

Posting Block

You can set the posting block on the physical inventory count document during creation, as shown in Figure 20.2. Because often a delay exists between a material movement and the posting of the movement, discrepancies may arise between the physical warehouse stock and the book inventory. To remove discrepancies during the physical inventory count, you should set the **Posting Block** indicator on the initial screen of the count document. The posting block is automatically removed when the counting results are posted for the physical inventory count.

Some text fields, such as the **Phys. inventory no.** and **Phys. Inventory Ref.**, are available for an inventory controller to maintain additional details about the physical inventory process. Details maintained in these fields are then available in the header details of the physical count document. The same details will also be available in reporting.

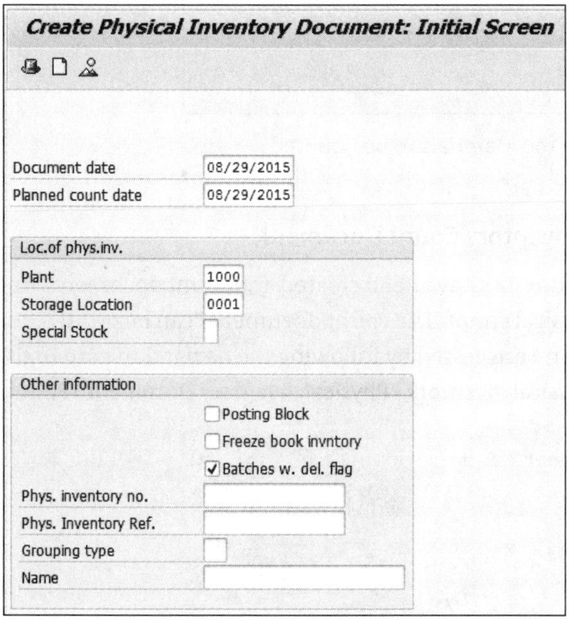

Figure 20.2 Creating a Physical Inventory Count Document

Freeze Book Inventory

If an inventory count hasn't been completed, the book inventory balance can be frozen in the physical inventory document with the **Freeze book invntory** indicator. This option prevents the book inventory balance from being updated by any goods movements, which could lead to incorrect inventory differences.

Including Deleted Batches

The **Batches w. del. flag** option allows the count document to include batches of a material that have been flagged for deletion. To ensure these batches are included in the count, the indicator must be set on the initial entry screen. The material to be counted is added line by line for the count document, as shown in Figure 20.3. These line items won't show a quantity of current stock.

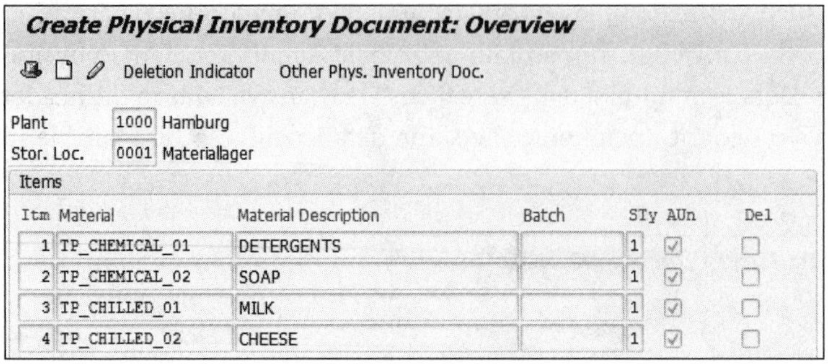

Figure 20.3 Detail Screen Showing the Materials to Be Counted

20.2.3   Printing the Physical Inventory Count Document

After the physical inventory documents have been created, the count documents can be printed out for the actual physical count. The count documents can be printed out using Transaction MI21, which can be accessed by following the navigation path **Logistics • Materials Management • Physical Inventory • Physical Inventory Document • Print**.

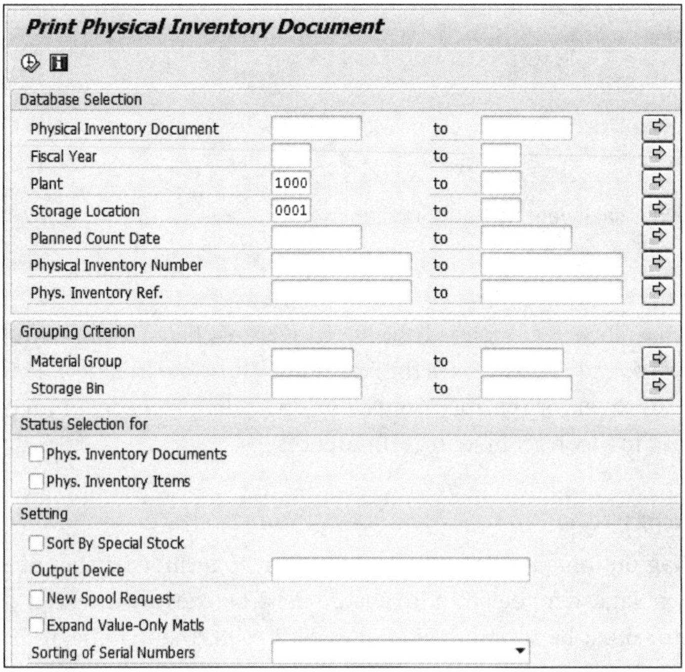

Figure 20.4 Selection Screen for Transaction MI21

Selection criteria can be entered to determine which count documents should be printed our; for example, Figure 20.4 shows selection criteria including **Planned Count Date**, **Plant**, **Storage Location**, and **Physical Inventory Document** numbers. After the selection has been determined, the count documents can be printed out.

Figure 20.5 shows an example of a printed physical inventory count sheet. The physical count document is given to the person who will count the materials in the physical area of the plant described on the document. The line items on the count document show the materials to be counted, and the person performing the count will write the quantity they counted on the document.

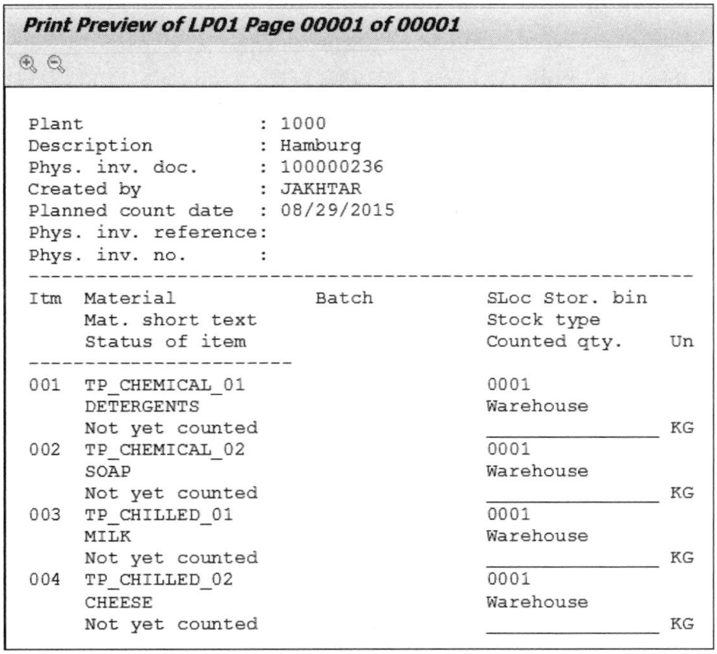

```
Print Preview of LP01 Page 00001 of 00001

Plant                  : 1000
Description            : Hamburg
Phys. inv. doc.        : 100000236
Created by             : JAKHTAR
Planned count date     : 08/29/2015
Phys. inv. reference:
Phys. inv. no.         :
----------------------------------------------------------
Itm  Material              Batch           SLoc Stor. bin
     Mat. short text                       Stock type
     Status of item                        Counted qty.     Un
-----------------------
001  TP_CHEMICAL_01                        0001
     DETERGENTS                            Warehouse
     Not yet counted                       ______________   KG
002  TP_CHEMICAL_02                        0001
     SOAP                                  Warehouse
     Not yet counted                       ______________   KG
003  TP_CHILLED_01                         0001
     MILK                                  Warehouse
     Not yet counted                       ______________   KG
004  TP_CHILLED_02                         0001
     CHEESE                                Warehouse
     Not yet counted                       ______________   KG
```

Figure 20.5 Example of a Printed Physical Inventory Count Sheet

In the next section, we'll examine how the completed count documents are entered into the system and what happens if a recount is required.

20.3 Counting and Recounts

After the physical inventory count sheets are printed out, they can be distributed to the personnel allocated for the counting process, and the count can begin.

With more emphasis on the accuracy of material counts, many companies now only use highly trained employees to count materials accurately.

Companies with the high inventory accuracy believe that giving employees direct responsibility for counting inventory and resolving discrepancies will significantly improve the physical inventory process. In this section, we'll cover entering the count, the difference list, how to reconcile missing material, and recounts.

20.3.1   Entering the Count

After the count has been completed, the physical count must be entered into the SAP system. The count quantities from the count sheets are transferred to their respective physical inventory documents. An inventory user can use Transaction MIO4 or follow the navigation path **Logistics • Materials Management • Physical Inventory • Inventory Count • Enter**.

An inventory user transfers the quantity from the inventory count sheet into the line item in Transaction MIO4, as shown in Figure 20.6.

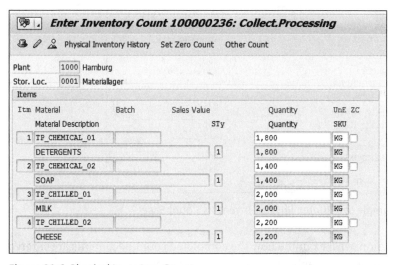

Figure 20.6 Physical Inventory Count

After the inventory count has been entered, the transaction is posted. The posting releases the posting block, if one had been placed on the physical inventory document. The count can be posted, and the physical count has been completed at that point.

If an inventory user made an error when entering the count document, they can use Transaction MI05 to change the physical count. An inventory user must know the physical count document number to perform this transaction. After changes have been made, the count can be posted if an inventory user or the supervisor is satisfied.

20.3.2   Difference List

The count can be compared against the book inventory by using Transaction MI20. This transaction allows an inventory user to enter a material and the physical inventory document. The transaction can be accessed by following the navigation path **Logistics • Materials Management • Physical Inventory • Difference • Difference List**.

After the **Plant** and **Physical Inventory Document** number in the example have been entered, the report can be executed. The resulting report shows the materials relevant to the selection, as shown in Figure 20.7.

List of Inventory Differences

I◀ ◀ ▶ ▶I 🔍 🖨 🥡 📑 📑 🖗 ∑ 🅘 🔁   Post Difference   Change Count   Enter Count   List of Unposted Docs

PhysInvDoc	Item	Material	Batch	Plnt	SLoc	Book quantity	Qty Counted	Difference qty	BUn
☐ 100000236	1	TP_CHEMICAL_01		1000	0001	1,040.000	1,800.000	760.000	KG
☐ 100000236	2	TP_CHEMICAL_02		1000	0001	10,000.000	1,400.000	8,600.000-	KG
☐ 100000236	3	TP_CHILLED_01		1000	0001	10,000.000	2,000.000	8,000.000-	KG
☐ 100000236	4	TP_CHILLED_02		1000	0001	10,000.000	2,200.000	7,800.000-	KG

Figure 20.7 Differences List for Physical Inventory Documents

The report, shown in Figure 20.7, identifies the book quantity (**Book quantity**), the counted quantity (**Qty Counted**), and the difference (**Difference qty**), if any. After the differences have been identified, the count can be repeated to check the differences, or the differences can be posted when approved by management.

20.3.3   Missing Material

Management must decide how to resolve inventory differences. The physical inventory procedures within SAP system show where material discrepancies occur, but management must decide how to find the missing material. Many companies have designed an auditing process to aid the physical inventory process in investigating the discrepancies. In many instances, an adjustment is made to the book quantity of the missing product, and then an offsetting adjustment is made days later when the material is found. In any case, missing materials cause additional work, disrupt the production schedule, and may lead to excess inventory of this material.

Some companies create *variance locations* to move lost and found material to and from, as a way of showing the variances without creating adjustments. A variance location must be closely monitored, and an ongoing procedure for finding the material discrepancies is important.

20.3.4   Recounts

If management doesn't accept the discrepancy, or the discrepancy is above a certain tolerance, then those materials need to be recounted. A recount allows users to recount the material in the location on the physical inventory document. Transaction MI11 (Recount Physical Inventory Document) can be found by following the navigation path **Logistics • Materials Management • Physical Inventory • Physical Inventory Document • Recount**.

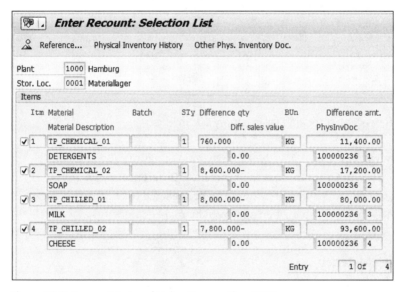

Figure 20.8 Recount Entered Using Transaction MI04

The recount transaction allows an inventory user to enter the physical count document number and view the detail lines. The detail information, shown in Figure 20.8, shows the materials relevant to the count document as well as the physical count quantity and the difference from the book quantity.

After the recount document has been printed out, a recount can be performed. When the recount is complete, new material quantities can be entered into Transaction MIO4. At this point, the count can be posted from Transaction MIO4 or through Transaction MIO7.

In the next section, we'll review the processes involved after the recount process is complete and discuss the process of posting the count document.

20.4   Physical Inventory Posting

The count and recount process results in a document that includes a final inventory figure for each counted material. This figure is the best and most accurate total produced by visually counting the material in the plant.

After the supervisor organizing the count approves the document, the count document can be posted in the SAP system.

20.4.1   Posting the Count Document

After a count has been entered, the document can be posted using Transaction MIO7, which can be found by following the navigation path **Logistics • Materials Management • Physical Inventory • Difference • Post**.

The physical document number must be entered, along with the posting date and the threshold value, which is an optional field that holds the maximum amount to which inventory differences are allowed for the inventory document.

The detail lines of the count document, shown in Figure 20.9, identify the difference quantity (**Difference qty**) and the difference value (**Diff. Sales Value**). For example, as shown in Figure 20.9, line item 1 shows that **Material TP_Chemical_01** has been counted, and the quantity counted is **760** pieces greater than the book quantity. The difference in value is also shown, in this case, $11,400. An inventory user can post the differences unless the difference value is greater than the threshold value, assuming a threshold value had been entered.

20

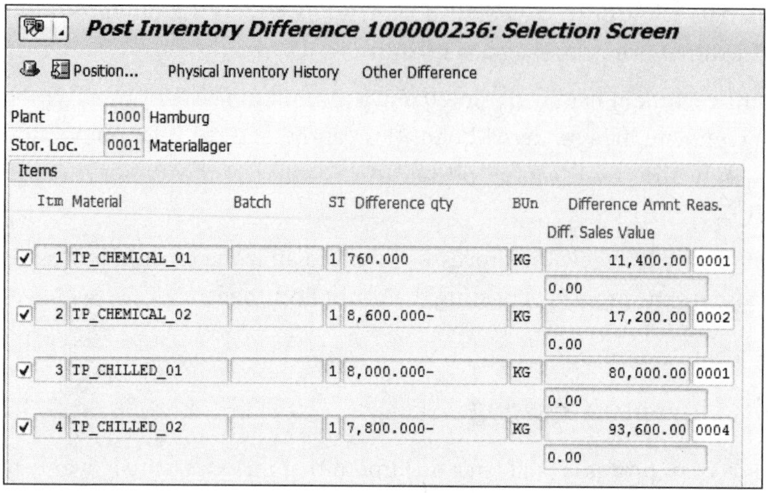

Figure 20.9 Detail Lines for Recount Document before Posting in Transaction MI07

Configuration Tip

You can define the limits or tolerances of value differences in local currency found during the physical inventory process at the following two levels:

- Maximum amount per physical inventory document
- Maximum amount per document item

Follow the configuration menu path **Materials Management • Inventory Management and Physical Inventory • Physical Inventory • Define Tolerances for Physical Inventory Differences**.

For each line item on the count document, the user posts the difference and a reason code to clearly show why the count doesn't correspond with the book quantity. Reason codes can be configured for each movement type required using Transaction OMBS or by following the navigation path **Materials Management • Inventory Management and Physical Inventory • Physical Inventory • Record Reason for Goods Movement**. The internal movement type used for posting inventory differences is movement type 701.

Figure 20.10 shows the configuration for the **Reason for Movement** used for identifying differences posted in the physical inventory documents. As shown in Figure 20.10, a number of common reasons have been configured for movement type **701**, including **Incorrect Barcode**, **Incorrect RFID**, **Incorrect Labeling**, and so on.

During an SAP implementation project, the MM consultant should ask the company to list out all the possible reasons they may have for posting material quantity differences during the physical inventory process. The consultant then configures these reasons and makes them available in the SAP system.

Tips & Tricks

In the same configuration menu path, you can control whether maintaining a reason for a movement is mandatory or optional during the physical inventory adjustment process (posting inventory differences).

Change View "Reason for Movement": Overview

M...	Movement Type Text	Reason	Reason for Movement	
701	GR phys.inv.: whse	1	Wrngly plcd in stor.	
701	GR phys.inv.: whse	4	Incorrect Barcode	
701	GR phys.inv.: whse	5	Incorrect RFID	
701	GR phys.inv.: whse	6	Incorrect Labeling	
702	GI phys.inv.: whse	2	Poor quality	
702	GI phys.inv.: whse	3	Damaged	
703	GR phys.inv: QI	1	Wrngly plcd in stor.	
704	GI phys.inv: QI	2	Poor quality	
704	GI phys.inv: QI	3	Damaged	
707	GR phys.inv.:blocked	1	Wrngly plcd in stor.	
708	GI phys.inv.:blocked	2	Poor quality	
708	GI phys.inv.:blocked	3	Damaged	

Figure 20.10 Configuration of Reason Codes for Physical Inventory Goods Movements

20.4.2   Posting a Count without a Document

If a count is made without a physical count document, the count can be entered directly into a transaction and then be immediately posted, as shown in Figure 20.11. On this screen, the required basic information has been entered to post a count's **Count date**, **Plant**, and **Storage Location**. Transaction MI10 can be accessed by following the navigation path **Logistics • Materials Management • Physical Inventory • Difference • Enter w/o Document Reference**.

An inventory user can add individual line items that have been counted and enter the amount for each line item. If a **Variance** in percentage was entered on the initial screen, then the user will be warned if the amount entered is greater than the allowed variance.

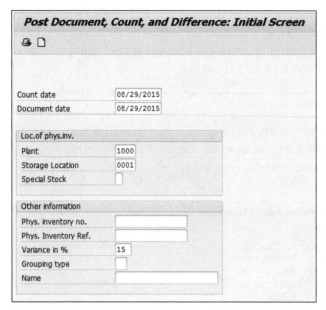

Figure 20.11 Entry Screen for Transaction MI10

After the material line items are entered, as shown in Figure 20.12, the document can be posted, and the values from the document will become the book quantity for those materials. The stock quantities for the materials can be checked using Transaction MMBE or Transaction MB52.

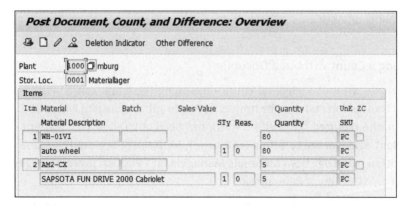

Figure 20.12 Counted Material Line Items for Transaction MI10

20.4.3   Accounting of Inventory Differences

When inventory differences are posted, the total stock is automatically adjusted to the counted quantity on the document. When the document is posted, the differences will correspond to either a goods receipt or goods issue.

If the counted quantity is smaller than the book inventory, the stock account is credited with the value of the inventory difference. The accounting entry is posted to the expense from physical inventory account. Subsequently, if the counted quantity is greater than the inventory balance, the stock account is debited with the value of the inventory difference. The accounting entry is posted to the income from the physical inventory account.

Configuration Tip

If your company also uses warehouse management (WM) functionality in SAP S/4HANA, SAP Extended Warehouse Management (SAP EWM), or embedded SAP EWM in SAP S/4HANA, then you can have SAP S/4HANA automatically create physical inventory documents on goods movement. This capability is especially helpful when inventory differences are posted in WM or SAP EWM as a part of the physical inventory process and must also be reflected in SAP S/4HANA in the form of physical inventory documents.

To set up the automatic creation of physical inventory documents for goods movements, use Transaction OMCC or follow the configuration menu path **Materials Management • Inventory Management and Physical Inventory • Goods Issue/Transfer Postings • Generate Physical Inventory Documents for Goods Movements**. On the screen that appears, first click the **Plant** button and ensure that the relevant plant has the **Trans./Event Type** as **WV**.

Go back and this time, click the **Movement type** button and select the **Generate phy.inv.doc** checkbox on all relevant movement types for which the system should automatically create a physical document on goods movements.

In this section, we discussed the posting of the physical count document used in counting material in the warehouse. However, in Section 20.4.2, in some instances, a physical count can be entered without a count document. Check with the supervisor of physical counts to work out policies for physical counts and determine whether counts without documentation can be posted.

Let's now cover the configuration basics and associated business processes for physical inventory, especially the most prevalent physical inventory method—cycle counting.

20.5   Cycle Counting Method of Physical Inventory

As explained earlier in Section 20.1, in the cycle counting method, materials are logically divided into various categories to separate high-value or high-consumption materials from others and thus require more frequent inventory counts. After this logical division, each material is assigned a relevant category in the SAP system.

In the following sections, we'll cover the necessary configuration steps, the master data, and the business processes associated with the cycle counting method of physical inventory process.

20.5.1   Configuration Basics

To configure the cycle counting indicator and its frequency, use Transaction OMCO or follow the configuration menu path **Materials Management • Inventory Management and Physical Inventory • Physical Inventory • Cycle Counting**.

Figure 20.13 shows the plant-level indicators for cycle counting of physical inventory (**CC Phys. Inv. Ind.**). Each indicator denotes the time interval at which physical inventory must be carried out for a material. The *float time* defines (in days) how much deviation is allowed between the planned physical inventory process and actual count.

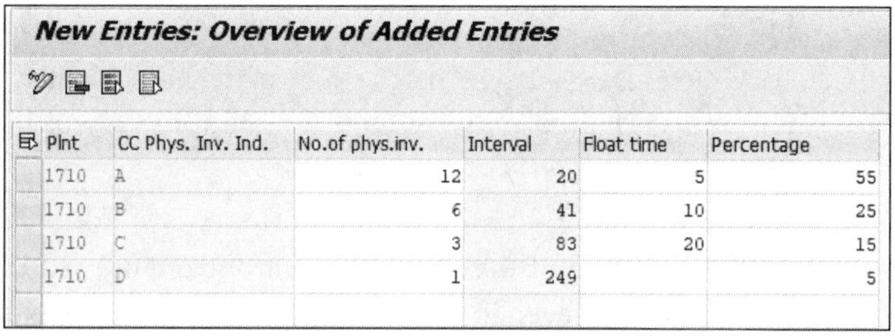

Plnt	CC Phys. Inv. Ind.	No.of phys.inv.	Interval	Float time	Percentage
1710	A	12	20	5	55
1710	B	6	41	10	25
1710	C	3	83	20	15
1710	D	1	249		5

New Entries: Overview of Added Entries

Figure 20.13 Configuration of Cycle Counting Indicators for Physical Inventory

For example, for a cycle count with indicator **A**, the **Float time** is defined as 5 days. So, if the physical inventory is slated or planned to take place on May 1 but didn't happened until May 6, then irrespective of the category, the system will automatically mark this material for physical count in the next cycle counting run. The **Percentage** column denotes the split of materials according to various consumption categories and must be always equal to 100. For example, if 200 materials are slated for a cycle count, then the first five materials with an **A** category defined in their respective material masters and with the highest consumption values will represent a 55%.

Figure 20.14 shows the assignment of the **A** indicator in the field **CC Phys. Inv. Ind.** to the material **EWMS4-502** for the **Plant 1710** in the **Plant data/stor. 1** tab. Notice the configuration undertaken in the previous step in the dropdown list shown on the right-hand side of the screen. Selecting the **CC fixed** indicator will disable the system from automatically changing the cycle counting indicator during ABC analysis. This indicator should only be selected if the cycle counting inventory indicator must remain the same regardless of its requirement or consumption values.

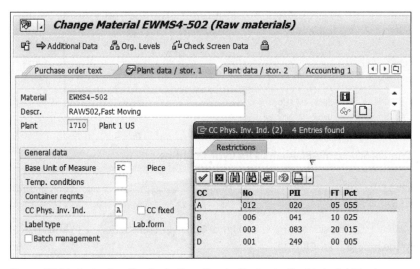

Figure 20.14 Assigning the Cycle Counting Indicator in the Material Master

20.5.2   Business Processes

During cycle counting, an ABC analysis is performed to analyze a material's requirements, such as its planned independent requirements (PIRs), sales orders, and dependent requirements, as well as requirements from stock transport orders for interplant transfers. An alternate ABC analysis can be based on the consumption values of materials during a specific period.

Access the screen shown Figure 20.15 either via Transaction MIBC or through the menu path **Logistics • Materials Management • Physical Inventory • Special Procedures • Cycle Counting • Set Cycle-Counting Indicator**. On the initial screen, enter the selection parameters as shown and choose the **Consumption/Usage** radio button for a given period. Click **Execute** or press F8.

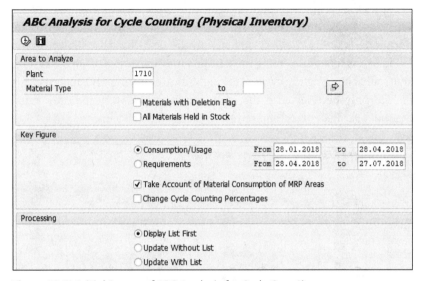

Figure 20.15 Initial Screen of ABC Analysis for Cycle Counting

---

Tips & Tricks

You can also access the screen shown in Figure 20.15 via Transaction SE38 and then executing the program RMCBIN00.

Figure 20.16 shows that that material **EWS4-502** and another material **38** are slated for cycle counting. Notice the column **%** denotes the percentage splits we previously configured.

Note

To create a physical inventory document automatically, use Transaction MICN or execute the program RM07ICN1 using Transaction SE38. This program automatically checks the due dates for inventories for all cycle counting materials.

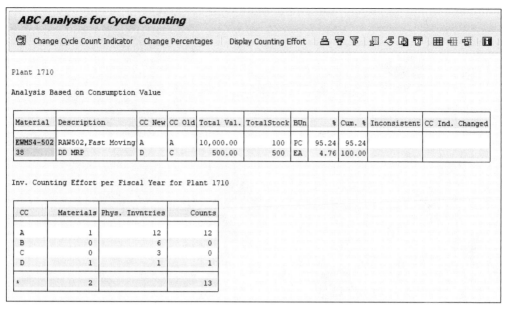

Figure 20.16 ABC Analysis for Cycle Counting

20.6   Summary

In this chapter, we explained various aspects of performing a physical inventory in the traditional manner, with counts and recounts. We also discussed the less conventional method of entering counts directly into the system without physical inventory count sheets. Physical inventory is an important part of inventory management despite being a simple process to follow.

If the physical inventory isn't accurate, and errors are made, then others parts of the business are affected. Therefore, you should investigate all potential count differences to ensure that the count is accurate and that the difference isn't just due to a counting error. The physical inventory process could also provide insights into theft, which a company must address to reduce the loss of inventory value.

In the next chapter, we'll discuss invoice verification, which produces a number of touchpoints with financials (FI).

20

Chapter 21
Invoice Verification

Invoice verification is the process through which vendors are paid for materials delivered. The procedure can involve a three-way matching process between the company's purchase order, the goods received note, and the vendor's invoice.

Invoice verification is part of the accounts payable (AP) process where vendors are paid for materials or services they've provided to the customer. Invoice verification is important to both vendors and customers because this process ensures that the quantities and the pricing are all correct and that neither party has made an error. The standard method of invoice verification is the three-way match. In this chapter, we'll describe this process as well as evaluated receipt settlement (ERS), which is a two-way match between the purchase order (PO and the delivery note, whereby a vendor is paid without an invoice being sent to the customer.

Let's discuss the two types of invoice verification: purchase order-based invoice verification and goods receipt-based invoice verification:

- **PO-based invoice verification**
  In PO-based invoice verification, the system allows invoices to post with reference to a PO, even though goods haven't yet been delivered. The line items of the PO are copied into the invoice posting screen at the time of invoice verification. The invoice can be posted both before and after the delivery of goods. This scenario is usually used in the imports procurement process where the vendor often needs to be paid in advance against an invoice before the goods are actually delivered.

> **Note**
>
> A PO's line item details are shown on the **Invoice** tab. This tab includes the **GR-Based Invoice Verification** indicator, which should be deselected for PO-based invoice verification.

- **Goods receipt-based invoice verification**

  In this scenario, the SAP system allows you to post invoices only after the goods receipt has been posted in the system. Invoices are matched with the received quantity of a PO. For multiple deliveries, the system provides each delivery on a separate line.

In the first section of this chapter, we'll discuss the traditional process for invoice verification, using a three-way match. Then, we'll go on to discuss ERS, document parking, price or quantity variances found while processing invoices, setting up tolerance limits to control variances, blocking invoices, and releasing invoices. More invoice verification business processes, such as down payments, retention money, invoice reduction, subsequent credit and debit processing, credit memos, and taxes will also be covered.

21.1 Standard Three-Way Match

This method uses the PO supplied to the vendor, the goods receipt or delivery note supplied by the vendor, and the invoice sent to the company from the vendor. In a successful three-way match, the quantity and price of all three documents will match, and the payment to the vendor will be sent via check or bank transfer at a date agreed to by both parties. In this section, we'll describe the process of entering an invoice, simulating the posting, and preforming the actual posting.

21.1.1 Entering an Invoice

The receipt of an invoice at the AP department triggers the invoice verification process. The invoice can either be a fax or a hard copy invoice or communicated via electronic data interchange (EDI). An invoice can be entered into the system using Transaction MIRO or by following the navigation path **Logistics • Materials Management • Logistics Invoice Verification • Document Entry • Enter Invoice**. The initial entry screen for Transaction MIRO is shown in Figure 21.1.

Most companies still use the traditional three-way match to process invoices and pay vendors. However, as more efficiency is being sought in the supply chain to reduce costs, other techniques are being introduced. Figure 21.1 shows a typical screen layout in Transaction MIRO. The following list explains the most important fields in this transaction:

- **Hold**

  Click this button when you have insufficient information for posting the invoice but want to save the partially entered data. Held invoices can be posted later when entering the missing information.

- **Simulate**

  Before posting an invoice, you can check the different general ledger (G/L) account postings using the **Simulate** button.

- **Messages**

  Click this button to see the information, warning, or error messages issued by the system.

- **Transaction**

  In this field, you can select one of the four options available from the dropdown list: **Invoice, Credit Memo, Subsequent Debit**, and **Subsequent Credit**. Based on the selected option, the screen layout will change.

- **Balance**

  This field shows the balance between the PO value and the invoice value and is for display only.

- **Basic Data**

  This tab contains several fields, such as **Invoice date, Posting Date**, and **Amount**.

- **Invoice date**

  The date is printed on the invoice, while the **Posting Date** is the date on which you want to post the invoice, and the **Amount** is the amount mentioned in the vendor invoice (a mandatory field). You can also enter references and tax amounts in their respective fields. If you select the **Calculate tax** checkbox, the system calculates taxes based on the selected tax code.

- **PO reference**

  Under this tab, from the leftmost dropdown list, you can select the PO to which an incoming invoice should refer. The options include **Purchase Order/Scheduling Agreement, Delivery Note, Bill of Lading**, and **Service Entry Sheet**.

- **Layout**

  Also located under the **PO Reference** tab, you can select a layout from the **Layout** dropdown list. The layout plays a vital role for invoice reduction because the system will display the fields based on the layout.

The invoice entry screen requires a user enter the details from the incoming invoice. A completed Transaction MIRO screen is shown in Figure 21.1. The PO number

21

4500000002 was entered for the invoice, which shows a total amount 15,500.00 USD as well as the quantity (100 PC) of material ordered and delivered. Click on the **Details** tab, and the screen shown in Figure 21.2 will appear.

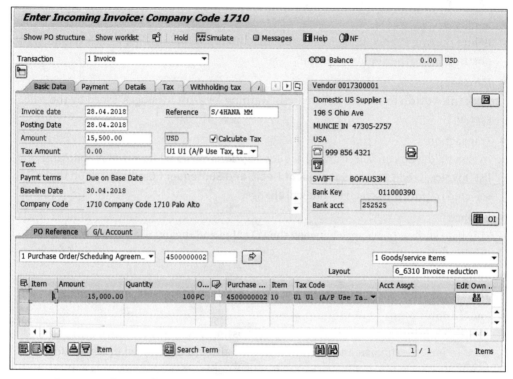

Figure 21.1 The Initial Transaction MIRO Screen

Figure 21.2 shows some more details from the invoice. An unplanned delivery cost (**Unpl. Del. Csts**) of 500.00 USD was entered to account for the transportation and materials handling charges that the vendor invoiced to the company for payment.

Report RMMR1MDC

Report RMMR1MDC (using Transaction SE38) is available within the invoice verification process and enables the automatic settlement of planned delivery costs. To invoke the report, use Transaction MRDC or follow the navigation path **Logistics • Materials Management • Logistics Invoice Verification • Automatic Settlement • Automatic Delivery Cost Settlement**.

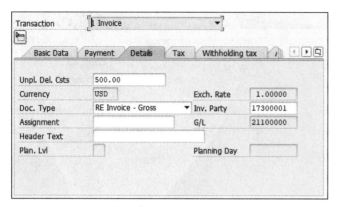

Figure 21.2 Details Tab to Enter an Unplanned Delivery Cost

Display List of Invoice Documents

Invoice verification includes Report RMMR1MDI (Display List of Invoice Documents), which does exactly what its name suggests and can be executed using Transaction SE38. New to the existing Transaction MIR6 (Invoice Overview), extended selection criteria and display options are now available. For example, on the initial screen, you can make selections by one-time vendors, gross invoice amounts, and entry dates. In the output list, the report shows both posted and held invoices.

21.1.2   Simulating a Posting

After a PO's details have been transferred to the invoice, and if a user believes the invoice can be posted, the user can test the posting of the invoice by simulating the posting by accessing the header menu and selecting **Invoice Document • Simulate Document**.

A simulation is a trial posting. Even if the invoice can be posted, the simulation won't actually post the invoice. If the simulation process can't post an invoice, a message will be posted to a message log. The message log shows errors and warnings. The messages indicate what issues are preventing the posting. In this case, errors can be due to tax codes, amount inconsistencies, and the tax jurisdiction.

Figure 21.3 shows the accounting entries from the invoice simulation process.

Click **Post** to post the invoice, and the system will create an invoice document number, which in our example is 510000001.

21

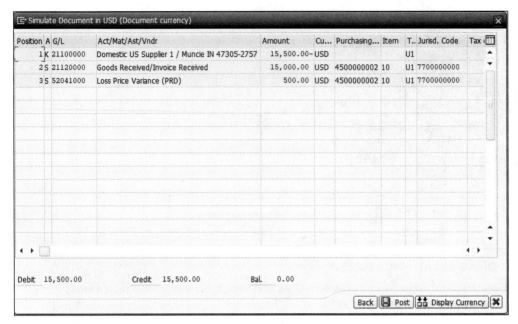

Figure 21.3 Invoice Simulation

21.1.3   Invoice Posting

After the message log has been cleared, nothing can prevent the invoice items from being posted. When the posting is complete, the information is passed through to the payment process in financials (FI). The payment process updates G/L accounts relevant to the posted document.

> **Prepayment of Vendors**
>
> In an SAP system, you can prepay vendors within the invoice verification function, for example, to pay highly favored vendors in advance. The function enables payment after issue of the invoice and full exploitation of the date of required payment and existing cash discounts, by posting the vendor liabilities, taxes, and cash discounts in FI in advance. The system executes the payment of the invoice regardless of the relevant goods receipt and the outcome of the invoice verification check.
>
> When the system posts an invoice, some standard checks are also executed. If the system already posted a prepayment document, you can only make restricted changes to the header fields of the invoice.

To execute the payment program, use Transaction F110 or follow the navigation path **Accounting • Financial Accounting • Accounts Payable • Periodic Processing • Payments**.

To schedule the payment's processing, you'll use the Schedule Manager via Transaction SCMA. The Schedule Manager can run a number of periodic tasks to be executed on a regular basis, for example, daily, weekly, or monthly. Most companies process invoices on a daily or a weekly basis.

21.1.4 Invoice Parking

Document parking allows you to enter the invoice but not to post it. An invoice document can be defined as parked. An invoice should be parked if it isn't ready for posting, which can happen for a number of reasons. For example, the invoice may need changes to ensure successful posting, or the balance of the invoice may not equal zero. The main reason that documents are parked and not simply placed on hold is that the invoice in a parked status can be modified, whereas an invoice that is just held remains in its current state.

An invoice can be parked using Transaction MIR7 or by following the navigation path **Logistics • Materials Management • Logistics Invoice Verification • Document Entry • Park Invoice**.

Transaction MIR7 is similar to Transaction MIRO for entering an invoice. The main difference is that, when you're parking an invoice, the document doesn't need to be correct or to balance equal to zero because the invoice isn't going to be posted. The document is parked and can be modified as needed.

After entering information into Transaction MIR7, if you decide that the invoice doesn't need to be parked or that all of the information needed to post the invoice is now entered, the invoice can be posted. You can select **Invoice Document • Save as Completed** or press $\boxed{\texttt{Ctrl}}$ + $\boxed{\texttt{F8}}$.

21.2 Duplicate Invoice Check

In some situations, a vendor might mistakenly send an invoice twice, resulting in duplicate invoices being posted in the SAP system. For this scenario, the SAP system provides the duplicate invoice check functionality, which prevents incoming invoices from being accidentally entered and paid more than once.

To set up this functionality, follow the menu path **Materials Management • Logistics Invoice Verification • Incoming Invoice • Set Check for Duplicate Invoices**. For each company code, select whether to activate or deactivate the check criteria for the company code, reference document number, and invoice date. The system will check for duplicate invoices only using the selected criteria. For example, if you've selected **Check reference** for a company code, then posting two invoices in the same company code with the same reference number will result in a "Duplicate Invoices Found" message.

In the next section, we'll discuss one use of invoice verification processes, evaluated receipt settlement (ERS).

21.3 Evaluated Receipt Settlement

ERS is the process whereby the goods receipt and the PO are matched and posted without any invoice—in other words, a two-way match. The vendor doesn't send an invoice for materials defined for evaluated settlement. This process isn't standard to most companies because the evaluated receipt settlement process requires a significant level of cooperation and trust in a vendor. However, this method can be particularly beneficial to companies that purchase materials between different parts of the organization. The evaluated receipt process reduces the need for sending and matching invoices between departments.

The benefits of ERS include the following:

- No quantity or price variances with invoices
- Purchasing process completed sooner
- Vendors paid on receipt of goods
- Favorable material prices from vendor

Let's now cover how to set up and run the ERS process in the SAP system. We'll cover the master data setup required as well as the ERS business process.

21.3.1 Master Data

In the master data, first, you'll need to set two indicators in the business partner (Transaction BP). As shown in Figure 21.4, choose the **FLVN01 (Supplier)** from **Display in BP role** dropdown list for BP **17300034**. Next, click on the **Purchasing** icon located on the top-right. In the **Purchasing Data** tab in the lower half of the screen, select the

GR-Based Inv. Verif. checkbox. Scroll down the same screen and select the **AutoEval-GRSetmt Del.** checkbox to activate ERS.

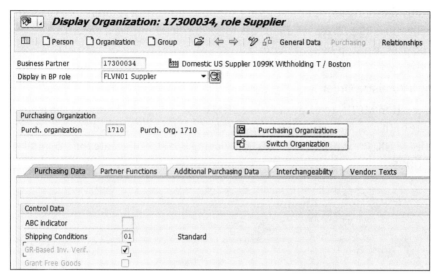

Figure 21.4 Goods Receipt-Based Invoice Verification in a Business Partner

In the second master data step for ERS, in the purchasing information record, shown in Figure 21.5, use Transaction ME11 (or Transaction ME12 for changes) to ensure that the **GR-Bsd IV** checkbox has been selected. Make sure the **No ERS** checkbox is deselected.

Figure 21.5 Goods Receipt-Based Invoice Verification in a Purchasing Information Record

21.3.2 Business Processes in ERS

The ERS business process starts with creating a PO for which the ERS will be activated followed by receiving some or all of the expected goods with reference to the same PO. Finally, the ERS process is run. In the following sections, we'll cover these business processes in a step-by-step manner.

Creating a Purchase Order

Use Transaction ME21N to create a PO for BP 17300034. Figure 21.6 shows the **Invoice** tab, where both checkboxes—**GR-Bsd IV** and **ERS**—have been selected. Create a PO for a quantity of 100 PC and a price of 100 USD. Saving the PO will create the PO number 4500000005.

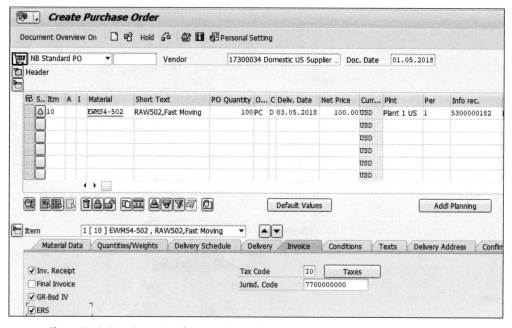

Figure 21.6 Creating a Purchase Order with ERS and Goods Receipt-Based Invoice Verification

Performing a Goods Receipt

Use Transaction MIGO for a goods receipt for 50 PC (partial receipt of goods) on PO number 4500000005, as shown in Figure 21.7. The PO is now ready for ERS processing.

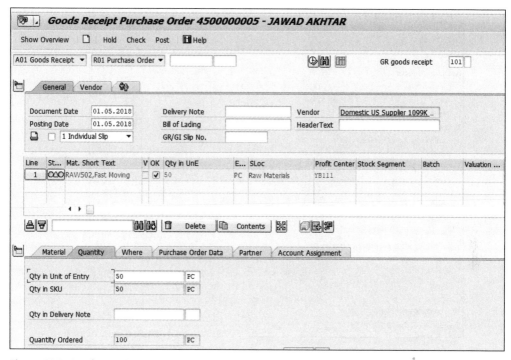

Figure 21.7 Goods Receipt

Running the Evaluated Receipt Settlement

The ERS process can be scheduled or run on an ad hoc basis. Transaction MRRL can be found by following the navigation path **Logistics • Materials Management • Logistics Invoice Verification • Automatic Settlement • Evaluated Receipt Settlement**.

The selection screen, as shown in Figure 21.8, allows a user to restrict the program to a certain **Plant**, **Vendor**, or a date range. After the selection has been made, the program can be executed. As shown in Figure 21.8, a selection has been made to restrict processing to one particular vendor, **17300034**, and to perform a test run by selecting the **Test Run** indicator. This indicator was subsequently unselected at the time the ERS process is run.

> **Tips & Tricks**
>
> We always recommend using the **Test Run** option first to test for any errors or issues that may arise during the ERS process.

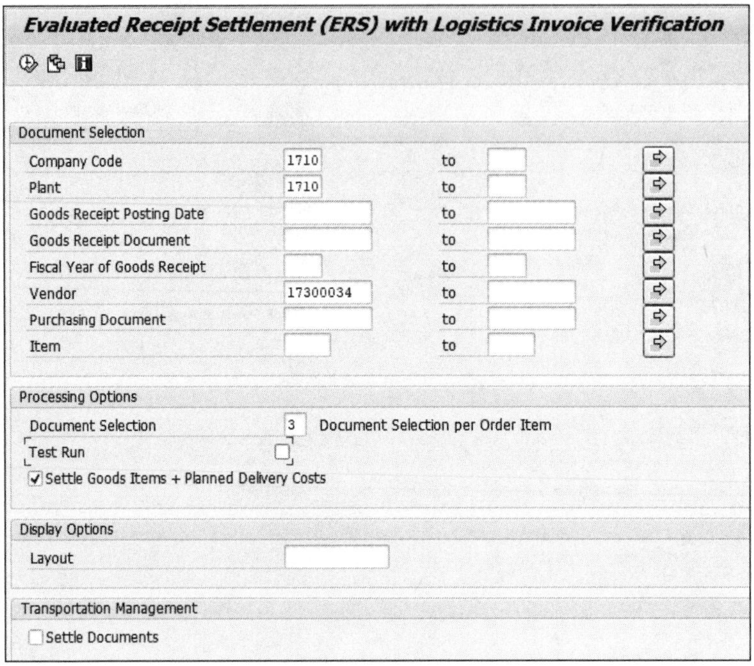

Evaluated Receipt Settlement (ERS) with Logistics Invoice Verification

Document Selection

Company Code	1710	to	
Plant	1710	to	
Goods Receipt Posting Date		to	
Goods Receipt Document		to	
Fiscal Year of Goods Receipt		to	
Vendor	17300034	to	
Purchasing Document		to	
Item		to	

Processing Options

Document Selection   3   Document Selection per Order Item

☐ Test Run

☑ Settle Goods Items + Planned Delivery Costs

Display Options

Layout

Transportation Management

☐ Settle Documents

Figure 21.8 ERS with Logistics Invoice Verification

Figure 21.9 shows the ERS with the logistics invoice verification (LIV) worklist wherein an **X** in the **ERS-Pstable** (postable) column denotes an invoice that can be created using the ERS process. If an invoice posting error arises in ERS, the system will show the relevant error, which must be first corrected for system to create the invoice. Thus, a "test run" of ERS will enable the business user to address potential errors that may otherwise prevent successful invoice posting via ERS.

To create an invoice via ERS, select the line item and simply save.

Evaluated Receipt Settlement (ERS) with Logistics Invoice Verification

	ERS-Pstable	Vendor	Reference Document	Fisc.yr.ref.doc	Item	Purchasing Document	Item	Reference	Doc. No.	Year	InfoText	FI Doc.
	X	17300034	5000000056	2018	1	4500000005	10					

Figure 21.9 ERS Worklist

Figure 21.10 now shows the columns **Inv. Doc.** No. 5100000004 and the associated **Accounting Document** 5100000003.

Figure 21.10 ERS with Invoice Document Number Posted

Configuration Tip

During the ERS process, if you encounter error message M8 446, you can change the attributes of the message by following the configuration menu path **Materials Management • Logistic Invoice Verification • Define Attributes of Systems Messages • Invoice Verification: Customer-Specific Message Categories**.

Note

To create invoices automatically, you can define ERS as a batch job. Use Transaction SE38 with program RMMR1MRS to schedule a batch job and the required variant. The system will automatically pick up the deliveries due to ERS and post the invoices.

21.4   Credit Memos and Reversals

Credit memos are used to adjust the amounts owed to a vendor. Credit memos differ from subsequent debits/credits, which don't change the invoiced quantity but only post the amounts. Companies use credit memos when an invoice is posted for more than the received quantity. With a credit memo, the invoiced quantity is updated.

For example, let's say a vendor has sent your company an invoice for a larger quantity of material than was delivered, and this invoice ended up getting posted to the system. In this scenario, a vendor credit memo is posted with reference to the PO for the excess quantity. The credit memo updates the G/L accounts and the PO history.

Credit memos are also used during the reversal (cancelation) of an invoice. In an SAP system, canceling an invoice isn't possible, but invoices can be reversed by posting a credit memo. Credit memos will update the same G/L accounts (with opposite debit/credit entries) that the invoice originally posted to.

Let's move on to discussing how to post a credit memo in the system.

21

Credit memos are posted via Transaction MIRO. Select **Credit memo** from the **Transaction** dropdown list and enter the PO number and **Posting Date**. The system will propose the total invoiced quantity and amount from the PO. With partial reversals, you can change the quantity and amount.

An invoice and a credit memo can also be used to cancel each other out. For example, if you've posted an incorrect credit memo and you want to reverse (cancel) it, you'll need to post an invoice document by using Transaction MIRO with reference to the PO.

21.5 Taxes in Invoice Verification

Most invoices are taxable, which means that you'll need to verify that taxes can be entered for value-added tax (VAT) amounts according to various tax procedures. During the purchase and sale of goods, taxes are calculated and paid to the vendor or charged to customers, respectively. For VAT, tax is calculated based on the difference between the purchase price and the sales price. The tax amounts collected from customers are paid to tax authorities.

When posting an invoice in the system, you can select the tax code and enter a tax amount. Alternatively, if you want the system to calculate the tax amount, select the **Calculate tax** checkbox in the invoice transaction screen (Transaction MIRO). The system will calculate the tax based on the tax code defined for each line item. Tax codes can be configured in the system for various types of taxes.

Tax codes and tax procedures are configured by the person responsible for financial accounting (SAP S/4HANA Finance). MM allows you to maintain default values for tax codes by following the menu path **Materials Management • Logistics Invoice Verification • Incoming Invoice • Maintain Default Values for Tax Codes**.

In this step, you'll define the default tax codes for each company code. Click on the **New Entries** button and enter the company code, the default tax code, and the default tax code for unplanned delivery costs.

21.6 Goods Receipt/Invoice Receipt Account Maintenance

A goods receipt/invoice receipt (GR/IR) account is an intermediate account used for clearing goods receipts and invoices. A GR/IR clearing account is cleared for a PO item when the delivered quantity and the invoiced quantity are the same. When quantities are different between a goods receipt and the invoice receipt for a PO a balance will be posted on the GR/IR account.

- If an invoice quantity is more than the quantity delivered, a balance amount appears on the GR/IR account, and the system expects additional goods receipts.

- If the goods receipt quantity is more than the invoiced quantity, a balance amount appears on the GR/IR account, and the system expects additional invoice postings.

If no additional goods invoice receipts are expected, you must manually clear the GR/IR account. For example, let's say 100 pieces of a material at $100 each have been delivered, as requested in the PO. However, an invoice was posted for only 80 pieces, and no additional invoices are expected from the vendor. The quantity difference of 20 pieces results in a balance of $2,000 in the GR/IR account. When you clear the GR/IR account with the GR/IR account maintenance transaction, the system will create an accounting document and clear the GR/IR difference of $2,000.

You can clear a GR/IR account via Transaction MR11. On the screen that appears, enter selection criteria and execute the transaction. If you selected the **Prepare List** processing option, you'll see a list of the POs causing the balance in the GR/IR account. This list displays the PO number, line item number, quantity difference, value difference, and so on. Select the appropriate line and click on the **Post** button to clear the difference in the GR/IR account, as shown in Figure 21.11.

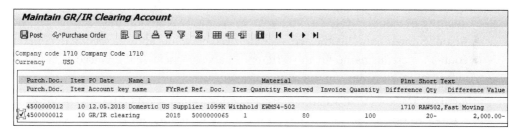

Figure 21.11 GR/IR Clearing Account

Now, the GR/IR clearing document is updated in the PO history. If GR/IR account maintenance has been executed for a PO item, the account maintenance document is displayed in a separate transaction in the PO history.

If an unexpected goods receipt or invoice receipt for the PO item occurs after account maintenance (the GR/IR clearing process), you can cancel the account maintenance document using Transaction MR11SHOW or by following the menu path **Logistics •**

Materials Management • Logistics Invoice Verification • GR/IR Account Maintenance • Display/Cancel Account Maintenance Document.

Enter the document number and press ⌈Enter⌋. On next screen, click the **Reverse** button and save. A reverse accounting document will be created that will also be updated in the PO history. You can now post the goods receipt or invoice receipt against the PO.

21.7   Invoice Reduction

If the invoice amount sent by a vendor is too high, and you want to post an invoice with the correct amount (which is a reduced amount), you can use the invoice reduction functionality via Transaction MIRO. The system handles this discrepancy by generating a credit memo.

For example, let's say you follow a procedure to post invoices for delivered materials and their quantities. Sometimes, however, you receive invoices for both delivered quantities and pending delivery quantities due to a vendor error. During the invoice posting, the manufacturing company may want to reduce the invoice amount so that the amount doesn't include the undelivered quantity. The SAP system functionality for invoice posting with reduction allows you to post invoices that contain a greater quantity/value due to a vendor error. While posting the invoice, you can reduce the quantity or value. In this case, the system creates two accounting documents: The first document contains the actual quantities and value, and the second document contains a credit memo for the difference between the actual invoiced quantities/ values and the system-suggested quantities/values.

Figure 21.12 shows that, according to the goods receipt for 70PC, the system correctly created an invoice of 7,000 USD (via three-way matching) for the PO 4500000007. From the **Layout** section located in the lower right-hand side of the screen, choose **Invoice Reduction** from the dropdown list. The system will bring up three fields specific to vendor invoice reduction process:

- **Correction ID**
  Field to denote the reason for invoice reduction. Choose **Supplier Error** from the dropdown list.

- **Invoice Amount Acc. To Supplier**
  Field to enter the amount as per the supplier invoice. Enter an amount of 10,000 USD.

- **Invoice Quantity Acc. To Supplier**

  Field to enter the quantity as per the supplier invoice. Enter a quantity of 100 PC.

> **Note**
>
> These three fields are located in the far right-hand side of the screen and require scrolling. These fields are aligned to show them in Figure 21.12. You can set a variant so that these fields appear in such a way that makes data entry easier and faster.

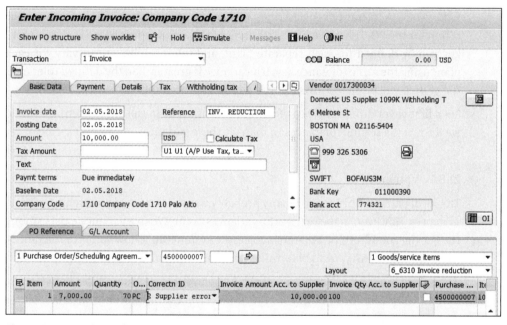

Figure 21.12 Invoice Reduction Process

> **Configuration Tip**
>
> You can also create customized reasons for invoice reduction process by following two steps:
>
> - Activate the business function LOG_MM_CI_1 by using Transaction SFW5.
> - After you activate the business function, you'll get a new customizing option. Follow the menu path **Materials Management • Logistics Invoice Verification • Incoming Invoice • Maintain Reasons for Invoice Reduction**. Create reasons for invoice reduction as required.

Once invoice reduction details are maintained, the system will display a popup message of the reduced invoice amount, at which point you can post the invoice.

In the next section, we'll cover various tolerance limits.

21.8 Tolerance Limits

The system can post an invoice if the variance is within the stated tolerance limits. The different types of tolerances are called *tolerance keys*, which are predefined in SAP system. A tolerance key describes a variance between the invoice and the goods receipt or the PO. Tolerance limits are assigned to each tolerance key. Each tolerance key can be defined for each separate plant, and tolerance limits can vary for each plant using the same tolerance key. If a variance is greater than the defined tolerance, the system will block the invoice from payment processing.

Let's first cover different types of variances that occur in the SAP system, and then we'll cover the setting tolerances to manage these variances.

21.8.1 Variances

The AP department of your company probably wants exact invoice matching with no variances. However, in the real world, variances occur. When a variance exists among the PO, the goods receipt, and the invoice, the system can follow variance tolerances, which you can configure, to determine whether the invoice should be posted or not.

An invoice has a variance if items, such as quantities or values, differ between the invoice and other documents. Four types of variances are associated with invoices:

- **Quantity variance**
  Difference in the quantity delivered and the invoice quantity
- **Price variance**
  Price difference between the PO and the invoice
- **Quantity and price variance**
  Difference in price and quantity
- **Order price quantity variance**
  A variance occurs when an invoice is entered and the matching process finds one of these four scenarios. Setting the tolerance limits on the four variance types can prevent unnecessary invoice blocks.

21.8.2   Tolerance Keys

The standard tolerance keys defined in the SAP system are noted in Table 21.1.

Tolerance Key	Tolerance Key Description
AN	Amount for item without order reference.
AP	Amount for item with order reference.
BD	Form small differences automatically.
BR	Percentage order price quantity unit variance (invoice receipt before goods receipt).
BW	Percentage order price quantity unit variance (goods receipt before invoice receipt).
DQ	Exceed amount: quantity variance.
DW	Quantity variance when goods receipt quantity equals zero.
KW	Variance from condition value.
LA	Amount of blanket purchase order.
LD	Blanket purchase order time limit is exceeded.
PP	Price variance.
PS	Price variance of the estimated price.
ST	Date variance.
VP	Moving average price variance.

Table 21.1 Tolerance Keys for Posting Invoice Differences

To define the tolerance limits, use Transaction OMR6 or follow the navigation path **Materials Management • Logistics Invoice Verification • Invoice Block • Set Tolerance Limits**.

After a tolerance key is defined, tolerance limits can be entered. Set these limits by selecting **Goto • Details**. Figure 21.13 shows the details for each **Company Code/Tolerance key**, including the upper and lower tolerances, which can be configured for both a price value in the specified currency and a percentage value. For example, the tolerances for **Company Code 3000** show that the **Lower Limit** for the tolerance has an **Absolute** variance allowed of 20 USD and a maximum **Percentage** tolerance of 10%.

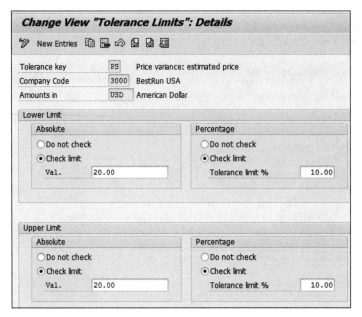

Figure 21.13 Tolerance Details for the Tolerance Key PS

On the **Upper Limit,** the tolerances are the same. Thus, if an invoice is entered for 300 USD but the PO is for 290 USD, the absolute variance is triggered because the variance is 10 USD above the 20 USD tolerance. Refer to Table 21.1 again for an understanding of the available tolerance keys.

If the **Do not check** indicator is selected, the system won't check the invoice for this type of variance.

If a variance is found, the AP department can then block an invoice from being paid. We'll cover how blocking invoices work in Section 21.9.

21.8.3   Supplier-Specific Tolerance

For a particular purchase, the total amount of money on the supplier invoice and the total amount suggested in the system may differ, meaning that their values are different from one another. This variance may occur due to a price difference in any one or more line items. For invoices with more than 100 line items, finding exactly the line items causing the variance can be quite cumbersome. Let's discuss business scenarios where this situation can occur and how the SAP system can deal with such scenarios.

Let's say a vendor is responsible for supplying several components required by an automotive manufacturer. Usually, the POs can contain up to 200 line items, and sometimes, the vendor invoice total amount and the system-suggested total amount don't match. In this scenario, quickly identifying the line item or items responsible for the variance can be time consuming.

Instead, you can post a variance in an invoice without reference to a specific line item. This scenario is called *total-based invoice reduction*. Let's say your business also has another requirement, which can be customized in the system: In the event of a small difference in total amount, the system should accept the vendor invoice and post the difference into a small differences G/L account. The small difference G/L account is a profit and loss (P&L) account type. You can do this in one of two ways:

- Total-based invoice reduction
- Total-based invoice acceptance

In total-based invoice reduction, the system creates two accounting documents: The first contains the invoice posting, and the second contains a credit memo for the difference amount.

For example, let's say the vendor's invoice contains 100 line items for a total amount of $100,500. However, while posting this invoice, the system suggests a total amount of $100,000, a variance of $500. Because 100 line items exist on the invoice, identifying the line item responsible for the difference would be time consuming; therefore, the invoice should be posted using the total-based invoice reduction functionality.

In *total-based invoice acceptance*, the system posts the difference amount into a non-operating expense or revenue account. The process steps in total-based reduction and total-based acceptance are similar to the standard invoice verification process. You post an invoice via Transaction MIRO and enter the invoice amount and PO number. The system will show the difference in the **Balance** field, and if this difference is within the tolerance limits, the status will be green.

The system decides whether to proceed with total-based reduction or total-based acceptance by checking the relevant tolerance limits. If an invoice difference is within the acceptable limits (per the tolerance limit defined in the system), the invoice is posted using the total-based acceptance scenario. If the invoice difference is outside of these limits, the system checks the difference limits for total-based invoice reductions. If the difference is within these limits, the system posts the invoice with total-based reduction. If, however, the difference exceeds these limits, the invoice can't be posted with the difference amount.

In the next section, we'll discuss how to block invoices in SAP system.

21

21.9   Blocking Invoices

When an invoice is blocked, the invoice amount can't be paid to the vendor. An invoice can be blocked in a number of ways:

- Manual block
- Stochastic or random block
- Block due to variance in an invoice amount
- Block due to variance in an invoice item

After an invoice is blocked, all of its individual line items are blocked, which may be problematic when many line items exist but only one line item is causing the variance. At this point, the finance department will need to investigate the variance to unblock the invoice for payment.

Payment won't be released when invoices are blocked for payment. When resolved, the invoice can be released for payment processing. Let's discuss the various options available to either manually block an invoice or to have the SAP system automatically blocking and invoice.

21.9.1   Manual Block

You can set the manual block during the entry of the invoice in Transaction MIRO. The manual block (**Pmnt Block**) field is on the **Payment** screen of the document header, as shown in Figure 21.14. Once set, the entire invoice is blocked for payment.

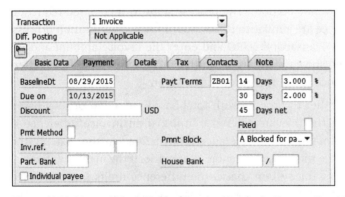

Figure 21.14 Manual Block Field of Invoice Header in Transaction MIRO

You can also set the manual block indicator in the appropriate line item. Doing so, however, won't just block that line item but will block the entire invoice from payment.

Note that the line item will show the blocked indicator (**Man Blk**), but the manual block field won't be changed until after posting.

21.9.2   Stochastic or Random Block

A stochastic or random block allows you to check invoices at random or according to a threshold value defined in configuration. Setting the stochastic block is a two-step configuration activity.

The first configuration step for activating stochastic blocks can be found by following the navigation path **Materials Management • Logistics Invoice Verification • Invoice Block • Stochastic Block • Activate Stochastic Block**.

In the second configuration step, you'll set a threshold for each company code and maintain a percentage that represents the degree of probability the invoice will be checked.

When configuring threshold values and probabilities, you should understand how a stochastic block works. If the total value of the invoice is larger or the same as the configured *threshold value*, the probability of that invoice being blocked is greater.

However, if the total value of the invoice is smaller than the threshold amount, the probability that the invoice will be blocked is calculated proportionally to the *percentage* configured.

For example, let's say you've configures the **Threshold value** for the company code (**CoCd**) 1710 to be $6,000 USD and the **Percentage** to be 50.00%. Each invoice entered over $6,000 USD has a 50% probability of being blocked. If an invoice of $3,000 USD is entered, then this invoice has a 25% chance of being blocked because it's half the value of the **Threshold value**. If the degree of probability should be the same for all invoices regardless of value, the **Threshold value** should be configured to zero.

To configure threshold values for stochastic blocks, follow the navigation path **Materials Management • Logistics Invoice Verification • Invoice Block • Stochastic Block • Set Stochastic Block**.

21.9.3   Block Due to an Amount of an Invoice Item

Sometimes, companies decide to block all invoices that have line items with large values. This safety feature can ensure that vendors aren't paid on invoices that have incorrectly been sent by the vendor or incorrectly entered by finance users, for example, by adding an extra zero.

The first step in configuring this kind of block is to activate the block due to item amount in the IMG. The configuration can be found by following the navigation path **Materials Management • Logistics Invoice Verification • Invoice Block • Item Amount Check • Activate Item Amount Check**.

After the **Check item amount** indicator has been activated for a company code, the detailed configuration of the item amount can commence. The first part of the configuration can be found by following the navigation path **Materials Management • Logistics Invoice Verification • Invoice Block • Item Amount Check • Set Item Amount Check**.

This configuration allows you to determine which invoice line items should be checked by the system. The item amounts for invoice items are checked on the basis of the item category and the **Goods Receipt** indicator, depending on the configuration.

The final step of the configuration is to set the amount at which the invoice is blocked, as shown in Figure 21.15. Using Transaction OMR6, the amount depends on the company code and the tolerance key. As shown in Figure 21.15, for **Company Code 3000**, an **Absolute** upper value has been configured, 10,000.00 USD.

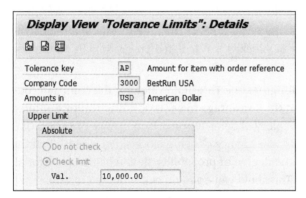

Figure 21.15 Upper Limit Configuration for the Block Due to the Amount of an Invoice Item

21.10 Releasing Blocked Invoices

After an invoice has been blocked, a procedure must be set up to ensure that the invoices can be released when the reason for the block is no longer valid. An entire invoice is blocked even if only one line item is causing the block. Therefore, before an invoice can be paid out for all of the line items, the invoice must be released by canceling the blocking indicator that was set when the invoice was originally posted. The automatic release of blocked invoices deletes all blocks that no longer apply to the invoices the user has selected for review.

To release the invoices automatically, use Transaction MRBR or follow the navigation path **Logistics • Materials Management • Logistics Invoice Verification • Further Processing • Release Blocked Invoices**.

In the parameter selections screen, select any of the following three reasons that lead to invoices being blocked:

- Blocked due to variances
- Manual payment block
- Stochastically blocked

If your AP department decides that it wants to review all invoices before release, then Transaction MRBR allows a user to flag that the release of the invoices must be made manually. In this case, the program will display all of the relevant blocked invoices for the selection criteria you've entered.

The detailed display for the invoices shows the reasons for the blocked invoices and highlights where the block is still in place but no longer valid. A user can then choose to release any invoices manually, as shown in Figure 21.16. In our example, one invoice line can be released. To release an invoice, simply select it and click the release icon (green flag).

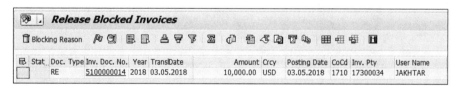

Figure 21.16 Releasing Blocked Invoices Identified by Transaction MRBR

The next two sections cover two functionalities: down payments and retention money.

21.11   Down Payments

A down payment is a type of payment made in advance during the onset of the purchase of goods and services. A down payment typically represents only a percentage of the full purchase price; in some cases, the down payment isn't refundable if the deal falls through. Financing arrangements are made by the purchaser to cover the remaining amount owed to the seller. Making a down payment and then paying the rest of the price through installments is a method that makes expensive assets more affordable in some cases.

For example, let's say a leading heavy-engineering manufacturer is involved in manufacturing boilers, heat exchangers, wind turbines, and so on. Whenever your company wants to buy any specific machinery or plant equipment from this manufacturer, you'll need to make an advance payment (down payment). The remaining balance of the total payment is paid upon the delivery of the goods.

In the following sections, we'll cover how to configure and set up down payments in an SAP system. The only configuration step required is the activation of the business function LOG_MMFI_P2P using Transaction SFW5. You can activate it yourself or engage an SAP NetWeaver consultant.

21.11.1   Creating a Purchase Order with a Down Payment

When down payments are activated, the **Payment Processing** tab appears in the purchase order, not just at the header level but also at the item level. Using down payments at the header or the item level depends whether an overall PO is subject to a down payment (that is, at the header level) or if any specific item within the PO needs a down payment (that is, at the item level).

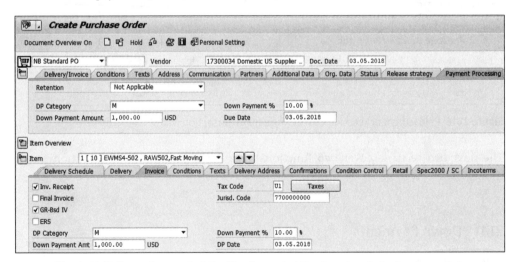

Figure 21.17 Down Payment at the Header and at the Item Level of a Purchase Order

For this example, maintain the down payment details in both the header and the item levels: The **DP Category** is **M**, while the **Down Payment Amount** is **1,000** USD. The **Down Payment** is **10%** of the PO, and the **Due Date** is maintained as **03.05.2018** (May 03, 2018). Save the PO and be sure to release it if a release strategy is in place. In this example, the system creates PO number 4500000009, as shown in Figure 21.17. Also, maintain the same down payment details at the item level of the PO as for the header level of the PO.

21.11.2 Monitoring Down Payments

Access the screen shown in Figure 21.8 using Transaction ME2DP or follow the menu path **Logistics** • **Materials Management** • **Purchasing** • **Purchase Order** • **Reporting** • **Down-Payment Monitoring for PO**. On the initial **Down-Payment Monitoring for PO** screen, click **Execute** or press [F8], and the screen shown in Figure 21.18 will appear.

Figure 21.18 shows the down payment worklist, which contains the PO 4500000009. To initiate the down payment process, choose the line item as shown and then either click on the create icon [ ] or, from the top menu, choose **Goto** • **Create Down Payment** to create a down payment request.

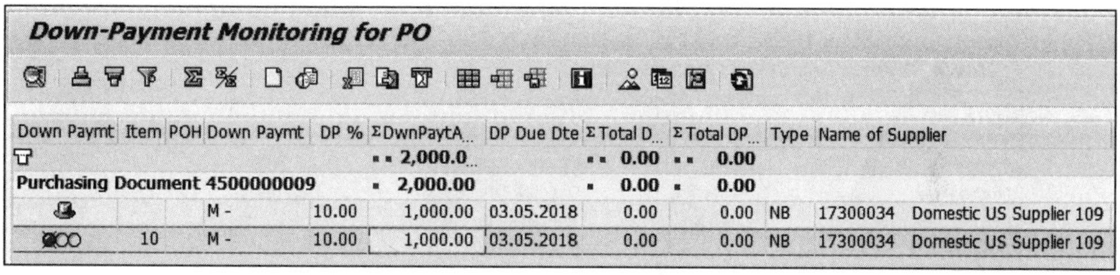

Down-Payment Monitoring for PO

Down Paymt	Item	POH	Down Paymt	DP %	ΣDwnPaytA	DP Due Dte	ΣTotal D..	ΣTotal DP..	Type	Name of Supplier	
					▪▪ 2,000.0..		▪▪ 0.00	▪▪ 0.00			
Purchasing Document 4500000009					▪ 2,000.00		▪ 0.00	▪ 0.00			
		M –	10.00		1,000.00	03.05.2018	0.00	0.00	NB	17300034	Domestic US Supplier 109
	10	M –	10.00		1,000.00	03.05.2018	0.00	0.00	NB	17300034	Domestic US Supplier 109

Figure 21.18 Down Payment Worklist

In the next screen that appears, the system automatically copies all the down payment data, whether from the header level or from the item level. Choose the **Down payment** request radio button and click **Execute**.

Figure 21.19 shows the down payment request for PO 4500000009. Remove the tax code **UI** from the column **Tx** and click **Execute**. The screen shown in Figure 21.20 will appear.

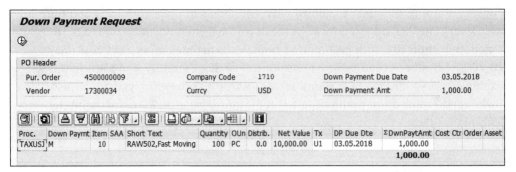

Figure 21.19 Processing Down Payment Request

21.11.3   Creating a Down Payment Request

As shown in Figure 21.20, enter the posting and the document dates, followed by the **Vendor Account**, which in this example is **17300034**. Maintaining the target special G/L indicator (**Trg.Sp.G/A Ind. A**) is also required. Save the document. On the next screen, click on the **DP History** (the multicolor bars icon shown in Figure 21.18) to see the complete details and history of the down payment including the down payment request number that the system created.

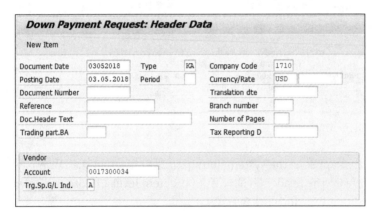

Figure 21.20 Creating a Down Payment Request

21.11.4   Purchase Order with Down Payment History

Access the screen shown in Figure 21.21 via Transaction ME23N and, in the item details of the **Purchase Order History** tab of the PO 4500000009, notice that down payment request 1700000001 has been created.

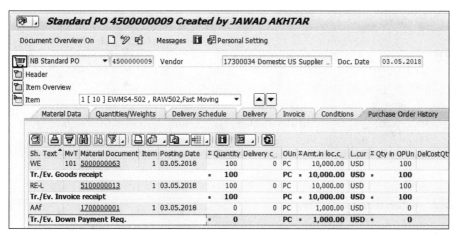

Figure 21.21 Purchase Order History with Down Payment Request

Perform the goods receipt against the PO using the Transaction MIGO and then post an invoice (via Transaction MIRO), as we'll cover in more detail in the next section.

21.11.5 Invoice Verification with Down Payment

In the invoice verification process, using the Transaction MIRO for the PO 4500000009, the system will display a popup informing you that a down payment request exists for that PO, as shown in Figure 21.22.

Figure 21.22 Information Message on a Down Payment during Invoice Verification

---

Tips & Tricks

Since the down payment process integrates with SAP S/4HANA Finance, a good approach might be to engage an FI consultant to check the completeness and correctness of financial entries. The FI consultant can use Transaction F-47 to create a down payment request or use Transaction F-48 to create a down payment directly in the system. The vendor line item display report (Transaction FBL1N) can also bring greater integration confidence between MM and FI.

21.12   Retention Money

Retention money is the part of an invoice amount that is retained until a defined due date, such as the end of a warranty period, to ensure that the delivery of materials or the performance of services fulfills the requirements defined in the contract. You can retain parts of the invoice amount until a specific due date to ensure the fulfillment of the contract when materials are delivered or services performed.

Using retention money functionality entails the following considerations:

- Retention money can't be used together with the prepayment of an invoice.
- An amount split isn't possible for retention.
- If you've activated valuation areas for the Material Ledger, you can't define retentions for PO items with these valuation areas.
- Retention can't be used together with installment payments.
- If multiple account assignments exist, different tax codes can't be used.
- Delivery costs aren't included when retentions are calculated.

As shown earlier in Figure 21.17, the **Retention** field at the header level of a purchase order includes associated options available in a dropdown list. The retention money functionality is also available at the item level of a purchase order.

Note

As with down payment functionality, we suggest engaging an FI consultant to set up and configure the retention money functionality in the SAP system.

To configure retention money, activate the business function `LOG_MMFI_P2P` through Transaction SFW5. To define the default due date for retention and other relevant settings, follow the menu path **Materials Management • Logistics Invoice Verification • Incoming Invoice • Retention • Define Default Due Date for Retention**. You can use the **Date Category** and **Warranty Duration** fields to control the validity period.

21.13 Summary

In this chapter, we described the processes involved in invoice verification. The entry of the invoice is a simple process. However, after the invoice is entered, the AP department must decide whether the invoice is correct and how to proceed if an invoice doesn't match the information in the PO or the goods receipt. Blocking invoices is quite a common occurrence, so understanding how different types of blocks work and why they are in place is important. We also covered other associated invoice verification business processes and scenarios.

In the next chapter, we'll discuss balance sheet valuation. A balance sheet is a financial statement that a company often refers to because it shows a financial snapshot of the company.

21

Chapter 22
Inventory Valuation and Account Assignment

Balance sheet valuation is the calculation of the material value for use in balance sheets. The method employed may depend on country-specific tax regulations, state and federal legal requirements, corporate financial practices, and internal accounting policy procedures.

A *balance sheet* is a financial statement of a business at a specific point in time. The balance sheet reports on the source of funds to a business and how those funds have been used or invested. The use of funds section of the balance sheet includes two areas: fixed assets and working capital. *Fixed assets* are assets that can be depreciated, such as machines and buildings. *Working capital* refers to the funds used to provide the flow of materials and services to achieve sales and to satisfy the customer. Working capital can include two areas: current assets and current liabilities. *Current assets* are cash, payables, receivables, and material in the warehouse. The material includes raw material, work in process, and finished goods. The *stock value* is the lowest cost or the net realizable—or saleable—value.

Whenever a valuated material is received into stock or issued from stock, the value of the total stock is changed and recorded in the financial accounts. This process is called *inventory valuation*. Inventory valuation in the SAP system is carried out based on the standard price or moving average price. In this chapter, you'll see how you can customize the various valuation methods to meet different business scenarios. Before we get into the details of each valuation method and their customization, however, you'll need to understand valuation areas.

A *valuation area* is the organizational level at which materials are valuated, such as at the plant or company code level. When the valuation area is at the plant level, you can valuate a material in different plants at different prices. When the valuation area is at the company code level, the valuation price of a material is the same in all of the plants of the company code.

In this chapter, we'll discuss the major concepts involved in inventory valuation, including valuation procedures, material price changes, and split valuation. We'll also discuss the configuration and business processes of using last in first out (LIFO) valuation, followed by an explanation of first in first out (FIFO) valuation. Finally, we'll cover lowest value determination based on market prices, range of coverage, and movement rate. Let's begin this chapter with split valuation.

22.1   Split Valuation

Split valuation enables you to valuate the substocks (part of the total stock) of a material in different ways. A number of reasons might justify valuating substocks separately, such as:

- The material has different origins (i.e., comes from different countries).
- The material is acquired via different types of procurement (i.e., external procurement versus internal procurement).
- The material has different categories of quality (i.e., damaged, poor quality, or good quality).

Let's say a car manufacturing company procures engine valves from both a domestic vendor and an overseas vendor. Naturally, the vendor prices for the material are different; therefore, the company needs to valuate the stock separately. Similarly, a stainless steel manufacturer will like to valuate its procured raw materials as different grades steel.

Split valuation is used only with the moving average price control, and materials subjected to split valuation can be valuated only via the moving average price method.

In this section, we'll use an example of a stainless steel raw material procured in three different grades: Grade A, Grade B, and Grade C.

The material is designated for split valuation based on the grade of material (steel). Raw material (steel) can be purchased from the same vendor or a different vendor, but the differentiating factor will be the grades of steel procured. While posting the goods receipt, an appropriate valuation type (either Grade A, Grade B, or Grade C) must be selected for each vendor.

With split valuation, you can see the total stock quantity and stock value at plant 1000 as well as the material valuation based on different grades of the material. The stock value of the material procured for Grade A will be slightly lower than Grade B of the same material. The stock quantities and stock values of split-value materials are cumulated at the valuation area (plant) level.

This example introduces two essential concepts in split valuation: valuation category and valuation type.

The *valuation category* indicates whether a material's stock should be valuated as one unit or in parts. This category also a key that indicates the criteria for defining partial stock and determines which valuation type is allowed.

A *valuation type* is a key that identifies split-valuated stocks of a material and indicates the characteristic of a partial stock. The valuation category is assigned in the material master record, and the valuation type is selected during material transactions, such as goods issues and goods receipts.

In the following sections, we'll start by covering the necessary configuration required to set up split valuation, followed by setting up the master data in which the configured split valuation objects are assigned. Business processes, such as, purchase orders and goods receipts, of split-valuated materials will be covered next. The section will conclude with showing a couple of stock reports of split-valuated materials.

22.1.1   Configuration Steps

Configuring split valuation requires the steps we'll describe in the following sections.

Activating a Split Valuation

To activate split valuation, follow the menu path **Material Management • Valuation and Account Assignment • Split Valuation • Activate Split Valuation.**

Allowing split valuation doesn't mean that you must only valuate the material on a split valuation basis. Split valuation is used only when the valuation category is assigned in a material master record.

Configuring a Split Valuation

To configure split valuation, use Transaction OMWC or follow the menu path **Material Management • Valuation and Account Assignment • Split Valuation • Configure Split Valuation**. On the screen that appears, choose **Global Types**. The screen shown in Figure 22.1 will appear.

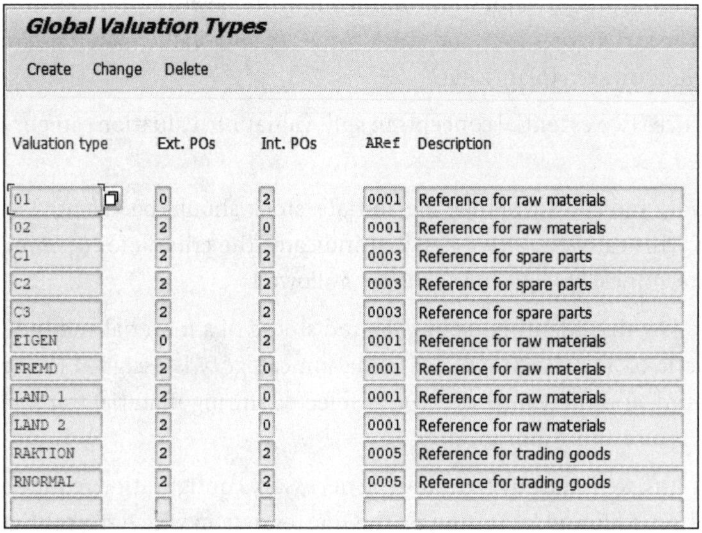

Global Valuation Types

Create   Change   Delete

Valuation type	Ext. POs	Int. POs	ARef	Description
01	0	2	0001	Reference for raw materials
02	2	0	0001	Reference for raw materials
C1	2	2	0003	Reference for spare parts
C2	2	2	0003	Reference for spare parts
C3	2	2	0003	Reference for spare parts
EIGEN	0	2	0001	Reference for raw materials
FREMD	2	0	0001	Reference for raw materials
LAND 1	2	0	0001	Reference for raw materials
LAND 2	2	0	0001	Reference for raw materials
RAKTION	2	2	0005	Reference for trading goods
RNORMAL	2	2	0005	Reference for trading goods

Figure 22.1 Global Valuation Types

In this step, you'll create valuation types and define their attributes, as shown in Figure 22.1. To create a new valuation type, click on the **Create** button and enter the valuation type "Grade A." Define the following attributes:

- **Ext. POs**
  This attribute indicates whether external POs are allowed.

- **Int. POs**
  This attribute indicates whether internal POs (i.e., production orders) are allowed.

- **ARef (account category reference)**
  This attribute is used to group valuation classes. Specify for which account category reference this valuation type is allowed.

Figure 22.2 shows the new valuation type Grade A. Repeat the same steps twice for creating two more valuation types, Grade B and Grade C.

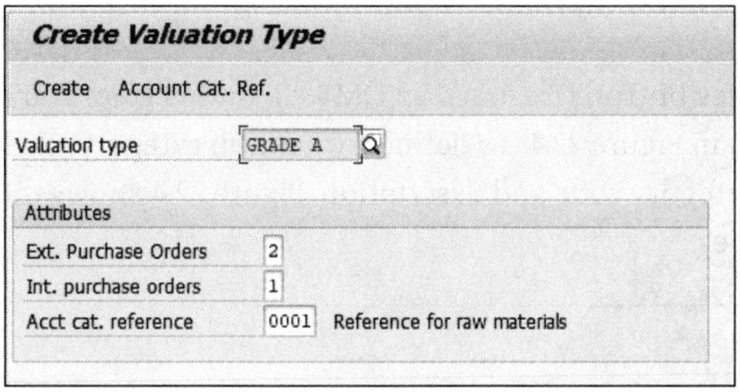

Figure 22.2 Creating a New Valuation Type

Then, as shown in Figure 22.2, click the **Account Cat. Ref.** button so that the screen shown in Figure 22.3 appears. On this screen, the account reference (**ARef**) shows that account category 0001 has several associated valuation classes (**Val. Class**): 0710, 0720, 3000, 3001, 3002, and 3003. Place your cursor in the **ARef 0001** field and click **Choose**, which will assign the newly created valuation type **Grade A** to account reference **0001** (reference for raw materials).

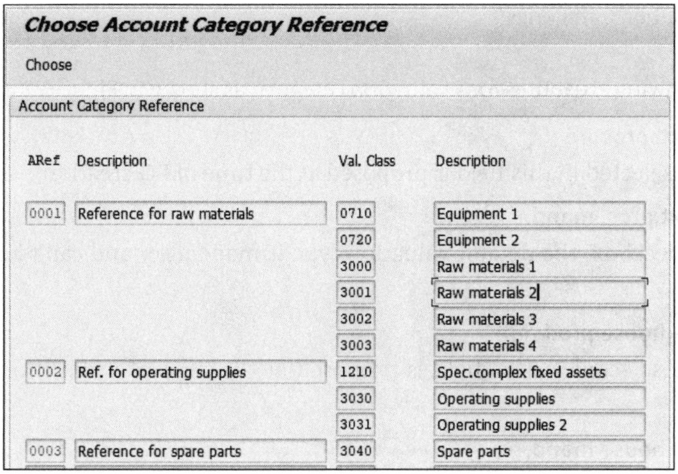

Figure 22.3 Account Category Reference

Repeat the same assignment steps for Grade B and for Grade C. Once completed, you'll see that all three valuation types—**Grade A**, **Grade B**, and **Grade C**—have the account reference (**ARef**) **0001** and appear on the screen shown in Figure 22.2. Save your entries and go back.

Creating Global Categories

Now, click on the **Global Categories** button (Transaction OMWC). In this step, you'll create global categories, as shown in Figure 22.4. To define a valuation category, click on the **Create** button. Enter the category code and description. Figure 22.4 shows the list of available valuation categories.

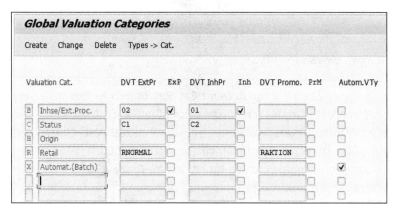

Figure 22.4 Global Valuation Categories

You can define the following attributes for a valuation category, as shown in Figure 22.4:

- **Default: val.type ext. procure**
  The valuation type selected in this field is proposed at the time of PO creation.

- **Default: val.type ext.proc. mand.**
  If you select this checkbox, the default valuation type is mandatory and can't be changed in the PO.

- **Default: val.type in-house prod**
  The valuation type selected in this field is proposed at the time of production order creation.

- **Default: val.type in-house mand.**
  If you select this checkbox, the default valuation type is mandatory and can't be changed in the production order.

- **Determine val. type Automat.**
  If this checkbox is selected, the system will automatically determine the valuation

type at the time of the goods receipt. This indicator is only useful for materials that are managed in batches. A valuation record is automatically created for each batch.

As shown in Figure 22.5, create a new **Valuation Category G** with a short description **Steel Grades**.

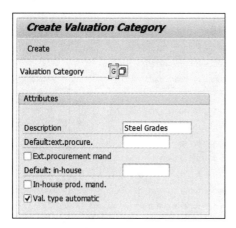

Figure 22.5 Valuation Category

In the next step, you must activate valuation types for the valuation category by clicking on **Types -> Cat.**, as shown in Figure 22.6.

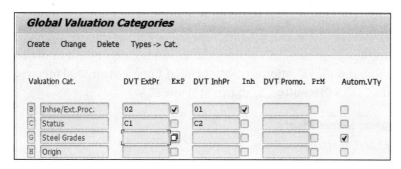

Figure 22.6 Global Valuation Categories

The valuation types **GRADE A, GRADE B**, and **GRADE C** are assigned to the **Valuation Cat. G** (Steel Grades) by clicking on **Activate** button located at the bottom of the screen, as shown in Figure 22.7.

Next, click on the **Cat. -> OUs** button shown in Figure 22.7 so that the screen shown in Figure 22.8 appears.

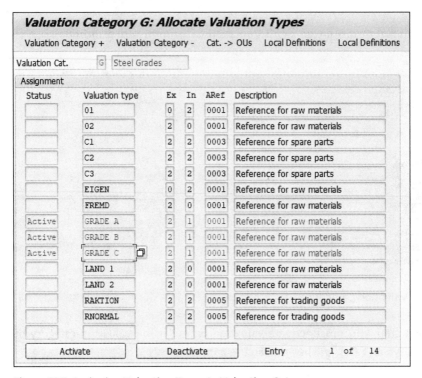

Figure 22.7 Assigning Valuation Types to Valuation Category

Figure 22.8 shows the option to restrict or limit the valuation category and valuation types assignment to specific valuation area(s) or plant(s). Choose **Plant 1000** followed by clicking on the **Cat. -> OUs** button, as shown in Figure 22.8.

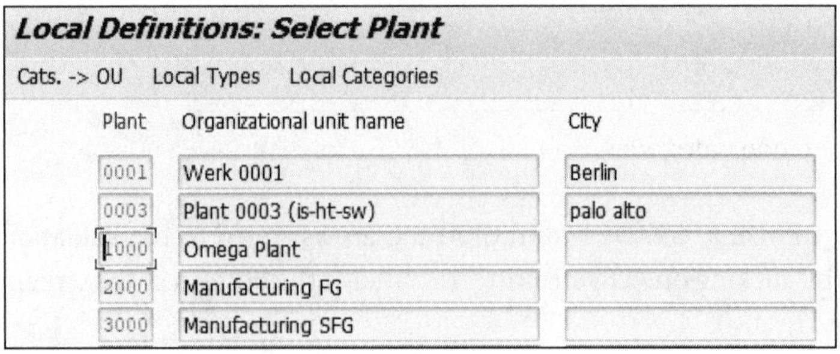

Local Definitions: Select Plant

Cats. -> OU   Local Types   Local Categories

Plant	Organizational unit name	City
0001	Werk 0001	Berlin
0003	Plant 0003 (is-ht-sw)	palo alto
1000	Omega Plant	
2000	Manufacturing FG	
3000	Manufacturing SFG	

Figure 22.8 Local Definitions: Selecting a Plant

Figure 22.9 shows the available valuation categories that can be activated or deactivated. For this example, click on the **Activate** for the **Valuation Category G** (Steel Grades).

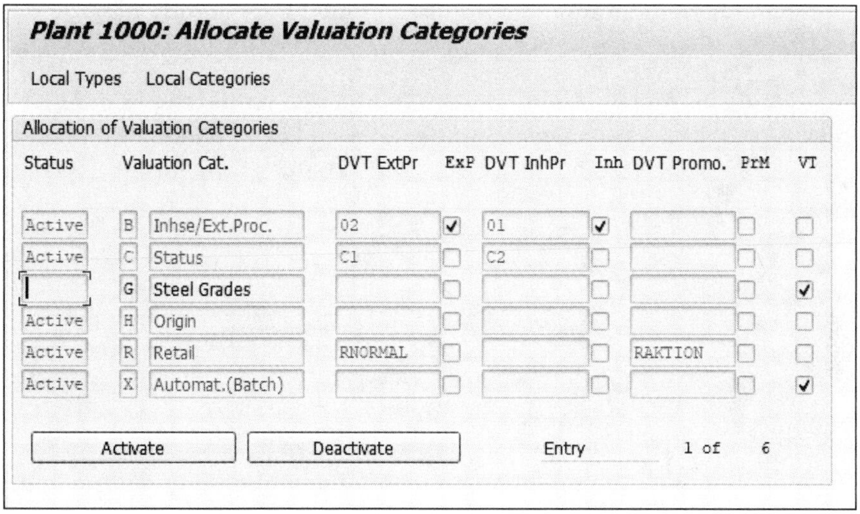

Figure 22.9 Activating a Valuation Category

At this point, we've completed the configuration settings required to set up split valuation. In the next section, we'll now assign the configured objects into master data.

22.1.2   Master Data

To understand how the process of split valuation is carried out in the SAP system, let's begin by assigning a valuation category in the material master record. After the split-valuation configuration is complete, you must assign a valuation category to the material master record in the **Accounting 1** tab (Transaction MM01). You can choose the relevant valuation category from the dropdown list. For example, the newly configured valuation category **G** can now be assigned to the material **10000084** in plant **1000,** as shown in Figure 22.10. Save your entries.

Note that simply assigning the valuation category **G** in the material 10000084 will *not* activate the three valuation types, Grade A, Grade B, and Grade C we configured earlier.

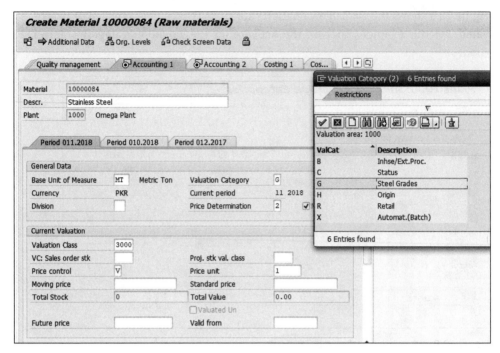

Figure 22.10 Assigning a Valuation Category

Access the screen shown in Figure 22.11 via Transaction MM01, enter the same **Material 10000084**, and click on the **Org. Levels**. In the popup that appears, enter **Plant 1000** followed by the **Valuation type Grade B**. Choose the **Accounting 1** tab from the **Select View(s)** button, which opens the screen shown in Figure 22.12.

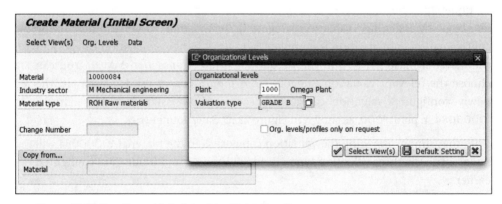

Figure 22.11 Creating a Material with a Valuation Type

Figure 22.12 shows an extension of the material 10000084 but this time shows the **Val. Type GRADE B**. (Compare this figure with Figure 22.10 to see the difference between the two.) You can maintain other details on this screen, such as price control V (moving average) and valuation class. Repeat the same steps to create material 10000084 with valuation types Grade A and Grade C.

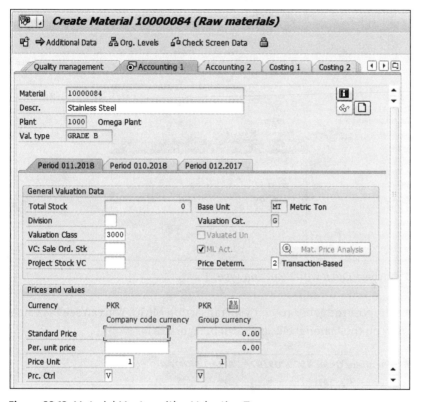

Figure 22.12 Material Master with a Valuation Type

22.1.3 Business Processes

Create a PO via Transaction ME21N and enter the material, quantity, plant, vendor, and other required data, as shown in Figure 22.13. Choose the valuation type on the **Delivery** tab of the PO. You can change the default value and select the required valuation type.

For our example, create two line items in the PO for two grades of steel (Grade A and Grade B) with the purchase price for Grade A being slightly less than Grade B. Save the PO, and the system will create PO number 4500000197.

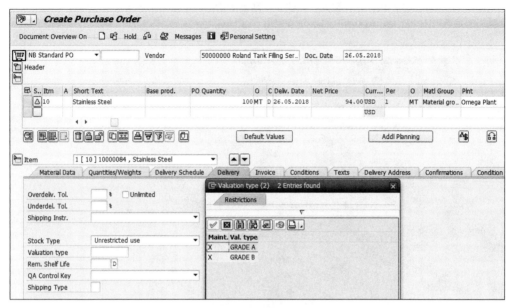

Figure 22.13 Purchase Order with Valuation Type

In the next step, post the goods receipt via Transaction MIGO. You can see the valuation type entry on the **Material** tab, as shown in Figure 22.14.

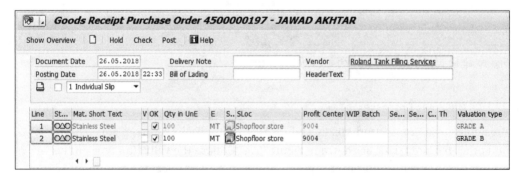

Figure 22.14 Goods Receipt of Two Materials with Different Valuation Types

22.1.4   Reports of Split-Valuated Materials

You can view the valuation price in the material master **Accounting 1** tab via Transaction MM03, which will show you the valuation price at the *plant* level, as shown in Figure 22.15. The stock quantity is the sum of all the quantities of various valuation types (steel grades in this case). The moving price denotes the moving average price of material 100000084 of various valuation types.

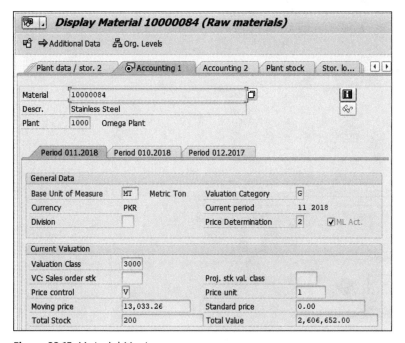

Figure 22.15 Material Master

If you select a valuation type at the organizational level, the system will display the stock valuation for the selected valuation type.

For example, for material 10000084, the value is assigned for split valuation based on steel grades. In the material master record, the stock valuation for a plant will be the total valuation procured, both Grade A and Grade B, as shown in Figure 22.16 ❶ and ❷, respectively. The valuation price for each valuation types is also different in these cases.

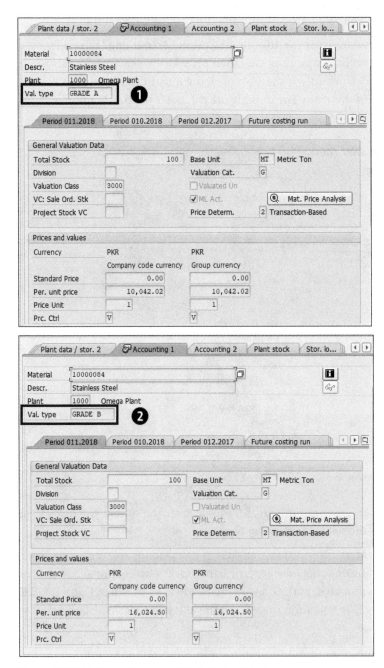

Figure 22.16 Material Masters of Both Valuation Types

Access the screen shown in Figure 22.17 via Transaction MMBE and enter the material 10000084 and plant 1000. You'll see the current stock of split-valuated material 10000084 by their respective grades.

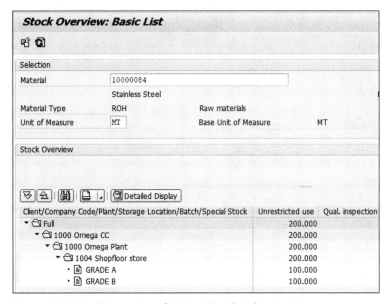

Figure 22.17 Stock Overview of Material with Valuation Types

In this section, we covered split valuation. In the next section, we'll cover account determination procedures in the SAP system.

22.2   Account Determination

Various transactions in MM are relevant for accounting, such as goods receipts, goods issues, and invoice receipts. In such cases, the system always creates an accounting document and posts the amount in the appropriate general ledger (G/L) accounts. G/L accounts are automatically determined with the help of automatic account determination settings. Consider, for example, a manufacturing enterprise that stores stock materials purchased from vendors. Whenever a material is received in a storage location with reference to a PO, the company wants its system to automatically determine and update the stock G/L account. Similarly, whenever an invoice is posted, the system should automatically determine the vendor G/L account and post the liability.

22

The SAP system provides automatic G/L account posting via the automatic account determination process. When you post a goods receipt against a PO, the system creates an accounting document (along with the material document) and G/L account postings are made. The system determines which G/L accounts should be debited and credited based on configuration settings for automatic account determination.

Before we discuss these configuration settings, let's cover the definitions of a few essential terms:

- **Valuation class**

  A valuation class is used to determine the G/L account for the materials stock account. In automatic account determination, you must create valuation classes and assign them to material types. While creating material master records, you must select the appropriate valuation class in the **Accounting 1** tab. The valuation class list in the material master record will depend on the material type. For example, in a standard SAP system, material type ROH (raw material) has three valuation classes: 3000, 3001, and 3002.

- **Transaction key**

  Transaction keys are used to determine accounts or posting keys for line items that are automatically created by the system. They're defined in the system and can't be changed.

Now that you understand the key terms in automatic account determination and how it will work in your business, we'll move on to describe the configuration and business processes involved.

22.2.1 Configuration with the Automatic Account Determination Wizard

Automatic account determination can be configured either with or without the automatic account determination wizard, a tool provided by SAP to help you with the automatic account determination functionality. To configure automatic account determination with the help of the wizard, follow the menu path **Materials Management • Valuation and Account Assignment • Account Determination • Account Determination Wizard**.

The wizard will ask a number of questions and, based on your answers, finds the correct settings and saves them in the corresponding SAP tables. With the exception of a few restrictions (as documented in the wizard), the wizard undertakes the following steps:

1. Defines valuation control
2. Groups valuation areas
3. Defines valuation classes
4. Defines account grouping for movement types
5. Manages purchase accounts
6. Configures automatic postings

We'll explain how to set up automatic account determination without the wizard because this manual and step-by-step approach to account determination will help you understand and work with the wizard. Further, account determination without the wizard enables you to create more complex customizations.

22.2.2   Configuration without the Automatic Account Determination Wizard

We'll now follow a step-by-step approach to setting up account determination in the SAP system. We'll cover the necessary configuration steps involved, followed by how to assign the configured objects in the master data. Business processes involving account determination and that use the master data are covered next. We'll also cover the accounting entries that happen as the result of stock posting. Finally, we'll also demonstrate, with an example, how to troubleshoot account determination errors that may arise during stock posting.

1. **Define valuation control**

   For account determination, you can group together valuation areas by activating the valuation grouping code (also known as the *valuation modifier*), which makes the configuration of automatic postings much easier. A valuation grouping code can be made active or inactive by choosing the respective radio button.

   To define valuation control, follow the menu path **Materials Management • Valuation and Account Assignment • Account Determination • Account Determination without Wizard • Define Valuation Control**.

   By default, the valuation grouping code is active in the standard SAP system.

2. **Assign valuation grouping codes to valuation areas**

   The valuation grouping code makes it easier to set automatic account determination. Within the chart of accounts, you'll assign the same valuation grouping codes to the valuation areas you want assigned to the same account. As shown in Figure 22.18, valuation grouping code 0001 has been assigned to valuation area 1000 and company code 1000. If another valuation area is also using the same set of G/L

22

accounts as valuation area 0001, you can assign valuation grouping code 0001 to that valuation area.

To assign valuation grouping codes to valuation areas, follow the menu path **Materials Management • Valuation and Account Assignment • Account Determination • Account Determination without Wizard • Group Together Valuation Areas**.

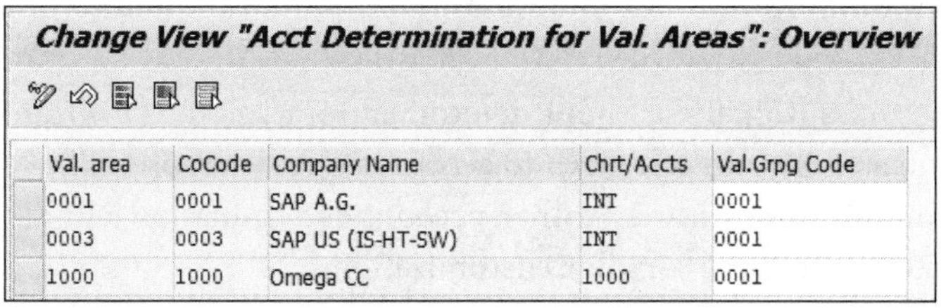

Change View "Acct Determination for Val. Areas": Overview

Val. area	CoCode	Company Name	Chrt/Accts	Val.Grpg Code
0001	0001	SAP A.G.	INT	0001
0003	0003	SAP US (IS-HT-SW)	INT	0001
1000	1000	Omega CC	1000	0001

Figure 22.18 Valuation Grouping

3. **Define valuation classes**

   In this step, you'll define the valuation classes allowed for each material type. Then, you'll assign the account category reference to the material type. As shown in Figure 22.20, account category references 0001 and 0002 are defined, and for each account category reference, one or more valuation classes can be assigned. Account category reference 0001 has been assigned to material type ROH, and valuation classes 3000, 3001, and 3002 have been assigned to account category reference 0001. Consequently, valuation classes 3000, 3001, and 3002 have been assigned to material type ROH. While creating the material master record for material type ROH, you can select any of these valuation classes. Similarly, for material type HALB, you can select valuation classes 7900 or 7901.

   In this section, through an example, we'll create the new valuation class 3004 and cover all the associated configuration settings required to ensure an end-to-end business process working.

   To define which valuation classes are allowed for a material type, use Transaction OMSK or follow the menu path **Materials Management • Valuation and Account Assignment • Account Determination • Account Determination without Wizard • Define Valuation Classes**. On the screen that appears, you'll see three options: **Account Category Reference**, **Valuation Class**, and **Material Type/Account Category Reference**. Follow these steps:

   - Click on **Account Category Reference** and, if needed, create an account category reference, as shown in Figure 22.19.

Change View "Account Category Reference": Overview

New Entries

Account Category Reference

ARef	Description
0001	Reference for raw materials
0002	Ref. for operating supplies
0003	Reference for spare parts
0004	Reference for packaging

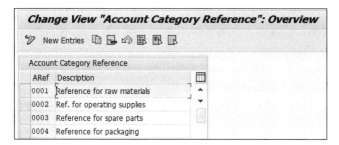

Figure 22.19 Account Category Reference

- Click on **Valuation Class**, shown in Figure 22.20, and then click on the **New Entries**. Create a new valuation class (**ValCl**) **3004** (with **Description Raw Materials-Steel**) and assign the valuation class to account category reference (**ARef**) **0001**, as shown in Figure 22.20.

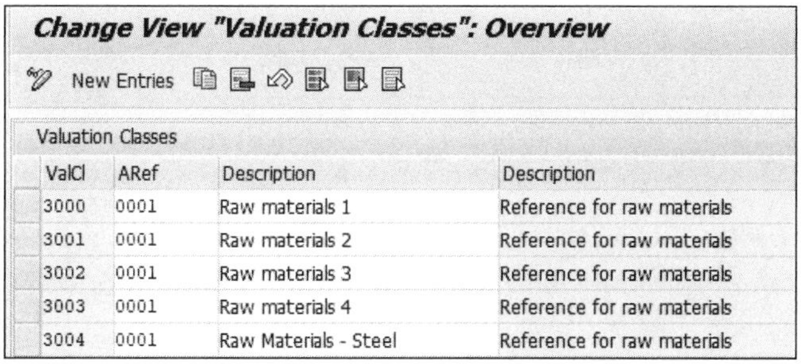

Change View "Valuation Classes": Overview

New Entries

Valuation Classes

ValCl	ARef	Description	Description
3000	0001	Raw materials 1	Reference for raw materials
3001	0001	Raw materials 2	Reference for raw materials
3002	0001	Raw materials 3	Reference for raw materials
3003	0001	Raw materials 4	Reference for raw materials
3004	0001	Raw Materials - Steel	Reference for raw materials

Figure 22.20 Valuation Classes

- Click on **Account Category Reference** and maintain a mapping between the material types and account references. For material type (**MType**) **ROH**, assign the account reference (**ARef**) **0001**, as shown in Figure 22.21.

Change View "Account Category Reference/Material Type": Overview

Account Category Reference/Material Type

MTyp	Material type descr.	ARef	Description
PROC	Process materials	0009	Ref. for finished products
PROD	Product groups	0008	Ref. for semifinished products
ROH	Raw materials	0001	Reference for raw materials

Figure 22.21 Account Category Reference with Material Type

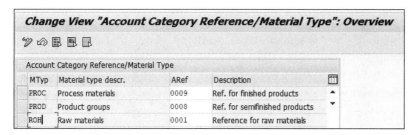

4. **Define account grouping for movement types**

   Now, you can assign an account grouping to movement types. The account grouping is a finer subdivision of the transaction/event keys for account determination. For example, during a goods movement, the offsetting entry for the inventory posting (Transaction GBB) can be made to different accounts, depending on the movement type. The account grouping is provided for the following transactions:

   – Transaction GBB (Offsetting Entry for Inventory Posting)

   – Transaction PRD (Price Differences)

   – Transaction KON (Consignment Liabilities)

   The account grouping in the standard system is only active for Transaction GBB. To define account groupings for movement types, follow the menu path **Materials Management • Valuation and Account Assignment • Account Determination • Account Determination without Wizard • Define Account Grouping for Movement Types**. Define the account grouping code, the movement type, and the transaction/event key combination, as shown in Figure 22.22.

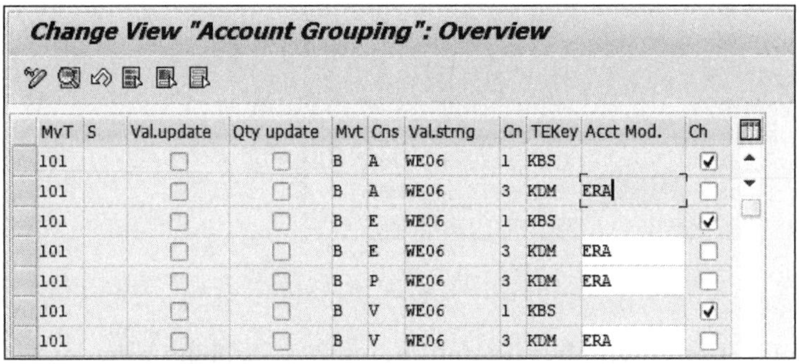

MvT	S	Val.update	Qty update	Mvt	Cns	Val.strng	Cn	TEKey	Acct Mod.	Ch	
101		☐	☐	B	A	WE06	1	KBS		☑	
101		☐	☐	B	A	WE06	3	KDM	ERA	☐	
101		☐	☐	B	E	WE06	1	KBS		☑	
101		☐	☐	B	E	WE06	3	KDM	ERA	☐	
101		☐	☐	B	P	WE06	3	KDM	ERA	☐	
101		☐	☐	B	V	WE06	1	KBS		☑	
101		☐	☐	B	V	WE06	3	KDM	ERA	☐	

Figure 22.22 Movement Types and Account Modifiers Combinations

> **Note**
>
> Value strings group together the various transactions used in account determination. For example, you can see the value string **WE01** by following the Customizing menu path **Materials Management • Valuation and Account Assignment • Account Determination • Account Determination Without Wizard • Define Account Grouping for Movement Types**. On this screen, if you double-click on any entries that contain WE01, you'll get a list of transactions, along with their descriptions. The transactions that appear in the value string are hard-coded in the system, so you should never try to change them.

5. **Configure automatic postings**

In this step, you'll enter the system settings for inventory management and invoice verification transactions that result in automatic posting to G/L accounts. A *transaction/event key* is a key to differentiate account determination by business transaction. For example, we must differentiate G/L account posted by goods receipt transaction and posted by invoice receipt transaction.

You don't need to define these transaction keys; they are determined automatically from the transaction of the movement type (inventory management) or from the transaction of invoice verification. All you need to do is assign the relevant G/L account to each posting transaction.

To assign G/L accounts to transaction/event keys, use Transaction OMWB or follow the menu path **Materials Management • Valuation and Account Assignment • Account Determination • Account Determination without Wizard • Configure Automatic Posting**. Click on **Cancel**, as shown in Figure 22.23.

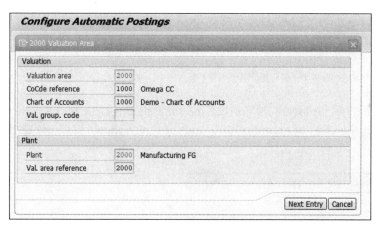

Figure 22.23 Configuring Automatic Postings

To assign a G/L account, click on **Account Assignment** (not shown) in Figure 22.23. You'll see a list of transaction keys; double-click on the key for which you want to set the G/L accounts. You'll need to define the valuation grouping code (also known as the *valuation modifier*), valuation class, and G/L account, as shown in Figure 22.24. You can then check your settings using the simulation function.

22

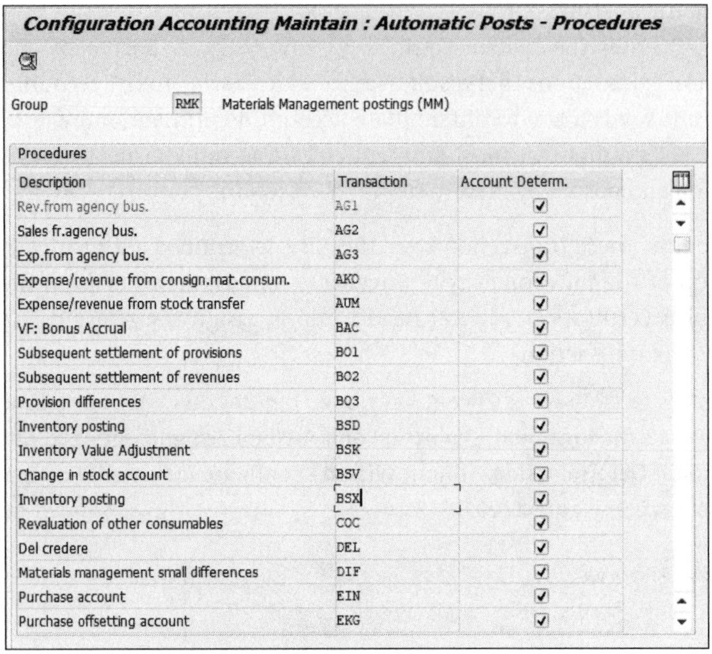

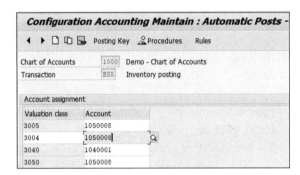

Figure 22.24 Automatic Account Posting Transactions

Choose **Transaction BSX** for inventory posting and for assigning G/Ls. In the popup that appears, enter the **Chart of Accounts 1000**, and the screen shown in Figure 22.25 will appear.

Figure 22.25 Transaction BSX with Valuation Class 3004 and G/L Account

Figure 22.26 shows the **Transaction BSX** for **Inventory posting**. Click **New** and enter the newly created **Valuation Class 3004** and assign the **Account 1050008**.

Go back to the screen shown in Figure 22.23, and this time, useTransaction WRX (for GR/IR clearing account) and maintain the G/L account of the newly created **Valuation class 3004**, as shown in Figure 22.26.

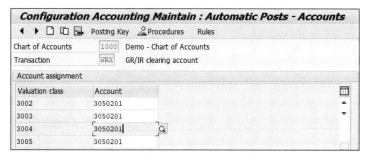

Figure 22.26 Transaction WRX with Valuation Class 3004 and G/L Account

Let's now look at the business processes and the associated master data setup and transactions, not only to check that the newly created valuation class 3004 works correctly, but also the associated G/L accounts.

22.2.3 Master Data Setup

Access the screen shown in Figure 22.27 via Transaction MM01. In the **Accounting 1** tab of the material master **10000087**, assign the newly created **Valuation Class 3004**.

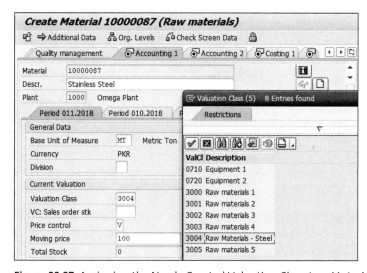

Figure 22.27 Assigning the Newly Created Valuation Class to a Material

Now, let's discuss the G/L account determination as they relate to goods receipt and goods issue postings. Post a good receipt of the material 10000087 with reference to a PO via Transaction MIGO. Then, display the goods receipt document and go to the **Doc. info** tab. Click on the **FI Documents** button, which will display a list of financial documents created for the goods receipt document, as shown in Figure 22.28. Select the accounting document to see the details of that accounting document, as shown in Figure 22.28.

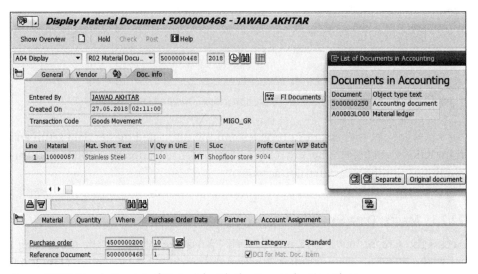

Figure 22.28 Goods Receipt of Material with the New Valuation Class

As shown in Figure 22.29, you'll see the G/L account postings, which are determined based on the automatic account determination configuration. G/L account 1050008 (inventory raw material stock account) is debited, and GR/IR account 3050201 is credited.

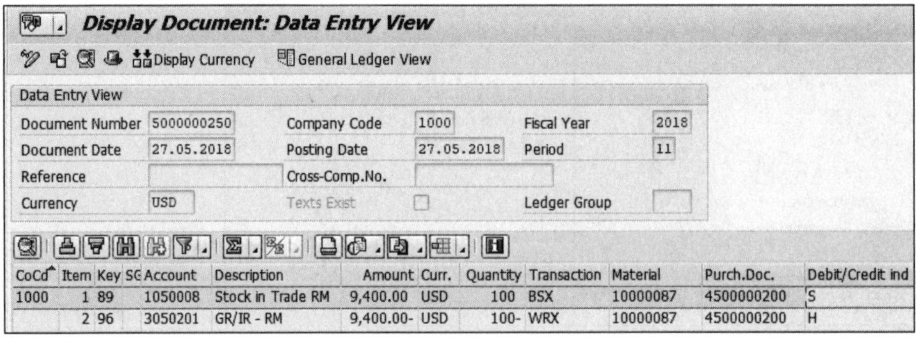

CoCd	Item	Key	SG	Account	Description	Amount	Curr.	Quantity	Transaction	Material	Purch.Doc.	Debit/Credit ind
1000	1	89		1050008	Stock in Trade RM	9,400.00	USD	100	BSX	10000087	4500000200	S
	2	96		3050201	GR/IR - RM	9,400.00-	USD	100-	WRX	10000087	4500000200	H

Figure 22.29 Accounting Entries of Goods Receipt

22.2.4   Troubleshooting Errors

Let's now examine what happens when the system brings up an error message because of missing or incomplete settings for the account determination process. In this example, we'll try to issue out the same material 10000087 against a cost center that we set up in the previous section.

Go to Transaction MIGO and use movement type 201 (goods issue to cost center). Select the cost center, plant, storage location, material, and quantity and click on the **Check** button to see whether the system can post the document.

Figure 22.30 shows the red traffic light as well as an error message that prevents transactions from being posted. Click on the message display icon under **LTxt**, which brings up the screen shown in Figure 22.31.

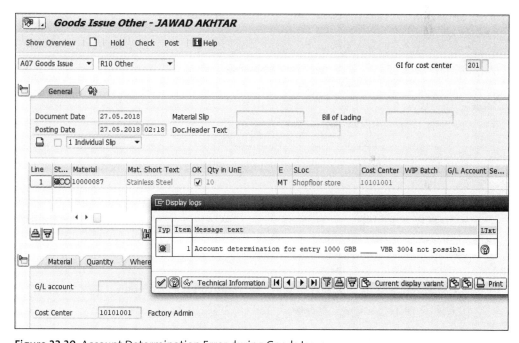

Figure 22.30 Account Determination Error during Goods Issuance

Figure 22.31 shows the account determination for the entry **1000** (the valuation area), the offsetting entry for inventory posting **GBB___VBR** for the **Valuation Class 3004** is not possible. To troubleshoot this error while staying on the same screen (and assuming you have the necessary authorization), click on **Account Determination**. The transaction can also be assessed using Transaction OBYC.

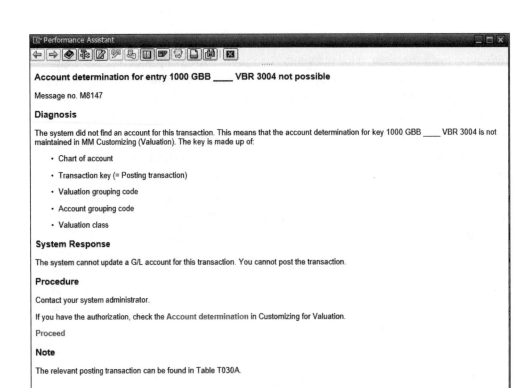

Figure 22.31 Detailed Error on Accounting Determination

Access to the screen shown in Figure 22.32 is possible when the system prompts you to enter or select relevant objects, such as the chart of accounts (**1000**) or the transaction (**GBB**). On this screen, maintain relevant G/Ls to **VBR** and the recently created **Valuation Class 3004**. Save your settings.

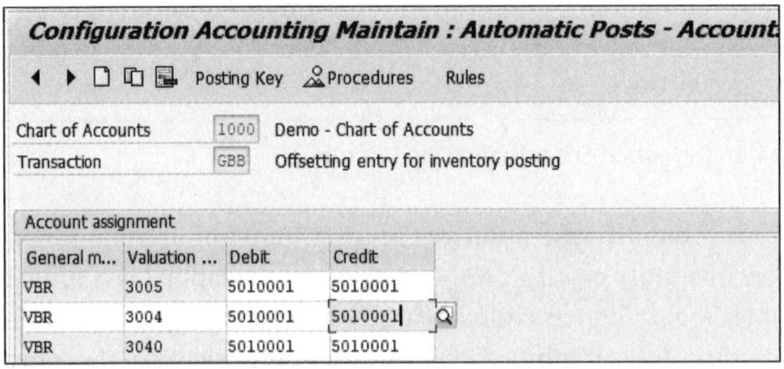

Figure 22.32 Assigning G/Ls to Transaction GBB-VBR

On clicking the **Check** button again, as shown in Figure 22.33. This time, the traffic light (or the status) turns green, and the system can post the goods issue for the cost center.

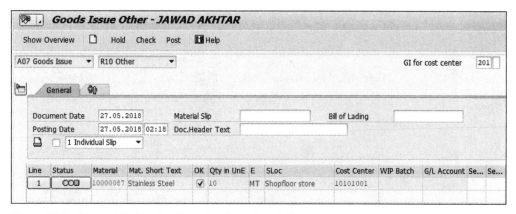

Figure 22.33 Account Determination after Error Resolution

Figure 22.34 shows the accounting entries of the transaction just saved (goods issuance for cost center).

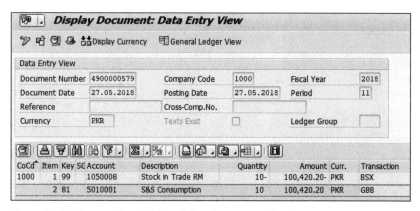

Figure 22.34 Accounting Entries of Goods Issuance for Cost Center

> **Note**
>
> During the course of an SAP implementation project, an MM consultant normally has a template (an MS Excel file) filled with important account determination assignment that is created in coordination with an FI consultant.

Table 22.1 shows a selective list of important transactions used in the automatic account determination.

Transaction	Description
AKO	Expense/revenue from consumption of consignment material.
AUM	Expenditure/income from transfer posting.
BSD	Supplementary entry for stock.
BSV	Change in stock.
FRL	External service.
FRN	External service, delivery costs.
BSX	Stock posting.
DIF	Materials management (MM) small differences.
EIN	Purchase account.
EKG	Purchase offsetting account.
FR1	Freight clearing.
FR2	Freight provisions.
FR3	Customs clearing.
FRE	Purchasing freight account.
FR4	Customs provisions.
GBB	Offsetting entry for inventory postings.
KBS	Account-assigned purchase order.
KDG	MM exchange rate differences.
KON	Consignment payables.
KTR	Price difference offset entry.
LKW	Accruals and defer account (Material Ledger).
PRD	Cost (price) differences.

Table 22.1 Transactions for Account Determination

Transaction	Description
RAP	Expense/revenue from revaluation.
PIP	Pipeline liabilities.
RKA	Invoice reductions from logistics invoice verification.
PRV	Material Ledger closing entries for the multilevel price variances.
PRY	Material Ledger closing entry, as well as during the rollup of single-level price differences.
UMB	Material Ledger closing entries (Transactions CKMLCP or MR22) when a material price is changed and/or revaluated.
LKW	Accruals and deferrals accounts in the Material Ledger. If you choose not to revaluate inventory, the LKW account is the offset for the PRY, PRV, KDM, and KDV transaction keys.
KDV	Transaction key for the exchange rate differences in the Material Ledger.
KDR	Differences due to exchange rate rounding.
COC	Revaluation of other consumption (only relevant for Brazil).
GBB-AUI	Material Ledger closing entries to credit the cost centers with the delta value between the plan activity type price and the actual activity type price. This transaction key is used to offset transaction key PRV, which receives the variances as a lower-level price variance.
	GBB-AUI is also used by the work in progress (WIP) revaluation function. For WIP revaluation, the delta between the plan and actual activity type prices is also credited to the cost centers that performed the activities using the account assigned to GBB/AUI and offset by the transaction key WPA.

Table 22.1 Transactions for Account Determination (Cont.)

As we covered earlier this section, a combination of GBB-VBR will lead to successful posting of a goods issuance against a cost center, including the associated financial entries. We'll cover a few more GBB-specific transactions.

Different business scenarios may involve postings to inventory accounts that you also want posted to different G/L accounts as well. The SAP system uses transaction key GBB (offsetting entry for inventory posting) where you can configure different G/L accounts for offsetting entries in different business transactions. The transaction

22

key makes extensive use of account grouping codes to differentiate business transactions, as follows:

- BSA: Used for posting initial opening stock balances.
- AUF: Used for posting goods receipt from a production order and for other settlement purposes if G/L accounts for account grouping code AUA are not configured.
- AUA: Used when a production order is settled to financial accounting.
- VQP: Used when a sample goods issue to quality management (QM) is posted without an account assignment.
- VQY: Used when a sample goods issue to QM is posted with an account assignment.
- VBR: Used when internal goods issue (e.g. cost center) occurs as a consumption account.
- VAX: Used when a goods issue from non-valuated sales order stock is made, that is, the sales order item does not carry costs and revenues.
- VAY: Used when a goods issue from non-valuated sales order stock is made, that is, the sales order item carries costs and revenues.
- VNG: Used when inventory stock or material quantities are scrapped.
- ZOB: Used when a goods receipt without reference to a purchase order is posted, that is, when the SAP purchasing functionality is not active or not used.
- ZOF: Used when a goods receipt without reference to a production order is posted, that is, when PP is not active or not used.

In this section, we covered the account determination process. The next section covers an inventory valuation method, last in first out (LIFO).

22.3   Last In First Out Valuation

Last in first out (LIFO) valuation is based on the principle that the last deliveries of a material to be received are the first to be used. In this case, then no value change occurs for older material when new materials are received. Because of the LIFO method, the older material isn't affected by the higher prices of the new deliveries of material. Thus, the older material isn't valuated at the new material price, which prevents the false valuation of current inventory.

LIFO valuation enables the increased amount of material stock per fiscal year to be valuated separately from the rest of the material stock. This option is important so that new material is valuated at the correct amount, while old stock remains valuated without being affected by the new material price. A positive variance between the opening and closing material balances of a fiscal year is known as a *layer* for LIFO valuation. A layer can be valuated as a separate item. The total of a material is the sum of all layers.

A layer is dissolved if a negative difference exists between the opening and closing stock balances at the end of a fiscal year. This situation happens, for example, if all the new stock is consumed plus some of the existing stock. In the following sections, we'll discuss how to configure, prepare for, and run a LIFO valuation.

22.3.1   Configuration

The first configuration step is to ensure that LIFO is activated by using Transaction OMWE, which can be found by following the navigation path **Materials Management • Valuation and Account Assignment • Balance Sheet Valuation Procedures • Configure LIFO/FIFO Methods • General Information • Activate/Deactivate LIFO/FIFO Valuation**.

The LIFO method also depends on the movement types being set up as relevant for LIFO. As shown in Figure 22.35, for example, two records have been flagged as LIFO (the **LIFO** indicator has been checked). Both records flagged as LIFO are for movement type (**Mvmt Type**) **101** and movement indicator (**MvtInd.**) **B**. This transaction can be accessed using Transaction OMW4 or by following the navigation path **Materials Management • Valuation and Account Assignment • Balance Sheet Valuation Procedures • Configure LIFO/FIFO Methods • General Information • Define LIFO/FIFO Relevant Movement Types**.

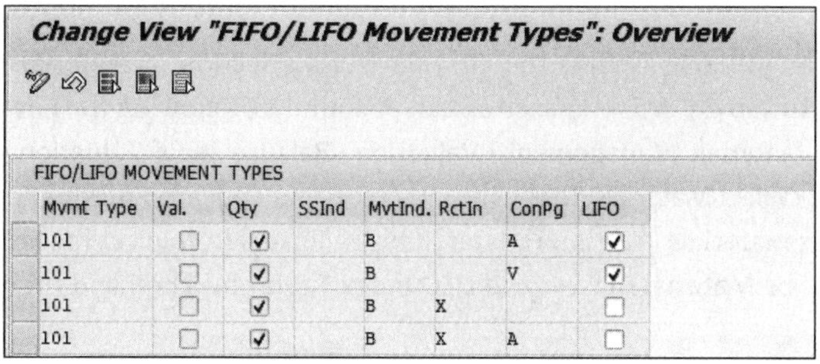

Change View "FIFO/LIFO Movement Types": Overview

FIFO/LIFO MOVEMENT TYPES

Mvmt Type	Val.	Qty	SSInd	MvtInd.	RctIn	ConPg	LIFO
101	☐	☑		B		A	☑
101	☐	☑		B		V	☑
101	☐	☑		B	X		☐
101	☐	☑		B	X	A	☐

Figure 22.35 Movement Types Configured as Relevant for LIFO Valuation

22.3.2   Preparation

To instigate a LIFO valuation, a number of preparation steps must be completed. These steps include ensuring the materials are defined for LIFO, setting up the base layers for valuation, and setting up the basis for comparison, as we'll discuss in the following sections.

Material Master Records

To prepare for LIFO valuation, you must ensure that the materials you want to value are flagged for LIFO. The flag is located within the material master on the **Accounting 2** tab, as shown in Figure 22.36.

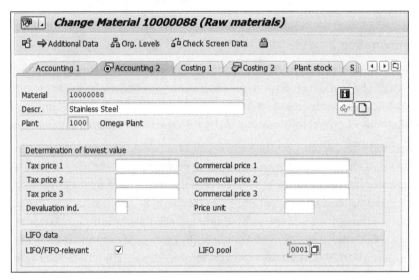

Figure 22.36 Selecting the LIFO/FIFO-relevant Checkbox in the Material Master

You can use Transaction MRL6 to update the LIFO flag for a selection of materials, material types, plants, and so on. This transaction can be found by following the navigation path **Logistics • Materials Management • Valuation • Balance Sheet Valuation • LIFO Valuation • Prepare • Select Materials**. In the initial screen that appears, enter selection parameters such as materials, plants, or material types. Ensure you select the **Set** radio button as well as the **Material Master and LIFO Index Table** checkbox and then click **Execute**.

Figure 22.37 shows the list of materials, including the material 10000088 in plant 1000, marked for LIFO valuation.

Flag Materials and Form Groups

29.05.2018 Flag Materials

Material no.	ValA	Unit	MTyp	LIFO	New LIFO	Pool	New Pool	LIFO Index
10000084	1000	MT	ROH	3	3			Record exists
10000085	1000	MT	ROH	3	3			Record exists
10000086	1000	MT	ROH	3	3			Record exists
10000087	1000	MT	ROH	3	3			Record exists
10000088	1000	MT	ROH	X	1	0001	0001	Record exists
10000104	1000	KG	ROH	3	3			Record exists
10000105	1000	KG	ROH	3	3			Record exists

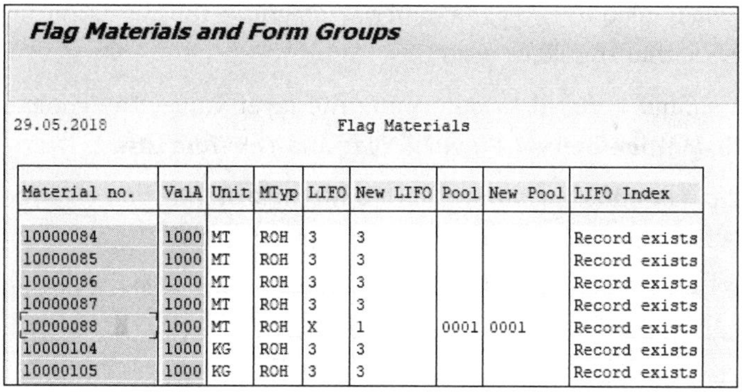

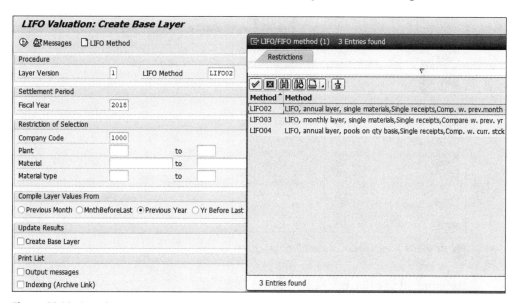

Figure 22.37 Materials Marked for LIFO Valuation

Base Layers

The measurement of material value changes is based on comparing different layers. Before LIFO can be started, the base layer should be created from information on the older existing materials. The base layer can be created using Transaction MRL8 or by following the navigation path **Logistics • Materials Management • Valuation • Balance Sheet Valuation • LIFO Valuation • Prepare • Create Base Layer**, as shown in Figure 22.38.

Figure 22.38 Creating a Base Layer

22

In Transaction MRL8, you'll need to enter the materials to create the base layer for and enter the LIFO method that should be used.

Select the values that should be used to determine the layer value. The choices include **Previous Month**, **MnthBeforeLast**, **Previous Year**, and **Yr Before Last**.

After setting the initial parameters, including the **LIFO Method LIFO02**, press F8 or click **Execute**, and the screen shown in Figure 22.39 will appear.

Figure 22.39 shows the list of materials whose base layer has been created starting from the base year 1994 (this base year was set in Customizing).

LIFO Valuation: Create Base Layer

27.05.2018   C R E A T I O N   O F   B A S E   L A Y E
Year: 1994
Period: 01
Stock for Previous Year

LVaL	Material	Quantity	Unit	Gross value	Crcy
1000	10000002	12	MT	80,150.00	PKR
1000	10000052	101	EA	1,507.00	PKR
1000	10000080	230	EA	22,080.00	PKR
1000	10000104	1,040.000	KG	15,565.00	PKR
1000	10000138	58.824	KG	1,983.74	PKR
1000	10000140	2,130.000	KG	2,847.81	PKR
1000	10000153	52.000	KG	533.30	PKR
1000	10000154	200	EA	20,000.00	PKR
1000	10000174	99,010	L	13,861,400.00	PKR
1000	10000176	29.744	KG	446.16	PKR
1000	20000000	9,997	EA	553,833.80	PKR
1000	30000037	4,920	EA	777,360.00	PKR
1000	30000081	10,617.225	KG	10,617,225.00	PKR
1000	40000004	9,448	MT	442,606,109.92	PKR
1000	40000006	40	MT	1,860,428.00	PKR
1000	40000007	50	MT	2,325,535.00	PKR
1000	40000008	39	MT	1,833,450.06	PKR
1000	40000009	50	MT	2,350,576.50	PKR
1000	40000010	50	MT	2,333,785.00	PKR
1000	40000011	65	MT	3,033,920.50	PKR
1000	40000090	5,195	MT	259,750.00	PKR
1000	40000103	99,883	EA	9,988,300.00	PKR
1000	40000104	99,999	EA	9,999,900.00	PKR
1000	40000105	100,000	EA	10,000,000.00	PKR
1000	40000126	508	EA	25,400.00	PKR

Figure 22.39 Base Layer Created for Materials

Determination of Basis for Comparison

Before running a LIFO valuation, a basis for comparison needs to be determined. During LIFO valuation, the stocks are compared at a particular point in time with the total of the layer quantities. These periods are defined in the SAP system:

- GJE: The stock at the end of the previous fiscal year is compared with the total quantities in the existing layers.

- VOM: The stock at the end of the previous period is compared with the total quantities in the existing layers.

- VVM: The stock at the end of the period before last is compared with the total quantities in the existing layers.

- CUR: The current stock is compared with the total quantities in the existing layers.

22.3.3   Running a Last In First Out Valuation

After all of the configuration and preparation has been completed for the LIFO valuation, the transaction can be executed to run the valuation. The following transactions can be run:

- Transaction MRL1 for a single material level
- Transaction MRL2 for the pool level
- Transaction MRL3 for comparison of lowest values

You can find these transactions by following the navigation path **Logistics • Materials Management • Valuation • Balance Sheet Valuation • LIFO Valuation • Perform Check**.

In Transaction MRL1, you can choose the LIFO method, the selection criteria, and the value determination for the new layer. As shown in Figure 22.40, the **LIFO Method LIFO03** has been chosen.

In the **Restriction of Selection** criteria fields, the **Company Code 1000** has been entered. The value determination for the new layer has been selected as **Total Accounting Period**. After these settings have been entered, the transaction can be executed, and the result for **LIFO method LIFO02** is shown in Figure 22.40. Different LIFO methods will produce different reports.

22

> **Note**
>
> Many more LIFO reporting and evaluation options are available for inventory valuations and can be explored by following the menu path **Logistics • Materials Management • Valuation • Balance Sheet Valuation • LIFO Valuation**.

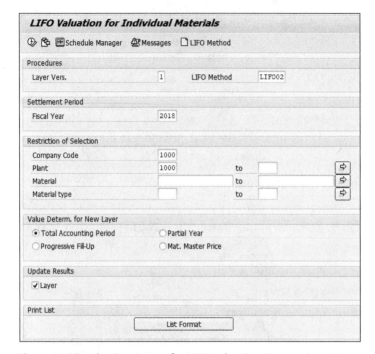

Figure 22.40 Selection Screen for LIFO Valuation Transaction MRL1

As shown in Figure 22.41, materials are listed on the report that now has LIFO valuations based on the LIFO02 method. The newly created base layers are denoted by green rows, the removed base layers are denoted by red rows, and materials with no changes to their base layers remain as gray rows.

LIFO Valuation for Individual Materials

LIFO Valuation for Individual Materials

LVaL	Material	Material description	Total Stock	BUn	Total Value	Crcy	Price	per
Year	Period	Change	Old Layer Qty	New Layer Qty	Old Layer Value	New Layer Value	Layer Price	Remarks
1000	40000006	DEF. BARS 19.1MM 12 M STR8 A-615	40	MT	1,860,428.00	PKR	46,510.70	1
1994	1		40	40	1,860,428.00	1,860,428.00	46,510.70	
1000	40000007	DEF. BARS 20MM 12 M STR8 A-615	50	MT	2,325,535.00	PKR	46,510.70	1
1994	1		50	50	2,325,535.00	2,325,535.00	46,510.70	
1000	40000008	Demo Material 1	39	MT	1,833,450.06	PKR	47,011.54	1
1994	1		39	39	1,833,450.06	1,833,450.06	47,011.54	
1000	40000009	Demo Material 2	50	MT	2,350,576.50	PKR	47,011.53	1
1994	1		50	50	2,350,576.50	2,350,576.50	47,011.53	
1000	40000010	DEF. BARS 19.1MM 12 M U/B A-615	50	MT	2,333,785.00	PKR	46,675.70	1
1994	1		50	50	2,333,785.00	2,333,785.00	46,675.70	
1000	40000011	DEF. BARS 20MM 12 M U/B A-615	65	MT	3,033,920.50	PKR	46,675.70	1
1994	1		65	65	3,033,920.50	3,033,920.50	46,675.70	

Figure 22.41 Result of LIFO Valuation Transaction MRL1

> **Note**
>
> Now that we've covered end-to-end business processes of inventory valuation by LIFO method, you can follow the following customization path to make any specific changes to LIFO customization. The customization menu path is **Materials Management • Valuation and Account Assignment • Balance Sheet Valuation Procedures • Configure LIFO/FIFO Methods • LIFO**.

This section has shown how materials can be flagged as LIFO. We've examined the LIFO valuation method in which the material that is purchased or produced last is sold, consumed, or disposed of first. The next section reviews the reverse of this method, the first in first out (FIFO) method.

22.4   First In First Out Valuation

First in first out (FIFO) is a valuation method in which the material that is purchased or produced first is also sold, consumed, or disposed of first. Companies with materials that are batch-managed, have an expiry date, or degrade in quality over time will often use this method. Using this method presupposes that the next item to be shipped out will be the oldest of that material in the warehouse. In practice, this method usually reflects that underlying commercial method pursued by companies is rotating inventory.

Newer companies commonly use FIFO for reporting the value of merchandise to bolster their balance sheets. As the older and cheaper materials are sold, the newer and more expensive materials remain as assets on the balance sheet. However, as the company grows, it may switch to LIFO to reduce the amount of taxes it pays to the government. In the following sections, we'll cover the same steps for FIFO as we did for LIFO.

22.4.1   Configuration

The configuration steps for FIFO are similar to those for configuring LIFO valuation. The first configuration step is to ensure that FIFO is active by using Transaction OMWE, which can be found by following the navigation path **Materials Management • Valuation and Account Assignment • Balance Sheet Valuation Procedures • Configure LIFO/FIFO Methods • General Information • Activate/Deactivate LIFO/FIFO Valuation**.

Lastly, configure the movement types being set up as relevant for FIFO. The configuration can be found using Transaction OMW4 or by following the navigation path **Materials Management • Valuation and Account Assignment • Balance Sheet Valuation Procedures • Configure LIFO/FIFO Methods • General Information • Define LIFO/ FIFO Relevant Movement Types**.

22.4.2   Preparation

After the configuration for FIFO is complete, the materials relevant for FIFO must be selected using Transaction MRF4. On the screen, you can set the FIFO valuation flag for a number of selections, for example, for a single **Material** or a range of materials, a **Plant**, a **Material Type**, or a **Material Group**. In our example, all the materials of **Company Code 1000** will be flagged for FIFO. This transaction can be found by following the navigation path **Logistics • Materials Management • Valuation • Balance Sheet Valuation • FIFO Valuation • Prepare • Select Materials**.

22.4.3   Running a First In First Out Valuation

After all the configuration and preparation has been completed for the FIFO valuation, Transaction MRF1 can be executed to run the valuation, as shown in Figure 22.42.

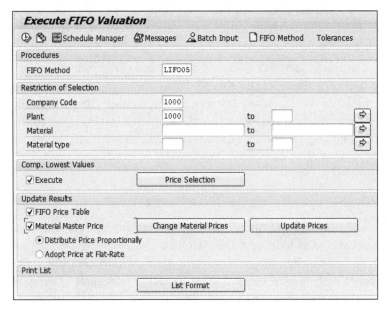

Figure 22.42 Selection Screen for Transaction MRF1

The transaction can be found by following the navigation path **Logistics • Materials Management • Valuation • Balance Sheet Valuation • FIFO Valuation • Perform Check**.

After the transaction has been executed, the FIFO valuation is performed for the selected materials, plant, and so on, and a report is displayed, as shown in Figure 22.43.

Execute FIFO Valuation

Execute FIFO Valuation

FVaL	Material	Material description	Total Stock Comp		Total Value	Crcy	Gross FIFO value	Total Val. Net Value
1000	80000061	CARTON CHOCO 4 CRUNCHY BEANS 24X24	10,547	EA	1,582,050.00	PKR	1,582,050.00	0.00
							PKR	1,582,050.00
1000	80000062	BOX CHOCO 4 CRUNCHY BEANS POUCH	10,995	EA	960,126.76	PKR	960,126.76	0.00
							PKR	960,126.76
1000	80000063	POUCH CHOCO 4 CRUNCHY BEANS RS. 5	190.000	KG	47,500.00	PKR	47,500.00	0.00
							PKR	47,500.00
1000	80000064	CHOCO 4 - (POUCH) - (24X24)	10,549	CAR	3,164,700.00	PKR	3,164,700.00	0.00
							PKR	3,164,700.00
1000	80000065	TAPE	10,998.609	KG	1,649,791.35	PKR	1,649,791.35	0.00
							PKR	1,649,791.35

Execute FIFO Valuation

VaAr	G/L Acct	Book Value	Crcy	Net value layer	Difference	Diff %	Gross FIFO value	Difference	Diff %
1000	1040001	563,617.60	PKR	563,617.60	0.00	0.00	563,617.60	0.00	0.00
1000	1050001	2,224,929,137.88	PKR	2,224,929,137.88	0.00	0.00	2,224,929,137.88	0.00	0.00
1000	1050002	3,426,944,149.39	PKR	3,426,944,149.39	0.00	0.00	3,426,944,149.39	0.00	0.00
1000	1050003	252,645,439.35	PKR	252,645,439.35	0.00	0.00	252,645,439.35	0.00	0.00
1000	1050004	163,315,904.43	PKR	163,315,904.43	0.00	0.00	163,315,904.43	0.00	0.00
1000	1050008	23,417,045.71	PKR	23,417,045.71	0.00	0.00	23,417,045.71	0.00	0.00
* 1000		6,091,815,294.36	PKR	6,091,815,294.36	0.00		6,091,815,294.36	0.00	
**		6,091,815,294.36	PKR	6,091,815,294.36	0.00		6,091,815,294.36	0.00	

Figure 22.43 Result of FIFO Valuation Transaction MRF1

22

> **Note**
>
> Many more FIFO reporting and evaluation options are available for inventory valuations and can be explored by following the menu path **Logistics • Materials Management • Valuation • Balance Sheet Valuation • FIFO Valuation**.

In this section, we showed how materials can be flagged for FIFO. You've seen that FIFO is a valuation method where the material that is purchased or produced first is sold, consumed, or disposed of first. In the next section, we'll review lowest value determination, which uses the valuation method of the lowest value principle.

22.5   Lowest Value Determination

Lowest value determination uses the valuation method of the lowest value principle (LVP). Simply put, LVP indicates where the material is valued at the lowest value held on the system.

Three types of value determination can be used to calculate the material value:

- Based on market price
- Based on range of coverage
- Based on movement rate

22.5.1   Lowest Value Determination Based on Market Prices

To determine the lowest value based on market prices, the SAP system searches for the lowest price from among the different prices stored for each material. The procedure looks at the material price from the following:

- POs
- Scheduling agreements
- Goods receipts for POs
- Invoices for POs
- Purchasing information records

Transaction MRNO can used to run the lowest value based on market price and can be found by following the navigation path **Logistics • Materials Management • Valuation • Balance Sheet Valuation • Determination of Lowest Value • Market Prices**. The selection screen, shown in Figure 22.44, allows you to enter a range of **Material, Plant, Material Type**, or **Valuation Class**.

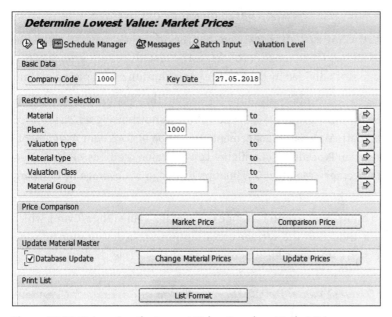

Figure 22.44 Determine the Lowest Value Based on Market Prices

After the selection criteria have been entered, the transaction can be executed. The results, shown in Figure 22.45, display the new prices of materials and the percentages change.

Determine Lowest Value: Market Prices

1 Determine Lowest Value: Market Prices 27.05.2018

CoCd	ValA	Material	Val. type	Material description	Comp.Price	New Price	Price Unit	Change in Percent	Suppl.	Itm	Price	Source	Rank	Purch.Doc
1000	1000	10000081		Limestone (CaCO3)	10,683.00	10,683.00	1	0.00		1	10,683.00	PO Price	1	450000019
1000	1000	10000082		Stainless Steel	10,042.02	10,042.02	1	0.00						
1000	1000	10000082	0000000308	Stainless Steel	10,042.02	10,042.02	1	0.00						
1000	1000	10000083		Stainless Steel	12,552.53	12,552.53	1	0.00						
1000	1000	10000083	GRADE A	Stainless Steel	10,042.02	10,042.02	1	0.00		1	10,042.02	PO Price	1	450000019
1000	1000	10000083	GRADE B	Stainless Steel	15,063.03	15,063.03	1	0.00		1	15,063.03	PO Price	1	450000019
1000	1000	10000084		Stainless Steel	13,033.26	13,033.26	1	0.00						
1000	1000	10000084	GRADE A	Stainless Steel	10,042.02	10,042.02	1	0.00		1	10,042.02	PO Price	1	450000019
1000	1000	10000084	GRADE B	Stainless Steel	16,024.50	16,024.50	1	0.00		1	16,024.50	PO Price	1	450000019
1000	1000	10000085		Stainless Steel	12,552.53	12,552.53	1	0.00						
1000	1000	10000085	GRADE A	Stainless Steel	10,042.02	10,042.02	1	0.00		1	10,042.02	PO Price	1	450000019
1000	1000	10000085	GRADE B	Stainless Steel	15,063.03	15,063.03	1	0.00		1	15,063.03	PO Price	1	450000019
1000	1000	10000086		Stainless Steel	15,063.03	15,063.03	1	0.00						
1000	1000	10000086	GRADE A	Stainless Steel	15,063.03	15,063.03	1	0.00						
1000	1000	10000087		Stainless Steel	12,651.48	10,042.02	1	20.63-		1	10,042.02	PO Price	1	450000020
1000	1000	10000088		Stainless Steel	10,042.02	10,042.02	1	0.00		1	15,000.00	PO Price	1	450000020
1000	1000	10000104		White crystalline powder	14.97	14.97	1	0.00						
1000	1000	10000105		White crystalline	0.00	0.00	1	0.00		1	30.00	Info Rec. Price	1	530000014

Figure 22.45 Determination of Lowest Price Report

22.5.2   Lowest Value Determination Based on Range of Coverage

With this method, the SAP system checks whether the price for a material should be devaluated because it has a high range of coverage. The system defines a *range of coverage* as the average stock divided by the average consumption over a period of time.

You can configure the percentage discount for devaluating materials by company code. To define the devaluation, use Transaction OMW5, shown in Figure 22.46, or follow the navigation path **Materials Management • Valuation and Account Assignment • Balance Sheet Valuation Procedures • Configure Lowest Value Methods • Price Deductions by Range of Coverage • Maintain Devaluation by Range of Coverage by Company Code**.

The configuration allows you to enter a range of coverage value (**Rnge/Cvrg.**), which is the average stock divided by the average consumption, and a devaluation percentage (**Deval. %**) for each company code (**CoCd**).

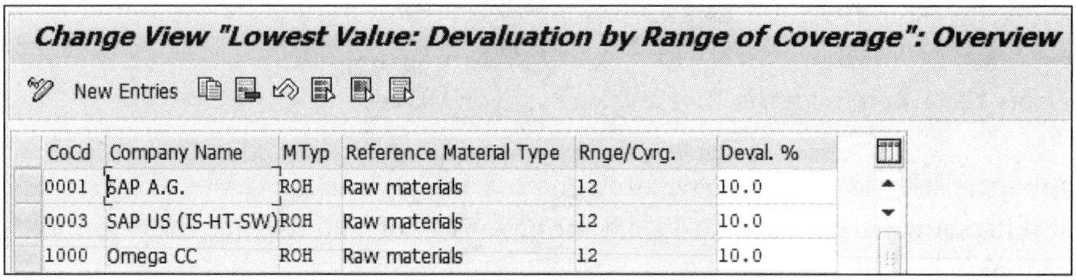

Change View "Lowest Value: Devaluation by Range of Coverage": Overview

🖉   New Entries

CoCd	Company Name	MTyp	Reference Material Type	Rnge/Cvrg.	Deval. %	
0001	SAP A.G.	ROH	Raw materials	12	10.0	
0003	SAP US (IS-HT-SW)	ROH	Raw materials	12	10.0	
1000	Omega CC	ROH	Raw materials	12	10.0	

Figure 22.46 Configuration for Devaluation by Range of Coverage

Transaction MRN1 can be used to run the lowest value based on range of coverage and can be found in the navigation path **Logistics • Materials Management • Valuation • Balance Sheet Valuation • Determination of Lowest Value • Range of Coverage**.

The selection screen, shown in Figure 22.47, allows you to enter a range of coverage. The values in the coverage for the lowest value determination can include **Material**, **Plant**, **Valuation Type**, **Material Type**, **Valuation Class**, and **Material Group**.

After entering selection criteria, as shown in Figure 22.47, the transaction can be executed. The results display the range of coverage, which determines the devaluation percentage and the calculated new value, as shown in Figure 22.48.

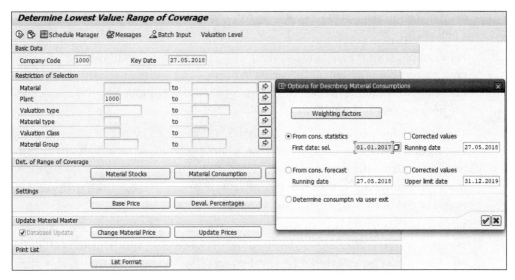

Figure 22.47 Selection Screen for Transaction MRN1

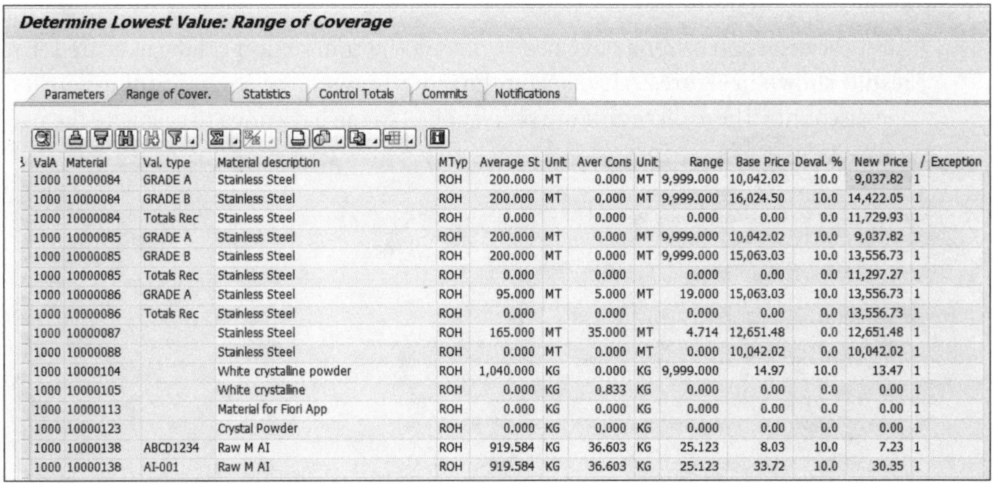

Figure 22.48 Results from Transaction MRN1

22.5.3   Lowest Value Determination Based on Movement Rate

In using the lowest value based on movement rate, we can determine the value of the material based on the slow movement or non-movement of a material. The system defines the movement rate as a percentage, where the total quantity of receipts is divided by the material in stock and then multiplied by 100 to convert the figure into a percentage.

For example, if your company has stock of 400 units of material ABC in a valuation area, and only 40 movements occurred in the period, then the movement rate is calculated as movements divided by the stock (40/400), multiplied by 100 to calculate the percentage, which in this case is 10%.

The devaluation percentage is configured in Transaction OMW6, similarly as using Transaction OMW5 for range of coverage, where a percentage is configured per company code. Using the previous example, if a decision was made that a slow-moving material is anything with a movement rate of below 15%, then the material ABC would be a slow-moving stock. Thus, the stock is devalued.

Transaction MRN2 is used to run the lowest value based on movement rate. The selection criteria is the same as shown earlier in Figure 22.47, which includes **Material**, **Plant**, **Valuation Type**, **Material Type**, **Valuation Class**, and **Material Group**. This transaction can be found by following the navigation path **Logistics • Materials Management • Valuation • Balance Sheet Valuation • Determination of Lowest Value • Movement Rate**.

After the selection criteria have been entered, the transaction can be executed. The results shown in Figure 22.49 displays the indicator with the corresponding percentage discounts. These discounts are then applied to the base price to calculate the new lowest price.

Determine Lowest Value: Movement Rate

| Parameters | Movement Rate | Statistics | Control Totals | Commits | Notifications |

ValA	Material	Val. type	Material description	MTyp	Stock Qty	Unit	Qty cons	Unit	% Iss	Devaluat. ind.	Base Price	%	New Price	/
1000	10000084	GRADE A	Stainless Steel	ROH	200.000	MT	0.000	MT	0.00	1	10,042.02	20.0	8,033.62	1
1000	10000084	GRADE B	Stainless Steel	ROH	200.000	MT	0.000	MT	0.00	1	16,024.50	20.0	12,819.60	1
1000	10000084	Totals Rec	Stainless Steel	ROH	0.000		0.000		0.00		13,033.26	20.0	10,426.61	1
1000	10000085	GRADE A	Stainless Steel	ROH	200.000	MT	0.000	MT	0.00	1	10,042.02	20.0	8,033.62	1
1000	10000085	GRADE B	Stainless Steel	ROH	200.000	MT	0.000	MT	0.00	1	15,063.03	20.0	12,050.42	1
1000	10000085	Totals Rec	Stainless Steel	ROH	0.000		0.000		0.00		12,552.53	20.0	10,042.02	1
1000	10000086	GRADE A	Stainless Steel	ROH	95.000	MT	5.000	MT	5.26	0	15,063.03	0.00	15,063.03	1
1000	10000086	Totals Rec	Stainless Steel	ROH	0.000		0.000		0.00		15,063.03	0.00	15,063.03	1
1000	10000087		Stainless Steel	ROH	165.000	MT	35.000	MT	21.21	0	12,651.48	0.00	12,651.48	1
1000	10000088		Stainless Steel	ROH	0.000	MT	0.000	MT	0.00	0	10,042.02	0.00	10,042.02	1
1000	10000104		White crystalline powder	ROH	1,040.000	KG	0.000	KG	0.00	1	14.97	20.0	11.97	1

Figure 22.49 Calculate New Lowest Price Based on Movement Rate

In this section, we examined the lowest value determination, which uses the LVP valuation method. In the following section, we'll discuss the concept of price changes in detail.

22.6   Material Price Changes

Material prices can change over a period of time due to changes in the market price. The SAP system includes functionality to accommodate these changes, and stock valuation is revaluated as per the current market price. For example, let's say a stainless steel manufacturer wants to change the valuation price of a material (stainless steel) due to a change in the market price.

The company has 100 MT in stock with a stock value of $10,000. The material is maintained with the valuation method standard price, and the price is $100/MT. The market price of stainless steel has since been reduced to $60/MT, and the company would like to update its stock valuation per the current market price. Valuation prices can be changed based on business requirements for three scenarios:

- A price change during the current posting period
- A price change during the previous posting period, with changes not carried over to the current period
- A price change during the previous posting period or year, which changes carried over to the current period

Keep in mind that changing the material price doesn't involve changing the material master record; a price change is an accounting transaction in which the total stock for a valuation area is revaluated.

Let's discuss these three different types of price changes.

22.6.1   Price Changes in the Current Posting Period

A material price change in the current posting period changes the material price and creates an accounting document. Let's say we have a material with a stock balance of 100 pieces, a price of $12/piece, and a total stock value of $1,200. Now, if the market price changes from $12/piece to $20/piece, you'll need to revaluate your stock valuation as per the current market price and post a price change document. After you've posted the price change document in the system, an accounting document is created; the stock G/L account is debited $800 (the difference between the original value of $1,200 and the new value of $2,000); and the expense/revenue from the revaluation G/L account is credited $800. The material price change is now complete, and the price stands at $20/piece.

22

22.6.2   Price Changes Not Carried Over

A material price change in the previous period or year changes the material price only in the previous period; in other words, the current price and valuation remain the same.

In this scenario, the price change transaction creates two accounting documents: one for the previous year and one for the current year. For example, when you change the price from $12 to $20 in the previous period or year, the previous period's stock account is debited $800, and revenue from the revaluation account is credited $800. To keep the price in the current valuation period the same, the system then posts one more accounting document for the current period, the stock account is credited, and the expense from revaluation account is debited.

22.6.3   Price Changes Carried Over

In this scenario, the price change in the previous period or year is carried forward to the current period. For example, let's say the price of a material has changed to $20. In the previous period, the material price was $12, and total stock was 100 pieces. In the current period, the material price is $15, and the total stock is 120 pieces.

As with the previous scenario, this transaction will create two accounting documents: The first accounting document is posted for the previous period, and the second accounting document is posted for the current posting period:

1. **First accounting document (posted for previous period)**
   The material price is increased by $8 (the new price is $20, the old price was $12); therefore, the stock value will be increased in the previous period by $800 (increased price of $8 × stock quantity of 100 for the previous period). $800 ($8×100) is debited to the stock G/L account, and $800 is credited to the revenue from the revaluation G/L account.

2. **Second accounting document (posted for current period)**
   For the current posting period, the stock quantity is 120 pieces, and the price is $15. Therefore, the calculation for the accounting posting will be as follows:
   - Reversal of price change in the current period: Reversal of the amount posted in the last posting period via the first accounting document:
     - Stock G/L account: $800 credit
     - Expense from revaluation account: $800 debit
   - Carryover price change into the current period: Because the new price needs to be carried over to the current period, the price difference amount results from the change in price from $15 per piece to $20 per piece in the current period:

- Stock G/L account: $600 debit (120 pieces × $5 is the price difference)
- Revenue from revaluation account: $600 credit
  - Net effect of the previous calculation: The net value is calculated from the previous two calculations and posted via the second accounting document:
    - Stock G/L account: $200 credit
    - Expense from revaluation account: $200 debit

The accounting document posted in the current posting period has credited $200 to the stock G/L account and debited $200 to the expense account from the revaluation account.

Now that we've discussed the three possible price change scenarios, let's look at the business process of price change and the configuration steps involved.

22.6.4 Business Process

You can change prices via Transaction MR21. To check the new valuation price and value of the stock in the material master accounting view, use Transaction MM03. You can post a material debit/credit via Transaction MR22.

This scenario is required primarily when materials are valuated with standard price control.

22.6.5 Configuration Steps for Price Changes in the Previous Period/Year

For a price change in the previous period or year, you must define whether the change also applies to the current period by following the menu path **Material Management • Valuation and Account Assignment • Configure Price Change in Previous Period/Previous Year**. Select the **Price Carryover** checkbox to activate the price change carryover.

22

22.7 Summary

In this chapter, we discussed how material is valued using the LIFO and FIFO methods and lowest value determination. Companies refer to the method of their material valuation in annual reports, and all of these methods are used. No one method is the most correct, and your company should choose whichever method is best suited at the time. As described in this chapter, newer companies often use FIFO to inflate their stock value, whereas mature companies can use LIFO to reduce their tax payments. Although not a core MM subject, you should have a good understanding of how material is valuated in SAP system. The majority of material stored in a plant or warehouse has value assigned to it. Valuations such as LIFO and FIFO drive how material is moved out of the plant, so the MM consultant should be aware of what valuation methods are commonly used and how these valuation methods work.

In this chapter, we also covered split valuation and account determination, including when the Material Ledger is implemented. Chapter 23 will examine the Material Ledger in further detail.

Chapter 23

Material Ledger

The Material Ledger leverages what's called the full absorption costing method through which all manufacturing costs are absorbed by the units produced. The unit cost of a product typically includes materials, direct labor, and both fixed and variable manufacturing overhead. The Material Ledger is part of product cost controlling (CO-PC), which manages inventory at actual cost and in multiple currencies and valuations.

Companies use the Material Ledger to manage inventory in both standard cost and actual cost. *Standard cost* is an estimated or predetermined cost that represents the total cost of performing an operation or producing a good or service under normal conditions. In a standard costing method, the standard cost is used throughout the month to value any material movement transactions. At the end of the month, the Material Ledger then calculates the actual costs for the period, taking into account all material movements and invoices associated with the raw materials, actual costs of the confirmations to the production orders, and any *price difference*. This actual periodic cost is an actual weighted moving average available through the Material Ledger.

In this chapter, you'll learn how to design, configure, implement, and use the Material Ledger efficiently. Practical examples of integrated processes from making, buying, and selling to month-end closing steps provide an effective reference guide to build or increase your knowledge of actual costing with the Material Ledger while making your day-to-day tasks clear and comprehensible.

23.1 Material Ledger Overview

The Material Ledger is part of product cost controlling (CO-PC) in controlling (CO) and serves as a subsidiary ledger for materials. CO is the management accounting component in SAP and contains several subcomponents: cost center accounting, overhead accounting, product cost controlling, and profitability analysis (CO-PA). As an MM consultant, having a decent understanding of how the Material Ledger works is important.

> **Note**
>
> While delivering the Material Ledger to a company, you should maintain close coordination with SAP FI and CO consultants so that MM integration with FI and CO is ensured. To understand how the Material Ledger integrates among MM, FI, and CO components, refer to the SAP PRESS E-Bite: *Introducing the Material Ledger in SAP S/4HANA* by Rogerio Faleiros and Paul Ovigele (2018, *www.sap-press.com/4648*).

Product costing is a complex process in any industry and is used to manage costs related to a manufacturing process. In SAP, product costing integrates with many other components and provides basic information for business processes used by various other SAP functional areas such as valuation of goods in materials management (MM), costs to determine price in sales and distribution (SD) pricing procedures, and ultimately setting the standards to measure production efficiency in manufacturing orders in the production planning (PP).

You must understand what standard costing is and how it is used in SAP system before diving into the Material Ledger. Standard costing is the process by which, for planning purposes, a company makes a preliminary target estimate of what a unit of product should cost for a determined period. In an SAP environment with standard costing, all material movement transactions such as purchases of raw materials, production, and transfers across different plants (sites/locations) of the company are recorded at standard values throughout the month.

The Material Ledger's primary function is to handle actual costing by collecting *price differences* against standards that result from goods and invoice receipts related to purchased orders and production variances, for example. At month end, these price differences are allocated back to the cost of the products—from raw material to finished products—across multiple levels of the production structure by using the multilevel cost rollup function in actual costing with the Material Ledger. This process allows companies to have a clear view of the actual performance of the production process in relation to targets while also providing invaluable insight into process inefficiencies. Variances to standards are captured separately in the general ledger (G/L) in SAP S/4HANA Finance. However, if you use the Material Ledger, these variances are not only tracked separately in SAP S/4HANA Finance; they can also be reconciled by product and plant, thus helping you to carry out analysis and comparisons against targets.

The fact that the Material Ledger carries the variances across several manufacturing levels adds a great deal of transparency on the value-added processes. The Material Ledger is a hybrid of a standard cost and a monthly weighted average cost. The *actual weighted average cost* is called the *periodic unit price* (PUP). PUP changes periodically as a result of goods movements and invoice entries. The PUP is used to revalue inventory at month end. PUP is available only if the Material Ledger is active for the material and the **Settlement Price Control 3** indicator is set.

You must also be familiar with the concepts behind actual costing with the Material Ledger before we look at its configuration. The Material Ledger does not exist in isolation; it extends standard costing functionalities and is mainly designed for use in manufacturing where the goods are produced or processed for use or sale.

The main purpose of the Material Ledger is to manage product costing and inventory in multiple currencies and valuations using actual prices. On a high level, actual costing with the Material Ledger involves three steps:

1. Preliminary valuation at standard cost and the recording of price differences
2. Price determination, the calculation of the PUP for single and multilevel products
3. Revaluation of inventory with the PUP

A great feature of the Material Ledger is *multiple currency valuation*. A total of three currencies and two valuation views are possible:

- *Local currency* for legal valuation in the currency of company code
- *Group valuation* for corporate group valuation for reporting purposes
- *Profit center* for profit center valuation or for transfer pricing functionality

If your company doesn't use the Material Ledger, normally, the valuation is carried out in a single currency, the company code currency. The Material Ledger enables valuation in two additional currencies for group valuation flow and reporting. Typically, if a company operates in many different countries, then the second currency or valuation is set as a group currency so that information in a single currency across different regions, i.e., U.S. dollars or Euros, can be easily consolidated. The third currency (profit center valuation) is commonly used in multinational companies to represent the transfer price for valuation of intercompany transactions across different locations and regions. This combination of currency and valuation is called a *valuation approach*.

23

In an actual costing environment, all goods movements within a period are valued at standard cost, which is called the *preliminary valuation*. At the same time, price and exchange rates differences are collected in the Material Ledger. Any material movement originated during a goods receipt or invoice receipt of a product is recorded in the Material Ledger. Business transactions relevant for valuation are translated using *historical exchange rates*, directly at time of posting.

Currency amounts that come from stock valuations, invoice verification, material cost estimates, and order settlement are translated into the other currencies in the respective areas and updated in the Material Ledger, as follows:

- **Invoice receipt postings**
  Amount is translated into the currencies managed in the Material Ledger at the current exchange rate. In standard SAP, exchange rate differences are calculated by comparing the exchange rates at goods receipt and invoice receipt. You can change these settings through the **Invoice Verification** configuration menu.

- **Settlement of production order**
  Values are not translated in the Material Ledger but transferred directly from the two currencies or valuations from the Material Ledger. The amount in the third currency is translated from the company code currency using the average rate.

- **Marking a standard cost**
  Results are not translated in the Material Ledger but are transferred directly from the standard cost estimate. The amount in the third currency is translated using the amount in the company code currency and the exchange rate at time of marking.

> **Note**
>
> The translation procedure we've mentioned could cause some discrepancies in the price of a material from one currency to another over a period of time. You can define how translations should occur in the FI configuration, including whether translations should be made starting from the *transaction currency* (the currency in which an individual document had been generated in the system) or from the company code currency. What exchange rate type will be used can also be determined in this configuration; typically, the average rate is used.

Material Ledger data collected throughout the period is used in the price determination during the periodic actual costing run to calculate the actual weighted average cost for the month (the periodic unit cost) for each material. All actual costs for the month are absorbed, and prices and exchange rate differences are rolled to the next level of production to determine the true actual cost for the period in question.

In addition to the actual costing functionality and the valuation of inventory in multiple currencies, one function of the Material Ledger is the *actual cost component split*. An actual cost component split groups actual costs into buckets across multiple manufacturing levels, thus providing your company with a view of the major relevant elements of the total cost, such as labor costs, raw material costs, freight costs, etc. The Material Ledger uses the same standard cost component structure for the cost component split at actual cost. Having this information available for each product and plant combination can help your company do important cost analysis more effectively by comparing actuals to standard costs as well as understand the breakdown of their costs with the functions provided by the Material Ledger. Using actual cost component split data can help your company make decisions more easily, such as whether to make or buy because the Material Ledger provides great detail into manufacturing and purchase costs.

Since actual costing information is updated at the level of the *procurement alternatives* and procurement processes (different options for procuring a material), you can also compare different sources of supply to analyze actual costs.

The actual cost component split available for cost of goods manufactured can also be transferred to controlling, profitability analysis (CO-PA), so you can have both the standard and the actual cost of goods sold (COGS) in CO-PA as well as the total cost and the cost component breakdown. The *actual cost in CO-PA* is calculated by revaluing the cost of goods sold for the period once the actual cost is known. Updating the actual cost of goods sold in CO-PA allows you use gross margin reports with different dimensions to analyze sales results using up-to-date information, thus identifying the most profitable products, for example, and working towards cost reduction to stand out in today's highly competitive business environment.

23.2   Business Processes

In this section, we'll dive into the main functions of the Material Ledger and examine how they relate and integrate with finance (FI) and logistics functionalities, such as MM, PP, and SD. We'll also cover key design definitions required for a sustainable Material Ledger solution.

23.2.1   Inventory Valuation Method

Price control indicates the valuation method for a material in a specific plant. Two types of *price control indicators* exist: standard price (S) and moving average price (V). A price control is assigned to a material in the **Accounting 1** tab of the material master, as shown in Figure 23.1.

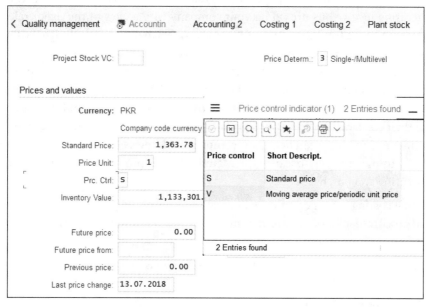

Figure 23.1 Price Control in the Material Master

- The *standard cost* is an estimated cost, fixed for a period of time according to your company's definition. Generally, this price follows the company's budget cycle and is based on an estimated, expected target unit cost for a product but may change more often based on internal decisions. Standard price and standard cost terms are used interchangeably and is also common in companies that run SAP.

- *Moving average price* is a weighted average cost that changes according to each goods receipt and/or invoice receipt (if invoice differs from purchase price).

Although moving average price reflects the most up-to-date data, using this price can cause other valuation problems if a stock shortage exists or the stock level is too low for the price difference to be posted, which leads to unrealistic prices because the remaining inventory is adjusted with the total invoice price difference. In a stock shortage situation, the system cannot allocate the variance (which can be positive or negative), and the variance remains on the purchase price difference account in the G/L because the system cannot allocate it to the inventory.

When working with moving average price, the timing on which the transaction occurs is critical. For an adequate valuation of the transaction at actual cost, a high dependency exists between the time at which the goods receipt and invoice receipt are posted and the time a material is issued from inventory. The same principle applies for variances related to the settlement of manufacturing orders.

As mentioned earlier in Section 23.1, when using the Material Ledger, materials with standard price control will be adjusted to an actual weighted moving average price at month end, which becomes your periodic unit price (PUP).

Note

In a Material Ledger environment, typically all finished products and semifinished products are set as standard price (price control S). Materials, such as raw materials or packing materials used in the production process of manufacturing a semifinished or finished product, are set at the moving average price.

Maintenance, repairs, and operations (MRO) materials are set with moving average price (price control V) because these materials are not used in a manufacturing process and therefore are not relevant for standard cost valuation.

Let's look at the impact of a material with standard price control through an example.

Let's say you have a raw material set to use a standard price and this material is consumed by a manufacturing cost center during the month. At month end, when actual costs are calculated and posted during the Material Ledger's post-closing step, the cost center will receive an additional amount related to the price difference apportionment. Further, the cost center that had already been completely absorbed will now have an under/overabsorption balance, which requires a manual journal entry to clear out the cost center.

If you use the Material Ledger, make sure the right price control design is in place. You should also avoid having materials with standard price consumed to a cost center or to a non-manufacturing cost object to avoid rework at month end. Materials with a standard price should always be used in a production process along with an appropriate cost object, such as a production order, a process order, sales order stock, etc., so that all price differences and revaluations of consumption are fully absorbed automatically by the system, thus preventing the need for additional manual clearing processes.

23

23.2.2 Material Price Determination

Material price determination indicates how the valuation of a material should occur after each business transaction for a material relevant to valuation. If the Material Ledger is active, this field must be set up in the material master using an appropriate combination of price control and material price determination.

The following price indicator options are available in the material master (**Accounting 1** tab) for price determination. **Accounting 1** tab contains current valuation data of a material. As shown earlier in Figure 23.1, note the field **Price Determ.** and the following dropdown options:

- **2: Transaction-based**
  Select this option to keep your inventory price control indicator as V (moving average) or S (standard price). If the material has price control S, the moving average is calculated for information purposes only, and this price is not used for valuation as the price control is standard. Materials with the transaction-based indicator option are not considered later in a multilevel actual costing.

- **3: Single/Multilevel**
  If you select this option, the price control has to be S (standard price). A moving average (period unit price) is calculated at month end. Single/multilevel price determination allows you to calculate single and multilevel price differences and carry these values over throughout a multilevel manufacturing production structure.

An appropriate combination of price control and price determination for a multilevel actual costing is shown in Table 23.1.

Price Control	Price Determination Indicator
V (Moving average)	2 (Transaction based)
S (Standard price)	3 (Single/Multilevel)

Table 23.1 Material Price Determination

23.2.3 Multiple Currencies

Defining multiple currencies is a critical step when designing product cost systems with the Material Ledger. Choosing the appropriate valuation that meets the needs of your company must be carefully deliberated. The multiple currency function is only available if the Material Ledger is active. Once the Material Ledger is configured and activated, *you cannot change* these settings. So, make sure you have the correct currency and valuation combination *before* you activate the Material Ledger.

You can manage a maximum of three valuation approaches in two currencies in a parallel valuation. All valuation approaches that you maintain in the currency and valuation profile must also be managed in the Material Ledger. The system checks whether the valuation approaches in CO, the Material Ledger, and FI, as well as the settings for the company codes, depreciation areas, and plants, are consistent with the valuation profile. In the Material Ledger, you can use a combination of currency types defined in the FI and CO components. As mentioned earlier, the combination of currency and valuation is called as a multiple valuation approach. SAP recommends using the group currency as the controlling area currency to ensure information is compatible among the MM, FI and CO components.

For illustration, a few examples of currency type and valuation combination setups are shown in Table 23.2 for group valuation and in Table 23.3 for a profit center valuation.

Valuation View	Currency Type
Legal	10 (Company code currency)
Group	30 (Group currency)
Group Valuation	31 (Group currency, group valuation)

Table 23.2 Parallel Valuation: Example of a Group Valuation

Three possible scenarios could be considered when choosing the currency for company level and group level reporting:

- **Legal (company code currency)**
  Currency code 10 is local currency of the company code, which represents the legal entity in SAP. An example of a local currency is USD (American dollars).

- **Group (group currency)**
  Currency code 30 enables reporting across multiple legal entities with different company code currencies. An example of a group currency different from our local currency is EUR (Euro).

- **Group valuation (group currency, group valuation)**
  Currency code 31 can be a different currency, perhaps based on a valuation for the corporate group (typically for profit elimination).

23

Valuation View	Currency Type
Legal	10 (company code currency)
Group	30 (group currency)
Profit Center	32 (group currency, profit center valuation)

Table 23.3 Parallel Valuation: Example of a Profit Center Valuation

- **Profit center (for usage of transfer pricing functionality) in group currency**
  Currency code 32 is used for profit center valuation, which manages transfer pricing for intercompany transactions (internal transfers of goods between profit centers valued with a specific price, for management purposes).

23.2.4   Price Differences

You must know the definitions of the various price differences in SAP when using the standard cost valuation method approach. A comprehensive understanding of the concepts of these differences will help you grasp the Material Ledger quickly while building up your knowledge using both standard and actual costing processes in SAP.

Purchase Price Variances

A purchase price difference or purchase price variance (PPV) occurs when the purchase price from external procurement, at the time of the goods receipt, differs from the standard cost of the material set up in the material master. Invoice receipts can also create price differences if the price differs from the purchasing document. The price difference amount is collected at the material and plant levels and stored in the Material Ledger. Subcontracting activities and subsequent charges can also create purchase price variances.

Exchange Rate Differences

Exchange rate differences occur when the exchange rate of the goods receipt with reference to a purchase order differs from the exchange rate at the time of invoice receipt. The same concept applies when the invoice receipt is performed before the goods receipt.

Manufacturing Variances (In-House Production)

Manufacturing variances represent the variance (remaining balance) of the cost of production on the production order and is calculated based on the difference between the total of the debits minus credits. Debit entries on production orders occur when the consumption of materials (i.e. raw materials or semifinished products) and activity type confirmations are charged to the order. When the production is complete and the products are moved into inventory, the order is credited. If the order status indicates final delivery or technical completion, then the balance on the order is a variance. However, if the order is not yet completed, the balance is considered work in progress (WIP).

The production order variance is transferred to FI and the Material Ledger when the order settlement is carried out. Production order variances can also be stored in the Material Ledger as price differences.

Stock Transfer Variances

Stock transfer variances occur when material movements are posted using the standard cost method. In other words, when transferring a product between two plants with different standard costs, a price difference is created, and the receiving material carries the variance.

Initial Entry of Stock Balances

An initial entry of stock balances using external values can also create a difference if the value posted is different from the current standard price. Typically, this activity is only relevant when migrating from a legacy system to an SAP system.

23.2.5   Debit and Credit of a Material

Debit and credit entries made directly to a material using Transaction MR22 are also treated as differences and are captured in the Material Ledger. Adjustments are required when a high price difference needs to be corrected to prevent a distortion of the material price and when reversing the original entry that caused the difference is no longer possible. An example would be a goods receipt with an incorrect price unit or base unit of measure (UoM) that thus caused a high price difference identified after the material had been consumed. Another example is, when closing the Material Ledger, non-distributed differences may need to be fixed. These differences may have appeared after material price determination due to a shortage of inventory.

Now that you have a good understanding of the concepts behind the Material Ledger and the factors influencing its use, let's delve into the configuration basics in the following section.

23.3   Configuration Basics

In the following sections, we'll cover the main steps involved in configuring and activating the Material Ledger. Ideally, this configuration activity is led by the CO consultant while MM and FI consultants provide the necessary support in integration-related scenarios and processes.

23.3.1   Activating Valuation Areas

SAP recommends activating the Material Ledger for all plants that belong to the same company code to ensure consistency with FI and MM. The valuation areas that will have the Material Ledger activated are configured using Transaction OMX1 or by following the IMG menu path **Controlling • Product Cost Controlling • Actual Costing/ Material Ledger • Activate Valuation Areas For Material Ledger**.

Double-click on **Activate Material Ledger** to configure the activation of the Material Ledger. Select the **ML ACT** checkbox. In the **PRICE DETER** field, specify the material price determination type to be used when creating material in the plant you are activating. Enter "3" (single level and multilevel price determination), as shown in Figure 23.2. You can enter "2" for materials that will be set up with the moving average price control (V) while creating the material master's **Accounting 1** tab.

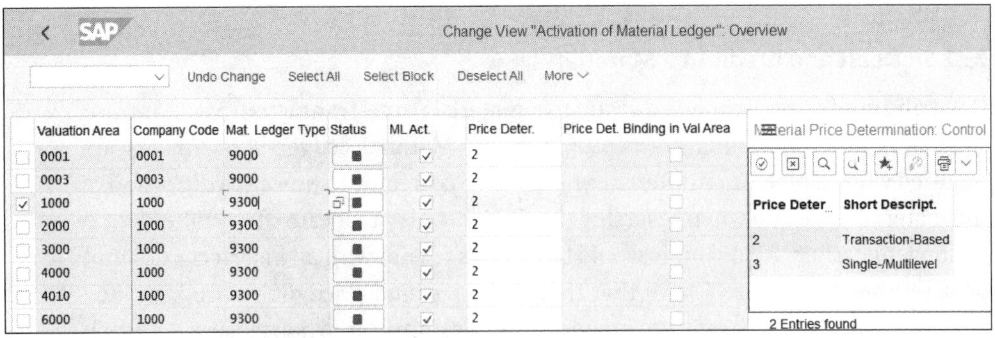

Figure 23.2 Activating the Material Ledger

Tips & Tricks

You can also make the price determination binding in the valuation area when a material is created. If you set this field, all materials in the valuation area cannot have the price determination changed. Do not set this indicator if you want to change the price determination at any future time.

Before activating the Material Ledger, you should also check relevant settings, such as currencies and account determination, to ensure completeness. Account determination is covered in Section 23.3.4.

Using Transaction CKM9, the option **Check Material Ledger Settings**, you can review the Material Ledger settings. This step is important once you complete the Material Ledger configuration but before the startup step, as shown in Figure 23.3.

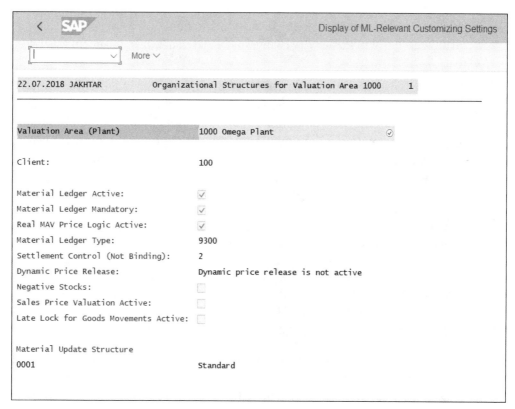

Figure 23.3 Checking the Material Ledger Customizing Settings

23.3.2   Assigning Currency Types

Next, you'll create Material Ledger types to define the available currencies. You can define up to three currency types to each Material Ledger type. Valuation areas and plants that belong to the same company code should use the same Material Ledger type. Make sure that the currency settings in FI and in the Material Ledger are correct before starting up the Material Ledger in production. You cannot change currencies, currency types, or Material Ledger types after go-live.

To keep information consistent across MM, FI, and CO, SAP recommends using a group currency as the controlling area currency. However, a company code currency can also be used.

23.3.3   Maintaining Number Ranges for Material Ledger Documents

A *Material Ledger document* records the changes that result from business transactions relevant for valuation. Each business transaction, such as a goods movement, invoice receipt, or material price change, has a Material Ledger document associated to it.

A Material Ledger document must be clearly identified in the system. This is achieved by saving each transaction in the Material Ledger under a unique number range reserved in FI for the Material Ledger. Usually, you won't have to create new groups. If new groups are created, they must be assigned to the correct number range for a new group of Material Ledger documents. Standard SAP has the following groups for Material Ledger documents segregated by transaction type:

- Material Ledger update (Group 01)
- Material Ledger closing (Group 02)
- Material Ledger price changes (Group 03)
- Single-level Material Ledger settlement (Group 04)
- Multilevel Material Ledger settlement (Group 05)
- Material Ledger repair (Group 06)
- Material Ledger closing cumulative valuation (Group 07)

To configure and maintain material number ranges, use Transaction OXM4 or follow the IMG menu path **Controlling • Product Cost Controlling • Actual Costing/Material Ledger • Maintain Number Ranges For Material Ledger Documents**.

23.3.4 Automatic Account Determination

Before discussing the automatic account determination settings specific to the Material Ledger, you must understand the integration among inventory management (IM), product costing, and accounting. Typically, material master setup for material movement transactions in SAP are plant-specific, which means they are managed at the material type level and the valuation area/plant level. Materials relevant for valuation are set up with accounting views and costing views. When a material is created, a *valuation class* must be assigned to the **Accounting 1** tab in the material master. A valuation class is a four-character code that groups and further classifies a material type. Valuation classes are usually determined by accounting because they define the G/L accounts used for material movement transactions with financial impact. Examples of valuation classes are raw materials, packaging materials, finished products, spare parts, etc.

For each material movement, such as a goods receipt from a purchase order, a delivery of a product to a customer, or a stock transfer between plants for an IM transaction relevant to financial and cost accounting, postings made to G/L accounts in the FI component must be identified by an accounting document. The G/L account is derived automatically from a default combination of configuration settings of material type, valuation class of material, and (in the case of split valuation) the valuation type and movement type.

The mechanism to automatically determine the G/L account for each business transaction is called *automatic account determination*. This functionality can minimize user inputs (and thus user error) because users won't have to determine the appropriate G/L account numbers. The account determination configuration table contains different settings so the system can find the appropriate posting account using a variety of data. Some important terms to understand related to automatic account determination are:

- **Chart of accounts of the company code**
  The automatic account determination must be defined individually for each chart of accounts.

- **Valuation grouping code of the valuation area**
  The valuation grouping code allows you to set various account determination settings within a chart of accounts when a chart of accounts is to run differently for certain company codes or plants (valuation areas). As a result, you can assign a different G/L account for the same valuation class under two different company codes within the same chart of accounts.

- **Transaction or event key (internal processing key)**

  A transaction key, event key, or processing key is a key used to differentiate account determination by business transaction. For example, let's say you must differentiate the G/L account posted by the goods receipt transaction from the G/L account posted by the invoice receipt transaction. These transaction keys are determined automatically from the transaction (invoice verification) or the movement type (inventory management). When configuring account determination, all you'll have to do is assign the relevant G/L account to each posting transaction.

- **Account grouping**

  An account grouping is used only for offsetting entries, such as consignment liabilities and price differences. An additional key called the account modification key can be assigned to each transaction event key, which provides a further breakdown of the posting transactions, such as physical inventory adjustments, consumption account to a cost object, goods issue to sales, etc. An account grouping is assigned to each movement type in IM that uses the posting transaction offsetting entry for inventory posting. G/L accounts must be assigned for every account modification key (grouping code). For example, transaction key event GBB contains account modification keys BSA, INV, VBR, and VAX.

- **Valuation class**

  The valuation class allows you to define automatic account determination depending on the material. For example, let's say you want to post a goods receipt of a raw material to a different stock account than for finished goods, even though the original transaction entered is the same for both materials. This feature can be achieved by assigning different valuation classes to the materials and by associating different G/L accounts to the posting transaction for every valuation class.

Automatic account determination is configured using Transaction OBYC or by following the IMG menu path **Materials Management • Valuation And Account Assignment • Account Determination • Account Determination Without Wizard • Configure Automatic Postings**. You can go straight to **Configure Automatic Postings** if you've already maintained other prerequisite settings, such as grouping codes, valuation classes, etc.

> **Note**
>
> Refer to Chapter 22, where we covered automatic account determination in a step-by-step manner.

Table 23.4 lists the transaction keys used in conjunction with the Material Ledger for Transaction OBYC.

Transaction Key Description	Transaction Key	Account Modification Key
Stock postings	BSX	
Price difference postings	PRD	PRA PRF PRU
Multilevel price difference (Material Ledger settlement)	PRV	PNL PPL
Single-level price difference (Material Ledger settlement)	PRY	PNL PPL
Exchange rate difference with open items	KDM	PNL PPL
Exchange rate difference from Material Ledger lower levels	KDV	
Price difference from inventory revaluation	UMB	
Price differences from stock transfer	AUM	
Revaluation of activity types	GBB	AUI
Revaluation of other consumables	COC	
WIP from material price differences	WPM	
WIP from activity price differences	WPA	
WIP from material price differences write-off	PRM	
WIP from activity price differences write-off	PRA	
Accruals and deferrals in the Material Ledger	LKW	

Table 23.4 Material Ledger-Related Keys in Transaction OBYC

We'll provide brief explanations for each of the keys next.

Inventory Posting (BSX)

Transaction key BSX is used for all postings to inventory accounts at standard cost throughout the month. At month end, when the Material Ledger is closed and the actual cost is known, the price difference portion related to the closing inventory is posted to the same inventory account, unless you choose not to revalue the inventory. The revaluation amount is identified by a specific document type (ML—Material Ledger Settlement), so that you can easily filter the entries related to Material Ledger revaluation.

Price Differences (PRD)

Transaction key PRD is used to post price differences that arise from material movements with a value that differs from the standard price set in the material master or in invoices. Examples include goods receipts against purchase orders and invoice receipts (if the invoice price differs from the PO price and the standard price). Price differences can also arise, for materials with moving average price, if not enough stock exists to cover the invoiced quantity or variances from order settlement. The settings for transaction event key PRD can be done with or without an account modification key. For more visibility into the various types of price differences according to specific business processes, distinguish the variances by G/L account. In this way, you can monitor the variances throughout the month and facilitate the reconciliation process at month end.

Transaction event key PRD can be further split into the following account modification or account grouping categories:

- None (blank): Variances related to purchase price variances
- PRA: Variances related to goods issues movements
- PRF: Variances related to production order variances
- PRU: Variances related to stock transfer postings (external amounts)

Price Differences: Multilevel (PRV)

The PRV transaction key is used in the Material Ledger closing to post multilevel price differences to inventory or to write off differences related to revaluation of consumptions, for example, cost of goods sold. A further breakdown of accounts is possible by using account modification keys:

- PNL: Transfer PRD to the next level
- PPL: Take PRD from a lower level

Price Differences: Single Level (PRY)

The PRY transaction key is used in the Material Ledger closing to post single-level price differences to inventory or to write off differences related to revaluation of consumption, for example, cost of goods sold. Similar to PRV, a further breakdown of accounts is possible by using account modification keys:

- NL: Transfer PRD to the next level
- PPL: Take PRD from a lower level

Exchange Rate Differences for Open Items (KDM)

Transaction key KDM is used for posting exchange rate differences that arise from a purchase order invoice posted with an exchange rate different from the goods receipt for materials with standard price or that arise from stock undercoverage/shortage for items valued by moving average price.

Exchange Rate Differences from Material Ledger Lower Levels (KDV)

Transaction key KDV is used in the Material Ledger closing to settle multilevel exchange rate differences to inventory or to write off exchange rate differences related to revaluation of consumption, for example, cost of goods sold.

Price Difference from Inventory Revaluation (UMB)

When a new standard cost is released, the system writes the results of the new cost estimate to the material master record as the current standard price. The standard price is then active for financial and cost accounting and is used to value the material until the next time a standard cost estimate is released.

When updating the new standard price (releasing the cost estimate), materials with an on-hand inventory balance are revalued once the new standard cost is released. As a result, the new inventory balance is the new unit standard price multiplied by the total quantity. The difference between the new inventory balance and the previous amount creates a revaluation, which is posted to the account assigned to the transaction key event UMB (gain/loss from revaluation). Postings related to inventory revaluation originating from the release of a cost estimate are cleared from the UMB account when the Material Ledger for the previous period is closed. As a result, the amount posted to this account is transferred back to inventory to determine the actual unit cost and then offset against transaction key PRY. Therefore, the balance of the UMB account related to inventory revaluation should always be zero at month end.

23

Transaction key UMB is also used with debit and credit postings using Transaction MR22. However, in this situation, the balance on the account is not cleared out at month end; only the offsetting account, transaction key PRD, gets cleared. You may need to create a journal entry to adjust the balance from this account depending on the transaction you're trying to adjust.

Price Differences from Stock Transfer (AUM)

Transaction key AUM is used to post price differences that arise from materials with different valuation when doing material-to-material transfers or in transfer postings that involve two plants when a complete value of the issuing material cannot be posted to the value of the receiving material. The receiving material will carry the variance. This situation applies to both materials with a standard price and materials with a moving average price control.

Activity Price Revaluation (GBB-AUI)

Transaction key GBB-AUI is the account used to post the over/underabsorption of a manufacturing cost center. This revaluation occurs during the actual costing run posting. The variance is allocated proportionally to its corresponding materials based on the quantity that was absorbed from the cost center to the production orders in the course of the month through an activity type or business process.

Revaluation of Other Consumables (COC)

Transaction key COC is the account used to post price differences related to single-level consumption not revalued using the original cost element. For example, a consumption of material to a cost center, where the movement type is not set up to be revalued using the original account and the cost object. The calculation of this revaluation is done when performing the revaluation of consumption step in the actual costing run at month end.

WIP from Activity Price Differences (WPA)

Transaction key WPA is the account used to post the Material Ledger revaluation from the WIP revaluation step on the actual costing run. These price differences stem from the actual price calculation of activity type or business process assigned to the work-in-process inventory. With WIP revaluation activated, you'll have to maintain the accounts in the account determination for the revaluation.

> **Tips & Tricks**
>
> You can use the same WIP G/L account configured in the **Posting Rules in WIP Calcu-lation and Result Analysis** in Transaction OKG8 to use both the WIP at standard cost plus the variances from the Material Ledger in the same account, which may help you analyze your overall WIP balances.

WIP from Material Price Differences (WPM)

Similar to transaction key WPA, the G/L account assigned to transaction key WPM is used to post the Material Ledger revaluation from the WIP revaluation step on the actual costing run. These price differences relate to material consumed to process orders still in process and thus should be assigned to the work-in-process inventory.

Again, since you activated WIP at actual cost, this transaction key must be main-tained with the appropriate G/L accounts. Regarding the G/L account for this process, the same principles from transaction key WPA apply for material revaluation. By using the same G/L account as transaction key WIP, your total WIP is assigned to a single account, which can facilitate further analysis. Different G/L accounts can also be used for this purpose, but note the account must be a balance sheet account.

WIP from Material Price Differences Write-Off (PRM)

Transaction key PRM is the account is used to cancel the WIP from material price dif-ferences posted initially to a transaction key WPM account. This entry only occurs when the production order is complete. This account is the offset account for trans-action key WPM. The G/L account is usually a profit and loss (P&L) statement account, which is typically not created as a cost element.

WIP from Activity Price Differences Write-Off (PRA)

Transaction key PRA is the account used to cancel the WIP from activity price differ-ences posted initially to a WPA account. Similar to PRM, this entry only occurs when the production order is complete. Therefore, this account is the offset account for transaction key WPA. The G/L account is usually a P&L statement account, which is typically not created as a cost element. The same account defined for transaction key PRM could be used here.

23

Accruals and Deferrals Account in Material Ledger (LKW)

Transaction key LKW is the account used when you don't want to revaluate the value of the closing inventory with the Material Ledger variances (price and exchange rate differences). Instead, all price differences are posted to this account. In countries where actual costing is a legal requirement, this transaction key should not be maintained.

Now that you've completed all the configuration settings for the Material Ledger, as well as all the relevant automatic accounting determination configuration steps, let's move on to activating the Material Ledger and setting valuation areas as productive.

23.4   Activating the Material Ledger

Activating the Material Ledger is a critical step, and you must make sure all Material Ledger-related settings are properly defined. Here is a quick checklist:

- Confirm that all currency settings are correctly configured for FI and in the Material Ledger.
- Confirm that the attributes of material types are correct; the only materials that will be converted to the Material Ledger are materials relevant for valuation. Make sure that all plants you want to activate in the Material Ledger are set as active for the Material Ledger. SAP recommends activating the Material Ledger for all plants belonging to the same company code because invoice verification cannot enter invoices that contain materials from plants with the Material Ledger active and with inactive Material Ledgers.
- In a new SAP implementation, the Material Ledger startup occurs before you start creating material master records.
- Also remember that, from the moment Material Ledger is activated in IMG to the end of the production startup, you cannot perform any goods movements in the affected plants in a testing or live system. A best practice is to perform the configuration in a development system and then migrate to other systems. You also cannot create material master records until the startup is complete.

> **Note**
>
> The relevant Material Ledger settings we just discussed can be reviewed using Transaction CKM9 or by following the IMG menu path **Controlling • Product Cost Controlling • Actual Costing/Material Ledger • Activate Valuation Areas For Material Ledger**. We highly recommend that you run this transaction before the production startup so that you can review any incomplete or incorrect settings, as shown in Figure 23.4.

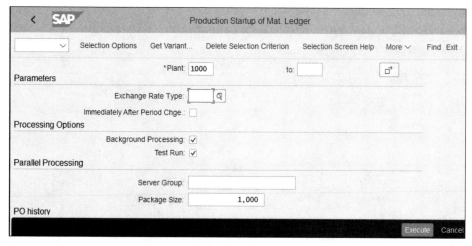

Figure 23.4 Production Startup of the Material Ledger

Figure 23.5 shows the Material Ledger settings in the **Accounting 1** tab of material master. The **ML Active** checkbox indicates that the Material Ledger is active on this material-plant combination. The valuation class 7920 associated with the material master and the price determination method (**Single-/Multilevel**) are also shown.

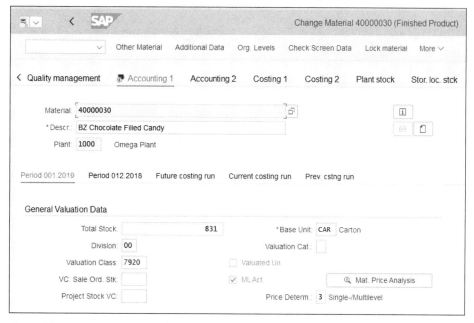

Figure 23.5 Accounting 1 Tab of the Material Master

Figure 23.6 shows the scrolled-down part of the **Accounting 1** tab of the material master, including more details such as the price control (**Prc. Ctrl**) to the company code and group currency details.

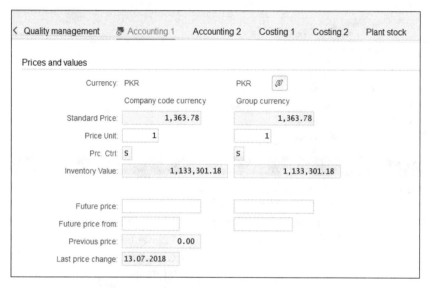

Figure 23.6 Price Control and Currencies Details of the Material Master

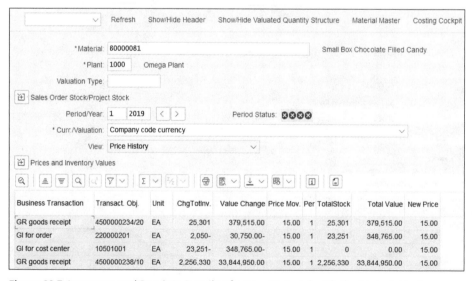

Figure 23.7 Issuances and Receipts Details of a Raw Material with the Material Ledger

As shown in Figure 23.5, click the **Mat. Price Analysis** button located in the lower right-hand side of the screen. All goods receipts and issuances of the material 80000081 in plant 1000 are recorded at an individual item level, and any price change is noted as well, as shown in Figure 23.7.

23.5 Reporting in the Material Ledger

The screen shown in Figure 23.8 is accessed using Transaction CKM3N and displays the results of a good receipt of a raw material purchased in the Material Ledger as well its issuances.

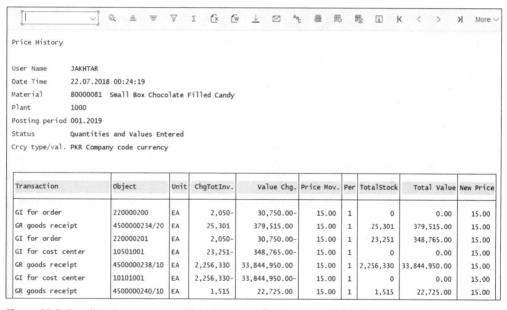

Figure 23.8 Receipts, Issuances, and Price History of a Raw Material Using Transaction CKM3N

The screen shown in Figure 23.9 is accessed using the same Transaction CKM3N but this time the details are for the finished good material.

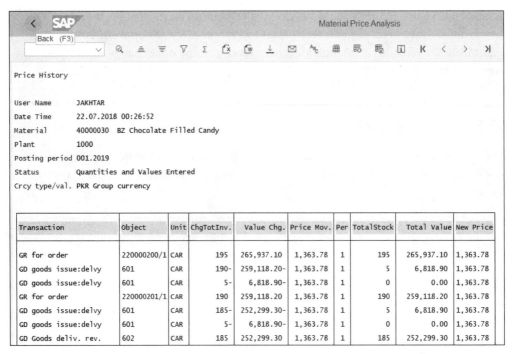

Figure 23.9 Receipts, Issuances, and Price History of a Finished Good Using Transaction CKM3N

As shown in Figure 23.10, Transaction CK11N has a different format to review the standard costing results. The view displays the standard cost-by-cost component. Be sure the standard cost component split will be performed because this split will be used to value the material movement transactions, including the cost of goods sold. The cost component split flows to CO-PA, which will allow you to review your cost of sales using the cost component breakdown. This great functionality provides detailed information in CO-PA, which can greatly help support your company when analyzing and reporting cost of goods sold, profitability, or gross margin in CO-PA. You can choose to report your cost of goods sold by nature of expenses or total, as well as profitability by product or any other characteristics available in CO-PA.

The screen shown in Figure 23.11 is accessed using Transaction MIGO and displays the material document 5000000468. The popup on the right-hand side shows that the system has not only created a material document, but also a financial accounting document and a Material Ledger document.

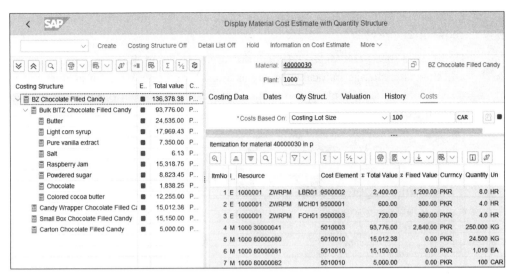

Figure 23.10 Material Cost Estimate

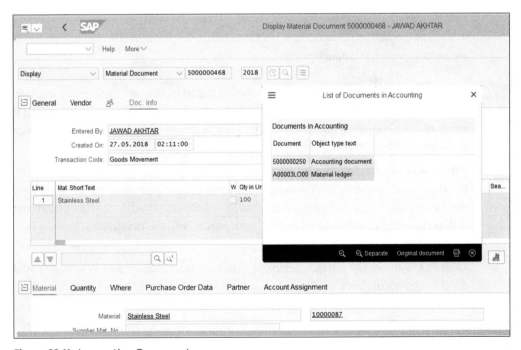

Figure 23.11 Accounting Documents

23

Click on the Material Ledger document A00003LO00, which brings up the screen shown in Figure 23.12.

Figure 23.12 shows the Material Ledger document showing the change to inventory and the value change in local currency as a result of a goods receipt against a purchase order. You can explore more details by clicking on the various buttons located at the top of the screen.

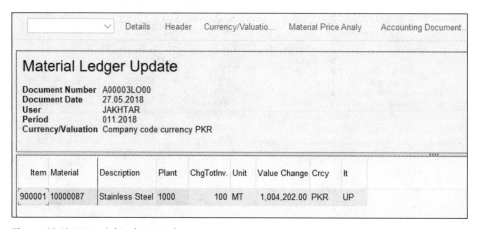

Figure 23.12 Material Ledger Update

Figure 23.13 shows the Material Prices Analysis report of the same material we saw in the previous figure. Notice that the last column **Price (New)** shows price changes that resulted from receiving goods against various purchase orders at different prices of the material 10000087.

Finally and briefly, let's review the cost center report using Transaction S_ALR_ 87013611 for manufacturing cost centers to ensure a zero balance. In this way, we'll ensure that any over/underabsorption has been fully absorbed during the actual cost rollup. Fill in the controlling area, fiscal year, period, and the manufacturing cost center group or values.

Figure 23.14 shows the various financial entries as the result of activities performed during the production process.

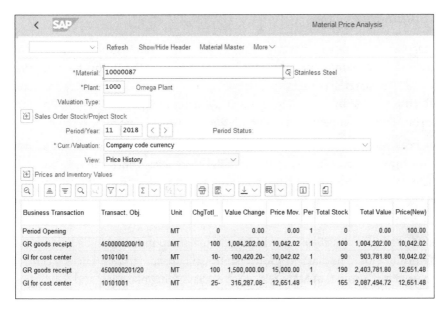

Figure 23.13 Material Price Analysis

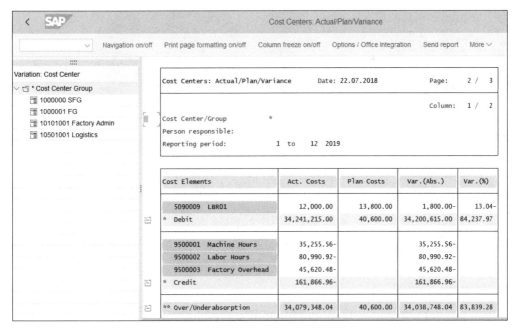

Figure 23.14 Cost Centers Analysis: Actual/Plan/Variance

23

23.6   Summary

In this chapter, we dealt with the Material Ledger, which retains the actual costs of materials and at the same time considers and records all of the factors behind price fluctuations. The Material Ledger can also hold values in three currencies at the same time, which is needed by companies frequently using or reporting in different currencies. The Material Ledger is now a default option available in SAP S/4HANA.

A number of benefits can be enjoyed using the Material Ledger, including the ability to keep inventory records in up to three parallel currencies, which can help consolidate businesses that are part of a large multinational company. Another benefit is that the Material Ledger provides information that can be used to decide on the most advantageous currency for the purchase of materials.

Chapter 24 examines classification, which we touched upon earlier in discussions of batch determination. The classification system isn't specific to MM but is a central function used in a number of MM areas, such as classifying materials and batches.

Chapter 24

Classification System

A classification system helps you search for information in the SAP system based on user-defined parameters and criteria. The standard features and available options are sufficient to set up the classification system in almost no time; hardly any configuration is involved. The classification system is also used across SAP's logistics functionality.

Classification systems occur everywhere. The Dewey Decimal system used in libraries is a classification system, zoologists use the Linnaean system for animal classification, and the US government uses the Standard Occupational Classification (SOC) System for classifying workers into occupational categories, to name only a few. SAP's classification system is a cross-component functionality that can offer significant benefits to business users through maintaining additional information about an SAP object that can't be maintained elsewhere. Classification can also be put to use as a powerful search tool.

Classification finds extensive use and application throughout logistics in SAP S/4HANA. Various options for categorizing and organizing your master data for quick and easy searches, whether material master, equipment, Document Management System (DMS) document, or batch, are available.

You can independently implement and integrate the classification system with your existing business processes at any time deemed necessary. For example, let's say your company already runs the SAP S/4HANA but has massive master data volumes that could benefit from better categorization and organization for easy and quick searches. Or, another example, let's say you have materials for which no provision exists in the material master to enter the material's attribute/characteristic details. For example, in the steel sheets re-rolling industry, six specific quantity and qualitative attributes are used to produce several variations of materials. No provision may exist to enter these specific attributes in the material master, but with the classification system, this information can be captured and used.

24

You can implement the classification system as a standalone, independent project. Integrating the classification system with the existing business processes consists of three main activities:

- Creating characteristics
- Creating classes and assigning characteristics
- Assigning classes to the relevant master data

In this chapter, we'll begin with covering the classification system, which includes characteristics and classes. We'll cover how to create characteristics and the associated options and controls available. Then, we'll not only show you how to create classes but also how to assign existing characteristics to classes. We'll also show you the significance of maintaining the correct class type. Finally, we'll assign the classification system to SAP objects and then show you how to maintain classification information and use classification for search functions.

24.1   Classification Overview

The following definition of a classification system from the Public Work and Government Services Department of Canada states:

> *A classification system is a structured scheme for categorizing entities or objects to improve access, created according to alphabetical, associative, hierarchical, numerical, ideological, spatial, chronological, or other criteria.*

The classification system in SAP S/4HANA let you put this definition to practical use. A *characteristic* in the classification system is the specific field in which a business user maintains specific information to categorize or catalog an SAP object. A *class* in the classification system acts as a catalog that holds all the characteristics. Classes are eventually assigned to SAP objects, such as a material, a customer, or an equipment master.

24.1.1   What Is the SAP S/4HANA Classification System?

The classification system in SAP S/4HANA fits the definition presented earlier because it's a structured framework primarily used for searching objects based on a series of characteristics that describe the object. The object can be a material, an equipment, batch, and so on.

The classification system can be an extremely powerful tool if constructed in a strategic manner with a significant amount of planning. Classification systems that are ignored by users probably evolved over time with no planning and are cumbersome and difficult to maintain. The more planning you put into creating a classification system, the more likely it will become a worthwhile tool.

Some companies employ outside consultants to review the materials they have and develop a structured naming and classification framework based on the description and use of the material. Although potentially an expensive and time-consuming project, your company could start implementing a classification system with rules and procedures already in place. For example, industry standards, such as Petroleum Industry Data Exchange (PIDX, *www.pidx.org*), offer business benefits to the global hydrocarbon industries when SAP classification is used to classify the rather large number of maintenance spare parts used in the industry.

24.1.2   Describing an Object

In developing the classification system, three areas will need to be addressed:

- Objects
- Characteristics
- Classes

You'll need to examine the object to be described and define a set of standard descriptions or characteristics. For instance, for a technical object like a pump, various characteristics can be used to describe the pump, including the pump's horsepower, the outer casing material such as steel, and its usage such as for pumping water or brine. These descriptions are called characteristics, and each characteristic has values or a range of values. For example, if we again consider the pump as an object and look at the characteristic "horsepower," a valid value might be "40hp." The value can be an exact figure, or the value can be configured as a range, if required.

The characteristics are grouped together in a class. The class contains a number of characteristics that are of similar values. The class is the entity assigned to the material in the material master.

A class is associated with a *class type*. The class type is a key used to assign a class to an object. For example, if a class is assigned to class type 001, then the class can only be assigned to those objects relevant for class type 017, that is, the material.

In this section, we provided an overview of the classification function in SAP S/4HANA. In the next section, we'll review how to create a characteristic and how to use characteristics in classification.

24

24.2   Characteristics

As described earlier, a characteristic describes an object, and a characteristic can have values or a range of values that are valid for each characteristic. In this section, we'll begin by covering the steps required to create a characteristic and the available options. We'll also cover the associated configuration settings that can help you effectively create characteristics and put relevant controls in place.

Inherited Characteristics

A characteristic is inherited when a characteristic and its value are passed from a superior class in the class hierarchy to the subordinate classes. The main advantage of inheritance is that the end user doesn't need to enter the characteristic in the subordinate classes because it has been entered once in the superior class and then inherited.

24.2.1   Creating Characteristics

After your company has decided on a set of descriptive characteristics for an object, the next step is to create the characteristic. Transaction CT04 is used to create the characteristic and can be found by following the navigation path **Cross-Application Components • Classification System • Master Data • Characteristics**.

In this tab, information related to a characteristic is defined, such as its description, data type, number of characteristics, decimal places (if any), and unit of measure (UoM). Table 24.1 describes some the important fields available in the various tabs shown in Figure 24.1.

Field Name	Field Description and Value
Description	Description of the characteristic, for example, pump capacity.
Chars Group	Groups together similar characteristics in one group.
Status	Status of the characteristics, for example, *released*, to indicate the object is ready for use.
Data Type	Indicates the type of data this characteristic has; for example, date, time format, or numeric format.
Number of Chars	Indicates the number of characters a value of this characteristic can contain.

Table 24.1 Details of Individual Fields of a Characteristic

Field Name	Field Description and Value
Decimal Places	Indicates the number of decimal places if the format is numeric.
Unit of Measure	Unit of measure of the characteristic (quantitative/numeric), if any.
Single-value/Multiple Values (radio button)	Option if a single value or multiple values are allowed for a characteristic. An example of using multiple values is when you can select a surface finish (coarse, pitted, or uneven). For multiple values, the system offers a checkbox for each value to select from the dropdown list.
Negative Vals Allowed (checkbox)	Select if negative values are allowed. Negative values for a characteristic cannot be entered unless this checkbox is selected.
Entry Required (checkbox)	Select if the user must enter a value for this characteristic. If not selected, then entering a value is optional.

Table 24.1 Details of Individual Fields of a Characteristic (Cont.)

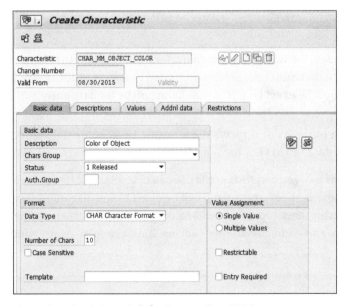

Figure 24.1 Basic Data Tab for Transaction CT04

You'll then switch over to the **Values** tab and maintain values for this characteristic. For example, let's say a characteristic provides an option to record the pump's value, which can then be searched in the material master along with any other characteristic. Select the **Additional Values** checkbox to ensure that values other than the prefixed 10, 20, or 30 are also allowed for entry as an input value. You can select the **Default values** checkbox (the **D** column) on any specific value, which will then automatically appear when the characteristic is used and therefore reduce data entry. However, you can overwrite the default value if necessary.

Click on the **Addnl data** tab to see more options. You can enter the relevant DMS documents number, document type, document part, and document version, if any. The various checkboxes and their functions can be described as follows:

- **Not ready for input**
  You can't enter a value in this characteristic. In other words, a preassigned default or calculated value automatically fills the characteristic field, and the user has no option to make an entry.

- **No Display**
  The system won't display a characteristic.

- **Display Allowed Values**
  If several values are already available from the **Values** tab of the characteristic, the system displays those values to facilitate the user during data entry.

- **Unformatted Entry**
  If this checkbox is selected, the system sets the characteristic's field length to a maximum of 30 so users can make multiple entries, separated by colons. If not selected, then the system displays the exact length of the characteristic for data entry.

- **Proposed Template**
  If selected, the system proposes or displays the template to facilitate data entry. Click back to the **Basic data** tab to view the template details.

Finally, on the **Restrictions** tab, you can restrict the use of a characteristic to a specific class type or types; otherwise, the characteristic will be available for use in all class types. For example, entering class type "001" will restrict this characteristic to this material class only. Save the characteristic by clicking the **Save** icon or pressing `Ctrl` + `S`.

Note

If you create a characteristic with a date format and eventually use this characteristic in a class, the system will *not* provide the standard option of bringing up a calendar from which to choose a date. Users will have to manually enter the date. If you want to enable the calendar option in the dropdown of the date characteristic, you'll need to engage an ABAP consultant.

Tips & Tricks

You can't assign the same characteristic more than once in the same class and class type. You can, however, assign the same characteristic to different classes of the same class type or to different class types, provided no restriction on their usage has been defined.

The standard system offers the option of using two separate batch input programs to upload large numbers of characteristics, to create classes, and to assign characteristics to classes.

24.2.2   Configuring Characteristics

A number of elements must be examined when configuring a characteristic. These elements are described in the following sections.

Characteristic Defaults

A number of configuration steps must be performed to allow characteristics to operate according to your requirements. The first step is to set default settings for a characteristic. If a certain field must contain a specific value, you can configure a default value required each time a characteristic is created. The configuration for the defaults is shown in Figure 24.2.

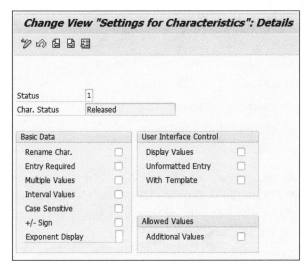

Figure 24.2 Configuration Screen to Set Defaults for Characteristics

To access the transaction and configure the default settings, by following the configuration navigation path **Cross-Application Components • Classification System • Characteristics • Define Default Settings**.

Characteristic Status

A characteristic can be set to different statuses, which are predefined in SAP S/4HANA: **Released, In preparation**, or **Locked**. A configuration transaction is available for you to create new statuses as needed. For example, a status can be configured that allows for review.

To configure the characteristic status, you can access the transaction by following the configuration navigation path **Cross-Application Components • Classification System • Characteristics • Define Characteristic Statuses**.

Value Templates

SAP S/4HANA includes a number of templates that can be used for entering information into characteristic values. You can also configure new templates for a specific characteristic value.

Many characters are configured for use in the templates, which can be found by following the configuration navigation path **Cross-Application Components • Classification System • Characteristics • Define Template Characters**.

Figure 24.3 shows the characters that are defined for use in the templates. The **Usage** field determines how the character is used. The options for the **Usage** field are as follows:

- 1: Numeric character that is valid for numeric and character formats.
- 2: Alphanumeric character that is valid for character formats.
- 3: Character that is valid for the character format.
- 4: Preliminary sign that is valid for the character format.
- 5: Separator that is valid for the character format.

Access the transaction by following the configuration navigation path **Cross-Application Components • Classification System • Characteristics • Define Templates**. You can configure new characteristic value templates or modify existing templates. Figure 24.4 shows various templates configured for use with characteristics.

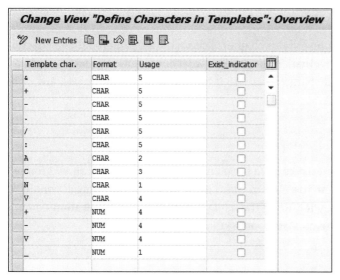

Figure 24.3 Configuration to Define Characters for Characteristic Templates

Change View "Templates": Overview

Counter	Template	Description
10	___,___.___	Numeric template
20	___,___,___._E-33	Template with fixed exponent
30	___._ MILLIMETER	Numeric template
40	___._E-SS	Scientific template
50	_._____E-__	Standard exponent display
60	CCAA----CCCCCAAA	Character template
70	TT,MM,JJJJ	Date template
80	HHMMSS	Time template
90	NN,NN	Software version
100	AANNN	

Figure 24.4 Configuration That Allows the Creation and Modification
of New Characteristic Value Templates

In this section, we examined how to create a characteristic and how characteristics are used in classification. In the next section, we'll review how to create and use classes.

24.3   Classes

As described at the beginning of this chapter, a class contains a number of characteristics that are grouped together. In the section, we'll cover how to create a class and
assign previously created characteristics to it as well as cover class types, and class
hierarchies.

24.3.1   Creating Classes

After the relevant characteristics have been created, characteristics can be grouped
together by assigning them to a class. A class can be created using Transaction CLO2,
shown in Figure 24.5, or by following the navigation path **Cross-Application Components • Classification System • Master Data • Classes**.

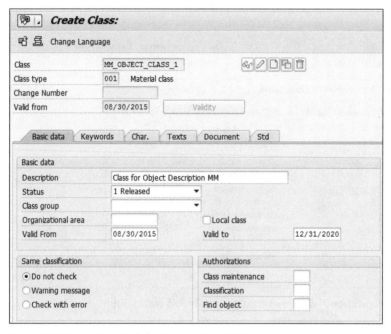

Figure 24.5 Basic Data Tab for Transaction CLO2

The **Basic data** tab requires a **Class type**. The class type is discussed in the next section. On the **Keywords** screen within Transaction CLO2, you can enter keywords that

can be used to search for the specific class. After the basic data has been entered, specific characteristics that should be assigned to this class can be entered in the **Char.** (characteristics) tab, as shown in Figure 24.6.

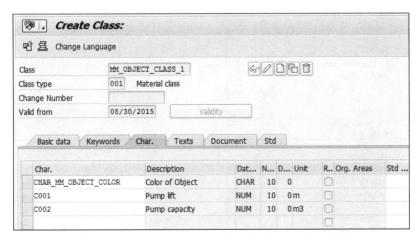

Figure 24.6 Characteristics Assigned to a Class in Transaction CL02

24.3.2   Class Types

A *class type* is an indicator to identify which objects are relevant for a class. Each class must belong to a class type. In this section, we'll take you to the necessary configuration settings you'll need to maintain to create classes. These configuration settings also offer options to maintain company-specific or business-specific controls, so that only the relevant users can access the required information.

As mentioned earlier, when creating a class, the class must belong to a class type. A class type represents the type of objects the class is being created for. As shown in Figure 24.5 earlier, the class MM_OBJECT_CLASS_1 has been assigned to **Class type 001**, which is the class type defined for a material master object. Consequently, the characteristics in the class will pertain to a material. If the user creating the class had entered class type 002, the characteristics would be describing a piece of equipment because equipment is the object defined for class type 002. Figure 24.7 shows some of the class types available when creating a class.

24

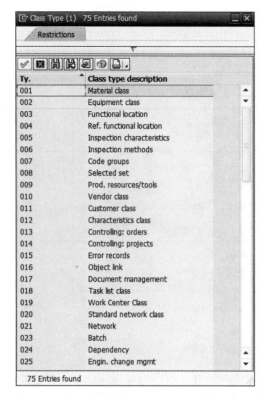

Figure 24.7 Class Types and Objects Assigned to Class Types

Many class types have already been defined in SAP S/4HANA. However, on occasion, you might need to create a new class type. Perhaps you have a client with a unique combination of objects, for example, a material/equipment combination that has no defined class type. If the client needs to describe this combination of objects, then the class requires a new class type so that the correct tables are accessed.

The class type refers to an object. When creating a new class type, the correct object must be selected. If the object isn't currently listed in configuration, it can be added.

The configuration for object types and class types can be found by following the configuration navigation path **Cross-Application Components • Classification System • Classes • Maintain Object Types and Material Types**.

A new object can be added in this transaction, as shown in Figure 24.8, by selecting **Edit • New Entries** and then choosing a new object to include. Most SAP S/4HANA objects will already be included in this transaction.

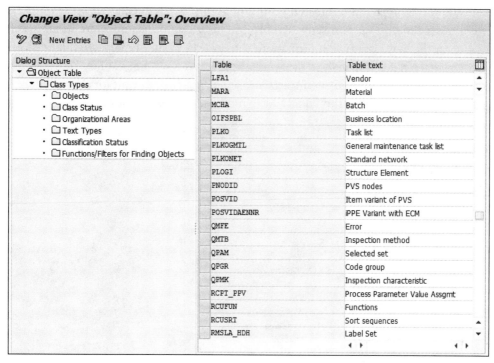

Figure 24.8 Partial Object List for the Class Type

To create a new class type, selects the object to be linked to the class type. Clicks on **Class Types** in the dialog structure to display the current class types for that object, as shown in Figure 24.9.

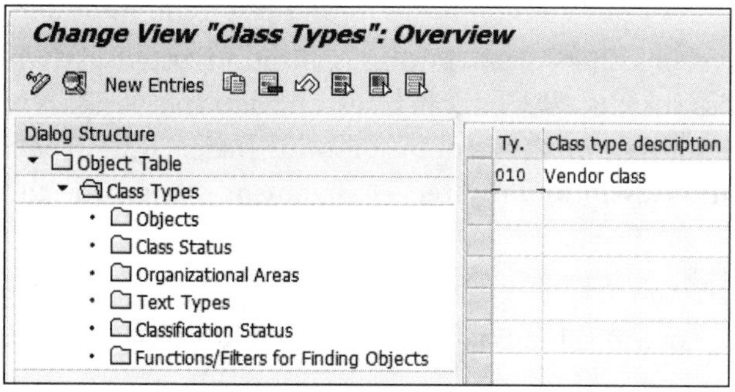

Figure 24.9 Class Types Currently Assigned to the Object

A new class type can be created for this object by selecting **Edit • New Entries** or by pressing the F5 key. A screen will appear, as shown in Figure 24.10, where you'll enter the new class type information. The new class type (**Type**) should be a three-character value. Normally, a new class type begins with the number "9." However, check with your data governance group for any policies relevant for classification. A class type description should be added in the second textbox for the new class type also.

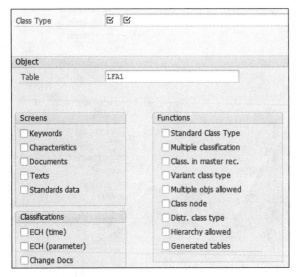

Figure 24.10 New Class Type Entry Screen

24.3.3   Class Hierarchies

As with other classification systems, the SAP S/4HANA classification system can create a hierarchy within the class structure. A class can be assigned to another class to create a class hierarchy using Transaction CL24N or by following the navigation path **Cross-Application Components • Classification System • Assignment • Assign Objects/ Classes to Class**.

As shown in Figure 24.11, classes **MM_Object_Class_2**, **MM_Object_Class_3**, and **MM_ Object_Class_4** have been assigned as subordinate classes of **MM_Object_Class_1**.

The class hierarchy can be seen using Transaction CL6C or by following the navigation path **Cross-Application Components • Classification System • Environment • Reporting • Class Hierarchy**.

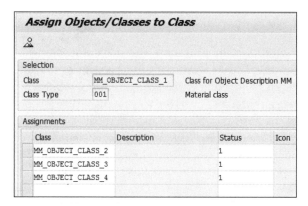

Figure 24.11 Assigning Classes to a Class Using Transaction CL24N

In the next section, we'll describe how to define object dependencies in classification.

24.4 Object Dependencies

Object dependency in classification refers to limitations that can be placed on objects to ensure that the correct classification occurs. Object dependencies can force specific values for one characteristic if a certain value in another characteristic has been selected. For instance, let's say a characteristic called *Color* has values *Red*, *Blue*, and *Green*, and another characteristic called *Finish* has values *Matte*, *Gloss*, or *Semi-Gloss*. You can define a dependency that states that, if the value *Green* is selected for *Color*, only *Gloss* can be selected for characteristic *Finish*. This dependency prevents incorrect characteristic values from being chosen.

To create a dependency, follow these steps:

1. Within Transaction CL02 (Classes), display the characteristics.

2. To create a dependency between characteristics, select the characteristic required and then choose **Environment • Change Characteristic**.

3. The display shows the change characteristic transaction. Choose **Extras • Object Dependencies • Editor**.

4. A dialog box appears where you can choose **Precondition, Selection Condition, Action**, or **Procedure**. After you select the appropriate object dependency, the dependency editor appears.

5. In this editor, create the dependency based on normal syntax.

24

843

> **Note**
>
> Advanced functions in the classification system, such as the precondition, action, and selection conditions, are known as *object dependencies*. Object dependencies enable you to maintain logical dependencies and group various characteristics with each other. For example, when you place an order for a new Ford Mustang car in black, you can only choose gray or black seat covers. With a red Ford Mustang, the available seat cover options are different. You can also use the classification system when to integrate variant configuration in your business processes. Refer to the SAP PRESS E-Bite: *Introducing Advanced Variant Configuration (AVC) with SAP S/4HANA* by Sefan Kienzle (2018, *www.sap-press.com/4606*).

In the next section, we'll examine how the classification system can be used as a search tool to find objects that have been classified.

24.5   Finding Objects Using Classification

The standard feature of the classification system is to make the selection of objects easier because objects can be found using values that have been entered for that specific object. In this section, we'll begin by showing you how to assign a class to an SAP object, such as the material master. Assigning a class to the material master will also bring up the characteristics associated with that class. Since the characteristics are how business users maintain SAP object-specific information, we'll show you how to search for specific SAP objects using the classification system.

24.5.1   Classifying Materials

For materials management (MM) in SAP S/4HANA, the most common function involving classification is creating the material master. When a material is created, one of the creation screens involves assigning classes to the material. In Transaction MM01 (Create Material), the classification screen allows a class or classes to be assigned to a material, as shown in Figure 24.12.

A class can be selected and then assigned values for the characteristics, as shown in Figure 24.13. A material can be assigned to any number of classes.

As shown in Figure 24.13, the **Material 400-522** has been assigned to class **MM_OBJECT_CLASS_1**. This class has three characteristics assigned. When the class is assigned to the object, in this case, **Material 400-522**, values can be assigned to the characteristics. Of the three available characteristics that can have values assigned, only two have been entered. The characteristic **Color of Object** has been assigned the value **Green – Color Code B9098**, and the characteristic **Pump capacity** has been assigned the value of **20 m3**.

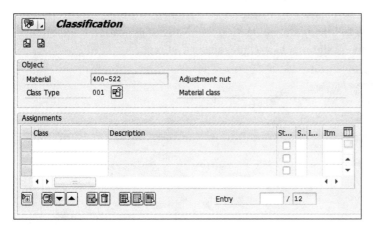

Figure 24.12 Assigning Classes for a Material in the Material Master Creation Transaction MM01

Figure 24.13 Selecting Characteristic Values Associated with the Class Assigned to the Material

24.5.2   Classifying Objects

An object can be assigned to a class or classes. This method is used when creating material masters or when assigning many objects to a single class as shown in Figure 24.14. Transaction CL20N allows the classes to be assigned to an object. This transaction can be found by following the navigation path **Cross-Application Components • Classification System • Assignment • Assign Object to a Class**.

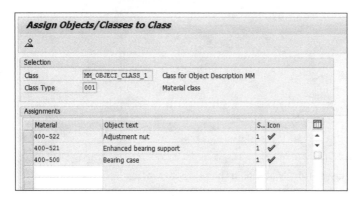

Figure 24.14 Assigning Classes to a Single Object Using Transaction CL20N

Transaction CL24N allows many objects to be assigned to a single class, which saves time if a new class needs to be assigned to many objects as shown in Figure 24.15. This transaction can be found by following the navigation path **Cross-Application Components • Classification System • Assignment • Assign Objects/Classes to a Class**.

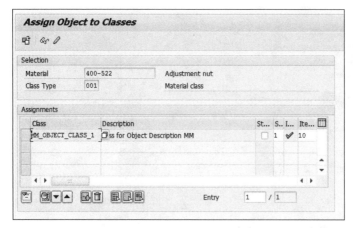

Figure 24.15 Assignment of Objects to a Single Class Using Transaction CL24N

24.5.3 Finding Objects

After implementing the classification system by creating characteristics and classes, assigning classes to objects and assigning values for the objects, the system can be used to find objects.

The key to finding an object is to use the characteristic values to find the object or objects that fit the value. The search criteria entered by end user, and the characteristics/values assigned are compared with the characteristic values assigned to the objects.

Transaction CL30N can be used to find objects using characteristic values. This transaction can be found by following the navigation path **Cross-Application Components • Classification System • Find • Find Objects in Classes**.

The initial screen will ask you to enter a specific class and class typeMatchcode selection is available if unsure about the class name. The detail screen shows the characteristics for the class that was chosen, and values can be entered against those characteristics. The transaction is then executed by selecting **Find • Find in Initial Class** or by pressing F8.

The transaction returns all objects that have the characteristic value that you entered, as shown in Figure 24.16.

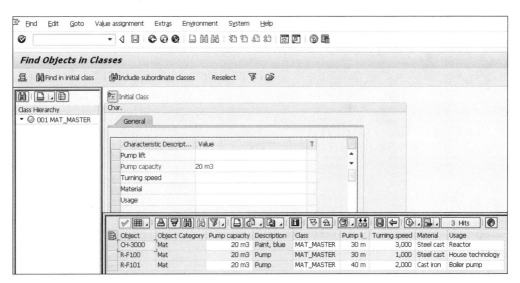

Figure 24.16 Objects Found Using the Characteristic Value Entered in Transaction CL30N

24.6   Summary

In this chapter, we described the classification system in SAP S/4HANA in detail. The classification system is a great tool for finding material that may appear to be similar to other materials but can be found easily using the characteristic value that has been assigned to it via the classification of the object. Classification is a long-term process that requires a significant level of commitment from the client and then ongoing maintenance to ensure that new materials, equipment, and other objects are classified when they are entered into SAP S/4HANA. If the classification system is correctly defined and implemented, a powerful and comprehensive search tool will be available.

Chapter 25 describes the functionality found in the Document Management System (DMS), which is a part of the central SAP functions and not part of MM. This powerful tool can help a company link documents to objects, such as a material inside the material master record

Chapter 25
Document Management System

The Document Management System (DMS) is a cross-application component that completely integrates with several areas within SAP S/4HANA. The DMS acts as a single source of information for business process owners as they perform their daily business functions.

The ability to secure and make available a company's digital assets continues to be of paramount importance as we move into an even more "plugged-in" society. SAP's answer is the Document Management System (DMS), which allows companies to safely store all the important documents in a central repository. You can implement DMS as a standalone project after SAP S/4HANA has already been implemented or while implementing other SAP S/4HANA functional areas.

Due to the nature of DMS and how it connects with most SAP S/4HANA functional areas, understanding and using SAP's classification system is essential. Before you read this chapter, we highly recommend that you first read Chapter 24, where we covered classification, which supports the foundation of working with DMS, in detail.

In this chapter, we'll first discuss the configuration basics for DMS, and then we'll move on to discuss how the DMS configuration is eventually reflected in master and transactional data. We'll also discuss several DMS features and functionalities.

25.1 Configuration Steps

In this section, we'll cover the configuration steps necessary to set up DMS.

25.1.1 Defining a New Number Range

To create a new number range of DMS document type, follow the menu path **Cross-Applications Components • Document Management • Control Data • Define Number Ranges for Document Numbers**. Click **Execute,** and a list of existing number ranges, shown in Figure 25.1 will appear.

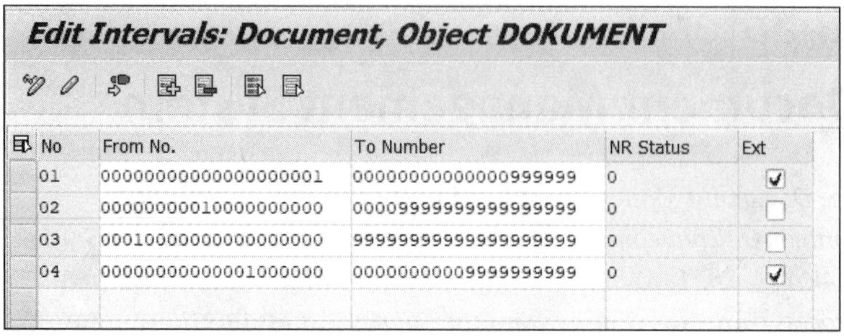
Edit Intervals: Document, Object DOKUMENT

No	From No.	To Number	NR Status	Ext
01	00000000000000000001	00000000000000999999	0	✓
02	00000000010000000000	00009999999999999999	0	☐
03	00010000000000000000	99999999999999999999	0	☐
04	00000000000001000000	00000000009999999999	0	✓

Figure 25.1 Available Number Ranges in the DMS

Table 25.1 provides details about the functions of some important fields shown in Figure 25.1.

Field Name	Field Value and Description
No.	Unique identification of the number range interval, indicating the number range sequence. For example, using number range interval 01 ensures that all created DMS documents have a number range starting from 1 and ending with 9999999.
From number	Number from which this sequence should start.
To number	Ending number to this sequence.
NR Status	Current running number that the system automatically updates, if any.
E.	Selecting in this checkbox indicates that this number range is an external number range. An external number range allows you to manually enter a number within the defined number range while creating a new DMS document. An internal number assignment is always in an increasing incremental order.

Table 25.1 Details of Individual Fields for Maintaining Number Range Intervals

To create a new number range interval, select **+Interval**, as shown in Figure 25.1. In the popup that opens, insert a new number range (for this example, enter "07"). Define the identifier as "0" and then define the number range **From number** 10000000 and **To number** 9999999 (after checking that the number range doesn't already exist in the **Existing Number Ranges** list). Click **Continue** and then save your entries. The new interval you just defined will show up in the **Intervals** list, as shown in Figure 25.2.

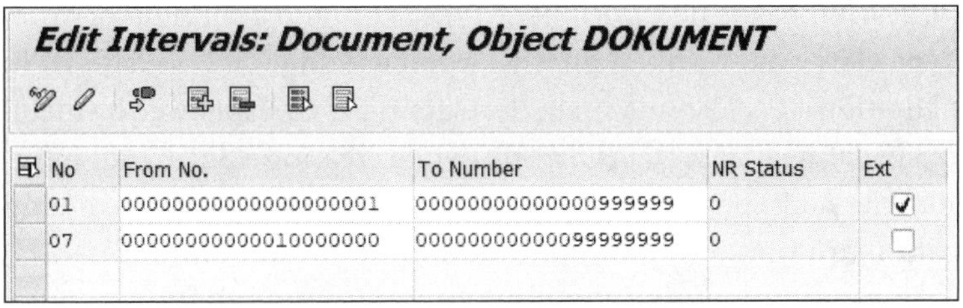

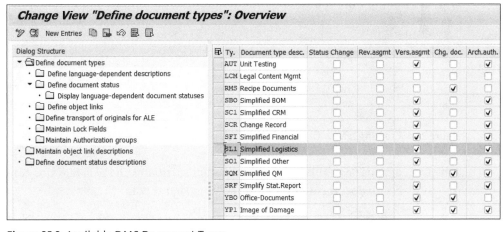

Figure 25.2 Defining a New Number Range for the DMS

25.1.2   Defining the Document Type

The system identifies every document in the DMS with a document type. A *document type* controls number ranges, field selection, the class to use, and objects (e.g., material master) that can be linked to a document type.

To create a new document type, follow the menu path **Cross-Applications Components • Document Management • Control Data • Define Document Types**. Click **Execute,** and the screen shown in Figure 25.3 will appear.

Figure 25.3 shows several DMS document types available. To create a new document type, we recommend copying an existing document type to save time and maintenance. For our example, use the standard available document type **SL1** to create a new document type **LC1**. Select document type **SL1** and choose the **Copy** function.

Figure 25.3 Available DMS Document Types

As shown in Figure 25.4, enter the new **Document Type** "LC1" and a short description in the field **Doc. Type Desc**. Maintain the Internal **Number Range** "07" as defined in the previous configuration step. Also, maintain the **Class Type** "017" followed by maintaining the previously defined **Class LC**. As a result, while creating a document information record (DIR), the **Additional Data** tab (Section 25.3.1) is available to maintain additional information in a DIR.

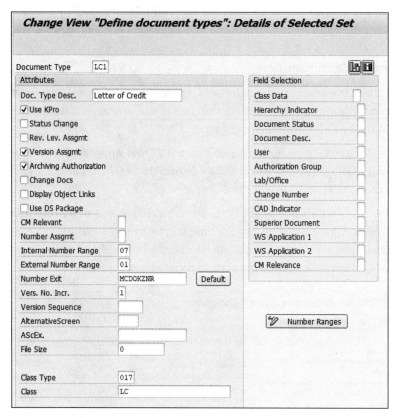

Figure 25.4 Creating a New DMS Document Type

Table 25.2 contains descriptions of some important attributes and field selection controls available for document type LC1, as shown in Figure 25.4.

Field	Field Description
Use KPro	Ensures that the original files are stored in defined storage systems (content repositories) via the Knowledge Provider. In standard DMS, you can store two original files without activating the Knowledge Provider. In addition to having the SAP NetWeaver team implement the Knowledge Provider, be sure this checkbox is selected so that you can upload multiple original files in a DIR.
Rev. Lev. Assgmt	Ensures that the system automatically assigns a revision level to a document the first time a business process owner releases a document with reference to a change number.
Version Assgnmt	Controls the automatic assignment of document versions.
Archiving Authorization	Controls whether the system can archive original application files for a DIR of this document type.
Change Docs	When you change a document, the system creates a change document and logs all field entries.
Internal Number Range	When you create a DIR, the system automatically assigns a number from this internal number range. For example, we can assign the previously created internal number range interval **07** (Section 25.1.1).
External Number Range	An option to assign an external number (manually) to a DIR. Even if you assign an internal number range to a DMS document type, you'll still have to assign an external number range.
Vers. No. Incr.	Controls the increment for document version numbers.
Class Type	Uniquely identifies the class type. For DMS, this class type is **017**, which we'll assign in this field.
Class	Identifies a class within a class type. For our example, we'll assign the previously created class **LC** here. Refer to Chapter 24 on classification.
Class Data	Ensures the availability of the **Class** and **Class Type** fields on the **Additional data** screen for the selected document type. This field also controls the navigation function **Extras • Classification** while creating the document in DMS.
Hierarchy Indicator	Assigns a document hierarchy, that is, the ability to assign one document under another document in hierarchical order (Section 25.2.4).

Table 25.2 Field Details of the Document Type Configuration Screen

25

Field	Field Description
Document Status	Modifies the **Document Status** field on the **Basic data** screen for the selected document type.
Document Desc.	Modifies the **Document Description** field on the **Basic data** screen for the selected document type.
User	The system incorporates (by default) the user name of the person creating the DIR.
Authorization Group	Controls the authorization group for each DIR.
Lab/Office	Indicates the laboratory office information in the DIR.
Change Number	Controls the engineering change number (ECN) of the DMS document type. Through ECN, the system traces and records all changes made.
CAD Indicator	Controls the CAD integration with the SAP.
Superior Document	Superior document information can be maintained in this field to establish a link with another related document. A superior document has one or more subordinate documents, thereby forming a document hierarchy. Refer to Section 25.2.4 for more information on document hierarchies.
WS Application 1 and 2	Use these fields to call up a workstation application, such as Word or Excel, during the creation of a DIR. If the first application doesn't work, then you can specify an alternate program. For example, if Word isn't working, then Notepad can be used to open a text file.
CM Relevance	This field indicates the document's relevance to change management.

Table 25.2 Field Details of the Document Type Configuration Screen (Cont.)

Note

A Knowledge Provider, mentioned in Table 25.2, is a set of SAP services implemented to manage document attributes, document storage, document retrieval, versioning, status management, and integration of full-text retrieval via TREX.

You can select one of the available options for use in the field selection controls, such as mandatory, optional, or hidden, on the right-hand side of Figure 25.4.

25.1.3   Document Status

Document status enables you to control who views and controls a document that has a specific status. For example, a document with an obsolete status can be restricted from viewing, or documents with a released status may not allow any further changes to a DIR.

To create a new document status, follow the menu path **Cross-Application Components • Document Management • Control Data • Define Document Status**. On the screen that appears, you'll see existing document statuses for document type LC1. To delete any unnecessary document statuses, select the relevant document statuses and choose **Delete**.

On the screen that appears, choose **Doc. St.** (document status) **FR** (which stands for released) and then click the details icon (magnifying glass).

Figure 25.5 shows the detailed screen that appears for the document status FR for document type LC1. Table 25.3 provides details on the control functions of some of the important fields.

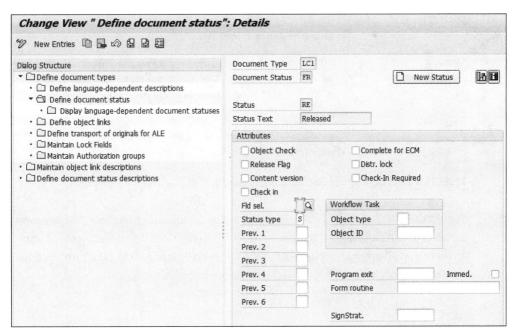

Figure 25.5 Detailed Screen of Document Status FR

Field Name	Field Description
Object Check	Checks the availability of the assigned object while creating the DIR.
Release Flag	Determines if a document with the *released* document status is released for other enterprise processes.
Complete for ECM	Controls whether a document with this status is effectively complete for engineering change management (ECM) purposes.
Distr.Lock	Controls whether a document can be distributed in this status.
Fld sel.	Determines how the log field is processed for documents of this combination of document type and document status. The dot (.) value indicates it's an option to enter the log to this status.
Status type	Controls the initial or secondary status. For details on various available statuses, see Table 25.3
Prev. 1	When a business user changes the status of a DMS document to a new or different status, the system checks whether the sequence of the status that was changed is adhered to.
SignStat.	You can integrate digital signatures in DMS. A digital signature is an electronic signing functionality where users enter their SAP password to digitally sign an SAP object.

Table 25.3 Field Controls of Document Statuses

Table 25.4 lists the available statuses that act as controlling functions. For example, status **O** doesn't allow any changes to be made to the DMS document, while status **C** ensures that all original documents of the DMS document are checked into the document repository before the DMS document can be saved.

Status Abbreviation	Description
W	Initial status
P	Primary status
T	Temporary status
O	Original processing status
S	Locked status
A	Archive status
[blank]	No special status type
C	Check-in status

Table 25.4 Status Abbreviations and Control Functions

25.1.4   Object Links

An *object link* ensures that all the DMS documents attached to an object, such as a purchase order or quality management (QM) notification, are automatically available as a reference. Object links are defined per DMS document type. One DMS document type can have multiple object links. For example, DMS document type LC1 can have object links to both material master and purchase requisition line items in MM, while DMS document type ZO2 can have object links to change numbers only.

Some examples of object links and their applications in business functions include the following:

- **Material master**
  All documents associated with the material master automatically become available whenever used in a standard SAP business function, such as a purchase order.

- **QM notification**
  All documents associated with QM notification automatically become available.

To create an object link, follow the menu path **Cross-Application Components • Document Management • Control Data • Define Object Link**. You'll see preexisting object links for document type **LC1**. These links are available because you used the copy function to copy document type SL1 to LC1, and all dependent entries, including object links, were also copied. You can delete the object links you don't need by selecting the relevant document statuses and clicking the **Delete** icon.

25

Select **Object EBAN** and choose **Details**, which brings up the screen shown in Figure 25.6 displaying the object link of **Object EBAN**, which belongs to document type LC1.

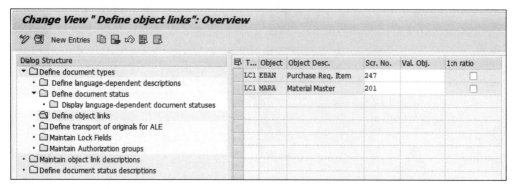

Figure 25.6 Object Links in the DMS

Table 25.5 provides details about some important fields.

Field Name	Field Description and Value
When New Version	When a business user creates a new version of a DMS document with reference to a previous DMS document, three options available for copying object links. The first option is that the business user is prompted to select whether the object link (e.g., link to purchase order) must also be copied from the source version to the target version. The second option is that the system automatically copies the object link. The third option is that all object links are ignored (and not copied automatically into the target version) in the new DMS document.
Document Version	With this checkbox, you can display either only the current version or all available versions of a DMS document.
1:n ratio	This checkbox controls whether more than one of a specific document type can be assigned to one object. If this checkbox is selected, you can assign a document type to more than one object.
Deletion block	Selecting this checkbox prevents the deletion of a DIR when it's linked to an SAP object.

Table 25.5 Field Details of an Object Link

Several object links exist to cater to various business processes in all SAP S/4HANA components. Table 25.6 shows some of the standard DMS object links available in SAP S/4HANA.

Object	Description
CR_DOC	Change Record Header
CR_ITM_DOC	Change Record Item
EBAN	Purchase Req. Item
EKPO	Purchase Order Item
EQUI	Equipment Master
LCMDOC	Legal Content Management Document
MARA	Material Master
PMAUFK	Maintenance Order
PMQMEL	Maintenance Notification
PRPS	WBS Element
QALS	Inspection Lot
QMTBDOC	Inspection Methods
SLCSRS_QST	Supplier Evaluation Response
STKO_DOC	BOM Header
STPO_DOC	BOM Item
VBAP	Sales Document Item

Table 25.6 Selective Objects for the Object Link

Tips & Tricks

If the standard object link in an SAP S/4HANA doesn't fulfill your organization's business needs, then you can customize a new object link. A DMS functional expert can collaborate with an ABAP programmer to develop a new object link. Click the blue information icon ⓘ, as shown in the top-right corner of Figure 25.5, and follow the instructions on how to create a customized object link.

25

At this point, you've completed configuring DMS in SAP S/4HANA. We'll now cover the document information record in the next section.

25.2 Document Info Record

Documents created in DMS are often referred to as document info records (DIRs). DIRs contain all the information, as well as the control functions, of DMS and are used interchangeably with the term "DMS documents."

In the SAP system, DMS uses a DIR to link the document to an object in SAP. The two important parts of the DIR are as follows:

- **Document part**
  A document part is defined as part of a document that is maintained as a separate document. This separation may be required if the original document is large and can be divided into relevant sections. For example, let's say a large specification document has relevant information for many materials; the specification can be divided into separate parts for each materials.

- **Document version**
  A document version describes the version number of the document. This number is particularly important for keeping the document current in situations where modifications may have been made to specifications, engineering drawings, and so on.

In the following sections, we'll show you how to create a new DIR using the document type LC1 we just configured. We'll also show you how to create a new version of a DIR and assign originals, which are basically attachments, to a DIR. Finally, we'll also show you how to create an object link of a DIR to an object such as a material master.

25.2.1 Creating a Document

Let's now create a new DIR. To create a new DIR, use Transaction CV01N or follow the menu path **Logistics • Central Functions • Document Management System • Document • Create**. Figure 25.7 shows the initial screen to create a DIR. Enter the **Document Type** LC1, which was previously configured. You don't have to assign a document part number or version because the system automatically assigns the initial number to the DIR.

You can also create a new DIR with reference to an existing or previously created DIR by entering the relevant DIR details in the **Template** section shown in Figure 25.7. Press ⌈Enter⌋, and the screen shown in Figure 25.8 will appear, displaying the detailed screen for the document type LC1.

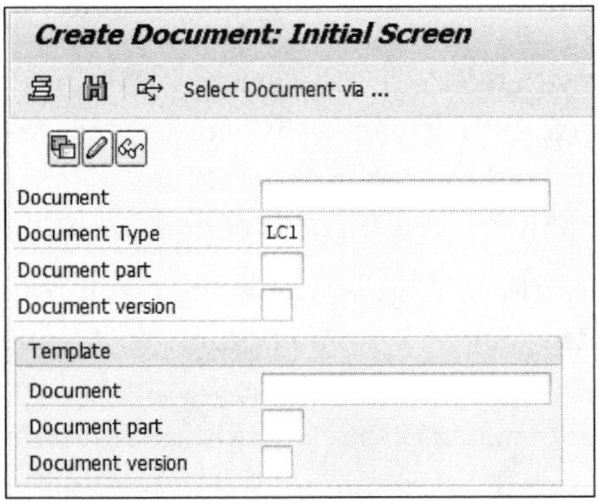

Figure 25.7 Initial Screen of DIR

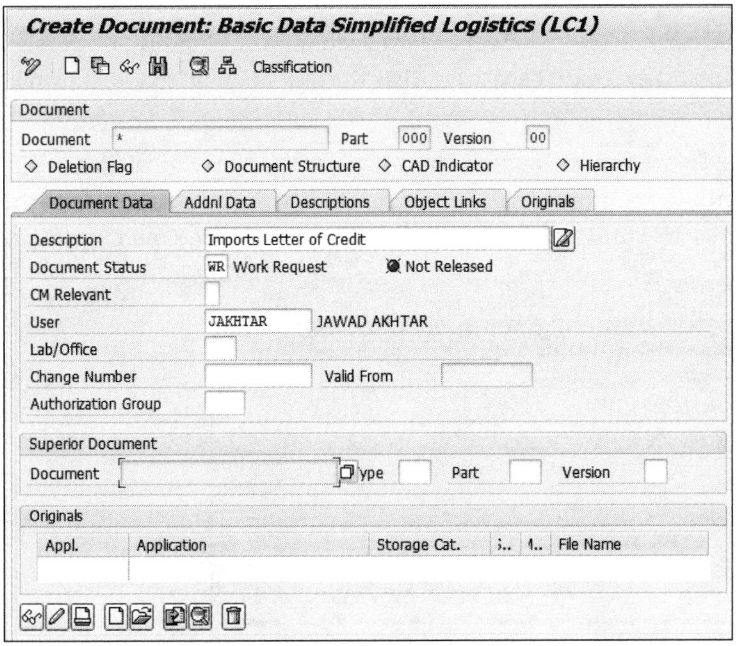

Figure 25.8 Maintaining Originals in DIR

In the **Document Data** tab, enter a short description of the document. This description is then searchable. Next, as **Document Status** was configured to as a mandatory field, it must be set as "WR." However, if an optional field, then you don't have to provide a status. (To mark the status as mandatory, choose the **Document Status** field, as shown earlier in Figure 25.4). Next, the default **User** name is of the person creating the DIR.

25.2.2   New Version of DIR

Creating a new version of a DMS document with reference to an existing DMS document is easier. A DMS document can have up to 999 parts and 99 versions. Often, creating and maintaining different versions of the same document (DIR) is useful for maintaining visibility to the changes made to the various versions of the same DIR.

To create a new version of a DIR, use Transaction CV01N or follow the menu path **Logistics • Central Functions • Document Management System • Document • Create**. For our example, enter the previously created DIR, document **type**, document **part**, and document version 00. Because document version 00 already exists, the system prompts you to create a new version.

25.2.3   Assigning Originals to DIR

To assign or upload original files, whether a Word document or a PowerPoint presentation from the network or a local hard drive, click the new original icon 🖉 shown in Figure 25.8.

A popup, shown in Figure 25.9, will appear where you'll assign the original files to DIR. Enter a short description of the original file and then define the menu path where the original file is stored. Use the **Original** dropdown list to define a file's menu path and click **Continue**.

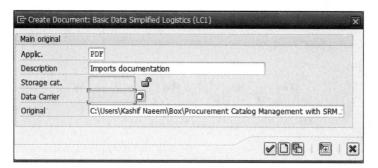

Figure 25.9 Maintaining Originals in DMS

The next screen contains an original file called *Procurement Catalog Management with SAP SRM.pdf*. You can activate the lock function by right-clicking the lock icon (shown in Figure 25.10) and then selecting the check-in option that follows. Checking in ensures that the original file is now saved securely in an SAP S/4HANA server and is accessible to everyone with the relevant authorization. With several icons available for the original stored files, the functions to change, display, download, or print are all available. We suggest that you explore the functionalities of these available icons. If KPRO isn't implemented, then you can attach only two originals here.

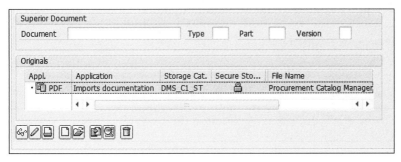

Figure 25.10 Original Document Checked In

25.2.4   Document Hierarchy

A document hierarchy provides a way to structure and streamline access to different DMS documents based on predefined business needs. A document hierarchy follows the principle of superior and subordinate documents. A superior document can also be a document folder that contains all of the relevant subordinate documents.

In the DIR, look for the **Superior Document** section. In the superior document, which is also a DIR, assign a superior document to a DIR, the **Hierarchy** indicator will turn green to denote that the current DIR is part of a document hierarchy.

If you double-click the green **Hierarchy** indicator, the system will take you to a detailed document hierarchy screen. On this screen, you can see the document hierarchy in both text and graphical versions. For a graphical display, choose **Hierarchy graphic**.

25.2.5   Assigning Object Links

Object linking ensures that all documents attached to an object are automatically made available. You can assign the material master (Figure 25.11) and the line item of a purchase requisition (Figure 25.12) to the DIR. Notice that, earlier in Section 25.1.4, you defined this object link in configuration for document type LC1.

25

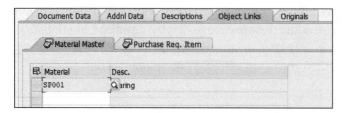

Figure 25.11 DIR Object Link with the Material Master

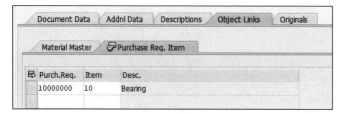

Figure 25.12 DIR Object Link with the Purchase Requisition Line Item

Save the DIR by pressing $\boxed{\text{Ctrl}}$ + $\boxed{\text{S}}$ or by clicking **Save**. The system generates the DIR document number, using the internal number range that we configured earlier. The screen shown in Figure 25.13 displays whether the document number range was correctly configured and assigned, then all DMS documents of document type LC1 follow the incremental number from the defined and assigned number range.

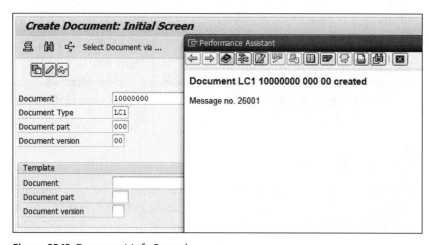

Figure 25.13 Document Info Record

Now that the DIR is created in the system, let's now quickly check out the two object links that we maintained: one for material master and the other for purchase requisition line item.

Access the screen shown in Figure 25.14 via Transaction ME53N (Display Purchase Requisition) and purchase requisition 10000000. Select the line item 10 and click on the documents icon 🗐. In the lower right-hand side, a popup will appear displaying the DIRs linked to the purchase requisition's line item 10.

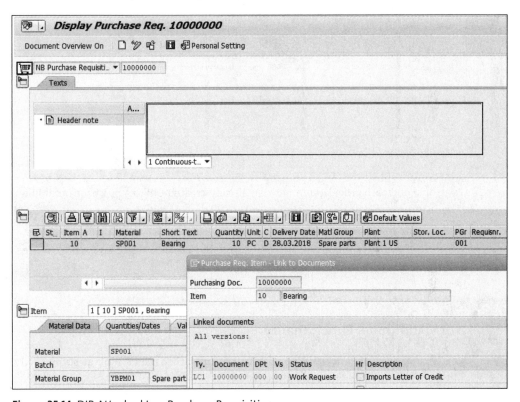

Figure 25.14 DIR Attached to a Purchase Requisition

Next, access the screen shown in Figure 25.15 via Transaction MM03 (Display Material) and click on the **Additional Data** button followed by clicking on the **Document data** tab. DIR 10000000 links up with the material master SP001.

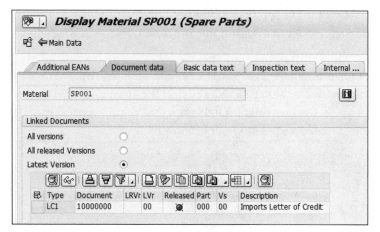

Figure 25.15 DIR Attached to the Material Master

Tips & Tricks

You can create an object link from a DIR, and vice versa. For example, if you are working on a purchase order, you can link an already-created DIR to a purchase order line item, thus creating a cross-link between the DIR and the linked objects.

Note that, to link an SAP object with a DIR, the object must already exist in the system. Similarly, to link a DIR with an SAP object, the DIR should already exist to create a cross-linking.

25.3   Additional Functionality

Now that we've covered document information records, let's look at some of the additional features and functionalities of DMS.

25.3.1   Additional Data (Classification System)

Let's discuss how the classification system integrates with DMS. This integration enables business process owners to record and maintain any additional information that doesn't fit in any specific business process or in any SAP objects, such as a purchase order or a sales order.

Choose the **Addnl.** (additional) **Data** tab, which opens the screen shown in Figure 25.16. On this screen, you'll see all the characteristics that were previously created and assigned to class LC. This class was also assigned to document type LC1 in the configuration settings (as shown earlier in Figure 25.4). Enter a value for each characteristic. Thus, DMS provides an option of entering characteristics information, which can then be used later for searching for DIRs containing some or all of the characteristic values.

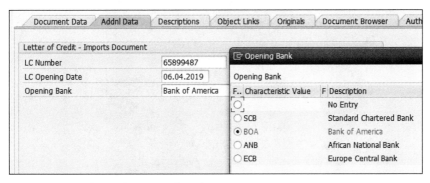

Figure 25.16 Additional Data or Classification in DMS

Note

Using classification in DMS also offers the advantage of incorporating advance classification functions, such as setting up actions and preconditions, which can ensure better data entry controls.

25.3.2 Long Texts

DMS also offers a feature that allows the incorporation of long text (of unlimited length) that's searchable by keywords. Any department of any organization can create a short (or long) description stored in DMS, which can then be used for search purposes. For example, the details of an entire inspection method can be incorporated in long text. Similarly, a summary of a presentation or an important report, which otherwise wouldn't fit anywhere else, can be incorporated into long text for subsequent searches. DMS offers standard long text search capability without the need to implement or install any additional component. Additionally, with this standard functionality, no search engine installation (such as TREX) is needed.

25

Use Transaction CVO2N or follow the menu path **Logistics • Central Functions • Document Management System • Document • CHANGE**. Enter the document number and the document type. On the next screen, click on the create long text icon ![icon], and the screen shown in Figure 25.17 will appear. Double-click to start incorporating long text in DMS, which can be of unlimited length and which will eventually be available for searching for combinations of keywords. In our example, we'll search for the word "Malaysia" using the search function in DMS.

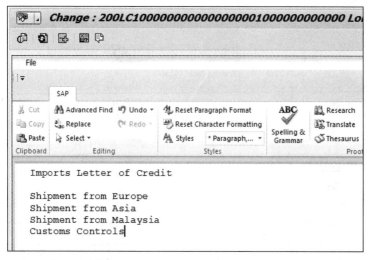

Figure 25.17 Long Text in DIR

25.3.3 Search Functions

DMS offers search functionality with a large number of options, including by document type, document number, document status, object link, classification, and short description.

For our example, you'll first incorporate long text in a DMS document and then use a keyword within the long text to search for relevant DMS documents.

To search for keywords in long text, use Transaction CVO4N or follow the menu path **Logistics • Central Functions • Document Management System • Document • Find**. The screen shown in Figure 25.18 displays the keyword, **Malaysia**. On this screen, you can also select either the **And** or **Or** operator to include multiple keywords as well as the **BUT NOT** operator to exclude certain keywords.

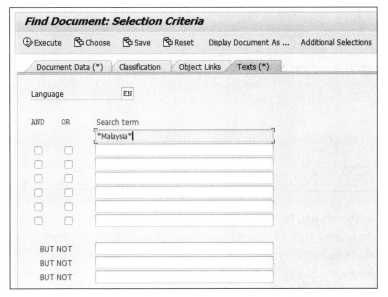

Figure 25.18 Search Function in the DMS

> **Note**
>
> Figure 25.18 shows various tabs that basically enable the available search options, such as using the classification function or object links to search for relevant DIRs.

The output of the search results to the preceding query contains a document that meets the criteria, as shown in Figure 25.19—the same DMS document number 10000000 with version 01, as shown earlier in Figure 25.17, where originally we had entered the long text.

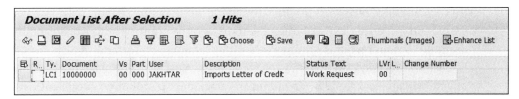

Figure 25.19 Search Results of Keyword(s) in Long Text

> **Note**
>
> An important aspect to note is that all characteristics associated with a DMS document type are available not just as search results, but also as reporting. Simply select the **Change Layout** to hide or display the desired fields.

25.3.4   Document Distribution

DMS documents created in an SAP S/4HANA can be distributed or sent to different recipients. These recipients can be internal SAP S/4HANA users or external email addresses. If the DMS documents are sent to the same set of users frequently, then you can create a recipients list. To start document distribution, use Transaction CVI4 or follow the menu path **Logistics • Central Functions • Document Management System • Environment • Document Distribution • Recipient List • Recipient for List**. On the initial screen to send out a DMS document, enter the document number, document type, document part, and document version. Click **Execute**.

In the detailed screen for document distribution that appears, manually enter two recipients near the bottom of the screen. However, notice that for one recipient, two different types of deliveries will be made: **RML** and **RMA**. For RML, the original DMS document is sent as a hyperlink that the business user clicks to view the file. For RMA, the original is delivered as an attachment.

Click **Execute**, and the document will be immediately sent. The job order number is created, and the system displays a message that appears when the document distribution has been successfully executed.

25.3.5   Distribution Lists

If a standard set of recipients to whom the DMS documents are sent on a regular basis exists, you can create a distribution list to reduce the effort of individually adding users. A distribution list is synonymous with a mailing list. To create a distribution list, use Transaction CVI1 or follow the menu path **Logistics • Central Functions • Document Management System • Environment • Document Distribution • Recipient List • Create**.

25.3.6 Document Management in Batches

To activate the **Documents** tab in the batch screen, follow the menu path **Logistics – General • Batch Management • Batch Master • Activate Document Management for Batches**. You'll also need to maintain the object link to the batch for the specific DMS document type. The relevant objects to link are **Object** MCH1, and **Screen no** 264 and **Object** MCHA, and **Screen no** 265.

25.4 Summary

In this chapter, we described the processes included in the DMS. Most companies have developed or are developing strategies regarding their documents. Having hard-copy documents moving around an organization can cause delays, errors, and miscommunication. Scanning documents on receipt, for example, invoices from vendors, is one way to reduce the time between approvals and payments to vendors. Knowledge of the DMS in SAP is paramount when advising clients on best practices for purchasing and other areas where document management can be an issue.

In the next chapter on the Early Warning System (EWS), we'll cover the user-defined alerts available in the system to help business users get timely notifications.

25

Chapter 26

Early Warning System

The Early Warning System (EWS) is made up of user-defined alerts that are triggered whenever any deviation or exception to an important business process occurs, thus allowing you to take timely action to minimize disruptions to your logistics and supply chain.

The Early Warning System (EWS) is built on the same SAP S/4HANA logistics info structures as standard analyses, with the added flexibility monitoring and receiving alerts for specific exceptions important to your business processes. For example, whenever the stock of a critical raw material falls below a user-defined stock level, the system should immediately alert procurement and production planners through EWS for timely resolution. EWS provides real-time updates and can be tailored to individual needs, and the frequency with which the system should share alerts can be customized.

EWS enables business users to define specific alerts to ensure no (or minimal) disruption to logistics and supply chain operations. Not only can you change predelivered exceptions, you can also delete exceptions that are no longer needed.

In this chapter, we'll explain how the EWS can help you, and then we'll provide the steps you'll need to follow to get the EWS up and running in your system. We'll begin with creating the exceptions that you wish to monitor, followed by grouping together various exceptions to create a comprehensive list of all exceptions belonging to an exception group. Next, we'll set up the schedule or the frequency with which the system should issue an alert for the exception. Then, we'll use an example to show how a business user performing a specific business process can trigger an alert in the system. The chapter concludes with EWS reporting.

26

26.1   Overview

In many instances in materials management (MM), EWS can come in handy, depending on what's important to your business. In this chapter, you'll learn how easily and intuitively setting up EWS can be by following the steps in a logical sequence. If your business requirements change at any time, you can make changes or even delete the EWS that you've set up. Some examples of where you can use EWS are as follows:

- When the vendor repeatedly fails to deliver acceptable quality raw material
- When the safety stock of a material falls below the defined limit
- When a vendor continues to make late deliveries of critical components
- When inventory of precious metal exceeds a certain value
- When quality specifications of an important raw material are out by more than 3%
- When you record production scrap at greater than 5% of total production
- When sales figures show a decreasing trend for a high-running, high-profit item for the past three months

EWS monitor key figures, that is, quantities and values, over a defined time period. These key figures can be stock levels (quantity), packing material wastage (quantity), rejected raw materials after quality inspection (quantity), the price of raw material (value) showing an upward trend, or when the total value of inventory (value) exceeds the defined threshold.

In any of these situations, you can configure EWS for the individual exception so that you'll receive alerts and can react immediately. While you can set up EWS for use with any logistics functionality, we'll discuss using in MM specifically. The relevant info structures available for MM are listed in Table 26.1.

Info Structure	Description
S038	INVCO: batches
S039	Inventory controlling
S090	WM: stock placements/removals
S091	WM: quantity flows
S094	Stock/requirements analysis

Table 26.1 Standard Info Structures for Inventory Controlling and Purchasing

Info Structure	Description
S011	Purchasing groups
S012	Purchasing
S013	Vendor evaluation
S015	Subsequent settlement: evaluation
S074	Subsequent settlement: operative
S111	Index: document adjustment
S170	Payment document data
S171	Payment item data
S172	Vendor billing document data
S173	Vendor billing document item
S174	Services

Table 26.1 Standard Info Structures for Inventory Controlling and Purchasing (Cont.)

Note

When EWS is set up for any logistics functional area, the relevant info structures are automatically made available by SAP S/4HANA. For example, if EWS is set up in MM, all MM-related info structures become available.

26.2   Early Warning System Setup

To set up EWS, you'll choose the relevant info structure from Table 26.1, choose the characteristics, and select the key figures. You'll also need to define the requirements of each key figure and configure the follow-up function. In summary, the required steps are:

1. Create an exception.
2. Group the exceptions.
3. Set up the periodic analysis.

> **Note**
>
> If several exceptions exist for the same info structure, you can combine them by creating a *group exception*, which is a list of individual exceptions. Like the first step, the follow-up function for this step involves determining whether an email alert to an individual is sufficient or whether the exception should be communicated to an entire distribution list.

The third and final step is periodic analysis, in which you'll define the frequency with which the system monitors for exceptions and issues alerts. Let's start with the first step in the following section: creating an exception.

26.2.1   Creating Exceptions

An *exception* is important data that you want to monitor from a business point of view. Creating an exception requires the following steps:

1. Choose characteristics.
2. Define the key figures.
3. Define the characteristic values.
4. Choose requirements.
5. Define the requirements.
6. Define the follow-up processing.

For our example, we'll create an exception called ZMM15, using info structure S039 (Inventory Controlling) taken from Table 26.1. For this exception, we'll specify that the system should issue an alert whenever the material QS8X60 reaches a stock quantity below 2,000 PC (the stock quantity is the key figure). If the system records an exception in the system, we want the exception highlighted with the color red, a popup message should open, and an email alert sent to the SAP inbox.

To set up the exception, use Transaction MC/1 or follow the menu path **Logistics • Logistics Controlling • Inventory Controlling • Early Warning System • Exception • Create**, as shown in . Follow these steps to create the exception:

1. For this example, enter "ZMM15" as the **Exception**, enter a short description, and enter "S039" as the **Info structure** (info structure S039 [Inventory Controlling]). Click the **Characteristics** option.

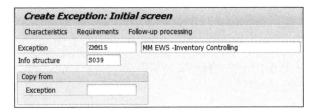

Figure 26.1 Characteristics Setup in EWS

2. In the selection screen, as shown in Figure 26.2, click the **Choose characteristics** button to select the characteristics on which you want to activate the EWS.

3. In the popup screen that appears, select **Material**, and move it to the left column by clicking the left icon ◀, and then click **Copy**.

4. For each characteristic shown in Figure 26.2, provide the corresponding value or a range from which to choose. Choose characteristic **Material** and **Charact. values** at the top of the screen.

5. In the popup window that appears, shown in Figure 26.2, enter the desired value or range of materials for which the system should monitor EWS. For this example, enter "QS8X60" for **Material**. Click **Copy**.

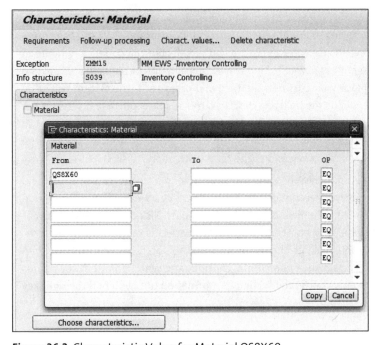

Figure 26.2 Characteristic Value for Material QS8X60

Now that the value for the characteristic material is defined, the next step is to define the requirements—that is, the information that you need EWS to monitor in day-to-day business processes. Choose **Requirements** to define requirements for the material. For this example, choose one key figure for the material, as shown in Figure 26.3, by following these steps:

1. On the **Requirements** screen, select **Choose key figures**, and from the popup that opens, select the key figures that will form the basis of your EWS alerts. For our example, select the **Total Stock** key figures by moving them from the right-hand side to the left-hand side by clicking the left arrow icon ◀.

2. Click **Continue**.

3. Define the **Period to analyze** fields, which stipulate the past and future periods on which the EWS must evaluate deviations. By defining **Previous periods** as "12," you're stipulating that all key figures for the past 12 months that meet the conditions must be considered during evaluation.

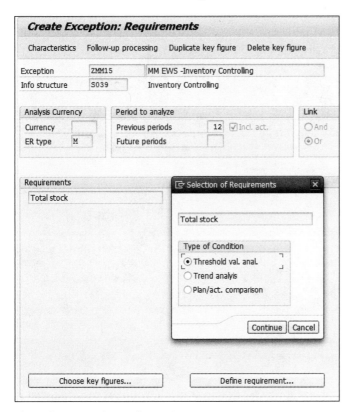

Figure 26.3 Key Figures for EWS

4. After selecting the key figures, click **Define requirement...**, shown in Figure 26.3, to specify the limits or other details that form the basis for EWS alerts. The requirement must be defined for each key figure. The options available are **Threshold val. anal.**, which requires a value to be specified, or **Trend analysis**, which is used to monitor positive or negative trends and requires you specify the percentage of deviation in the trend. The **Plan/Act** button enables alerts to business users whenever a user-defined deviation between planned and actual values occurs.

26

5. For the key figure **Total Stock** in Figure 26.4, place your cursor in the key figure and double-click it. (Alternatively, you can click **Define requirement...**, and the popup shown in Figure 26.3 will appear.)

6. As shown earlier in Figure 26.3, select the **Threshold val. anal.** radio button and click the **Continue** button. In the popup shown in Figure 26.4, enter "< 2000" and click **Continue**. This step stipulates that you want to monitor the material quantity whenever its inventory falls below 2,000 PC.

> **Note**
>
> All standard operators, such as less than (<), greater than (>), equal to (=), and not equal to (≠), are available when setting threshold values.

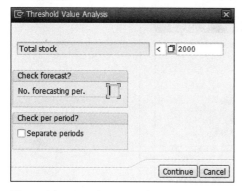

Figure 26.4 Requirements for Key Figures

The next step in defining an exception is to define the follow-up processing—that is, what and how the EWS informs you that an exception has occurred. For this example, click **Follow-up processing** to bring up the screen shown in Figure 26.5.

On this screen, we've specified that, whenever the exception occurs, the details should be marked in red and sent as a table to the specified mail recipient. Furthermore, the same information must be communicated by email to the correct SAP inbox.

> **Tips & Tricks**
>
> Select both the **Active for std** (standard) **analysis** and **Active for periodic analysis** checkboxes shown in Figure 26.5, which will be subsequently checked whenever you run analysis reports in EWS.

Figure 26.5 Follow-Up Processing to Define the Requisite Parameters

26.2.2   Group Exceptions

If you want to monitor more than one exception from the *same* info structure in EWS, grouping them together in an exception group is convenient and practical for ease of reporting. For example, if a material's scrap is monitored for its upper tolerance limit with the color red and its lower tolerance limit with the color yellow, then grouping these two different exceptions can provides these details in one list or report in EWS.

> **Note**
>
> For this example, exception grouping isn't used. However, the concepts and other details covered in this chapter should be sufficient for you to quickly set up exception grouping. Exception grouping is found in the same menu path as EWS.

26

26.2.3 Setting Up Periodic Analysis

Now that exceptions have been defined, the last step in setting up EWS is to define the frequency with which the system should alert the person who set up EWS (e.g., every eight hours, daily, once a week, or once a month). For our example, we'll set up periodic analysis for the exception by setting up a variant and defining the frequency of the analysis.

To get to the **Periodic Analysis** screen, as shown in Figure 26.6, use Transaction MC/7 or follow the menu path **Logistics • Logistics Controlling • Inventory Controlling • Early Warning System • Periodic Analysis • Area to Analyze • Create**. Then, follow these steps:

1. Enter "ZMM15" as the **Exception** for periodic analysis and then click **Create**.

2. A popup window appears asking for the name of the variant to create. Enter "ZMM15" as the variant. Click **Create** to open the **Variants: Change Screen Assignment** screen.

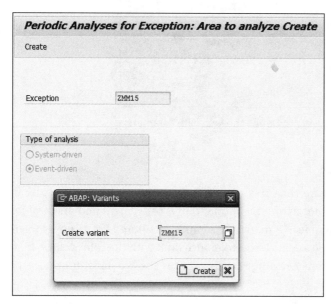

Figure 26.6 Setting Up Periodic Analysis

3. Define this variant as applicable for the individual screens (**For Indiv. Selection Screens**), which means that the parameters of the variant, such as material QS8X60, are automatically available for selection on the EWS screen for info structure S039, number 1000. If you select the **For All Selection Screens** radio button, then these parameters are available for all of the different screens of EWS by default.

4. Click **Continue** to open the **Edit Variants** screen shown in Figure 26.7. You can define the initial screen parameters for your variant here. For our example, define that the system should automatically select material **QS8X60** and make the material available by default.

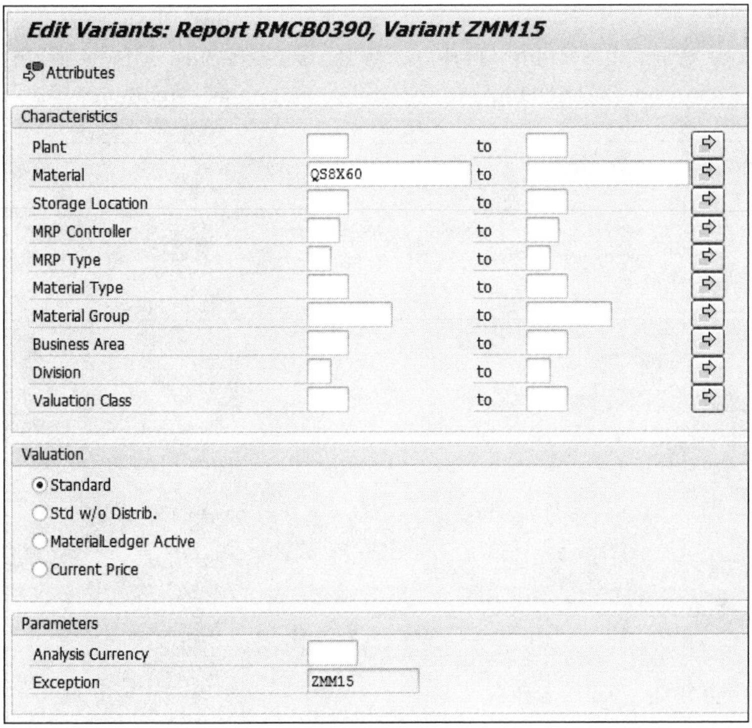

Figure 26.7 Editing Variants in EWS

After defining the parameters, click **Attributes**, where you can provide a meaningful description of the variant. This description is communicated whenever EWS needs to alert an exception. For example, the meaningful description, "Critical raw material shortage," immediately alerts the recipient to respond. Contrast this message with the more generic and vague description, "Late deliveries." This approach also helps if the same alert is sent to many people on a distribution list. For this example, enter a description like "MM EWS – Inventory Controlling." Finally, click **Save** to save the periodic analysis.

A message appears to confirm that the variant is saved with all of the values on the selection screen.

26.3   Scheduling an Early Warning System

You'll now need to define the scheduling information on exception ZMM15 to determine how frequently the system should analyze it for potential exceptions. To bring up the initial screen for scheduling the exception, as shown in Figure 26.8, use Transaction MC/B or follow the SAP menu path **Logistics • Logistics Controlling • Inventory Controlling • Early Warning System • Periodic Analysis • Schedule**. After entering "ZMM15" as the **Exception**, click **Schedule** to schedule your analysis frequency.

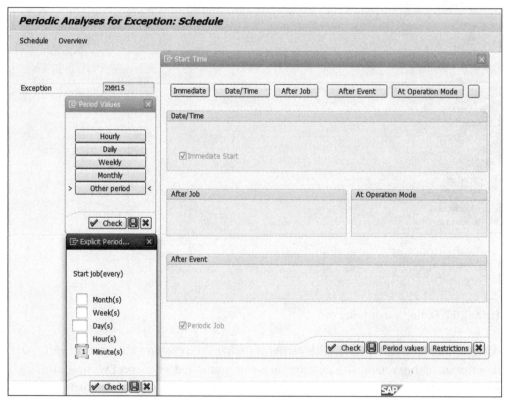

Figure 26.8 Defining Schedule Details for EWS

Figure 26.8 shows two options: either schedule the analysis of the exception group immediately or define the analysis as a periodic job and then define the period values. Click **Other period** and enter "1" (**Minute**) in the resulting popup.

The option of scheduling the job immediately ensures that any new exceptions are immediately reported. However, if the **Date/Time** option is used, for example, then exception monitoring and reporting start on that specified date and time only, as a scheduled job. The second option of scheduling a periodic job helps ensure that system resources aren't unduly overburdened.

> **Tips & Tricks**
>
> The scheduling frequency should be practical as well as within a reasonable gap—for example, daily. Under the **Daily** scheduling option, all exceptions for the entire day are consolidated into one issued alert, thus allowing the person who set up the alert to address to all the day's exceptions in one sitting.

Click **Save** to save your scheduling details. A message will appear to confirm that the background job for exception ZMM15 has been successfully planned.

In the next section, we'll show you how the EWS works in the system, what happens as users perform day-to-day business functions, and how the system alerts users when an exception occurs. Business users can continue to perform and report their daily activities in the SAP S/4HANA, such as performing goods receipts against purchase orders, goods issues for consumption, reporting daily production with scrap percentage, and recording the results of quality inspection lots.

26.4   Early Warning System in Action

In this example, the business process owner (the inventory controller) consumes material QS8X60 so that its stock falls below 2,000 PC. As soon as that happens, EWS will alert the person who set up the alert. For this example, the alert is sent as a popup, and an email is sent to the SAP inbox.

Access the **Stock Overview: Basic List** screen shown in Figure 26.9 by using Transaction MMBE for material QS8X60 in plant 1000 (Hamburg). Notice that the available unrestricted stock quantity is 3,680 PC. Now let's consume enough of this material so that its stock falls below 2,000 PC.

To consume the stock of material QS8X60 against the cost center, use Transaction MIGO and enter movement type 201 (Goods Issuance for Cost Center). On the screen shown in Figure 26.9, enter an issue or consumption **Quantity** of "3,000" PC so that the overall stock of material QS8X60 falls to 680 PC. Save your entries as shown in Figure 26.10. This transaction should trigger the EWS.

26

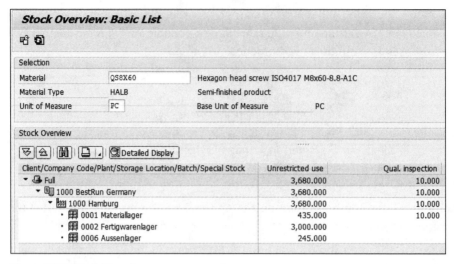

Figure 26.9 Stock Overview

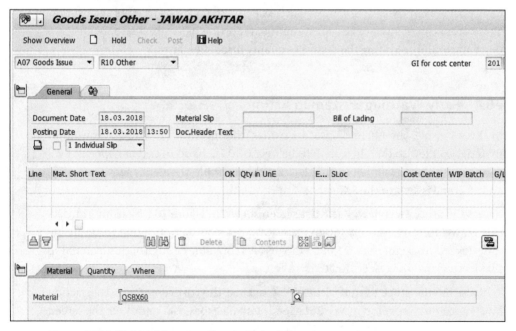

Figure 26.10 Material Consumption to Reduce Inventory

After you save the entries, click **Back**. The system issues a popup message, as shown in Figure 26.11, to alert you of the deviation (exception) that has occurred.

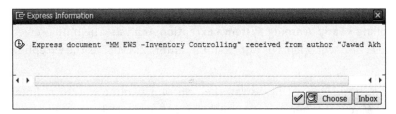

Figure 26.11 EWS Popup Alert Issued Immediately When an Exception Takes Place

Notice that, in the popup, the system brings up the same text "MM EWS – Inventory Controlling" that we defined during the initial stages of setting up EWS.

The system also delivers the same exception message in the SAP inbox. You can use Transaction SBWP to check your inbox for unread documents that contain EWS alerts too. Also, since keeping track of all the EWS popups isn't always possible, you can go to the SAP inbox and address the alerts there, as shown in Figure 26.12.

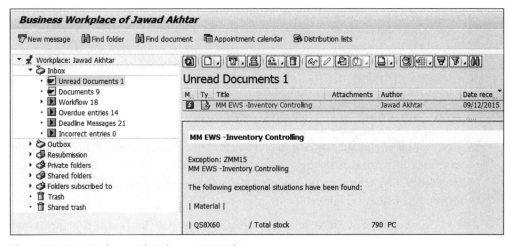

Figure 26.12 SAP Inbox with Relevant EWS Alert

26.5   Exception Analysis

You can also analyze exceptions with EWS in logistics. While alert monitoring is certainly an invaluable EWS tool to promptly alert you about any deviations and exceptions, you'll often need detailed information about the exception to address it. Fortunately, EWS is supported by MM, which ensures that comprehensive details related to all exceptions are instantly available.

Use Transaction MCYG or follow the menu path **Logistics • Logistics Controlling •
Logistics Controlling • Early Warning System • Exception Analysis**. The initial screen
for exception selection will open. For our example, enter "ZMM15" as the **Exception**
for analysis.

Click **Execute**, and the system will display the selection parameter screen. Enter
"QS8X60" for the **Material**. When you execute the exception analysis report by press-
ing [F8] or clicking **Execute**, the system displays the results, as shown in Figure 26.13.
This exception analysis shows the defined key figure with data as separate columns.
Furthermore, the entire row of the **Material** column is red, as originally defined.

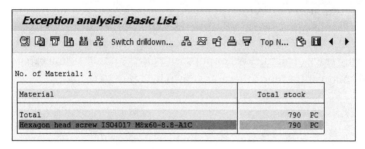

Figure 26.13 Exception Analysis Report of EWS for Material QS8X60

26.6   Summary

This chapter explained how quickly and easily a business process owner in any relevant area of work can set up EWS without any extensive functional or technical
knowledge. EWS alerts can be modified, deleted, or updated anytime, as necessary to
reflect the business need.

In the next chapter, we'll cover special procurement types in the SAP S/4HANA.

Chapter 27
Reporting and Analytics

Timely, accurate, and comprehensive information helps companies make better and faster business decisions. You can immediately start using a large number of information systems, standard reports, standard analyses, and SAP Fiori apps available in the SAP system for logistics in general and for materials management (MM) in particular.

In this chapter, we'll provide guidance on how to leverage a large number of standard reports available in all areas of the SAP system. We'll cover standard reports, such as information systems, which are available for day-to-day reporting, as well as a large number of standard analyses available to help business process owners make better decisions. After you become familiar with the features and functions for reporting, including tools and icons, navigating to unexplored areas of reporting will be easier. SAP S/4HANA's embedded analytics enable dashboards to be used to measure and improve important logistics and supply chain key performance indicators (KPIs).

In this chapter, we'll cover the information systems of materials management (MM), including several functions particularly beneficial to business users, such as the ability to create various graphs from the data. After we cover the options for reporting with real-time information in information systems, we'll discuss how to report on historical data with standard analyses available for MM, as well as some of the associated features, such as time series and ABC analysis.

27.1 The Basics of Reporting

To take full advantage of your SAP system, you must become familiar with the icons and other features frequently used in reports. Because these icons and functions are the same in all the information systems and analyses, you'll be able navigate quickly to get the desired information or even find tips and tricks to manage the display and availability of data, as needed.

27

Table 27.1 includes a selected list of icons available when you run information systems or standard analysis, including a brief description of what an icon does when clicked.

Icon	Icon Detail	Details/Application
	Refresh	Refresh data
	Change	Change object, such as inspection lot
	Display	Display object, such as inspection lot
	Maintain Selection Options	Select operands, such as greater than, less than, and so on
	Get Variant	Choose a previously saved layout
	Deselect All	Deselect all previously selected values
	Select All	Select all lines or key figures
	Check Entries	Check entered data before execution
	Cancel	Cancel and return to previous screen
Multiple selection..	Multiple selection	Checkboxes to make multiple selections
	Insert line	Insert line between values
	Delete line	Delete a selected line
	Aggregation	Summation
	Sub-total	Apply subtotal after a total on a key figure is first performed
	Do Not Choose All	Deselect all
	Choose All	Select all
	Hide Selected Field	Hide a field or column from display
	Show Selected Field	Display a field or column
	Time Series	Time line of key figures
	Execute F8	Run the transaction or report

Table 27.1 Select List of Icons Used in Reporting

Icon	Icon Detail	Details/Application
	Display Key Figures	Display all key figures
	Graph	Graphical representation
Switch drilldown...	Switch drilldown	Switch key figures display
	Sort in Ascending Order	Sort selected column in ascending order
	Sort in Descending Order	Sort selected column in descending order
	Import from Text File	Import/upload from notepad
	Copy from Clipboard	Copy data from notepad
	Delete Entire Selection Line	Delete the selected entry
	Move	Move field from one location to another
	Mail	Send by email
	Drilldown By	Drill down by characteristic
	Hierarchical Drilldown	Change drilldown level
	Other Info Structure	Switch to other info structure (when already in one info structure)
	Download	Download the data in various formats
	Change Layout	Change or select layout
	Filter	Set or delete filter
	Print	Print or print preview of reports
	Multiple Selection	Available on every parameters selection screen
	Find/Search	Search for any term
	Search Again	Search the same details/values again
	Calculate	Perform calculation

Table 27.1 Select List of Icons Used in Reporting (Cont.)

27

In the following sections, you'll learn how to leverage the standard reports and standard analyses available in MM.

27.2   Purchasing Reports

In this section, we'll navigate you through some of the important features and functionalities for purchasing reports and general evaluations. This section starts out with covering the options available for initial parameter selection including multiple selections. Then, we'll delve into the output of purchasing reports and the data manipulation options available once you've run a report.

27.2.1   Purchasing Documents

Purchasing document reports consist of the most up-to-date information about a specific object and is based on the transactions that business users have performed as part of the business process. For example, when you execute the purchase order (PO) selection, the system displays the current status of various POs, including those whose deliveries are made but awaiting invoicing from vendors. If you run the same report again after six hours, for example, after business users have recorded more goods receipts or vendor invoices, the system shows up-to-date (and different) information. This information reflects the accurate and up-to-date status of various activities and business processes.

In the following sections, we've divided the large number of available options for parameter selection into several figures for ease of understanding and comprehension.

Figure 27.1 shows the **Purchasing Documents per Document Number** screen of purchasing documents (Transaction ME2N). On this screen, you not only have several options to choose from in the **Program selections** area but by also choosing the dynamic selections icon (tri-color screen), the system brings up far greater options to choose from. For example, it's possible to have a parameters selection that is specific to a purchasing document header or item.

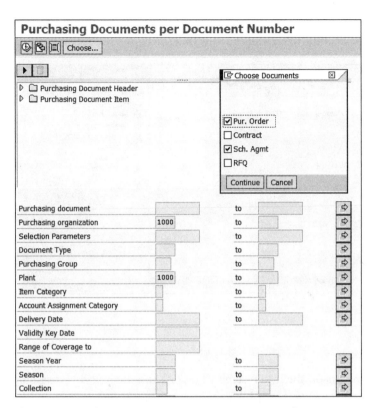

Figure 27.1 Purchasing Documents per Document Number

27.2.2   Multiple Selection

So far, you may have noticed that on the selection screen of a report, the option is available to enter any parameter in a range or an interval. For example, for the **Plant** field ⇨, you can enter only a selection interval. But what if you want to exclude a certain plant within the plants range on the selection screen or include two plants in addition to those given in the plants interval? All this and several other options are available via the **Multiple Selection** option available in all information systems and reports, as shown in Figure 27.2.

Click the multiple selection icon ⇨, as shown in Figure 27.2, for any parameter, and in the resulting screen, four tabs allow you to include or exclude single values or even an entire range. You can enter information in each of the four tabs, and the ensuing output (report) will show the desired results. You'll also find available icons to further facilitate the business user, such as copying data from a clipboard, adding or deleting

27

a line within the values, or using the multiple selection icon. The multiple selection icon enables you to select multiple values by selecting the requisite checkboxes.

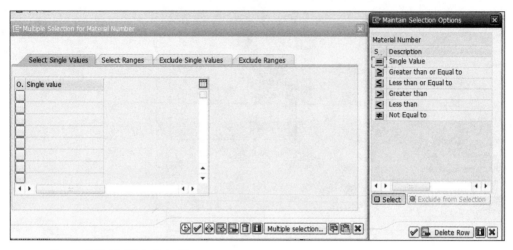

Figure 27.2 Multiple Selection

27.2.3   Report Output

After entering parameters on the initial screen, you execute the report by pressing [F8] or clicking **Execute**. An example of such a report is shown in Figure 27.3.

Item	Type	Cat	PGr	POH	Doc. Date	Supplier/Supplying Plant	Material	Short Text	Matl Group	D	I	A	Plant	SLoc	Quantity	OUn	Quantity	SKU	Net Price	Crcy	Per	Quantity	OpenTgtQty
10	ZLDP	F	002		24.01.2017	40000000 S/4HANA Business Partner	10000104	White crystalline powder	0001					1000	1,000.000	KG	1,000.000	KG	10.00	PKR	1	0.000	0.000
Purchasing Document 4500000065																							
10	ZLDP	F	002		24.01.2017	40000000 S/4HANA Business Partner	10000104	White crystalline powder	0001					1000	10.000	KG	10.000	KG	15.00	PKR	1	0.000	0.000
Purchasing Document 4500000066																							
10	NB	F	004		24.01.2017	40000000 S/4HANA Business Partner		Services	0002	D	K		1000		1	AU			15,000.00	PKR	1	0	0
Purchasing Document 4500000067																							
10	ZLDP	F	P01		25.12.2016	40000000 S/4HANA Business Partner	10000052	Screw	MG03					1000	100	EA	100	EA	15.00	PKR	1	0	0
Purchasing Document 4500000068																							
10	ZLDP	F	P08		26.01.2017	40000000 S/4HANA Business Partner	70000000	Trading Test	MG09					1000	100	EA	100	EA	100.00	PKR	1	0	0
Purchasing Document 4500000069																							
10	ZLDP	F	P08		26.01.2017	40000000 S/4HANA Business Partner	10000080	Demo RW	MG04	L			1000	1001	100	EA	100	EA	15.00	PKR	1	0	0
20	ZLDP	F	P08		26.01.2017	40000000 S/4HANA Business Partner	10000080	Demo RW	MG04				1000	1001	100	EA	100	EA	15.00	PKR	1	0	0
Purchasing Document 4500000070																							
10	NB	F	P08		27.01.2017	40000010 Ramzan Bros.	10000123	Crystal Powder	0001				1000	1001	1,000.000	KG	1,000.000	KG	10.00	PKR	1	0.000	0.000
Purchasing Document 4500000071																							
10	ZLDP	F	P08		07.02.2017	40000000 S/4HANA Business Partner	10000138	Raw M AI	01				1000	1001	37.647	KAI	44.291	KG	50.00	PKR	1	0.000	0.000
Purchasing Document 4500000072																							
10	ZLDP	F	P08		07.02.2017	40000000 S/4HANA Business Partner	10000138	Raw M AI	01				1000	1001	9.412	KAI	11.073	KG	10.00	PKR	1	0.000	0.000
Purchasing Document 4500000073																							
10	NB	F	P08		08.02.2017	40000020 Aslam & Sons	10000140	Raw Materila for MEAT	01					1000	100.000	KG	100.000	KG	47.88	PKR	1	0.000	0.000
Purchasing Document 4500000074																							
10	NB	F	P08		22.02.2017	40000000 S/4HANA Business Partner	80000000	Demo Packaing	MG04				1000	1001	100	EA	100	EA	15.00	PKR	1	0	0
20	NB	F	P08		22.02.2017	40000000 S/4HANA Business Partner	80000000	Demo Packaing	MG04				1000	1001	100	EA	100	EA	15.00	PKR	1	0	0
Purchasing Document 4500000075																							
10	NB	F	003		28.02.2017	40000040 ABC LTD	20000020	Computer	MG50					1000	5	EA	5	EA	55,000.00	PKR	1	0	0
20	NB	F	003		28.02.2017	40000040 ABC LTD	20000020	Computer	MG50					1000	3	EA	3	EA	45,000.00	PKR	1	0	0
Purchasing Document 4500000078																							

Purchasing Documents by Document Number

Print Preview

Figure 27.3 Purchasing Documents

In this report, you'll explore a few important options that are available, such as aggregation, setting a filter, or totaling and subtotaling a key figure. Some of the common and obvious options, such as sorting in ascending or descending order of information and changing or displaying objects, aren't covered.

Fields Selection

Figure 27.3 shows only a limited number of columns and information, whereas you can display and manipulate an enormous amount of information and even save the display layout, if you routinely use it. Click the change layout icon ⊞ ⌄, as shown in Figure 27.3.

> **Tips & Tricks**
>
> As shown in Figure 27.3, you can place your cursor on any column and right-click to display all of the available options—not just for that column, but for the entire report.

Aggregation

You can aggregate or sum up (total) any key figure or quantity. With the total icon already in place for a key figure, you can then use the subtotal icon ⅜ ⌄ to subtotal any number of characteristics and key figures, as shown in Figure 27.4.

Purchasing Documents by Document Number

Item	Doc. Type	Cat	PGr	POH	Still to be invoiced	Currency	Doc. Date	Supplier/Supplying Plant	Material	Matl Gro
				••	295,503.18	EUR				
					121,489,004.61	PKR				
					1,341,356.80	USD				
	ENB			•	61,000.00	PKR				
					1,081,684.80	USD				
10		F	P14		1,081,684.80	USD	17.06.2018	50000000 Roland Tank Filling Servi	10000068	01
10		F	003		61,000.00	PKR	14.07.2018	40000020 Aslam & Sons	80000082	01
	EUB			•	0.00	PKR				
10		F	P08		0.00	PKR	07.01.2017	2000 Manufacturing FG	40000060	MG52
	FO			•	0.00	PKR				
					35,000.00	USD				
10		F	001		0.00	PKR	11.12.2017	40000030 Mubeen & Sons		0005
10		F	001		0.00	PKR	11.12.2017	40000000 S/4HANA Business Partner		0005
10		F	001		0.00	PKR	11.12.2017	40000000 S/4HANA Business Partner		0005
10		F	001		0.00	PKR	11.12.2017	40000000 S/4HANA Business Partner		0005
10		F	001		0.00	USD	17.05.2018	50000000 Roland Tank Filling Servi		0005
10		F	001		35,000.00	USD	18.05.2018	50000000 Roland Tank Filling Servi		0005
	LP			•	20,000.00	EUR				
					0.00	USD				
10		L	004		0.00	USD	09.06.2018	50000000 Roland Tank Filling Servi	10000091	0004
10		L	004		20,000.00	EUR	09.06.2018	50000000 Roland Tank Filling Servi	10000084	01
	NB			•	73,503.18	EUR				
					119,046,138.14	PKR				
					219,322.00	USD				

Figure 27.4 Summation

As shown in Figure 27.4, first use the total option on the **Still to be invoiced** by select-ing it and clicking the total icon ⅀. Then, select the **Doc. Type** column followed by the **Still to be invoiced** column, and click the subtotal icon 🖳 ▪. The system displays the various summation levels by square dots on the right-hand side. You can then also choose the individual summation level by clicking the summation icon shown in Figure 27.4 located at the bottom of the screen.

Filters

As shown in Figure 27.5, you can also click the **Net Order Value** field or use **Maintain Selection**, which brings up the popup windows. Select the **Greater than or Equal to** option, and click **Continue**.

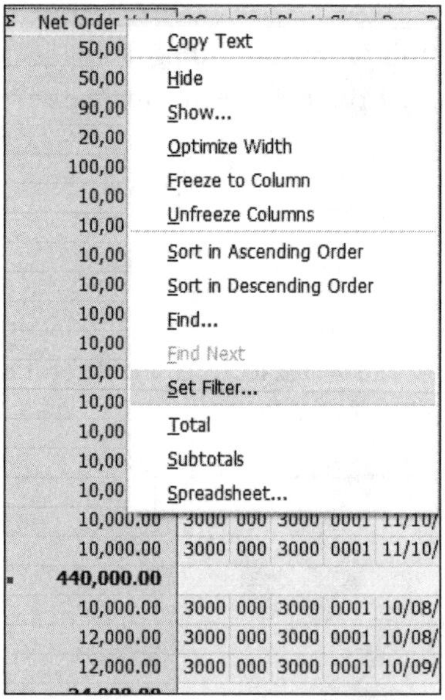

⅀	Net Order						
	50,00	Copy Text					
	50,00	Hide					
	90,00	Show...					
	20,00	Optimize Width					
	100,00	Freeze to Column					
	10,00						
	10,00	Unfreeze Columns					
	10,00	Sort in Ascending Order					
	10,00	Sort in Descending Order					
	10,00	Find...					
	10,00	Find Next					
	10,00						
	10,00	Set Filter...					
	10,00	Total					
	10,00	Subtotals					
	10,00	Spreadsheet...					
	10,000.00	3000	000	3000	0001	11/10/	
	10,000.00	3000	000	3000	0001	11/10/	
▪	**440,000.00**						
	10,000.00	3000	000	3000	0001	10/08/	
	12,000.00	3000	000	3000	0001	10/08/	
	12,000.00	3000	000	3000	0001	10/09/	

Figure 27.5 Filter Settings

As shown in Figure 27.6 you enter "10,000.00" in the **Net order Value** field so that the report now shows only those purchasing documents having net order values greater than or equal to 10,000.00 USD.

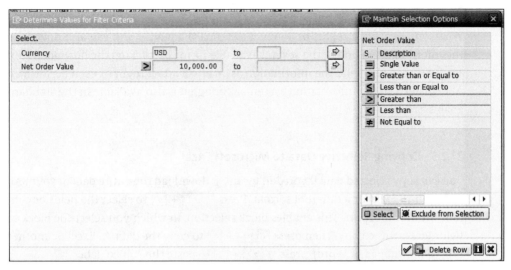

Figure 27.6 Active Filter

The red arrows shown in Figure 27.7 indicate that the list is sorted in descending (upward red arrow) or ascending (downward red arrow) order.

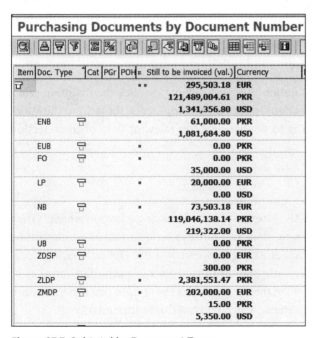

Figure 27.7 Subtotal by Document Types

27.2.4   Downloading

When you execute a report or conduct a standard analysis, you can also download the information in one of the several available forms by clicking the download icon 🗐 . You can also send the information as an email attachment or even perform an ABC analysis in the information system, although it's also available in the standard analysis reports.

27.2.5   Copying Selective Data to Microsoft Excel

You can copy selected data if you don't want to download the entire data of your SAP system into Excel or a different format. Press [Ctrl] + [Y] to select the fields or content within the report. This enables block selection, in which you select the block of fields you want to copy. Then press [Ctrl] + [C] to copy the data. In Excel or another program (Notepad or Word), press [Ctrl] + [V] to paste the copied data.

27.2.6   Printing

The print option is available by clicking on the print icon 🖨 within the report. It's important to note that all parameters used in the generation of the report in the information system also become part of the printout, including the filters, and so on.

27.2.7   Maintaining Selections

A frequently used option is **Maintain Selection**. When you click the maintain selection icon 🗐, the **Maintain Selection Options** screen appears. A shortcut to the **Maintain Selection Options** screen is to double-click the relevant field of the selection screen of any report.

27.2.8   Maintaining Variants

Maintaining a variant in the SAP system is similar to saving a layout, which is then available for repeated use when needed. You can also set a variant as the default by managing your layout options. For example, when you use the purchasing documents report, perhaps you always use plant 1000 and always set the date range as 30 days away. Instead of entering all of these parameters every time you run the report, you can save these details as a variant, which you can then subsequently select.

There are two areas where you can maintain variants. The first one is on the **Initial Parameters Selection** screen of any report, information system, or analysis when defining the selection parameters. Simply enter the information once in the parameters selection screen, and proceed to save the variant by choosing **Goto • Variants • Save as Variant**. On the **Variant Attributes** screen that appears, give the variant a name and a short description, and then choose whether to make each field required, hidden, or protected from data entry. With the variant saved, next time you just need to choose **Goto • Variants • Get the variant**. You can also delete incorrect or unwanted variants.

The second option to save a variant is when you've already executed an analysis or a report. The system displays all list fields, and once you've made the required changes (for example, any filter set, any sort of a column in ascending or descending order, or any aggregation), you can then click the select layout icon 🔄 and select the **Save Layout** option from the dropdown list. In the ensuing popup window, enter the name of the layout and a short description. Here, again, you can change or delete the saved layouts, if needed.

27.2.9   PO History

Refer again to Figure 27.3 and click on the PO history icon 📖, which brings up all the transactions that succeed after a PO was created. Figure 27.8 shows the PO 4600000008 in which goods receipt and invoice receipt was recorded.

Sh. Text	MvT	Material Document	Item	Posting Date	≡ Quantity	Delivery cost qua	OUn	≡ Amt.in loc.cur.	L.cur	≡ Qty in OPUn
BzWE		5000000400	2	13.02.2018	0	1	EA	50,000.25	PKR	0
BzWE		5000000400	3	13.02.2018	0	1	EA	50,000.25	PKR	0
Tr./Ev. Delivery costs					▪ **0**		**EA** ▪	**100,000.50**	**PKR** ▪	**0**
WE	101	5000000400	2	13.02.2018	1	0	EA	4,500,000.00	PKR	1
WE	101	5000000400	3	13.02.2018	1	0	EA	4,500,000.00	PKR	1
Tr./Ev. Goods receipt					▪ **2**		**EA** ▪	**9,000,000.00**	**PKR** ▪	**2**
BzRe		5105600952	5	13.02.2018	0	2	EA	100,000.50	PKR	0
Tr./Ev. Del. costs log. inv.					▪ **0**		**EA** ▪	**100,000.50**	**PKR** ▪	**0**
RE-L		5105600952	2	13.02.2018	1	0	EA	4,500,000.00	PKR	1
RE-L		5105600952	3	13.02.2018	1	0	EA	4,500,000.00	PKR	1
Tr./Ev. Invoice receipt					▪ **2**		**EA** ▪	**9,000,000.00**	**PKR** ▪	**2**

Figure 27.8 Purchase Order History

In this section we covered some of the standard reporting available in the SAP system. The data in the reports are up-to-date at the time of running or executing them.

27

In the next section, we'll cover standard analyses available in the all of logistics and supply chain.

> **Note**
>
> Chapter 17 on inventory management covers the associated inventory management reports in detail and therefore isn't repeated in this chapter.

27.3   Standard Analyses: Purchasing

Using standard analyses, users can draw on information from the standard info structures available in the SAP system. The difference between reports, such as purchasing document reports, and standard analysis is that, in information systems, the information is dynamic and changes whenever a business user performs a relevant business functions. In standard analysis, the system draws from historical information to enable the business user to make better business decisions. In other words, information from information systems flows into analyses.

> **Note**
>
> You can access standard analyses for all the logistics areas in the SAP system from the central location in the logistics controlling (CO) node by following the SAP menu path **Logistics • Logistics Controlling**.
>
> You can then navigate to the relevant component's standard analyses option. The SAP components for which standard analyses are available are logistics, inventory controlling, purchasing, sales, shop floor control, quality management (QM), shipment, and plant maintenance (PM).

In the following sections, we'll cover a standard analysis of MM. We'll also show a few features and functionalities available only in analyses and not in information systems, such as time series analysis and ABC analysis.

27.3.1   Standard Analyses in Materials Management

To access the standard analyses of MM, use Transaction MCE7 or follow the menu path **Logistics • Logistics Controlling • Purchasing Information System • Standard Analyses • Material**.

On the initial screen that appears, enter selection parameters such as **Purch. Organization** 1000 and click **Execute**. The screen shown in Figure 27.9 will appear.

Figure 27.9 shows key figures of different materials such as the **PO value**, the **Order quantity**, and the **Invoice Amount**. Click the **Switch drilldown...** button, and in the popup window that appears, choose **Month**.

Material Analysis (PURCHIS): Ranking List

Switch drilldown   Top N

Top 20: GR value pstg. date

Material	PO value		Order quantity		GR quantity		GR value pstg. date		Invoice Amount	
Total	115,627,431.92	PKR	120,114.796	***	118,050.364	***	204,793,076.68	PKR	143,886,386.27	PKR
70000004	0.00	PKR	8	EA	8	EA	126,200,001.00	PKR	126,200,001.00	PKR
70000001	0.00	PKR	2	EA	2	EA	30,000,000.00	PKR	0.00	PKR
10000242	0.00	PKR	1,810	MT	1,810	MT	10,136,000.00	PKR	0.00	PKR
10000206	0.00	PKR	210	MT	210	MT	8,820,000.00	PKR	8,820,000.00	PKR
	13,200.00	PKR	44.000	***	37.000	***	2,980,111.00	PKR	7,259,536.00	PKR
10000084	0.00	PKR	300	MT	200	MT	2,606,652.00	PKR	0.00	PKR
10000085	0.00	PKR	200	MT	200	MT	2,510,505.00	PKR	0.00	PKR
10000083	0.00	PKR	200	MT	200	MT	2,510,505.00	PKR	0.00	PKR
10000087	0.00	PKR	200	MT	200	MT	2,504,202.00	PKR	0.00	PKR
100000038	30,635.00	PKR	24.508	KG	1,500.000	KG	1,875,000.00	PKR	0.00	PKR
100000034	45,562.40	PKR	35.048	KG	1,300.000	KG	1,690,000.00	PKR	0.00	PKR
10000086	0.00	PKR	100	MT	100	MT	1,506,303.00	PKR	0.00	PKR
80000050	0.00	PKR	30,010	EA	30,010	EA	1,500,500.00	PKR	0.00	PKR
100000036	14,700.00	PKR	4.900	KG	500.000	KG	1,500,000.00	PKR	0.00	PKR
100000035	35,748.96	PKR	35.048	L	1,200	L	1,224,000.00	PKR	0.00	PKR
10000091	113,068.87	PKR	490	MT	100	MT	1,068,300.00	PKR	0.00	PKR
10000081	0.00	PKR	100.000	KG	100.000	KG	1,068,300.00	PKR	0.00	PKR
10000082	0.00	PKR	110	MT	100	MT	1,004,202.00	PKR	0.00	PKR
10000070	0.00	PKR	5,000.000	KG	5,000.000	KG	850,000.00	PKR	0.00	PKR
10000054	0.00	PKR	60	EA	30	EA	507,466.68	PKR	823,041.91	PKR
Rest	115,374,516.69	PKR	81,171.292	***	75,243.364	***	2,731,029.00	PKR	783,807.36	PKR

Figure 27.9 Material Analysis

Figure 27.10 shows monthly view of the data from a few key figures. You can display a large number of fields, as shown in Figure 27.10, just like in original document reports or in information systems. To display hidden fields, click the choose key figures icon , and a popup window will appear. The left-hand side of the popup window shows the fields that the system already displays, whereas the right-hand side shows a large number of fields for you to choose from. Also, filters are available for key figures—**All**, **Exponential numbers**, and **Quantities**—which, if selected, can help you quickly identify and select the desired fields for the report.

As shown in Figure 27.10, place your cursor on the key figure **GR Value Posting date** and choose **Top N**.

27

Material Analysis (PURCHIS): Ranking List

Switch drilldown   Top N

Top 100: Invoice Amount

Month	PO value		Order quantity		GR quantity		GR value pstg. date		Invoice Amount	
Total	115,627,431.92	PKR	120,114.796	***	118,050.364	***	204,793,076.68	PKR	143,886,386.27	PKR
02.2018	0.00	PKR	2,032.000	***	1,142.000	***	156,557,201.00	PKR	126,200,001.00	PKR
09.2017	5,000.00	PKR	1,211.000	***	212.000	***	8,925,000.00	PKR	8,820,000.00	PKR
05.2018	0.00	PKR	43,359.000	***	43,241.000	***	18,617,755.84	PKR	6,971,886.00	PKR
04.2018	5,000.00	PKR	697.000	***	638.000	***	415,814.10	PKR	976,583.57	PKR
07.2018	767,756.76	PKR	28,187.392	***	34,751.000	***	7,168,265.00	PKR	410,265.00	PKR
03.2017	0.00	PKR	1,368.000	***	1,331.000	***	35,825.00	PKR	270,340.00	PKR
06.2017	0.00	PKR	20	EA	10	EA	0.00	PKR	101,000.00	PKR
05.2017	0.00	PKR	500	EA	500	EA	50,000.00	PKR	50,000.00	PKR
10.2016	46,675.70	PKR	51	MT	51	MT	46,675.70	PKR	46,675.70	PKR
04.2017	100.00	PKR	1,811.000	***	1,652.000	***	37,618.30	PKR	21,985.00	PKR
06.2018	114,794,721.32	PKR	5,138.040	***	128.000	***	1,233,775.00	PKR	17,650.00	PKR

Figure 27.10 Monthly Breakdown of Material Values

Figure 27.11 shows the goods receipt value by value of materials in a twenty-month time period. You can enter any number to view the top numbers of key figures.

Material Analysis (PURCHIS): Ranking List

Switch drilldown   Top N

Top 20: GR value pstg. date

Month	PO value		Order quantity		GR quantity		GR value pstg. date		Invoice Amount	
Total	115,627,431.92	PKR	120,114.796	***	118,050.364	***	204,793,076.68	PKR	143,886,386.27	PKR
02.2018	0.00	PKR	2,032.000	***	1,142.000	***	156,557,201.00	PKR	126,200,001.00	PKR
05.2018	0.00	PKR	43,359.000	***	43,241.000	***	18,617,755.84	PKR	6,971,886.00	PKR
12.2017	3,000.00	PKR	31,829.000	***	31,823.000	***	11,669,500.00	PKR	0.00	PKR
09.2017	5,000.00	PKR	1,211.000	***	212.000	***	8,925,000.00	PKR	8,820,000.00	PKR
07.2018	767,756.76	PKR	28,187.392	***	34,751.000	***	7,168,265.00	PKR	410,265.00	PKR
06.2018	114,794,721.32	PKR	5,138.040	***	128.000	***	1,233,775.00	PKR	17,650.00	PKR
04.2018	5,000.00	PKR	697.000	***	638.000	***	415,814.10	PKR	976,583.57	PKR
05.2017	0.00	PKR	500	EA	500	EA	50,000.00	PKR	50,000.00	PKR
10.2016	46,675.70	PKR	51	MT	51	MT	46,675.70	PKR	46,675.70	PKR
04.2017	100.00	PKR	1,811.000	***	1,652.000	***	37,618.30	PKR	21,985.00	PKR
03.2017	0.00	PKR	1,368.000	***	1,331.000	***	35,825.00	PKR	270,340.00	PKR
01.2017	0.00	PKR	2,613.000	***	1,464.000	***	11,651.00	PKR	0.00	PKR
12.2016	0.00	PKR	102.000	***	102.000	***	11,506.00	PKR	0.00	PKR
03.2018	2,000.00	PKR	200.000	***	100.000	***	6,000.00	PKR	0.00	PKR
02.2017	2,978.14	PKR	363.364	***	275.364	***	5,489.74	PKR	0.00	PKR
01.2018	0.00	PKR	620.000	***	620.000	***	1,000.00	PKR	0.00	PKR
12.2020	0.00	PKR	0	MT	0	MT	0.00	PKR	0.00	PKR
01.2020	0.00	PKR	0	MT	0	MT	0.00	PKR	0.00	PKR
12.2019	0.00	PKR	0	MT	0	MT	0.00	PKR	0.00	PKR
06.2019	0.00	PKR	0	MT	0	MT	0.00	PKR	0.00	PKR
Rest	200.00	PKR	33.000	***	20.000	***	0.00	PKR	101,000.00	PKR

Figure 27.11 Ranking List

27.3.2   Key Figures

Sometimes, you may just want to see all of the key figures of one characteristic. Double-click any entry of the characteristic, and the system displays all of the key figures of that characteristic. In our example, the characteristic is the material and all of the key figures shown in Figure 27.12 for vendor 50000000. You can also download this data or send this data via email.

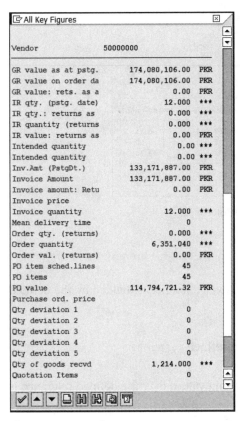

Figure 27.12 Key Figures

27.3.3   Other Info Structures

You can also navigate to the **Other info structure** screen within the standard analysis by clicking the other info structure icon ⊞. In the ensuing popup window, enter the name of the new info structure or use the dropdown menu to select an info structure. If any custom-defined info structures will also be available for selection.

27.3.4   Standard Analysis: ABC Analysis

Access the screen shown in Figure 27.13 by selecting the key figure **Value Stock Receiving Quantity** by placing your cursor over it and choosing **Edit • ABC Analysis** from the menu bar. In the popup window that appears, choose the **Strategy** for the ABC analysis as **Total ValueOverTol (%)** and click **Continue**.

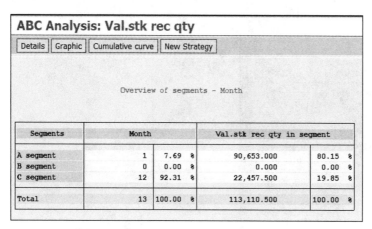

Figure 27.13 ABC Analysis for Values with Overtolerance

The options in ABC analysis are as follows:

- **Total ValueOverTol (%)**
  The total value of all the characteristics over tolerance is divided by the defined percentage.

- **Number vendors (%)**
  The number of vendors is divided by the defined percentage.

- **Valueover Tol (absolute)**
  The actual number of characteristics having values over the defined tolerance is divided up in either A, B, or C segments.

- **Number vendor**
  The number of materials is divided up in either A, B, or C segments.

ABC analysis enables you to select the right strategy and then divides key figures into the top three groupings. You also have the flexibility of defining the percentage of a key figure to be listed in the A, B, or C segments.

As shown in Figure 27.13, you have the flexibility of overwriting the system-suggested segment sizes for A, B, or C. Click the **Graphic** button to open the **SAP Business Graphics** screen shown in Figure 27.14.

Figure 27.14 show a graphical representation of the ABC analysis. The blue vertical bars denote the A, B, or C segments of characteristic values of segment A, while the yellow bars represent segment C.

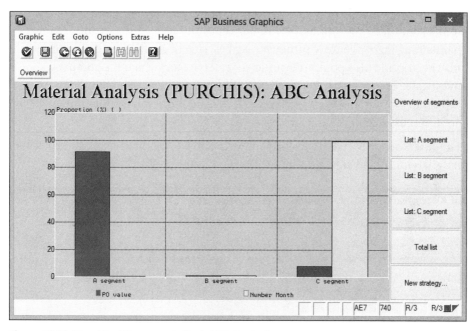

Figure 27.14 Graphical Representation: ABC Analysis

27.4   Standard Analyses: Inventory Management

Now that you're familiar with several features of purchasing reports, you should be able to take advantage of several standard analyses also applicable to inventory management.

27.4.1   Inventory Turnover

This metric is one of the most commonly used KPIs in inventory management, as inventory turnover typically reflects the overall efficiency of the supply chain. The formula for inventory turnover is: *Cost of goods ÷ average inventory*

Inventory turnover is the number of times inventory must be replaced during a given period of time, and this number specifies how often the average valuated stock is consumed or sold (turned over). Low inventory turnover reflects excess inventory or an overstock situation, the presence of dead stock, and liquidity problems, which put increased pressure on working capital.

In comparison, high inventory turnover is usually seen as a positive sign, since this number indicates the company is rapidly consuming or selling goods. While this maintaining high inventory turnover may be a sign of good inventory management practice, it could also point to insufficient safety stock, which the company should investigate. To improve inventory turnover, companies can look into shortening lead times by sourcing from local, instead of distant, suppliers; fine-tuning the service levels used; and refining forecast accuracy for materials.

Using Transaction MC44, Figure 27.15 shows the inventory turnover of the top twenty materials for the key figure average value stock value (**AvgValStockValue**).

Material Analysis: Inventory Turnover: Ranking List

Top 20: AvgValStckValue

Material	VlStTn-Val	AvgValStckValue	Tot. usage val.	AnTtlStkTrn-Val	AnValStkTrn-Val	Average usage	
Total	0.06	3757506,593.71 PKR	226,491,517.31 PKR	0.05	0.05	730.379	***
30000112	0.00	1928919,287.43 PKR	6,764,747.00 PKR	0.00	0.00	1	MT
40000189	0.01	980,501,351.14 PKR	14,321,023.50 PKR	0.01	0.01	750.500	MT
40000004	0.00	442,606,109.92 PKR	0.00 PKR	0.00	0.00	0	MT
10000206	0.06	37,356,912.33 PKR	2,274,838.85 PKR	0.06	0.06	27.625	MT
30000038	0.60	35,650,113.91 PKR	21,467,138.10 PKR	0.55	0.55	14.007	MT
70000024	0.43	32,601,356.79 PKR	14,041,185.00 PKR	0.39	0.39	256.460	EA
70000004	1.64	31,744,898.26 PKR	52,128,571.72 PKR	1.49	1.49	1	EA
10000204	0.05	30,305,000.00 PKR	1,430,000.00 PKR	0.04	0.04	17.875	MT
10000205	0.02	30,175,553.57 PKR	594,750.00 PKR	0.02	0.02	7.625	MT
40000140	0.06	17,233,240.39 PKR	985,504.96 PKR	0.05	0.05	5.375	MT
70000023	0.44	15,548,025.00 PKR	6,769,525.00 PKR	0.40	0.40	251.188	EA
10000174	0.00	13,861,400.00 PKR	0.00 PKR	0.00	0.00	0	L
70000001	0.00	12,857,142.86 PKR	0.00 PKR	0.00	0.00	0	EA
30000081	0.00	10,617,225.00 PKR	0.00 PKR	0.00	0.00	0.000	KG
40000105	0.00	10,000,000.00 PKR	0.00 PKR	0.00	0.00	0	EA
40000104	0.00	9,999,900.00 PKR	0.00 PKR	0.00	0.00	0	EA
40000103	0.00	9,988,207.14 PKR	100.00 PKR	0.00	0.00	1	EA
80000031	0.00	7,500,000.00 PKR	0.00 PKR	0.00	0.00	0	PC
10000072	0.00	6,438,513.21 PKR	105.00 PKR	0.00	0.00	0.002	KG
80000030	0.00	5,992,380.00 PKR	0.00 PKR	0.00	0.00	0	PC
Rest	1.21	87,609,976.76 PKR	105,714,028.18 PKR	1.10	1.10	1,014.919	***

Figure 27.15 Inventory Turnover

> **Note**
> You can now calculate average inventory turnover (Transaction MC.B), which shows the average total consumption per day divided by the average stock.

27.4.2   Dead Stock

Dead stock is stock that hasn't been consumed during a given time period. To deal with excessive dead stock, revisit the safety stock level maintained in the system to lower the level to where dead stock is kept to a minimum or eliminated, but where you won't face a disruption in the supply chain. Safety stock is the minimum stock level of a material kept in inventory to account for any supply disruption or sudden demand surge. Figure 27.16 shows the standard analysis of dead stock and can be accessed via Transaction MC50. On the initial screen of Transaction MC50, the selection parameters provide several options you to determine what constitutes or defines dead stock of materials.

```
Key Figure: Dead Stock

 [ ABC analysis ] [ Classification ] [ Single-line ] [ Sort in desc. order ] [ Sort in asc. order ]

All plants cumulated                  Analysis date   14.07.2018

Analysis: Dead stock

Number of selected materials:     5

Dead stock value               0.00  PKR

 Material        Short text                              Dead stock value       %    cum.%
                 Current stock         Average stock     Dead stock

 10000000        RAW SCRAP HMS                              0.00 PKR    0.00 %  0.00 %
                    15,296.715  MT      1,154.401 MT        0.000  MT
 10000001        RA II                                      0.00 PKR    0.00 %  0.00 %
                       100.000  KG          2.431 KG        0.000  KG
 10000002        RAW SCRAP SHREDDED UNPROCESSED             0.00 PKR    0.00 %  0.00 %
                     1,593.425  MT        155.652 MT        0.000  MT
 10000003        RAW SCRAP BUNDLES UNPROCESSED              0.00 PKR    0.00 %  0.00 %
                       892.740  MT         81.212 MT        0.000  MT
```

Figure 27.16 Dead Stock

Tips & Tricks

Be sure to explore the buttons, such as the **ABC analysis** button or the **Classification** button, located at the top of Figure 27.16, which can provide more information about key figures under review.

27.4.3   Slow-Moving Items

Slow-moving items denote stock that isn't obsolete or dead but that has moved very little during a time period. Therefore, periodically evaluating the last usage of slow-moving items and lowering its safety stock and minimum stock levels as low as possible may make sense.

The screen shown in Figure 27.17 is accessed via Transaction MC46 and displays, in number of days, when a material was last consumed or if the material hasn't been consumed at all.

Key Figure: Slow-Moving Items		
ABC analysis Classification Double-line Sort in desc. order Sort in asc. order		

```
All plants cumulated                  Analysis date   14.07.2018

Analysis: Slow-moving item

Number of selected materials:    269

Stock value          6,502,753,356.54  PKR
```

Material	Short text	Days since consumpti
80000062	BOX CHOCO 4 CRUNCHY BEANS POUCH	67
80000064	CHOCO 4 - (POUCH) - (24X24)	67
80000065	TAPE	67
10000076	Wastage Glass	63 (no consumption)
10000078	Broken Glass	63 (no consumption)
40000022	TROY 300ML PS-05 (1X6)X8	63 (no consumption)
40000023	B - TROY 300ML PS-05 (1X6)X8	63 (no consumption)
10000002	RAW SCRAP SHREDDED UNPROCESSED	61
10000071	Iron(III) oxide Fe2O3	55
10000072	Chromium(III) oxide Cr2O3	55
10000073	Sodium Oxide	55
10000075	Calcium Oxide	55
10000081	Limestone (CaCO3)	49 (no consumption)
10000082	Stainless Steel	49 (no consumption)

Figure 27.17 Slow-Moving Items

27.4.4   Range of Coverage

This key figure reflects the number of days during which the current stock will cover future stock issues and is based on past stock and issue values. In other words, the range of coverage indicates how long existing inventory will last, assuming that the average future stock issues will be the same as those in the past. The usage-based range of coverage is calculated as follows: *Current stock ÷ average usage per day*

The requirements-based range of coverage is calculated as follows: *Current stock ÷ average requirement per day*

This inventory management KPI can help your company spot materials with excess coverage and to take action to reduce unnecessary inventory. The opposite is also true: by identifying a potential shortage situation early on, corrective measures can be taken. The screen shown in Figure 27.18 is accessed via Transaction MC42 for usage value-based range of coverage.

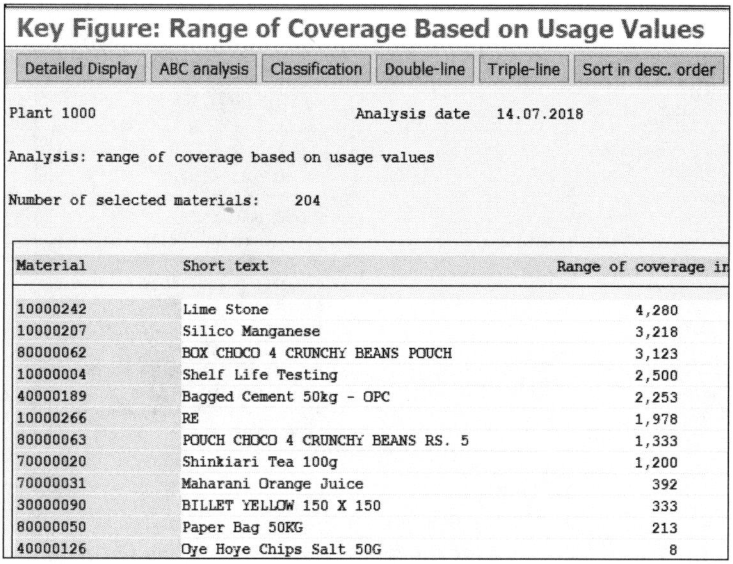

Key Figure: Range of Coverage Based on Usage Values

| Detailed Display | ABC analysis | Classification | Double-line | Triple-line | Sort in desc. order |

```
Plant 1000                        Analysis date   14.07.2018

Analysis: range of coverage based on usage values

Number of selected materials:     204
```

Material	Short text	Range of coverage in
10000242	Lime Stone	4,280
10000207	Silico Manganese	3,218
80000062	BOX CHOCO 4 CRUNCHY BEANS POUCH	3,123
10000004	Shelf Life Testing	2,500
40000189	Bagged Cement 50kg - OPC	2,253
10000266	RE	1,978
80000063	POUCH CHOCO 4 CRUNCHY BEANS RS. 5	1,333
70000020	Shinkiari Tea 100g	1,200
70000031	Maharani Orange Juice	392
30000090	BILLET YELLOW 150 X 150	333
80000050	Paper Bag 50KG	213
40000126	Oye Hoye Chips Salt 50G	8

Figure 27.18 Range of Coverage Based on Usage Values

> **Note**
>
> For a range of coverage based on requirements, use Transaction MC43. Further, for insight into the average range of coverage, use Transaction MC.C.

27.4.5   Stock Value

Knowing current stock values helps your company identify which items tie up the most capital in the organization. This information can support any inventory optimization initiative. Analysis can be based on either the current stock value or the average stock value. Whereas the current stock value is calculated by multiplying the stock level with the current price, the average stock value is calculated by multiplying the average stock level with the current price. The screen shown in Figure 27.19 can be accessed via Transaction MC48 for the stock value key figure.

27

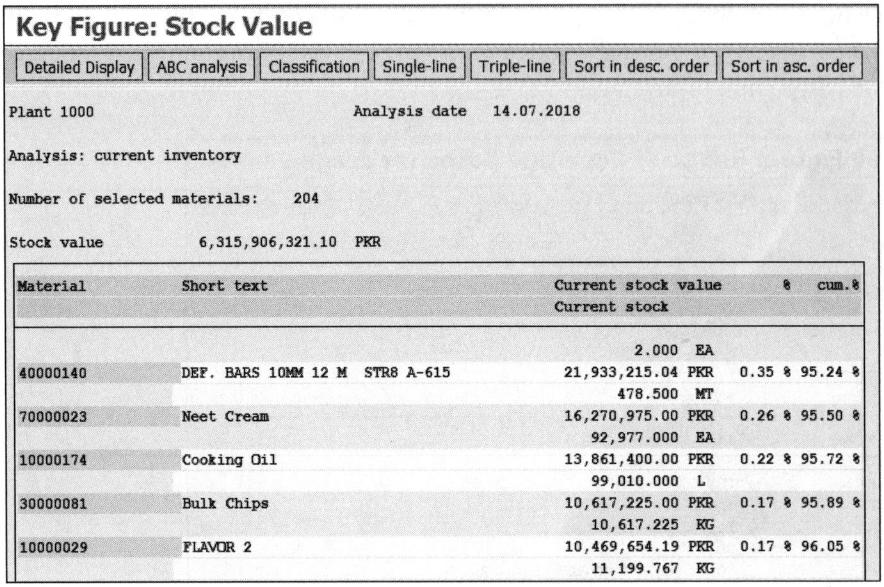

```
Key Figure: Stock Value
[Detailed Display] [ABC analysis] [Classification] [Single-line] [Triple-line] [Sort in desc. order] [Sort in asc. order]

Plant 1000                          Analysis date   14.07.2018

Analysis: current inventory

Number of selected materials:    204

Stock value         6,315,906,321.10  PKR
```

Material	Short text	Current stock value Current stock	%	cum.%
		2.000 EA		
40000140	DEF. BARS 10MM 12 M STR8 A-615	21,933,215.04 PKR	0.35 %	95.24 %
		478.500 MT		
70000023	Neet Cream	16,270,975.00 PKR	0.26 %	95.50 %
		92,977.000 EA		
10000174	Cooking Oil	13,861,400.00 PKR	0.22 %	95.72 %
		99,010.000 L		
30000081	Bulk Chips	10,617,225.00 PKR	0.17 %	95.89 %
		10,617.225 KG		
10000029	FLAVOR 2	10,469,654.19 PKR	0.17 %	96.05 %
		11,199.767 KG		

Figure 27.19 Stock Value

The screen shown in Figure 27.20 displays the average stock value key figure and is accessed via Transaction MC49.

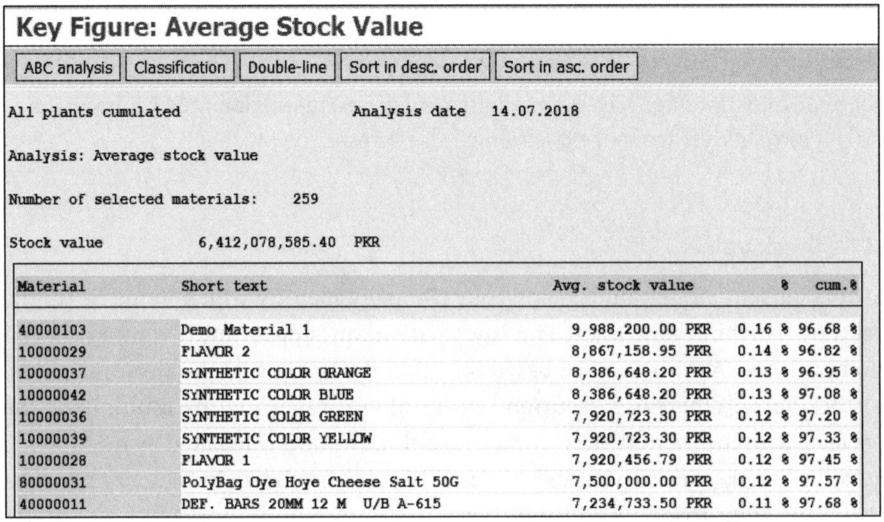

```
Key Figure: Average Stock Value
[ABC analysis] [Classification] [Double-line] [Sort in desc. order] [Sort in asc. order]

All plants cumulated                Analysis date   14.07.2018

Analysis: Average stock value

Number of selected materials:    259

Stock value         6,412,078,585.40  PKR
```

Material	Short text	Avg. stock value	%	cum.%
40000103	Demo Material 1	9,988,200.00 PKR	0.16 %	96.68 %
10000029	FLAVOR 2	8,867,158.95 PKR	0.14 %	96.82 %
10000037	SYNTHETIC COLOR ORANGE	8,386,648.20 PKR	0.13 %	96.95 %
10000042	SYNTHETIC COLOR BLUE	8,386,648.20 PKR	0.13 %	97.08 %
10000036	SYNTHETIC COLOR GREEN	7,920,723.30 PKR	0.12 %	97.20 %
10000039	SYNTHETIC COLOR YELLOW	7,920,723.30 PKR	0.12 %	97.33 %
10000028	FLAVOR 1	7,920,456.79 PKR	0.12 %	97.45 %
80000031	PolyBag Oye Hoye Cheese Salt 50G	7,500,000.00 PKR	0.12 %	97.57 %
40000011	DEF. BARS 20MM 12 M U/B A-615	7,234,733.50 PKR	0.11 %	97.68 %

Figure 27.20 Average Stock Value

27.4.6   Usage Value

By executing an analysis on the consumption (usage) value of a portfolio of materials, your company can determine which items have a high level of usage value and a high capital lockup. This information can provide insights into which materials are the big movers in the company and can also help identify potential slow-moving items. The screen shown in Figure 27.21 is accessed via Transaction MC45.

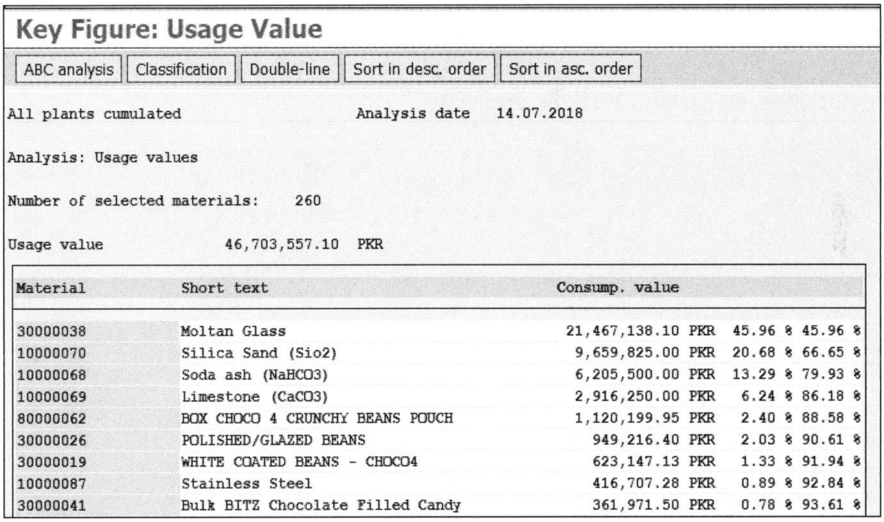

```
Key Figure: Usage Value

 ABC analysis    Classification    Double-line    Sort in desc. order    Sort in asc. order

All plants cumulated                Analysis date   14.07.2018

Analysis: Usage values

Number of selected materials:     260

Usage value              46,703,557.10   PKR

 Material        Short text                          Consump. value

 30000038        Moltan Glass                       21,467,138.10 PKR  45.96 %  45.96 %
 10000070        Silica Sand (Sio2)                  9,659,825.00 PKR  20.68 %  66.65 %
 10000068        Soda ash (NaHCO3)                   6,205,500.00 PKR  13.29 %  79.93 %
 10000069        Limestone (CaCO3)                   2,916,250.00 PKR   6.24 %  86.18 %
 80000062        BOX CHOCO 4 CRUNCHY BEANS POUCH     1,120,199.95 PKR   2.40 %  88.58 %
 30000026        POLISHED/GLAZED BEANS                 949,216.40 PKR   2.03 %  90.61 %
 30000019        WHITE COATED BEANS - CHOCO4           623,147.13 PKR   1.33 %  91.94 %
 10000087        Stainless Steel                       416,707.28 PKR   0.89 %  92.84 %
 30000041        Bulk BITZ Chocolate Filled Candy      361,971.50 PKR   0.78 %  93.61 %
```

Figure 27.21 Usage Value

27.4.7   Requirement Value

The requirement value key figure provides insight into materials that have a high level of requirement value and which are, therefore, possible candidates for high capital lockup in the future. The requirements value of a material is derived from the current price of valuated requirements within a period of time (in the future) and is accessed via Transaction MC47.

27.5   SAP Fiori Apps

SAP Fiori is SAP's next-generation, web-based user experience for working with SAP systems, and each app is shown as a tile in the SAP Fiori launchpad. A large number of SAP Fiori apps are available in SAP S/4HANA, and the apps library is constantly

27

expanding. Apps for master data, transactional data, reporting, and analytics using SAP components are available in the SAP Fiori apps reference library.

Figure 27.22 shows the initial screen of SAP Fiori launchpad, where individual apps are represented as tiles. Apps can be group together based on different roles, such as the materials planner or the inventory controller. Apps can also be grouped together based on functional areas, such as MM or QM, as shown in Figure 27.22. Due to highly intuitive nature of apps, users can quickly get up to speed through use. Further, most master data and transactional data apps, and even several reporting apps, in SAP Fiori still have the look and feel of SAP GUI (graphical user interface) by using the same menu options, menu bars, buttons, and icons.

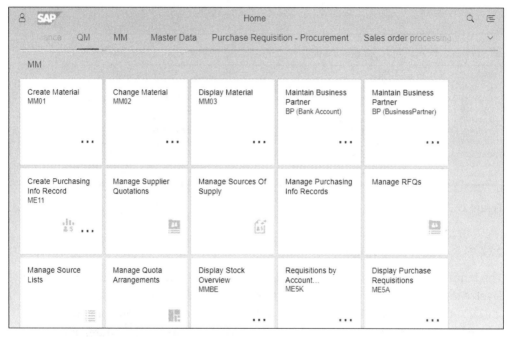

Figure 27.22 SAP Fiori Launchpad

Let's cover some of the SAP Fiori apps useful in MM.

27.5.1   Monitor Material Coverage

Figure 27.23 shows the **Material and Production Planning** SAP Fiori app group. Click on the Monitor Material Coverage app so that the screen shown in Figure 27.24 appears.

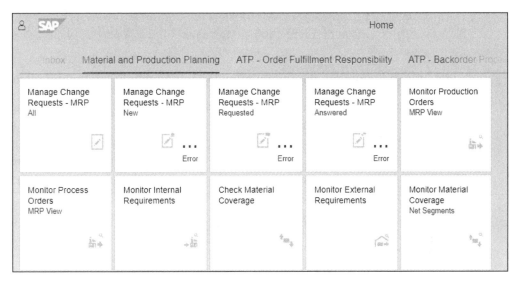

Figure 27.23 Role-Based SAP Fiori App Tiles

As shown in Figure 27.24, the Monitor Material Coverage app displays some materials with the green bars, which represent comfortable stock availability. The red bars represent a situation where the inventory or materials planner should pay greater attention to avoid stockouts or the unavailability of a required material on a desired date. One such material that needs special and immediate attention is material 40000030, which is showing a shortage of 13.07.2018 (July 13, 2018) of 10 CAR (cartons).

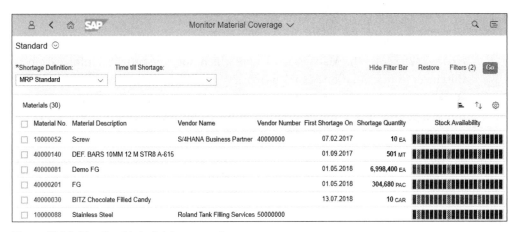

Figure 27.24 Monitor Material Coverage App

The dropdown list on the left-hand side provides options for the inventory planner to filter materials based on different criteria. After a new filter is applied, click on **Go**.

27.5.2   Inventory Turnover Analysis

Figure 27.25 shows the Inventory Turnover Analysis app, which provides the same information we saw earlier in Figure 27.15, which was the SAP GUI version, versus the SAP Fiori app shown here. You can even explore related apps for more or different analysis by clicking on the **Related apps** link located on the right-hand side of Figure 27.25. Further, the option to zoom in or out from the data, to display the data as an MS Excel table, or even to download the data are all available.

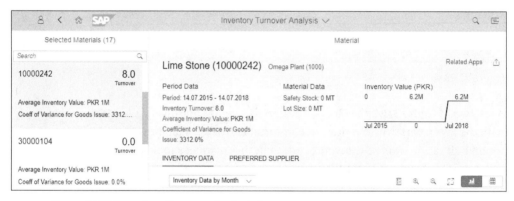

Figure 27.25 Inventory Turnover Analysis App

27.5.3   Manage Stock

Figure 27.26 shows the Manage Stock app, which not only provides information on the current stock situation of various stock types such as unrestricted-use or blocked stock but also provides an option for an inventory controller to perform business transactions on the same screen. For example, to add more unrestricted-use stock of material 10000002 in plant 1000 and storage location A001, click on the icon next to the unrestricted-use stock 110.000. A popup will appear where more quantity of material can be added, and on saving the information, the system will display a message of the material document number created by this transactional step.

Figure 27.26 Manage Stock App

27.5.4   Material Documents Overview

Figure 27.27 shows the Material Documents Overview app, which has a similar look and feel of SAP GUI Transaction MB51. The top half of the figure offers several filters that you can use to display only the required information, as shown in the lower half of the screen.

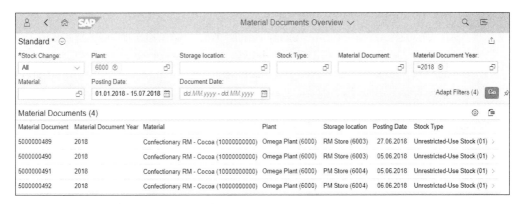

Figure 27.27 Material Document Overview App

27.5.5   Material Stocks on Posting Date

Figure 27.28 shows the Material Stocks on Posting Date app, which is same as the SAP GUI Transaction MB5B. The available options include displaying totals or subtotals or displaying the data in ascending or descending order. You can also navigate to detailed data of a line item, such as the material document (**Mat. Doc.**), by double-clicking on the line item.

27

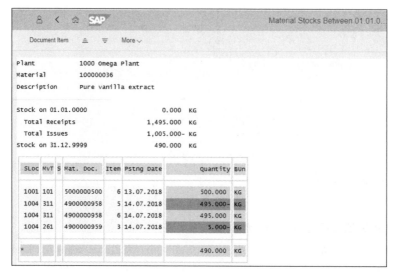

Figure 27.28 Stock by Posting Date App

27.5.6 Supplier Evaluation by Time

Figure 27.29 shows the Supplier Evaluation by Time app, which displays the score calculated for each supplier and its associated variance as a percentage. Drilldown capabilities are available on the left-hand side to view this information from different perspectives, such as by material group or purchasing group.

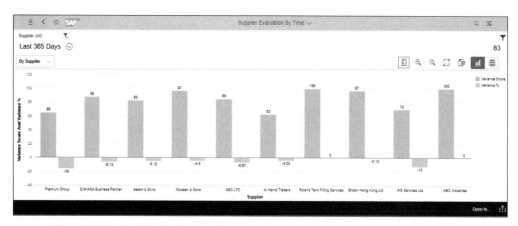

Figure 27.29 Supplier Evaluation by Time App

27.5.7 Purchasing Group Activities

Figure 27.30 shows the Purchasing Group Activities app, which displays trends in various procurement activities that have been undertaken, such as the number of purchase orders, contracts, and scheduling agreements created as well as the deliveries received against these procurement activities. Drilldown capabilities are available on the left-hand side to view this information from different perspectives, and you can also set filters on characteristics and key figures.

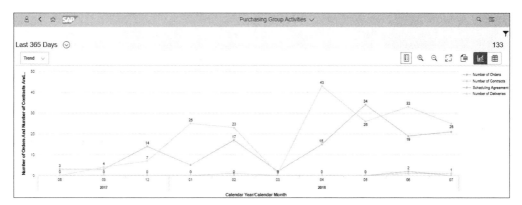

Figure 27.30 Purchasing Group Activities App

27.5.8 SAP Fiori Library

As we mentioned earlier this section, the SAP Fiori library is constantly expanding at a rapid pace for both SAP S/4HANA on-premise and SAP S/4HANA Cloud.

Go to *http://bit.ly/SAPFioriAppsLibrary* to search and explore the latest SAP Fiori apps. Figure 27.31 shows the initial screen of the SAP Fiori library, where you can search for relevant apps on the left-hand side. App details will appear on the right-hand side of the screen. To make relevant apps available for use, reach out to an SAP Fiori consultant with app details and the specific role or group that will use these apps.

27

Figure 27.31 SAP Fiori Apps Library

27.6   Summary

In this chapter, you learned how to leverage information systems, standard reports, and analyses in MM as well as the next-generation SAP S/4HANA Fiori apps. The information covered in this chapter can certainly help you use the same reporting tools and features in other logistics and supply chain components in an SAP system.

As we've seen, MM in the SAP S/4AHANA system is quite comprehensive and offers in-depth and practical solutions for a large number of business processes and scenarios for a diverse range of industries. Not only that, MM offers options that enable you to implement and integrate MM in all the important business processes. However, the actual return on investment for the SAP system implementation can only be ensured when you strive to understand how various SAP system components are integrated with each other. Those of you working in more supply chain management roles have seen how MM is vital to many processes in the logistics and supply chain. To achieve flawless integration during an SAP system implementation, you'll need to maintain extensive collaboration and intense coordination among the various stakeholders in the company.

Appendix A

Movement Types

Table A.1 lists the most common types of movement types used for goods issuance, goods receipt, and transfer postings available in the SAP system.

Goods Issuance (Consumption) and Goods Receipt		
Movement Type	Special Indicator	Movement Type Text
101		Goods receipt for purchase order into warehouse/stores
102		Goods receipt for purchase order into warehouse - reversal
103		Goods receipt for purchase order into GR blocked stock
104		Goods receipt for purchase order -> GR blocked stock - reversal
105		Release GR blocked stock for warehouse
106		Release GR blocked stock for warehouse - reversal
107		Goods receipt to valuated blocked stock
108		Goods receipt to valuated blocked stock - reversal
109		Goods receipt from valuated blocked stock
122		Return delivery to vendor
161		Returns for purchase order
201		Consumption for cost center from warehouse
261		Consumption for order from warehouse

Table A.1 List of Standard Movement Types Available in SAP

Goods Issuance (Consumption) and Goods Receipt		
Movement Type	**Special Indicator**	**Movement Type Text**
262		Consumption for order from warehouse - reversal
331		Withdrawal for sampling from quality inspection
351	K	Transfer posting to stock in transit from unrestricted-use
501		Receipt w/o purchase order into unrestricted-use stock
503		Receipt w/o purchase order into quality inspection stock
531		Receipt of by-product into unrestricted-use stock
551		Withdrawal for scrapping from unrestricted-use stock
561		Receipt per initial entry of stock balances into unrestricted-use
Transfer Posting		
Movement Type	**Special Indicator**	**Movement Type Text**
301		Transfer posting plant to plant (one-step)
311		Transfer posting storage location (one-step)
321		Transfer posting quality inspection to unrestricted
323		Transfer posting quality to quality within plant
541		Transfer posting to stock with subcontractor from unrestricted-use stock
542		Transfer posting to stock w. subcontracting from unrestricted-use - reversal

Table A.1 List of Standard Movement Types Available in SAP (Cont.)

Appendix B
The Authors

Jawad Akhtar is an SAP logistics and supply chain management expert with a focus on business sales and delivery. He earned his chemical engineering degree from Missouri University of Science and Technology in the United States. He has more than 20 years of professional experience, 16 of which have been spent working with SAP systems. He has experience working on several large-scale, end-to-end SAP project implementation lifecycles, including rollouts. He works with SAP clients to help them identify the root causes of business issues and address those issues with the appropriate SAP products and change management strategies. He now focuses on next-generation SAP products such as SAP S/4HANA, SAP Integrated Business Planning (SAP IBP), SAP Ariba, and SAP C/4HANA.

Akhtar is also a technical advisor to SAPexperts, an ASUG speaker, and a contributor to SearchSAP, where his "Ask the Expert" column shares real-life lessons and best practices gleaned from SAP implementations, discusses ways to avoid common project pitfalls, and features various SAP products that solve key business issues.

Martin Murray was a respected logistics consultant and worked with IBM for more than 15 years. He joined the computer industry upon his graduation from Middlesex University in 1986. In 1991, he began working with SAP R/2 in the materials management area for a London-based multinational beverage company, and in 1994, he moved to the United States to work as an SAP R/3 consultant.

Index

C

I

Q

R

S

- Configure embedded and decentralized EWM in SAP S/4HANA

- Get step-by-step instructions for implementing key warehouse processes, from goods issue to kitting

- Explore your options for integration and reporting on your warehouse

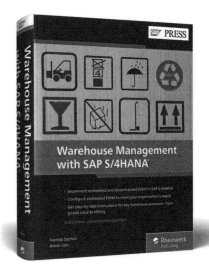

Namita Sachan, Aman Jain

Warehouse Management with SAP S/4HANA

Embedded and Decentralized EWM

Are you ready for warehouse management in SAP S/4HANA? With this implementation guide to EWM in SAP S/4HANA, lay the foundation by setting up organizational and warehouse structures. Then configure your master data and cross-process settings with step-by-step instructions. Finally, customize your core processes, from inbound and outbound deliveries to value-added services and cartonization. SAP S/4HANA is now ready for you!

approx. 875 pp., 2nd edition, pub. 03/2020
E-Book: $79.99 | **Print:** $89.95 | **Bundle:** $99.99

www.sap-press.com/5005

- Run your sourcing and procurement processes in SAP S/4HANA

- Configure purchasing, sourcing, invoicing, evaluation, and more

- Analyze your procurement operations

Justin Ashlock

Sourcing and Procurement with SAP S/4HANA

Your comprehensive guide to SAP S/4HANA sourcing and procurement is here! Get step-by-step instructions to configure sourcing, invoicing, supplier management and evaluation, and centralized procurement. Learn how to integrate SAP S/4HANA with SAP Ariba, SAP Fieldglass, and more. Then, expertly run your system after go-live with predictive analysis and machine learning. See the future of sourcing and procurement!

approx.750 pp., 2nd edition, pub. 03/2020

E-Book: $79.99 | **Print:** $89.95 | **Bundle:** $99.99

www.sap-press.com/5003

- Configure and run inventory management in SAP S/4HANA

- Plan, execute, and optimize goods receipt, stock transfers, and more using SAP Fiori applications

- Analyze your inventory, from KPI monitoring to custom queries

Bernd Roedel, Johannes Esser

Inventory Management with SAP S/4HANA

Jump-start your inventory operations in SAP S/4HANA! Review basic inventory practices and consult step-by-step instructions to configure SAP S/4HANA for your organization's requirements. Then put the system to work! Run the SAP Fiori applications that guide your core inventory workflows: inventory planning, goods receipt, core inventory, production planning, and inventory analysis. This hands-on guide to inventory has the details you need!

494 pages, pub. 09/2019
E-Book: $79.99 | **Print:** $89.95 | **Bundle:** $99.99

www.sap-press.com/4892

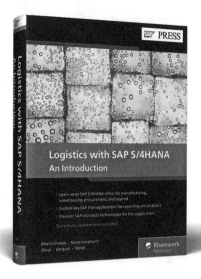

- Learn what SAP S/4HANA offers for manufacturing, warehousing, procurement, and beyond

- Explore key SAP Fiori applications for reporting and analytics

- Discover SAP Leonardo technologies for the supply chain

Bhattacharjee, Narasimhamurti, Desai, Vasquez, Walsh

Logistics with SAP S/4HANA

An Introduction

Transform your logistics operations with SAP S/4HANA! With this introduction, see what SAP has in store for each supply chain line of business: sales order management, manufacturing, inventory management, warehousing, and more. Discover how SAP Fiori apps and embedded analytics improve reporting, and explore the intersection between your supply chain processes and new SAP Leonardo technologies. Take your first look at SAP S/4HANA logistics, and see where it will take your business!

589 pages, 2nd edition, pub. 01/2019
E-Book: $69.99 | **Print:** $79.95 | **Bundle:** $89.99

www.sap-press.com/4785

- Learn what SAP S/4HANA offers your company

- Explore key business processes and system architecture

- Consider your deployment options and implementation paths

Bardhan, Baumgartl, Choi, Dudgeon, Lahiri, Meijerink, Worsley-Tonks

SAP S/4HANA

An Introduction

Whether you're already en route to SAP S/4HANA or taking your first look, this book is your go-to introduction to the new suite. See what SAP S/4HANA offers for your core business processes: finance, manufacturing, sales, and more. Learn about your reporting, extension, and adoption options, and consult customer case studies to learn from current customers. From the cloud to SAP Leonardo, get on the cutting edge of SAP!

647 pages, 3rd edition, pub. 12/2018
E-Book: $59.99 | **Print:** $69.95 | **Bundle:** $79.99

www.sap-press.com/4782

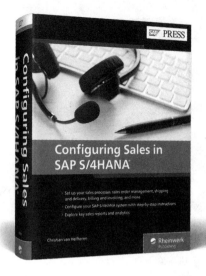

- Set up your sales processes: sales order management, shipping and delivery, billing and invoicing, and more

- Configure your SAP S/4HANA system with step-by-step instructions

- Explore key sales reports and analytics

Christian van Helfteren

Configuring Sales in SAP S/4HANA

SAP S/4HANA Sales is here! Business partners, the material master, and critical sales workflows all require careful configuration—this guide has the expertise you need. Learn about key business processes for sales order management, billing and invoicing, available-to-promise, and more. From setup and configuration to your reporting options, this book has you covered!

766 pages, pub. 12/2019

E-Book: $79.99 | **Print:** $89.95 | **Bundle:** $99.99

www.sap-press.com/4907